The Collected Works
of Esther Kreitman

LJP

The Library of the Jewish People

The Library of the Jewish People *presents primary, original voices of significant writers and thinkers in the fields of Rabbinics, the Arts, and Politics. These foundational Jewish writers will engage, inspire, and teach present and future generations.*

The Collected Works of Esther Kreitman

First Edition, 2026

The Library of the Jewish People

POB 8531, New Milford, CT 06776–8531, USA
& POB 4044, Jerusalem 9104001, Israel
www.ljp.pub

Der Sheydim-Tants (Warsaw: Brzoza, 1936); translated by Maurice Carr as Deborah (London: W.and G. Foyle, 1946; republished London: Virago, 1983, New York: St. Martin's Press, 1983, London: David Paul, 13 August 2004, ISBN 978-0-9540542-7-4, and New York: Feminist Press, 1 May 2009 ISBN 978-1-55861-595-3).

Brilyantn (London: W. and G. Foyle, 1944); translated by Heather Valencia as Diamonds (London: David Paul, 15 October 2009, ISBN 978-0-9548482-0-0).

Yikhes (London: Narod Press, 1949); translated by Dorothee van Tendeloo as Blitz and Other Stories (London: David Paul, 1 March 2004 ISBN 978-0-9540542-5-0).

ISBN 978-1-61329-254-9, *hardcover*

Printed and bound in the PRC

THE LIBRARY OF THE JEWISH PEOPLE

ESTHER KREITMAN

COLLECTED WORKS

EDITOR, ANITA NORICH

Contents

Publisher's Preface

Esther Kreitman (born Hinde Ester Singer, 1891–1954) was an important Yiddish translator and writer, who has for too long been overshadowed and shunned by her two famous brothers, Isaac Bashevis and Israel Joshua Singer. She was also distanced from her mother, and trapped in an unhappy marriage.

Kreitman produced an impressive corpus of novels, short stories, and essays, modelled on her own experiences as a woman living across Europe through two World Wars and the Great Depression. Her writing tackles important societal, historical, and economic injustices, giving a voice to the poor and furthering the feminist cause.

The Library of the Jewish People is pleased to present in full Esther Kreitman's Collected Works, including never-before translated short stories and other works, thereby honoring her work in her own right and doing justice to this hitherto neglected writer.

We are happily obliged to thank the editor of this volume, Anita Norich, for enlisting her deep knowledge of Kreitman's life and her tireless efforts to locate, translate and edit her works; our Managing Editor, Uri Bollag, for bringing this volume to completion; Rachel Miskin and Ruth Pepperman for editing the texts; Tomi Magerman for the typography; and Tani Bayer for designing the covers worthy of this author.

The Library of the Jewish People will continue to bring both well and lesser-known writers from the fields of Rabbinics, art, and politics to contemporary English speakers. While we are saddened to think about how much esteem Esther Kreitman could have enjoyed during her lifetime without the familial, societal, and economic burdens, we are grateful to be enriched by her writing and hope that this volume will contribute to her finally receiving her place among the towering figures of Yiddish writing during the twentieth century.

Matthew Miller, Publisher
Jerusalem, 2026

Timeline

	Esther Kreitman	Jewish Context	Global Context
1891	March 31: Hinde Esther Singer is born in Biłgoraj, Poland. Her parents are Pinkjas Mendl Menachem Zynger (a hasidic rabbi) and Basheve Zylberman.		
1893	Birth of her brother, Israel Joshua Singer, who would go on to become a noted Yiddish writer.		
1897		First Zionist Congress held in Basel, Switzerland. General Jewish Labour Bund in Lithuania, Poland, and Russia (Algemeyner Yidisher Arbeter-bund in Lite, Poyln un Rusland) founded in Vilna, Russian Empire.	
1903			Publication of *Q.E.D.*, the first novel of Gertrude Stein.
1904	Birth of her brother, Isaac Bashevis Singer, who would go on to become a noted Yiddish writer.		
1906	Birth of her brother, Moshe Singer, who would go on to become a rabbi.		
1912	Marries Avraham Kreitman, a diamond cutter, and moves to Antwerp, Belgium.		
1913	Birth of her son, Maurice Kreitman. He too would become a writer, better known by his pseudonym, Maurice Carr.		
1914		The World War will lead to the collapse of empires, the rise of communism and the creation of new states, all of which will have profound impact on Jewish life.	Outbreak of WWI.

1915		Birth of Saul Bellow.
1917	UK government issues the Balfour Declaration, pledging themselves to help establish a Jewish National Home in the Land of Israel. The last days of the Russian Empire sees the abolition of the Pale of Settlement and the formal granting of de jure equal rights to Jews. Bais Yaakov school system for Orthodox girls founded by Sarah Schenirer in Krakow, Poland. The initiative is approved by Yisrael Meir Kagan (the Chofetz Chaim) the leading Ashkenazi Orthodox thinker of the age. It revolutionizes education for Jewish girls and young women. Before this there had been no organized education for women in the Orthodox world. The Bolshevik revolution, initially supported by many Jews, will lead to a long period of persecution of Jewish culture and religion in the USSR and its satellite states.	Russian Revolution of October sees the Bolsheviks seize power in a coup. The Russian empire is replaced with the Union of Soviet Socialist Republics.
1918		World War I ends.
1919	Poland's ambiguous relationship with its Jews – which represented the leading Jewish community of the world in terms of population and cultural and religious influence – leads to the Polish parliament passing antisemitic laws discriminating against its Jewish citizens. There is active support for Zionism, including military training.	Republic of Poland is founded. One of the few countries in Europe at the time to allow women to vote.
1920	Britain receives the Mandate for Palestine, transforming the unilateral Balfour Declaration into binding international law.	
1921	Israel Joshua Singer publishes Pearls, a short story that brings him to the attention of the literary world.	
1925	Isaac Bashevis Singer publishes *In Old Age* (*Oyf der elter*), his first published work, winning the literary competition of the Literarishe Bleter.	

1926	Collapse of her marriage. Starts to divide her time between London and Warsaw, eventually settling permanently in the British capital before the outbreak of WWII.		
1928		Creation of the Jewish Autonomous District (Birobidzhan) by the USSR as a Yiddish-language "homeland" for the Jews of the Soviet Union.	
1929			Wall Street crash and beginning of the Great Depression that lasts until World War II. Birth of Adrienne Rich, who would go on to become a leading American poet, essayist, and feminist.
1932		Israel Joshua Singer publishes *Yoshe Kalb*..	
1933			January 30, Adolf Hitler becomes Chancellor of Germany.
1934	Her brother Israel Joshua Singer moves to the United States.		
1935	Her brother Isaac Bashevis Singer moves to the United States.	Regina Jonas ordained as first female Reform rabbi.	
1936	Publishes her novel, *Dance of the Demons* [*Der Sheydims Tants*], which was first serialized as *Dvoyrele* [*Deborah*] in 1934.	By 1939, there are more than three million Jews in Poland, constituting about 17 percent of world Jewry, and about 10 percent of the Poland's population. In the larger cities it is about one third.	Birth of A.B. Yehoshua.
1939			September 1: Germany invades Poland. WWII begins.
1940	Her experiences in the Blitz are recalled in her collection of short stories, *Yikhus*, published nine years later.		"The Blitz" bombing campaign of Britain by Germany begins. It lasts for eight months. Despite killing more than 40,000 people, it is ultimately unsuccessful in breaking British morale or limiting production of war materiel.

1941		The systematic mass murder of Jews begins. Initially carried out by shootings, it eventually evolves into industrialized murder by gassing in extermination camps. The Lubavitcher Rebbe, Rabbi Menachem Schneerson, arrives in New York after escaping Nazi Europe .	June 22: Operation Barbarossa, the German invasion of the Soviet Union, begins.
1944	Publishes her novel *Diamonds* [*Brilyantn*]. Death of her brother, Israel Joshua Singer, in New York.		
1945		By the end of WWII, almost six million Jews – one third of world Jewry – have been murdered. More than 90 percent of the Jews of Poland have been annihilated.	May 8: Unconditional surrender of Germany and end of WWII in Europe. Japan fights on until August 15.
1946	Kreitman learns of the death of her mother and brother Moshe. They had probably been forcibly evacuated to Kazakhstan from Poland by the Soviet regime, thus evading murder in the Holocaust. However, such evacuees often lived under very harsh conditions, which may have led to their death. Esther never learned the details of their fate.		
1947	Visited in London by her brother Isaac Bashevis Singer. He refuses to help her emigrate to the US and also refuses her financial help.	November 29: The UN General Assembly adopts the Partition Resolution. War breaks out between Jews and Arabs in the Land of Israel. The war continues until March 1949.	
1948		May 14: The State of Israel is declared.	
1949	Publishes *Yikhes* [Lineage] a collection of short stories.		
1954	Dies in London, UK, at the age of sixty-three.		
1962		Isaac Bashevis Singer publishes *Yentl the Yeshiva Boy*. The central character, a woman who seeks education and intellectual growth, is often considered to be based on his sister.	

General Introduction

Anita Norich

Esther Kreitman (1891–1954), or Hinde as she was called in the family, was a translator and the author of two novels, a collection of short stories, and uncollected stories and essays that appeared in the London and Belgian Yiddish press and beyond. She was born in Bilgoray, Congress Poland, and died in London. She spent several years in the small town of Leoncin where her father served as rabbi, then at the Hasidic court in Radzymin where her father taught, and in Warsaw before moving to Antwerp and then London. In 1912, a marriage was arranged for her with Avram Kreitman, a diamond cutter. They lived in Antwerp until they and their infant son went to London at the outbreak of World War I. The marriage was not a happy one and the couple spent significant periods of time apart. Kreitman returned to Poland twice between the two world wars, once in 1926 and again in 1929. At the end of World War II she went to Paris and was deeply moved to find Yiddish culture flourishing there despite the traumas suffered by its activists.

Hinde was the oldest child in a famous and, from all indications, discordant family of writers. Her parents, Pinchas Mendl and Batsheva, emerged from the radically different religious worlds of Eastern European Jewry: Pinchas Mendl was an adherent of Hasidism, characterized by its devotion to a *tzaddik* [a righteous man] and by its enthusiastic, emotional expression of religious devotion; Batsheva was the product and follower of *misnagdim* (literally: opponents; specifically opponents of Hasidism), characterized by their devotion to rationalism, learning, and a distaste for what they regarded as the excesses of Hasidic practice. Six children were born into this family: Hinde, the Yiddish writer Israel Joshua Singer (1893–1944), two daughters who died in early childhood, the Yiddish Nobel Laureate Isaac Bashevis Singer (1904–1991), and Moshe (1906–1944), the only son to remain within the family fold, following his father into the rabbinate and perishing with his mother and wife in Russia during the Second World War. The three Yiddish writers all produced autobiographical novels or memoirs, and, despite their differences, they all described their parents in remarkably similar terms, pointing to what they perceived as the reversed gender roles in the family. Pinchas Mendl was described as sentimental and was repeatedly called a *batlen*, an impractical, unworldly man; Batsheva was consistently described as a more aloof parent, an intelligent, learned woman, more worldly and much less emotional than her husband, "*a froy mit a mansbilishn kop*," as I. J. Singer wrote – "a woman with a man's head."

Kreitman was, by all accounts, the unhappy product of this mismatched pair and was equally mismatched with her own husband. Within the Singer family, Hinde was regarded as something of an embarrassment, an hysteric subject to nervous breakdowns or, as Isaac Bashevis Singer wrote, an ill woman who was either mad or epileptic or possessed by a dybbuk, the wandering soul of Jewish legend – usually male – who enters the body of another – usually female – and must be exorcised. That last diagnosis is the only one we can definitively reject, but it is also the most revealing one. (What the family thought of as her "fits" were most likely petit mal seizures.)

The dybbuk signals transgression and for Bashevis there could be no more apt image for this transgressive woman who wrote Yiddish literature, speaking in a voice that sounded strikingly like that of modernist male writers.

Kreitman was an active participant in the London literary magazine *Loshn un lebn* (Language and Life) and in socialist politics. Her book publications began with two translations from English to Yiddish, both produced in Warsaw during her second visit there. In 1929 she published Charles Dickens's *A Christmas Carol* (*Vaynakht*), following it in 1930 with George Bernard Shaw's *Intelligent Woman's Guide to Socialism and Capitalism* (*Di froy in sotsyalizm un kapitalizm*), which had appeared in English only two years earlier. Her choice of texts to translate only underscores the pervasive myth of her contrariness since it could not be supposed that these titles would meet with a particularly warm reception from the Yiddish readers for whom they were intended. The letterhead she printed in London attests to her interest in translation. One of her London addresses (56 Lordship Park, Stoke Newington, N.16) appears under the heading: Commercial, Patent & Legal Translations. Her husband's lack of employment meant not only that the family moved often, but also that she had to find other work, primarily in handiwork trades.

Kreitman's novel *Der sheydim tants* (1936) was first serialized under the blander title, *Dvoyrele* (in London's *Di post*, 1934). It was translated by her son, Maurice Carr, in 1946 and contained significant changes intended, no doubt, to make it more accessible to a postwar English audience. The novel traces the life of a teenager who is denied the educational and social advantages her brother enjoys and is finally married off to a hapless diamond cutter. Her second novel, *Brilyantn* (1944), appeared in Heather Valencia's English translation as *Diamonds* (2010). It is the story of a diamond merchant and his family in Antwerp in the years before the family's flight to London as World War I approaches and depicts their changed circumstances once in London. Kreitman was also publishing short stories and essays during the two decades before her death. Many of these were collected in a volume entitled *Yikhes* [1949; Lineage], translated by Dorothee van Tendeloo in 2004 under the title *Blitz and Other Stories*. The characters in these stories live in the towns and villages of Poland or in London whose topography and sites Kreitman describes in detail. Variant translations of two of these stories are included in an appendix to this collection. Translations of her other short stories and essays appear in this *Collected Works of Esther Kreitman* for the first time, as do letters addressed to her by George Bernard Shaw and Stefan Zweig and essays by her son and granddaughter.

The parallel geographical trajectories followed by the author and her protagonists have led critics to read Kreitman's work as autobiography, but also as ethnography, history, or feminist screed. It can be more productively understood as works whose characters are deeply engaged with their historical and social contexts. Kreitman writes about the economic and political realities of people's lives, about their political and sexual awakening, and about women who rebel against the strictures of their lives. She is always attentive to the plight of women in traditional Jewish life, to the poor, and especially to the injustices of capitalism. She is equally attentive to those who are ill or denied an education or suffer through the horrors of war.

We can only speculate about why Esther Kreitman never signed her name with the "Singer" added to the translations of her work into English and other languages. Was she simply taking her husband's name as was customary? Did she seek to distance herself from her unhappy family life? Was she asserting her independence, her unwillingness to be linked to the brothers who rarely acknowledged that she was a writer? Her reputation has both gained and suffered from this association with I. J. Singer, born two years after her, and I. B. Singer, born eleven years after him. Critics invariably refer to her as their less famous sister and use a range of adjectives that amount to the same thing: she is most often described as a writer overshadowed, eclipsed, neglected, forgotten, or ignored. But in her own day, and more recently, her reputation must rest on her writing rather than on her brothers. When they or other male writers of Yiddish prose declared their independence from the strictures of traditional Eastern European Jewish life and letters, they were heralded (or vilified) as modern men creating a new literature and new forms of Jewish expression. Kreitman responded to the same influences, refracted through the different perspectives made by gender and social status, and the more fluid ones of temperament and consciousness. Rather than analyzing her nerves or her marriage it is most appropriate to analyze her literary work in its social context and to recognize her significance to our understanding of modern Yiddish literature.

The Dance of the Demons (Deborah)

דער שדים-טאַנץ

A novel
ראָמאַן

Translated by Maurice Carr

Introduction

Anita Norich

The Dance of the Demons' Yiddish text was first serialized in 1934 in the London journal, *Di post,* under the title *Dvoyrele,* then published in 1936 as a book under its current title, *Der sheydim tants.* It was translated in 1946 by Esther Kreitman's son, Maurice Carr. The novel depicts a young woman's desire to escape the constraints of a restrictive religious environment, a family in which she is regarded as little more than a household drudge, and the madness (or depression?) that threatens to overwhelm her. In addition to this personal and psychological turmoil, Kreitman traces the emergence of its protagonist's modern political and cultural consciousness, a consciousness that had long been the hallmark of modern Yiddish literature but was now noteworthy because it was associated with a female character.

The protagonist, Deborah, envies her mother's learning. She envies, in fact, all learning, whether secular or religious, and reads whatever is available – psalms, secular poetry, grammar books, Karl Marx, storybooks of every kind – whenever she can steal time from the demands of her highly regulated domestic life. Deborah rebels against the Talmudic injunction quoted by her father in the novel: *kol hamelamed 'et bito torah ke'ilu melamdah tiflut* [whoever teaches his daughter Torah, it is as if he taught her something frivolous – i.e., things unnecessary and wrong for her to know].

Gender roles are inverted in the tensions the novel traces between the generations. These tensions are usually figured in Yiddish literature in a son's rebellion against the law of the father and against the patriarchal religious authority that is at odds with the emerging sense of the modern, independent self. In *The Dance of the Demons,* the tensions are similar, but the conventions of the genre are refashioned by the daughter's rebellion which is primarily directed at her mother who represents all authority and knowledge in the household. Deborah seeks her own path through learning, sexuality, politics, or art. Neither her weak and ineffectual father nor her overpowering mother can guide her on that path.

Kreitman links class and gender, condemning the powerlessness and silence to which they consign women and the poor. She offers a resonant connection between the status of Hasidim (like Deborah's and Kreitman's own father) and women in Jewish life. Both are childlike, subject to the supervision of masterful figures; both crave belief in something; both are ignorant and need to be educated. By the novel's end, this naive subjection is replaced by an insistence on individual responsibility for the self and for others, and by a clearly articulated, though not yet realizable desire for a more equitable social order.

The novel's fragmented characterizations of people, places, and events is more pronounced in the Yiddish original than in this English translation. Differences between the English and Yiddish texts raise intriguing questions about the process of translating this novel, a process about which neither author nor translator left any record. Kreitman's own translations from English to Yiddish make it quite clear that her command of English was excellent. There are frequent instances in her Yiddish text of calques from English, words or expressions it would have been unlikely for her to have heard in her native Poland but that she incorporated from her adopted language (e.g., "*Frosts kunstmoleray*" [Frost's artistry], referring to Jack Frost, "*brekhn dos ayz*" [breaking the ice]). It seems likely that she would have been able to influence the English translation of her novel. In fact, at various points in the text, one can imagine the mother peering over her son's shoulder. One – or both – of them undoubtedly took the liberty of editing parts of the text. One – or both – thought that the perspective of a Yiddish novel in 1936 could not remain unchanged in its postwar 1946 English version.

Differences between the Yiddish and English texts attest to the editorial revisions that accompanied this process of translation. By 1936, Jews in traditional dress were forbidden to walk in Warsaw's Saxon Gardens, but the 1946 English text links that prohibition with the horror that had just ended. The Yiddish text has those dressed in modern garb strolling freely in the Gardens "*vi zey voltn gor keyn yidn nisht geven*" [as if they weren't even Jews]; in the English text there is a sign in the Gardens warning "Jews Wearing Gaberdines and Dogs not Admitted." More radically, the English text erases any sign of the German culture that had, by 1946, become synonymous with genocide. In the English version, Deborah takes great comfort in reading Russian and, especially, the verses of Pushkin, but in Yiddish she is comforted and inspired by German's Gothic script and by Goethe's poetry, which she and her brother recite from memory. This rare moment of camaraderie is excised in the English text, as if to erase any hint that exposure to German culture might unite these characters as nothing in their Jewish lives could.

This translation is a product of its time and place and, frequently, the British idiom or Cockney accent that substitutes for a Warsaw-inflected Yiddish reminds us of the distance between turn-of-the century Jewish Warsaw and mid-century London. The English text's allusion to "the artful dodger" is missing – and meaningless – in Yiddish. Intertextuality in the Yiddish alludes to talmudic or biblical texts; in English, the intertextual reference here is to Dickens's *Oliver Twist*. When the Yiddish text refers to Deborah's grandfather as a *misnaged*, the English text erases this unfamiliar term, substituting a lengthy explanation about *tzaddikim* and Hassidim. *Goyim un goyes*, or the more pejorative *shkotsim un shikselekh* used to refer to non-Jews, becomes simply "men and women" or "youths."

Deborah speaks more in the Yiddish version, both to other characters and to herself. We hear her express her thoughts and feelings. In the English version, the emphasis is on everyone else's judgment of Deborah. The English also softens her mother's view of Deborah a bit. Lamenting, as Deborah does in English, that she is "so little thought of by her mother" is not the same as feeling, as she does in Yiddish, that her mother doesn't like her [*zi gefelt nisht der muter*]. Similarly, her mother's sarcastic, dismissive *khokhume mayne* [my genius] is changed into the English phrase "Mummy's little darling." These are certainly not errors, but rather deliberate changes made with a new audience in mind.

The most extensive changes appear in the novel's opening chapter where virtually every page discloses the editorial process, the felt need to explain Jewish ritual and lore to an English audience, and the desire to protect some part of the now-decimated Eastern European past from the harshest criticism it received in Kreitman's Yiddish novel. *Der sheydim tants*'s first chapter does not begin with the invocation of the Sabbath we have in English. It offers a considerably longer depiction of the family, one in which Deborah's father is even more dependent on his wife's practicality and her knowledge of religious texts, her mother is even more disdainful of her husband, and her brother even freer to roam away from this unhappy family. In Yiddish, Kreitman describes a home in which may be found everything "*akhuts abisl azoyns, vos zol shmekn mit heym*" [except anything at all redolent of home]. Such omissions in the English moderates the unremittingly bleak view of Deborah's home. It may also help explain the increased focus on Deborah's psyche. There is, after all, some possibility for addressing, perhaps even remedying psychological distress, individual trauma, childhood unhappiness. There was, in 1946, no redress to be imagined for the world of Eastern European Jewry.

Chapter 1

It was the Sabbath. And even the wind and the snow rested from their labors. The village of Jelhitz, a small cluster of wooden cottages and hovels, stood hidden away from sight at the edge of the Polish pinewoods – to all appearances nothing more than one of the many snowdrifts covering the land. But within, Jews were comfortably asleep in their beds after the heavy Sabbath dinner.

All was silent in the village, but nowhere was the quietude so impressive as in the large house by the synagogue which stood facing the common meadowland and the frozen river. Here lived the rabbi, Reb Avram Ber, and unlike most of his flock, he did not snore in his sleep. As for Raizela, his wife, her breathing was so gentle, that whenever Deborah peeped into the bedroom to see whether her parents were astir yet, the fourteen-year-old child grew anxious, wondering whether her mother was breathing at all.

The warmth and the shadowiness of falling dusk were cozy inside the rabbi's house, but Deborah, as she sat beside the tiled stove, reading, felt lonely and sorry for herself to the point of tears.

Earlier in the day she had overheard her father say:

"Michael is showing great promise in his studies, the Lord be praised! One day he will be a brilliant Talmudist."

Michael was her younger brother who, in accordance with the centuries' old custom of Orthodox Jews, was being brought up to spend all the days of his life in the study of the Talmud.

"And Father, what am I going to be one day?" Deborah then

suddenly enquired, half in jest, half in earnest, for, as long as she could remember, never had a word of praise fallen to her lot.

Reb Avram Ber was taken aback. It was an accepted view among pious Jews that there was only one achievement in life a woman could hope for – the bringing of happiness into the home by ministering to her husband and bearing him children. Therefore he did not even vouchsafe Deborah a reply, but when she pressed him, he answered simply:

"What are *you* going to be one day? Nothing, of course!"

This response did not at all satisfy Deborah. It was quite true that most girls grew up only to marry and become drudges, but there were exceptions, such as her own mother, Raizela, who was highly educated, a real lady, and as wise as any man.

To be sure, in his heart of hearts Reb Avram Ber disapproved of his wife's erudition. He thought it wrong for a woman to know too much, and was determined that this mistake should not be repeated in Deborah's case. Now, there was in the house a copy of Naimonovitch's Russian Grammar, which Deborah always studied in her spare moments, but whenever her father caught her at this mischief he would hide the book away on top of the tiled stove out of her reach, and then she would have to risk her very life to recover it. She would move the table up against the stove, set a chair on the table, herself on the chair, and after all that trouble, clouds of dust and loose leaves from torn books, disused feather dusters and God knows what else would come fluttering and tumbling down – everything, in fact, except the Russian Grammar. Nevertheless, during her fourteen years of life, she had managed to learn all its contents by heart, and still she was dissatisfied. How tediously morning changed into afternoon and evening into night! How wearisome was her housework, and yet, beyond that, she had few real interests. She was forever lacking something, herself hardly knowing what. A strange yearning would stir in her, an almost physical gnawing sensation, but it had never before been so painful as on this wintry Sabbath afternoon, when all was quiet within and the world outside was muffled with snow.

She sought refuge in daydreams. She recalled how the family had first come to Jelhitz many years ago, arriving at nightfall; how the bearded pious Jews, in long gabardines, black top boots and peaked cylindrical caps – a fashion surviving from the Middle Ages – came forward with lighted candles to greet their new rabbi, crying in unison:

"Blessed be thy coming!"

What a splendid figure Reb Avram Ber had cut in his rabbinical garb – black buckled shoes, white stockings, satin gabardine and broad-brimmed black felt hat.

As she remembered all this, and saw again the smile – grateful and almost childish – that had settled in Reb Avram Ber's longish fair beard, hot tears slowly trickled down her flushed cheeks, senseless tears for which she could find no justification.

When Michael burst into the room and found his sister crying, a psalter in her hand, he laughed so boisterously that his parents woke up in the next room. Michael and Deborah were never on very friendly terms. And he snatched this opportunity of poking fun at her, calling her a fool for staying indoors, for poring over the Psalms with tears in her eyes like a miserable old sinner whiling away dull old age with penitence. As for himself, he had been out on the river, which stretched away frozen, hard as a sheet of steel, with snow-covered fields all around, with a blue, transparent, Sabbath sky hanging above, wonderfully silent. After his exertions, Michael's cheeks were flushed, his ears tingling with frostbite, and the bright gleam in his eyes flashed with ever-changing tints – now black, now brown, then coppery. He had come back brimming over with life, and his sister, who always stayed indoors and meekly bore the stagnation of their home life, seemed to him now more pitiful than ever.

He became more subdued when his father entered the room.

"Have you been getting on with your studies, Michael?" Reb Avram Ber asked with a sleepy yawn.

"Yes, Father."

Deborah gaped. She endeavored to catch Michael's eye, but he was reading some religious tract very studiously, and there was nothing in his now thoughtful face to betray his lie. Good God, what a wicked boy! And what was worse, he thought himself so clever and dared to make fun of her. She had a good mind to give him away. But Reb Avram Ber was asking her for a glass of hot tea, and seemed to have forgotten all about Michael by now.

Anyhow, not that her own conscience was any too clear! Exchanging one of her father's religious books for a work of fiction was surely an even more heinous sin than going for a slide on the ice on the Sabbath. If her father was to know of it, he would – she could not imagine what he might not do…Good God! How awful to exchange a holy book for a story book! Conscience-stricken herself, she kept her tongue, but as she poured out the tea she reflected that had she been a boy instead of a girl, she would not have found herself driven to commit such iniquities. She would have spent all her time in the study of the Talmud. But hers was a dreary lot, and even when she erred, life was still maddeningly dull. As for the bookseller, he only came down to the village once in every four weeks, on market day.

That was the only day which broke the humdrum silence of the village. When she woke up on market day, to the rumble of spring-less peasant carts and the sound of strange voices, a thrill passed through her, as though having gone to sleep in an isolated hut far from all human habitation she had suddenly awakened to find herself in new surroundings, where life simply tumbled over itself. Indeed, Jelhitz was unrecognizable on market day. Gone was the sovereignty of the ragged goats that otherwise rambled about the village as if they were the masters of all they surveyed. All was transformed. Even the leaning houses seemed to wear an air of alertness on market day. Peddlers did not leave by candlelight, in the dark before dawn, to tramp the surrounding farms. None of the menfolk idled their time away in the warmth of the synagogue, relating strange tales of events in the unknown beyond. The very womenfolk had no time for the least tittle-tattle. The blanket of snow that stretched away from Jelhitz to the forest and to the horizon was broken by countless footsteps and wheel ruts. And peasants, in carts and on foot, crowded into Jelhitz, driving cattle before them, or dragging unwilling pigs behind them, with their wives accompanying them in festive attire. While competing merchants from nearby villages brought their own wares – anything from lace veils to top boots, carved crosses to sheepskin jackets, sweetmeats to quack medicines. Gypsies were there, and conjurors, and drunkards, and idlers and loungers. And lastly came the bookseller, whom Deborah sought out with more eagerness than the rest, only to be bitterly disappointed. For, as it always turned out, he had nothing of real interest. His was a burden of holiness: prayer books, prayer shawls, ritual fringes, and a miscellany of religious tracts. Only by chance would a profane book get mixed up with this spiritual load. So during the intervals of waiting she would have to read "The Fate of the Enchanted Princess" or "The Tale of the Three Brothers" ten times over, and in the end return to the wrinkled pages of the psalter after all!

The wintry light was beginning to fail by the time Raizela joined the family in the living room. She got out of bed and immediately climbed on to the couch by the window, where she spent most of her waking hours, absorbed in philosophic and religious books. Absentmindedly the family drank their tea, all of them except Deborah preoccupied with their reading. And yet, though they all seemed to be unaware of each other's presence, every one breathed a breath of gentle disapproval on his neighbor. Michael was grieved to have to stop indoors under his parents' eye, and indeed, as soon as he could, he slipped out unnoticed. Deborah felt slighted by them all. And husband and wife were displeased with one another on an old, old score.

Raizela was accustomed to a different life from that which she had been leading during the past ten years in Jelhitz. She had been brought up in a house of plenty – plenty, in the material as well as the spiritual sense of the word. Her father was one of the best-known rabbis in Poland and perhaps the most learned Jew of his day. His very presence commanded the reverence of all who saw him – even of such plain folks as live by the sweat of their brow and usually feel nothing but contempt mingled with hatred for those who do no work but "wear out the seats of their pants" over the Talmud. He was very tall, with a dark lean face, magnificent black silky beard and large black eyes which showed a fine sense of humor that was eternally being stifled by a stern sense of duty and of the Holy Presence. He rarely spoke, only studying from early morning till late at night, with many scholars, or rather disciples, some of them middle-aged men, at his side, and around him in the house moved his many sons and daughters and grandchildren. It was the custom of pious Jews to marry off their children at the age of fifteen or so, and then to keep them at home until they became self-supporting.

Also Raizela, his favorite daughter, had been wed at the age of fifteen. And the husband chosen for her, a youngster a year older than herself, was Reb Avram Ber, because of his great learning and the renown attaching to his name. Some of his ancestors were among the great of Israel, household names in the Jewish world, and moreover he claimed descent from King David. So it had seemed a promising match. However, Reb Avram Ber turned out to be a failure. True, there were few to compare with him in learning; but he was unworldly, needed looking after like a child. Beyond the realm of the Talmud, he was just a simpleton.

He went on with his studies in his father-in-law's house until he was himself a father of two children, and still he gave no thought to the future. At length it was decided that Reb Avram Ber must set up for himself. The only course open to this simple-minded young man was to become a rabbi, but in order to qualify for such a position in a town of any importance he was required by the law of that time to pass an examination in the Russian language and in other temporal subjects, so that he might combine the functions of registrar of births, marriages and deaths with that of rabbi.

After much persuasion, Reb Avram Ber was finally torn away from the Talmud and made to journey to the town of Plotck, where he took up residence with a tutor who specialized in preparing future rabbis for the official examination. With thoughtless willingness he paid the full fee in advance; with thoughtless reluctance he turned to his new subjects. And still all might have gone well, but for the chance arrival of another future rabbi – a handsome young man with cute, twinkling eyes, a cynical mouth and a delightfully pointed silken little beard. This young man was soon on friendly terms with the tutor's wife and, among other things, told Reb Avram Ber that this woman wore no wig, as prescribed by Jewish law, according to which no married woman may expose her hair lest the charm of her tresses provoke sinful thoughts. In any case, Reb Avram Ber was tired of the whole business. He simply could not concentrate on the new, queer education. Nor did he relish the tutor's continual reproaches about not doing as he was told. He was weary to death of the uncongenial surroundings generally, but when his eyes were opened and he saw that the tutor's wife was not wearing a wig as prescribed by Jewish law, that was the last straw.

For once in his life he became a man of action – and he ran away. Lacking courage to return to his father-in-law's house, he decided to go into the "wide world." The "wide world" was the nearest village to Plotck. The Jewish inhabitants, finding a stranger in their midst, shook hands with him, bade him "Peace!" then asked him who he was, what was his business, whence had he come, whither was he going. And many more questions besides did they ask him, as the custom is. But Reb Avram Ber answered briefly. He merely begged the beadle to announce that a preacher had arrived and would deliver a sermon immediately after the evening service.

Reb Avram Ber was well versed in parables, and his rambling sermon, full of deep knowledge of the law, was mingled with many fascinating tales which held his audience spellbound.

"His words flow sweet as wine!" said the womenfolk, not a little impressed by his good looks.

"A great scholar!" declared the menfolk.

Thus it was he went from village to village, until he at last came to Jelhitz, which had been without a rabbi for some time past. And Reb Avram Ber found great favor in the eyes of the Jews of Jelhitz. The community of three hundred souls determined not to let this erudite young man continue on his travels. After several heated meetings, at which everybody tried to speak at the same time, Reb Avram Ber was appointed rabbi of Jelhitz.

But Raizela never forgave him his escapade. And on this wintry Sabbath afternoon it all came back to her. The family were in great distress. The stipend paid by the community was far from adequate, and driven by the sheer force of circumstances, Reb Avram Ber was that evening going to ask for an increase.

Earlier in the week he had consulted her how to go about it. She was his adviser in all secular matters. Reclining on her couch, ailing and feeble, she would turn his problems over in her mind and drop words of counsel.

"Whatever you do, don't be apologetic," she had said in a quiet voice that seemed to heighten her frailty.

"Oh no, I'll be very firm with them this time," replied Reb Avram Ber.

Raizela's thin lips spread into a faint smile. She could not help thinking that her husband looked rather ridiculous, promising to be firm, with his blue eyes so gentle, with so pleasant a smile playing on his face.

Reb Avram Ber, usually short-sighted and unobservant of what was going on around him, had by this time learnt to interpret that flickering little smile as a bitter reproach to himself for his past errors, and whenever he noticed it he began to defend himself stoutly, as though her thoughts had been audible. And then, when Raizela made no reply, he invariably transferred to his father-in-law that flush of anger which had risen in him momentarily against his wife.

He blamed the father for having encouraged the daughter to study, for having supplied her with reading-matter (Orthodox books, of course, though afterwards it was whispered that she read all sorts!) and for generally having taken her – a mere female – into his confidence.

With that the "scene" always ended, and calm was restored to the home. But now, on this wintry Sabbath afternoon, when any talk on worldly matters was out of place, husband and wife were again having the same old quarrel, even though not a word passed between them. And Reb Avram Ber felt relieved when the time came for him to put on his overcoat and go into the synagogue, only a few steps away, for the evening service.

In a hushed murmur the sound of prayers reached the house. Deborah listened intently. In her imagination she saw the all too familiar bearded faces of the congregation in the candle-lit synagogue, and she wondered what the heads of the community would say to her father's request. She did not expect him back for some time. But Reb Avram Ber returned immediately the service was over. He looked very grave, and he brought bad news.

One of the villagers' children, who had been slightly ill for some time, had suddenly taken a turn for the worse. The father, Mendel, nicknamed "Big" Mendel, one of the wealthiest men of the tiny community, was traveling to the town of R– to ask a *tzaddik*, a holy man, who dwelt there, to pray for the recovery of the infant. Another villager, whose wife was with child and was troubled with presentiments of disaster, was accompanying "Big" Mendel, in order to beg the *tzaddik* to drive out the evil spirits responsible for the presentiments, and Reb Avram Ber proposed to go too. He would thus have to postpone his request for an increase in his stipend until some other, more propitious time.

Raizela was displeased. Like her father, she was not a believer in *tzaddikim*,* professional holy men, who, because of their purity, were reputed to stand in closer communion with God than the ordinary mortal. She often tried to enlighten Reb Avram Ber, ridiculing in her quiet way the possibility of any man being holy by profession, the sophistry of such a man wielding occult powers to heal and to wound, to create and to destroy, in return for temporal might and wealth. These *tzaddikim* lived in great style, holding court like kings

* The plural form of *tzaddik*.

and branching out into great dynasties, the sons inheriting the holy spirit from their fathers.

But Reb Avram Ber was not to be deflected from his faith. He was a staunch follower of the *tzaddikim* and their movement of Hasidism. He never doubted that the *tzaddikim* were righteous men, and he loved the cult of Hasidism, which declared that life being God's most precious of all gifts, it would be sinful for man not to delight in this gift. He loved to serve God by being merry, and he loved to travel to the courts of the *tzaddikim*, where he met other Hasidim, pilgrim believers, from all parts of the country and from all stations in life, where he could mingle with his fellow men in an atmosphere of mystical rejoicing; where he could join in the dancing, the singing and the prayers of the masses; where he heard strange new stories, picked up haunting new melodies and received fresh inspiration for even more steadfast application to the Talmud and the mystical Kabbala.

With eager anticipation now he dressed up in his warmest greatcoat, tucking his beard into the lapels, and by the time "Big" Mendel's conveyance had drawn up outside the window, he had quite forgotten about the financial straits of the family and his promise to be firm.

"Big" Mendel entered with pale face. Usually beaming, he was very grave now, and he chilled everybody's heart. Reb Avram Ber hastily bade the family goodbye. Raizela was cross and returned her husband's farewell without even raising her eyes from the book she was reading.

The wheels crunched on the snow outside, and Reb Avram Ber was gone.

Chapter 2

It was on a Thursday, about ten o'clock in the morning – Raizela had just made her mind up to send off a telegram, for never before had Reb Avram Ber spent such a long time at the *tzaddik*'s court – when the door opened and in walked Reb Avram Ber himself, beaming with joy, his whole person wrapped in an air of mystery. He entered wiping the perspiration from his face with a red-spotted handkerchief, although the weather was still cold and wintry. His eyes sought a chair. Deborah brought him a stool and placed it opposite her mother lying on the couch. Reb Avram Ber seated himself, unbuttoned his overcoat, removed his hat, adjusted the velvet skull-cap on his head, stuffed his handkerchief back into his pocket, and exclaimed:

"I have news for you!" And then – "All's well, the Lord be praised! All's well!"

He turned to Deborah, in whom he hoped to see a bright reflection of his own happiness. Deborah, finding her father in such high spirits, anticipated that he had brought home a larger sum than usual, given to him as a parting gift by the *tzaddik*, and she rejoiced. They were in a bad way, deeply in debt. And she waited impatiently for him to name the amount. Then, recollecting that he had mentioned "news," she was all agog to be let into the secret. But as if on purpose to tantalize her, all at once Reb Avram Ber turned very deliberate. He released his beard, took out his pipe in leisurely fashion, knocked it on the leg of his stool, filled it with tobacco, pulled large puffs of smoke to get it to light properly, and at length he said:

"How would an offer of fifteen rubles a week, with free accommodation, appeal to you, I wonder?"

Raizela's eyes opened wide with astonishment. She looked at him for some time and made no answer.

"Aha, you are surprised? Well then, let me tell you all about it."

Deborah sat down on the edge of her mother's couch in silence. She did not know whether it was best to look solemn, like her mother, or happy, like her father.

"Now you've heard of the new yeshiva, the Talmud academy, which the *tzaddik* is building at R–?"

"Yes, I've heard. I know all about it," Raizela answered sharply, angry with Reb Avram Ber for having caused her so much anxiety by his prolonged absence.

Reb Avram Ber explained that he had been offered the post of principal lecturer at the yeshiva. Strangely enough, she did not seem at all pleased with the prospect of fifteen rubles a week. She had no faith in the *tzaddik*, and she told Reb Avram Ber as much in plain words.

"You're always the same!" said Reb Avram Ber, waxing angry. "I do believe you wouldn't trust your own shadow!"

Here was he out of breath after tearing through the village high street, the sooner to bring her the glad tidings, and now nothing but disappointment – no response whatever.... But he was soon appeased. She was poorly, she should have been spared the worry of the past few weeks, he excused her in his heart.

"As you know," he continued, "for some reason or other the *tzaddik* treats me with the greatest consideration. Whenever I pay him a visit, he showers gifts on me and insists on my accepting them. And if it wasn't for his kind help from time to time, I don't know where we should be. Well naturally, the moment he saw an opportunity of giving me a secure livelihood, he was delighted. I was the very man for the job. The *tzaddik* has a heart of gold, really he has. When he asks me how I am getting on, and I tell him that you are ailing, that the children too are in delicate health, and that our livelihood is only so-so, it simply breaks his heart."

Raizela gave a faint smile. Reb Avram Ber noticed it.

"Well then, *you* tell me why he insists on giving me money! Does he profit by it in any way? Now I ask you, why?"

"Since you ask, I shall tell you. The *tzaddik* of R–, you see, unlike most other *tzaddikim*, has very few learned Hasidim among his followers, not to mention rabbis of course. Well naturally, he likes to see a full-blown rabbi mingling with his crowd once in a while. Don't you always tell me how reluctant he is to let you go, and how he keeps delaying your departure as much as ever he can? Only that explains why he is so eager for your company, and that is why he invites you to come, the oftener the better, though every visit you pay him is so much extra expense to him. You know quite well that a *tzaddik* always accepts gifts, but never offers any. It's obvious! You don't see it – I do!"

Reb Avram Ber reached for his beard again, and began striding hastily up and down the room.

"You're a skeptic! You're no better than your father! You are calumniating a holy man. A skeptic is capable of blaspheming our very Father in heaven and the Messiah. I always said that your father made a very great mistake in giving you an education."

Now, as ever, Reb Avram Ber transferred his wrath to his father-in-law....

Thereafter never-ending discussions took place between father and mother. As the town of R– was of course much larger than the village Jelhitz, both Deborah and Michael hoped that for once Father would have his own way. Then they would at last be rid of sleepy little Jelhitz, and with Reb Avram Ber installed as head of the yeshiva at R–, a new and glorious life would begin.

Reb Avram Ber scarcely applied himself to his studies. He was forever arguing with Raizela, who never once wavered in her opinion that the *tzaddik* was not a man to be trusted – she had the less faith in him because of his gifts! On the other hand, Reb Avram Ber did his best to convince her that here indeed was the finest possible proof of the *tzaddik*'s great-heartedness, holiness and generosity, quite apart from the fact that the post had to be filled by someone – and the academy was going to be one of the finest in the whole of Poland and even Lithuania.

"Moreover, the rabbi of that town is almost eighty, and when his time comes, will have no heir to succeed him. Not that that matters. May he go on living to a great old age, until the coming of the Messiah!"

Deborah and Michael were in entire agreement with their father.

The most prominent members of the Jelhitz community began calling on Reb Avram Ber in an endless succession, in an endeavor to deter him from taking the proposed step. They made him many tempting promises, invented all sorts of fairy tales, and insisted that for a long time past they had been thinking of increasing his stipend; but finding him adamant they tried their luck with Raizela. In honor of their visit Raizela sat up on her couch, heard out patiently all they had to say for themselves; she nodded her wise head and inwardly thought that they were liars no less than the *tzaddik* himself.

Very soon a go-between, acting on behalf of a young man of a neighboring village who had cast an eager eye on the vacancy which Reb Avram Ber would leave, began making ever more frequent appearances in the home. Michael rejoiced anew each time the man called, although in himself the stranger was not such as to rejoice one's heart, for there was a wild, greedy-needy look in the fellow's eyes; his beard was unclean and tufted; he wore a gabardine which was so old, it must have belonged to a distant ancestor – apart from being greenish, greasy and shiny through age, it was bespattered with mud up to the girdle; and over his top boots he wore a pair of sloppy, squelching galoshes, which he did not trouble to remove even when coming into Reb Avram Ber's study. He announced himself by wafting a strange aroma into the house, partly due perhaps to the evil-smelling pipe and cigarette ends rolled in ordinary newspaper which he was in the habit of smoking. Deborah and Michael could not bear the sound of his voice, nor his manner of arguing, nor the way he gesticulated with hairy hands and filthy fingernails. But most repugnant of all was his grin, revealing his teeth – brown, chipped and in parts black as coal. And as if that in itself were insufficient, a slight foam would play on his mouth whenever he grew excited. No, there was nothing very aesthetic about him. Yet how they exulted to see him!

Strangely enough, neither Deborah nor Michael ever dreamt of feeling disgusted with Hannah, the "daily woman," notwithstanding that the greasy folds of her dress absolutely clung to her hips in their stickiness: to her they were accustomed. Indeed, Deborah was perfectly content if she was left in peace by Hannah, who was forever muttering and grumbling about never receiving a helping hand, forever nagging at that "lazy idle girl" who refused to run an errand but gave herself a holiday the moment she, Hannah, entered the place. Of late Deborah had in fact avoided the woman, not that she minded the work. But for some time now Hannah had been at loggerheads with the world, testier than ever. As she dragged herself from one task to the other, dark clouds continually frowned and threatened down from her aged face. The dark furrows around her neck had grown even deeper, and the swollen wrinkles in her cheeks and round the corners of her mouth even flabbier. Her tiny beard had greyed of late together with the wisps of hair showing through her wig. She would give the family no more cooked dinners. No use reasoning with her, pleading with her. She would listen, shake the empty skin bag under her chin, mutter something through her drawn, toothless mouth, and take not the slightest heed.

In the end Raizela decided that, weary as she was of Jelhitz, she had after all but little to stake: she would therefore entrust herself to the mercy of the Lord, and maybe everything would turn out for the best. That settled, she curled herself up more resolutely on her couch, wrapped herself tighter in her black velvet jacket, continued her reading more intensively than ever, and left the matter entirely in Reb Avram Ber's hands – an occurrence which was without precedent.

Unexpectedly, Michael began to chum up with Deborah. He knew that she felt about the matter as strongly as he did, and would therefore sympathize with him. He went to her complaining how unreasonable was the attitude of their mother in refusing to meddle in the whole affair; thanks to her lack of interest, it would be a long time before anything was settled, if ever. Both brother and sister were filled with longing to leave the stagnant, sleepy village behind them, to get rid of old Joel, the beadle, of the everlasting loneliness and dreariness, of the unpleasantly familiar atmosphere, of Hannah, of the long, empty days, and above all – of mother's couch, which they hoped Rev Avram Ber's successor would take over together with the rest of the furniture.... Although Reb Avram Ber visited the *tzaddik* twice in the course of three weeks, and on each occasion returned with renewed enthusiasm – the roof was well-nigh finished, students were beginning to arrive, they were meantime studying in the *tzaddik*'s own synagogue, the *tzaddik* was now promising twenty rubles a week – in spite of all this, both Deborah and Michael were still very dubious, for did they not clearly see how indifferent their mother was to the whole business?

However, one fine morning after Purim, when the door opened and in walked a stranger, short, stout and middle-aged, with an expensive fur collar on his huge black greatcoat, and in his wake a pale young man, tall and thin, with sharp, nervous eyes overcast by dark, bushy eyebrows, with long black sidelocks (which he was in the act of disentangling from the rest of his hair), only then did Michael begin to feel a certain conviction that negotiations were well advanced, and he could not resist sharing his glee with Deborah, who was even more exultant than he.

Reb Avram Ber received his visitors with a hearty welcome – "Peace unto you!" – as was his custom. He pulled up chairs for them at the table in person. The short stout man sat down with a thud, unbuttoned his greatcoat, caught his breath, glanced at his solid gold watch and returned it to his waistcoat pocket. The pallid young man looked around him as if seeking a place to deposit his suitcase, and finally he stood it under the table, seated himself respectfully and glanced across at his father-in-law. Suddenly the go-between appeared as if from thin air (he had come in quite unobserved), and he too took a seat – without being asked. Also he unbuttoned his overcoat, and having made himself quite comfortable, gazed up at the ceiling. Only when Reb Avram Ber had told Joel to tell the woman to be good enough to bring in tea, did the fellow suddenly remember his duty of introducing the guests. Whereupon Reb Avram Ber again asked them how they were, and how did they like the village. The conversation turned on Jelhitz and the benefice. It transpired that the young man had only four hundred rubles at his disposal – his entire worldly fortune. Reb Avram Ber felt awkward and disappointed. Only four hundred rubles! And he had himself heard Raizela say that at eight hundred rubles the house with the goodwill of the benefice would be a real bargain. Those were her very words, and now she refused to have anything to do with the whole business; but without her he was completely at a loss. He grew weary of the conversation, and in the end started debating a point in the Talmud.

The color suddenly rose to the pallid young man's face. He stood up and he sat down. He warmed up to the discussion. His eyes began to glow; he tingled all over. New life welled up within him, there was nothing apathetic about him now, he was quite a devil of a young man.... Serenely Reb Avram Ber stroked his beard, serenely he sipped his tea, serenely he listened to all the young man's arguments, and then at one stroke he shattered them out of existence, mercilessly dashing to pieces the intricate structure of logic which the young man had built up with so much toil and care.

The short stout man followed every movement, every gesture of his son-in-law. He could not make out what those two were wrangling about: why was the rabbi so cold-bloodedly tormenting his, Gimpel's, son-in-law, and why had the latter got so excited? He smiled, not that he saw anything to be pleased about or otherwise. As for the go-between, he did not even watch the pair.

"Bah!" he said.

Meanwhile Joel had slipped into the kitchen for a chat with old Hannah, trying to coax a little bit of prophecy out of her as to whether anything would come of it all.

The go-between began to calculate his hoped-for commission,

chalking various sums on the table; then he counted the tassels of his ritual fringes; he was bored.

The young man was feverishly engaged in untwining one end of his silken braided girdle. Almost with anger he tugged at his youthful sprouting beard. He rose and began striding hastily over the room, to and fro, backwards and forwards. Suddenly he paused in front of the bookcase. Mechanically he took out a volume, *Pri Megadim*, and pored over it a while, without seeing a word. His thoughts were far, far away. He continued his pacing up and down, and then stopped at the window. He looked out, with his deep-set eyes opened wide, as if there on the crumbling roadway lay the solution to his knotty problem. Now he was simply tearing his girdle into shreds. His father-in-law went up to him and rescued the girdle from out of his hands.

"Caiman, what are you doing? You're spoiling your girdle."

Already Reb Avram Ber was sipping a second glass of tea. Reb Avram Ber was at home in the Talmud. He had no need to get excited.

"Yes, yes, it is so!" Reb Avram Ber agreed with his own thoughts.

But at that moment a smile spread over Reb Caiman's face. He took out his handkerchief, wiped his face, and delivered himself of so powerful a dissertation, that at first Reb Avram Ber was at a loss for a reply, let alone for an argument with which to shatter his opponent. Finding himself in difficulties, Reb Avram Ber rose to his feet, reached for his beard and this time he too became a little heated. A struggle for life or death ensued.... In the end a smile settled on Reb Avram Ber's face.

Exhausted, the young man sat down. Abashed, defeated, completely disarmed now, he also smiled, but sad was the smile.

"You showed great knowledge, Reb Caiman. I see that you are a great Talmudist, the Lord be praised. Indeed, you showed great insight," said Reb Avram Ber. He could afford to show tolerance towards the vanquished. "Tell me, where did you study?"

"In Suddiger."

"Ah, I presume you are a Hasid of the Suddiger *tzaddik*? So! And your father-in-law, which *tzaddik* does he give allegiance to?" asked Reb Avram Ber, not wishing to ignore Gimpel altogether.

Reb Caiman looked across at his father-in-law. The latter did not quite grasp what Reb Avram Ber meant. Reb Avram Ber guessed that Gimpel gave allegiance to no *tzaddik*, and exchanging a glance with Reb Caiman, they dropped the question.

By this time the broker had lost all patience.

"Reb Caiman's father-in-law," he began, taking advantage of the momentary pause, "wishes to take over the benefice and the house."

Reb Avram Ber could not help smiling.

"Really? How wonderful!"

Reb Caiman also smiled. His father-in-law was to take over the benefice – that was excellent!

Gimpel looked first at one, then at the other. What was the joke? Funny creatures, those two! First they disputed, then they exchanged knowing smiles. But not to be outdone, he grinned broadly. The broker alone would not smile. He wiped his mouth with the flat of his hand, and got ready for some practical work.

"Saving your reverence," he said, "but it's getting late. It's time we came down to business!"

Rev Avram Ber excused himself. He retired to Raizela's room. Raizela wrinkled her forehead. She gazed at him with her large, gloomy eyes.

"So you are really going to take the leap?" she said.

"Why, of course! And, please God, we shall have no reason to regret it. The only trouble is that the young man is short of money."

"Nonsense! The young man may be short, but his father-in-law has plenty. If you were to agree to seven hundred rubles, that would be very moderate indeed. And we must not forget that in a few years we shall be needing a dowry for our daughter. Besides, the house alone...."

She could say no more. A lump rose in her throat, stifling her words. She had spoken softly, and her voice had sounded hollow, as if it came from nowhere. She lay back on the couch. Reb Avram Ber stood there a while, waiting for her to go on. She said nothing further. At last he returned to his study, paced up and down several times, and then repeated word by word Raizela's point of view.

"Seven hundred rubles!"

He felt better. Thank goodness that was over!

Gimpel whispered into Reb Caiman's ear that he was not in a position to make up the difference of three hundred rubles. The go-between wriggled like a worm. On the quiet he told Reb Avram Ber how shocked he was to hear the price – perfectly extravagant! – and on the quiet he tried to talk Gimpel into believing that this was the greatest bargain one could hope to come across in a lifetime.

Reb Avram Ber told Joel to call in Raizela. This annoyed her. Preparing a little speech for Reb Avram Ber when he had to face the village council, well, that was one thing, but haggling with a merchant on his behalf was another – no, she would not lower herself to that. She scribbled down a few words and sent them in with Joel. Reb Avram perused the scrap of paper. A smile settled in his beard.

"Well, gentlemen," he said, "I shall now accept six hundred rubles, and here's good luck!"

"Amen!" howled the go-between, as if he had suddenly had a tooth wrenched out.

Gimpel began to bargain with renewed fervor, in an attempt to bring the price down lower still. But Reb Caiman spoke several urgent words in his ear, and he stopped. He then demanded to be shown round the house. He wished to inspect it. Now this was Michael's responsibility. From behind the kitchen window, Deborah gloated over them. Finished with the exterior, Gimpel insisted on being shown round all the rooms. Here Deborah came to Michael's aid, and together they passed from chamber to chamber. Gimpel critically examined the walls, the ceilings; he knocked at the stoves, as if they were doors; rattled the windows. Only the panes and echoes responded as he endeavored to find fault. Even so, he now felt pleased with himself. At last he was in his element. Now *he* was the man of the moment. Afterwards, it was arranged to summon the elders of the Jelhitz community, in order to talk the matter over with them and obtain their approval that very same evening.

Joel, the beadle, returned tired and perspiring, quite out of breath.

"Phew! My word, I've had a run for my money – rushing all over the place! I had to keep calling and calling before I could find anyone at home."

"Well, and did they promise, to come?"

"I should say so! Ha, you leave it to Joel! My good point is that I know exactly what to say. Of course, I never told them what they were wanted for. He, he! I know the right thing to say, just leave it to me! He, he, he!"

"What do you think, Joel, will this young man appeal to them?"

"Will he appeal to them? Of course he'll appeal to them! He's a gent, that's what he is! The only trouble is that they don't feel like parting with you at all."

"Well, yes, but you can't expect me to stick in this hole of a village forever," said Reb Avram Ber, as if apologizing to Joel, and he told the beadle to ask the woman to be so good as to bring in a glass of tea.

Joel warmed his hands over the coals of the samovar, and thought it a pity that Hannah was getting older every day, and the older – the crosser. Nevertheless, he liked the idea of having a little flirt with her, of tickling her under the chin, of placing his ancient hand on the back of her parched, wrinkled neck, and he did not stop at the mere idea. Hannah nearly overturned the samovar, and as was her wont when Joel became frolicsome, she scolded him most vehemently, told him that he was nothing but an old fool, while memories came back to her of times which seemed to be of yesterday and of long, long ago.

Towards evening the elders began to arrive one by one, until Reb Avram Ber's study overflowed with them. Most conspicuous of all were the two Mendels, "Big" Mendel and "Little" Mendel. The former was tall but with a bad stoop (as if ashamed of his great size!), and his head, supported by a brown curly beard, reared itself above the whole assembly. He wore a fur collar and long fur gloves, which hampered him as every now and then he tried to twirl the ends of his long drooping moustache. He had apparently just returned from the forest and had not had time to change. Then "Little" Mendel – a tiny fellow, with a tiny pinched nose perched on a tanned face, with a tiny roundish beard, and with two sparkling black eyes that were quite immense for so miniature a creature. These eyes of his never kept still for a second. At one moment they would penetrate into your innermost soul, read all the secrets hidden there, and at the next, in passing, they would peep in to see what was happening within your neighbor. He was quick to find his bearings, and knew everything. You could not deceive him. Dressed in a somewhat worn black cloth coat, a pair of childish galoshes (which, like the broker, he did not take off when coming into the room – lest they should be gone by the time he went out), enveloped in a large red woolen scarf taken from his own shop (where the stocks verily reached the low ceiling), he did not in appearance betray that great wealth with which the villagers credited him. He was held in great esteem because of this belief – and he knew it.

The two Mendels formed the core of the congregation. The rest had come more or less for the sake of propriety. They said very little, but listened attentively to what the two had to say. Today, possibly for the first time in his life, Reb Caiman was suffused with a deep red from the nape of his neck to the tips of his ears, for "Little" Mendel, contrary to his custom, gave him a long and searching look before he could make up his mind about him. However, by way of compensation, he darted only a fleeting glance at Gimpel and immediately recognized his man. Gimpel returned the glance with interest. He could not make out why that tiny mite had stared so curiously first at his son-in-law and then at himself. What did that little doll mean by it?

"Gentlemen!" said Reb Avram Ber, looking down first at "Little" Mendel and then up at "Big" Mendel, then at the general assembly. "Gentlemen, as you see, I must leave you. It is so ordained by God, for man does not make the slightest movement, does not stir his little finger, without that it has previously been determined in the heavens. I–," said Reb Avram Ber; but at this point "Big" Mendel exchanged a look with "Little" Mendel, whereupon the rest of the throng looked round themselves significantly and waited for one of the Mendels to speak. Reb Avram Ber's study was filled with the sound of breathing. No one uttered a word. Reb Avram Ber took advantage of the silence and continued:

"You see this young man, Reb Caiman, here? Well, Reb Caiman is, the Lord be praised, a profound Talmudist. More, he is – one might say – a sage, well versed in our Holy Knowledge. We have only just had a discussion, and I must admit that he wore me out."

Reb Caiman gazed intently into an open book lying on the table and never lifted his eyes. Gimpel gathered that he had reason to be pleased with what Reb Avram Ber had said concerning his son-in-law, and he looked at Reb Avram Ber with an expression of animal gratitude. All eyes turned upon Reb Caiman. Reb Caiman smiled faintly in recognition and quickly lowered his eyes again. "Big" Mendel, "Little" Mendel and – for the sake of appearances – the rest of the elders, approved Reb Avram Ber's negotiations with Reb Caiman for the disposal of the benefice. Joel brought in a bottle of whiskey and beakers. The health was drunk of the old and the new rabbi. The crowd wished them both luck, and chatted a while. Reb Caiman exerted himself to exchange a few words with the elders of his new flock.

Before taking their leave the villagers went into Raizela's room, paid her their respects, wished her happiness, and one by one they left for home.

That evening left a deep impression on both Deborah and Michael. They remembered it all through the years to come.

As soon as the villagers had departed, Reb Caiman drew himself erect and squared his shoulders, as porters do after throwing down a heavy load from their backs. From under his black bushy eyebrows he threw a look of gratitude to Reb Avram Ber.

"Well, Reb Caiman, you will soon be assuming your new duties. I am sure you will be a success."

Reb Avram Ber held out his hand. Reb Caiman took it and pressed it with such warmth, that even Joel felt the glow of that handshake.

Raizela came in. Pale, thin, and with those large grey eyes of hers, she looked like a Talmudist who spends his days and nights and years in study, rather than a woman. Even the black dress and velvet jacket she had on scarcely betrayed her. Reb Avram Ber pulled a chair up for her and politely bade her be seated, as if she were his guest.

"You know, of course, that the elders, that is to say, Reb Mendel and er…" Reb Avram Ber had almost said "Little" Mendel, but he checked himself in time. He racked his brain for the correct surname, but could not remember it. At last he cried out gleefully, "and Reb Mendela Shvairdsharf, they have both, the Lord be praised, given their consent."

"I know. Congratulations!" Raizela said quietly to Reb Caiman and Gimpel. The latter watched her with the expression of a cow when it turns its head to discover by whom it is being milked. A thought crossed his mind that she it was who was now depriving him of a little fortune; then another thought, that possibly he could bring the price down once more if he tried. He tried.

It had always been the broker's misfortune that when a transaction was all but completed – all that remained for him to do was, seemingly, to stretch forth his hand and pocket the commission – then some hitch occurred unexpectedly and everything ended in smoke. For this very reason he had viewed the present negotiations with a skeptical air, notwithstanding his mannerism of chalking up on the table the interests that would accrue from the commission. At Gimpel's essay, and flushed as he was with his rare success, he now became so confused and flustered, that spots began to dance before his eyes. He lost his head entirely. Catching sight of Raizela's wan features, he decided that she was to blame for everything: calculating and cruel, she would at a touch destroy all the fruits of his victory. He failed to see that it was Gimpel who had started his haggling all over again.

Clutching his ritual fringes, the broker frenziedly lashed the air and cried out, "For shame, Madam! It is very wrong of you! The rabbi himself will tell you so. Saving your reverence, but it really is very, very wrong of you! Very! Why, what we're offering you is a little fortune!"

"This is no marketplace!" Raizela said to Gimpel with cold contempt, and made as if to walk out.

Seeing Raizela rise from the table, the broker became so alarmed, that he flew to the door, planted himself there firmly, prepared to let no one pass, and he screamed almost at the top of his voice:

"For shame! We are Jews, aren't we? Well then, we must settle the matter peacefully, here and now – and let's get it over!"

Raizela smiled her wise smile. She wanted to please him, this poor comical man. So she sat down again. Gimpel scarcely dared to breathe. Fear mingled with respect, an unaccountable feeling of awe dumbfounded him now as he looked at her once more.

"Well, here's luck!" Joel suddenly interposed, drowsily rubbing his eyes.

"Here's luck!" the company echoed his words, all except Raizela, and thereupon it was agreed that Reb Avram Ber was to receive a deposit within the next few days, the balance to be paid at the date of moving. And the price, of course, remained as stipulated by Raizela – six hundred rubles.

Only on his way back to the inn did Gimpel, who was a keen bargainer and indeed always bought cheaper than his competitors, begin to wonder why he had withered under Raizela's gaze, accepting her demands without a whisper. What had made him so afraid of her?

"A very funny woman!" he remarked to his son-in-law, with a pang of regret.

"A very clever and a worthy woman!" retorted Reb Caiman, and softly, quite softly, he added, "Of course, she comes of good stock… the daughter of a learned man.… What a difference!…"

Chapter 3

When the last of the strangers had gone, the family grouped themselves in a corner of the living room to discuss the events of the day in unwonted intimacy. Raizela felt as if some great change had, of its own accord, descended upon their modest way of life, and she could not accustom herself to the thought that it was she who had consented to it all. Nevertheless, had the occasion arisen, she would again have given her consent – and again rather reluctantly.

A bittersweet mood took possession of them directly the strangers left, a sort of yearning for the past and a misty vision of the future. Even Deborah and Michael's jubilations were forced. No one, however, revealed his feelings to the other, nor gave the slightest hint of them. The family talked far into the night, recalling every incident, laughing heartily over many of them, and outwardly everybody seemed quite cheerful.

It was four o'clock when they went to bed. In spite of the lateness of the hour, sleep would not come. Only towards dawn did the first snores rise up from the beds, and a faint odor of perspiration and warmth filled the air.

Deborah was unable to fall asleep even towards dawn. She tossed about in her bed, smothered herself up completely in the feather bed, but to no avail. If she could only talk to the night watchman out on his beat and induce him to stop pacing backwards and forwards on the crumbling roadway outside her window, perhaps by offering him some of her father's tobacco. Every crunching step he took in his heavy boots was simply torture to her. In the heated turmoil of her mind she imagined that it was he who prevented her from falling asleep.... How terribly dark and thick the air was, as if the night had poured barrels of pitch over the whole world. And it seemed to be getting darker still. What a long, long night! And they had gone to bed so very late. She dug herself into the hot bedclothes, tucked her head in and drew up her legs, so that her hair and knees rested upon her belly, but that did not help.

"No wonder Mother calls me a silly wild goose! No wonder! The rest of them are all asleep. They didn't work themselves up into a frenzy. Deborah, you're mad!" she cried into a mouthful of bedding. "Go to sleep, will you?"

In the end, when all her self-remonstrances proved unavailing, she slipped out of bed, lit the tiny paraffin lamp and tried to read a fragment of newspaper which one of the elders had forgotten on the table and which she had hidden away as a rare treasure. The shadows on the wall trembled. A stifling sickly stench spread over the room. She turned down the offending wick, hid the paper under her pillow, and when the light of morning was waxing strong, she finally dozed off.

It was midday when the family awoke. They dressed in haste.

"Dear, dear, what a time to get up! Pish, pish!" said Reb Avram Ber.

Deborah awoke gaily. The few hours of sleep had refreshed her. All that had passed yesterday came back to her. Well, the momentous step had been taken.

Hannah came in. Deborah caught her round the waist and impetuously danced her round the room. Hannah flared up. Her seared face assumed an even grimmer expression than usual.

"Let me be!" she cried, pushing her away. "I'm in no dancing mood, not me! And what's the matter with you, anyway? What have you got to dance about? Nothing, believe me!"

Deborah stepped back in confusion. Hannah's words had pricked her like a needle. She wandered away gloomily, but since Michael was still on the most friendly terms with her, it was not long before she left off moping because Hannah would not share her joy, and after breakfast brother and sister repaired to the river like true comrades (an occurrence without precedent), there to build plans for the future. She quite forgot that such a woman as Hannah existed.

There on the river, which still stood frozen and firm although spring was at hand, Michael gave boisterous expression to his great, great joy.

The Passover holiday was over. The family were packing. The home was topsy-turvy. Michael refused point blank to have any truck with his old overcoat: he would leave it behind. Deborah pointed out that it might come in useful, but Michael paid no heed.

"Rot!" he said. "Who wants a shabby old coat like this? Old rags!"

He was now wearing his new gabardine. What did he care if he might soil it? Not a bit! Deborah protested. Why had not *she* put on her new frock? Had they not had all their new clothes made specially for their new home?

Raizela was no longer reclining on her couch.

Reb Avram Ber was helping Joel to transfer the books into large wooden packing cases. He was perspiring freely, and constantly mopped his face and beard. Joel was working sluggishly, as if he did it only to keep up appearances. Soon he would be beadle to Reb Caiman, soon he would have new duties thrust upon him and he deemed it best to spare his strength.

However, a few villagers showed up and offered to lend a hand. They abused him for his laziness, then told him to get out of their way, and they set to work with a will. Reb Avram Ber watched them, and wiping the sweat from his forehead, he marveled at their skill. He smiled with contentment as he smoked his pipe and breathed huge clouds of smoke.

"Pish, pish!" he exclaimed with admiration. "Just look at them!"

He stroked his beard.

The villagers did not trifle. Clip-clap! Clip-clap! – and there stood the cases all nailed up and fastened with rope, and there were the bedclothes and other household articles packed in huge wickerwork baskets or bundled up in sacking. Reb Avram Ber felt so grateful to them. How could he ever thank them? His gentle face simply shone with pleasure, there was such a good-natured look in his eyes, and his smile was so infectious, the very pipe in his mouth seemed to be smiling too. Inspired by Reb Avram Ber, the villagers flocked into the kitchen to offer their help there. They would not allow Raizela to touch a thing.

"No, you know how delicate you are," they said to her, "You must be careful. If only Deborah will be so kind as to tell us what to do, you can leave it to us – we'll do it!"

Hannah was indisposed. Her head bandaged up with a filthy handkerchief, she lay upon Raizela's couch and from this point of vantage watched the villagers at their labors.

"Let 'em get on with it! It'll do 'em good! Oh Lord, give them my headache, will you?"

She was in a black study, her mind racked by doubts as to whether the new rabbi's wife would engage her. But she consoled herself with cold comfort. She sighed:

"Ah well, something is sure to turn up. Anyway, one last shirt and one last hope are worse than useless!"

Mottel, an orphan who was supported by the community so that he might study in the house of worship and who, when assistance failed him, took his meals at Reb Avram Ber's table, was busy too. He was rejoicing, for yesterday Reb Avram Ber had informed him that he might accompany the family to the town of R– and there enter the new yeshiva. He was showing great industry and constantly busied himself over tasks which brought him close to Deborah. Occasionally their eyes met. Once he had even touched her hand. A shiver had gone thrilling through his body. It was as though something were running down his spine. He too was dressed up in a "new" gabardine, one that Reb Avram Ber had obtained on his behalf from "Big" Mendel's clerk. He also had a new hat. They were rather a tight fit for him, but then he looked quite the young spark in that grey gabardine, with its tails and two grey buttons on the back. As for his spectacles, he had given them such a brilliant polish that day, that no matter what Deborah did, she could not help seeing herself reflected in the lenses.

A crunching of wheels and a clinking of harness announced the arrival of Abbish. He had two carts, one for the passengers and another for the luggage. Almost the whole village had assembled outside the rabbi's house. The boys had a day off from school and they were kicking up a shindy. They clambered onto the carts, stood up on the spokes of the wheels, got cuffs and kicks from Abbish and his man Itchela, but what did they care? It was better than being whacked by the schoolmaster.

Already Abbish was hitching up the rope on top of the tarpaulin that covered the chattels in case of rain. He gave the final touches, and now they were off. Michael exulted. How his pals and even the grown-ups envied him! He was enjoying himself. A cluster of small boys was hanging on to the tailboard. Michael drew Abbish's attention to this churlish conduct. Abbish felt for his whip and the youngsters all scattered, but were all back again the moment he turned his head. The wheels plowed through and churned up the earthen village roadway.

Raizela was by now weary of nodding her head to right and to left, weary of smiling in acknowledgment to farewells and parting blessings showered upon her by humble women who had been lacking in courage to come and say goodbye personally and did so now *en passant*. Half the village, at the very least, men and women and children, escorted the family a goodly distance, all the way to the meadows by the river. They walked step by step with the horses, talking and laughing, giving counsel and blessings. The horses accompanied the uproar, with the rhythmical stamp! stamp! of their newly-shod hoofs. And at every renewed outburst of womanish sentimentality, they lifted their heads and uttered a loud neigh, as if they too wished to put in a word, or give their blessing or perhaps even give some counsel – counsel to the women that they were overdoing things, that it was no good going on forever. In the end the women themselves realized that it was no good going on forever, and at last after a few final exchanges, they turned for home. Abbish climbed up on to his seat, made himself comfortable, swished his whip over the horses' heads and cried:

"Gee up! Come on now, me hearties!"

This was what the horses had been waiting for. High-spirited after many days of inaction, they let themselves go, and how they galloped! The cart swayed and jumped and with a great clatter and thunder of hoofs it seemed to leave the ground and simply flew through the air. Reb Avram Ber became alarmed lest it should overturn, and Abbish was obliged to slow down somewhat.

Soon the village was out of sight, but after going only five or six miles they came upon a Jewish hamlet, Senzimin. Here they stopped, for Reb Avram Ber would not dream of passing without so much as saying goodbye to the inhabitants who were his parishioners. Abbish pulled a wry face. But he had to yield: Reb Avram Ber was the master!...

During the halt the horses gulped down a pail of water each, then buried their muzzles in the thick grass and resigned themselves to the inevitable. It was no use showing impatience: Jews would be Jews, and *would* have their own Jewish way! Deborah fretted. She would have loved to be off again, to draw ever nearer and nearer to R–. But the menfolk of Senzimin, and more so the womenfolk, were people with secret longings and yearnings of their own, and had to give expression to these feelings once in a while. After all, surrounded always by peasants, cattle and sheep, they never saw a new Jewish face from one year's end to the other, except when they went to Jelhitz for the High Holy Days, and now that such a golden opportunity had presented itself – the rabbi himself and his family (God bless them!) here in the hamlet – were they going to let the occasion pass without due celebration? It was not as if they saw a really respectable Jew every day of the week or every week of the month. What if Hershl Stock did tramp into the hamlet regularly each week, with his exposed chest all hairy, like a peasant, with his muddy top boots slung over his shoulder, with his long shaggy beard and his hand gripping a stout, knotty stick that had a large nail protruding at one end, looking for all the world like a highway bandit, but coming only to buy pigs' bristles – could one call him a Jew? Was he a Jew worthy of the name? So the present occasion was indeed one to rejoice over, and they made the most of it.

The greatest joy and honor fell to the lot of "Uncle" Jonah, whose custom it had been to bring Raizela some gift early each autumn, such as a sackload of potatoes, carrots, beetroots and other vegetables which would keep during the winter. To be sure, it was no mean privilege to have the rabbi greet you and clasp your hand before turning to the other farmers of the hamlet, and to give you such a radiant smile that it made you tingle all over. His good wife, leaving him in a state of bewildered festivity, meanwhile slipped into her cottage, rummaged about in the pantry and soon returned with a round of dried yellow cheese made almost entirely from cream, and with a pound of yellow butter patted in between two newly plucked green leaves. Both the butter and the green leaves were moist with silvery drops of water so bright and pure, it verily made everybody's mouth water.

Youngsters from afar, noticing that something was afoot in the hamlet, something which might very well concern themselves, promised their Christian comrades a lump of sweet white Sabbath bread, and entrusting herds of cattle, sheep and goats to their care, rushed home to welcome – whom, they did not know.

Other women followed the example set by Jonah's wife. They brought to light whatever treasures they had: a pot of cream, or homemade preserves, or a bottle of raspberry juice, things that were not to be touched in the ordinary way but were kept in reserve for special occasions, such as a wedding or (God forbid!) an illness. Raizela protested. She thanked them, but what would she do with all these delicacies? She pleaded with them; but they were deaf to her entreaties. They simply put the gifts into the cart, tucked them up in straw, and hoped that the rabbi and his family would enjoy these refreshments on their journey.

The horses having drained the remaining water in the pails, again held their heads out uncomfortably as Abbish led them by the halter. Again there was the stamp! stamp! of powerful hoofs, again a shower of blessings and counsels, but now these homely folk were waving the last farewell. When the hamlet was left behind, Reb Avram Ber suggested that he and Raizela should move over onto the other cart.

"We won't get bumped about so much," he said.

Raizela consented: she would be able to get on with her reading in greater comfort. So Itchela adjusted some soft bundles for them to sit upon.

The "children" now had the cart all to themselves. That was magnificent. Magnificent was hardly the word for it!

The air was laden with the scent of fresh grass. The trees were showing leaves already – so bright and green and tender. On some trees there were full-grown leaves hanging among hosts of heavy reddish buds which seemed ready to burst into blossom and to cover the dark, lush boughs at any moment. The sky here was infinitely loftier than in Jelhitz or even Senzimin, and was steeped from horizon to horizon with a brilliant golden light. The sky rested motionless over the world. And if, at times, a tiny white cloud emerged, it was powerless to stir, for all was at peace. The sun poured its rays down upon the bare fields, pierced the scattered trees and splashed its brilliance over the peasant huts and hovels which, strewn over field and meadow, and half sunken into the ground, looked like strange plants growing out of the spring earth ready whitewashed by nature. They hugged their shadows tight. All was at rest. All was radiant, fresh and alive with the life of early spring.

"God bless your labors!" Abbish called out to peasant men and women engaged in plowing and sowing with an intent and eager air. Small thin-legged horses were stubbornly dragging shiny plows, under which the soil sprang up black as soot. Every movement of the laborers rippled with health and vigor.

"May God give you health!" the peasants responded, making the sign of the cross.

Reb Avram Ber could not understand Polish, but he guessed that greetings were being exchanged. And he felt a keen desire to say something himself. He might have managed a few words in Russian, for had he not once spent two whole weeks studying the language? There were still a few phrases he remembered. Suddenly he was overcome by a passionate feeling of love towards those strangers in the fields, at their health-giving and useful toil.

"Man was created for labor," he quoted.

Everything around him was so full of love and beauty. His feelings mastered him, and he began to sing joyfully: "How glorious and pleasant, most holy, are Thy…" He forgot that it was the season of *Sefira,* when music is forbidden, but Raizela immediately pulled him up. Reb Avram Ber broke off, the sudden interruption leaving a trace of sadness on his face. But no man, least of all Reb Avram Ber, could remain downcast for very long on such a glorious day.

The carts rolled on. The peasants were lost to sight; the hammock suspended between two trees, the sleeping child, the linen spread out on the ground for bleaching, vanished. The fields were now vast and solitary: not a soul was to be seen. The soil was black and furrowed, but already it was showing signs of birth – tiny green corn blades.

Reb Avram Ber felt restless. His heart thumped and trembled in exultation. He began humming again, but checked himself.

"*Sefira, Sefira!*" he murmured.

Suddenly he felt he would like to embrace Raizela and kiss her. But, for one thing this was not the place – absurd to think of it! – and for another, Raizela was so deep in thought, she looked so terribly solemn.… The cart swayed on and on, and after a time Reb Avram Ber dozed off. Raizela's eyelids too were drooping and viscid. She had strained her eyes with reading. (Incidentally, she had noted and taken in the wondrous beauty of the day as sensitively as the others and perhaps even more so.) She fell asleep.

Michael was whistling as loudly as ever he could. He sat on the driver's seat, beside Abbish, and fingered the reins. Every now and again he egged the horses on in a truly professional manner, although they still trotted along with great briskness and needed no constant "Gee-ups!" or clicks of the tongue by way of encouragement. However, since it gave Michael pleasure to do so, Abbish was not going to deprive him of his fun.

All this time Mottel kept squirming as if he had the itch. Empty though the cart was, he could not settle down. He was continually edging towards Deborah. Now he sat so close to her that she could feel the warmth of his young boyish body. A shiver ran through her and a sensation which she knew she ought to be ashamed of, to conceal. So she crimsoned, and thus only revealed her guilt all the more. She moved away; but Mottel persisted. He wriggled and writhed and sidled up. He hardly noticed the beauty of the scenes through which they were passing. Deborah engulfed him completely. Suddenly he whispered something to her, so softly that she heard it only by the promptings of her instinct. She made no reply, but moved away. Mottel snuggled up against her. Suddenly she felt that he had enclosed her hand in his big palm, and it scorched her, it was burning hot. She tore her hand away and flushed crimson all over. Her eyes filled with mist. And how fortunate it was that she had kept her presence of mind, for at that very instant Michael turned his head. If he had caught them in the act!...

Another three hours went by, and already the sun was low in the skies. Faraway horizons grew still remoter. Small wisps and whole mountains of burnished copper clouds moved in stately fashion over the clear blue sky, growing larger and shinier with every passing minute. Distant treetops seemed to catch fire and to approach. Peasants began to make for home across the footpaths, hatchets and saws in hand or slung over their shoulders. Some called out a friendly word of greeting, others just stopped to watch the two carts go by. Felling trees in this early hot weather was no joke, and coarse linen shirts were clinging, quite drenched, to aching backs. Large drops of sweat were poised on bulging temples. Youths uttered long, low whistles every now and then in exultant anticipation. They felt the pangs of hunger through the livelong day. The cattle too were unable to eat their fill in the meadows, with the grass so young. Hence they were all wending their way home with hearty appetites. The girls had gone before them to prepare supper, and from low chimneys there rose white coils of smoke and blue coils of smoke – a promise of cooked food, hard welcome beds and sweet sleep.

At length Abbish decided to halt. Itchela slipped the nosebags over the horses' heads. But the animals chewed the fodder reluctantly, every now and then lifting their heads out of the bags to turn them this way and that, as though with an air of disapproval. They had their tongues hanging out and halfheartedly tried to swallow the morsels caught in saliva. Their viscid nostrils dilated as if endeavoring to sniff something in the air. Itchela came back from a nearby pond, with a bucket of water in either hand. The horses snorted, reared, and almost overturned the buckets as they thrust in their eager heads. In a moment the buckets were emptied. The water was still dripping freely from their muzzles, when Itchela was back with two more – this time for his own horses, and Abbish immediately set off to get a fresh supply himself. On this occasion the water did not meet with such a lively reception, but it was accepted nevertheless. Abbish replaced the bags, Itchela did likewise, and seeing with what relish the horses were now munching their oats, it whetted their own appetites.

Abbish tossed a hefty lump of black rye bread over to his mate, followed by a large piece of dried sausage, and the two of them did themselves justice. Raizela called up to Michael. She handed him a parcel. What treats that parcel contained! – pancakes, cheese, gingerbread, large juicy pears, all kinds of fruit juice, and what not. Reb Avram Ber muttered grace after grace over each separate victual. As for Raizela, she seemed too busy responding "Amen!" to partake of very much herself. Abbish wiped his moustache, picked the crumbs out of his beard and thanked the "children" for all the delicacies to which they had treated him. He handed Itchela a flask of water, climbed up on to his seat and gaily called out to the horses:

"Now get a move on, me beauties!"

But apparently Abbish had never been that way before, for with the best will in the world the horses could not now comply with his behest. The road ended abruptly in a stretch of soft clay. For quite an hour the wheels struggled in the mess, now sinking to the axle, now dragging themselves out again, only to go under once more, until at last the outskirts of the forest were reached, which all this while seemed so close at hand, one had only to put one's fingers out to grasp the twigs of the foremost trees.... A sorry illusion, for the fight took a whole hour, and with every inch of ground gained, the going got heavier – a veritable little wilderness barring meadow from forest.

"Come on, you cripple, shift yourself!" a burly young giant with a large round face and sinewy arms bawled at a small emaciated horse which had got stuck and seemed to be using its prominent ribs rather than its legs as it strained at the cartload of clay to which it was harnessed. It was doing its best to please its master, a bony peasant with a clay-besmeared face and clayey beads of sweat as big as peas on his upper lip, but the peasant flogged the animal furiously. The young giant who was looking on, himself fresh and still bursting with energy after the day's toil, put his hack and saw on to the cart, and digging himself in, put his shoulder to the cart. It bumped out of the ruts and was soon standing safely on firm ground.

Abbish was whacking his horses for all he was worth. The young giant glanced over his shoulder at him. "Jewish horses!" he muttered, and slinging his hack over his shoulder, went on his way.

Abbish lost his temper. He cursed Itchela for ill-treating the horses.

"They're not yours, are they, you big lout? You don't care if you cripple them, do you? If you weren't such a lousy, clumsy blockhead, we'd have been miles away by now."

He conveniently overlooked the fact that he was in the lead himself.

The ordeal was over at last. At last they had entered the forest. They all retook their places in the carts, which stopped a while to give the horses a rest. Abbish wiped the sweat off himself and off his horses with the same dirty piece of cloth. The animals blinked and looked back at him with gratitude in their yellow eyes.

The forest was entirely ablaze. The tops of the fir trees loftily reached for the sky, which although still a translucent blue, was scarcely noticed here.

Abbish was back on his seat, and he sent Michael packing.

"You get off of here, and stay where you belong, and stop making yourself a nuisance!" he fumed, quite forgetting that this was not Itchela whom he was addressing. Michael did as he was told. He had had enough anyway.

Already the outer belt of forest, on which clearing work had been begun only the week before – and it was still pretty dense – was in full retreat. The sturdy pines and slender firs were recoiling, and above the sky had emerged once more over a wide belt of whitewashed saplings – and the going was good. A pale slice of moon had come out, and soon sparkling stars were assembling, playful, frolicsome and young – just like the saplings.

But then they came to a dismal stretch of woodland. Here the corpses of once living trees stood all in disorder, their knotty backs bent, the tracery of their branches disheveled, their hideously drooping boughs all bare, so that they inspired one with dread, with terrible forebodings. These trees looked like crafty, hulking old men, and their boughs like trembling hands stretched forth, secretively, to capture something in the gathering dusk. Fear crept over Deborah, fear mingled with loathing, and she was glad when they finally came into the forest proper.

On either side of them it stretched dense and dark. The track, beaten by hoofs which had passed this way before, grew narrower and darker the deeper it penetrated into the forest. The air was perfumed, far sweeter than any honey.

"Ah! Ah! Have you ever smelt anything like it?" an unspoken question hovered on all lips, but there was no breath to spare for speech. Everybody was silent and drank in the scented May air of a Polish forest at night.

"Look, a rabbit!" cried Deborah.

Michael turned his head, but too late – the rabbit had vanished.

"What a shame, you should have seen it! It simply flew along as if it had wings. It did look dainty!"

"Ha, ha! Ever seen a rabbit look dainty?" Michael scoffed. "You're a real joke, you are!"

"You should have seen it!" Deborah persisted.

"Oh, give the rabbit a rest! I don't want to see it," said Michael, while his gaze eagerly sought the ground.

Reb Avram Ber, having said his evening prayers, decided that it would be safest for them to travel all in one cart overnight. He tugged the hem of Itchela's jacket, Itchela turned his head and listened. The uncouth fellow did not appear impressed, he disposed of Reb Avram Ber's fears with a wave of the hand, but had to yield in the end and he shouted over to Abbish to stop. Again Raizela climbed down from one cart and on to another. She did not seem very pleased about it. Abbish shared her displeasure.

"A forest," said Abbish, "is a very funny place. To dillydally in it is asking for trouble. The Polish forests aren't so safe as they used to be, especially at night. No, sir!"

Raizela gave him a searching look, but did not comment on his heavy sarcasm.

"That's the reason why I said it was best if we all traveled together. And we ought not to fall asleep, either," said Reb Avram Ber.

"If we do that, maybe robbers will seize us, take all our belongings and rip our guts open!" Itchela put in teasingly.

"If you keep awake," said Abbish, trying to make good Itchela's clumsy jest (that fellow was a lout!), "if you keep awake, you can always ransom your lives."

"Very comforting!" thought Raizela.

"If you don't keep awake, you may get up in the morning and find your heads lopped off, and worse still, find all your belongings gone," chimed in Michael with a great air of bravado, but he turned his face to hide the signs of fear on it.

"Michael, hold your tongue!" Reb Avram Ber admonished him, in his "sternest" manner. "Open not thy mouth unto Satan," he added in a soft, tremulous voice.

"Be quiet, idiot!" said Raizela.

Deborah shrank into her coat. Mottel closed his eyes.

Michael now deeply regretted the words he had uttered. Somehow, they seemed to have intensified the hazards and perils.

When they were all in the one cart, Abbish cracked his whip, and they proceeded at a trot through the very heart of the forest. The heavy odors of the night were intoxicating. The cart rocked, swayed, and the passengers, in spite of their resolve not to fall asleep, let their heads droop one by one, raising them every now and again in an attempt to resist slumber, but weariness triumphed, and they slept soundly.

It was only when the carts had come to a standstill at R –, that everybody woke up with a start.

Chapter 4

The sun came up like a clot of blood, with promise of another brilliant sunny day. Deborah felt bewildered. When had they left the forest? She rubbed her eyes. Surely she had not dropped off to sleep?

They were in R–. The one-storied houses of the main street, where Abbish had pulled up to enquire from Reb Avram Ber the whereabouts of the *tzaddik*'s court, looked to her like soaring skyscrapers in her drowsy state of mind. The town slept. The windows were all draped, some with rich curtains or embroidered blinds, others with cheap but clean half curtains, others again with sheets and even pinafores. Here and there the light of a lamppost glowed feebly, ineffectively.

Somewhere on a bench in the open lay the sleeping figure of an old Jew – or was it a gentile? She could not tell. He lay there all of a heap, with his head between his hands. Deborah shuddered. Never before had she seen such a pitiful sight.

Fulsher, Jelhitz's own madman, came to her mind. Even he had his couch in a loft up in the synagogue. True, there were occasions when he never went to bed, but stood slamming the door all through the night, crying that it was his mother (who was long dead) that was pushing the door and pinning him down by his lungs and his liver every time he tried to get away. He would weep and whine, complaining that his mother was too quick for him. Ghostly, the bang-bang of the door and the frenzied shouting would ring through the night-smothered village. Only with the first streaks of morning would he leave off and, exhausted, sink down into oblivion in the doorway of the synagogue. Well, he was a madman; but the huddled up person on the bench over there, one could tell – even as he slept – that that was no madman. Such a wave of pity passed over her for the poor destitute white head of hair, that a pang of hate was born in her, hatred of the town where such a sight was possible.

The carts passed slowly through the tortuous streets, and after much pother turned into a small square courtyard. Abbish and Itchela between them unloaded the cart and carried the goods away through one of the doorways in the courtyard.

"Hallo, Deborah, what are you gaping at? Don't you see, this is the end of the journey?" said Reb Avram Ber.

Deborah hardly paid any attention. She stumbled along and gazed upwards at the veiled windows. So many rooms in that one house alone, and yet there was an old man sleeping out in the street. Her people were calling her, so she went in.

"Anyhow, it's a good job there's that bench by the pump for him to sleep on," she thought, trying to console herself, but it was no use. In the end she decided that he must be a lunatic too, and she was comforted.

Soon she was engaged in viewing the rooms of their new home. All was so different from Jelhitz. The ceilings were whitewashed, but not the walls; these were painted over with a pattern of brown flowers on a blue background. Brown flowers! She could not help laughing. No wonder they were brown, growing on brick walls....

She paid a visit to all three rooms and the kitchen. It was a splendid flat, with large windows, lofty and airy.

"What are you wandering around for, Deborah? You'd better help your mother arrange something to sleep on. She is so tired. And you could do with some more sleep yourself. It's only about five o'clock."

Deborah undid the bundles of bedding and rigged up two "couches" on the floor. Her mother laid herself down. Reb Avram Ber said his early morning prayers and followed her example. Ah, it was good to be able to stretch one's limbs once more! Deborah lay with her head resting on her mother's pillow.

Their first day in the small town of R–, the day which had been the focus of so many of Deborah's dreams, passed away quite unexcitedly. The family just drifted into their new life, and the only strange sensation was a certain unpleasant feeling of loneliness....

Reb Avram Ber was the first to awake.

"Where's Michael?" he said, rousing Deborah.

Raizela heard him in her sleep.

"Oh dear, what's happened to him?" She wrung her hands. "Where could Michael have got to? He'll lose himself in this strange place."

As he was nowhere to be found in the courtyard, nor in any of the closets, there would have been quite a hue and cry, had not Michael turned up at that very moment, his face all beaming. He failed to see the black looks which were given him, in which joy mingled with dark threats. He rushed into the room where Mottel was lying and gave him a kick. Mottel opened a pair of sleepy, rather bad-tempered eyes, which stared at him in amazement.

"What a lot of sleepyheads!" cried Michael, actually referring only to Mottel. He said "a lot," because it added emphasis. "If you had only seen what I've seen! Crumbs, what a town! What a town! Just like Jelhitz, and I don't think!"

"Where have you been, eh?" asked Reb Avram Ber, trying to be stern.

"Nowhere!"

"Where's nowhere?" interposed Raizela crossly.

"I was in the courtyard."

"But you weren't in the courtyard!"

"I was!" persisted Michael.

"Well, what's the use? So long as he's back, the scamp!"

Reb Avram Ber felt that it was incumbent on him to act the host here. He conducted Raizela round the rooms. Although he had seen them before, he studied them with fresh interest and drew her attention to all the good points. Raizela did not show the least sign of pleasure. She looked vexed and grieved, although there was nothing she could find fault with. All was admirable. The walls were freshly done up, the ceilings spotless and smooth – vastly superior to Jelhitz, but somehow the place did not appeal to her. At least in Jelhitz one had had something tangible to disapprove of.

"Good, eh?" inquired Reb Avram Ber with much satisfaction.

An ancient knee thrust open the front door, and the owner of the limb appeared, bearing a tray in his flabby old hands that trembled palpably. The tray was crowded with tumblers, spoons, a jugful of warm milk, a bowl of sugar, several gingerbreads and a steaming kettle. The old man staggered up. He deposited the tray, rectified his crooked back somewhat, and still panting breathlessly, fumbled for something in his pocket.

"The *tzaddik*, that is to say the old lady, his mother, sends you these refreshments, with her compliments," he said, helping himself to a pinch of snuff.

"Thank you," said Raizela.

"He, he! No need to thank *me*! If the *tzaddik*, that is to say, the old lady, his mother hadn't sent me – he, he, he! – I can assure you I wouldn't have brought you all this of my own accord!"

Even Raizela condescended to smile. Reb Avram Ber was delighted.

"Well, Reb Baruch, do you think we shall be comfortable here?"

"Why, of course you will, of course! I wish I was in your shoes. You know, the *tzaddik* himself sent in word to his mother, telling her to tell the – atchoo! – the beadle to tell the cook to hand me… Atchoo! Atchoo!!"

Michael was struggling with inner mirth – this was evident from the concerted twitching of his features. He was either going to laugh or to make some very witty remark. But he was afraid to chance it in front of a newcomer in a new town.… He held his peace.

"Take a seat, Reb Baruch!" Reb Avram Ber invited the old man to join them, forgetting the while that there were no chairs.

The old man glanced about him.

"Why, you've nothing to sit on yourselves."

"That's all right, we'll soon remedy that," said Reb Avram Ber, himself pushing a box up.

They all settled down on cases and bundles of bedding. Deborah poured out the tea. Mottel felt that it was good to be alive today. He was like one of the family. Reb Avram Ber pressed the old man to accept a glass of tea. Raizela moved away on to the farthest bundle, and eagerly drank from her glass – her throat was parched. The old man, feeling Reb Avram Ber's friendly gaze fixed on him, began telling them all about the yeshiva. Reb Avram Ber exulted. Every now and then he cast a glance at Raizela to see if she was impressed.

The repast over, Reb Avram Ber passed his red-spotted handkerchief across his moustache. Their visitor, helping himself to more snuff, also wiped his mouth dry – with the flat of his hand. Then he accompanied Reb Avram Ber to the synagogue.

"Good morning!" the old man stuttered at the door, just managing to hold back a sneeze.

"How about you, Mottel? I expect to see you at the synagogue soon. And you too, Michael, I don't want you to dawdle," said Reb Avram Ber from the threshold.

Mottel slipped into the kitchen where Deborah was sulking in a corner. Mottel knew the cause of her bitterness: he had overheard Raizela scold her without any justification whatever, whereas Michael, who had been playing truant, had been let off without so much as a word. Favoritism, thought Mottel, not without indignation.

"How do you like it here?" he asked, because he wanted to say something to her, and immediately a thought struck him that this was a stupid question, for as yet they had seen nothing of the place either to like or dislike.

"So-so!" Deborah answered him morosely.

"What's the matter?" Mottel persisted, feeling more awkward than ever. Perhaps he ought not to have asked any questions?

"Do you believe in luck?" Deborah asked.

Now that was a peculiar question! It was so unexpected.

"Why, yes!" he said. And perhaps there was no such thing after all? Anyhow, none of it had ever come his way.

About two in the afternoon a rosy-cheeked girl with short chubby arms and gay eyes knocked at the door.

"The *tzaddik*'s mother has asked me to come along and help you put things straight," she announced.

This was a welcome visit.

Reb Avram Ber came home for a few brief minutes to have his lunch, and then went off to the yeshiva to deliver his first lecture.

"It would be a pity to waste any time," he told Raizela apologetically.

The maid set to work with a will. Now she was cleaning the windows and soon she was scrubbing the floors. Deborah offered to lend a hand, but quite offended her. Raizela was not a little amused by the girl's vanity. It was inconceivable that she always toiled with so much zest, but that she was no slattern like Hannah, that much was clear.

"Now I'll go and fetch the dinner," she said, unpinning her tucked up frock. She combed her hair with a broken comb, wiped her face on the edge of her pinafore and studied her reflection in the gleaming windowpanes. She returned with a heavy load of many dishes. The tablecloth, which Deborah had found for her, she spread out over several cases pushed together, and this hilly table she laid with massive silver cutlery and a fine porcelain dinner service. Nothing was omitted, not even the pepper pot.

While going about her task, with a more leisurely air now, she informed Raizela that the *tzaddik*'s wife – the "young one," as she called her – was a real diamond, and that his mother, the "old one," ought to take a lesson from her in good manners. If she, the maid, had been born under a lucky star and had not been an orphan, she would have entered the service of the young one and not the service of the old one. She collected the tea things, and after being very strongly pressed by Raizela, departed with fifteen kopecks in pocket.

A few days later, Laizer Nussen, the elder of the *tzaddik*'s five personal attendants, and the most insolent, the most blackguardly of them all, appointed himself – quite against Reb Avram Ber's will – as his right hand. He got hold of Reb Avram Ber's money for the purchase of furniture, ordered goods according to his own taste, consulted no one but himself, and spent just as much as he thought he would. Raizela hated the fellow; but such trivial matters as love and hate impressed Laizer Nussen not at all. He was nothing if not hardheaded and practical. Raizela's cautions to Reb Avram Ber not to trust him proved of no avail. He simply had to trust him, for such was Laizer Nussen's wish, and when Laizer Nussen wished a thing, he had his way with folks far wilier than Reb Avram Ber.

However, when the time came round for erecting the furniture, Laizer Nussen considered his duties at an end and he charged Reb Baruch to accomplish the task with the help of Zelik, the *tzaddik*'s manservant.

In spite of the fact that old Baruch was forever protesting that by rights none other than himself was the elder of the *tzaddik*'s personal attendants, and that had the father of the present *tzaddik* survived (his memory be blessed!), none other than he, Baruch, would have lorded it in the court, with Laizer Nussen a mere nobody – but the old *tzaddik* (his memory be blessed!) had departed this life many a year ago and was probably now holding court in paradise – in spite of all this, Baruch was under the orders of Laizer Nussen, always at his beck and call, and all he could do to express his rightful indignation was to take a pinch of snuff. To be sure he also found consolation in whiskey taken neat. But old Henya, Baruch's wife, always maintained that it was only since he had been deprived of his mantle of glory by Laizer Nussen that he had taken to tippling, and she denied the assertions of certain old inhabitants who would have it that Baruch had been addicted to his drop of whiskey even at the best of times. Anyhow, a grand old man was Reb Baruch, never drunk, though always drinking, and even though oftentimes, when he drifted away into dreams of the days gone by, when he romanced over tales of yore, he would lie on a shocking scale, giving the most fantastic descriptions replete with the minutest details to stamp them as authentic, still you could not help liking him and, what was more, become deeply absorbed in his yarns. One look at Reb Baruch was enough! It was fascinating to see him go into raptures, see his dim old eyes light up again and a smile play on his lips, himself fully believing in all those strange events and miracles which happened in the lifetime of the old *tzaddik* (his memory be blessed!) when he, Baruch, had bossed it in the court, with Laizer Nussen still unborn. Deborah adored these yarns, as she did the teller of them. And she positively came to hate Laizer Nussen for having usurped old Baruch's authority. Even Raizela was well disposed to him. She only used to marvel how so old and flabby a man, with one foot in the grave, came to be possessed of so fertile an imagination.

Zelik put up the beds – wooden beds with carved tops – beds that were remarkable in many ways. For one thing they looked distinctive, and for another they were dirt cheap, costing (as Laizer Nussen said) next to nothing. Actually, of course, twenty-five rubles for a couple of beds was a tidy bit, but then (as Laizer Nussen said) there are beds and beds. What beds! What a polish and a glitter, and the workmanship put into the carvings!

"Don't you like them?" said Laizer Nussen to Raizela. "What, you think the wood cheap? Well, what of it? You don't mean to tell me that it's the wood that counts. Rubbish, you're not going to fight the beds! Ah, may the Lord grant you good health and happiness in them!

"What's that? They'll start groaning later on when you get into them? Nonsense! Give them a dose of oil and they'll soon be cured. Ha, ha! Surely they're no better than mortal men," Laizer Nussen philosophized, and took his leave after repeating his instructions to Zelik.

Baruch rendered help by croaking to the rhythm of Zelik's hammer and by handing up the wrong tools. When the pincers were wanted he delivered a screwdriver. This rather annoyed Zelik, but he refrained from rudeness. After all, Baruch was one of the *tzaddik*'s personal attendants and an old man besides. Indeed, Baruch had grandchildren who were of the same age as Zelik. Furthermore, he had a warm corner in his heart for the old man.

When he had done with the beds and had given them a shaking to test their strength, Zelik turned his attentions to the wardrobe; this too had its good points, if one looked for them.

"It's just a bit on the narrow side," said Zelik, "and it's too much of a featherweight. Why, you could carry it off on your back."

However, the table eclipsed and atoned for everything: it was large and robust, with a high polish through which biggish ink stains were visible – apparently second-hand, but that was a detail. It was a table not to be compared with other tables. When a man could sit at a table like that, with its legs planted firmly on the floor like a bear's paws, with its edges a mass of carving, with its polish positively dazzling, and yet the whole so massive, so solemn, it gave him added inspiration for the study of the Talmud (said Laizer Nussen), and even food, when served on such a table, gained added relish. On the other hand, the kitchen table was brand new. So was the kitchen bench. The dresser was spick and span and had a commanding position opposite the door. As for the bench, that was finished off at either end with scallops. In each scallop a hole had been bored most artistically, and from under each hole a brass button sent forth a golden glitter.

"A pity they're not varnished. If I were you I'd have them varnished," said Zelik thoughtfully to Raizela. "Like this, they'll get dirty in no time."

"Don't be an ass!" Baruch put in, to the accompaniment of a pinch of snuff. "Varnish shmarnish! It's when they get dirty that you want to varnish them, not before! Ass!"

Zelik categorically refused to accept any beer money.

"May you enjoy it all in the best of health," he said and, collecting his tools, went off. Baruch followed him out, and now once more the family were installed in a home of their own, for which the Lord be praised.

Raizela had everything new: new furniture, a new home, a new town, a new life.... But with all this newness something else that was new stole over her – a new feeling of gloom, which depressed her without cause, a sense of oppression that grew heavier day by day, whilst Raizela's purse grew lighter day by day. Not that this was the source of the strange misery lurking in their new home, which Deborah tried for the time being at any rate to keep as prim as possible.

On the other hand, Reb Avram Ber daily returned from the yeshiva with fresh tidings of joy: students were flocking in from all parts of the country; the yeshiva was already one of the most important in Poland;

soon there would be no vacancies for fresh arrivals, and they would have to be turned back, unless a new wing was added to the building.

On the previous Sabbath, at his usual banquet, the *tzaddik,* while expounding the law, had introduced many Scripture texts, allusions and insinuations in his sermon to demonstrate how great were the heavenly rewards bestowed upon the charitable of the land who enabled poor Jewish students to pursue their studies of the Talmud. He begged – nay, commanded – every inhabitant of R– to make certain of securing such heavenly reward by inviting students to share the family board for at least one day in the week, as is the custom among pious Jews. This noble deed could be rendered nobler still by well-to-do people who could afford to share their board with students several days during the week. The *tzaddik* stated that for the time being the students were being fed in the communal kitchen established in the court, that the kitchen would be maintained hereafter as heretofore, but that to further the work of the yeshiva, it was essential that outside assistance should be volunteered, and solemnly he charged his followers to participate in his most holy mission. Solemnly two rows of beards pointed downwards at the long table. Solemnly the throng of Hasidim standing around the table shook their heads. After this the *tzaddik* returned to his usual preachings, and went off into celestial raptures.... The *tzaddik*'s appeal soon spread all over the town, and Jews freely offered their hospitality to the students – not for several days in the week, to be sure, but a large number invited students home for one day in the week.

Reb Avram Ber delivered his lectures day by day. Michael attended in the company of students many years his senior, but he was not a jot behind them. Deborah had plenty of housework to keep her occupied. Raizela alone found the time hanging heavy on her hands. Somehow she could find no relish in any of the books she picked up; she had not settled down yet, had not become accustomed to the feel of the new couch, which incidentally, like herself, had a very feeble constitution.

"You know, you would be well advised to pay a call on the *tzaddik*'s wife. It would make a delightful change. She's quite an exceptional person – a person of real dignity. She comes of a very good stock – the Balzaker *tzaddik* is her father – and she's very clever. Moreover, she's a learned woman," said Reb Avram Ber, and as he said these last few words, he scanned Raizela's face to see how they would impress her. Raizela smiled. She reflected that it would be well if some fitting occasion were to arise.

It arose very simply. One sunny morning the *tzaddik*'s wife sent her maid in with an invitation to Raizela. The girl did not look like a servant at all, dressed as she was in a neat white frock with a little white starched pinafore over it, and patent leather shoes on her tiny feet; nor did her face betray her – a pretty blonde with a captivating smile. As she entered, she simply brought new life into the place.

"The *tzaddik*'s wife begs you to be good enough to call on her for tea this afternoon," she said to the accompaniment of such a radiant smile, that even Raizela's thin lips parted.

The *tzaddik*'s wife, clad in a long black silk dress, with a long string of costly pearls round her white, plump throat, rose to her feet when Raizela entered, also clad in a black dress, but without a string of pearls on her thin, skinny neck. She came forward to welcome her visitor, bade her be seated, and directly created a favorable impression on Raizela. The woman's frank, clever expression, especially the eyes, were bound to please, and certainly Raizela was a keen judge of character. For the rest, everything in the chamber was set out so originally, with so much good taste, the mistress and her surroundings harmonized so perfectly, that the effect could not but please. The drapings on the walls, the silk curtains by the door and windows, dark blue and quiet; the furniture simple and yet artistically splendid – all was at one and endowed with her spirit. The atmosphere in the chamber was caressingly gentle: it did one's heart good, soothed the heavy spirit, dispelled oppressive thoughts, and characterized the individual who had known so well to arrange it all. Raizela felt at ease – in her own element. This was the milieu she was always pining for.

The *tzaddik*'s wife showed her a copy of a newly-published book which had reached her only that morning and which had been sent to her by a nephew, who incidentally was its author. Afterwards she led her to the bookcase, opened the glass panel and introduced her to what she called her "friends" – a rare collection of books in which she took great pride. She considered herself something of a connoisseur, and proved as much to Raizela by indirect means.… In front of this imposing array of books, Raizela felt sorely tempted, as though she had suddenly entered a large garden full of all kinds of fragrant flowers, none of which she could pluck, even though the mistress politely offered them to her. The *tzaddik*'s wife closed the bookcase again. They returned to their seats, and the maid with the pleasing frank face served tea and biscuits on an engraved silver tray which was deeply wrinkled with age. The spoons, the sugar bowl, the tongs, all bore the same blazonry as the tray and all showed the same signs of antiquity, bearing tribute to their common descent from an old and powerful family.

"Why, you haven't touched your tea yet. Please don't let it get cold. Would you rather have some fruit juice?"

"Oh no, thanks, please don't trouble!"

"As I was saying, we can never be lonely when we have our books. That is, of course, the right type of books," the *tzaddik*'s wife resumed, speaking for Raizela as well as for herself and again hinting that Raizela could have free access to the library if she wished. "You see, I know all about you. The rabbi (Reb Avram Ber) has told me all, and a passion for books is a fault we both of us share."

Raizela smiled with real pleasure.

When she returned home and told Reb Avram Ber where she had been, adding that she had found the *tzaddik*'s wife pleasant company, Reb Avram Ber stroked his beard with such an air of rejoicing, he could not have been more pleased if an unknown uncle had left him a million rubles.

"And what a wonderful collection of books she has!" said Raizela as an afterthought.

"You see! Didn't I always tell you that you would be far happier here than in Jelhitz. You never had anyone to exchange a word with in Jelhitz, but here you already have such a splendid friend. She's a very fine woman! So gentle…"

"True!" Raizela agreed.

"At present you only have a first impression. You'll think even more highly of her when you get to know her well," said Reb Avram Ber, his face wreathed in smiles, and he went on to say how the *tzaddik*'s wife was so esteemed by her husband's Hasidim, that many of them would not dream of paying him a visit without calling on her to pay her their respects.

"That shows how much they think of her. And to tell you the truth," added Reb Avram Ber, dropping his voice as though he feared the walls might hear him, "I've come to the conclusion that she's more deserving of respect than is…" Reb Avram Ber did not finish the sentence.

But Raizela understood. She was silent.

In the yeshiva all went smoothly. It stood in a corner of the spacious courtyard of the *tzaddik*'s residence full of majesty with its new bricks a fiery red and its corrugated iron roof glowing beneath the sun's scorching breath. The large windows were all flung wide open, and from them issued a sweet, melancholy chant which floated over the courtyard, turning and twisting and swelling, till it reached the street; then suddenly it withdrew, curling itself up secretively, full of mystery, but soon it rang out again boldly through the whole courtyard, and above all the voices that melted into one chant could be heard Reb Avram Ber's gentle and fatherly "*Yesh omrim*…."

Mottel rejoiced in the unexpected opportunity that came his way one morning when Reb Avram Ber, having left his pipe at home, picked on none other than Mottel to go and fetch it for him. Mottel, now taking his meals in the communal kitchen, had not been to Reb Avram Ber's house for a long time. He had hoped that one day he would receive an invitation, but that had not occurred to Reb Avram Ber at all, for he saw the boy every day, and how was he to guess that Mottel was simply burning with desire to see Deborah? Mottel set out for the pipe like a pirate for hidden treasure, but fate was against him. It so chanced that on the very same morning Deborah had decided to go along to catch a glimpse of the *tzaddik*. She had not yet seen him in the flesh, and having learnt that he was due to deliver the first of a series of weekly lectures at the yeshiva, she lay in wait for him in one of the many doorways of the spacious courtyard. The place was quite empty, save for a few old women who waddled in like ducks, then waddled out again, leaving a void once more, and for an excited-looking youth, bearing a strong resemblance to Mottel, who rushed out of the yeshiva as though the building were on fire.

Time wore on and still nothing happened, until she began to think that she had come on a fool's errand. A faraway clock struck the hour – eleven peals floating through the quiet air. The last stroke had scarcely died away when the *tzaddik* suddenly appeared in the courtyard with one of his personal attendants. His tread was firm and strong, and his boots met the cobbles fairly and squarely, resounding through the huge square courtyard like the pounding of a horse's hoofs. Deborah recoiled, as though afraid of profaning a holy presence, but on giving him a second furtive look, it was a feeling of alarm and not of awe that took possession of her. The man frightened her by his very size. Never in all her life had she seen such a gigantic Jew. What a height! What a girth! And what a belly! Never before in all her life had she seen such a tremendous creature. His shiny black silken gabardine was unbuttoned, and on his projecting paunch the white ritual fringe garment with its wide black stripes billowed out as though filled with a strong breeze. His beard was terribly long, it reached down to his waist. And his face was a shining red mass of flesh – utterly coarse! There was nothing holy about his appearance, in spite of the great length of beard. There was a crafty and self-satisfied twinkle in his luminous eyes. Deborah gaped. Could this really be the *tzaddik* himself? She compared him with the image of her grandfather, of her father. How utterly different! There was no comparison. A strange *tzaddik* indeed!

Suddenly, as she stood musing over the *tzaddik*, vainly trying to recover from her amazement, she became aware of two blazing dark eyes fixed upon herself with a look that touched her to the quick; a tall and lean young man was approaching, clad or rather wrapped up in a long, shabby gabardine encircled by a half-torn sash. He went by swiftly, seeming to float over the ground. His eyes were large and deep-set in a lean pale face all cheekbones. In passing, the eyes gave her another flash, which stirred her to the depths, and then this young man too vanished in the doorway of the yeshiva.

"Now that's a funny looking *tzaddik*!" said Deborah to herself, trying hard not to think of the young man. Perhaps she had been mistaken? Perhaps that big fat man was only one of the attendants? But no, an attendant would not be wearing a silken gabardine on a weekday, nor would he have on a rabbinical fur hat. That hat was easily thrice as big as her father's and how comically it was perched on the head. Both the hat and the head had a knowing air, as though the two of them were in a conspiracy.

She laughed aloud.

Now, that young man with the blazing eyes looked more like a real *tzaddik*. At this thought she crimsoned. But undeniably there was something deeply spiritual and intellectual about that lanky figure.

On the way home she stopped at the butcher's to get some chops for dinner.

Later on in the day, when she attempted to picture the *tzaddik* to her mother, a new surprise lay in store for her. Raizela showed not the least sign of astonishment. She just listened with an amused smile.

"Well, that's splendid! I am glad to hear that the *tzaddik* is looking hale and hearty. Splendid!"

That was her mother's sole comment. It was all very weird....

Chapter 5

The weeks passed into months, and Raizela's purse dwindled until it was positively consumptive. There was scarcely enough money left to buy food with, and still the *tzaddik* neglected to pay any stipend. By this time even Reb Avram Ber, who had imagined all along that it was the *tzaddik*'s intention to make payment in a lump sum, began to grow uneasy and at length he approached him about it (although he had to fight a bitter inner struggle before he could bring himself to do so).

"Give me a call at five o'clock, and then we shall see what we can do for you," was the *tzaddik*'s reply, as though he were answering an appeal for charity.

Reb Avram Ber smarted, but did as he was told. One must live.... There was the family to think of....

The *tzaddik* asked him to take a seat. Then he informed Reb Avram Ber that shortly he would be going away to take the waters. In a peremptory tone of voice he charged Reb Avram Ber to keep the yeshiva up to the mark and to maintain discipline among the students. After that he turned to the subject of the communal kitchen, intimating that in the absence of his mother, who was accompanying him to the watering-place, the establishment would be run by Laizer Nussen's wife. Money would be provided by himself for the purpose. Next he discoursed on a knotty talmudic problem, racking his brains all the while for some subterfuge to escape his obligations. Then came a brooding silence; in the end he vanquished his own reluctance. He rose to his feet, drew aside a dark green plush curtain and vanished into a chamber, the existence of which Reb Avram Ber today discovered for the first time. He heard the *tzaddik* jingle a bunch of keys, and there was a turning of heavy locks. When the *tzaddik* emerged, he hurriedly stuffed two paper notes into Reb Avram Ber's hand together with some silver coins. Reb Avram Ber handed them over to Raizela after evening prayers – five and twenty rubles in all. This restored confidence in the home.

"He seems to prefer paying a lump sum," said Reb Avram Ber.

"I don't see how you make that out," Deborah put in.

"Why, there's over a hundred rubles owing already."

"Don't be silly. This is obviously just something to get on with," Reb Avram Ber reassured her. "I'm certain he'll let me have the rest before he leaves."

Meanwhile, in the *tzaddik*'s court preparations were in full swing for the coming departure. Again several weeks went by without Reb Avram Ber receiving any further payment. The family were beginning to feel the pinch; each passing day brought them nearer to destitution. Reb Avram Ber could not understand it at all; but the *tzaddik* could – only too well! He held forth on the achievements of the yeshiva almost daily, impressing on the public how holy a mission this was and how it was incumbent on them to do everything in their power to support the institution's material welfare. He quite worked himself up into a frenzy when appealing to the inhabitants of the town to accommodate in their homes as many of the students as possible, in order to lighten the burden on the communal kitchen. The whole court was echoing with appeals. Now at last he was on the point of departure, and still Reb Avram Ber heard nothing from him. When Reb Avram Ber, after many broken resolutions, finally brought himself to speak to the *tzaddik* about it, the *tzaddik* airily dismissed his request with a promise to attend to the matter in the near future. Time wore on, and still nothing happened. For some reason or other, the proposed journey was put off, no one knew why. Reb Avram Ber remained hopeful.

Then, when all preparations were complete down to the last detail, the *tzaddik*, surrounded by a veritable army of personal attendants and manservants, even including a ritual slaughterer, took his departure without giving any notice, and Reb Avram Ber was left behind empty-handed. The *tzaddik*'s mother went off with her own personal suite, his wife left soon after with hers. When bidding goodbye to Raizela, she asked her whether she was going away this summer. Somehow the *tzaddik*'s wife had guessed that all was not going well with the family, and she purposely put this question to test her suspicions. The whole truth of the matter, that her husband had left Reb Avram Ber absolutely penniless, was so improbable as not even to enter her mind. Raizela said in reply that she had not quite made her mind up yet. From this the *tzaddik*'s wife inferred more than Raizela would have had her infer. She sent for Reb Avram Ber, offered him a loan of twenty-five rubles, informed him that she would have a talk with the *tzaddik* about his obligations, although she could not say that she exerted any very great influence with him, and – but here her voice faded into a murmur inaudible to Reb Avram Ber....

There was unrest in the yeshiva. There was anger at the yeshiva. The hospitality extended by the townsfolk to the students was far from sufficient for keeping them fed day by day or even every other day. As for the communal kitchen, the soup served there grew thinner from mealtime to mealtime, as did the students. They began to look haggard through undernourishment. Many of them left the town. Reb Avram Ber was, of course, powerless to hold them back. Nor could he infuse those who remained with any zest for their studies. So the Talmud suffered too.... Laizer Nussen's wife showed no inclination to expend any of her own money on the kitchen. The trifling sum the *tzaddik* had left in her care was soon consumed. The students clamored for food, but there was none to be had. The butcher, the baker, the grocer – every one of them, to a man, refused to grant any credit. They were not going to give their goods away and then have to go cringing to the *tzaddik* for their due, following him about like beggars seeking alms, such was their unassailable argument.

The yeshiva went to pieces. If a student had a home to go to, he did not think twice about leaving. Reb Avram Ber's mind began to wander: it was all like a nightmare and he saw no means of shaking it off.

Again Raizela spent whole days on end reclining upon her couch. Deborah had become not merely the housekeeper but the family charwoman and washerwoman. She was taught her work by the neighbors, who never wearied in telling her that an honest day's toil never did anyone any harm, it was good for a girl, and what was good for their own daughters was good for her too. Deborah came to hate them. It was obvious that the neighbors took great pleasure in seeing her upon her knees, and she wondered why it should afford them so much joy. What gratification was there in the sight of her scrubbing a floor?

Mottel again took his meals – such as they were – with the family. He abused the *tzaddik* most vilely (not, however, in the presence of Reb Avram Ber, who would not allow it in spite of everything). Michael came home from the yeshiva every evening with a new store of jokes at the *tzaddik*'s expense. These witticisms grew funnier and more biting as the plight of the students became worse. Michael was himself the author of many of them. He also gave imitations of the *tzaddik* making a propaganda speech on behalf of the yeshiva, his voice quavering rapturously and his hands flung above his head in a frenzy of holiness. In this Michael was inimitable, and his efforts were greeted with hysterical laughter. It was the sole ray of cheerfulness that pierced the heavy gloom. Thanks to Michael, not only Deborah and Mottel, but also Raizela would laugh, thus forgetting her troubles for a little while.

Also, the young man with the luminous dark eyes and prominent cheekbones, the one whom Deborah had seen go by on that disturbing morning when she had been out to catch a glimpse of the *tzaddik*, now frequented their home as the personal guest of Reb Avram Ber. Deborah felt that there was something mysterious about him. For one thing, he consistently refused food, always saying that he had just finished a meal somewhere or other. Discussion, that seemed to be his passion – talmudic debates with her father. She did not know the reason why, but whenever he visited the home everything seemed to brighten up, all worries were forgotten and life became delightful. He introduced a strange, as it were rarefied atmosphere in the house, dispelling all cares. And yet in himself he was far from cheerful. He seemed to be of a rather gloomy disposition. Even Raizela was impressed by him, saying that it was a joy to hear him talk, although of course he barely exchanged a word with the womenfolk. He was extremely aloof, keeping himself to himself even when he was at a person's side. Deborah came to the conclusion that he must be fanatically religious. As for earning her mother's admiration, that was indeed an achievement, which caused Deborah both pain and pleasure – pain because she was herself so little thought of by her mother, and pleasure because … simply because it pleased her! She had once overheard Raizela sing his praises to Reb Avram Ber.

"A young man of exceptional spirit," her mother had said. "He obviously has great powers of intellectual concentration, and there is nothing boastful about him. It's quite a treat to have him here."

"Well, he's far away the most brilliant student we have, you know. He's a wonderful boy. I only wish I had the means, I'd take him as a husband for our daughter."

That always made Deborah laugh. It would be quite a joke, getting engaged. Ah, how her former friends would all envy her! And that woman Surka in the grocery shop would not dare to be so rude to her any more. Deborah could just fancy herself as a bride. …

Only in some ways he seemed rather unreasonable. Why was it that he could never walk along deliberately like other people? What made him rush so? And what thing was it that his eyes were forever seeking? When he discussed the Talmud with her father, why did he have to be so intent and cutting? At such times his eyes seemed to become an even deeper black, and they bulged from their sockets, flashing fire. But even when he was only listening his eyes were different from other people's. But there was a strange beauty in them, and they held some secret also. Peculiar eyes! He was handsome. If he were better dressed, she thought, he would be exceedingly handsome. …

Undeniably her spirits rose to festive heights in his presence. She would become so absorbed, that she never even noticed Mottel's jealousy. He would turn green with envy when that radiant look came to her face directly the stranger entered. Now, she had a liking for Mottel too. He supplied her with books, and had talks with her whenever he got the chance. He once lent her a book which he cautioned her to read in dead secret. She must never in all her life tell anyone about it, nor in any circumstances divulge its source. He impressed upon her that this was the only type of book an enlightened person should read. Not only did one derive much benefit from the reading of such books, it was one's sacred duty to read them. And then he confided to her, as a solemn secret, the fact that it was the dark-eyed stranger who distributed this literature. This came as a terrible shock to her. But little by little the surprise wore off. Mottel told her incidentally that the stranger was a freethinker. She never repeated a word of all this. She had given her oath not to. But it was most unfair of Mottel to have let out such a secret in the first place. Perhaps that was why she felt more attracted to the stranger....

As the summer wore on, a number of fires broke out in the *tzaddik*'s court. They were not of a very serious nature, and were soon extinguished. But they developed into a little epidemic, hardly a week passing without its fire. Here an overturned candle was found blazing on a table. There a dropped cigarette end had set the wooden floor smoldering. Next the cloth on the mantelpiece over the grate in the communal kitchen caught light. Flames might shoot up anywhere. No one could understand it and there was a great deal of speculation. Nothing like it had ever happened before. However, as the fires were always quickly got under control, with little serious damage done, the Lord was praised for His clemency as well as being thanked for His little mercies in providing the townsfolk with a topic of conversation on these drowsy summer days when no one had any inclination for work and besides there was none to be done. The *tzaddik* and everybody else that mattered were away, the flow of Hasidim had ceased for the time being, the communal kitchen was as good as closed. Actually, therefore, the fires were a blessing in disguise, occupying the minds and tongues of neighbors lolling in the narrow streets and courtyards under a fierce sun which sent the whole town to sleep.

Deborah found more variety in life than ever she had done in Jelhitz. There the days used to pass with a greater sense of security, with no expectancy of strange things to come; from morning to night and from night to morning time used to go its irksome way with unbroken monotony. Now life was unsettled, harsh circumstances played havoc with it. Trouble and cares descended on the family from all quarters, came swarming in like vermin from the walls of a rotten building, creeping forth from every chink, and each time one chink was stopped up, two others appeared in its place.…

But matters came to a head when one morning a woman dressed all in black came to their door and, announcing herself as the landlady, vociferously demanded the rent. Now that was something they had not bargained for at all. All this time Reb Avram Ber and his family had labored under the illusion that the house they were living in was the property of the *tzaddik*, and that, in accordance with his promise, they were entitled to their flat rent free. He had never said a word about the payment of rent and of course no such possibility had ever entered their minds. It transpired, however, that Laizer Nussen had paid for the first quarter in advance; and the next payment was now overdue. The house actually belonged to this widow in mourning, who at the end of each quarter would come down from Warsaw to collect her rent. Madam was a shrew. She did not believe in sparing anyone's feelings. Raizela assured her for the hundredth time that it was the *tzaddik*'s liability, not theirs, and that he was sure to pay in full on returning from his holidays. But the woman refused to listen to reason.

"Whatever arrangement you have with the *tzaddik* is *your* affair, I'm not interested. All I know is that you live here and therefore you must pay the rent," she said with an air of finality, and nothing would move her.

"But why didn't you ever show up before, why didn't you get in touch with us in the first place? Then we should have avoided all this unpleasantness," Raizela pressed the woman, but she, taking a seat by the window, unbuttoned her costly black coat, detached the black veil from her black hat, put her black kid gloves upon the table, crossed her black silk-stockinged legs, and settled down as if she would wait forever – unless she got her rent, that is.

Reb Avram Ber was lecturing in the yeshiva at the time. Deborah ran to fetch him. She told him the story hastily, in as few words as she could.

"Mamma is quite distracted. Something must be done quickly. The woman won't go away, she won't go away!"

"Hm!" Reb Avram Ber muttered, looking first one way, then the other, as if he had lost something. "Oh merciful God, creator of the heaven and earth and all that in them is, do not forsake me! Pray help me, help me!" Reb Avram Ber pleaded, like a child pleading with its father, and shattered by the news – the last thing he could have expected – a broken man, he hastened home.

"Good morning!" he said, partly addressing the woman, but with his eyes fixed anxiously on Raizela.

The woman stirred.

"Pray be seated, be seated," Rev Avram Ber said, still the perfect gentleman.

She kept her seat.

"Couldn't you possibly give us a few weeks' respite? God willing, we shall not keep you waiting very long, and I assure you that not a single groschen will you lose."

Neither Reb Avram Ber nor Raizela had kept their wits about them sufficiently to realize that this woman had no legal claim upon them, since Laizer Nussen had rented the flat on the *tzaddik*'s behalf. The woman knew this full well, but was trying her luck. She might as well get her money now as later.

"You see, I am a widow. God grant that you may never be one yourself! Just a poor widow," she explained to Reb Avram Ber. "And it wouldn't be right to keep me waiting for my money, now would it? A lonely widow, that's what I am, and I have no one to care for me. And that's why I…"

"Up above," said Reb Avram Ber, and he involuntarily raised his eyes heavenwards, "up above, widows and orphans are guarded over."

He uttered these words with such fervor, that the set of the woman's mouth, with its heavy furrow on either side, softened somewhat, and a glistening moisture even entered her eyes. She rose from her chair, put on her hat and lowered the crepe over her face.

"Well, then I have your promise, Rabbi, that you will let me have payment within the next four weeks?"

"Yes, God willing! But I never said how many weeks. For all I know I may be able to let you have the money before then – everything is possible with the Lord! – but maybe it will take rather longer than that. He is almighty!" Reb Avram Ber added, as though speaking to himself.

The woman slipped a black glove on to her fingers, making her apologies to Raizela the while. Had she not been a widow.…

"Now what are we going to do?" Raizela demanded of Reb Avram Ber, who, as it happened, was at that very instant putting the same question to God Almighty. "The strange part about it is that this woman should have left us in peace all this while. It's not like her to miss any of her tenants. Of all our afflictions, I never dreamt, never imagined, that this one would be coming to us. Never! Well, I suppose we owe that woman a tidy sum of money now."

"Yes, but the *tzaddik* promised to give us free accommodation, and I scarcely think he would care to compromise himself with such a woman, who would certainly not hesitate to damage his good name. She's the more dangerous because she does not live in these parts, and I think that when he comes back he'll let her have the rent without further ado."

This did not seem altogether unreasonable to Raizela, but was there any certainty?

"Have you anything in writing to support your claim?" Raizela inquired, merely for the sake of saying something. She knew full well that Reb Avram Ber had no such thing and would scorn the very idea of it.

"Of course not! You don't imagine I would ask the *tzaddik* for a written agreement!"

"Of course not," Raizela repeated Reb Avram Ber's words, and turned away from him. She picked up a book, but not a single word could she understand, nor could she repress the nervous tremors of her emaciated body which, like a thing apart from herself, quivered violently and would not be soothed.

"Will you have something to eat, Father?"

"I have not said my morning prayers yet," Reb Avram Ber replied, as he wandered up and down the room with knitted brow. He kept tugging at his beard and muttered something inarticulate to himself all the time.

"Do be calm," he said finally, approaching Raizela. "The Lord will not forsake us. Believe me, everything will turn out for the best. These troubles will pass, and meantime you mustn't destroy yourself with worry."

His plea remained unanswered. He went back to the yeshiva.

"Deborah, can you hear someone screaming? I wonder what's happened?"

"It's nothing, Mamma. It's only that woman again, kicking up a row."

"Yes, but I can distinctly hear Polish?"

"It's her all right! Only she's giving the neighbors a piece of her mind in Polish. I suppose she thinks she'll get her rent quicker that way," Deborah explained, and could not help laughing.

Then a thought crossed her mind that the woman might yet return. She did not mention this fear to her mother, but all mirth was stifled. Nervously, she followed the woman's screams all through the house.... Thank God, they had ceased!

"Ugh, what a horrid woman! Don't you think so, Mamma?"

Raizela made no reply.

So it had come to this! This! The image of the woman all in black still haunted her, still sat on that now vacant chair by the window.

In Jelhitz, at least, Raizela had had a little nest of her own, a little peace and security. There she had never had any cause to tremble lest a threatening black crow might descend upon the home to scare the family out of their wits. There the roof over their heads had been their own, and it all came back to her how, by a strange chance, a long cherished ambition had been realized, how a house had been built up on the foundations of a passing thought. It had all happened most unexpectedly, and the memory of it now rose clearly in her mind.

It had all started with the wealthy villager Hershl Shveiger taking it into his thick head that Solomon, his son (who was no less thick-headed than the father), must at all costs become a scholar. And when, on approaching Reb Avram Ber, he obtained a ready promise that the boy would be taught all that he possibly could be taught, Hershl Shveiger was seized with such transports of delight, that he pressed Reb Avram Ber to accept an advance fee of one hundred rubles. That was how it began. Then she, Raizela, humorously told Reb Avram Ber that she would invest the money in a cottage, and she immediately forgot all about this chance remark. But Reb Avram Ber passed it on to "Big" Mendel, who laughed heartily, and jokingly informed the congregation after prayers in the synagogue that the rabbi was going to build himself a house for a hundred rubles. "How's that for a brainwave?" he asked, and everybody chuckled. But Reb Joseph Cahn, a man who owned vast tracts of forest and who only came down to the village to attend divine service on the anniversaries of his parents' deaths, took this jesting in bad part. Without saying a word at the time, he silently made a resolve to translate this dream house into reality, and a few days later he sent down a huge load of timber with his compliments to Reb Avram Ber. Now Reb Joseph Cahn was a man of great influence, and when he did a thing, everybody else did the same, and soon gifts were pouring in from all quarters. Someone sent in a load of tiles, a timber merchant drove up with a cartful of beams, a few of the villagers gave cash. Within a short time there was more than enough building material, and all that Raizela had to pay for was labor, locks for the doors, window panes, cement and other small sundries. And thus a joke gave rise to a handsome cottage! But matters did not end there, for fortune had deigned to smile and it so chanced that Joshua Glisker, who managed the squire's estates, one day told the squire the curious tale of how the rabbi was building himself a house for a hundred rubles. The squire was very much struck with it. He laughed merrily, and taking Joshua Glisker along with him, paid the rabbi a call.

Raizela saw it all again in her mind's eye as she lay huddled up now on her couch. She had only just got out of bed. Reb Avram Ber was away at the synagogue at the time, when in walked Joshua Glisker to announce that the squire was desirous of speech with the rabbi. This news quite startled her. What business could the squire have with the rabbi? It occurred to her that in all probability he was engaged in a dispute with some Jewish merchant, and having lost his case in the courts, now wished to arrange for Jewish arbitration, for this was a customary procedure with the Polish gentry. It transpired, however, that the squire had no disputes with anyone. All he wanted was to speak to Reb Avram Ber on a matter touching his person. Joshua Glisker knew what this matter was, but not a word could she wring from him. He was determined to lend a sharper edge to the surprise that lay in store. Now, she remembered her introduction to the squire who, tanned and humorous-eyed, opened wide his grey eyes with astonishment on seeing that this was the rabbi's wife, but he immediately made a deep bow and allowed the smile, which always lurked on his stern face, to come to the surface, in an endeavor to cover up his surprise.

Reb Avram Ber hurried home from the synagogue, white as a sheet. He was quite distressed, especially as the squire had not stated the purpose of his visit. But when the squire greeted him with a smile from afar, and finding that Joshua Glisker was there too, Reb Avram Ber was somewhat comforted.

Puzzled as she was herself, her puzzlement grew when the squire, after first shaking hands with Reb Avram Ber, briefly stated that he had heard the story of the house that was to be built and wished to offer a site for its erection, free of charge and exempt from all tax. She remembered how the squire had firmly declined their invitation to step inside, for which she was very thankful, because the place was in such fearful disorder. How, after he was told that they would like to erect their house next door to the synagogue, the squire's face became wreathed in smiles and he commended the rabbi on his good taste in choosing to live on the outskirts of the village facing the meadow.... Thereupon they all trooped off in a procession – herself, Reb Avram Ber, the squire with his manager, and a large brown long-haired dog that kept wagging its tail, as if the animal too was delighted with Reb Avram Ber's good taste.

A smile came to Raizela's lips as she saw again Reb Avram Ber shrinking into himself and dodging this way and that to avoid the dog which, unfortunately for him, happened to be in high spirits and gave vent to them by dashing from person to person. Then Joshua Glisker produced a wooden yardstick, which had been folded up in his pocket, and squatting on the ground, he made various measurements, drew chalk lines, uttered comments and looked out of a corner of his eye all the while, as though to say:

"If you please, I'm a business manager; but if the occasion arises, I'm equally good as a surveyor, and pray tell me, is there any task in the world I could not do better than any other man?"

And there stood the squire, tall, erect, fair-headed, his hair glinting in the sun, his nose longish and, as it were, smiling. He bored holes in the ground with the end of his cane to mark the chalked-in grassy plot, then turned to her and said that she could consider this her property for all time. Reb Avram Ber, moved by gratitude, clasped the squire's hand and pressed it with all the warmth he could muster. Then a red-haired youth with stupid wooden features brought up two sleek black horses with extraordinarily thin legs, narrow heads and docked tails. How adroitly the squire and his manager jumped on to the animals' backs, and, after a final deep bow to herself, went off in such a gallop, that Reb Avram Ber was lost in amazement for a long while after.

"Dear, dear, just look at them!" he said.

Raizela broke into a smile on her couch, but only for an instant. The heavy curtain of gloom enveloped her once more, choking her, numbing her. And now it had come to this! This! Now she was at the mercy of a pitiless shrew, whose very presence chilled one's heart....

What little shelter the family had had was all swept away. It had been thoughtlessly dissipated. Nothing was left to them but a few sticks of furniture. And what did the future hold in store now?...

After many trials and tribulations Reb Avram Ber succeeded in obtaining a loan of ten rubles and with this he silenced the woman in black when, sure enough, four weeks later, she turned up to get whatever she could from the family and to find out if the *tzaddik* was back in town....

Chapter 6

Towards the end of summer two sturdy grey thoroughbreds came dashing through the streets and alleys of R–, to pull up with a great flourish in the courtyard of the *tzaddik*'s house where preparations were in full swing for the reception of the holy master. And everybody knew at once that he had come, he had arrived!

Reb Avram Ber, who happened to be leaving the yeshiva at the time, unwittingly came face to face with him. But the *tzaddik* gave no sign of recognition, and accompanied by two of his personal attendants, went straight indoors to seclude himself in his sanctum.

A crowd of sightseers quickly gathered in the courtyard – Jews, old and young, and women and children, with even a few gentiles. And reverently they eyed the *tzaddik*'s horses which, with their heads plunged deep into their nosebags, calmly went on chewing their oats, without so much as condescending to give the rabble a glance.

Towards the end of summer he returned, with all his suite, from the watering place. His mother came back too, with her own suite. Only his wife had been left behind: she had not finished taking her cure yet.

Once more the court began to throb with life.

Again the *tzaddik*, with just a little less fat on him, his face scorched by the sun and the skin of his shiny nose in tatters, mounted the "throne." Again his attendants went about the court with an intent and mysterious air.

No longer were common maidservants to be seen reposing on balconies on high, no longer did they gaze down from the holy of holies, carrying on flirtations with romantic young men on the cobbles below. The old life began anew. Tiny men kept dragging big baskets of victuals into the court. Restaurants re-opened their doors. And Hersh Laib's talkative wife again stood airing her old grievance to her old audience about her husband's irksome duties. His was the distasteful task, as the *tzaddik*'s youngest attendant, of taking the *tzaddik* to the closet. It was not the right sort of work, she protested, for so handsome a fellow with such tidy habits and such a lovely curly little beard....

"The *tzaddik* is tired and he can receive no visitors," was Laizer Nussen's stern reply to all those – personal friends even – who presented themselves to welcome the *tzaddik* on his arrival.

"The *tzaddik* will now receive visitors," was the news which a little later rejoiced the hearts of those personal friends who were just thirsting for a glimpse of the holy man's greasy sunburnt face.

Reb Avram Ber was not among them, even though officially he was still the *tzaddik*'s closest confidant. He had no desire to see the man, still less inclination to bid "Peace!" unto him at a time when sorrow, distress and bitterness racked his own soul. Because of this man, he had lost his old naive confidence in humanity. Reb Avram Ber was vaguely aware of this, and withal unconsciously, deeply mourned the loss. Because of this man, also, he knew for the first time a terrible feeling of self-disgust. He could not face Raizela without a sense of shame, without wincing. It agonized him horribly to see her suffering, suffering in silence. Never had he brought anything upon her but suffering! First he had taken her out of a house of plenty to lead a cramped, miserable existence in Jelhitz, then he had persuaded her to accompany him to a "promised land," but here, instead of a change for the better, destitution had come upon them: the *tzaddik* had shattered their lives, taking them away from a position where their bread and butter was assured and literally leaving them to starve, as if they were nothing better than toys, playthings for the *tzaddik* to do with as he pleased....

On the third day after his homecoming the *tzaddik* sent for him.

"Peace unto you, *tzaddik*!"

"Peace be unto you! Now tell me, what have things been like in my absence?"

Reb Avram Ber lost his temper. He was overwrought. The *tzaddik's* fat, beefy face and sanguine complexion got on his nerves. Reb Avram Ber had changed.

"Things have been unsatisfactory, as was only to be expected."

"Why, what on earth do you mean?"

"And what on earth do *you* mean by looking so surprised? The students were left unprovided for, they were hungry and ran away. 'No bread, no Torah,'" Reb Avram Ber retorted with ill-concealed anger. He was about to make a direct demand to the *tzaddik* for a settlement of the outstanding debt. The *tzaddik* felt it coming, he had foreseen it. Plunging suddenly into deep meditation, he began pacing the room. Without stopping, he harangued Reb Avram Ber:

"Yours was a precious trust. I left the yeshiva completely in your trust, and I must hold you responsible for what has happened. Had you used your full powers, there would not have been this mass desertion on the part of the students. Within a few weeks you have managed to reduce the yeshiva to a miserable skeleton of its former self. It's a pity, a terrible pity!"

"But the students were left to starve. There was no money in the cash box to keep the communal kitchen going, and failing charitable support from the townspeople, the position was hopeless."

"Pshaw, nonsense!" the *tzaddik* exclaimed, and his face turned as red as if it had been boiled.

He resumed his pacing of the room. From the back pocket of his gabardine the end of a large handkerchief peeped out and kept wagging up and down like a scornful finger. A silver snuff box was clutched in his hand. He made a gesture, as if dismissing an unpleasant thought from his mind, and turned his back on Reb Avram Ber without a word. There was nothing left for Reb Avram Ber to do but to go. He went, in silence.

Again several uneventful weeks went by. Some of the old students returned to the yeshiva. New ones were recruited, especially among young married men of the upper middle-class, eager to escape the black looks of angry fathers-in-law, whose hospitality they enjoyed. Having been given wives at a very early age, in accordance with ancient tradition, and then carefully looked after until such time as they might be able to support themselves, when they came of age they often resisted strongly any attempts to be converted into responsible husbands, and large numbers of such young men flocked to the yeshiva to take the air and to continue their leisure in the beautiful hygienic building. Some of them actually were serious students. As for those young men who thought nothing of going without food for days on end, they had not left the yeshiva in the first place. The *tzaddik* found a new ornament for himself in the form of a magnificent-looking rabbi who knew all the tricks and who fleeced the *tzaddik* with all the cunning he could muster.

Michael's hatred of the *tzaddik* was quenched. The man was simply a prosperous sharper and Michael accepted him as such. This realization greatly tickled his fancy, lending an even keener edge to his everlasting jokes at the *tzaddik*'s expense. This new air of detachment made his witticisms irresistible and they flashed like lightning through the blackest of clouds, piercing the heaviest of gloom. Thanks to his gift of mockery, Michael became the most popular student in the yeshiva, though the youngest.

"Come on, Michael, do your stuff! We're just about fed up to the neck!" his companions would demand entertainment, as if he were a professional clown.

Michael was never caught unawares and before long he had the yeshiva resounding to shrieks of laughter. Ha, ha, ha! Ha, ha, ha!

"Good, Michael! Bravo!"

Reb Avram Ber, in spite of everything that had happened, continued to deliver his lectures with unflagging zeal. He and his family had nothing to eat, but still he went on giving his lectures day after day.

And now the High Holy Days were at hand. The strips of sunlight, which all through the summer had settled expansively in between the benches and desks of the lecture hall, began to shrink with each passing day. The sky above hung lower over the rooftops. But the hot weather lingered on, as though oblivious of any change in the seasons. Indeed, the heat became more stifling than ever.

One Friday afternoon, when the cooks in the court were hard at work and when Deborah had finished her scant preparations for the Sabbath, while Michael was resting on the grass in a meadow outside the town, close by a bridge over the river, where the sight of girlish bare feet and of naked sunburnt arms bearing baskets of mushrooms kept his eyelids from drooping, and Raizela was reclining at home on her couch, feebler than ever, when Reb Avram Ber had just come back from the ritual bath house, with water trickling from his beard and sidelocks – all at once a smell of burning filled the *tzaddik*'s court.

His mother was the first to notice the fumes. Clad in a trailing black silk dress, with a big flowery bonnet on her head, she ran out into the center of the courtyard to raise the alarm, screaming herself hoarse before she could make herself understood. Soon the whole atmosphere was contaminated with this acrid odor, but the cause of it was a mystery until suddenly the large open windows of the yeshiva began to belch forth huge clouds of smoke. Panic broke out. Crowds flocked into the courtyard from the numberless doorways and from the street gate. The people shouted, they flung up their arms in despair, until an insistent voice suggested that the fire brigade should be sent for. By the time they arrived, the impenetrable black mass of smoke inside the yeshiva had begun to vomit up half-smothered flames and sparks. Within a few minutes the entire court stood brightly lit up.

The *tzaddik*, accompanied by Hersh Laib, the youngest of his personal attendants, arrived on the scene. He had been to take a ritual bath, and gleaming drops of water still lingered on his long beard and his sidelocks were dripping. His face and bare throat were flushed as if they had been scalded with boiling water; in contrast, the color of his shirt was dazzlingly white.

"My good people, what's the matter with you? Why don't you do something?" He uttered a cry like a wounded creature, and as if to set an example, he began to sprint across the courtyard with the agility of a boy of twelve – there was nothing of the fat old man about him now – making straight for his sanctum.

A great uproar ensued.

Someone shouted out: "The *tzaddik*!"

The multitude began to chant: "The *tzaddik*! The *tzaddik*! The *tzaddik* has gone into his sanctum! Help! Save the *tzaddik*!"

Jews ran helter-skelter with disheveled beards and outspread hands to join the *tzaddik* in his peril. Women ran helter-skelter to join the *tzaddik* in his sanctum. Bundles of bedding, clothing and all sorts of knick-knacks tumbled helter-skelter from windows outside the danger zone, sparks shot up helter-skelter from the stifling fumes, and helter-skelter came the *tzaddik*, back from his sanctum, with a large leather portfolio under his arm and his mother hard on his heels.

And climbing on to a heap of bedclothes, he sat down, surrounded by his valuables and the salvaged holy scrolls, which had been carefully wrapped in cloth like coddled babes – sat motionless like a statue in bronze.

The firemen were unable to make much impression on the blaze. The flames went from strength to strength, growing more brilliant as they ate their way through the building gluttonously, pausing only now and then to lick their meal with relish. The *tzaddik*'s mother stood wringing her hands. The sky, aglow with the setting sun, was now illumined by two conflagrations. In the narrow street outside the court there was a constant wailing. Women, overcome by fear that the whole town might be swept by the flames, fainted away on the pavement. Youngsters shrieked. The menfolk carried them away from the scene of the fire.

Still the *tzaddik* sat upon his pile of valuables, and nothing could move him. All the worthies of the town tried their powers of persuasion on him, pleading with him, imploring him to accept their hospitality, but he refused to climb down. Then the common folk approached him, after everybody else had failed, but it was no use. Reb Avram Ber was quite heartbroken at the pitiful sight. He inwardly pledged the *tzaddik* forgiveness, but what did forgiveness avail the *tzaddik* who was clinging stubbornly to his perch like an outcast? Like a creature forlorn he sat there, surrounded by his treasures. The manuscripts and priceless diamonds, which were locked up in his portfolio, he stealthily transferred to his deep bosom pocket. His mother, whose diamonds they were, loyally remained at his side, and thus they sat hour after hour keeping guard.

Later on when twilight descended on the courtyard (the rest of the town was long since wrapped in darkness), he arose and, with a congregation of a few score Jews behind him, said his evening prayers. The womenfolk and the gentiles withdrew respectfully, and contemplated the awesome scene from afar. Above, the sky was perfectly dark, now that both conflagrations were extinguished. The holy scrolls were taken into the little old synagogue, which stood quite unscathed. The court as a whole had not suffered much damage, but the yeshiva was destroyed completely; the sole visible trace of it was a tangle of girders, a heap of black rubble mixed with wet cinders, the whole studded with glowing embers. The *tzaddik* had his property taken back indoors, under his personal supervision. His eyes, though so deeply embedded in flesh, were keen and all-seeing.

For a very long while to come the *tzaddik*'s personal attendants and the local restaurateurs would pour wondrous tales into the ears of the faithful, how the *tzaddik* had braved the flames, how, imbued with a holy spirit of martyrdom, he had staked his life on salvaging the rare manuscripts and tokens that had been bequeathed to him by his father (whose memory be blessed!) and many other marvelous things did they recount; many were the miracles that the *tzaddik* had wrought on that memorable Friday afternoon.

His persistence in clinging to the pile of valuables in the courtyard was interpreted in a variety of ways. One school of thought insisted that his action was a demonstration of submission to the heavy hand of Providence. But others insisted that he had behaved thus through sheer modesty. A third explanation was that having been temporarily rendered homeless together with the holy scrolls, the *tzaddik* had taken this opportunity of publicly lamenting the exile of the children of Israel. As for the fire, although there was much speculation, no one knew for certain how it had started. There were murmurs that the yeshiva had been deliberately burnt down, that one of the students did it in revenge. It was known that feelings had run high among the students when the *tzaddik* went away to take the waters, while he left them to starve. And many of the townsfolk thought this theory reasonable. Others pooh-poohed it. The whole thing remained a mystery.

The High Holy Days were but a few days away. And this was the *tzaddik*'s busy season. A multitude of Jews from far and near came flocking to him to secure his blessing.

The court and the narrow streets around it were packed. There was a coming and going of people from morning to night. The town saw many strange faces – the careworn, perspiring faces of hardworking Jews. Many of these strangers were wearing their working clothes. Cobblers smelt of leather, tailors had threads all over them, and millers were coated from head to foot in flour. They had had neither the time nor the inclination to change. The pilgrimage to R– was a luxury they could ill afford, although the journey only took a few hours from Warsaw and other populous Jewish centers. When a man has a family to feed, he must keep his nose on the grindstone all the time, and the *tzaddik* must wait. But on the eve of the High Holy Days hard hearts softened. The voice of the soul made itself heard above the din of the daily round. What was the use of satisfying the flesh, if the soul went hungry? The flesh would perish, the soul would live forever. And Jews, hearing the call, jumped on to carts and into trains, and came flocking to the *tzaddik* (God bless him!) to ask him to pray for them, to ask him to save their souls which, hidden under shabby working clothes, were pining for spiritual succor. And everybody rushed about as if in a trance.

The *tzaddik*'s personal attendants were overwhelmed, in a perfect sweat over their dual task of writing out cards of introduction for the visitors and quietly pocketing tips.

Meanwhile hasidic devotees who at all seasons heard an inner voice say – *it is not this frivolous mundane existence which matters, it is not lowly flesh a Jew must care for, but the soul, aye, the great and mysterious hereafter when the soul shall live forever;* devotees who were not in the habit of snatching a mere day off to see the *tzaddik,* but would come to rejoice in his holy presence time and again; such devotees sauntered about the court with an air of perfect leisure, like men at home. And loftily they viewed the common herd waiting in the queue with piously inflamed faces to see the *tzaddik* – to see him for a fleeting moment, hand him a donation and then fly off home again to their wives and children, to their mean occupations in the quest of nothing better than bread and butter.…

Every single inn in the town was packed, there was not a bed to be had anywhere. The prices of foodstuffs were soaring hourly. The innkeepers and their families were run off their feet by day, and when night came they had no pillow to lay their heads on. Traders forsook their usual posts in the marketplace and invaded the streets around the court, where business was flourishing. Loudly they cried their wares, consummating the general din and confusion:

"Buy, my good people, buy, buy! This is your last chance before the prices go up! Come on, what would you like?"

"Ten groschens for two boiled eggs! Boiled eggs, straight from the fowl, all new-laid, all hot!"

"Lovely apples! They're a tonic! Pears, four groschens a pound! Four groschens only!"

"Anybody wanna 'ot cheese cake? Speak up! I'm givin' em away for nothin'! That's right, put down five groschens and see for yourself!"

This last wisecrack was being shouted at the top of her voice by a woman of gigantic stature, who was doing a roaring trade. It caught Michael's fancy while he was out sightseeing. In the flood of craziness that was pouring through the town, this mountain of a woman with her amused smile seemed like an island of common sense which would never be submerged. Never before had Michael seen such a torrent of hurrying fools! They were streaming in, to cleanse their souls in the mud!...

Michael missed none of the sights and then went home to play act the more comical scenes for his mother. He mocked the humble mien of those waiting in the queue, beseeching Laizer Nussen to accept their money; how Laizer Nussen quelled them with a glance, even while he pocketed their coins.

"Michael, will you do me a favor and shut up," said Raizela. "I've a terrible headache, and I'm not going to have it made any worse through listening to your everlasting nonsense about the *tzaddik*. Keep quiet!"

"All right, Mamma, but you should have seen Laizer Nussen. You ought to have seen him, he was wonderful. He had the whole mob completely under his thumb, and they all insisted on having their cards of introduction written out by him. The other personal attendants were ignored, and stood by helpless, and were they looking blue! Watch, Mamma, this was the expression on their faces! As for poor old Baruch, he was perfectly wretched. Poor fellow, he hasn't done a stroke of business all day. The mob had all made their minds up to be fleeced by Laizer Nussen and by no one else."

Deborah was angered by Michael's derision of the "mob." Ignorant and simple-minded, they were bamboozled, made naught of; but no one ever tried to enlighten them, no one ever ventured to expose the *tzaddik* and his confederates for what they were, and so the "mob" continued to lavish luxuries upon him in all innocence.

"But you can't expect these plain honest people to know any better," she argued with Michael. "Wasn't Papa just the same? Didn't he used to think a lot of the *tzaddik*?"

Deborah felt hurt for her own sake as well as theirs.

She shared their fate. She was a drudge, treated with contempt by those upon whom she danced attendance, and if ever she tried to shake off her responsibilities, protesting that she was made for something better, they asked her with a sneer:

"Don't you think housework is good enough for you? Well, why don't you study the Talmud, and one day you'll be a rabbi maybe?"

Such was life, Deborah mused bitterly. People were derided, but never shown their errors.

As for Michael, this crazy rush to the *tzaddik* was to him nothing but an inevitable manifestation of incorrigible human folly, and he was duly amused. He left Deborah to get on with the moralizing.

"Mamma, why doesn't someone tell the common people the truth about the *tzaddik*? Why shouldn't they know that he's a scoundrel?"

"Yes, but who's going to tell them?"

Deborah reflected.

"Why doesn't Papa do it?"

"Don't be absurd!" said Raizela, and she relapsed into her former pensiveness.

"No, go on, Mamma, tell me, why can't Papa do it?"

Raizela was silent for a while. Then she remembered that she had not answered Deborah's question.

"What is the use of telling them the truth, if they're not going to believe you in any case?" said Raizela. "They would certainly go into a frenzy and might even assault you. You see, they're rather feeble-minded, and they can't help clinging to one support or another. If it wasn't the *tzaddik*, it'd be somebody else. They must have an idol to pay homage to. The *tzaddik* is their golden calf."

"They put a ruble in the slot and out comes the fattened calf!" Michael put in through the open door of the next room.

"And what a calf!" said Raizela.

"A regular bull!" Deborah laughed.

"Who's a bull?" demanded Michael, rushing in again to join the conversation. "You can't call the *tzaddik* a bull. He's a slaughterer, and his crowd are cattle. Cattle, that's what they are, and that's what you are, too!"

"Stop! That will do! I don't want to hear another word about the *tzaddik* and his flock. It's no affair of ours."

"But how is it that learned Jews believe in him as well?" Deborah persisted.

"Enough, I say!"

"No, but tell me, Mamma, why is it?" Deborah went on undaunted.

"It's because the so-called learned Jews who hang round this *tzaddik* are really only mediocre Talmudists. He has a big, but a poor, following, and so with what little knowledge they have they shine here and play the part of venerable men who are the confidants of the *tzaddik*. Elsewhere they would receive hardly any attention at all."

"Yes, but even so, would they still remain loyal if they were to be told that the *tzaddik* is a downright liar?"

"For goodness sake, stop! You're an utter fool!" Raizela snapped back at her, having completely lost her patience. "No wonder it is written in the Talmud that *an ignoramus will ask questions for the mere sake of asking*," she turned to Michael with a smile.

Deborah did not understand this Hebrew quotation, but instinctively gathered the gist of it. She turned away shamefaced and with a vow that never again would she humbly serve the "great," only to be scoffed at, like those poor crowds that were struggling to see the *tzaddik*....

Almost every night, in bed, she firmly resolved to give up her duties of keeping house, and to become a student instead. Ever since childhood she had longed to receive an education, to cease being the nonentity of the family. She would learn things, gain understanding, and then not only would Papa be a great Talmudist, not only would her mother possess a boundless store of knowledge, not only would Michael be a brilliant student, but she, Deborah – the girl who, as her father had once said, was to be a mere nobody when she grew up – would be a person of real consequence. She would make her own life. But these thoughts were all very fine at bedtime. When she got up the next morning, she was drawn irresistibly into the usual drab routine, and each day was like a wretched repetition of the one that had gone before it. Again she managed the home, again she assumed the burden of responsibility that weighed so heavily on her childish shoulders. She was lacking in courage and too sentimental to leave her ailing mother to get on with it, and so – without being told, without being thanked – she went back into harness again, fretting and suffering all the more for her vain hopes of freedom – freedom that seemed within her grasp.

She did not even have any friends to go out with, to relax once in a while. Two former chums, both of well-to-do families, had one day come upon her while she was on her knees, scrubbing the floor, with her dress tucked up like a charwoman, and since then they had never been to see her again, nor did she ever attempt to renew the friendship herself.

It was, to be sure, a comfort to have that Russian book to fall back on, which Mottel had lent her. He had taken her into his confidence and told her all his secrets. He was studying Russian surreptitiously, and one day he had met her in the meadow and gone over Pushkin's verses with her. By now she very nearly knew the whole book by heart. Mottel himself was bubbling over with enthusiasm.

"The Russians," he said, "are wonderful. They write marvelous stuff. Why, you wouldn't find poetry like this in any other language!"

Books took her out of herself. The drab surroundings became festive. She lived in a new and spiritual world. But she could hardly find the time for such diversion; there was always something to do in the house. She did not protest. What was the use, since there was no one who could possibly step into her shoes? It sorely grieved her, nevertheless. Why should she, above all, bear the brunt of the hard times they had fallen upon? It would not have hurt so badly if the family had shown her some appreciation, instead of taking it for granted that she was their lowly maidservant who must have aspirations for nothing better, whose dreams were the dreams of a fool. Such thoughts had been tormenting her for a long time past, and she was forever seeking consolation in the moth-eaten yellow pages of Mottel's books.

Sometimes, however, even the poems failed her, her harrowed mind would not be soothed, and then she would run out of the home and post herself in the gateway of the house. Or she would lean up against a lamppost which stood a few yards away and which had not been lit up for years, and she would watch the children at play, gaze after the passersby who came and went, intent on their trivial tasks, completely absorbed in their humdrum, humble lives. Healthy-minded people. They got on with their work steadfastly, and it never entered their minds to ask what it was all about. What did they live for? Why? Why?

Chapter 7

The High Holy Days were over. Gone was the sacred, sweetly mournful atmosphere, and in its stead came trivial, commonplace gloom. All was quiet within the *tzaddik*'s court; sickly quiet. At times a soft, drowsy singsong issued from the ancient little synagogue, but it sounded as though a weary mother were lulling her sick child to sleep, or as though a half-sobered drunkard were wistfully singing to himself.

From morning to night innkeepers lay dozing on the benches outside their establishments, or roamed the streets of the town sighing that business was bad.... The sun shed warmth and light. Ignoring the calendar, it blazed away day after day; the sharp cobblestones of the winding alleys were burning hot to the touch of bare feet, and it seemed as though the obstinately lingering summer would never make way for winter. But little by little, time had a telling effect on the seasons. Dawn would be late in coming, the day would rise sluggishly with sticky eyes; drops of dew were poised on every window like tears. Although it would still be stiflingly hot in the afternoons, the sun never rose high in the sky, but hugged the rooftops as if it were slinking away....

A dread spirit of hopelessness haunted Reb Avram Ber's home. Quite suddenly Reb Avram Ber had become the most practical-minded member of the family. He could plainly see the approach of winter. (There was no such season as autumn or spring to Reb Avram Ber's way of thinking.) Coals were needed, warm clothing – and a hundred and one things besides. Slowly, without haste, the grip of winter was going to close its hold, and he found himself powerless to lift a finger in self-defense. If the yeshiva had not been burnt down, there might still have been a little hope. As things were now, the *tzaddik* could wash his hands of Reb Avram Ber and could leave the family to their plight – a sorry plight indeed! And while they had become inured to hardship, Reb Avram Ber clearly realized that a new chapter of destitution was opening – a chapter that would be darker than ever before, for not only was all their money spent, but their strength, too, was spent. Here was Raizela so feeble – like a guttering candle which needed but a breath of wind to blow it out! How would she survive it all? Reb Avram Ber was terribly downcast, and he could only pray to God for mercy.

The *tzaddik,* to be sure, had pledged himself on more than one occasion to have the yeshiva rebuilt. But that was not much use, when the family stood in need of instant relief. Reb Avram Ber, after a lengthy and bitter inner conflict, had again brought himself to approach the *tzaddik.* Whereupon the *tzaddik* had declared that a remedy must be sought, that the Lord never forsook any of His children, and, with these words, the interview had come to an end....

True enough, Raizela's father had begun to send in a little money from time to time. But there is an old Jewish saying that "You cannot fill a torn sack."

Winter set in. The rooftops put on their gleaming blankets of snow. An orphaned little tree in the *tzaddik*'s courtyard grew stiff; its poor frozen twigs pointed like helpless, accusing fingers at the rime forever lying in the gutter. The cobbles glittered in the coldly brilliant sunshine. And all day long crows kept cawing in front of the windows, lending even greater emphasis to the wintry atmosphere in the homes of the poor.

Reb Avram Ber was hardly ever to be found at home nowadays. Raizela never stirred from her couch. She was always reading. Deborah began to look haggard and tense, and her expression held something of nervous fear in it. She was easily exasperated, fretting terribly over every trivial mishap, while her mind seemed too numb to take in the really substantial troubles. Even Michael had, in the course of a few weeks, turned far too taciturn and grave for a boy of his age and more particularly for his nature. If ever he did crack a joke, it was so biting, so cynical, it made his companions wince. Quite suddenly he had grown into a man – a bitter man of fifteen.

Reb Avram Ber tried hard to secure a new benefice, but without success, in spite of the proverb which he kept repeating to himself – *He who searches shall also find....*

And, as ill fortune would have it, the winter turned out to be most severe. The slippery pavements and heaps of snow, frozen hard as iron at intervals along the gutters, helped to remind Deborah whenever she ventured forth that her flimsy little coat was most unseemly.

There were occasions when Michael would tear himself away from it all and go down to the river to have a slide. But it was not like olden times. Even his mirth was joyless now. He had reached the age of understanding – he could no longer pretend that life was a game. He had begun to think seriously of earning a living for himself, but did not know which way to turn. For his part, he would have become an apprentice to a tailor, or an errand boy, but at home he did not even dare breathe any such suggestion. It would only have created a scandal. And it was really a weird notion: was he, Michael, going to become a common drudge? Still, the desperate urge to do something remained, giving his early-matured brain no rest. His face had become pale and gloomy. Somehow he looked very much taller than he had done only a short while ago, and his habitual stoop had become very pronounced.

The panes in the windows and doors were everlastingly adorned with the handiwork of Jack Frost. The home was bitterly cold. Whenever a fire was lit it refused to burn properly. The coals seemed to know that they were in a poor man's grate and, therefore, took no pains. The winter went on and on, but – like all earthly things – it came to a finish at last.

It was early spring. Already the snow was thawing and forming puddles and streamlets everywhere. In the river on the outskirts of the town huge lumps of ice were afloat. Once more Jews were to be seen about, with their gabardines spattered with mud up to the waist. A Passover atmosphere was abroad. Spring's warm breath sweetened the air. Once more Jews' thoughts turned to *matzos*, to charity, and other sacred things. And with the coming of spring, with the lengthening of the days, and the sun mounting higher and higher in the sky, a bright ray pierced also the gloom in Reb Avram Ber's home.

Quite by chance Reb Avram Ber one day made the acquaintance, in the synagogue, of a wealthy man who had come to ask for the *tzaddik*'s blessing. Introducing himself, this visitor explained that he was a comparative stranger to the place, for hitherto there had been in his own home town a resident *tzaddik* who, unfortunately, had passed away recently, without leaving an heir. Now it appeared that this stranger, who had attached himself to Reb Avram Ber, was a very rich man indeed – the leading light of his own community – and it was his earnest wish that a new *tzaddik* should be found, to keep up the dignity of his home town. It was more convenient, anyway, to have a *tzaddik* on the spot, and so a search was going on for a holy man, although so far none had been found. No established *tzaddik* would dream of moving from one place to another. On the other hand, there was no room for an impostor.

"No room for an impostor!" the wealthy visitor said with an air of finality as he unfolded his story to Reb Avram Ber.

It occurred to Reb Avram Ber that if the vacancy had been for a rabbi, this would have been a heaven-sent opportunity. He said as much half regretfully, and thought no more of it. But there was such an earnest, simple smile on his face as he spoke that the other man was touched. At that very instant Reb Avram Ber endeared himself to the stranger for all time, and a thought, a hope was born.

"Well, actually we need a rabbi too for, you see, our former *tzaddik* (blessed be his memory!) was also our acting rabbi. But this is where the hitch comes in. Opinion among us is divided, for unfortunately there are a lot of snobs in our town – as there are in every other town. They all happen to be supporters of the *tzaddik* of Ger, and they never used to think much of our own *tzaddik*. They were his sworn enemies in fact, and used to jeer at him and ridicule him. And now that he has departed this life they don't want to have a new *tzaddik* at all, but mean to install a rabbi of their own choosing. You would hardly believe it, but the candidate they have put up is a son-in-law of our former *tzaddik*. This upstart fellow is a man after their own heart because he, too, is an ardent Hasid of the *tzaddik* of Ger, and was never on good terms with his own father-in-law. Do you follow me? That's one side of the picture. The rest of us, that is everybody except the handful of snobs, dislike this upstart son-in-law, and we won't have him at any price." Here the narrator's gorge began to rise.

"Of course, we're more numerous and powerful than the arrogant scum that always floats on top and, believe me, in the end we'll have our own way. The snobs don't stand a chance. What we want is not merely a rabbi, but a rabbi and *tzaddik* combined. Now tell me, would you care to assume that position? Will you come and live with us?"

"Of course I won't!"

"And pray, why not?"

"Simply because I am not a *tzaddik*."

"All right, we'll appoint you as one."

"God forbid! *Tzaddikim* are not appointed by their fellow men, but by God."

"Well, then, allow me to inform you that you have as much right to be a *tzaddik*, and are as holy as any *tzaddik* on earth," the stranger unhesitatingly declared his ardent faith in Reb Avram Ber. "I know that you are. However, if my first suggestion doesn't appeal to you, how about this? Become our rabbi, and as for being our *tzaddik*, you will decide about that after you have been living among us for a while."

Being a shrewd businessman, this wealthy visitor had a clever little plan at the back of his mind for outwitting the snobs. He interrupted Reb Avram Ber, who had begun to speak.

"Yes, yes, I know. I know more about you than you imagine. For a number of years you were the minister of Jelhitz and you were very highly esteemed there."

"Yes, but who told you?"

"Never mind! There are a lot of people who have spoken to me about you in this place, and they all think just as highly of you."

Reb Avram Ber smiled; he strove hard not to succumb to this flattery, but to no avail.

"I take it that you would be willing to become our rabbi pure and simple," the stranger went on in his masterful way. "As for my original proposal, you could decide about that later on. Meantime, it would put the snobs in their proper place!"

Again he began to foam at the mouth about the "snobs."

"No, but I would never dream of settling down to strife and discord," Reb Avram Ber protested, unhappy at the thought that what might have been a chance of salvation should turn out to be no more than a wretched temptation.

The stranger fell more and more deeply under Reb Avram Ber's spell. He had quite lost his heart to him. But he kept his head, and inwardly dismissing Reb Avram Ber's objection to strife and discord – life was all strife and discord! – he begged Reb Avram Ber to hold himself in immediate readiness to travel when summoned by the elders of the community.

"On receiving our invitation you will know for certain that all opposition has been eliminated, and there will be nothing for you to fear," he said in conclusion.

By now Reb Avram Ber had an unpleasant taste in his mouth, but as he did not imagine there was anything serious in this man's talk, he answered casually:

"Well, when matters have progressed thus far, we shall think it over."

"Please God, they will progress thus far, and a good deal farther! I assure you! And now you have my word of honor that when we do send for you, all difficulties will have been removed."

A fortnight later Reb Avram Ber received from his new-found friend a letter that bore also the signature of several other members of the community, to the effect that they wished to appoint him as their minister; that they desired the honor of a visit from him, and if he were willing to come, two members of the congregation would be sent to escort him; that these two estimable members would bring to Reb Avram Ber an official letter of invitation signed by the whole congregation, and, moreover, in the unlikely event of his ultimate rejection of their offer, all the expenses he had incurred would be refunded to him, and that willingly! …

At home there was great rejoicing. Reb Avram Ber, of course, was not a little pleased, but one point sorely troubled his conscience – was he not depriving another man, the "upstart" son-in-law, of his livelihood? Raizela knew nothing about the "upstart" or the "snobs," since Reb Avram Ber had omitted all mention of them. He sent back a letter to say that he was willing.

The next thing was that one fine morning a comfortable carriage, drawn by two prosperous-looking horses, drove up into the courtyard of Reb Avram Ber's house and two men got out who were muffled up in their greatcoats as if it were mid-winter. The carriage immediately made off again, and it was a long time before the neighbors at the windows could stop staring at the gateway through which so rare a sight had come and gone.… The two muffled-up men enquired after Reb Avram Ber.

Raizela was taken by surprise. She climbed down from her couch, asked the visitors into the sitting room, begged them to take a seat and motioned to Deborah to go and fetch her father at once.

On hearing the news, Reb Avram Ber quite forgot his pangs of conscience about the "upstart" son-in-law. He was full of glee.

"So they've really come, have they? Thank God!"

He added something in an undertone, which sounded like a prayer, and he made straight for home, beaming all over as he entered.

"Pray be seated, be seated!" The visitors sat down again.

Reb Avram Ber asked Deborah to get the samovar ready. Raizela stayed where she was for courtesy's sake, but after a little while excused herself and returned to her couch.

Meanwhile, Deborah had picked out the best spoons and had polished the tumblers until they glittered like crystal. It was with the utmost zest that she poured out the reddish, transparent tea, and watched the visitors imbibe it. They were both very diffident, and needed Reb Avram Ber's gentle persuasion before they would take off their coats. Each of them unwound an incredibly long blue scarf from a bashfully rigid neck. Reb Avram Ber then pressed them to take lunch with the family.

That morning Deborah asked for more groceries on credit than she had ever done before, and in return she was obliged to answer all the shopkeeper's searching questions as to who the visitors were, was it their own carriage they had arrived in, what business brought them hither, were they or were they not relatives, when were they likely to leave or did they intend to stay with the family for good, and no matter how niggardly Deborah tried to be, in the end the shopkeeper's thirst for knowledge was well-nigh satisfied.

After lunch the carriage reappeared in the courtyard. The visitors donned their long scarves once more and advised Reb Avram Ber to put on the warmest clothes he had, for the cold was bitter, they said, out in the open country. Helping him to climb in, they wrapped him up as cozily as they could, not forgetting themselves, and off they went.

Michael had got wind of the visit and rushed home hotfoot, but he was too late. The carriage had gone.

"Serves you right!" Raizela teased him. "If you hadn't been wasting your time, but had been in the synagogue studying as you should be, you would have seen and known all."

A fortnight passed without word from Reb Avram Ber, apart from the brief postcard which he had sent off on arrival at his destination.

Meanwhile it was getting close to Passover. Raizela received a few rubles from her father, and was quite at a loss what to do with the money, for there were so many ways in which she could have used it. However, the grocer was pressing strongly for payment, and Deborah flatly refused to go into the shop unless she was given the money to clear the debt. Matters had come to such a pass that she would have to hang around watching newcomers being served while she was ignored, and in the end the goods would be flung at her like charity. So Deborah had her way, and again the family was left penniless.

Already the mild spring breezes were heavily laden with the savory odor of hot *matzos*. The Jewish quarter of the town was full of soap and water, of beetroot soup, of all manner of vegetables, of anxiety, distress and headaches as to the wherewithal for the sacred celebrations – in short, full of the coming Passover. Every cobblestone, every shriveled-up bush and tree seemed to be in Passover mood. The porters of the town had all washed their faces clean, and wore paper hats on their heads, with new pieces of sackcloth round their shoulders. Whistling tuneful ditties, they were to be seen coming out of underground bakehouses with immense baskets of *matzos* on their heads, followed by flushed, anxious-looking housewives. Very Orthodox Jews were to be seen with little bags of *shmira,* which they nursed tenderly like coddled babes.

The town was full of cheerful bustle. Even the everyday cares and troubles gained a new flavor of their own. Jews hurry-scurried with their gabardines flapping in the breeze. The peasants who came to market made a splendid profit on their cartloads of potatoes, live poultry and eggs. As for eggs, the prices that were being paid on that Passover eve were positively fantastic! The crush was terrific in the marketplace. The stallholders were shouting frantically. The peasants who brought their produce to town were besieged by eager buyers.

In Raizela's home, however, there was no hint as yet of the coming Passover. Taciturn as usual, she lay on her couch, poring over a book, with her little feet tucked under her as though she were quite oblivious of the fact that there were only ten more days to go. The air was full of a silent sorrow – it hung there like a curse, which everybody thought fit to ignore. One question tormented everybody: What could have happened to Reb Avram Ber? Why had he not answered any of Raizela's letters?

At last, only six days before Passover, Reb Avram Ber came back. Now, as once before in Jelhitz, he sat down on a stool in front of Raizela's couch and said – but this time with bated breath – that all would be well, the Lord be praised, if only…if only…she, Raizela, were willing.… Whereupon Raizela's eyes opened wide in astonishment, and she gazed at her husband with a terrible suspicion: did this man mean to drag her through the mire again?

"Let me explain the position," said Reb Avram Ber, feigning composure, but the extreme uneasiness that possessed him was betrayed by every wrinkle in his face. "It's not a rabbi the community are looking for after all, but...."

Raizela's eyes opened wider still.

"But?..." she echoed.

It was quite five minutes before Reb Avram Ber found his tongue again.

"But... a *tzaddik*."

"What?"

"Well you see, this is the position. Their former rabbi also served as a *tzaddik*. He made a very comfortable living, and was highly respected. What they're after now is someone to take his place."

"So what of it?" Raizela cut in impatiently. All this talk about the former *tzaddik* seemed to her quite irrelevant.

"So they have asked me..." Reb Avram Ber resumed, in such a gentle whisper that Raizela had to incline her ear to catch what he was saying. "They have approached me.... In fact, they tell me that they have heard say that I come of a very illustrious family, and I may add that my own reputation is not unknown to them either; indeed, they are very favorably disposed to me, and they promise me a comfortable living. Really, they treated me with the utmost respect and consideration. The whole community absolutely begged me to come to them as their...you see, they want a new *tzaddik*."

"And still I don't know what you're driving at," said Raizela. "What if they do want a new *tzaddik*? How does that concern you? You don't mean to tell me that their official invitation to you to become their new rabbi was no more than a scrap of paper, or is that what you're trying to say?"

Reb Avram Ber felt the blood rushing up into his head.

"Not exactly, but the difficulty is this: a son-in-law of the former minister has staked his claim as the sole rightful successor, and says he is not going to make way for a stranger. To try to oust him would mean settling down in an atmosphere of strife, and what's more, this son-in-law has a small, but voluble, following in the town. He is himself a Ger Hasid, and all the other Ger Hasidim in the neighborhood are strongly on his side. Whereas they used to scoff at the father-in-law, and mocked him at every turn, they think highly of the young man, and they say they'd sooner have bloodshed than see him go. With the exception of this small opposition, the official invitation to me was actually signed by practically the whole community. And these good people tell me that in the long run they will triumph over the dissenting minority, but patience is needed. Meantime, they want me to come and live with them. All our troubles are going to be over soon, thank God! I can trust these people, they are all honorable men, and I have nothing to fear from them. 'To begin with, you will be our *tzaddik*, or rather our leader,' they say to me, 'and then in due course you will become our rabbi.' At first I wouldn't hear of it, but after a while I became convinced that I would not really be compromising the son-in-law's chances, because he's quite unacceptable to the congregation as a whole. Whatever happens, the benefice is certain to go eventually to an outsider. There can be not the slightest doubt about that. And don't for one moment imagine that these good people are trying to deceive me. No, they're in dead earnest! In fact, do you know what they did? They gave me fifty rubles to help us over the Passover holiday. Of course, I didn't want to take the money. But it was no use my arguing. They absolutely forced the money on me, although I never gave them any definite decision, because I wasn't sure of your attitude. 'Please,' they said to me, as if I were doing them a favor, 'please accept this and prepare a Passover festival fit for a king!'"

Raizela was steadfastly silent.

Reb Avram Ber at last got tired of sitting down. He stood up and began pacing the room, mopping his brow with his spotted yellow handkerchief as he went. A quarter of an hour passed by. Half an hour. Still she said not a word, did not even attempt to say anything, but only followed his every movement with a melancholy look in those big grey eyes of hers, which scorched him like glowing embers.

Deborah came in. She had been out shopping. On catching sight of her father she became flushed with pleasure.

"Hallo, Papa! When did you get back? Why don't you take your coat off? It's quite warm in here. Shall I pour you some tea?"

And without waiting for a reply she busied herself at the samovar. Soon a gleaming glass of tea stood at the head of the table.

"How are you, Papa?"

"I'm all right, Deborah, I'm all right," said Reb Avram Ber, gratified to find himself spoken to at last.

"Is everything fixed up?" she asked, unable to curb her curiosity any longer.

"More or less!"

And at this Reb Avram Ber stole a glance at Raizela, who still lay on the couch in the same position as before, with that strange, faraway air, which gave him the creeps. There was something unnatural in the folds round the corners of her mouth. They seemed to betoken a peculiar smile, or was it an expression of anguish? Or did that grimace mean that she was crying? Or maybe she was smiling and crying at the same time? Her whole body was trembling palpably.

A sensation of warmth filled Reb Avram Ber's breast, and soon this excessive warmth made him feel sick. He began to choke. Spluttering, he asked Deborah to fetch him a glass of water. She handed it to him, and wondered what on earth could have happened. Only now did she notice that her mother was all aquiver. Reb Avram Ber sipped a little water, then folded his hands behind his back and began to march up and down the room once more as if he had broken a journey and must resume it in haste.

"Oy, oy, oy! God Almighty, I pray to you to save us! Oh, merciful Father, what else is there left for me to do?" He turned suddenly on Raizela, as if she were his merciful Father. "Would you rather see us starve to death? Be reasonable! You know quite well that I don't think myself a *tzaddik*. They have asked me to become their spiritual leader, that's all, their leader. Surely I'm good enough for that, good enough to teach simple honest Jews the rudiments of the Talmud and be to them a sort of spiritual leader...."

Still Raizela was speechless.

"Tell me, what harm is there in that? Speak, is there anything else left for me to do?"

He pleaded with her as with a hard taskmaster, but she ignored him. In those two deep folds around her mouth there reposed a smile which seemed hard, cynical even; yet at the same time it was also pitiful and full of entreaty, like a childish pout. Suddenly, quite unlike her usual self, she burst out laughing, and laughed boisterously like a woman possessed.

"Oh dear me, it's funny to hear you! You have only just entered the profession, and already you have all the cards up your sleeves. You're up to all the tricks of the trade," she said with so much derision, with such deep contempt in her voice, that Reb Avram Ber squirmed like a mean little worm. "To begin with you said that these *good people* wanted you as a *tzaddik*. Now your memory has failed you and you have changed it round to a 'spiritual leader.' You've made a very pretty display of yourself. And now tell me, how can you complain about the *tzaddik* of R– if you're of the same kidney as he is?"

As she put this question to him she eyed him with the severity of a judge preaching at a prisoner.

It was Reb Avram Ber's turn to be speechless now. He did not know what to say in reply. He felt disgusted with himself. He realized that she was quite justified in speaking to him the way she did. It was sickening of him to have ever contemplated doing such a thing. A host of persuasive tongues and his own wretchedness had nearly succeeded in seducing him. And he was touched with gratitude towards her for having saved him from such a mean temptation.

"She is always in the right," he said to himself. "Always! Her good sense never fails her!"

And with a sense of relief, as if a heavy burden had been removed from his breast, he sat down and began to sip the tea with enjoyment, although it had long since grown cold.

"Are you asleep?" Reb Avram Ber enquired a few hours later, rousing Raizela in the other bed.

"No!" Raizela whispered, still in her uncommunicative mood.

"You know, you're perfectly right. Listen, I've thought it all over very carefully, and I've come to the conclusion that there can be no doubt about it: you're perfectly right! I'm only human, and knowing the terrible plight we're in, my head was turned. I'm going to turn down their offer, and as for the money they've given me, I'll borrow a bit of it to tide us over the holidays, and I'll send the rest back immediately. I suppose something will turn up. God won't forsake us. And maybe you could go away with the children and live with your father until something does turn up. It'll make things a lot easier for you, and it will also give me more freedom to travel and look for a new position."

Raizela was reconciled.... And Reb Avram Ber, tired out and relieved, fell asleep with a great sense of comfort.

It was only on the following morning that Deborah and Michael were told that their father's journey had been fruitless. Deborah considered it a "pure misfortune," but she had little time to spare for idle speculation. The Passover festival was right on top of them, and there was much to be done. Moreover, her father handed her a sum of money to do things in style, and that was certainly a comfort. After a long and assiduous search for domestic help she led home in triumph a decrepit old charwoman, and combining their efforts they set to work with a will....

The woman shuffled about the rooms with an aimless air, but there was great skill in her bony misshapen hands – like the leafless branches of a tree – as she scrubbed the tables, the chairs and the floors. Her every movement was accompanied by the quivering of her fleshless, wrinkled second chin and by an everlasting sigh. Now and again she stopped to wipe her red diseased eyes, and told Raizela her troubles, complaining how poor she was and how her miserable little home was devoid of all trace of the coming festivities.

"If you can't go about begging, you've only yourself to blame, is what I say! You work yourself to death, and no one's going to thank you for it, neither! Such is life!" she philosophized, and as she wiped her fingers on her livid face the smears she produced on her nose were for her the sole trace of the coming festivities.

Reb Avram Ber ordered *shmira* for himself and for Raizela. *Matzos* were delivered in good time. Everything was got ready in the twinkling of an eye. It all happened in the nick of time. Nor was the charwoman forgotten by Raizela, so that in the end the smears on her nose were as nothing compared with the many good things she took home.

Michael kept aloof from all the turmoil. He lay at his ease on a synagogue bench (in a different neighborhood far away from the *tzaddik*'s establishment) and diligently tried his hand at "making faces" (which was how Reb Avram Ber termed Michael's efforts at portraiture, to which he had recently taken with great enthusiasm). When he came home for his meals he did not stay for very long, because the charwoman simply drove him out of the place. However, in the evening, when she had finished and was preparing to go home, she afforded him ample compensation. He happened to wander into the kitchen and found her, with her dress still tucked up, gloating over her numerous parcels in brown paper stacked on the newly scrubbed floor. It occurred to him that she would make a splendid study, and no sooner had the thought struck him, than out came his pencil and paper. No one paid any heed to what he was doing, least of all the charwoman. But when he no more than asked her to turn her head a little and to raise her skirt somewhat, she fixed such a startled gaze upon him, and her face became so expressive, that Michael had reason to thank her for the rest of his life, for this was his first and last sketch which he never destroyed.

Immediately after the holidays Reb Avram Ber sent back thirty rubles, together with an apology. He wrote to say that he was sorry he could not accept the congregation's friendly offer, and was even more sorry about his inability to send back the money in full. He promised to make good the deficiency at the first possible opportunity. In response to his letter, the two estimable gentlemen who had visited him once before came again in person; but all their arguments, all persuasion, failed utterly. Reb Avram Ber gave them a categorical refusal. The men went away deeply mortified. Heavens, what a humiliation! They could not for the life of them see what good reason Reb Avram Ber could have for turning his back on plain, but honorable Jews who wished to appoint him as their *tzaddik*, who sincerely wished to pay homage to him and to provide him with a comfortable living. He had objected to being named a *tzaddik*. That was a detail about which they would raise no difficulties. He had preferred to be called a "spiritual leader." Very well, then, a "spiritual leader" he would be! But now, it seemed, no concession would satisfy him.

"We're not good enough for him, that's what it is! If only the snobs had asked him to be their *tzaddik*, he would have fallen over himself for joy!" the two disappointed men told each other, with no little ill-feeling, as they drove away.

Two days later there was an exchange of correspondence between son-in-law and father-in-law. Reb Avram Ber began by writing a very long letter. Apart from the usual respectful title, he now addressed his father-in-law as, "One of the most illustrious children of Israel," and so on and so forth. He described fully the plight the family was in. He then made it perfectly clear that he, Reb Avram Ber, had always done everything that lay within his power to provide for his wife and children, and that he was in no way to blame for what had happened, for everything in life was predetermined by Providence, which no man, no matter how strong he was, could resist. Therefore, Raizela and the children would have to go and stay with her father for a short while, until matters would improve, and Reb Avram Ber had faith that they would improve before long. God would surely not neglect him. This epistle elicited a reply in which Reb Avram Ber was merely addressed as, "My esteemed and worthy son-in-law" – and the rest of the usual title was lacking. The reply then went on to say briefly that "my beloved daughter" and the children would be welcome – God forbid that it should be otherwise – only the fact of the matter was that Reb Avram Ber had been born a simpleton, had remained a simpleton, and would always be a simpleton....

Chapter 8

The following week a strange thing happened. On the very day that Raizela and the children were to have gone away to stay in her father's house, Reb Avram Ber brought home a visitor – a swarthy, bright-eyed man with a long, well-cared-for and, as it were, sensible beard.

"Good afternoon!" said the stranger in a very pleasant tone of voice.

His friendly greeting met with a chilly response from Raizela. She imagined that this was another of those bright specimens with whom Reb Avram Ber was always getting himself into trouble. Not that it mattered, for she was returning to her parents' roof, and it would be a very long time indeed before Reb Avram Ber would induce her to come and live with him again. Her cup of bitterness had overflowed! But when Reb Avram Ber called her into the next room she could not be rude and refuse so, hiding her reluctance, she joined the company. Reb Avram Ber pulled up a chair for her and began to tell her in his enthusiastic way that Reb Zalman (this being the visitor's name) hailed from Warsaw, but had come down to R– for a few days to see the *tzaddik* on a certain matter touching the yeshiva, and that this same Reb Zalman was of the opinion that Reb Avram Ber could, if he so wished, get an appointment as a rabbi in Warsaw.

"Which would, of course, be splendid!" said Raizela, smiling her most skeptical smile, but, in spite of herself, the very suggestion gladdened her heart, even though she had as much hope of its coming true as she had of the samovar, that stood upon the table, joining in the conversation. Still, she found it rather pleasant to listen to Reb Zalman as he held forth over his glass of tea. According to him, there was in Warsaw a certain neighborhood in which a rabbi was badly needed. It had a dense Jewish population, and as none of the "official" rabbis – that is, those appointed by the central rabbinical authorities – lived within reasonable distance of this district, Orthodox Jews found themselves greatly inconvenienced. For instance, if any doubts arose as to whether food was kosher or not, a mistress might order her maid to consult a rabbi. But this maid, being lazy – and most servants were lazy – might not do as she was told and then – horror of horrors! – the holy laws of Moses would be transgressed. Now Reb Zalman had a great many friends in this particular neighborhood, and he was more than certain that with a little persuasion from him they would willingly subscribe towards a stipend for Reb Avram Ber. Incidentally, being an arbiter in Jewish law, Reb Zalman was well acquainted with some of the official rabbis, and a possibility not to be ruled out was that he might even obtain a grant for Reb Avram Ber from the central authorities. He would draw their attention to the evil practices at present rife in the neighborhood through the lack of a rabbi, and so on and so forth....

Within a very short time Reb Zalman was perfectly at home not only with Deborah, who had meantime refilled the glasses, and not only with Michael, who sat opposite him and made a poor pretense of studying a religious tract, but was familiar also with the four walls, and with the tea on the table, and was familiar even with Raizela, who listened to all he said, having come to the conclusion that he was by no means a fool.

"Finally, I'm going to make the *tzaddik* do his bit to help. He needs my favor, as it happens, and if I press the matter on him he won't refuse. Not that he's likely to quibble with me, in any case," he added with complete self-assurance. "What I'm going to ask – or rather demand of him – to do is to circularize his many Hasidim in the neighborhood, telling them to give me their full support. Believe me, if you take my advice, you'll never have cause to regret it. Warsaw is a thoroughly

Jewish city, if ever there was one! What's the good of your hiding yourself away in a poky little town like this?"

The latter remark came as a shock to Deborah. How could anyone call R– a poky little town? Surely he would not have said any such thing if he had ever been to see Jelhitz!

"I don't mind telling you Warsaw is a wonderful city to live in," Reb Zalman went on with an expansive air, as if he owned the place. "Good old Warsaw! It's the city of golden opportunity. If a man can't do any good for himself in Warsaw, he's not likely to prosper anywhere! There are quite a number of 'unofficial' rabbis in Warsaw. We call them 'private' rabbis. And they all manage to make a comfortable living. And there's no reason why you shouldn't do the same. In fact, you would be in a better position than the others, because the need for a rabbi in your district is very real."

Reb Zalman did not leave it at that, but carried on as if his own future were at stake, as if his very existence depended upon whether or not Reb Avram Ber was to be happily established in Warsaw. And he spoke with so much forcefulness, withal so quietly, and there was such unshakeable confidence in his candid brown eyes, that his plan unfolded itself like a living thing, like a flower opening its petals in the sunshine, and everybody at the table was seized with a sudden urge to get up and run off to Warsaw at once. He spoke with great reasonableness, measuring every detail carefully, leaving nothing to chance, and in the end there was no room left at all for argument or doubts. It was decided that Reb Avram Ber should travel up to Warsaw with Reb Zalman and there try his luck. Meanwhile Raizela and the children were to postpone their departure for the time being.

"I'm sure you're not in a hurry to get back to your father's house. That always remains as a last resort," declared Reb Zalman.

Deborah was delirious with excitement. It was all like a dream which could hardly come true. But what if her father was really to return from this new trip and say: "All's well, the Lord be praised! We're going to live in Warsaw!" What then? It would simply be wonderful! So much better than going to live in Grandfather's house! No, she had not forgotten the holiday she had once spent there with her mother some years ago. What a life it had been! There was Grandmother always on the go, always busy making jam and fruit juice, and gooseberry tarts and preserves. There was that old-fashioned oven in the kitchen, in which a tremendous fire was kept going from morning to night; it was never allowed to die down for a single instant.

Of course, it was a house full of plenty, but it was more than that – a house full of untouchables. All the cherries, the gooseberries, the black currants, all the plums, raspberries and blackberries were put away for the wintertime and were not to be touched. Anyone might have thought that summertime was a season of slavery, and that all the delicious things which grew ripe in the sunshine were only intended to be left over and enjoyed in the winter. It was so silly!

In other respects, her grandmother was not really a bad sort. Anyway, she fed her family on the fat of the land – fish and meat and soup in plenty. And she seemed to take real pleasure in seeing everybody stuff himself like a turkey. It quite upset her if ever a dish was refused. But no tidbits on the sly! Oh, no, she wouldn't stand for that! And that was just what Deborah loved best of all, preferring it above all the elaborate dishes served so plentifully at table. If ever Deborah helped herself to a solitary gooseberry she was at once denounced as a greedy wretch, a hopeless case, a puss, a cat, and, in fact, all sort of things!

And to make matters worse, first thing every morning Grandmother would march off to say her prayers in the synagogue – and where Grandmother went there went her bunch of keys. All the cupboards would be locked. And if Deborah happened to be starving, well, she could go on starving! There was nothing to do but wait for Grandmother to finish saying her prayers. Of course, when breakfast did come up, it was a meal fit for a king – black currants and cream, delicious hot rolls and coffee with a really glorious aroma – but the maddening part about it all was that Deborah must never take anything of her own accord....

Then, when Thursday came round, discipline would become so very strict as to turn the home into a veritable prison, for that was the day when "Long" Malka, the outside domestic help, took charge, and she was not a woman to be trifled with in any form or fashion. To think of all the work that woman had to get through on a Thursday! Grandmother was not much good at baking, and she simply had to have the assistance of "Long" Malka. And "Long" Malka knew it, and how she lorded it in the house! She behaved like the czar. For not only did she bake the plaited loaves, she also had the butter cakes to do, and the fruit cakes, and the egg cakes, and the oil cakes, and the rolls, and the gingerbreads. And when that was finished, she had to knead still more dough, and roll it flat and cut it up into noodles. Well, a woman who could do all that was a perfect treasure in the house. So ill-betide Deborah if she got suspiciously close to the kneading trough, or was suddenly tempted to make off with a hot gingerbread. That treasure of a woman could not have created more fuss if it had been her own property that was being pilfered. Not that the fuss finished there. In fact, that was where it began. After "Long" Malka had done shouting (and could she shout!), Grandmother would start moralizing. Then came a sermon from an aunt who had been supported under the parental roof with an ever-growing family ever since she had got married twenty years ago, and for this reason – or rather in spite of it – considered herself one of the household authorities. Next, uncle would indulge in some good-natured chaffing and, last of all, came a terrible reprimand from Mother.

And just by way of a finishing touch, every Friday morning her grandmother would give her a big basket of victuals and tell her to distribute them to the respectable poor of the town. There would be a loaf – as big as "Long" Malka's head – for each family and half a pound of meat. It might be raining cats and dogs, or the sun might be scorching like the fire in the kitchen hearth on a Thursday, never mind that, she must sally forth with the basket, get rid of its contents and come back for more – sometimes there would be a few pieces of boiled fish as well, for the very respectable poor – and God help her if she tried to wriggle out of this noble and charitable deed!

Now the trouble with Grandfather was quite of a different order.

He spent every moment of the day in his private study, poring over the Talmud and composing his books, and no one ever saw anything of him. On those rare occasions when he came out to stretch his limbs she simply longed to have a word with him, or at the very least to hear him speak (for, as it happened, she loved him passionately), but he had a strange incomprehensible language all of his own, made up entirely of "Nu!" and "Nu-O!" These "Nus!" and "Nu-Os!" had something very profound in them, which would quite overawe the love she bore him, so that in the end her respect for him would outweigh her love. Raizela was the only person in the house he ever spoke to. And in the presence of him who was so wise, so exalted, Deborah, who was so small, so frivolous, could only feel deeply ashamed of herself. If he ever smiled at her, she only felt like going away and hiding herself in a corner, for the moment he condescended to notice her he could not but see how mean she was – just a mere worm by comparison with himself.…

Then again, there were her cousins to consider – the cheeky brats! Throughout her stay they had treated her like an impostor, as if they alone, having been born and bred in the house, were the genuine grandchildren, whereas she was only a stranger, and what did she mean by intruding? True enough, she *was* a guest, and as such her grandmother thought fit to present her with a complete new outfit of clothes. But that was a blessing in disguise, for thereafter the air turned hot for her. Her cousins dropped all pretense of politeness, and quite overwhelmed her with their envy. They mocked her, and ridiculed her, and made her life a misery, so that she came to detest the fine new clothes, and would much rather have gone without. And in the end, when Raizela was sent away by her parents to a watering place to take the cure, and Deborah – poor child! – was left to fend for herself, she might just as well have gone and hanged herself on the highest bough of the highest tree she could possibly find!…

Of course, things would be changed now. Even so, the prospect of going to live in Warsaw was infinitely more attractive.… But why fool herself? Was such a thing really possible? Certainly, she had heard people speak a great deal about the wonderful city of Warsaw. For instance, "Little" Mendel always went to Warsaw to get the best materials for his shop. And Joseph Cahn's son, it was said, was a student in the university at Warsaw. But that a rabbi should be wanted in Warsaw, and that none other than her father – a man whom both her grandfather and her mother rated as being a homely simpleton – should fill the vacancy, now surely that was a crazy notion. And yet Reb Zalman maintained that it was a possibility – nay, a probability. Well, perhaps it was, and perhaps it wasn't!

Michael took it all for granted, and he was exceedingly happy. As a matter of fact, he had lately had a lot of funny ideas in his head about going to Warsaw on his own. He had quite made his mind up to throw up his studies, run away from home and find a job for himself in the big city. But now, it seemed, without waiting for him to act, opportunity had come knocking at the door quite unexpectedly. And by way of celebration he began to whistle aloud. Reb Avram Ber looked up with a startled air.

"Who's that? Is that you, Michael?"

Michael hung his head a little and apologized, with a gentle smile on his reddening face, saying that he was quite unable to account for his whistling; it was in no way deliberate, and he was just as surprised to hear the sound as they were. Both Reb Avram Ber and Raizela assured Reb Zalman that this was the first time the boy had ever done it in the home.

"Well, is everything settled?" Reb Zalman asked, pushing back his chair and rising to his feet.

Reb Avram Ber eyed Raizela for confirmation. She began to ponder. After all, it seemed a feasible plan, and they had nothing to lose. Further, if it were to materialize, they would not have to be dependent for their livelihood on such a narrow circle of people as they had been hitherto. As for returning to the parental roof, that could certainly wait. Reb Zalman was perfectly right.

"Tell me," said Reb Avram Ber, rather losing his patience, "shall we take a chance?"

"Yes, I think so. No harm in trying."

Deborah fluttered. Perhaps, when she got to Warsaw, she might come across that brainy student with the lean face and the luminous eyes, that young man whom she had first seen when she had gone to catch a glimpse of the *tzaddik*, and who would always bestow such a strange look on her. She had almost forgotten his name. *Simon* – that was it! Shortly before the yeshiva had been burnt down he had suddenly disappeared, and Mottel told her that he had gone away to the capital. The memory of him was so painfully vivid, that she quite lost her presence of mind and she asked her father if Simon was now in Warsaw.

"Whom do you mean? Oh, I know! I've no idea where he's got to at all. Someone brought him a letter at the yeshiva one day, he went off in a hurry to the station and that was the last we saw of him. He did not even trouble to come back and say goodbye. I imagine he must have received some bad news. Perhaps someone in the family was taken ill. I often wonder where he is. But tell me, what do you want to know for?"

Deborah crimsoned.

"Oh nothing, I only asked!"

"Well, that's settled. We shall make the trip tomorrow morning," said Reb Zalman, bidding the family good night.

"He's a sensible fellow," Raizela observed, after the door had been closed behind him, "but how he loves to exaggerate!"

"He's a man you can trust implicitly," said Reb Avram Ber. "Kind-hearted and clever. And a very shrewd businessman. Knows everything, knows everybody, goes everywhere and has never let anyone down. In fact, he's always willing to lend you a helping hand. He's ever so popular. We've known each other for years and years."

"Is he a Hasid?"

"No, he isn't. It's business that brings him here to see the *tzaddik*. The two of them have been associating for years."

Raizela gave a grunt of disapproval. Her confidence in Reb Zalman was suddenly dissipated. However, the suggestion was still worth trying. She was none too keen on going back to eat of her father's bread again.

About ten o'clock on the following morning Reb Avram Ber, shepherded by Reb Zalman, took the train for Warsaw, and in a fortnight's time he returned with the glad news that he had actually rented a flat for them to move into.

"Really? Without asking?"

"Well, Reb Zalman said that there was no need for me to ask," Reb Avram Ber apologized. "And honestly, I think it was best not to. 'To delay is fatal,' Reb Zalman says to me. 'Decision is everything. Don't dillydally! Once a man starts to hesitate, he usually spoils all his plans.' You know, Reb Zalman tells me that the *tzaddik* is going to pay all the removal costs. He made the *tzaddik* promise. I say, Deborah, could you give your father a glass of tea?"

"So we have a promise from the *tzaddik*? Now *that* is something to bank on," said Raizela with a laugh.

"You wait and see! This time everything is going to turn out for the best."

"I hope so!"

As he sipped his tea, Reb Avram Ber recounted his experiences.

"The type of Jew you meet in Warsaw is more genial, more generous in every way, if you know what I mean."

"Not so narrow-minded and less self-centered," Raizela hazarded.

"Absolutely!" said Reb Avram Ber, his enthusiasm bearing on Raizela's good sense rather than on the noble qualities of the people he had met. "Money is to them of little consequence. They can make it and they can spend it. Now you saw Reb Zalman! He's a typical example. If they conceive a liking for anyone, they'll go to any lengths to help him. I think I was lucky, because they all seemed to take a liking to me. You should have seen the reception I was given in the synagogue. They got out a bottle of brandy and drank my health. And everybody welcomed me with such warmth, there was so much good fellowship all round, anyone might have thought these people had known me all their lives. They were honestly delighted to see me. I could tell by their faces.... And, you know, they really must have a rabbi in that neighborhood, for they tell me the present state of affairs is simply shocking. Shocking! One man, who seemed to be rather important, came up to me and said, 'Glad to meet you! It's a good job we're going to have someone at last to set our house in order, because it's wicked to be without a rabbi. And I think you're just the right sort of person for us – an honorable man with no hypocritical nonsense. You know, not the sort of rabbi who cares only for his fee, and who when someone turns up for a free consultation sends out word to say that he's asleep and can't be disturbed. Not that sort! You're a man after our own heart,' he says to me, 'and I hope you will be comfortable with us and make a really good living.' And, God willing, so we shall!

"Reb Zalman has no end of influence with these people. He's quite one of the exalted. Everybody respects him immensely. He spent the whole evening with me in the synagogue getting up a list of subscribers. There wasn't a single person who dared refuse him, and he carefully avoided one or two people who looked rather doubtful. It was a real pleasure to watch him. He has all his wits about him, has Reb Zalman. And he has a high sense of dignity too. A great-hearted man! You can't imagine how helpful he was. I didn't know how to thank him!

"To begin with, he insisted on putting me up. And he introduced me to his wife. Now she's a wonderful woman, a perfect angel, that's what she is! The things she did to make me feel at home and comfortable! She was after me all the time – 'Help yourself to this, and help yourself to that!' And the bedclothes she gave me were fit for a king to sleep in. Even after I had gone to bed she sent her boy in to ask if I could do with an extra pillow. She couldn't do enough for me. And as for Reb Zalman, he actually devoted a whole week to flat hunting. I got quite tired going about with him, because no matter how many flats he saw, none of them was good enough. Very particular man, Reb Zalman. He kept picking and choosing, he couldn't have been more finicky if the flat had been for himself. He was out to find a place that would have every convenience, at a low rental. And that wants a bit of finding! He went to no end of trouble and he didn't seem to care a bit that while he was taking care of me, he was neglecting his business to his own detriment. At last he discovered just what he wanted. 'You see,' he says to me, 'he who searches shall also find.' He was so exultant, anyone might have thought he had found some hidden treasure. Of course, I suppose this flat really was better than the others we had viewed. But to tell you the truth, I never saw any difference myself."

Raizela smiled a patronizing smile which seemed to say, "Heavens, what a terrible simpleton you are!" Nevertheless, it now dawned upon her for the first time that her own skeptical outlook on life led to stagnation, to nothingness, and only such strong faith as animated Reb Avram Ber led to the highroad of life: it was only by utter simplicity and a childish belief in one's fellow beings that one could gain the whole world, with these qualities alone could one savor the true delights of life; indeed these qualities were in themselves the most beautiful thing that life had to offer, and a truly wise man was he who could accept this offering. What was the use of forever sitting in judgment on life and never being able to pass any sentence on it?

For a whole fortnight Raizela kept away from her couch and resumed the use of her legs. She helped Deborah to get everything ready for the journey, even taking the trouble to check up the linen when it was returned by the washerwoman. (They had specially hired a washerwoman for the occasion.) Deborah and Michael had never seen their mother so active before, and they wondered what had suddenly come over her. It rejoiced their hearts. Michael, inspired by her example, willingly lent a hand and he did not spend a moment in idle lounging as he had done before leaving Jelhitz. He simply worked wonders. At one moment he cut short a piercing whistle and burst forth into song instead. At the next he smashed a jug. Then he picked up a heavily laden trunk and ran all round the room as fast as he could go. Deborah, as usual, did most of the work, and all the while her mind was feverish with extravagant pictures of what Warsaw would be like, although even at this late hour she could not settle down to the thought that it was there they were really going to live.

But at last the great day dawned. Quite early on Tuesday morning a large cart drove up into the courtyard and the furniture was packed into it pell-mell. Then a second cart arrived for the rest of the household goods. When the flat was all empty and every voice there raised an echo, the finishing touches were put to the tarpaulins on the hoop frames of the carts, and after vainly scraping their hoofs against the cobbles – to the accompaniment of loud shouts of encouragement – the horses finally got going and the carts rumbled away out of sight. The family put on their wraps. Raizela went downstairs wearing a black velvet jacket over her long black dress and with a black silken shawl over her head, which overshadowed her face and made it appear gaunter than ever. Reb Avram Ber joined her, clad in his winter coat (although the weather was very mild) and with his old rabbinical hat on his head. It was good to see him wearing his rabbinical clothes again. He shook hands with the neighbors, and even gave the womenfolk a nod.

"Did you say goodbye to the *tzaddik*?" asked Raizela.

"Yes! I have forgiven and forgotten. Let us hope that God will forgive him too," said Reb Avram Ber, apparently not without his doubts. "Although I must say that he has taught me a useful lesson. Only now do I understand the true wisdom of, 'Put not thy trust in men, for thy support lies not in them.' Naturally, the world is full of good and kindhearted people, but we have only one Being to look to for support and that is to our Father in heaven. He is a loving and generous Father...."

Reb Avram Ber glanced up at the sky which was of a deep summer blue.

Now here came the *tzaddik*'s carriage and thoroughbred pair, which all the townsfolk knew so well. The *tzaddik* had particularly insisted that this, his own carriage, should convey Reb Avram Ber to the station.

"And have you said goodbye to his wife?" asked Reb Avram Ber.

"Why, of course!"

"And his mother?"

"No, I didn't feel like it."

"Didn't Deborah say goodbye to her either?"

"No!"

"Never mind!"

Laizer Nussen and old Baruch were in the *tzaddik*'s carriage, and Reb Avram Ber and Michael joined them. Raizela and Deborah got into a trap behind, a hired vehicle drawn by only one horse – a cumbrous-looking animal with fat bandy legs and bushy grey fetlocks.

The family nodded farewell to the small crowd which had gathered in the gateway. Deborah did not even forget to wave goodbye to those horrid women who had once taken such keen relish in teaching her the art of scrubbing floors. A brief shower of blessings – and they were off!

Deborah turned her head for a last lingering look at the familiar scene for which she knew nothing but loathing. Suddenly, she caught a glimpse of Mottel standing a little apart from the crowd. How pitiful was the smile on his face; he seemed on the verge of tears. It was a smile of bitter protest – protest at having been left behind, deserted. A great wave of pity surged over her; so, given the chance – and had she not been ashamed – she would have rushed back to say goodbye to him all over again and to explain to him that they themselves were no more than traveling into an uncertain future. But Mottel was soon out of sight, and in his stead came the image of Simon. Simon! Perhaps she would meet him in Warsaw, hurrying as he always hurried with his threadbare gabardine wrapped closely round his lean frame, with his eyes blazing, so dignified in spite of his shabby clothes, so spiritual!

Just as they were setting off, Michael had called out a friendly word of encouragement to Mottel, but Mottel had seemed quite deaf. He now stood stock still, gazing down the narrow street as if he half expected to see the carriages, which were bearing Reb Avram Ber and his family away, turn back to pick him up....

Michael was in great spirits.

"Gallop on, my good horses, and may you drop dead ere you take it into your silly heads to turn back!" he hissed through his teeth after the dramatic fashion of a hero of a novel which he had recently been reading on the sly. "Gallop on, you fat devils, you've only got a short distance to go. Take us to the station and no further!"

Then, relapsing into a more humorous mood, he said to Faivish, the coachman, "Ever thought of treating your horses the same way as you treat the *tzaddik*? If you put your mind to it, you could make the mob worship your horse as they worship the *tzaddik*, and they'd all come flocking round the animal to obtain its blessing. Bet you never thought of that!"

Faivish turned a pair of stupid startled eyes on him, and then a few minutes later he burst out into a loud guffaw.

"I say, you don't mean to tell me that you've digested that joke at last?" said Michael.

"What's that chap jabbering about? What joke?" said Faivish to himself and then he laughed again, as if he would split his sides.

"Ain't she a beauty," he gasped. "Can yer see 'er?"

"Whom?"

"Over there!" said Faivish, pointing his whip at an emaciated mare with an ugly sore patch on her flank harnessed to a heavily laden, rickety cart with an improvised top made up of torn sackcloth. She was a terribly dejected looking animal, holding her head very low, and her foaming mouth seemed to be doing more work than her legs which moved sluggishly as though loath to leave the ground.

"Beauty yourself! You ought to be ashamed of yourself laughing at a poor old skeleton that ought to be in its grave! Faivish, my boy, you won't be much more than a skeleton yourself by the time the *tzaddik*'s finished with you. You'll have a sore behind to sit upon, you'll be all skin and bones, a real old crock!"

However, there was no denying that Faivish was a first class coachman and knew how to handle his horses.

They pulled up with a flourish outside the station. With a very ceremonious air Laizer Nussen wrested from Reb Avram Ber a suitcase containing his manuscripts and took it into the waiting train, where he deposited it on the luggage rack. Then, fussing about over nothing in particular, he scolded old Baruch for being a lazy wretch; he asked the family again and again if they were quite comfortable and – with a last sweet smile at them all – took his leave. Baruch remained behind, and handed over to Reb Avram Ber a parting gift – a few pinches of snuff which he transferred into a little piece of paper with shaky hand, spilling some on the floor.

"There you are! Here's something no man can do without on a journey. You'll find it very stimulating. Look here, Michael, I've got some for you and all. I'm not so sure you deserve any, you rascal, but I'm going to give you the benefit of the doubt" – and he extended a pinch between forefinger and thumb – "Come on now, sniff it up like a man. Come on, stop fooling. Will you put that trunk on the rack for me, Michael? That's the idea!"

Michael sniffed it right up, and sneezed and laughed so much, he came near to choking.

"Atchoo! Atchoo!"

"You won't forget an old friend, will you? Drop us a line now and again, don't forget!" Reb Baruch shook hands with Reb Avram Ber. "And you" – he turned to Raizela – "don't let's have any more of your nonsense! From now on I want you to keep well and strong. As for you, Michael, you've got to become a reformed character. There'll be no *tzaddik* where you're going to, and I want you to concentrate on your studies, see?"

Michael chortled.

"Well, I'll be going," Baruch said at last. "Godspeed!"

He clambered down the carriage steps, his body sagging as though he were a rag doll. The train moved off, as if all this time it had only been waiting for Baruch to get off.

"Good riddance!" said Michael, but Reb Avram Ber silenced him.

"How they all ignore me! Even Baruch didn't think it worth his while to say a word to me," Deborah mused, and though she tried to dismiss the matter as of no importance, it hurt her to the quick. "Everybody dislikes me, everybody!..."

"Michael, get away from that door! Deborah, don't put your head out of the window!" Raizela kept saying, first in a tone of entreaty, then snappishly; but they just could not tear themselves away, for there in the distance was the spreading town, with its grey little houses like so many toys, with here and there a splash of red, and the whole dominated by three lofty steeples. All around, the green countryside was on the move, as though bewitched. The trees with their branches a mass of reddish buds, had such a strange air of stupid beauty as they rushed by frantic with haste: one might have thought they were late for an important appointment. Just overhead the smoke drifted past, puff after puff, and beyond that the sky showed a cool, pellucid blue. No wonder Raizela's nagging passed unheeded!

"Deborah!"

"What?"

"Mamma's asleep!"

"Hush, I know."

"Isn't it a grand view?"

"It's wonderful! What, are you trying to sketch it? I shouldn't waste my time if I were you. You'll only tear it up afterwards. You could save yourself a lot of trouble by tearing the sheet in the first place."

Strangely enough, Michael took no offense.

"Look, Deborah, you see that line where heaven and earth meet, that's called the horizon. Now you follow that right round as far as you can go. The more you keep your eyes fixed on it, the drowsier you get, and in the end you're sure to go to sleep."

"I bet you won't find me going to sleep!"

"Don't be a fool! You've only just started. You wait and see!"

"Hush! Daddy's asleep now."

"There, what did I tell you."

Michael, it seemed, no longer heard the call of art, for with sudden impatience he stuffed his pencil and the sheet of paper back into his pocket, and now they were both standing with their noses flattened against the window. Someone behind them shut the window opposite. They both turned their heads, and then as hastily resumed their former positions. By tacit agreement they were vying with each other to see the most sights; neither of them meant to miss a single ditch, or a bush, not to mention that green little hillock with its funny hump or the stagnant pool nearby, with its surface all covered in deep green moss.

"There must be a village close by," said Deborah.

"Why must there?"

"Don't you see those cows over there, and what about that flock of sheep? Look, there's the shepherd boy!"

The engine ahead suddenly emitted a piercing whistle. A cloud of smoke came gliding past the windows and drifted into the carriages. All the windows were shut to with a bang. The train came to a standstill with all the couplings jolting in succession. They had come to a station. Reb Avram Ber suddenly woke up. So did Raizela. A number of elderly men and women also woke up with a start. An inspector came on the scene, his official face all puckered up with official ennui.

"Tickets please!" he called out with a break in his voice, as though he were too weary even to clear his throat. Discovering no bilkers in this compartment he passed on to the next, hoping to meet with better luck there.

An old woman, with a huge shopping basket in her hand, got out of the train, holding on to the iron railing for dear life as she negotiated the three steps. At long last both her shopping basket and herself were safely deposited on the platform. An old man with a sack over his shoulder followed her just as cautiously. Then a bold youth, who was quite empty-handed, made a brave jump for it, but he caught his foot on the edge of the steps, and when he scrambled back to his feet a stream of blood was spurting from his nose.

"Serves him right!" said a huddled up old man, scratching his thin straggly beard.

The train moved off. It met with a very long goods train passing in the other direction. There was a change of scenery – scraps of woodland interspersed with numerous clearings. In one of them stood a small group of peasant huts. They were so diminutive that their chimney pots seemed to be almost on top of the ground, but there was life within, for every chimney had its fluttering ribbon of black smoke – deep black in contrast to the bright white of the distempered walls. Michael was actually waving to a peasant lass.…

And now, in the distance, a host of monster chimney stacks could be seen towering up as though they were leaning on the sky. These, too, were tipped with ribbons of smoke. A maze of grey buildings loomed up close at hand, and into this maze the train rushed headlong at full speed. On all sides passengers began hurriedly taking the luggage off the racks. The train stopped short with a spitting and hissing of steam. It seemed to Deborah that they could scarcely have left the village behind yet, for they had only traveled a very short distance. But all around were immense buildings – far bigger than anything she had ever seen even in R–. Could this be Warsaw?

"Where are we, Papa?"

"If I'm not mistaken, we're in Praga – a sister town of Warsaw."

"And have we got very far to go before we get to Warsaw?"

"No, we're practically there. This is where we get out."

"And does Warsaw look anything like this?"

"Yes, very much the same."

"Well, that's funny! It was only a short journey. And, do you know, I always used to think Warsaw was hundreds of miles away!"

"Yes, that's just like you! You're a great thinker, only you always think the wrong thing," said Michael with a laugh, and Deborah blushed.

What a terribly busy station! And it was all paved with smooth flagstones – just like the description of a big railway station in one of the novels she had been reading. The crowd was seething with excitement – all in a tangle like a swarm of bees. And no one ever stopped, except for a brief instant to snatch a paper from one of the news vendors. Why all this hurry? Had they all gone mad? Why couldn't they walk along sensibly like normal people? They were a queer lot!

Michael took the luggage off the rack, aided both by Reb Avram Ber and by Deborah. Raizela stood adjusting the shawl on her head. By now everybody had left the train, and the family got out on to the platform, where they huddled together with the luggage at their feet. An endless succession of porters came up to offer their services, but Reb Avram Ber shook his head at them, with a most apologetic smile, as if he craved their forgiveness for declining.

But here came Reb Zalman, a smile of welcome tucked away in his trim, long black beard. He was upon them before they could recognize him in the dense crowd.

"Hallo, how are you? Hallo, everybody! I only managed to get here in the nick of time. My droshky was held up in the traffic. I hope I haven't kept you waiting."

"Not at all. We've just got out of the train."

"That's splendid! I timed it perfectly. I don't mind telling you, I know all the railway timetables by heart. Now if you'll wait here for me, I'll go out and get a droshky," said Reb Zalman as breezily as ever, and he hurried off again.

Reb Zalman's arrival lent a homely little touch to the strange and, as it were, official atmosphere of the station. His very appearance somehow put the family at their ease, and it added firmness to the ground underfoot. They would not have dared to move away from this little haven where he had asked them to wait for him: to leave it was to step into the dread unknown.

"Isn't he a wonderful man? A blood brother couldn't have been more devoted! And don't forget that he's a busy man. He is putting himself out for our sake," said Reb Avram Ber.

"Yes, he's an extremely kind and sensible fellow," Raizela agreed.

It was not long before Reb Zalman was back. Business-like, he picked up a suitcase in either hand, refusing to call a porter.

"You don't want to throw your money away, do you? Instead of arguing, let's get going!"

He made Michael carry the remaining case, while Deborah took possession of the small bag. Reb Avram Ber and Raizela were left empty-handed, and thus they marched behind Reb Zalman as he strode on well ahead of them. Outside the station they were helped into the droshky by a cabby in a shabby uniform and with a weather-beaten face which looked as though it had been boiled tender.... Raizela and Deborah occupied the rear seat, with Michael sandwiched in between, while Reb Avram Ber and Reb Zalman faced them on the narrow tip-up seat opposite – a precarious perch for two grown men, but fortunately neither of them was on the bulky side. The cabby stood scratching his head a while, as if he were about to protest at having to take five fares, but in the end he said nothing and, climbing on to the box, set off at a brisk pace over the bumpy cobbles.

Soon they came to a bridge. The roadway across it seemed to be exceedingly well paved, for the droshky now sped along with the utmost smoothness. Before they had gone far, however, there was a holdup in the traffic ahead; their own droshky stopped, and so did a long line of trams, lorries, motorcars, droshkies, bicycles and peasant carts coming up behind. What a great number of peasant carts for such a big city, what were they doing there? And what was the meaning of this sudden stoppage? A little while ago everybody in the station and out in the streets had been hurrying along like mad, so what good reason could they have now for halting as if possessed of a single body and soul?

"Goodness gracious," said Raizela, "what queer goings on! At one moment you see everybody racing along as if we were in a gold rush, at the next everybody stops as if time simply didn't matter at all."

Deborah was delighted. Her mother and herself had been thinking alike. And as for the sudden standstill, nothing could have pleased her better, for on either side of the bridge lay the mighty River Vistula, its placid surface stained a deep red by the late afternoon sun. Then a boat sounded its horn. The sheet of sunlight was cut in half, and from under the bridge a pleasure steamer entered into view, bit by bit, with white foam frothing angrily all round it. A few dinghies, no bigger than toys, which she had not noticed in the water before, were caught up in the wake of the passing vessel, and how they bobbed up and down merrily, as if they were not in the least frightened of this terrible river! It all seemed quite unreal, like a dream. And now another steamer was coming up.

"Coo, what a big ship!" she said to Michael.

"A whale of a ship!" said Michael, and then he added with an air of bravado, "I wouldn't be afraid of climbing up its rigging. I bet you I wouldn't!"

Deborah laughed like a grown-up sister.

The waterside was lined with strings of barges. And as far as the eye could reach there were stacks of timber, heaps of rubble, assortments of scrap iron and no end of casks – casks of a monstrous size, the like of which she had never seen before. The barges, of course, were at anchor, but all the dumps of material lining the river bank looked as if they might drift away at any moment – they had no visible support.…

There was a sudden stir in the tangled line of traffic and, as if by a pre-arranged signal, it all came to life. They were on the move again, and a few minutes later they had crossed the bridge. The river was lost to sight, and now they came to broad streets with imposing houses rising up on either side.

"This is Warsaw proper," said Reb Zalman with a grave and important air. "How does it strike you? Some people, you know, think Warsaw the finest city in the world. That they do."

Reb Zalman was mentally clapping his hands for joy, but he could hear no echo, so he turned to the cabby:

"Well, driver, would you describe Warsaw as the finest city in the world?"

"Sure I would. Sure!" said the cabby with a sarcastic grunt, in plain Yiddish.

Deborah looked round as if she could not believe her own ears.

"What, is that fellow a Jew?" she gasped.

"Evidently," said Raizela, herself rather taken aback.

"He's a Jew we can be proud of, to judge by his looks – a man of real intellect," Michael put in, but Reb Avram Ber protested.

"You mustn't judge a man by his looks. Everybody has his redeeming features. And anyway I'm sure it's his uniform which is to blame for his coarse appearance."

"Maybe he's a gentile who has just picked up a few words of Yiddish," Deborah reflected in a loud voice. She could not persuade herself that the cabby with his clean-shaven chin and sanguine complexion was in fact a Jew.

"Nothing of the sort," the driver suddenly spoke up for himself, without turning his head. "I'm a Jew all right! And don't I know it! I 'ave to work like a 'orse to earn me miserable living, I do. I 'ave to be out in every lousy weather, I do! No wonder I look like a brute. 'Ave to work to earn me blooming living," he whined, and furiously lashed his horse....

"A good job he's taking it out of the horse. He might have taken it out of us," said Reb Zalman with a smirk.

Deborah was all eyes. She jerked her head this way and that. There were so many wonderful sights to be seen, she could not properly fasten her attention on any of them. At one moment she was pointing out one of the marvels, but at the next her eye was caught by another and even greater marvel. As the streets filed by, she felt a pang of regret at having missed so many good things. And opening her eyes wider than ever, she determined to see everything! As for Michael, he simply sat still and stared straight ahead of him. He had no alternative, for he was jammed in and could not move. But he had a vision of indiscriminate hustle; the town was like an inferno, in which humans swirled about endlessly, aimlessly, as though they had been placed by Satan himself in a boiling cauldron. If Warsaw had been hell, however, Michael would have rejoiced to go there....

"Market day in Jelhitz!" said Deborah, addressing no one in particular and bouncing on her seat. She had no time to spare for idle conversation. They had been driving along for quite a while, and still there was no slackening in the fierce city current – more streets, more shops, more crowds, more traffic. Where did it all begin, and where did it all end?

Then the droshky pulled up, and the cabby jumped off on to the pavement.

"Well, well, here we are! Let me introduce you to your new home. No, this isn't it! I say, driver, it's twenty-four we want!"

"All right, you've no need to 'oller at me! I ain't deaf," the cabby retorted sullenly, and tugging the halter he brought the droshky to a standstill at number twenty-six.

"No, twenty-four, my good man, twenty-four!" Reb Zalman shouted.

"All right, keep your wool on, keep your wool on!"

Michael, squeezing his way out between Deborah and Raizela, was the first to alight, and he helped the others down. He almost had to lift his mother out, as Raizela found that one of her legs had gone quite numb. When the neighbors first saw her they thought she was lame. Deborah, carrying the bag in one hand and a shawl in the other, kept guard over the luggage piled up on the pavement. Michael put his head into the droshky to make sure that nothing had been left behind. Meanwhile, Reb Zalman was engaging in a lively argument with the cabby, who was asking for more than his due. The cabby swore volubly, but finally clapped his big red hands together by way of assent, then examined the coins which Reb Zalman dropped into his palm, and after spitting on the money for luck, he buttoned it up in his large wallet, thrust it deep into the back pocket of his shiny trousers, buttoned up his blue greatcoat, climbed on to his box and, with a farewell flourish of his whip, drove away.

"Look everybody, a lot of country yokels are moving into our house!" cried a little girl of about twelve, with a feather-speckled pigtail.

Her companion, a red-haired girl with a freckled little face and a sore nose, which she was in the act of wiping with the back of her freckly hand, burst out laughing.

The newcomers gathered in the gateway also attracted the attention of the gossips chatting in the inevitable little grocery shop tucked away in a corner of the courtyard.

"D'ye know who that is, Malkela? It's our new rabbi, God bless him!

Ain't it nice to have a rabbi in our own house, ain't it an honor for us?" remarked an old woman with her livid face a network of wrinkles.

"Sure it is! They're movin' in 'cos I live 'ere. Ain't I an attraction?" said Malkela coquettishly, and tickled by her own waggishness, she waited for some response, but none came. "Ha, ha!" she chortled, all by herself; then drawing her tattered shawl firmly around her fleshless, narrow shoulders, she vanished into one of the doorways in the courtyard, with a jug of milk in her hand.

"I say, who's that skinny young woman over there, poor thing?" inquired a huge fat woman, pointing to Raizela; this fat woman had been busy picking a Dutch herring and had missed the conversation. "You ought to know," she went on when the shopkeeper merely answered her question with a scowl.

"I don't know nothing!" the shopkeeper declared venomously. "What I do know is that you're taking too much liberty in picking and choosing around here. Hi, take your fingers out of that sauce. If you don't think my pickled cucumbers are sound, you can go elsewhere. Ah, so you want me to book it up, do you? I thought so! Curse you, and go to hell!" the shopkeeper added when the fat woman was out of earshot. "Some of these here customers are about the limit."

Reb Zalman led the way into one of the innumerable doorways in the courtyard and up a dimly lit flight of stairs, then another and another, until everybody was quite out of breath. After a while they got accustomed to the gloom and could plainly see the steps – dirty grey steps worn smooth by countless feet and littered with rubbish. Once or twice the party paused to rest, then went on again, slipping on the refuse, until at last when they had reached yet another landing Reb Zalman announced that this was their destination. He fumbled in his pockets and produced the key. He inserted it into the lock of an impressive-looking brown door, and flinging it open as wide as he could, he cried:

"You are at home!"

Reb Avram Ber placed a chair for Raizela and she dropped on to it quite helpless.

"Well, isn't this a wonderful flat?" said Reb Avram Ber with his eyes fixed on Reb Zalman. "For this and for many other things we must thank Reb Zalman. A friend in need is a friend indeed, and no man could have a better friend than Reb Zalman."

Reb Avram Ber could not resist paying Reb Zalman this little compliment. It was very unlike him, for he invariably praised people behind their backs. The sincerity of it went to Reb Zalman's head, and also to his legs, for although he said "Pshaw!" and waved the compliment away with his hand, he felt his knees giving way for joy.

They all sat down to rest, either on chairs or on the luggage. Then Reb Zalman went away, taking Michael along with him, and in about half an hour's time he returned with a big parcel in his hands wrapped up in brown paper full of greasy stains. He told Michael to pull the table up into the center of the room and to set the chairs all round it – this was an unfamiliar table with unfamiliar chairs. Where did they come from? Reb Zalman spread a prosperous-looking starched tablecloth.

Just then there was a knock at the door. Reb Zalman admitted a portly woman in the early forties wearing a blonde, neat wig in which a costly clasp was fastened; her hands were white and smooth, and when she smiled her childish dimples showed very prominently, as did her artificial golden teeth. When Reb Zalman gave her a smile, she flushed like a child – even her double chin turned red – and she became quite flustered. Raizela tried to be pleasant to her, and asked her to take a seat, which she did, still completely at a loss, but in the end she managed to pull herself together; she rose to her feet again, held a whispered conversation with Reb Zalman and began to lay the table with a dinner service which she had brought along in a basket. Then she went into the kitchen and returned with a big dish containing soup, which she ladled out; without a word, she set down a cooked yellow fowl – a plump one, and like herself it had an embarrassed air; as though ashamed of its utter nakedness – not forgetting a cruet, sliced bread, a siphon of soda water and pickled cucumbers. Finally she laid the cutlery – all of massive silver, resounding on the table in massive silvery tones – and she begged Raizela to take every possible care of all these domestic treasures.

"You know how easily things get broken and mislaid…when everything's topsy-turvy…you know what I mean…" the woman apologized with a guilty air.

Raizela reassured her and endeavored to thank her, but could not think of anything to say. She was herself disconcerted to see this woman so embarrassed and ill at ease.

"I'm ever so grateful to you," she brought out at last.

"Not at all!" the other woman replied, and backed away to the door with obvious relief.

"She lives next door," Reb Zalman explained. "You'll find them a very nice couple. Extremely well off and ever so religious. Her husband is by no means an ignorant man, and what's more, he's an extremely decent fellow. Most generous. No one in need has ever been turned away from his door. If only they had a child, they'd be as happy as the day is long. It's a pity they can't have any children, such a pity!" Reb Zalman shook his head regretfully. "When she saw me the other day she promised she would get everything ready in good time, and as you see she has kept her word. Don't think, though, that she's an exception. The Jews of Warsaw are all like that. They're kindhearted, and know how to live and let live."

Once again Reb Zalman waxed enthusiastic over the nobleness of the Jews of Warsaw.

"Quite! Quite!" Reb Avram Ber exclaimed, stroking his beard to his heart's content.

Reb Zalman had dinner with the family, and as a matter of fact he seemed to be famished.

Soon after nightfall the menfolk went away to the synagogue, returning without Reb Zalman. Then late at night the removal vans arrived and the furniture was brought up by the dim light of the gas jets flickering on the brick walls of the staircase. The kindhearted husband of the kindhearted woman next door put in an appearance. He was short of stature, had a massive gold chain across his comfortable, gently heaving belly, and wore a grey coat which was a cross between a gabardine and a frock coat, and he padded about noiselessly in gleaming top boots. He smiled a good deal, and as he did so – like his wife – he revealed a mouthful of artificial gold teeth.

He greeted Reb Avram Ber with much warmth, and even shook hands with Michael, but treated the womenfolk to a mere nod of the head – it was a short, broad and friendly head. After a little polite conversation, in the course of which he praised Reb Zalman to the skies and reassured Reb Avram Ber that they would do everything they could to ensure his wellbeing, he divested himself of his coat, rolled up the starched cuffs of his immaculate shirt and helped to put up the beds, a task at which Michael had been struggling in vain for some time. A big blue vein came out on his low forehead, but at last he was finished. He put his coat on again, glanced at his massive gold watch, gave everybody a friendly nod and took his leave.

"Just past midnight," he remarked as he opened the door. "Good night, everybody!"

The family passed the night in a trance, so that they were very startled when, in the midst of their slumbers, they heard a loud, persistent banging at the door.

"Who's that? Why, look, it's broad daylight!"

They dressed in haste and opened the door to Reb Zalman.

"Well, you were certainly sound asleep," Reb Zalman greeted them with a laugh. "I've never known a night to pass so quickly myself. I see the furniture's come."

"Yes, it came late last night."

"Now this young man is going to put things straight for you," Reb Zalman declared, at which all eyes turned on a youth with an unwashed, pimply face, who had slipped in unobserved. Hearing himself introduced, the youth shuffled up from the door and began to shift the furniture about. Reb Zalman never budged until everything was in shipshape order. The jobber cursed him under his breath for being a "finicky old woman," and for wanting everything done in his own way. But at last Reb Zalman could find no more complaints to make; he went away to attend to his own business, and once more the family were established in a new home, once more they were strangers in a strange city.

"Hark at all that shouting down below!" said Raizela as she settled down on her couch.

"Yes, I wonder what it's all about. We never heard a sound last night," said Deborah, greatly puzzled. Putting her head out of the window she could see down below a number of men and women in rags and tatters who came into the courtyard to cry their wares and then went away again, usually without finding any customers.

"Hot rolls, hot rolls! All hot!"

"Old rags! Old boots, galoshes, hats, old rags! Don't throw your rags away, sell them to me!"

"Any windows to mend? Any windows to mend? Windows!"

"Cakes, cakes, cakes!"

"Good God, it's maddening!" Raizela cried, losing all patience.

"You won't notice it after a time. You'll soon get used to it," Reb Avram Ber pacified her. "Reb Zalman asked me to warn you about it beforehand, so that you shouldn't be upset, only I forgot to mention it. You see, all these good people are very poor and are trying to make an honest living. Most of them are Jews," Reb Avram Ber added with a sigh.

"So there's no lack of poverty anywhere – not even in Warsaw! Ah, well, you'll find plenty of misery everywhere...."

Chapter 9

In the flesh the Jews of Warsaw bore no resemblance whatever to the superhumans that peopled Reb Zalman's fancy. They seemed to be wholly ignorant, in fact, of the mighty reputation which Reb Zalman had built up for them, and never even pretended that they could earn money with the same ease as they could spend it. Deborah had imagined that they all lived in the lap of luxury, were all fabulously rich. But she was soon to be sadly disillusioned. She was soon to know that it was only a myth.… Now here was Deborah herself a citizen of Warsaw, but so hard up she could not afford to buy a hat, could not scrape together a few coins for such a simple thing as a hat, and was, therefore, obliged to stay indoors for three weeks on end, like an eager dog chained to its kennel. By the end of that time she was just about disgusted with the Jews of Warsaw.…

Reb Zalman's eldest daughter, Miss Rushka, who – according to her father – was of the same age as Deborah and was, therefore, expected to be her friend, had made it quite clear, when she paid her first call on the Sabbath after the family's arrival, that in the city of Warsaw it was most improper for a young lady to venture forth hatless into the streets. In would be counter to all the unwritten laws of decency. Consequently, Deborah stayed indoors. Funds were low, and anyway, her coat was too shabby for her to go out walking in it.

In the early days Miss Rushka had come again and again to find out how the hat problem was getting on, but one day her father, butting into the prim conversation like a boor, declared vehemently that Rushka herself had not worn a hat when she first came to Warsaw from the dear little village of Jilkovka, although at the time, some eight years ago – and here Reb Zalman put his foot into it badly – Rushka had been quite a grown-up young lady. At this she had almost burst into tears, and nothing more was seen of her again. Deborah was left to her solitude, and instead of getting fed up with Miss Rushka, she got fed up with herself.

It was all very well for Michael. He had no hat problem. He could go wherever he pleased. And even though his gabardine was out-at-elbows, he was not the sort to care. He had settled down in a little synagogue in the Gnoina Road, where he devoted himself to the Talmud, when he was not otherwise engaged in matching his wits against his fellow students. The rest of the time he spent sauntering over the streets of Warsaw, like a tourist, never knowing where he was going, but always finding his way home again. And that suited him to perfection!

Then one day Reb Zalman turned up with a broad-chested youth who had a remarkably expressive, swarthy face with large mournful eyes, and a big hump on his back that pushed his gabardine out to a sharp point, around which streaks of shine radiated like rays of light. Michael, who had just tucked his forelocks into his mop of hair and had brushed his gabardine in readiness for his daily stroll round the town, was stopped at the door by Reb Zalman, who declared that in future Michael must join forces with Joseph (this being the hunchback's name), who was going to make it his business to collect the subscriptions towards Reb Avram Ber's stipend.

"You see, things can't go on as at present," said Reb Zalman, explaining the deep logic of the situation. "The subscribers mean well, but very often they can't find the time to call in with their subscription, or else it slips their memory, or maybe they're hard up, but if you go to their door and ask for it, then you bring them face to face with realities and the cash comes rolling in...."

Michael did not resent the proposal. On the contrary. Here was a wonderful opportunity of getting to know a multitude of strangers in a strange city. As for going round the houses, knocking at the doors and pocketing other people's money, Michael could imagine nothing more enjoyable. Certainly more enjoyable than poring over the dry pages of the Talmud. But he soon changed his mind. After a couple of weeks, he met with ugly looks from the womenfolk, who protested that they knew nothing about their husbands' affairs; and servant girls would give both Joseph and himself a no uncertain piece of their mind for being so importunate and skeptical when told that there was no one at home. Sometimes Joseph and himself would take turns at knocking at a door which remained obstinately closed, and in the end one of the neighbors might appear on the scene and order them to clear out and stop disturbing the peace. As for climbing up the stairs and down the stairs, there was nothing very delightful about it after all. Moreover, an unsavory whiff of decay and poverty assailed the nostrils in every courtyard and on every staircase. And as the sun grew hotter, as spring changed into summer, the whiff changed into a stench that was positively sickening.

The uproar out-of-doors became more and more deafening. More and more children came pouring out of their squalid, overcrowded homes and refused to return until long after sunset. All day long they played games in the courtyards, all day long their shouts and cries resounded through the length and breadth of the city. Their shrill voices, happy and carefree now that dreary winter was over, almost stupefied the grown-ups, who were pretty noisy themselves. And there was still the endless procession of ragged men and women that were still as eager as ever to sell hot cakes and buy old rags and mend broken windows. The massive towering walls trembled under the impact of their assaults. Then the music! No sooner did the scratchy strains of a gramophone record issue forth from one of the windows, than inevitably a beggar turned up in the courtyard and set up his own gramophone in opposition. Military marches and arias, waltzes and ragtimes blared away at each other, striving with might and main to drown one another, and as they wrestled furiously, first one would come out on top, then the other. During the interval an old beggar woman might enter and burst into song like a nightingale.

She would be followed by more beggars, who all warbled the same melancholy Yiddish songs, and only varied their chanted appeals for charity:

"Kind folk, have mercy on a destitute ailing widow with six children; have mercy on my poor mites, they're waiting for me, waiting to be fed at my breast. Don't let them starve. Throw down all you can spare!..."

"Throw down all you can spare! I'm a cripple and an orphan. Look me over, but don't overlook me!"

Begging eyes – eyes dim and mournful and eyes bright and crafty – would be upturned to the wide open windows from morning to night.

Now and again a slut might sling her rubbish through the window into the courtyard....

Before long Michael had had more than enough, and he washed his hands of Joseph. A lone figure now, the poor hunchback bore his heavy hump from door to door, trudging through interminable streets and courtyards, climbing up endless stairs and down again, while Michael, relieved of all responsibility, strolled about with his hands in his pockets, enjoying the peace and quiet of elegant residential neighborhoods where the streets were lined with trees in blossom, where flowers were blooming in vases at the windows, and where every drawn blind told the same tale – the inmates had taken up residence in their country estates or had gone abroad....

Deborah's heart was filled with longing to see for herself those dreamlands where Michael could wander so freely, while she was kept a prisoner in her own home – all because of a miserable hat!

How happy she might have been if only she had been born a boy! It was not without good reason that her father had insisted, way back in Jelhitz, that girls were inferior creatures. Now why on earth could not men and women wear the same clothes? If she was to wear a gabardine like Michael, then, like him, she could go wherever her fancy took her.... However, instead of having to wait for so sweeping a reform, she found her hat problem solved one day.

It all began early one morning, when the family had passed some two months in their new home. There was a loud knock at the door, and when Deborah went to see who it was, she shrank back in amazement, for at first glance she thought the caller was the *tzaddik of* R– disguised in a lounge suit and with his chin clean-shaven.

"Can I have a word with the rabbi?" he boomed at her in a voice that was like the blast of a double bass. He had a belly that started halfway up his chest and finished halfway down his legs; his backside was like the dome of a great cathedral.

"Papa is at the synagogue."

"When d'you expect him back?"

"In about half an hour's time."

"Will it be all right for me to wait?"

At this Deborah turned deathly pale. Terror-stricken she conducted him into her father's study and asked him to take a seat. He raised a clenched fat fist, pushed his sleeve back, revealing a wide leather strap round his wrist, then compared the hands of his wristwatch with those of his big golden pocket watch hanging on a tremendous golden chain across his waistcoat, and after stroking his purple jaw awhile, he carefully lowered himself on to the chair, which croaked hoarsely as though it were in great pain. He eyed Deborah with a good-humored twinkle in his crafty, thievish little eyes.

"I think you're afraid of me, Missy," he said.

"No, not at all. I mean, it's ridiculous, why should I be afraid of you?"

He looked her up and down with an expert air.

"Go on, tell the truth! Aren't you afraid of me?"

"Of course I'm not," Deborah protested, backing out of the room, and she fled into the bedroom, where Raizela was still abed.

Speaking in a whisper she told her mother about the caller and what a fright he had given her. She begged her mother to get up at once, but Raizela only gave her a scornful look.

"Stop playing the fool! There are no cannibals living in these parts, and he won't eat you. Now go in and join him. Don't you know it's rude to leave a visitor all by himself?"

"But Mamma, you've never seen such a terrible looking fellow in all your life. Why, he's even bigger than the *tzaddik*!"

Raizela laughed noiselessly.

"Off with you now! Run in like a good little girl, like mummy's little darling!"

Deborah fussed about in her father's study, setting the books straight in the bookcase, dusting the table and collecting the scattered manuscripts which Reb Avram Ber had been working on during the night and which he had been too tired to put away before retiring. She pretended to be very busy, so as to avoid the visitor's gaze, but all the time she was intent on listening to the muttering of the chair as it groaned under its cruel burden. Luckily Reb Avram Ber had forgotten his prayer shawl, so he put in an appearance sooner than expected.

"Good morning, Rabbi!" the man bawled at him, rising to his feet with an exaggerated air of reverence, while the chair uttered a gasp of relief.

"Good morning!" Reb Avram Ber responded quietly, himself rather overawed. "Well, and what can I do for you?" he added as an afterthought, with eyes averted. And he motioned the visitor to a seat at the table. But as if to atone for his momentary lapse, he now looked the man full in the face, without a trace of restraint and so sweetly, that the visitor was instantly put at his ease and a wave of familiarity swept over him. Reb Avram Ber was both like a brother and a father to him now – a kindly father who was going to listen to a terrible confession from his erring son.

"Don't hesitate!... I'm prepared for the worst," Reb Avram Ber's kindly beard seemed to say. And his kindly eyes seemed to add: "Well, after all, even the best of us are only human, and we must learn to understand each other and to forgive. Yes, forgiveness is all!..."

The visitor, who was the chief of a powerful gang of criminals and a notorious figure in Warsaw's underworld, was suffering from a secret sorrow which he was eager to share with someone. Reb Avram Ber's expression was encouraging, and the gangster felt the words welling up to his tongue of their own accord. Still, it would have been easier to begin if he could only undo his collar and take a deep breath of air. Putting his finger down his neck, he found that he was in a sweat. However, when once he had got started, he knew, he would not stop until he had gone the whole hog. But the problem was, how was he to begin? He had another look at Reb Avram Ber's face, then cleared his throat, and just as he was putting his snowy white handkerchief back into his pocket, he had a brainwave. He would approach the matter in a roundabout way:

"Your holiness, what brings me here to you today is a question of Jewish law...."

"Ah, that's good! Proceed!" Reb Avram replied with gusto, rubbing his hands at the thought that this brutish creature was sensitive to questions of Jewish law. The Creator invested even the ugliest of creatures with a sacred soul. It was wonderful!...

"This is the position," the gangster continued, endeavoring to speak in a whisper, but every word he said could be plainly heard all over the flat. "You see, Rabbi, I'm a God-fearing Jew, that's what I am! A Jew every inch of me, and I run my house on strictly kosher lines. That's me! Home life is home life, and business is business! That's why I never let any of the boys come anywhere near my home. And let me tell you, that if they were to try and interfere with any of my children, or if they tried to play me yeller, I'd wring their necks and dump 'em in the Vistula. Get me? What I says to them is this: 'Boys, you all know me. My name's Berl Fass...' and that does the trick with them. They know that I'll always give them a square deal. I know that they'll always give *me* a square deal. Honesty, I says, is the best policy. So there you are! But you can't always be too clever. No, sir! You can go on dodging trouble all your life, till you think yourself the most artful dodger in town, and then – like a bloody fool – you go and trip up. That's what you go and do, you go and trip up! Now I'm not new at the game, and as for me being a booby, ask anyone you like: whatever they may say about me, they won't call me a booby. No, sir! But I'll tell you what happened.

"A couple of weeks ago a nice bit of stuff came up from the

country – and I jolly well had to hide it away somewhere or other. After all, it's my bread and butter. And 'tain't like old times, you know. No, sir! The police are pretty strict nowadays. They'll take a bribe all right, but it's got to be a big 'un. That it has. They've got their jobs to think of, they say, and the lousy sort of argument they put up to you nowadays is this: 'We want our fair share of the swag, and if you're not going to play the game, we'll jolly well answer the call of duty!' It's become a regular racket. I never liked the police, but if I was to tell you what I think of them now.... Anyhow, a feller has to use his wits, and I decided to ask no favors of these here newfangled coppers, and what I did was to lock the stuff up in my own house. D'you get me?"

"Yes, but how does all this relate to Jewish law?" asked Reb Avram Ber. He could not follow the story at all, and he looked Berl Fass up and down with unconcealed curiosity.

"Now I'm just coming round to that. I was just going to tell you of the hot water I got into. Did I get myself into a sticky mess! What a sticky mess! You see, I had a young feller working for me, you know, one of these here smart handsome blokes, and his job was to keep the girls in order. He knew his work all right, all the girls were crazy about him. He's a well-set-up young feller, with a mop of black hair and a beautiful little moustache. He has a little cane under his arm, and swaggers about like a bloody lord.... You know the sort I mean! He can make love to a girl quicker than you can wink. And what does my own daughter do? She goes whoring with him, that's what she does! Brings shame on her own father, makes a fool of her own father, that's what she does! What a misfortune! And when her husband gets to hear of it – and he didn't have to go far to find out, 'cos the other feller actually had the face to tell him about it, boasted about it, that's what he did – as I was saying, when her husband got to know, he went up into the air, just like that! He will have nothing more to do with her! He's finished! He's had enough! All he wants is a divorce, and nothing else'll satisfy him. But that's only the beginning of the story. The rotten part about it is that my daughter's expecting a baby. And what her husband says is, that he doesn't believe he's the father. He doesn't believe it a bit. He doesn't want to be the girl's husband, and he doesn't want to be the kid's father. So that's that! And it's no use trying to cajole or threaten him. He doesn't care if I stick a knife into him. And to think that only a year ago I spent a little fortune over a grand wedding reception. Lovely affair it was! I made my mind up to marry her off to a respectable, honest working man. A real decent fellow. You'd do the same for your own daughter, wouldn't you now, if you were wallowing in the mud right up to your neck?" Here he paused and placed his hand under his chin to illustrate how high the mud reached. "Well, it just shows you, you can't be too clever! You can't go on fooling God Almighty all the time. He's like the police: if He doesn't catch you now, He'll catch you some other time! No, you can't be too smart! And when you get what's coming to you, all you can do is go and kick yourself. I said to her, with tears in my eyes, 'You lousy bitch, what have you gone and done to your poor old father? What d'yer mean by playing your own father yeller, you dirty hussy?' She doesn't say a word, but just looks at you and looks at you, till it breaks yer heart. After all, it's yer own flesh and blood! The dirty double-crosser got round her 'cos he wanted to have the laugh of her husband, who was too stuck up to speak to the likes of him. Too standoffish, you know! It's a good explanation, but it makes no difference to the sticky mess we're in now. I don't mind telling you, I've had a bit of my own back already. I've given that double-crosser something to remember me by, and he's in the horspital now. As soon as he's out, I'll get one of my boys to finish the job for me. He'll be pushing up the daisies before the month's out. I'll fix him, I swear to God I will! But is there anything I can do in the meantime to put things right, that's what I wanner know! My son-in-law, the silly boob – he should have kept his eyes open – insists on having a divorce. All right, he can have a divorce! For all I care he can go and hang himself, if he feels like it. But what about the poor little mite? Why should the innocent little babe suffer? 'Tain't its fault! The poor thing's going to become an orphan, so to speak, with its father and mother both alive and kicking.... What can we do about it?"

Reb Avram Ber spat into his handkerchief and had a good mind to show his visitor the door. But in the first place he was very much afraid of him, and – more important still – it was his bounden duty to divorce the woman both from her lawful husband and from her paramour. It was an extremely serious case. Although Reb Avram Ber had been unable to make head or tail of the first part of the story he understood only too well the nature of the sin committed, and that by a married woman! Good God, it was monstrous! He felt sick at heart.

"How old is the child?" he asked.

"Not so fast! She's expecting it any day now. What I want your holiness to tell me is this: supposing it's a boy, can we go on with the circumcision ceremony without the father being present?"

"Of course you can! In fact, you *must go* on with the ceremony! Meanwhile, your daughter will have to obtain a divorce from each of the two men," Reb Avram gave his ruling. "And she must do it immediately, understand? There must be no delay!"

Berl Fass promptly got to his feet, growling like a wounded beast. Then, mopping his brow, he sighed aloud.

"Your holiness, will you do me the favor of seeing this business through and giving her the two divorces? Lord love us, I never knew I had two sons-in-law!"

It was some time before Reb Avram Ber gave his reply. He sat with his face buried in his hands.

"Very well, then! Be here with your daughter and her husband at ten in the morning, in four days' time. By then I shall have all the papers ready. Later on, you can bring the other man along."

"Thank you very much, Rabbi! I'm much obliged to you, I'm sure! God bless you, and may you never have any such trouble come your way as long as you live!"

And with this parting benediction, Berl Fass strode from the room with two great big tears filling his tiny little eyes.

Reb Avram Ber paced the room with his mind in a turmoil. It was unbelievable! What an abomination! Was flesh and blood really capable of sinking to such low, despicable depths? He could not get over it. He even felt disgusted with himself at having agreed to officiate at the divorce proceedings, although to refuse would have been to neglect a solemn duty. What harassed him was the thought that he would not have dared to say no to that ugly beast of a man, whatever the circumstances....

"What's worrying you?" asked Raizela, when Reb Avram Ber joined her.

"Nothing. Someone called in to consult me on a question relating to Jewish law," and suddenly he smiled in spite of himself – a fleeting smile which left no trace of mirth in his ruffled beard.

"But what on earth made him shout at the top of his voice?"

"Nothing to speak of!" Reb Avram Ber said with an impatient gesture, and Raizela guessed at once that it was something unfit for Deborah's ears.

Later in the morning she heard the whole story. Reb Avram Ber began to grumble about Warsaw.

"That's the sort of thing that can happen only in a big city. You never hear of such goings-on in the provinces. When so many people are herded together, they lose sight of their own individual value as human beings with a sacred soul...."

"I wonder why he picked on us, anyway?"

"I suppose he asked some stranger for the address of the nearest rabbi, and I was the unlucky one. I don't like it a bit!"

Reb Avram Ber heaved a sigh and offered every excuse he could think of, for having agreed to officiate.

"Still, it's wonderful, when you come to think of it: seemingly a brute, yet he believes in God and thinks it necessary to consult a rabbi. An evil man, a wicked man, but he still has a divine spark in him somewhere or other," Reb Avram Ber wound up on a more cheerful note, and away he went to the synagogue, this time with his prayer shawl safely tucked under his arm.

Four days later Berl Fass showed up precisely at ten. Within this short time he seemed to have aged quite a lot. In spite of all the fat on his face, he bore a haggard expression. Even his belly seemed to have shrunk. Shuffling along behind him came his daughter, a woman of about twenty-two – possibly rather younger than that – with a pale oval face and blazing jet-black eyes, her lips half parted under her retroussé little nose. Tastefully dressed in a blue cape, with a little black bonnet on her head, she looked very attractive and dainty. There was something very gentle both about her expression and her gestures. She was followed by her mother, a woman in her forties, with a long pinched nose, with freckles and warts all over her face, with an ugly set of decayed teeth and with her bleary eyes a vivid tear-stained red.

Reb Avram Ber closed the book he was reading, and told Berl Fass to sit down. A few minutes later the scribe arrived accompanied by Susskind, the beadle, who, although he was attached to the local synagogue, yet found time to help Reb Avram Ber out now and again. Susskind transferred a long wooden bench from the table to the back wall for the women to sit on. At last the lawful husband turned up – he was a powerfully built young fellow with a massive chin which, clean-shaven though it was, bristled with the black roots of his beard. He greeted the group at the table, but took good care to ignore his father-in-law and the two women opposite. Few words were spoken, as the possibility of a last minute reconciliation was altogether ruled out. The husband obstinately refused to sit down, but kept pacing to and fro, only stopping with a sudden jerk whenever he was addressed by Reb Avram Ber. He seemed terribly embittered, and if his demeanor was cold and dry, it was only because he was steeling himself with fists clenched, for there was an unholy little light in his eyes which betrayed his deep agitation, pain and fury. His young wife, for her part, was perfectly calm; only her mother kept sniveling and blowing her nose till the end, and till the end a large drop of moisture was suspended on the tip of her nose, as if that, too, were a tear.

Directly the proceedings were over the two parties dispersed. Berl Fass turned his head in the doorway to say that he would call in with the other man as soon as he had recovered sufficiently to leave hospital. After he had paid off the beadle and the scribe, Reb Avram

Ber had four rubles for himself. Never before had he done so well out of a divorce case.

Some weeks later the other man limped into Reb Avram Ber's study, leaning on a stout stick and his head all swathed in bandages. The young woman had meanwhile had her baby, and she was now very much paler and thinner. Clad in a close-fitting black costume she looked more girlish than ever. She did not have her mother with her this time, but her father was there, and there was nothing subdued about him now. A triumphant expression flashed and sparkled in his tiny eyes within their pockets of fat. Two burly men wearing caps took up a watchful position at the door. One of them kept fingering a bulky object in his trouser pocket, while his companion, a swarthy fellow with very short legs and extraordinarily broad shoulders, kept treading on the other's toe by way of a reminder that it was out of order to whistle here. So every now and then a merry whistle would trail off into a grunt of pain.

"This is the bloke I was telling you of, Rabbi! Ain't he a beauty? You wouldn't believe it, but he never wanted to come on this trip at all. He says she suits him grand the way she is now, without having any rabbis to put her right. That's what he thinks. But I got him to see my point of view, that I did, and he'll be seeing a lot more funny things by the time I've finished with him. Take a peep at those two kids at the door! You see them, Rabbi? I can trust 'em like I could my own father!"

Only now did Reb Avram Ber become aware of their presence.

"Please be seated," he said.

The two men exchanged an amused look.

From time to time the lover stole a peep, from under his bandage, at the young woman, who was unable to check the flow of tears coursing slowly down her pale cheeks. He did not seem to take much interest in what was going on, but did as he was told. (He had no option.) When all the formalities had been completed, Berl Fass triumphantly snapped his fingers at the two men in the doorway, who exchanged a knowing look, and then gave their chief a wink that spoke volumes. They had girdled their loins for the slaughter.

"Well, Rabbi, that's that! And when I'm satisfied with a nice bit of work nicely done, money's no object to me! No sir! Here you are, Rabbi, take ten rubles, and don't argue!" he exclaimed, putting the note down with such a mighty thump of his fist that all the furniture in the room jumped. "Don't argue!" he cried, although Reb Avram Ber never said a word. "You've earned every bit of it. Take it!"

"So long, Rabbi!"

"Good day!"

Berl Fass got hold of his daughter by her arm and bundled her out of the room.

"Come on, you bitch. And you, fellers, seize him!"

The limping man was hustled out by the two gangsters at a half run.

Reb Avram Ber looked all round him, as if to convince himself that the place was really empty. He sighed with relief. As he was on the point of passing into the next room, he was called back.

"You've forgotten the money on the table," said Susskind, the beadle, his eyes sparkling oddly from out of the hairy depths of his eyebrows and beard. Reb Avram Ber gave him a tip, producing the coins from numerous pockets all over his person (he never remembered to put his possessions into the same pocket). The beadle went away doubly satisfied, for he had the funeral of a rich man to attend later in the day.

"All over?"

"Yes, thank God!"

Raizela caught sight of the ten ruble note which Reb Avram was holding gingerly between his fingers.

"What! He gave you ten rubles?"

Reb Avram Ber deposited the note on the couch at her side.

"I really ought not to have accepted such a big sum, but I didn't dare breathe a word to him, because he behaved like a devil today. I do believe he has the devil in him."

"In the old days they used to stone a woman if she committed such a sin," said Raizela.

"It's terrible! I do hope that God will send us our daily bread through different channels…."

And Reb Avram Ber cast his eyes upwards, as though in prayer.

He returned to his study. Deborah brought him in a glass of tea. He eyed her tenderly, and eager to keep her at his side, he asked her to tidy up. She flicked the cigarette ash off the table, swept up and put the chairs straight.

"You're a darling! Do you think you could let me have another glass of tea?"

Deborah fetched him a second glass. He had taken a volume of the Talmud out of his bookcase, and only when he had become absorbed in its parched yellow pages did he find peace of mind once more.

Deborah had bought herself a hat. She need not stay indoors any longer and need not look to Michael for descriptions of the marvelous sights of Warsaw. In any case, she never believed a word he said: all he did was to spin fantastic yarns out of his head, so as to lend an even keener edge to her pangs of longing. On the Sabbath there was never any washing up to do after dinner (for this was the day of rest), and as for clearing the table, that was child's play, especially as there was a smart new frock hanging in the wardrobe, waiting to be put on for the first time, not to mention the hat which was breathtakingly *chic* – its beauty no one could deny, not even Miss Rushka. This young lady, in fact, was going to call on her and take her out for her first walk through the select part of Warsaw, the "real" Warsaw as Michael called it. And Deborah was in a great flutter and more exultant than she cared to show. Now here was a knock at the door. That, to be sure, was Miss Rushka!

"Hello, how are you? Won't you sit down?"

"Oh, no thanks, I don't mind standing," said Miss Rushka, promptly sitting down. "Oh, please don't bother! I've only just had my tea."

"Well, won't you help yourself to some fruit, then?" Deborah pleaded, as she put the hat on in front of the mirror.

Miss Rushka came to her aid.

"Not like that! Like this! There, it suits you much better that way," she said, jerking the hat into a rakish angle. "Don't you think so?"

Deborah solemnly nodded her head. The new hat solemnly nodded assent, and away they went down the stairs like a whirlwind. Miss Rushka was hard put to it keeping up with Deborah, who finally moderated her pace; it was only by a supreme effort that she succeeded in hiding a little of her impetuous excitement.

Out of doors the sun was shining brightly as if it appreciated the importance of the occasion. The street was full of animation, full of the breath of life. Carefree strollers thronged the pavements. While the elderly folk sauntered along at their leisure, young couples elbowed their way past in a hurry. There were girls with their boyfriends, and girls without their boyfriends. Girls with young men wearing the Orthodox gabardine, but with newfangled smart little caps and gleaming black top boots; girls with young men wearing lounge suits – anyone might have thought they were gentiles; and other girls with young men who looked like half-breeds, for they wore coats that were a cross between a gabardine and a frock coat, and had on stiff collars and stiff cuffs, which none but the wearers knew to be of papier mâché. There were women with their husbands and women without their husbands. Thin women and fat women. Men with long beards and short beards. And there were children of all ages and sizes.

Among the jostling crowd there were many sinful young people who were going to break the Sabbath; hurrying away into an unfamiliar neighborhood they would furtively mount a tram that would take them to the distant Bagatelle Gardens. The unorthodox were heading for the magnificent Saxon Gardens, where a notice, "JEWS WEARING GABARDINES AND DOGS NOT ADMITTED" barred the way for the others. Only the chosen subjects of the czar could enter there. As for the working men, for the most part they were off to the Kreszinski Gardens, where they had their traditional rendezvous. Nor was a mere stroll round the streets of the town to be sniffed at! This was the holy Sabbath, when work, unemployment, cares and troubles, creditors and all other pests were forgotten, when every man was his own master, and almost every home was supplied with food for the day. As for the evil city smells, no man in his proper mind took any notice of them. As for the dust that blew into one's eyes, and the awkward cobbles that harassed the feet, these things were so familiar that no one could have really and truly enjoyed his stroll without them.

The street they were in was like home to Deborah. The scene it presented on a Sabbath was, in particular, so familiar to her that she thought she could recognize every single face, every crack in the wall, every cobble. She could see it even with her eyes closed, after having spent so many watchful, wistful hours at the window. She knew by sight all those bareheaded, big-bosomed girls with the painted faces and the multi-colored shawls on their backs, who paced up and down on a weekday, and now, on the Sabbath, although they still wore the same clothes, yet had a festive air about them. These girls had strange habits: they beckoned to every man that passed them by. She often wondered why, and not knowing anything about rouge, she also wondered how they came by their high complexions.

Today Deborah's own cheeks were colored a deep red. She was quite giddy with joy. All that she had been longing for week after week was now within her grasp. Only… coming up to meet her was the old woman who kept the wine shop, and this old woman had a lot to say:

"Hallo, Deborah! I like your new clothes. Wish you well to wear them! How's Mamma? Did I tell you the other day…."

Deborah scarcely listened to the old woman's prattle, and only hoped it would not go on forever.

"Well, I won't detain you any longer," Deborah blurted out after a while, and escaped from the old gossip's clutches.

"This is Krulewski Street, you know," Miss Rushka announced.

"It's beautiful! And look how clean it is!"

"The best is still to come. We shall soon get to Marszalkowski Street, and I tell you that's going to thrill you! Let's turn the corner.

Now, here we are! It's wonderful, don't you think so?" Miss Rushka asked with deep pride.

Deborah did not know what to think. She was quite dazed. On the sunny side of the road the windows of the stores and shops were one blaze of reflected golden light, with pier glasses sparkling like slabs of crystal. From high velvet pedestals, streams of crepe de chine, batiste and delicate lace, fine as a spider's web, came gushing down like waterfalls in a fairytale. Lengths of cloth, tapestry, velvet, silk and muslin floated gently down to the floor from on high, as though supported by nothing more substantial than a gentle breeze. It seemed inconceivable that all these things would in time be cut up and used, still less that there were so many people wealthy enough to consume all these luxuries.

Deborah and Miss Rushka passed from shop window to shop window, each with its regal display of costly stuffs, flowers, furniture, objets d'art, paintings, jewelry. All was magnificent. Again and again Deborah found that she could not tear herself away. The brilliance was positively dazzling.

And how restless the traffic seemed by way of contrast! Wheel upon wheel, wheel after wheel, rolled by, with automobile drivers tooting their horns, with coachmen cracking their whips, with the continual patter of horses' hoofs on the smooth roadway, and elegant ladies and gentlemen leaning back so daintily in their coaches and carriages, coming and going, till it made Deborah's head reel. Without speaking a word, she feasted her eye on all these marvels, and the more she feasted the hungrier she grew. She now realized that Michael had not exaggerated in the least. On the contrary, his descriptions paled before the reality.

At twilight the scene, as Deborah saw it, surpassed all bounds of the imagination. Quite suddenly the shops lit up. The stuffs in the windows became fantastic to look at, unreal. The illuminated globes high up on the standards lining either side of the street trailed away into the distance like two strings of milky pearls suspended in mid-air. The luminous advertisements outside the cinemas kept vanishing and reappearing as if they were winking at the passersby. And from out of the cafes, which she had given scant notice before, issued the gentle strains of narcotic music.

The advertisements and signs detracted somewhat from the beauty of the scene, introducing the commonplace. And soon after the first blaze of splendor, the polish was dulled by the sudden influx of large crowds coming out of the parks. People began to jostle each other on the pavements and to gather round the shop windows like moths round a bright light, dispersing only when the light rudely went out. In some of the shops a dim light was left burning. As if by magic, the street had changed beyond recognition. The harmony of it was dissipated. Nonetheless, Deborah still went on admiring its many glories.

"I can tell you it beats everything that my brother led me to expect...."

Miss Rushka was gratified. Like Michael, she began to boast of all the other showplaces which Deborah had never seen.

"And what about the Saxon Gardens? I suppose you haven't been there yet, have you?"

"No."

"If you'd like to go, I'll take you there tomorrow. It's ever so classy! You find all the nicest people there, people with titles and money and everything.... Jews wearing gabardines are not admitted, and girls can't go in unless they wear a hat, so it just shows what a posh place it is. Have you got permission to go out whenever you want to?"

Deborah stopped to think. She really could not say.

"*I* have!" Miss Rushka put in, wrinkling up her nose in triumph.

"I don't suppose Mamma would have any objection. I suggest you call for me tomorrow."

"No, you call for me!"

"I couldn't find my way," confessed Deborah, not without reluctance. It was most unpleasant to be the innocent rustic.

They parted with a handshake. Rather than tell Miss Rushka that she had not the faintest recollection of the way home, Deborah wandered aimlessly about the back streets, which now struck her as being drab and dismal looking. She stopped several people and made inquiries, but experienced difficulty with her broken Polish and was confused by the directions given to her. She turned left and right, and right and left. In the end, when she had given up all hopes of getting home again, she ran down a gloomy alley, which seemed to have a menacing air about it, and suddenly found herself in the one street that she knew so well.

"Well, did you have a good time?" Raizela asked, smiling with amusement at the way Deborah stood staring with an air of bewilderment, as though she failed to recognize her own home, which she had left behind only a few hours ago.

Deborah was glad to hear her mother's voice. Yes, this was home! With a merry laugh she ran up to her mother to kiss and hug her.

"Oh, Mamma, I spent such a wonderful afternoon. We went to Marszalkowski Street, and it almost took my breath away. It's quite close, you know! Within walking distance. I was ever so surprised, because after what Michael told me, I imagined it was miles and miles away…"

"So you imagined that, did you?" exclaimed Michael, stirring behind the curtain at the window. She had not noticed him there before. "You judge all things by yourself. Because you're pretty at a distance and awful at close quarters you think everything else is the same. And even at a distance you're only pretty when you disguise yourself in pretty things. And what a disguise you've got on today! Phew! I say, how far did you get today? I bet you never went to the Allées! No, of course you didn't. That *is* miles and miles away. You'd get sore feet if you tried to walk it, and until you've seen the Allées you haven't seen Warsaw at its best, I don't mind telling you!"

Michael emerged from behind the curtain with a victorious smile, his supremacy still unchallenged.

"Come on Deborah, get yourself changed and let's all have tea," Raizela said.

Deborah took no notice. She felt not the least inclination to strip off her finery and dress up like the family drudge once more. Life at the moment was too sweet for such a humdrum task as puffing at the embers in the samovar. Again the old feeling of revolt against her mother took her by storm. It was not fair, why could not her mother ask Michael to prepare the samovar: he could do it just as well. But then, on second thoughts, she realized that she ought to feel grateful for all the splendid clothes they had given her, and without a word she went into the bedroom and returned with her sleeves rolled up all ready for work.

Reb Avram Ber put in an appearance, his face radiant with joy, as ever. He did not seem to mind a bit the passing of the dearly beloved Sabbath. Welcome though the Sabbath was, when its delights were over he found new delights. For one thing, there was the newly-made tea to look forward to (of course, the samovar could not be touched on the Sabbath). For another, there was the ceremony of blessing the new moon. And best of all, soon after sunset there was the end-of-Sabbath feast, when a man could sing and rejoice with his fellow men, and join with them in hoping for a bright future in the days to come. …

"May the new week bring new happiness," said Reb Avram Ber, in accordance with old Jewish custom. "Hallo, Deborah! I see you're busy. That's good! I hope you won't forget our friends next door."

And zestfully passing one palm of his hand over the other, he went away again to join the company in his study. Deborah gave the glasses a good polish, filled them and put them on a tray.

"Off with you, Michael, and join the feast. Your place is with the menfolk, and I shall be very glad to get rid of you," said Raizela.

"Very well, Mamma, I'm off! But not just yet. You'll find me joining the feast when winter comes round. In the winter you get a lovely portion of roast beef and delicious *borscht*. Now, that's in my line. But in the summer all they put on your plate is a scrap of herring, and I turn my nose up at that."

"Idiot!" Raizela scolded him with great good humor.

***

The next day Miss Rushka called again. Mother did not object in the least. Deborah was duly impressed by the Saxon Gardens. Although she had seen trees and grass and flowers in abundance in her lifetime, she had never been in a cultivated park before. Its urbane beauty – the many-hued flower beds in such perfect harmony, in spite of the sea of color; the shapely grand old trees; the long shady avenues – made a striking picture. Unlike yesterday's scene, instead of throbbing with excitement it soothed the nerves. Everybody in the park had such a calm and unruffled look, as though time were of little account. Spruce young couples sauntered along most peacefully, even if there was something in the way they clung to each other which betrayed feelings not quite so peaceful. Old gentlemen on the benches had their heads concealed behind newspapers, or sat smoking or polishing their spectacles. Tastefully dressed children played hide and seek, ignoring both their nurses and the soldiers who had their arms round the nurses. These children had no respect at all for grown-ups, not even for those wearing resplendent uniforms.

The thoroughfares around the park were far less noisy than they had been yesterday. There was less glitter also. Marszalkowski Street was half empty. Most of the shops were closed and had their blinds down. Elderly ladies and gentlemen, often with prayer books under their arm, were taking the air with a solemn and pious demeanor. Even the students and their young ladies were more subdued, larking about on the sly. The shop signs seemed to have dwindled into insignificance overnight. Only a few luminous advertisements were to be seen here and there, and they were scarcely noticeable in the daylight. A long line of cabs waited in idleness, with no one to disturb the drowsy cabbies, for this was Sunday, a holy day of rest.

"Miss Rushka, what about a trip to the Allées?"

"No, not today. We can go there next Saturday, if you like. You'll find the place absolutely dead today, but on a Saturday it's spiffing!"

Very well, then, next Saturday it would have to be. Miss Rushka's word was law.

***

Gradually, Deborah accustomed herself to life in Warsaw, until she gave it no thought, knowing that she was part of it, and it was part of her. As time went on, all things became commonplace, matter-of-fact and, at best, homely. Nothing surprised her, nothing overwhelmed her. Marszalkowski Street lost its magic. The tramps of both sexes huddled up in the porches and on the broad flights of stone steps in front of the churches ceased to torment her mind; they barely excited her pity. She never noticed them, as they lay there like shapeless bundles, and the only time she paid them any attention was when she was extra flush in money and could spare a few kopecks. Life at home settled down to a comfortable jog trot. Reb Avram Ber's position went from strength to strength. The Jews of the neighborhood fell into the habit of bringing their differences to Reb Avram Ber for arbitration, they paid their dues far more punctually, and there was little to complain of.

Michael drifted away from the synagogue and the Talmud, and picked up with young men, and occasionally even with girls of a different set. He began to frequent homes which would have shocked Raizela and Reb Avram Ber if they had known. But they never knew a thing, and Michael made the best of both worlds....

Reb Zalman remained the close friend of the family. Hardly a day passed without a visit from him. Having helped Reb Avram Ber to comparative prosperity, he was now anxious to help him in other ways, and thinking it over carefully he came to the conclusion that the one thing Reb Avram Ber still needed, and needed badly, was a husband for his only daughter, Deborah. That being so, Reb Zalman kept a lookout for eligible young men, and almost every other day he burst into the home with a wonderful new marriage proposal. At first he was singing the praises of a wealthy merchant who had a son. Whereas the wealthy merchant was not much of a Talmudist, although it would be very wrong to describe him as a downright ignoramus, the son was a man of great learning or, at any rate, would be one day if he kept up his studies. This son was perfect in every way, only just a little bit simple in the head, but that, Reb Zalman argued – and Reb Avram Ber concurred – could not be regarded as a fault, for the father was so wealthy that the son would be provided for amply for the rest of his life. Then, a few days later, Reb Zalman turned up with a discovery that beat everything: an absolutely priceless young man – no, verily a saint; a young man who really and truly was a great Talmudist, and had so far lived the life of an ascetic; his father was said to be a close friend of the great *tzaddik* of Ger; the father was by no means a wealthy man, but it was an honor – a great honor – to marry into his family. Ay! And then, by the end of the same week, Reb Zalman arrived triumphant: he had found the right match at last. A Lithuanian Jew, but a man one could trust nevertheless; as clever as clever could be, endowed with the gift of the gab; sure he had the gift of the gab, for he was a preacher; had pots of money; had divorced his first wife because she had borne him no children; an opportunity that would not come again. But alas, Deborah refused her suitors one and all.

She did not want to get married yet, and begged Reb Zalman to leave her in peace. She said she could wait, and could wait a long time. This was a setback for Reb Zalman. He would lie low for a couple of weeks, and then start again. After all, a girl must get married sooner or later, and better sooner than later, because if a girl never caught a husband while she was young, she might not get one at all in the end, especially if she had no dowry. Nice thing it would be for Deborah to become an old maid, a very nice thing! But what was the use of talking to her? One might just as well talk to a brick wall.

"Now try to understand me," Reb Zalman reasoned with her. "You know quite well that but for me you would have still been wearing your shabby old clothes, you wouldn't have been able to show your face in the street, and the home would still have been a den of misery. You'll do me the justice of admitting that I mean well, and that I have had more experience of life than you have. Do you think I'd press you if it wasn't for your own good? Believe me, I know your value, and know just what sort of husband you deserve."

"Admitted, Reb Zalman, but you can't expect me to go and marry the sort of person that appeals to you."

"Well, tell me who you think is good enough for you," Reb Zalman said with ill-concealed annoyance.

"No, the point is they're all too good for me," Deborah retorted, with the color coming into her cheeks. She felt the blood rushing up into her head.

"I know the sort of person you want," Reb Avram Ber joined in the conversation, losing his temper for once. "You want one of those newfangled husbands that don't wear the Orthodox gabardine, is that it? Depend upon it, I'll not give you any of these newfangled husbands that don't wear the Orthodox gabardine!"

Thus all Reb Zalman's labors proved fruitless, and Deborah remained a lonely spinster.

Chapter 10

As the summer wore on Deborah gave up her last lingering hopes of ever seeing Simon again. Meanwhile, the High Holy Days were drawing near, and Reb Avram Ber's home was thrown into confusion. All day long there was a coming and going of people who sought Reb Avram Ber's advice; his table was littered with reference books, and his brow was knitted in deepest meditation. Even the hunchback was in the swim: in the evening, when he returned from his daily round and emptied his bulging pockets, the pile of copper coins was larger than usual, often containing a sprinkling of silver.

However, what was at first no more than confusion developed into a perfect riot when Reb Zalman suddenly gave the family short notice of his determination to organize a temporary synagogue in their own home for the High Holy Day services.

"Now, you listen to me," said Reb Zalman. "It's good advice I'm giving you. We'll work out the seating accommodation, then you'll print some priced tickets, I'll distribute them among my friends, and if we don't sell them I'll eat my hat. You, Reb Avram Ber, will conduct the service. The little congregation will just love the intimate atmosphere, and it'll be a good thing all round. Now take my advice, and you'll never regret it!"

Raizela dubiously shook her head, raising all manner of objections, but in the end Reb Zalman had his own way. Reb Zalman inevitably had his own way. Thereupon bedlam was let loose. All the furniture was dumped into the bedroom, hired wooden benches and tables were introduced; loud-voiced workmen in aprons made themselves at home, rapping away with hammers for all they were worth and leaving all the doors wide open. Deborah toiled unremittingly. Even Michael was given some work to do. As for Reb Avram Ber, he kept passing from room to room, voicing his approval of all the tasks accomplished and gladly giving his blessing to all the suggestions made.

Raizela took no part in the proceedings, which were to her reminiscent of an unpleasant incident in her girlhood when, passing through the village high street one day, she had been caught up in a crowd of wildly excited people, and although she was not in the least interested in the pig on the rampage which was the cause of all the excitement, she had nevertheless had to endure all the commotion, shouting and pushing. It was not at her behest that the home was being turned topsy-turvy (as she stated quite definitely on more than one occasion). But when Reb Zalman, who was sacrificing his own time and personally had nothing to gain by the enterprise, assured her (with nods of approval from Reb Avram Ber) that a little fortune was at stake, and no one could afford to throw away a little fortune when winter was coming and provision must be made for it in all manner of ways, she pretended to see the light of reason. All the same, she never budged from her couch, except when it had to be moved from one place to another (and that was a most frequent occurrence).

The confusion which always prevails at that time of year became worse as the holy days approached, casting their shadows before them.... Reb Avram Ber had an endless procession of visitors. The home was bleak and bare. And the serried rows of tables and benches bore witness to the fact that the solemn festivals were at hand; very soon the Day of Atonement would break in all its fearfulness. This was a time of spiritual uplift, when every man must raise his soul from the sloth of the impure flesh and cleanse it. Such was the tale the unvarnished tables and benches told. As for the tickets pinned down on the tables, they told an altogether different tale. They bore witness to the fact that so far only very few seats had been booked, and the whole venture seemed doomed to failure. Instead of making a little fortune, Reb Avram Ber seemed likely to lose money: with only a few more days to go, no more than a handful of worshippers had reserved seats. The bedroom was crowded like a second hand shop, and the family had to do a lot of climbing to get into bed at all. There was no comfort even in the kitchen, where space had been made for needy folk who could reserve a seat for nothing if they wished, or could get one for next to nothing if they were proud as well as being poor.

Raizela eyed the unreserved seats (it seemed that the more expensive ones, in particular, would be quite deserted) with mingled mockery and grief. Reb Avram Ber was crestfallen at the unexpected fiasco, and keenly felt his wife's contempt. He rued his weakness in yielding to Reb Zalman's advice. It really was a shame to create such an awful disturbance in the home all to no purpose. The holidays would be spoilt, and more than ever he marveled at Raizela's wisdom and foresight.

"Foresight and wisdom go together," said Reb Avram Ber, when Reb Zalman called in to see how things were getting on.

"So they do," said Reb Zalman, "and I wouldn't lose heart if I were you. You just wait and see! At the last moment you'll have a tremendous throng come clamoring for seats. They'll be falling over each other for seats. And I'll tell you the reason why. Only people who move about a great deal, and are not firmly established, are likely to come here, as they can't be regular members of any one synagogue. And usually they're busy people, their minds are occupied in other ways; but at the last moment they suddenly wake up, they go hunting after a seat like mad, and that's when the money comes rolling in...."

Reb Zalman's words were prophetic. In the end most of the seats were taken, yielding an appreciable sum of money (but not a little fortune, by any means). Reb Zalman rubbed his hands with profound glee. He had only one regret.

"I must tell you, Reb Avram Ber, it's a pity you decided to offer free seats in the kitchen. Your duty to yourself and your family is more important than your duty to strangers," he said rather wistfully, but now that the harm was done, Reb Zalman did not actually take it to heart – far from it. "And now I'm going to tell you a little secret. Seeing that things were going badly, I put on an extra spurt, and knowing the ins and outs of Warsaw I got talking to the right sort of people, and that did the trick. Where there's a will there's a way, and when I buttonhole a man and put up a suggestion to him he never refuses."

Raizela smiled, for only a few days ago Reb Zalman had stated that strangers would come flocking in of their own accord. But Reb Avram Ber saw nothing to smile at; it never occurred to him that Reb Zalman was contradicting himself; all that mattered to him was that indubitably Reb Zalman was as good a friend as any man could wish to have, and pleasurably stroking his beard Reb Avram Ber asked Deborah to serve tea and biscuits.

It was only on the eve of the Day of Atonement that Raizela began to lend a hand. The poultry, which had been offered up to God with ancient ritual, now had to be cooked, and supper had to be ready before sunset, for at sunset the fast began. There was plenty to do. Meanwhile there was the soul to think of, for on the awesome Day of Atonement all its blemishes would be written down in the great book of judgment up in heaven. Reb Avram Ber was like a man possessed! On that one day poor Michael atoned for all his past sins, because his father kept a sharp eye on him; and how he chafed under the pious paternal yoke! His love for mischief went unrequited all through the day, for it was the eve of the frightful Day of Atonement.

The family had partaken of the ritual supper, drinking their fill of tea, soda water and tap water to tide them over the fast. And evening was coming on. Worshippers began to arrive with their prayer shawls and prayer books, handkerchiefs and slippers, smelling salts and sins. Every man had his own bundle and every woman had hers.

The sun was on the point of setting. Reb Avram Ber's study, where the holy ark stood up against the easterly wall, draped with a green velvet curtain richly decorated with golden embroidery, was full of the noiseless flutter of mysterious holy spirits. On the lectern, beside the ark, a cloth of the same material as the curtain was spread. The burning tall wax candles, embedded in sand containers, projected large vague shadows on the brown walls. Shreds of scarlet light, remnants of the setting sun, were fast losing their identity in the candlelight – at one with the rippling, watery shimmer.

Reb Avram Ber, clad in flowing white robes, with a white silk skull-cap on his head, stood swaying over the lectern softly chanting to himself. His lips scarcely moved, as though he were in a trance. His whole being was filled with raptures of holy fear and joy. There was something God-fearing even about the gentile whom Michael was showing round the place, and to whom he was explaining the tasks to be performed on the morrow. Raizela wore an old fashioned white silk dress (her wedding gown). Her demeanor was grave. Her tiny face, with its large wide open grey eyes, looked wonderfully innocent; her skin had become strangely translucent. Her frailty was painful to look at. Deborah, in a white little pinafore and with a white bow in her hair, looked like a big serious child. As for Michael, he was a picture of devoutness in his black silken gabardine and black velvet cap. He had not tucked his sidelocks away today, and they dangled very prominently in front of his large red ears.

At the last moment an old woman came tottering in, panting for breath. She was dressed in the clothes of a bygone age, and the green spangles adorning her black velvet spencer reflected the last fading gleams of sunset with a ghostly light. The black fringes of her ancient, beaded bonnet surrounded her tiny pinched features like a somber black frame – black for mourning. Picking a free seat in the kitchen, in front of the open door leading into the study, she hastily brought her wrinkled long fingers into play – tremulous, ineffective fingers which struggled painfully to undo the knots in her handkerchief, in which she had tied up her prayer book. It was a musty old volume (quite as ancient as herself), and came to pieces in her hands. After she had put its yellow leaves together again, she produced a bottle of smelling salts, and having convinced herself by a single sniff that the scent was strong enough to revive a corpse, she carefully wiped the one and only remaining lens in her spectacles that were suspended on a long black cord, and all was ready....

There was a sudden hush. The first prayer, *Tefilla Zaka*, was begun and soon over. Reb Avram Ber turned to the congregation, raised his forefinger and motioned to several of the male worshippers. They rose and surrounded the holy ark, pausing for an instant before they drew the curtain, as though they were steeling themselves for their sacred task. Stretching out their hands with great reverence they picked up a scroll each and posted themselves round Reb Avram Ber, who began to sing in a rich, pure voice, with everybody chanting after him:

"Al daz hamokem vaal daz hakool...."

And there was never a stray sound to mar the solemn chorus.

Next Reb Avram Ber intoned *Kol Nidrei.* A sound of weeping rose up in the living room, where the women were gathered; but of all of the lamentations none was so mournful as those issuing from the kitchen. Those wretched-looking women on the cheap and free seats sobbed as if their hearts would break. The woman in the black spencer wailed loudest of all. Incidentally, she was the only one among them who could read the prayers, and all through the service she sang a duet with the cantor. Reb Avram Ber was a baritone, the old woman in the spencer an alto. To hide their poverty the worshippers in the kitchen had put white bows into the shabby hair of their wigs and had covered their tatters with new white pinafores, and now to hide their ignorance they clustered round the woman in the spencer to repeat every word after her, but try as they might, they could conceal nothing. Although the old woman kept screaming at the top of her voice, it was impossible to hear a word of what she was saying. She might have been more distinct if only her tones had not been so shrill.... For lack of guidance, her companions began to mumble prayers of their own composition, and fell a-weeping whenever she did.

On the morrow Reb Avram Ber delivered both *Shahris* and *Musif.* He was on his feet all through the livelong day, but was almost oblivious to the strain. His voice flowed into attentive ears like pure, sweet wine into parched throats, revivifying, strengthening and intoxicating. The womenfolk wept and wept, and were all agreed (in between prayers) that this was the best cry they had ever had, every new outburst bringing new solace, as though the Lord Himself were lifting the heavy burdens from their hearts. Raizela forced back her flow of tears, only dabbing her eyes with the handkerchief that lay in readiness on the desk, when the tears brimmed over suddenly. Also Deborah kept wiping her eyes.

As the day wore on, the atmosphere indoors became more sultry. The candles softened, and when the streams of melted wax went dripping into the sand containers the candles, too, seemed to be weeping. The worshippers were all in their stockinged feet, and the odor of sweaty feet was blended with the scent of smelling salts. Faces turned deathly pale, and in the stifling heat vision became blurred, the walls began to turn round and round. But no one paid the slightest heed to bodily discomfort: the soul alone was being ministered to, and that day the flesh was sadly neglected. At last the scarlet tints of sunset were mingling once more with the yellow candlelight, and *Nilla* was being recited. At this point the womenfolk broke down completely, so that even the menfolk became infected and now and again one of them uttered a sob. But he stifled it as best he could, and soon regained his self-control. It would never do for him to go off into paroxysms like a mere woman!

The final evening prayer was a more ordinary affair, and soon over. The flesh now came into its own, and it rallied strongly.

"Come on now, get out of my way," the flesh said in its brutal fashion to the soul. "You've had all the attention you deserve, and a bit more than you deserve! You go to sleep again, and let me fend for myself...."

The soul said not a word in reply. With sweet reasonableness it appreciated the justice of the insolent demands of the flesh.

Immediately the service was over, the congregation hurriedly exchanged good wishes and broke up, making for home as fast as their enfeebled legs would carry them.

Deborah laid the table (also as fast as she could go). Strangely enough, Raizela, who usually felt too weak to stand, found new strength today. She actually helped Deborah to serve up supper. Reb Avram Ber was beaming. Michael was eating. Deborah was munching as she brought in the dishes.

When they were all seated round the table and had reached the last course, Deborah made an announcement that her leather belt was missing.

"I've looked for it everywhere, but I can't find it."

"Never mind," said Raizela. "You're sure to come across it sooner or later. I saw you wearing it this morning."

"Yes, Mamma, but later on I took it off. It was rather uncomfortable, so I put it down on a chair in the kitchen, and I think it's been stolen."

"Rubbish! As if anyone would steal on the Day of Atonement! I think the girl's crazy!" Raizela flushed with anger.

But Deborah keenly felt the loss of her belt, and she persisted:

"I don't care what you say, but I have my suspicions, and the person I suspect is that old woman who sat next to the door in the kitchen and kicked up such a row over her prayers!"

"Deborah, for God's sake stop it!" Reb Avram Ber intervened, greatly upset. "Fancy making such an accusation when you have no proof at all, and fancy doing it on the Day of Atonement! Dear me, I'm surprised at you!"

"But Papa, you must remember that the Day of Atonement is over now," Michael corrected his father.

"Hold your tongue! Listen, both of you, I won't have another word!" Reb Avram Ber was quite angry by now.

"Yes, Papa, you can depend upon me to keep quiet. All I want to say is this: it's disgraceful to suspect that woman. What on earth would she steal a belt for? I'm sure that if ever she was to yield to temptation, a spencer would be the cause of it, and then only if she could find a replica of the one she'd got on," said Michael, pretending to cough.

"And pray, how is it you know what she had on?" Deborah exclaimed triumphantly. "You were sitting next door and had no business to make eyes at the old women!"

"Idiot! How could I help noticing her? After all, she was the assistant cantor."

Michael could contain his mirth no longer. He could plainly see the comical woman in his mind's eye, and he hurried away into the kitchen to laugh it off in solitude. Meanwhile, poking around the saucepans he came on some stewed fruit which had been left over for dinner next day. He tasted it, found it delicious, and ate it all up.

On the morrow, when the workmen came to collect the benches and the desks, the belt came to light, very much trampled and soiled.

"Mamma, I've got it!"

"What?"

"The belt."

"Didn't I tell you?"

"There, that just goes to show that you have to make certain of the facts before you can cast any suspicions," said Deborah.

This gave Michael his chance:

"Well said, Deborah! Well said! The average person leaves off suspecting when he knows for certain, but you just begin!"

"Always poking his nose in where it's not wanted!" Deborah said with a laugh. In spite of herself, she admired his ready wit. Even as she had said it, she had realized that she was getting muddled, but how quick he was on the uptake!

Raizela also was laughing, quietly, and again Michael was pleased with himself.

The festive season was over, and this was the time of year when an old folk song haunted the air in town and village – an old familiar melody that evoked a smile here and a sigh there:

> Father, my Father, winter is drawing near,
> And Father, O Father, a Jew should know no fear.
> But look, O look, the snow is falling fast,
> And hark, O hark, at the spiteful wintry blast.
> See, there goes my roof, the water's coming through,
> Hurry, Father, hurry, send succor to a poor old Jew!

It was a Jewish leap year and nearly end of October. In the early morning the window panes would be covered with hoar frost. And now and then a little snow came fluttering down.

"We've laid in a supply of coals for the winter, our greatcoats are back from the tailor's," said Reb Avram Ber, "the nights are growing longer, and in the long winter evenings I shall be able to concentrate more than ever on the Talmud. All's well, the Lord be praised!"

Raizela wrapped herself up more tightly in her velvet jacket, and she, too, could concentrate better on her reading. The gems of wisdom in her books sparkled more brightly than ever in the wintry light.

Michael went on with his studies in a desultory way. He only came home for his meals, for all day and every day he was very busy doing nothing in particular with a set of friends who were occupied in the same way. He enjoyed the company of his boon companions, gaining their respect by his keen sense of humor, and he was perfectly satisfied with life in general and with himself in particular.

Deborah was the exception. She could not come to terms with the world around her. She was alternately gloomy and restless.

She felt that there was something lacking in her life. What that something was she could not tell. In former days her great obsession had been the glamor of city life. That passion now was satisfied: she had come to the greatest city in Poland. Soon after her arrival there, her one burning desire had been to get a hat and a new outfit of clothes, so as to go forth freely in the streets of the town. That desire, too, was satisfied. What else did she desire, what was it that gave her no peace?

How was it that her mother managed to strike such deep roots in life, although she hardly ever moved from her couch and fed her mind on her own thoughts? As for her father, he knew how to play with life and laugh with it. Then again, Michael found all things of absorbing interest; he never had to flounder about like a lost soul, but knew always what he wanted and took the shortest cut to get it. She alone was afflicted. She alone could find no place for herself.

When she did the housework she felt she was wasting her time.

She hated to be a common drudge. But whenever she went on strike and sulked in a corner, she was just bored to death. Of course, there were books to read. But somehow they had lost their magic, they no longer afforded her that complete sense of escape as of old.

As for Miss Rushka, that girl was a terrible bore. Deborah got on much better without her, and was highly pleased when Miss Rushka went off into one of her sudden tantrums and stayed away for no reason at all. However, when Deborah could stand the loneliness no longer, she would pay her a ceremonial visit. And one day she learnt from no less a person than Miss Rushka that there were evening classes in Warsaw, which were open to the public. So Deborah joined, and that gave her new zest in life. She would look forward to the evenings. She did not merely listen attentively to the lessons, but drank them in. Whenever the class was given to learn by heart, Deborah was invariably the first to master it. Moreover, she struck up an acquaintance with a girl who, although much older than herself, treated her like an equal. This friendliness Deborah very much appreciated, especially as Bailka (as she was called) was such a good-natured, cheerful soul, so interesting and clever. Gradually they both became friends and were much attached to one another.

From time to time Bailka would vaguely allude to some sort of "association," which was engaged in very important work and had a sacred mission to perform. Then, after a while, she began to speak more openly and asked Deborah if she would care to join the movement. Deborah knew nothing about the movement, but she was certainly prepared to join. She had complete confidence in Bailka. In fact, she began to look forward impatiently to the great day when Bailka would introduce her, as promised, to the comrades of the party.

"If you impress the comrades, as I hope you will, we shall be ever so pleased to have you in our ranks. We need men and women capable of the deepest loyalty and capable of great sacrifices. Democratic inclinations, while good in themselves, are not enough. Strength of character and firmness of will are wanted to back them up. …

Deborah was all eagerness. She had only the haziest idea of what it was all about, but as there were comrades, loyalty and sacrifices in it, it was in all probability a good thing. After all, she had read something about the comrades in Mottel's books. They were all great, noble men and women.

"For my part, I'm certainly going to recommend you," Bailka reassured her. "I tell you what, give me a call about six o'clock on Saturday night, and we'll talk things over, we'll go out for a walk and generally have a good time."

Deborah accepted the invitation with wide open arms.

One last puff at the embers of the samovar just before the end-of-Sabbath feast, and she was off to Bailka's!

"Hullo, Deborah, I'm glad you've come. Would you mind very much if I took you out for a walk? You know on weekdays I'm so busy that the only time I can take a bit of fresh air is on Saturday nights," said Bailka, as if to apologize for not asking her in, and for having come to the door all dressed up in her hat and coat.

They went for a stroll, Bailka talking and laughing vivaciously all the way. She told Deborah a great many jokes (which were far funnier than any of Michael's wisecracks). And she imparted such a strong sense of vigor, both mental and physical, that Deborah was carried away with enthusiasm. She was infected with her companion's gaiety, infected with her healthy laughter, and was even tickled to death when Bailka trotted out the stalest of stale jokes.

"What a wonderful creature you are!" Deborah addressed Bailka in her thoughts, and almost said it aloud.

Soon after seven o'clock they went indoors. Bailka lodged in a tiny room that was poorly furnished but scrupulously clean. It had one window and a small square table that was spread with a red cloth. She asked Deborah to sit down on the bed as the solitary chair was "feeling out of sorts today." They both had a good laugh at the expense of the poor broken chair, and then Bailka got busy at the gas ring. She poured out the tea and perched on the bed next to Deborah. As they sipped their tea Bailka told her more about the party, its program and the means they used for achieving their ambitious ends.

"We have comrades at work all over the country. Many of them are very young, but we also have elderly and highly experienced men, also elderly women. And, it may seem rather strange to you, but we also have many comrades from wealthy families, people who have sacrificed an easy life itself if need be. We have among us the sons and daughters of rabbis and even of *tzaddikim*. But, of course, the working class is our mainstay. They are the life blood of our movement: that goes without saying! You've heard of Karl Marx, haven't you?"

"Yes, to be sure, and I've read a little of his work."

"Tell me, what have you read?"

"Well, a good few chapters of his *Politische Oekonomie*. But it made very difficult reading. I went over some passages again and again, and even then I must confess that there were certain points which rather confused me."

"And what else have you read besides that?"

"A good deal about the Nihilists. All about Mikhail Bakunin and his comrade Maria, who was a dressmaker. And then the czar's own brother…or was it his uncle? I'm not quite sure…."

"And how did those books impress you? Did they convey any message to you, did they ever make you stop and think of the life going on all round you?"

"Yes, ever so often. But to tell you the truth, it seemed rather strange to think that only a small handful of people could ever defeat so much wickedness."

"And that, I suppose, is why you never thought of joining the party yourself? Or maybe you had another reason? I want you to be perfectly frank with me, because before you take the jump – and it can turn out to be a very dangerous jump for yourself and for others – it's best to know the whole truth and face up to it."

Deborah gave an account of herself, how she had been brought up in a tiny village and had recently been living in a provincial town, where she had never come into contact with people outside her own class; her mother was an ailing woman, and for that reason the entire responsibility of keeping house devolved on herself; it was only a few months ago that books of a revolutionary nature had first come her way; she loved her parents very much indeed, and felt very sorry for her mother, who was only in poor health, but was, in spite of her incessant suffering, the most interesting and the cleverest woman in all the world.

They had a long and earnest conversation. Deborah eagerly drank in everything that Bailka said. It was only now that she realized how insignificant was her own mental equipment: Bailka was so vital, full of intelligence and extremely well read; at the same time she was such a jolly and sensible little person, a wonderful mixture of common sense and idealism. Apart from her political activities, she had to work for a living, had to find her own food and clothes and rent, all of which she managed so well that she could even afford to pay for evening classes and to offer a friend a cup of tea. Deborah saw Bailka in a new, a glorious light, and unhesitatingly told her what she thought of her. Bailka chuckled.

"Oh, you're such a baby, so naive, but I like you all the better for that. Well, there's only one thing left for me to tell you now, Deborah, and that is to preserve complete secrecy. And when I say secrecy, I mean it – silent as the grave. When you've recovered from your first flush of excitement, when you're quite calm, think it over carefully, remember the risk you're running, and if you still feel you'd like to join, then you can count yourself as one of us. Now for some more tea, and, better still, something to eat. I bet you're hungry. I know I am. I could eat a horse! Will you join me at supper? Say yes or no. Don't be backward. We don't stand for ceremony here; if we never say much among strangers, we make up for it by being perfectly open among ourselves."

"All right, then, give me some supper, please," said Deborah, showing her mettle.

Bailka cut up a Dutch herring, flavored it with vinegar and sliced a loaf of bread. It was ages since Deborah had partaken of a meal with so much relish. As for Bailka, she, too, seemed to enjoy her supper, so much so that her bulging cheeks turned a bright red as she munched and munched.

"I say, Deborah, you've forgotten to tell me who gave you all those books to read. Was it one of our members?"

Deborah turned uneasy.

"You'll have to excuse me, but...but when I borrowed the books I promised never to tell anyone." She crimsoned with an air of guilt. "You understand, don't you? It's not my own secret, so I can't very well speak about it, can I?"

Bailka smiled a little humorously.

"That's the spirit. And if you have any secrets of your own, you must guard them just as jealously," she added in more serious vein. "Now you take this pamphlet, read it through and then let me have it back tomorrow, or else burn it. Yes, you'd better burn it, when there's no one looking, of course. Well, I have your promise that whatever happens you'll never breathe a word about all this to a single living soul, is that right? Mum's the word, even if in the end you decide not to join the party. In a more sober mood you may not think it worth your while, or you may disagree with our policy, but even then you must be silent, because I want you to understand that a single thoughtless remark may mean torture and Siberia to countless comrades. Once the secret police swoop, there's no knowing how many lives will be wrecked."

"I swear to it that I'll never say a word, even if it should mean torture and Siberia for myself. And as for joining, my mind's made up. I've set my heart on it. I feel that I am on the threshold of a new life, a beautiful life."

Bailka gave her a quick glance. No, there was nothing false in those false-sounding words. They expressed genuine emotion, they were the utterance of a person who was capable of real enthusiasm, who was possessed of a great store of pent up energy, and who, if properly guided, could render real service to the cause. Here was a youngster who only needed to be roused from her sickly stupor to start a new life and to do honest-to-goodness work side by side with the party comrades.

Bailka saw Deborah home almost to her doorstep. They parted with an appointment to meet the next day, which was a Sunday, at about five in the afternoon.

"So here you are! What makes you so late?" said Raizela.

"Late, am I?"

"Why, of course, it's half past eleven!"

"I suppose I was so busy talking, I never noticed how the time flew. Well, well, I never thought it was as late as all that. Is there anything you'd like me to do for you, Mamma, before I go to bed?"

"No, nothing!" said Raizela, and getting off the couch she went into her bedroom.

Reb Avram Ber had one of his reference books on the table, and after settling some query in his mind he, too, went into the bedroom. Evidently, the end-of-Sabbath feast had come to a close that night earlier than usual. Even Michael was abed, snoring loudly, and with a book tucked under his pillow. Secrets everywhere!

Deborah scrambled into bed. Reb Avram Ber's footsteps, as he paced up and down reciting the prayer, *Hear, O Israel*, were beginning to trail off. Yes, they had ceased, and now the home was all in darkness. She lit a candle on a chair at her bedside, and draping the back of the chair with her frock, threw the rest of the room into shadowiness.

She settled down to read. She consumed eagerly the contents of the booklet. It was a small tract, which summoned her to a stupendous struggle against the enemy. It described the fate of those comrades who, devoting all their energies to the cause, devoting the best intellect and the fairest ideals in the land to the sacred task, had fallen victims and were languishing in Siberia, repining in the prisons and fortresses, stricken men and women who were being driven to madness, whose lungs were being destroyed, whose nerves were being methodically shattered, who were becoming epileptic through the never-ending horrors and blind through the eternal darkness in the dungeons. It described the fate of heroic men and women who would not acknowledge defeat even in the throes of torture, and to whom the modern Inquisition was but a cruel passing joke. She read on. Her heart bled. Her eyes flashed. Her cheeks burned. Her breath was hot. She was filled with passionate hatred of the enemy, an overwhelming longing for revenge, and with love and enthusiasm for those men and women who struggled and suffered so bitterly.

When she had finished reading she felt that it was unthinkable for her to carry on with her present useless life, it was impossible to remain indifferent. Good God, how the storm was raging over the land, and all oblivious to it she had simply been eating and drinking and sleeping like a senseless brute, never lifting a finger to liberate the people from their yoke, never giving a thought to sweeping all the misery, filth, injustice and pain from off the face of the earth.… Good heavens, compared with the rulers sitting in high places the *tzaddik* of R– was quite a harmless, even a noble creature! For her the past was now dead, quite dead. The party would have to admit her into its ranks, she would refuse to take "No" as an answer. If they doubted her strength, she would swear to them by all that was holy that she would remain discreet, nay dumb! She would not spare herself in her task, she would make a superhuman effort. Yes, they would have to accept her, and there could be no turning back from the road that was clearly marked out for her.

She writhed and tossed about in her bed, and at long last, when she dozed off, sinister dreams haunted her slumbers. Every now and then she started up violently, her hand reached for the booklet under her pillow, and when she found that it was still there she was overcome with joy.

In the morning she built up the fire in the kitchen range as usual. The booklet went up in flames on top of a pile of newly-chopped wood drenched in paraffin. As she watched the flames at work a gloomy nervous frown distorted her face. She half imagined she could see the victims of the new Inquisition burning at the stake before her very eyes. The burning pages curled up. One or two straightened out again, and on the smooth black sheets the letters suddenly showed up white. Ghostly though they were, the words could be plainly distinguished. Deborah recoiled, terror-stricken. Her whole body was taut with gooseflesh: she shuddered. The charred remains of the booklet began to crumble.

By now her father was astir. He was coming in, probably to wash. Steeling herself, she approached the grate and poured more paraffin on to the fire which had died down after the first flare-up and was on the point of going out. It occurred to her that she had forgotten to clear up last night before going to bed. That might kindle suspicion! Thenceforth she attended to her household duties with greater diligence. In the first place it would not do to arouse suspicion… and then again, it was her bounden duty to help her mother who was feeble and unable to fend for herself. Seen in that light, her work was no longer drudgery, and it actually afforded her a certain feeling of comfort, even of pride.

Ten days later Deborah's name was enrolled on the list of members of the Socialist Party.

Now Deborah had been a comrade for fully a month, and with Bailka's guidance had become initiated into the workings of her "cell." She had taken her place in the ranks and was conversant with the daily routine. However, there was nothing hard and fast about the routine; the tactics required high individual judgment and the resourcefulness born of experience, because there was the constant possibility of police raids, accidental discovery, betrayal, espionage and other dangers. So Deborah had not up to the present been entrusted with duties of any importance. All the same, she was popular with her comrades, especially the young male comrades.

One Sunday afternoon the group foregathered in Bailka's tiny room to receive an important leader who was coming up from the provinces to address a conference which was going to be held later in the week and to which he was bringing much vital information. At this conference also he was to obtain revised instructions for a big scheme that was then afoot. For hour after hour Bailka kept talking about this comrade, his supreme qualities as a theoretician and his ingenuity in flouting the police under their very noses. She extolled him to the skies, and promised Deborah to introduce her to him, although it was doubtful whether Deborah would be allowed to stay on after the meeting proper had begun, because it was highly confidential and she was only a newcomer.

"But I'll ask our comrade when he arrives, and if he says 'Yes,' that will be good enough," said Bailka, and the rest of the company echoed her words: "If he says 'Yes,' that will be good enough."

So there sat Deborah, perched on the rim of Bailka's bed and, clutching the rim with her fingers, she listened attentively and solemnly to the conversation that flowed all round her: it flitted from one subject to another and always returned to the visitor whom they were expecting. He was late.

"I don't suppose anything can have happened to comrade Draiskin?"

"No, I'm not worrying about that. What does worry me is his health," said Bailka.

"Why, what's the matter with him?"

"I couldn't tell you. But he looks an awful sight, although he won't admit that there's anything wrong with him. 'Bailka,' he says to me, 'your brain's gone wrong and I despair of mending it.' He's full of jokes and carries on with his work as usual, but I don't like his looks."

"Well, it's up to him. He doesn't need a wet nurse," said a young girl who was of very slender build, frail as smoke, but who had a very determined, even grim-looking fold round the corners of her mouth. She rarely joined in the conversation, but when she did she spoke in a tone of complete finality.

"Here he is, he's coming!" Bailka exclaimed, and she pushed her way to the door.

"Whoa-back, Bailka! Not so fast! You want to be sure what you're doing," the grim-lipped little girl warned her.

"Don't talk rubbish. Don't you think I know his footsteps by now?"

She unbolted the door. A tall, stooping young man with a bony livid face walked in. He had wrapped his grey overcoat about him tightly so that it clung to his frame; he seemed to be doubled up with cold. His nose was pinched as though frostbitten. His jawbone was clean cut and sharp as a knife. But his eyes were very big and were blazing with warmth.

"Good evening, comrades!"

"Good evening!"

They moved up to make room for him.

"Thank you, comrades! Well, and how's everybody?"

"Fine!" they answered in chorus. "And how are you?"

"All right, except...."

The company held their breath.

"Except for the cold, it's bitter tonight. Sorry to have kept you in suspense. You can take it from me that everything's perfect. The machinery's well-oiled and running as smoothly as may be. We're going to bring off a big coup this time, comrades. But we've suffered one terrible loss this week. Old Hans suddenly had a stroke and died."

He took off his hat and coat and flung them on to the bed, at which everybody smiled.

"Oh, he did, did he? Poor fellow, he won't be able to go and tell any more tales out of school. Still, I suppose when he gets to hell he'll offer his services as an *agent provocateur* to the devil," said Bailka, and then giving Draiskin a look of remonstrance mingled with unbounded love and respect she took his hat and coat away and hung them up on a nail in the door.

"I'm sorry, Bailka! Fancy me forgetting to put my things away properly!"

"Yes, fancy that!" said the grim-lipped little girl sarcastically, and they all laughed.

"Look here...." Draiskin was about to say something, but he stopped short on catching sight of Deborah. His eyes turned questioningly to Bailka. Maybe Deborah would not remember him after all this time; but no, there was not much hope of that.

"Excuse me," he addressed Deborah, "Haven't I seen you before, in R–?"

"Yes, that's right."

"Well, what brings you here? Or, rather, how are you?" He quickly changed his tone.

"I'm very well, thank you," Deborah replied mechanically. Her surprise in recognizing, in this revolutionary leader, Simon, the brilliant Talmud student of the yeshiva at R–, had left her mind a blank.

"Well now, tell me more about yourself. And how's your father and your mother?"

"They're all right, thank you!"

"I take it you're in Warsaw now with your people? How's Michael getting on? Still has his keen sense of humor, I trust?"

"I don't think he'll ever lose that."

"Good! I like him, he's a bright lad."

Deborah kept silent.

"Bailka, where have you put my coat? What a nuisance!" he cried with a sudden show of impatience.

Bailka took the hint: she led the way to the door. While he was rummaging in his pockets he held a hurried conversation with her.

"What the devil is she doing here?"

"She joined the party."

"That's obvious, but how long has she been a member?"

"About a month."

"Extraordinary!" said Simon Draiskin, showing his displeasure. "Anyway she will have to go now. Can't have her here at the meeting. See that she leaves before we start! She's a nice kid, her intentions are certainly of the purest, but we can't have a newcomer butting in."

"I promised her that I'd try to get your consent."

"That settles it. Tell her I refused."

"Let her stay on my responsibility. I assure you she's absolutely reliable," Bailka pleaded.

"I don't doubt it. But see that she goes home immediately. Don't serve tea until she goes."

"All right!"

"Well now, tell me," he said, turning to Deborah, "how is life treating you?"

Deborah could think of nothing to say. Her head was quite empty. God, if only she could find her tongue!

"Tell me," Draiskin went on, "who converted you?"

"Me? Bailka did!" (Thank goodness for that!) "I'd like to know who converted *you*?"

"Me? Bailka did! She could convert anyone. But speaking seriously, I'm an old hand. Well, how do you find things here?"

"Fine! Only I'm a terrible greenhorn, I've been no more than a passenger so far."

"All in good time. Meantime you must adopt our policy of keeping ears and eyes – open; mouth – shut. Never mention my name to anyone at home, or anywhere else. You won't forget, will you?"

Deborah shook her head.

"It would be great fun, though, to see your father's face if he were to be told that his daughter and his disciple were both … both … *Lord have mercy on us*!"

He untwined his sidelocks from out of his mop of hair and turned his eyes upwards, as though in prayer. The company roared with laughter.

"Ha, ha!"

Deborah felt a burning sensation shoot through her breast. Her love for him at that moment was so painful!

"I suppose you weren't really in earnest when you used to come home with my father and carry on those discussions …"

"There you go supposing! That will never do!"

"Sorry! I'll learn sooner or later."

"But what till you do learn?"

"Till I do, silence!" Deborah responded, almost bursting into tears with humiliation.

Simon was anxious to be rid of her, and did not even trouble to hide it. Despite his sneering manner, he could not conceal his motives from Bailka. She guessed them by her feminine instinct, and she, too, was on the verge of tears – angry, jealous tears. There were innumerable comrades as young as Deborah, who were staking their freedom, their all for the cause, and likely as not they, too, had friends and dear ones to care for them, to love them.

Deborah began to put on her things. Simon brightened up.

"Going? Already?"

"Yes, I'm wanted at home. Mamma's none too well."

"Is she still ailing?"

"Yes, still ailing."

Bailka had told her that she must leave. She would so much have liked to stay on. Why could he not make an exception? Simon wrapped his roomy overcoat about him again, turned up his collar and saw her down the stairs.

"Goodbye! And once more, Deborah, not a word about our having met here. Not a whisper! You understand, don't you? The consequences might be very, very serious."

"Don't worry. I'm not the baby you think I am."

"Splendid, Deborah, splendid!"

All this while he was clasping her small, warm hand with his long, burning fingers. She knew forgiveness now. Most likely he had some very good reason for treating her the way he did.

"After all, how can I be so bold as to judge his actions?" she pondered. "Look at Bailka! She kept telling me again and again about comrade Simon, his heroism, his drive, his unswerving strength of character, but when I asked her where he lived she dried up and said, 'Everywhere and nowhere.' I soon recognized him, but it wasn't till he detached his sidelocks that he ceased being a stranger somehow. Then I saw him properly, *properly*!… "

His warm handshake had not only sent the blood racing in her veins, had not only made her flesh tingle, but had stirred her to the depths of her soul. He loomed up large in her mind's eye, dwarfing all else. Superficially facetious, he was, in fact, an earnest and a deep man – a great man, as Bailka had called him. She had sensed it long ago. Her first glimpse of him as he had hurried through the *tzaddik*'s courtyard had been sufficient to convince her of that. Even so, he was modest, had himself seen her down the stairs and had called her

"Deborah!" like an old acquaintance; although as far as party matters were concerned he treated her with severity; he was the leader and she the novice in whom he could place no trust until she had proved herself.

It was, she thought, nothing but Fate that had brought her into contact with Bailka. There were plenty of other revolutionary circles in Warsaw, where she might never have met him. Bailka said that there were more comrades engaged in underground work than most people imagined. By good fortune their paths had crossed. Under his inspiration she would work unremittingly for the common cause. Their ideal would be achieved in their lifetime. As they would sow, so also would they reap. She would faithfully serve him, fondly look after him. She would give him the strength for his great task. He seemed to be in a wretched state of health, much worse than in R–. He needed to be taken care of. The time would come when his name would resound through the world. The masses would point him out: this was the man, the great and holy man who had devoted the work of a lifetime for their weal, this was the man who had suffered selflessly for their sake. And always she would be by his side.... God only knows to what dizzy heights her soaring fancy might not have taken her, had she not suddenly come to earth with a bump: all at once she found herself sprawling on the pavement and close by she heard a voice, a lusty voice that was both strange and yet familiar, bawling through the night air:

"What d'yer mean by doing that, you big lousy stiff? Hey, what's the big idea?"

Just then she became aware of two large fleshy hands gripping her thighs, and these hands lifted her to her feet with so violent a jerk that she would have tumbled over again had not one of the hands caught her by the arm and steadied her.

"Thank you!" Deborah said to the man who had helped her up. He was a gigantic fellow with a tremendous belly, and he had curious, thievish little eyes which, while blazing ferociously, yet held a merry twinkle in them.

She tried to detach herself from his grasp, but he seemed to be unaware of her convulsive efforts to free herself.

"I've a good mind to break yer bloody neck for you, that's what I've a good mind to do! I could break every bone in yer bleedin' body for doing that, I could!"

By now Deborah had recognized the man: he was Berl Fass, the gangster chief who had once come to see Reb Avram Ber on a point of Jewish law. And her heart sank. She felt sick. She shivered. She racked her brains for some means of escape from this loathsome creature and the cluster of men surrounding him. But she was powerless to move. He was clutching her tightly by the arm. What was she to do? Should she scream for help? The pressure of his fleshy fingers was relentless. This physical contact overwhelmed her, nauseated her, and she was almost paralyzed with fear.

"I beg your pardon, Missy," said Berl Fass in his most genteel tones. "None of the regular boys would have done such a thing to you, that they wouldn't. Only this one here is a new one, just up from the country; he's just an ignorant piece of flop, that's all he is!"

Deborah would gladly have pardoned him many times over if only he had let go of her and allowed her to run away. Actually, she was not aware of the fact that she had been tripped up. She imagined that she had slipped on the icy pavement. It was a frosty night and the slush had frozen hard.

"Boys, let me introduce you! This 'ere Missy is the rabbi's daughter, that's who she is! And if any of you guys was to come cocky with 'er I'd flay you alive and rip yer bellies open! See? What you do with any other girl ain't no business of mine! No sir! Play abaht with 'em as much as yer like! Do to 'em what yer like. I ain't of the interferin' sort. But keep yer paws off the rabbi's daughter, get me? That's friendly advice, that is, and anyone as doesn't want friendly advice, will get something else comin' to 'im! And now, you come 'ere, you country yokel!"

He turned to one of the men, a lanky, pale-faced youngster with a murderous glint in his watery eyes. They were smiling eyes, cruel and mocking. This newcomer to the gang was leaning up against a lamppost, nonchalantly twirling a straw between his tobacco-stained bony fingers, but beyond that he gave no sign of life. The twirling straw seemed to absorb all his attention; he stood his ground and never as much as batted an eyelid. Berl Fass gave him a shrewd scrutiny. He observed the mocking little smile, and all at once flew into such a rage that his face turned purple and his eyes became bloodshot.

"So you won't talk, ha? There's gratitude for you! After all I've done for 'im, picked 'im out of the gutter. Well, well, that's just too bad!"

Berl Fass let go of Deborah's arm, and before she realized what was going on two immensely powerful slaps resounded through the clear, frosty night.

"And now sling yer hook! Why, if 'e'd a been one of my regular boys I'd 'ave murdered 'im, honestly I would! I'd 'ave stuck a knife in 'im! I ain't got no room for troublemakers. 'E's fired! Who's the boss 'ere, me or 'im?" said Berl Fass, turning to a one-eyed fellow, who was short but abnormally broad-shouldered, and who seemed to be the second in command. "Who's the boss 'ere, hey? If that feller starts any tricks, I'll squash 'im like a bug, that's what I'll do! Blimey, I've met 'is sort before, and what did we do to 'em? Tell me what we did to 'em!" Berl Fass went on, playfully jogging the one-eyed man whose face bore a perpetual expression as though he were winking knowingly. "We did 'em in, that's what we did to 'em! He, he, he!" he went on, chortling. "D'jer see 'im laugh, did yer? 'E's laughin' the other side of 'is face now!"

Berl Fass roared with satisfaction. He had suddenly sensed danger in the taciturn newcomer. The youngster's smile and, above all, his quiet manner testified to a strong ruthless character, deep cunning and leadership. Here was a possible rival. And Berl Fass rejoiced in the knowledge that he and no one else but himself was the undisputed boss, still in possession of his full powers, and he would see to it that no one stepped into his shoes in his lifetime.

"Ha, ha, ha!" he roared, and his mighty gust of laughter followed Deborah down the street.

"Goodness me, how pale you are!" said Raizela. She noticed, too, that Deborah was shivering all over.

"Pale, am I?" Deborah feigned surprise.

"Come here, let me have a look at you."

Raizela felt her forehead.

"Why, I think you're feverish! You must have caught a cold."

"Me feverish? No, but I fell over on my way home. It's so slippery out of doors."

"Dear me! It doesn't do for a girl to walk out late at night all by herself in a big city like Warsaw. What's the matter with you? You look so scared; what's happened?"

"Nothing, Mamma, I think you're imagining things."

"Come here and lie down! As if we never had enough trouble already!"

"No, I'll get the samovar ready. There's really nothing the matter with me."

"It's all right, we'll manage without you tonight," said Raizela, tucking her in.

Indeed, Deborah needed that rest badly. She was all atremble.

Reb Avram Ber also came up to her to feel her forehead. He, too, thought that she had a bit of a temperature; he, too, declared that she must not think of getting up; and assisted both by Raizela and Michael, he tackled the samovar.

Thus Deborah reclined on her mother's couch and comfortably watched them at their labors. In spite of her fright she could not help laughing at their industrious air as they all struggled with the solitary little samovar. These were revolutionary times, to be sure! She had changed places with her mother, and now Raizela was actually bringing her a steaming glass of tea....

Chapter 11

Soon after Deborah had taken her leave, a few more comrades – men and women, most of them very young – arrived singly, rapping at the door in the same prearranged fashion. Before long Bailka's little room was shrouded with smoke, and the atmosphere became unbearably hot and stuffy. Simon's cheeks flushed a peculiar red, and he kept struggling to overcome his suffocating little cough. For his sake, the company stubbed their half-finished cigarettes, but the window had to remain closed and veiled. The frail, grim-lipped little girl jotted down the minutes of the meeting in shorthand, and also took down some dictation from Simon. Bailka distributed the little packages of propaganda leaflets which Simon had brought in the lining of his coat, and with monotonous insistence she warned each comrade to use the utmost care in passing on this illegal literature to the public. One by one the comrades said good night, going abroad at the peril of their lives, until only Bailka and Simon remained, together with another comrade who had come up from the country specially to attend the meeting.

They had tea, and here the brewing of it was a complicated process. Bailka was preoccupied with improvising a bed on the floorboards. In the end she managed to share out equally the two pillows, the quilt and their three overcoats in accordance with the best socialist principles....

She turned the light out, removed the heavy cloth from the window and admitted the frosty night air through a tiny chink at the top. Now that the room was in darkness it seemed to be bigger and loftier. Simon settled down on his back, with legs propped up, in anticipation of a sleepless night. Bailka stretched her overcoat to its full length and patted it, as if to coax it into growing; but in the end she was obliged to curl herself up instead. The hour was late and not a sound was to be heard.

How she had grown, Simon's thoughts turned to Deborah. She was no longer a child, but a woman, a tempting and sensible little woman at that. He wondered: had it ever occurred to her that it was only for the sake of seeing her that he used to frequent their house at R–? Would she guess now?…

"What a splendid Romeo I would make!" he suddenly interrupted his own train of thought to indulge in self-mockery. "Well, well, Romeo, it's a good job for you that your Juliet doesn't care a hang for you, never did and never will. Credit her with more sense than that!"

But after all it was only natural for a poor fool to fall in love the moment the doctor told him that, for the sake of his health, he must cut women out of his life. Now, to be sure, was the ideal time to fall in love, he was overwhelmed with work, and on the verge of a physical breakdown. Ideal! Damn those jailers! They had well nigh knocked the life out of him during his last term in prison, and here he was actually thinking of love, romance.… He coughed.

But there it was – one simply could not help falling in love with her. For that matter, he was even in love with her father! Anyhow, she would never know of his feelings for her; however strong his passion might be, he would not betray himself. But, since he must deny himself all the joys of life, did that mean he must also endure all its suffering? Did that mean that the fear of what might happen to her because she was in the party must henceforth haunt all his thoughts? Why not get her pushed out of the party? All at once he was overcome by a fit of anger – and a fit of coughing. His bedmate stirred uneasily, as though he would wake up, but turned over instead and slept on peacefully. No, no, he was being less than just to himself. If he were certain that she would be of real service to the cause, he would be satisfied to let the matter rest. But the fact was that she would be of no value in any case. She would not be able to conform to strict discipline. Terrorism would sicken her. She loved humanity too indiscriminately. She was a reincarnation of Reb Avram Ber – in petticoats…

Now Bailka's bed was creaking. She kept moving about. And his own bedmate was snoring away rhythmically, repeating himself endlessly. Lucky fellow, thought Simon, dead to the world! But just then, as if to refute this, his comrade cocked up a leg and put out his hand with a comical gesture, as though he were waiting for someone to fall into his arms. Simon chuckled. Bailka turned over in her bed. The sleeper then uttered a grunt of disappointment and snored on.

Bailka dressed with the first pale flush of wintry dawn. At six o'clock she was astir, padding about with quick, short, noiseless steps like a kitten. It would be a pity to disturb Simon, for he had only just fallen asleep. She knew, because she had been awake most of the night herself. She put her own scant bedding over the two men, draping it over them gently like a loving mother. They could do with a little extra warmth, for the early morning air was very raw. Softly she closed the door behind her.

Downstairs, in a tiny shop tucked away in a corner of the courtyard, there were all sorts of sweetmeats to be had, early though the hour was, if only one could afford the money. Bailka bought a small loaf, a buckling, a jug of milk for Simon, and a quarter pound of granulated sugar.

"Good morning, comrade!" the young man up from the country greeted her from under the blankets.

"Good morning! Tell me if you want to get dressed. But it's ever so early, you know, and if I were you I'd go back to sleep. Or have a lie-in and get yourself warm before you dress."

She spoke in a whisper, so as not to rouse Simon. It was he who was snoring now, but not very loudly and by no means rhythmically – the snores came in fits and starts. Bailka discovered that she had run out of tea. By the time she got back the young man up from the country was all but dressed and Simon was wide awake.

"Good morning! Did you have a comfortable night?"

"Fine, thank you!" said Simon, and then he grinned at his bedmate. "That was a good performance you put up last night. You sound like a symphony orchestra when you snore, don't you?"

"Do I? It's no good asking me."

"Well, I'm telling you. You do! And I know a good symphony when I hear one," Simon laughed. "Now, comrade Bailka, may we have a little privacy?"

She went out.

Simon hurriedly pulled on his trousers, put on a pair of slippers and, readmitting Bailka, began to help make the bed. She laughed as the two men disputed hotly how it ought to be done, each demonstrating his own – the only proper – method: the result of their combined operations was that the bedclothes finally looked like a camel's hump.

"Go on, get away with you, you sluts! You just watch me. See? I say, comrade Simon, you'll catch cold. Why, you're running about half naked."

"Stop nagging!"

"Simon, be reasonable, stop splashing about in that icy water."

With the obstinacy of a child, Simon dipped his hands in the freezing water; with great relish he washed his emaciated neck and chest, bathed his yellowish face in handfuls of water, and plunged his black mop of hair under the chipped tap, splashing the water all over the place.

"Aah! Lovely!"

Bailka protested.

"Stop nagging, Bailka, and don't be so stupid! D'you think I'm going to knuckle under and walk about all day like a man in a dream, with a fuddled head and sticky eyes, just because you've taken it into your head to treat me like a deathbed case? Here I am alive and kicking, and believe me I'm not going to degenerate into a frowsy old tramp."

"No, that's past history," Bailka retorted laughingly, and the young man up from the country, who was busy pouring out the tea, applauded gleefully.

It was time for Bailka to go to work. She shook hands with the young man up from the country and wished him *bon voyage.*

"Of course, you're staying, aren't you?" she said to Simon, and she stood stock still, feasting her eyes on him. "Don't forget, I'll be home at eight sharp." With a hasty glance at the clock hanging on the wall she closed the door behind her and flew down the stairs.

Simon's comrade scribbled down some notes in his diary, and after a short discussion on the mission he had been entrusted with, he set out on the long return journey to his home village. Simon was left by himself.

He did his hair. It would be a good thing if he could persuade Michael to join the party. That youngster had guts whereas Deborah was a waverer. It would probably be as easy to talk her into Zionism as it had been to convert her to Socialism. She was the sort of person who had to cling to something or other – anything would do, but, of course, a lover would be best of all! True, she had the makings of an idealist – an idealist without a definite ideal. Could he be sure, though? Maybe she knew her own mind perfectly well? But oh, how she must be able to love! How she could love! She was born for that.

He completed his toilet. He did not fancy any food. He began to go through a stack of papers, some of which he crumpled up and put aside for burning. No, she must not remain in the party. Girls like Deborah were not wanted. Deborah and company were the martyrs of the movement, they always ended up in the torture chambers, without doing any real good. He put the kettle on to boil and poured himself out a glass of tea. He walked up and down the room, taking three steps each way, sometimes two. The tea was getting cold on the table. His throat was parched. He sat down to drink and to resume his reading. But her image kept staring at him from out of the documents. That girl had taken complete possession of his senses. She was everywhere now. Damnation! Those papers were a nuisance! After all, life was not all work.

"What if you were to put your arms around me and kiss me? Wouldn't that be lovely? Do be honest!"

Simon started. It was almost as if he had really heard Deborah's voice. He sipped his tea again.

"She'd never say a thing like that, because she doesn't care a damn for me. God, what a fool I am!"

There was one thing he knew for certain: he would get no work done today. A whole day would be wasted, and there was nothing he could do about it. He had had a bad night; maybe that had something to do with it. His bedmate had kicked up a hell of a row. However, there must be no repetition of this sort of thing, he must recover his grip on himself. "Simon, think of all the jails you've been in at His Majesty's pleasure; think how many seats in your trousers you've worn out in prison cells; remember the beatings, the damp and the dark; and remember above all that you're consumptive, and it would be worse than a joke if you started playing the great lover now. Be yourself!" Anyway, it was all nonsense, this business of falling in love. It was the sort of piffle a woman could indulge in, when she had time hanging on her hands. It was rubbish, pure and simple. What if Deborah was a very pretty girl? Was that sufficient reason for him to go off his head? She and everything about her appealed to him. Very well, next time he saw her he would look her over and rejoice....

What did the clock say? Half past ten! Was that all? Phew, it was a long morning! The time was passing at a snail's pace. Damn it! He might just as well look in on Reb Avram Ber and sound Michael. Michael would be a big fellow by now. He had always been on the tall side. And it would be a joke to see the old man again. Cheerful old boy, he was! Did your heart good to talk to him. He radiated good fellowship and could put new life into you. Nice chap, old Reb Avram Ber!

In this frame of mind he changed into his hasidic clothes. He donned his top boots, the parched leather crackling as he thrust his thin legs into them. He put on his black velvet cap, detached his sidelocks and, glancing at the little mirror on the wall, saw himself broken up into many fragments in the cracked glass. The broken reflection was grinning at him. A pity he had no mud to spatter on his gabardine; that, to be sure, would have lent the finishing touch.

He tried the door after him, and set out on his hunting expedition, with Michael as his intended prey. On the staircase he encountered a hasidic Jew who hailed him with a loud and familiar good morning, as though they had known each other a lifetime. Simon returned the greeting in a similar tone.

He wandered about the streets aimlessly. It was damp and messy weather, and the biting cold soon pierced him to the bone. His face turned a bluish hue. A public clock showed the hour at a quarter past eleven. He might as well drop in now. Even if it was a bit on the early side, there would be no harm done. Reb Avram Ber would make him just as welcome.

On that particular morning Reb Avram Ber was apparently making preparations for a very busy day, for he was actually at breakfast – long before his usual time – when Simon entered. The living room was warm and shadowy; its homely atmosphere savored of wintry comfort and snugness. Reb Avram Ber was in the act of stirring his coffee. He had only just given up a hopeless struggle with the piece of butter on his fried egg; this frozen, slippery piece of butter refused to melt, and even Raizela had failed to make any impression on it. She sat at the table, absorbed in a book, with a shawl over her angular shoulders and her face deathly pale.

Simon knocked at the door, which stood ajar.

"Good morning, good morning!" Reb Avram Ber exclaimed, holding out his hand long before Simon had reached the table. "Peace unto you!"

"And peace, also, unto you!"

"What a rare visitor, to be sure! Pish, pish!" Reb Avram Ber was exultant. He pulled up a chair for him. "Sit down, Simon!"

"Thank you!"

"Well, well, and where have you been hiding all this time? So you've been living with your parents? And when did you reach Warsaw? You came up by train last night? Bless my soul, what a rare guest! It's quite a time since I saw you last. You think it's two years? No, no, not as long ago as all that. Now tell me, how are you?"

"So-so!"

"How about your health?" said Reb Avram Ber, casting a suspicious eye over his visitor.

"Oh, nothing to worry about! I'm perfectly fit."

"Do you mean to tell me you don't recognize him," said Reb Avram Ber, turning to Raizela. "It's Simon – you know, he was at the yeshiva in R– the best student I ever had."

Reb Avram Ber's best student smiled.

"Why, of course! I just couldn't place you at first. How are you?"

"Very well, the Lord be praised. And how are you?"

"Poorly, as usual."

"Of course, you'll take breakfast with us, won't you? I suppose you said your morning prayers before you came out?"

"Why, of course!"

"That's good! Now, won't you say grace and bring your chair up closer?"

"Thanks, but I've had my breakfast and I just couldn't manage another meal."

"Are you sure?"

"Quite sure!"

"All right, then you'll have coffee with us. No one ever refuses coffee. Dear oh dear, oh dear, what a pleasant surprise," Reb Avram Ber kept murmuring over and over again; he could not get over it. "Have you been going on with your studies all this time? Don't I know how much you love the Talmud!"

By way of reply Simon undid his overcoat and instead of removing it he threw it across the back of his chair. The sudden change of air, this indoor warmth after the bitter cold out-of-doors, had taken his breath away and he was half-choking. But he had no regrets.

"The very image of his daughter," he kept saying to himself as he contemplated Reb Avram Ber's good-natured face, which expressed such genuine pleasure at this unforeseen visit.

Raizela went into the kitchen, her shawl slithering down from her stooping shoulders. She brought him in a cup of coffee herself.

"How is your father?"

"These are trying times for him."

Reb Avram Ber groaned:

"Can't he make ends meet? What a shame! Is he keeping in good health, though?"

"Hardly!"

"Oy, oy, oy!" Reb Avram Ber sighed with deep felt grief. "Life is one long struggle for Thy chosen race," he exclaimed, addressing Jehovah. There was not a trace of complaint in his voice; he was merely bringing a fact to the Almighty's notice. But that it pained Reb Avram Ber, of that there could be no doubt.

"Have there been any changes since I saw you last? I shouldn't be surprised if you were engaged, or even married?"

"No, no," Simon replied, and his face turned red. "Damn it," he thought, "the old boy is giving me a hint; I only wish I could take it! Come to think of it, he always did covet me as an eligible husband for his daughter. It would suit me perfectly. But no such luck!… What the devil! Here I am blushing like a maiden! What's come over me? I've degenerated into a regular softy. A little while ago I had firmly made my mind up that this business of falling in love was all moonshine, and now here I am starting to play the fool all over again. However, if I have to blush, this is the best place for it.…"

The beadle burst into the room in a great state of excitement, crying:

"He says he's not going to attend the arbitration. He says he won't have anything to do with it, and he's not going to waste his time by coming here."

"You should have explained to him that, as a Jew, he is in honor bound to attend an arbitration when summoned."

"Yes, and when I said that he pushed me out and slammed the door in my face, the boor! The ruffian!" the beadle fumed.

Reb Avram Ber grunted.

"Never mind, he'll think better of it."

"How's your daughter?" the beadle asked, as he helped Raizela to clear the breakfast things off the table. "I hear she was taken bad last night."

Simon's pulse quickened. He very nearly committed the mistake of asking Reb Avram Ber what was wrong with her, and that would never have done for a pious young man.

"You see, when she was coming home last night after visiting her friend she slipped over, and as we thought she was rather feverish we decided to keep her in bed for the day; but it's nothing serious."

"Michael asked me to get here as early as I could because Deborah was ill, and when I heard that I was quite alarmed," said the beadle.

"That's right, that's right!" Reb Avram Ber nodded his approval, not in reference to the beadle's alarm, but to Michael's initiative.

Simon was furious with himself.

"Don't you know that you're going to peg out soon?" he taunted his other self that had risen up within him in revolt. "You'll soon be in your grave, and no matter how much you protest you'll never be able to satisfy your wishes. You're a miserable dreamer. I tell you again that all your longings are so much nonsense, sheer lunacy! A delusion! And I'm going to knock some good common sense into you, even if I have to smash you in the process...."

Reb Avram Ber indulged in a little small talk with Simon, then eagerly passed on to a talmudic dissertation. At first Simon felt very little relish at the prospect of being drawn into a debate. These theological quibbles were so remote from life, and he had long since washed his hands of them. His links with the past were broken. His last term of imprisonment had been his undoing. Although his chest had given him trouble before then, his lungs had still functioned. In those old days he had it in him to lead a life of make believe with complete conviction. He was his own master, and could dismiss at will any absurd little thoughts or temptations that might willy-nilly creep into his mind. He had known how to hate like a full-blooded man and how to strain every nerve in the struggle against the parasites of society. When his duties took him to the town of R–, where he kept up communications with gentile comrades who would come to see him in hasidic garb to deliver reports sewn up in their silken gabardines, and to take away intelligences and instructions in the lining of their fur caps, and time had hung heavily on his hands, he had it in him to concentrate seriously on the Talmud, and he actually found it a not uninteresting way of whiling the time away. Of course, in those days he had a pair of lungs to breathe with – oh, if only he could take a deep, painless breath of air at present, just one breath – and he had been able to lead a dual life without much effort. Now everything was changed, and this talmudic discussion soon revealed how dull his brain had become. It all sounded rather weird and wonderful, and he got quite flustered. Bit by bit, however, the cells of his memory came to life again, and towards the end his arguments gained in swiftness, power, and coherence.

Reb Avram Ber could not but notice the transformation. He led the discourse onto a higher plane, and the two men became more and more involved in its intricacies. Gradually Simon entered into the spirit of the thing. The taut skin over his cheekbones flushed an unhealthy red, as though bloodstained. His large black eyes were blazing beneath his overhanging brows. He eventually detached himself altogether from immediate realities, and gesticulated violently as he spoke, and his fingers grimly clutched the edge of the table while he listened to Reb Avram Ber's rejoinders. Reb Avram Ber was fighting back for all he was worth. He reached for his beard, his trusted comrade in arms, and the two of them – Reb Avram Ber and his beard – struggled valiantly to set Simon's disquisition at naught. But they found it a very difficult task. Obviously Simon was determined not to yield, never would he suffer defeat. Then the argument ended as these arguments always did end, with victory for Reb Avram Ber. All covered in perspiration, Simon leaned back in his chair and he smiled the familiar wry smile of the vanquished. Reb Avram Ber resumed his seat and he, too, smiled – a pleasant smile of victory.

"I have the impression that you do not study quite so intensively as you used to when we were together," said Reb Avram Ber with a shade of reproach in his voice; but this sounded so fatherly, that for a moment Simon forgot that he was only acting a part, and he began to excuse himself in all earnestness.

"Not that it matters, because it's never too late to mend," Reb Avram Ber added hurriedly. This was by way of a tactful reminder to Simon that he must not neglect his studies in the future.

A woman knocked at the door; she had a slaughtered chicken under her arm, which she wanted Reb Avram Ber to examine, so that he might tell her whether it was kosher or not. And hard on her heels followed the man who had so boorishly refused to attend the arbitration, and who had now changed his mind. Simon put on his overcoat and buttoned it up.

"Well, goodbye Simon, and don't forget to call in again tonight. I should like to have another chat with you," said Reb Avram Ber, seeing him to the door, and then he turned to the two newcomers who were waiting for him impatiently.

Simon said good day to Raizela through the half open door of her room, and only when he reached the bottom of the staircase did it occur to him that he had forgotten to ask about Michael, the very thing he had come for. He wondered how he could make good his omission. Should he retrace his footsteps? No, he would have to call back later, in the evening. But he was not so sure that he would, for he suddenly sensed a wave of pity in himself – pity for Michael. Reb Avram Ber's home, that sweet home and all that was in it, he cherished now above all other things. After all, no great harm would be done if he were to drop Michael. The world was full of people, and one Michael more or less in the ranks of the party was not going to make all that much of a difference.

He bent his steps homewards – the little home he shared with Bailka for the time being. When he got there he found it bitterly cold. Without troubling to change, and keeping on his overcoat, he sat down on Bailka's bed. A great many thoughts, all rather blurred and incoherent, went flitting through his brain; some of them would not go away, and they all became entangled. They were mainly memories of R–. It had been good to be alive. He had been a real man then, high-spirited, strong and healthy. Although he had already done two terms of imprisonment as a "suspected character," he had emerged with nothing worse than a slight cough and occasional twinges which were easily ignored. What did he care about a little pain when he had all the air between heaven and earth to breathe? But now, now that air was denied to him, everything had changed. It was no use his trying to deceive himself. The fact of the matter was that his burning enthusiasm had faded, and he was doing party work now only because his reasoning powers, his plain common sense, prompted him to do so. He understood the cause, but did not *feel* it. And also the conviction of ultimate success was lacking, now that he saw the struggle in all its stark reality…"the going was bad, the mud was axle-deep, and the horse was weary" – oh, so weary!

Without troubling to change he set off for another ramble through the streets and singled out a restaurant which seemed to be fairly clean while having no pretensions to elegance. He went in and ordered dinner. The man who took his order wore a rather mysterious preoccupied air, for he too led a dual life – he was by turns sole proprietor of the restaurant and its sole waiter. He was short and rotund; on his comfortable paunch he wore an apron of a doubtful white, and he wore a big smile on his double-chinned face of a doubtful pink. He recited the menu by heart, all in one breath. Simon ordered a plate of soup, a portion of roast beef and a glass of tea with lemon.

The fat man nodded his head knowingly and departed, leaving Simon firmly convinced that dinner was about to be served. But for ten minutes nothing happened. To while the time away Simon picked up a newspaper from a chair nearby. Gradually it dawned on him that the news he was reading was all too familiar, so he glanced at the date. He laughed. The paper was of historical interest…well over a month old. Well, by the clock on the counter, he had been waiting for quite fifteen minutes. There was nothing for it but to go on waiting. Then some minutes later he rose and went in search of the lost fat man. He tried all the doors at the back, gazing down dark passages. Then he opened a curious little door, which he made haste to close again, but there was no sign of the man anywhere. Except for a kitten frisking about with a ball of paper, and a speechless, sore-nosed infant that stood warming its tiny hands upon the cast iron stove in the center of the restaurant, there was not a living soul in sight. The scanty assortment of cakes and pastries displayed on the counter had such an uninviting air that there was no risk of their being pilfered (and of this the fat man was apparently aware).

Simon lost patience, and just as he was about to walk out, in trotted the fat man with a plateful of potatoes and peas, which he set down with a great show of haste, and before Simon realized that this was not the dish he had ordered, the restaurant was again deserted. Simon was minded to protest that this was not what he wanted, but there was no one he could lodge a protest with. Even the child had vanished, and as for the kitten, it appeared quite unconcerned. Having no choice in the matter, he tackled the potatoes and peas, and then sat waiting once more; but this time the fat man reappeared after an interval of only five minutes. Having no more roast beef left for today, he had brought some nice fried liver. Simon was afraid it would give him indigestion; but restaurateurs are born, not made, and the fat man was master of the art of persuading diners to eat dishes not of their own but of his choosing.... Now, tea with lemon was different: that was something the fat man was prepared to serve at any time, and he therefore set it down on the table before Simon had scarcely started on his liver, so that when he came to drink it, it was ice cold. But that was his own fault.

"Look at him, taking all day to eat his dinner!" the fat man muttered to himself, as he watched Simon trying to cut the tough rubber-like liver. "What a nincompoop! I thought he'd finish it in a jiffy, and I never wanted to keep him waiting for his tea."

Simon paid for his meal and left the stuffy restaurant for the ill-lit streets. It had grown quite dark. The strips of greenish wet light that came tumbling on to the pavements from the square windows of green-walled soda fountain parlors, which now in the winter were given up to the sale of galoshes, only emphasized the general gloom.

What next? Eight o'clock was a long way off yet. He was beginning to feel the cold acutely. As he sauntered along, the scattered dimly-lit little shops and the huddled-up shabby old women with eyes tearful from the frost, who either sat selling hot *baygel* or held their hands out for alms as he passed, and the bright red of swollen cheeks and hands of a woman behind a pile of wrinkled red apples, all seemed to lend a keener edge to the cutting wind.

He went indoors again and changed. He felt his normal self, if rather less festive now. Goodbye to the talmudic student! Yes, it was time he got down to some honest-to-goodness work. But how was he to keep the cold off? He wrapped himself up in the blanket from off the bed, and to make things more cheerful, he turned up the wick of the paraffin lamp. But it gave off sickening fumes, and he had to turn it down again. Only now did he observe that he had forgotten to destroy the pile of crumpled up papers which he had put aside on the table. That was bad.

"Half a mo', we'll soon get nice and warm," he said to himself. He put the papers into the small iron stove. He found a few pieces of wood and managed to build up a fire.

Now he would be able to get some work done. But no, his mind was not functioning. He had a splitting headache. And the fried liver he had eaten was already giving him trouble. He could feel its pressure between his nether ribs. He should not have touched it. Damn those merchants! For the sake of profit they'd give you a dish of boiled pebbles and make you eat them. That species, that class must be exterminated ruthlessly, he said to himself aloud.... Meanwhile, the fire had developed into a merry blaze.

"But even merchants have to make a living," said a voice inside him.

"Well then, they must find productive work to do."

"But there's not enough work to go round," the voice inside him protested.

"Oh isn't there? Then there ought to be! And a remedy must be found. In a properly ordered society all natural resources will be fully exploited. There will be work and wealth and leisure for all. Poland, for example, is a fertile and rich country, and managed scientifically, it could easily be self-supporting. The same is true of other lands. If only we could change the system…I wish I hadn't eaten that liver!"

Bailka knocked, and he let her in.

"Good evening, comrade!"

"Good evening, comrade!"

"Well, how did you get on?" asked Bailka, taking off her hat and coat.

Simon made no reply.

"Wasn't he interested?"

"Look here, Bailka, I have decided to leave that blessed family alone. I don't want to get them mixed up in this business. I have my reasons, very good reasons. Before I convert others, I'm going to renew my own life and get down to work with my old driving power. D'you remember the bygone days? It would be a good thing if we could launch a really nationwide propaganda campaign – on new lines."

"What do you mean, new lines?" Bailka inquired, as she turned the minced meat, which she had brought home with her, into the frying pan. Very soon a savory odor of fried onions, hominess and healthy hunger filled the tiny room. "So you've had your dinner out, and you ate fried liver? And it was tough, eh? You'll have some tea with me? All right then, I'll pour you out a glass. You know, you should have refused that liver. You're just like a big baby!"

"Of course I'll have tea," Simon rejoined absent-mindedly.

"Have you still got a lot of work to do?" Bailka asked, as she keenly munched a mouthful of meat. Her cheeks were flushed and glossy, and her eyes feasted on Simon, as if to season her plain fare.

"Look, if we were to adopt new tactics, if we were to change our strategy entirely…"

"What do you mean, new tactics?" Bailka demanded as before.

"What do I mean? Supposing we were to abandon terror as an instrument of class struggle…"

For a moment Bailka stopped chewing.

"Yes, drop the old slogan that the end justifies the means. There is nothing in the doctrine of the Jesuits that is worthy of imitation. It's an old and obsolete idea and is as good as played out. Yes, long practice has proved it a failure."

"And what are the new tactics?"

"We must make a fresh start. A slow process, maybe, but a sure one. I'll give you a primitive example. Take the average man. Explain to him in a friendly way the injustice, confusion and absurdity of the present way of life. If he cannot understand you at first, don't lose patience, be tolerant, and carry on with the good work, convincing him with hard facts and logical theories. And when you have done this, remain on friendly terms with him, let him feel that you're his comrade, although your views differ from his. He'll come over to your side much sooner than you imagine."

"Yes, and meantime the downtrodden masses will groan helplessly in chains, and starve, while high society makes merry and carouses, enjoying perfect security."

"Why, of course, Bailka, that was the sort of answer I was expecting. But you can't devise a big plan like that and make it sound feasible on the spur of the moment. Anyway, it was no more than a passing thought. Although what I was trying to get at was this: if we could gain widespread sympathy for our cause by peaceful means, if we acted as an irresistible magnet attracting all the healthy elements of society, then the present social order would crumble in ruins and we could build up something worthwhile in its stead in a comparatively short time."

"Who's going to sponsor this new plan? Who's going to handle it."

"Bailka, your naiveté surprises me. You're being perfectly childish. I was only thinking aloud, so please don't pose silly riddles!"

"All right, but if you're going to preach tolerance, you'll have to be a bit more tolerant yourself and permit me freedom of speech," said Bailka with a merry laugh.

"Well said!" Simon felt pleased with Bailka. "You know, sometimes a single thought gets into your mind and no matter how stupid it is, you can't drive it away. It nags and nags."

"I think you're not feeling any too well today."

"Yes, as a matter of fact I am rather queer. I reckon it's the liver up to its tricks."

"Tell me, do you mean to stop in Warsaw for any length of time?"

"Yes, I'm going to settle down now for a while."

"Well then, I know where you can get a nice little room at a reasonable rent, and since I'm looking after you so well, may I give you some sound advice?"

"Don't bother, I know exactly what you're going to say: abstain from washing in cold water, abstain from eating liver, abstain from smoking, abstain from everything! In fact, don't move without Bailka's permission!"

"Well, if you want to treat it as a joke, you can, but I will say this much: you have no right to squander recklessly what little strength is left to you. It's not purely a personal matter. Your strength is our strength. We can't afford to lose it. That's the position, quite frankly. You must look after your health, not for your own sake, but for our sake. It's a pity, you know, that my mother isn't living in Warsaw. She'd take good care of you, she'd coddle you, and in a short time you'd be your old self again. You'd be able to get twice as much work done, and she'd simply love the idea of waiting on a God-fearing man, serving a talmudic student. She'd feel she was reserving a seat for herself in heaven. You'd be like a son to her, taking the place of that wretched daughter of hers who ran away from home to become a dressmaker, a common seamstress. Poor me, I'm the black sheep of the family, and in my home village if ever they mention my name they speak it with a curse."

"You forget, Bailka, that I'm not going to play the talmudic student any more. There may be exceptional cases when I shall have to do so, but as a rule I shall be my own normal self."

"Well, if that's how it is, then all you can expect from her is a torrent of curses for being a miserable sinner like myself," said Bailka, and she laughed till her bosom was all aquiver, so that Simon, who was gazing intently at her across the table, saw the woman in her as if for the first time, and he found that she was not really altogether unattractive.

"Have some more tea?"

"No thanks!"

They kept up the conversation for some time. Then Bailka made the beds. Having had so little sleep on the previous night they were both tired and eager for bed. She put the light out. But again sleep would not come to her; Simon dozen off almost instantaneously – she could tell by his breathing.

Bailka struggled pitifully with her passionate longings. She felt hot and kept wriggling about uncomfortably. How painful it was to lavish so much love and to receive no response, to labor on barren soil. She lay awake for a long time. It was past three in the morning when she left her bed. In her long nightdress she looked a tall and slim figure. She seated herself on the edge of Simon's bedclothes. She gazed into his pallid face which showed up strangely white in the darkness – it was more like a specter than a human face. For a long while Bailka kept gazing at it. She was carried away by an ecstasy of love that was almost too powerful for her to bear, and a warm, motherly sense of compassion encompassed her, such as might move a mother watching over her sick firstborn child on the threshold of death. She brushed his hair away, stroked it tenderly, and planted a light kiss on his forehead. Simon started up.

"Bailka? Is that you? What's happened? Why aren't you asleep?"

Bailka burst into tears like a helpless child.

"Is anything the matter? Aren't you feeling well?"

"Simon, don't try and pretend. You must know! Not that I have anything against you. But don't go out of your way to hurt me by ignoring my… my agony!"

"Now, now, Bailka, don't be childish!" He took her in his arms, gently stroked her hair. "Bailka, you know perfectly well that I'm… a sick man. You and I are working shoulder to shoulder for the same cause. You know perfectly well that I think very highly of you – in fact, I'm interested in you, ever so interested. You're a very nice comrade to have, one of the best. Your sound common sense, and your straightforward attitude to people and affairs… I like you for those qualities alone. Look, you'll catch cold. Go back to bed, Bailka."

He gathered her up closer in his arms, covered her over with the quilt which she had given him that night, having taken the overcoats for herself. She was trembling from head to foot with the cold, with tenderness that had for so long been pent up inside her common sense, with passions and emotions that would not yield even to the strictest of common sense.

They both forgot for the time being that he was stricken with a contagious disease, or wanted to forget.

Bailka rose at an early hour. She thought of leaving a note behind to say that she had not wished to disturb him. But it was not in Bailka's nature to play the coward. She did not go to work before her usual time. She prepared breakfast. They drank coffee together and spoke about the furnished room he would have to find for himself. They both behaved, as hitherto, without any trace of restraint, as if nothing had passed between them.

Simon made his home in Warsaw. He carried on with his regular party work. By giving lessons he was able to make a fair living, eking out the small allowance which he received from the party.

Deborah learned to love him more and more with each passing day. But Simon did not play the part of the lover at all.

His attitude to her was rather absent-minded, like a grown-up trying to be friendly to a well-behaved, if rather unintelligent, child. Finally, deeply shaken by each renewal of contact with her, he decided to exclude her as far as possible from the day-to-day routine of the party. In the end she would lose heart and stay away altogether. He argued with himself:

"She can never be yours, that much is certain. You have your work to do, and it is infinitely more important than hers – that's plain – so you must get rid of her."

In the early days Deborah persuaded herself that there was a good reason for her being barred from the confidential meetings: she had not had sufficient experience. Then it occurred to her that possibly she was under suspicion because her father was a rabbi and all her ancestors were clerics. As for Simon, who was tarred by the same brush, he was a man of great ability. His talents were indispensable and the party would have been so much poorer without them. But who was going to worry and take chances with a mere nobody like herself?

The fact that it was all Simon's doing did not once cross her mind. It only grieved and pained her to be ignored by him, to find herself spurned by a great man who had no patience for the lesser fry. Occasionally she even imagined that he was assuming this attitude towards her expressly to make her suffer. But if only she could bring herself to believe that, how she would have rejoiced! The plain truth of the matter was that he was scarcely aware of her existence. It was terrible to have to confess this to herself, but it was obvious. Of course, they had no common meeting ground. He was so much above her. But in what way did she compare unfavorably with the other comrades of the rank and file? What fault had she committed to lose that little prestige which she had held on first entering the party? And why had even Bailka cooled off towards her so suddenly? Why did Bailka go out of her way to avoid her? Why? Why?

Questions such as these harassed her mind all through the winter. Nowhere could she find any place for herself. And to make matters worse, at home they kept pestering her with marriage proposals which wore down her last lingering shreds of patience. The family and friends of the family began to look askance at her. Raizela came to regard her as an eccentric.

"Honestly, I don't know what's become of Deborah. She behaves so unnaturally. All day long she goes about with a vacant stare on her face, as if her mind were blank, full of queer, faraway thoughts, and then suddenly she will start to cry and then in the midst of her tears she will burst into song like an imbecile. And she stays out very late of nights. And I don't know if you've noticed it, but she's turned into a brazen-faced little hussy. At the slightest provocation she'll fly into a terrible rage and jump down your throat. It's all very, very strange.

I hardly dare to say in so many words what I fear has come over her. You think her nerves are on edge? Don't be silly! I don't think anybody could be more nervous than I am, yet you don't see me going about crying at one moment and bursting into song at the next. It's perfectly disgraceful. Very soon all the neighbors will be wagging their tongues. I do wish we could find a husband for her – marry her off and bring her to her senses...."

Deborah learned to detest her home. She realized only too well that the family had come to look upon her as an hysterical, irrational creature. She began to brood, and her every thought was – how to run away. Young people often left home on account of differences with their parents. When the rift between the old and the new generations became unbridgeable, a parting of the ways was inevitable. That was the course Bailka had taken. But she, Deborah, was not made of the same stuff as Bailka! Now, Bailka was a prominent member of the party, but as for herself, she was being spurned by the movement. It was one thing to contemplate action, but quite another to accomplish it. Anyway, she had nowhere to go, no means of escape.

Gradually, of her own accord, she held more and more aloof from the party and its members. She imagined she could detect something of derision in Simon's treatment of her, something that amounted to contempt. Finally, when she approached him one evening and asked him point blank why the party thought fit to pass her over, when more recent recruits than herself were being entrusted with duties of one sort or another, he told her nonchalantly:

"To be perfectly candid, you do not quite fit in with our requirements...."

This after days of self-torture, of agonizing vacillations before she could find it in her to throw caution and pride to the winds!

Moreover, as he made this "candid" reply, he averted his head and scanned a dog's-eared magazine which happened to be lying on the table, as if he did not as much as care to set eyes on her. At the time, also, Bailka sat reading a newspaper with unblinking absorption, as if she too wished to take part in this demonstration of complete indifference. It was the last straw. It was more than Deborah could endure. She could never understand how it was she managed to check herself from bursting into tears like a child in their presence. Possibly it was her perpetual fear of appearing childish that saved her. At any rate, she shed no tears while in Bailka's room.

The moment she got home she had a good cry. After the storm came calm, and she vowed never again to give him a single thought. Her love and affection gave way to hatred, not only for Simon, but for the whole clique around him. And her socialism perished....

If only she had been able to use her hands and could earn a living, no matter how meager, she would have flown from Warsaw, from her parents, from herself and above all from Simon. She had no wish ever to see him again, had no wish to live in the same city as he. And, as a matter of fact, in all probability she might never have met him again, for only a few months after he had settled down in Warsaw he was recalled to R– to reorganize the party machine which had broken down there.

Chapter 12

Meanwhile Reb Zalman, all undeterred, was arranging a match for Deborah, and one evening he arrived with a brand new proposal, one that was – in these hard modern times – almost too good to be true.

"I have a remarkable story to tell you, Reb Avram Ber, of the strange workings of Providence," said Reb Zalman, beside himself with excitement at the strange workings of Providence. "But before I begin, Reb Avram Ber, do you know Reb Baruch Laib, the principal of the Berishlitz yeshiva?"

"I should say so," replied Reb Avram Ber. "Everybody knows Reb Baruch Laib!"

"And tell me, did you ever make the acquaintance of his son?"

"Let me see now… I did meet him once in R–. He was going away to Belgium, I believe, and he came down with his father specially to say goodbye to the *tzaddik*. That's right, and I invited him to dinner. Yes, I know the young man you mean."

"Aha, now you just listen to this funny prank of Providence! Here you are, Reb Avram Ber, with a daughter on your hands, who is, shall we say, an up-to-date young lady, one of those modern young ladies who insists on having a husband dressed up in the newfangled European style. You, for your part, would not dream, of course, of considering any such suitor in a newfangled get-up. And for this reason all our proposals have been foredoomed to failure. Here you are, just about beginning to lose heart. So what must happen? Well it so happens that the other night Reb Baruch Laib drops in for a chat. We get talking about one thing and another, and suddenly it comes to me in a flash – just like that. The funny part about it is that I fancy Reb Baruch Laib was thinking on similar lines himself. Anyhow, guess what I did, Reb Avram Ber? I suggested a marriage between your daughter and his son. How's that for a brainwave? It's the old, old story of satisfying the wolf and saving the lamb, so to speak. Ha, ha, ha! Really, I must say that Providence weaves a very cunning net. I suppose you know that the town of Antwerp boasts of one of the most deeply religious Jewish communities in the world?"

"Well, I have heard something to that effect."

"No, but I beg you not to take it from hearsay! You take it from me! There is more true religion to be found in Antwerp than anywhere else. Here in Warsaw a great deal of wickedness is hidden away under Orthodox gabardines. Now in Antwerp, where everybody dresses in the modern style – after all, it's a foreign country, and when in Rome one must do as the Romans do – as I say, whereas they dress differently, at heart they're more Orthodox and infinitely stricter than most of the people here. They are Jews in the best sense of the word, and Antwerp is a thoroughgoing Jewish city if ever there was one. Everybody there studies the Talmud. The place is full of synagogues and hasidic circles – in a word, a replica of Warsaw! Take Reb Baruch Laib's son! He devotes several hours to the Talmud in a hasidic circle every evening as soon as he's finished his day's work."

"What's that? Do you mean to tell me he's a working man?"

"A working man, if you please! You don't imagine he's a tailor or a cobbler or something low-down like that! Allow me to inform you that by profession he is nothing more nor less than a diamond cutter!"

"What?!" Reb Avram Ber was left almost breathless.

"That's it, a diamond cutter! I need hardly tell you, therefore, that he does not exactly have to struggle to make a living. How goes the old tag? The man who chops the wood gets the splinters. And believe me, the man who cuts great diamonds gets the little diamonds. Besides, it's a gentle art, a noble profession. I must make a confession to you, Reb Avram Ber – I envy you greatly. I only wish Reb Baruch Laib had chosen to marry into my family. But no, Providence would have it otherwise! What Reb Baruch Laib has set his heart on is marrying into your family. He has heard say that you have a really fine daughter, good looking and clever. And maybe you, Reb Avram Ber, will guess who it was imparted this knowledge to him...." Here Reb Zalman smiled a significant smile. "The point is, Reb Baruch Laib is anxious to give to his son a wife who will be a good influence, who will help to keep his son the same as he's always been – a pious, upright and honorable Jew. That's the idea! After all, a girl that springs from such good stock as yours, Reb Avram Ber, is bound to set a shining example to any young man...."

Reb Avram Ber's hand reached for his beard. It was all very odd. But who could tell? Maybe there was something in it! The ways of Providence were inscrutable. At any rate, he would call in Raizela. She found the proposal quite reasonable.

"But does he know that we have no dowry to offer?"

"That's a detail which you need not worry about! I have already made it clear to Reb Baruch Laib what an honor it would be for his son to marry into your family. I'll even go a step further and say that, with a little management, I'll induce Reb Baruch Laib to provide the dowry himself. In fact, I'll go a step further than that, and make him bear the wedding expenses and all. You leave that to me. Once my mind's made up, nothing can stop me. I don't believe in delay, and tomorrow morning, please God, we shall write a letter to the young man asking him if he is willing to be married, and if his answer is yes, if only he gives his consent, then the whole thing will be almost too good to be true!"

The young man in faraway Belgium readily gave his consent. And why not? What could be better than marriage on such terms? Here was his father beseeching him to accept a fine dowry, wedding gifts, financial support after the wedding, and whatnot, with a wife thrown into the bargain! Better still, his father was accompanying the offer with a handsome remittance. And the girl was good looking, too, because he remembered having seen her in R–. Not at all bad! He would have been a dolt to turn the proposal down. No, he would never do such a silly thing as that. He was going to be a bridegroom! It was a soft job. He liked soft jobs. He hated hard work, and, above all, he hated looking for work!

When they approached Deborah on the subject, she considered it as a means of escape. If she could go abroad, then she would be able to live her own life. She would be under no more obligations as the daughter of an Orthodox rabbi, everything would be left behind, all her ties with the past would be severed. The past would be dead. So frantic was her impatience, so feverish her condition, that she failed to see any alternative to the dramatic gesture of giving herself away to a man whom she had never set eyes on – at least she could not remember him – an utter stranger about whom she knew nothing. She was conscious of only one thing: she must run away. And when Reb Zalman talked and talked, until she could bear to listen no longer, she said "Yes."

Her consent obtained, Reb Avram Ber waxed jubilant. Raizela was less effusive than he; she well concealed her satisfaction. But Deborah was the more deeply pained by her mother's attitude. It showed plainly enough that Raizela would feel no pangs at parting with her. It showed plainly enough that her mother was eager to see the back of her. Well, that being so, there was only one thing left for her to do, and that was to clear out! She had been given notice to quit! Did that really mean that her mother would never care to see her again, would never miss her? Yes, that was what it meant. It could mean nothing else, and her sense of surprise was even greater than her grief. She was a pariah. Simon wanted to have nothing to do with her. Her parents were quite willing, nay happy, to send her away to a distant land. The party had unceremoniously kicked her out. And she, poor fool, had been deluding herself all along that, despite all appearances, Simon was not really indifferent to her, that there was a mistake somewhere, that her parents loved her, that her mother's habit of preaching at her was prompted by motherly affection.

"Of course, the real truth of the matter is that she hates me, always has hated me, and is perfectly delighted at this opportunity of getting rid of me. That's what it all boils down to. I'm not good enough for her, I'm not her clever, artful sort. Not that I had to find it out for myself, for she's always telling me as much. And she's right! I am a fool! A sentimental idiot, I pity and trust those who taunt and persecute me, I live in a world of make believe, and they can see it all as a grand joke. My own mother pokes fun at me, so does Michael, and Simon, and everybody.... Everybody!"

She would go away and get married. As a means of escape from a home which was only a home in name, and which she hated like poison, as a last resort of getting away from parents who were eager to disown her, a marriage of convenience was surely no worse than the cowardice of dying by her own hand! As for the man whom she was going to marry, he did not matter at all! Why, not even her father had flinched. She could almost hear them all shouting at her, "Get out! We don't want you here!" And even her father did not care a damn. That her father loved her dearly was something she had never doubted. Now she saw the hard truth: she was all alone in the world. She began to weep and sob in a loud voice.

Raizela came running in from the bedroom as fast as her feeble legs would carry her.

"What is the matter, Deborah?"

For the moment Deborah really hated her mother. She wished for nothing better than to make her suffer. She did not trouble to reply, and finally when Raizela had repeated her question many times over and had become quite alarmed, Deborah calmly declared that she was not crying and would her mother oblige by leaving the room. Raizela gaped at her. She had never known Deborah to address her in this manner. She became furious, and without a word trudged back to her bedroom.

"It's too bad," she said to Reb Avram Ber, who had joined her to discover the reason for Deborah's sudden outburst. "That precious daughter of ours is doing her best to kill me. I shall be very glad to see this marriage through, and have her go away – in peace," she added.

"Of course you'll be glad, for its a wonderful match, for which the Lord be praised! It's a very serious matter nowadays, finding a husband for a girl without a dowry."

"What's more, she picks and chooses. No one's good enough for her."

"Yes, thank God, she has not disgraced us by running off with a freethinker, or doing something of that sort!" Reb Avram Ber rejoiced. "And at the same time she'll be marrying a man dressed in the modern style, just as she has set her heart on doing. Reb Zalman tells me that this young man in Antwerp is as good a Jew as you could wish for, God-fearing and a Talmudist. He's well off and will make a splendid husband. The Lord be praised!"

A few days later the family received a formal visit from a short, tubby woman wearing on her huge bust a jacket of black cloth trimmed with innumerable silk ribbons and with a very broad, prosperous-looking shawl of fine lace on her head. Behind her, and overlooking her, came a tall, lean, red-faced woman, likewise wearing a black jacket with silk ribbons, although her trimmings were far fewer and less glossy, and her shawl was narrow and rather mean-looking. And trotting along at their side like a puppy came yet another woman in a black jacket; but she was very skinny and tiny indeed, and she had no silk trimmings to boast of at all. The shawl on her head was as narrow as a thread, and her pinched little nose was even narrower still. She had watery little eyes, a pitiful little mouth with wrinkles and a pitiful little chin with more wrinkles. These three ladies were Deborah's prospective mother-in-law, the mother-in-law's sister and the sister's sister-in-law respectively, and they had all come to inspect Deborah.

The sitting room had been tidied up for the occasion. Raizela was wearing her black gown. The skin over her cheekbones was flushed. Deborah's face was glowing with fever. And the big paraffin lamp diffused its mellow light over her with a radiance such as befitted a young, innocent bride.

After a strenuous effort, her prospective mother-in-law managed to climb on to a chair. However, she did not succeed in getting comfortable and appeared to be only half way up. But this was all to the advantage of her lanky sister opposite, who was able to claim all the space for her long legs under the table. As for the sister's sister-in-law, she perched on her chair with her short legs dangling playfully like a child. Deborah took note of all these details. Suddenly she burst out into an uncontrollable fit of laughter. The three newcomers exchanged a look of amazement, and the marriage quest might have ended there and then if Deborah had not retrieved matters by responding sensibly, tactfully and modestly to all the questions which were later put to her, and if Raizela for her part had not informed the visitors that during the morning a very comical incident had taken place, which Deborah could not forget, and which kept provoking her laughter again and again.

Deborah passed muster. Some days later an engagement party was held.

Deborah's prospective father-in-law was a big, fat man with a very long and fiery red beard, and with a shiny forehead and beefy face in which his eyes were scarcely visible, lost in a tangle of fluffy side whiskers, jutting eyebrows and puffy lumps of flesh. All through the ceremony he did nothing but stare at the bride-to-be. The more he saw of her, the more he wanted to see, and he had his eyes glued on her to the very end. On the other hand, his wife, who once again was unable to get the best part of herself onto the chair, had her eyes glued on *him* to the very end.

When they presented Deborah with a long golden chain and hung it round her neck, she shivered at the touch of the cold metal and at the thought that the most vicious of dogs might safely be tied up with a chain such as this. She made no attempt to follow the flow of talk at the table, nor did she pay any heed to the shower of congratulations and blessings which fell all round her. Her thoughts all moved in one narrow channel: she was taking revenge on her parents, on Simon and on herself. Fully persuaded though she was that Simon cared for her not in the least, she experienced a perverse pleasure in this mean trick she was playing on him. At the height of the celebrations, however, when a plate was smashed to pieces on the floor and everybody began screaming, "Mazel tov, mazel tov!" a gloomy cloud, so dark and horrible, settled upon her, that even the guests suddenly noticed it for all their rejoicings. Everybody began to ask what was wrong: was she, God forbid, ill, or did she feel faint, or would she have a glass of water, or take a sip of brandy? And they begged her not to hide the truth from them. She reassured them that there was nothing the matter with her, but the deathly pallor of her face and the expression in her eyes belied her tongue.

At last the party dispersed. At last even Reb Zalman had taken his leave. And now the lamps were being put out. Deborah lay in her bed, fixedly gazing at the darkness enshrouding her. Her mind was a blank. She was incapable of thought, incapable of feeling. She had no regrets. She was not fully conscious of what had happened that evening. Already a clock somewhere in the distance was striking five. All things about her dwindled, growing smaller and smaller till they faded out of sight. She fell asleep. In the morning, as soon as he was awake, Reb Avram Ber hastened in with beaming face to renew his congratulations.

"Mazel tov, Deborah! May this be the beginning for you of a long, long life of happiness! Listen, Deborah, I cherish you in my heart now more than ever before. The Lord be praised for His graciousness! Well, Deborah, why don't you say something? Aren't you happy?"

She remained silent.

He brought a jug of water into her bedroom and slithered an enamel basin over the floor up to her bedside.

"Come, Deborah, hold out your hands and I'll pour the water for you."

"But what do I want to wash my hands in bed for? Can't I do that when I get up?"

"Don't you see, I want you to have breakfast in bed. I believe you were feeling rather faint last night."

He gave her a piece of honey cake which had been left over from the engagement party, and he brought her a glass of tea in bed. Deborah looked at the cake and winced, as if its sweetness were poisonous and its honeyed aroma stank in her nostrils.

"I can't touch it, Papa, I just can't. Take it away and leave me alone."

"What's the matter with you, Deborah? Don't you feel well?"

"Of course I'm feeling well, I feel splendid! And now let me go to sleep again, please! No, I don't want any tea either. No, I want nothing. Nothing at all."

"Maybe a little more sleep will refresh you," said Reb Avram Ber, and he went off to tell Raizela that for some reason or other Deborah was looking very pale and was refusing food.

"She must be tired," said Raizela. She was going to have some more sleep herself, and turned over with her face to the wall. "By the way, how did you manage to make tea?"

"I asked the beadle to buy a jug of hot water in the shop downstairs."

It was two o'clock in the afternoon when Deborah got out of bed. She moved noiselessly about the home, clearing up the mess of last night's party. Her face was extraordinarily pale, and her eyes were in mourning, sparkling with gloom and despair.

From that day onwards she felt like a stranger in the house – a superfluous stranger. Her father, her mother, her brother – she regarded them all as acquaintances who were accommodating her as an unwanted guest and were looking forward to the hour of her departure. She began to look forward to it herself. That sense of resignation, oppressive and bewildering, never took leave of her no matter where she went or what she did. She was bowed down under her burden of ponderous thoughts, of weird and hideous notions, which from that morning onwards harrowed her brain without cease, distorted her vision, poisoned the blood in her veins. A thousand times over and over again she reasoned with herself – she could easily break off the engagement; and a thousand times over and over again she refused to listen to reason. If her parents wished to see the back of her, she must not miss this opportunity of quitting. It was only bare self-respect. There was but one alternative, and that was for her to find a way of earning her own living. But how? What was she to do? She had never been taught a trade. She was a useless ornament. Stubbornly, and with ever-growing bitterness, she let things slide.

Her parents were puzzled. Raizela was inclined to think that Deborah's speechlessness had come about by way of a reaction to her former frivolous talkativeness. She was growing up. After all, she would shortly be a wife, and was probably feeling the responsibility. As for the color having gone out of Deborah's cheeks, Raizela gave this little thought. Herself always ailing and engrossed in her books, she scarcely noticed the change. She did mention it once or twice to Reb Avram Ber, but he thought that there was no ground for worry.

"I think it's more or less the normal thing. This is a difficult period in a girl's life, you know what I mean," he half explained, waving his hands in an effort to convey his thoughts to Raizela. "The only pity is that she seems unable to grasp how fortunate she is. Thank God, though, that things have turned out so well. Reb Baruch Laib, you know, travels all over Russia collecting donations for his yeshiva. The money pours in. He's a very good speaker, you see, and he gets very well paid for his work.... The great difficulty had been to find a suitable husband dressed up the modern way, that being what she had set her heart on. Well, that's the sort of husband she's going to have. So there you are!"

"But Papa, how on earth can you presume to know what I have set my heart on?" intervened Deborah, coming in from the kitchen, where she had accidentally overhead the conversation.

"Aha," said Reb Avram Ber with a smile, "we old people know more than you imagine!"

In the family circle they began to treat her with rather more deference, as if she were an independent person. Everybody tried to show her greater consideration, and her mother in particular was anxious to see her always well dressed. Her prospective father-in-law lavished many costly presents on her, but both he and his gifts left her quite cold. This peculiar attitude puzzled him and hurt his pride. His own womenfolk in particular were greatly astonished.

Deborah's unmaidenly conduct formed an everlasting topic of conversation with them.

"What a queer girl!" they murmured. "She's very clever and all that, but so unreasonable. I was a good girl in my time, to be sure, but I wasn't above taking a present if it was offered to me. Why, she's such a funny creature, she won't even put her jewelry on. She just doesn't seem to care a hang whether she gets a present or not...."

"She's shamming, that's what it is. You stop giving her presents, and then I bet she'll come begging for them. You take my tip," said the long-legged sister-in-law to Reb Baruch Laib.

Winter drew to a close, and gone were the long nights which afforded Deborah such ample opportunity to brood and brood, without her being able to hatch a single new thought. Spring was here again.... The streets of Warsaw thawed in the sunshine, and the slush coating the pavements and roadways became like one vast swamp. The Passover holiday was muddy, warm and sultry (that, at any rate, was how they impressed Deborah). And, like all earthly things, they, too, came to an end, and inevitably in keeping with the season the days began to grow longer and longer. The sun climbed ever higher and higher, gaining in power. And from out of their musty homes, where they had been hibernating, townsfolk came flocking into the open, to breathe, to fill their lungs with the summer air. Children were again everywhere in evidence, kicking up a shindy. Again the courtyards began to stink in the glowering heat. Once again the rag-and-bone merchants turned out in full force, filling the air with their monotonous cries from morning to night. The baker's wife again sat cursing in her corner at the gateway, where she sold hot bread rings from a huge basket. Deborah once more took up her position at the wide open window, looking out into the courtyard. She rarely ventured out of doors. She had only one interest in life: to watch the children at play. For hours on end she would follow their restless movements, their excitements and frequent little quarrels; there were occasions when she entered absolutely into the spirit of their lively games.

She declined to touch any of the housework. She did not mind a bit the confusion all round her; the home was in a terrible muddle, and for her part it could stay like that. Actually she was unfit for work. Of late she had begun to suffer from pains at the heart. The doctor who saw her said her heart was not affected – nerves were at the root of the trouble, merely that. Plenty of fresh air was what she needed, he said, and nourishing foods, and – above all – she must refrain from worrying. He prescribed a medicine, but it made no difference. Sometimes the pains eased, then again they grew more acute.

"An early marriage will cure her of all her ills," said Reb Zalman, when Raizela took him into her confidence. "As soon as she has a husband and a home to look after, nerves will be a luxury for which she will have no time to spare. It's a good job, I'm thinking, that her future father-in-law knows nothing about it. He would certainly break off the engagement at once."

"God willing, she will soon be herself again. Nerves are not a real illness," said Reb Avram Ber, by way of soothing Reb Zalman, and Raizela herself was somewhat comforted.

"Deborah, I hear you have become engaged to a wealthy young man abroad. Allow me to congratulate you!" were Bailka's first words at a chance encounter in the street. Her eyes were full of mockery.

"Well, he's not wealthy," Deborah managed to bring out after a long pause. "And nothing definite has been fixed yet. My parents are eager to see me married. You know what parents are, always trying to provide for their children's future. But I'm going to have some say in the matter myself."

"Oh, really? It's funny that I should have been told you were already engaged."

Deborah crimsoned.

"Who told you?"

"Oh, someone you wouldn't know."

That was a lie! But it clarified a great deal that had been obscure to Deborah. It explained why Bailka had been giving her the cold shoulder of late. "She thinks I am selling myself for money. I suppose she looks down on me as a future capitalist."

So that was why Bailka had shrugged her shoulders so impatiently at their last meeting, when Deborah had asked how comrade Simon was getting on. "How should I know?" Bailka had answered almost sullenly. Why not put an end to all this falsehood, this misery, and call the marriage off?

"By the way, Deborah, I've just received a letter from Draiskin. He tells me he's going to spend the summer in Warsaw. Last week, you know, he paid us a flying visit."

"Indeed?" Deborah blurted out. Then checking herself, she went on more calmly:

"Did he spend the day with you?"

"No, only a few hours."

Bailka was scanning her face, as if eager to detect something. Deborah tried to persuade herself that she was only imagining things. Surely Bailka could not have guessed, and yet there she stood, gazing into her eyes as though searching for some sign of emotion. "I believe I'm going mad. I'll finish up in an asylum. I'm moving in a crazy world full of mad fancies and with a mad longing to do myself a great injury."

"Listen, Bailka, I'm trying to find myself a job. Do you think I could get work at a dressmaker's? Could you help me in any way?"

Bailka burst out laughing.

"Well, it's easy enough to find work at a dressmaker's. But you have to know the work first, don't you see?"

"Bailka, tell me why you've turned against me in this strange way. If you're angry with me, why don't you say so? Don't you think it would be much better than playing this double game?"

"But, Deborah, don't be silly. I'm not angry with you, not at all. I'm rather upset about party matters, and believe me I have plenty of personal worries besides, so perhaps I don't appear quite as friendly as I might. But whatever else I may be, I'm not angry. You're not really to blame!" She immediately repented this latter remark. Deborah was asking:

"Why, what do you mean?"

"Nothing, of course! Don't be so suspicious, Deborah. There isn't a hidden meaning behind everything I say, as you seem to think. Now let's change the subject. Tell me, how is it you're looking so ill, not a bit like your old self? And how is it we never see anything of you these days?"

"*You're* imagining things now. I'm feeling perfectly fit. And as for why I keep away, probably you could explain that better than I could. It's surprising you should affect such complete innocence."

"Believe me, Deborah, it's no fault of mine. If I had any say in the matter, everything would be quite different. The others don't seem to understand you as well as I do." Bailka made excuses. She was moved to compassion by Deborah's appearance.

Deborah promised to call on her one evening, as of olden times, and never kept her promise, even though many a time she felt that it would have been a comfort to take Bailka into her confidence. She still had a great liking for her.

One day one of the comrades agreed to teach Deborah how to operate a silk winding machine. When she broke the news at home, there was an outcry of woe and a wringing of hands.

"What madness is this? Do you mean to say you're going out to work just when you're about to be married? Why, the girl's gone crazy, absolutely crazy!"

"Let them talk themselves blue in the face!" she thought. "All they care for is their own precious selves." When once she had learned the trade and could earn a little money, they would have no one to talk to.

During the first few days of her new venture all went well. Everything was perfect. The comrade who was giving her tuition, a frail young man with, as it were, solemn-looking shoulders and good-natured drowsy eyes, toiled unremittingly from morning to night. He had two assistants, an apprentice girl and his own sister, a plump little girl of about sixteen, both of whom sang at their work. Noisily the cog wheels turned round and round, beating time to the incessant songs. And the colorful silk threads whirled round and round to the music, gleaming and glittering and forever changing hue. At first all Deborah had to do was to follow closely the swift progress of the leading silken threads: to see how they responded to the action of the treadle, how they snapped whenever there was a sudden jolt, how the loose ends were caught between thumb and forefinger and knotted together again. Tying the knot seemed rather a ticklish business, yet even that was simple enough. Not only the young man, but his sister and the apprentice girl performed all these operations with apparent ease and great deftness. When the young man told Deborah for the third day in succession that she must still stand by as an onlooker, she thought he was merely wasting her time. She was convinced that she had learned all there was to know in a matter of hours.

She was highly delighted when he finally called on her to try her skill at the machine. But, as she soon discovered, there was a world of difference between merely watching and actually tackling the job. Whenever the thread snapped, the loose ends escaped her, no matter how strenuously she tried to catch hold of them, and even when she succeeded in grasping them after many exertions, she could not tie the knot properly. It would keep coming undone. When she at last made the knot secure it was always ugly and clumsy. And there was worse to come: as soon as the silk began to run strongly, without any breakages, and her hopes soared high, it refused to pass smoothly on to the bobbins in orderly fashion, as it did effortlessly with the other operators, but jumped about zig-zag and got into a hopeless tangle. Neither patient determination, painstaking concentration, nor repeated demonstrations and coaching by the comrade were of any avail.

"It's just as I thought – no one can possibly hope to pick up a skilled trade in a few short days," the comrade's aged mother commented as soon as it was plain that Deborah was at long last resigned to a true appreciation of the circumstances: they were only poor people, all dependent on the bread-winning eldest son, whose time was too precious to waste and certainly his stock of silk was too valuable to be spoilt.

"Well, well, do you mean to tell me your career has come to an untimely end?" scoffed Michael. "Or have you gone on strike? No,

I know what's happened: you've already made your pile and have decided to retire."

Deborah bit her tongue till it bled. She made no reply.

She began to look for a situation as a nursemaid. She had many interviews and was given countless promises, but never an engagement. Always she received a polite letter containing some excuse or other. But surely to goodness some girls did find employment as nursemaids, and wealthy ladies did need nursemaids for their pampered infants? It was a mystery.

Meanwhile time was growing short: the marriage was due to take place at an early date. Raizela took a very lively interest in getting the trousseau together. For once in her lifetime she all but denied herself the pleasure of reading. Day in, day out, a loud-voiced tradeswoman darted in and out of the house with endless samples of cloths, linens, silks, velvets, feathers, eiderdowns, trimmings and many other things besides. Deborah moved about the home like a stranger. She had no patience for the samples. What did matter to her were the newspaper advertisements under the heading, "NURSEMAIDS WANTED." And all the time she was afflicted with pains at the heart.

"We'll never get ready for the wedding if we wait for *her* to come down to earth," said Raizela, and she ordered lengths of material entirely on her own judgment, all of the highest quality. She was convinced that no one knew better than herself what would best suit Deborah.

Next Deborah had to pay a long succession of calls on her dressmaker and tailor. They took her measure and gave her innumerable fittings. Mechanically, Deborah did all they asked her to do; she no longer consulted her own wishes and had lost all her will power. So she was going to get married after all, and yet it was sheer madness! If she were to decline even now, what could her parents do to her? And even supposing no one would accept her as a nursemaid, nor yet as a servant, could she not remain as she was and cling to her home? Thus was the trend of Deborah's thoughts as she stood in front of the mirror, while the dressmaker adjusted the semi-finished clothes on her living dummy, putting pins in and taking them out again, undoing seams and sewing them up again, basting and chalking and talking. Deborah lifted her arm, lowered it, rested her foot there, rested it here: she obeyed orders.

"Dear me, you will be a radiant bride, to be sure!" the dressmaker hissed her flattery at Deborah from between clenched teeth, for she had a pin in her mouth.

"So I'm going to be radiant, am I?" said Deborah, with only a hazy notion as to why she had spoken.

"Bless your little soul, of course you will! Now just have a good look at yourself in that mirror. Why, you look like a born princess. Honestly, a queen at her best couldn't look any prettier. I hear you're going to settle in Germany. Am I right?"

"Belgium!" Deborah corrected her.

"Go on! Isn't Belgium somewhere in Germany?"

"No, of course it isn't!" Deborah smiled.

There was nothing to smile at, as far as the dressmaker could see. One was entitled to ask a question and receive a polite answer. All the same, it was not policy to argue the point with a client.

"Surprising your parents should let you go that far," the dressmaker resumed, taking the pin out of her mouth.

Deborah was silent. All at once she felt she was going to tear off the half-finished frock, dash it to the ground, and herself fall to the ground weeping and tearing her hair. She forced back a tear which sparkled in a corner of her eye for a fleeting instant, and then she turned her right shoulder towards the mirror (as requested by the dressmaker).

"Must be a love match, that's what it is," the dressmaker went on, trying to draw her client into conversation. Finding that she could get no information, she formed her own conclusions. "Nowadays parents have absolutely no control over their children. I hope you won't think I've been putting my nose in where it's not wanted, only knowing your father was a rabbi, it seemed rather funny he should allow you to go away and live in Germany."

"Shut up and go to hell! Fool, idiot!" Deborah fumed in her thoughts. "Please hurry up!" she said aloud, by way of reply.

The dressmaker said not another word, but she was most curious to know how the lovers had first met; she was simply burning with anxiety to find out. Some girls had all the luck. Here was a slip of a girl, there was not much to her, really, and yet she had had her love affair and was going abroad to marry him. Probably *he* was of the passionate type. Some girls had all the luck. Others, like herself, had no luck at all.

Deborah's reserve of patience finally gave out. As each passing day brought her closer to the impending wedding, her nerves became more and more inflamed. Now at last she began to protest, to entreat her parents to break off the engagement, or at least to arrange for her to meet the man she was supposed to marry.

"What's that? You want to put us to shame now that the wedding is only a few days off and all the arrangements have been made and everybody knows? Stuff and nonsense!"

At last she quietened down; she ceased tormenting herself; her strength deserted her, and she took to her bed with a nervous breakdown. The home was plunged into chaos and utter despair. Raizela stooped like an old woman as she went about her work. She fumbled all she did; everything she touched slipped through her fingers. And there was more to be done now than ever. Michael became her right hand, and he did for the remaining crockery. Reb Avram Ber walked about like a man in a dream: he was in a continual state of alarm lest Reb Baruch Laib, Deborah's prospective father-in-law, should get to know how things were.

But they succeeded in hushing the matter up (for which the Lord be praised!). The doctor, without actually saying so in as many words, led Reb Baruch Laib to believe that Deborah was indisposed with a feverish cold. After a while the doctor reached the decision that his patient's nervous disease was not to be cured by keeping her in bed. On the contrary, she must get up, take plenty of fresh air, mingle with the crowd, shun solitude of any kind, and – very important this – she must avoid dwelling on any painful thoughts which might be afflicting her; plenty of fruit was what she wanted, plenty of vegetables – and most important, said the doctor, pulling out his watch – on no account must she worry. In his opinion her indisposition was due to some trying experience, such as would leave a deep impression on a highly-strung adolescent mind. That was why she must do everything within her power to banish foreboding thoughts. Her condition did not give rise to anxiety; the illness could now be nipped in the bud; but to do so, it was essential that his advice be acted upon rigorously, and then he went on to give the most unprofessional sort of advice, the sort that left one flabbergasted, coming as it did from a medical man.

Some weeks passed. Deborah regained the merest semblance of a young, healthy woman. This, therefore, was the appropriate moment to marry her off. There had been several postponements of the wedding, but the happy event could not be put off forever.

"Do you mean to say you're worrying about what the doctor said? Can't you see the man's crazy?" said Reb Zalman at the family conference, scornfully shrugging his shoulders and flinging out his hands in mock despair.

Raizela and Reb Avram Ber were both obliged to acknowledge that the doctor was as mad as a hatter. Obviously no sane man would say to a bride, who had completed all her arrangements for the wedding and had her trousseau all ready, that she must find a job as a saleslady so as to keep her mind occupied, and if the man who said such things – a doctor at that – was not sane, clearly he was insane.

"*Goyim* will be *goyim*!" said Reb Zalman.

Again Reb Avram Ber and Raizela, were both obliged to acknowledge that *goyim* will be *goyim*.

"Have you ever heard of such a thing? Here's a girl on the threshold of her married life, with all her life before her, and some silly fool of a doctor comes along and has the impertinence to tell her to.... Why, it's monstrous! Monstrous! As if we wanted his advice! A doctor's job is to give you medicine and pills," said Reb Zalman, "and if we stand in need of advice, we shall know where to get it: we'll go and consult a *tzaddik*!"

"You're quite right. And, please God, she will be all the better for an early marriage."

Meanwhile, there were rumblings of revolt from another quarter: Reb Baruch Laib was greatly perturbed to see that Deborah had grown so much thinner. She had not been plump to start with; he now felt that he was being badly cheated. He voiced his protest vehemently, without beating about the bush.

"And you should see my other daughter-in-law, the one that's married to my eldest son. Why, she's a perfect beauty. I've never seen anyone with a rounder face and a rosier complexion – just like an apple." Thus Reb Baruch Laib.

"Yes, it's a pleasure to look at her. Why, her countenance is so handsome and bright and cheerful, you feel quite dazzled when you look at her. She's like a full moon." Thus Reb Baruch Laib's wife.

And the couple shook their heads in despair over Deborah.

"However, let's hope she'll impress the bridegroom favorably. That's all that matters really," said Reb Baruch Laib. He wondered, though: would she impress him, and how?

It was determined that they should all leave for Berlin on the following Sunday, and the wedding was to take place on the Tuesday after.

When that fateful Sunday came round, only six weeks after her nervous breakdown, an excited, jostling crowd of bosom friends, not to mention neighbors, assembled in Reb Avram Ber's home to bid farewell to the happy bride. They all drank a toast to the lovely bride and to the proud parents, and they ate and they drank and made merry (after first complying with the prim formalities of refusing to eat and drink and make merry), and they renewed their congratulations again and again to Deborah, her family and in-laws. They stood about laughing and joking and talking and jabbering, till the very walls seemed to be swaying dizzily. But it was the kisses that the womenfolk smothered her in which sickened Deborah most of all. Her cheeks and mouth were aching, limp and slobbery, and still the endless succession of smacking lips came on and on. Tireless lips, wet, ugly lips, that deafened her with kind hopes and blessings. They trusted most sincerely that Deborah would be very happy, and that her husband would prosper in that far-off land; one day, perhaps, he was going to be a millionaire – who could tell? Everything was possible with a man who dealt in diamonds. Why, they knew of girls who had been brought up in poverty and had found themselves outlandish husbands and were now living in the lap of luxury. Even so, all the guests were surprised that Raizela should agree to part with an only daughter, and all the guests said as much in very plain language.

Deborah pricked up her ears. Surprised, were they? Well, granted that her parents were eager to be rid of her, why on earth should she oblige by running away? How on earth had all this come to pass? Surely it was not too late to change her mind even now! Why not scream her refusal now, at the top of her voice, and dumbfound these hateful people who called themselves her parents, her well-wishers, her friends? Why not undo their wicked machinations and put them to shame? But what was it all about, anyway? She was not being sent into the wastes of Siberia. She was going first to Berlin, and then on to Antwerp. And possibly when she got to Berlin he might not like the look of her and might refuse to have her. There was still that chance of escape as Reb Baruch Laib had pointed out only a few days ago. But on that occasion, when she had offered to break off the engagement, Reb Baruch Laib had declined to hear another word, and had told her not to take every passing remark so seriously. So now she was traveling out to meet him. What would she do if, as ill luck might have it, he said "Yes"? He? Who was this *he* to whom she was going to give herself away?

"What a mad whirl my mind is in! If Simon were to know how things really are, he would save me from myself. God, what makes me always do the contrary of what I *want* to do? I know quite well that I am doing the wrong thing, and yet the moment I make up my mind one way, I act the reverse way. One mistake after another, one folly after another! Don't I know that I'm acting the fool, and yet I can't help myself. I just go blundering on and on…I must be raving mad!"

"Deborah, here's Mrs. Barski to say goodbye to you."

Deborah's throat was parched. She dreaded kissing Mrs. Barski. She kissed Mrs. Barski, and even smiled back sweetly at her.

No, there could be no turning back now. After yesterday's foolishness, she felt too sick at heart to care what might become of her. What an idiot she had been to go to the cafe and solemnly break the news to Simon that her parents were forcing her, against her will, to marry a man in Antwerp whom she did not know. Now he looked up and caught sight of her, what a tender expression had entered his eyes, how they had fondled her. As he gazed at her and sought her eyes, and his hand moved forward as if to clasp her own, she felt sure that he loved her. He spoke to her, and his voice was even gentler than his words:

"I wonder, Deborah, if you have ever suspected how strong even the frailest of us can be?"

He still went on looking at her in that ecstatic way, and she said jerkily:

"I don't understand. What do you mean?"

She was quite certain then that her instinct had not betrayed her when occasionally it prompted her to believe that Simon cared for her, that he loved her. Just then, however, some comrade joined them at the table, and she waited patiently, hopefully. At last they were alone again, and she blurted out the whole stupid story, trusting that he would be sorry for her, that he would try to dissuade her, or might even protest – now at length he would speak his mind – but, instead, she heard Simon say quite cheerfully:

"So you're going to get married. Ah, let me congratulate you!" She wondered if she had heard aright. But then he added: "You did very well to accept, Deborah. Yes, you did very well!"

So here she was again kissing an old woman whose face was disfigured with warts – brown warts and black warts, and some of them had hair growing out of the center. How disgusting those hairs were!

She was dying to wipe her hand across her mouth, but for some reason the old woman would not look the other way, the beast!

Was she really justified in throwing the blame on others? They had their own point of view, and she ought to have hers. It was all her own fault. What if Simon had shown indifference? That surely was not sufficient cause for her to run away from herself. Scorning all opposition, she could simply say, "I refuse to go!" and the whole terrible nightmare would end instantly.

But no, her parents would not have to throw her out bodily. She would go of her own accord. Now, what would Bailka have done in her place? Bailka would not have wavered.

They were helping her to climb into the droshky. They were off, heading for the station.

She had not even said goodbye to Bailka. What was Miss Rushka doing in the droshky? Surely it was unnecessary for the whole of Reb Zalman's family to see her off to the station. And what had come over Miss Rushka today that made her look so different from her usual self?

The procession of droshkies was speeding through the streets of Warsaw. Trip-trap, trip-trap! went the patter of the horses' hooves. A feeling of bliss, so exquisite that it hurt, took possession of her all at once. She had a strange craving to drink in all she saw, as if she had been away from the city for years. Every sharp cobblestone, every muddy stretch of pavement, every shabby building, every panting porter bent double under his staggering load, became suddenly a precious part of herself. Even the beggar women, who sat on the doorsteps nursing babies in torn shawls, and who kept pinching the flesh of these babies to make them howl piteously, were like dear, old, loving friends, from whom parting was difficult. And how quaint those red-nosed, aged-looking little girls with the swinging pigtails were today; how worried the expression on their faces, poor things!

The droshkies were held up in the traffic. A little distance away an old woman in tatters, her face a furrowed, formless jumble of skin and bones, was sitting over a basket, on a doorstep, calling out her wares. Sighting the droshky, she lifted up her basket appealingly. The contents were a sticky mess, for all the world like a heap of dung.

"Buy my gol'en fruit, ladies, buy, buy!" she droned feebly in a scarcely audible, nasal voice. She fingered the mess in the basket to make it look inviting, but only succeeded in squashing it the more.

Deborah peered into the basket. She wondered very much what the contents might be. It quite teased her. She hazarded a guess just as the droshky began to move on – over-ripe apricots. She felt so sorry for the old woman. Alms would not come amiss, even though Bailka was of the opinion that charity only helped to bolster up the existing rotten social order. Anyway, who was to blame for its rottenness? – Miss Rushka and Reb Baruch Laib! She tossed the woman a coin. The droshky gathered speed. She turned her head, and saw the old woman squabbling with a ragged urchin. The boy grabbed the money, spat the woman full in the face through his thick lips, and lifting one leg hopped away in triumph. What an outrage! But the droshky was now going at full speed.

"Well Deborah, you can say good riddance to Warsaw now," observed Miss Rushka.

"What do you mean, good riddance?" Deborah exclaimed hotly. She continued more calmly: "On the contrary, I think Warsaw a splendid city."

"Sure, Warsaw is the finest city in the world! There is no other city to compare with it, anywhere!" said Miss Rushka. "Why, I wouldn't leave Warsaw for all the diamonds in the world!"

Deborah moved away on her seat.

Miss Rushka's mother coughed uneasily, and lightly pinched her daughter in the fleshy part.

"I don't know so much! Some people love nothing better than to travel," she said, trying to make amends for her daughter's spitefulness, and then, to demonstrate her friendly feelings, she added: "Why, when I come to think that soon you will no longer be with us, it simply breaks my heart.…"

Deborah was silent.

Chapter 13

What a mighty contingent of uncles, aunts, brothers, sisters, cousins, nephews, nieces and bosom friends were gathered at the station to give the bridal party a right royal sendoff! How they all overran the platform, talking and shouting and kissing and sending their love to all the other relations that would be waiting at the journey's end!

"Remember me to the bridegroom, remember me to Rebecca, remember –."

Slowly the train moved off, with the engine roaring and spitting like a furious monster. Puff, puff, puff!

And the uncles, the aunts, the brothers, the sisters, the cousins, the nephews, the nieces and the bosom friends were left behind, waving their hands, their handkerchiefs and their umbrellas like mad. They were on the verge of exhaustion, but still they went on waving farewell and blowing kisses, as if they were quite insatiable. How they all loved to kiss and kiss again! Why did they address her with the familiar "thou," Deborah wondered. How was it that she had never addressed Simon as "thou"? The absurdity of this thought, which entered her mind so unexpectedly, both shocked and sobered her. She was waking up to the realities of the situation. With every fleeting instant the train was drawing closer and closer to a strange city, where a stranger would be waiting to claim her as his own, and she was leaving Warsaw, her home and her past. But, in spite of herself, she did not very much care now. It was all so false.

"Deborah, what about having a little lie-down?" her mother was saying.

That caused her to lose her temper suddenly. Would they never give her a moment's peace?

So it had come to this, after all. Somehow they had laid hands on her and were disposing of her just as they pleased, as if she were a corpse. And yet, here she was alive and in full possession of her senses. How had it come about? But perhaps – and at the thought, an icy shudder ran down her spine – she was not really in the full possession of her senses? Maybe she was living in a kind of trance, so that although she was able to see and hear and feel, she lacked the means to resist. What was to be done? One thing was certain: the train was bearing her on and on. Soon it would be too late. As if it were not too late already! She was helpless. Again she shuddered.

Someone was asking her something about smoking.

"No!" she said.

The gentleman in the corner seat opposite gave her an astonished look.

"No, I don't mind if you smoke. Not a bit!" she said, collecting her scattered wits.

"Thanks!" said the gentleman, politely doffing his hat, and now that he had removed it from his head he went a step further and tossed it on to the rack. He lit a cigarette, leaned back in his seat, crossed his legs, and having made himself quite comfortable emitted a large puff of smoke through his dark red lips. The smoke coiled upwards and vanished in a faint white haze. There followed another big puff, this time dense and bluish.

"Pardon me, Miss, but may I enquire what is your destination?"

"Berlin," Deborah responded peevishly. Why didn't that fellow keep to himself? What was the matter with him?

"Ah, so we're both going to the same place. I think Berlin is a wonderful city. Have you ever been there?"

"No!"

"Ah, then you've something to look forward to. I love Berlin. I once lived there for four solid years; that was when I was studying for my degree. What a time I had there! The best years of my life! Honestly, I feel quite excited when I think that just a few more hours and I'll be stepping out into the same old station, the same old streets! How we old people long to revisit the haunts of our youth. Of course, at your age you can't imagine any such thing. But as for me, I'm all eagerness to see my old digs again, where I once spent a few really happy years. It will be a pleasure to meet old friends again, and would you believe it, I'm even anxious to see the old professor again. He was a sarcastic little fellow! Ha, ha, ha! How everything changes and grows sweet in your memory after you've left it behind for years and years!"

Deborah was lulled into good humor. It was a pleasure to listen to his boyish talk. So frank and good natured. She wondered where he was now living. His words had a ring of sincerity. She would speak to him. Of course she would. It would bring on forgetfulness. It would take her out of herself.

"May I enquire," she said, using his own expression, "where is your home town?"

"Why of course you may!" he exclaimed with a smile, pleased to see that he had broken down her reserve. "My home is in Harkov."

"So you're a Russian?"

"Yes, that is so. I'm only going to Berlin for a short visit, to get myself some new instruments – surgical instruments. Berlin is the place for instruments – the best the world has to offer. Germany's ambition, you know, is to conquer the world, and one day I believe she'll do it. The Germans are making such tremendous progress in all the sciences, they march ahead with such gigantic strides, no other country in the world can keep abreast of them."

"I get it: *Deutschland uber alles*!" said Deborah, recalling how Simon had always scorned the Germans for their chauvinism.

"Well, they certainly know their own strength. They are fully conscious of their own power. They feel proud of themselves, and not without justification," said the doctor in his enthusiastic way.

"You certainly are passionately pro-German, aren't you?" said Deborah, the color mounting to her cheeks.

"No, I don't think I am. I love Germany, and I love Russia, only in a different way. Russia has got something big, something epic about her, if you know what I mean. But I will say this: after a taste of Western European civilization, you begin to wish that Russia were not so backward, so primitive. Anyway, I am a Jew first and last. And if I'm really interested in any country, that country is Palestine. If it ever becomes our own, however, I would prefer to see it developed on the German, rather than the Russian model. Russian soil, Russian natural resources – wonderful! Czarist policy, czarist barbarism – no thank you! Please let me continue. In some respects this country's way of life borders on complete lunacy, and unless we have a radical change, and that pretty soon, Germany will teach Russia a severe lesson."

"I take it you are a Zionist?"

"Of course I am! No Jew in his right mind can be anything but a Zionist."

"I don't agree with you. But to return to the point, I must say I'm very much surprised at the beautiful rosy picture you paint of the Germany of blood and iron. To my knowledge, the Germans may be wonderful instrument makers, but what they most excel at is militarism and antisemitism. I've been told, and I'm quoting a person of real authority now (Simon again!), that the Germans are the world's worst reactionaries. Really, I don't know how you can tolerate their slogan *Deutschland uber alles*! We all know that Russia is unruly. But Russia as she is today is a diseased country. And surely wrongdoing in the case of a healthy country, as of a healthy person, is less pardonable than in one that is ailing?"

"Yes, you're perfectly right there, Miss, perfectly right! Of course, from my own point of view Palestine really ought to be *uber alles.* Not that I'm so arrogant as to want even that," said the doctor, rather amused.

Deborah was carried away by that passionate zest for life and affairs which mostly lay repressed within her and which used to well up so irresistibly whenever she heard Simon speaking at party meetings.

"I wonder how you can say and think such things when you profess to hate tyranny and brutality! Do you really imagine that if Kaiser Wilhelm were to free the Russian people of their antiquated yoke and were to rule them with his own civilized iron rod, a new and a better Russia would be born? Would you care to see Germany perpetuate tyranny and brutality by modern scientific methods? For my part, I think that if any such thing were to happen, life would not be worth living!"

Deborah's tone became heated, her cheeks flushed and her eyes were flashing. Her blood was up and she appeared ready to proclaim war on the kaiser single-handed.

"Yes, Miss, but please, I beg of you, do not get so excited. After all, my personal views are of little account, and believe me I don't really care a hoot if we have Rasputin or Wilhelm as our ruler. I have no politics, and my only political concern is the welfare of our own people. For the rest, all tyrants can go to the devil. Moreover, it is far safer not to discuss such delicate subjects on Russian soil, for walls have ears, and whatever our views, we had best keep them to ourselves, for to Russia we must return."

These last words touched Deborah to the quick.

"I won't be coming back," she said softly.

The doctor did not hear her remark. He helped himself to another cigarette.

"Now, now Deborah, what manner of conduct is this? What on earth put it into your head to enter into conversation with a man you've never seen before? And of all things, fancy speaking politics to a complete stranger? How do you know he isn't a spy? For all you know, he may be an informer. Really, no respectable girl ever dreams of picking up casual acquaintances on a train. It just isn't done!" Reb Baruch Laib admonished her, the moment the doctor had withdrawn with a most affable bow like a man of true western culture, and had gone off down the swaying corridor intent on doing himself some good in the dining car. "Why, as I sat there listening to the conversation, I felt my hair rise on end. I felt I was about to have a fit; but I didn't dare interrupt in case I made matters worse. Good God, supposing we got ourselves into trouble with the authorities, that would be a nice thing, wouldn't it? Wouldn't it?"

Did that beast, who was supposed to be her father-in-law, presume to address her as though she were his own property? Did he too imagine that he was free to bully her and trifle with her life? Oh, oh, one more word from him and she would make him pay for all the persecution, all the humiliation she had ever suffered.

"Deborah, why don't you say something? You wouldn't like your father-in-law to feel that you're ignoring him, would you now?" Reb Avram Ber interceded.

Her father's gentle voice reminded her of her love for him.

"I have nothing to say, Papa. Any time a passenger speaks to me, I shall answer him. It's not a crime, only common courtesy."

"Yes, but remember you're a grown-up girl. A grown-up girl mustn't talk to a strange gentleman," Reb Avram Ber reasoned with her.

She smiled.

"Look at her, look, she's laughing at us!" cried Reb Baruch Laib. Beside himself with excitement, he was attempting to pace up and down the compartment.

"All this is quite uncalled for," Raizela put in, detaching herself from her book.

"Please, Mamma, you keep out of it. Why worry? You're soon going to get rid of me!" Deborah addressed her mother with unconcealed bitterness.

"Yes, thank God!" Raizela retorted, and she returned to her reading.

Reb Baruch Laib's wife, Tertsa-Roisa, was having a nap. As usual, she heard nothing, saw nothing. Her breath came easily, unctuously, and in the midst of her slumbers a good-natured little smile was playing on her parted, whitish lips – lips that were a wee bit askew in her fleshy face. Deborah happened to rest her glance on these tranquil features, and suddenly it occurred to her that if the bridegroom was anything like his mother, then at this very moment he too would be snoozing and smiling in his sleep while the train rushed onwards from Antwerp to Berlin.

Sated and beaming, the doctor ambled back from the restaurant car. He resumed his seat and one could tell by his amiable expression that he was hankering for an opportunity to launch out on another heart-to-heart talk; however, he would not repeat his first mistake, but would confine himself strictly to topics that were pleasant and happy and romantic. Not by any stretch of the imagination could he guess that the fat old man with the great belly, fiery red beard and glowering countenance, with blazing pinpoint eyes, was puffing and blowing so furiously all because he – a doctor and a gentleman – had chatted, innocently enough, with a fellow-passenger. In fact, he was not even aware that the young lady in question was a member of the fat old man's party. What he did notice was the fact that she was wearing her morose and unapproachable expression again.

For her part, Deborah was only too eager to continue the discussion and to broaden it, if only to teach her father-in-law a lesson. And, besides, it was a joy to converse with a person who treated one as an equal, who was intelligent without being self-important. Unlike most people he did not inspire in her that unaccountable embarrassment which created a barrier between thought and speech – an impassable barrier which fostered unnatural silence and misunderstanding. She watched the doctor light a fat cigar. He addressed a few words to her. Her answer came abruptly. Inwardly raging, she rose, went out into the corridor, and then, instead of returning, she sat down in the next-door compartment. Reb Avram Ber joined her.

"Thank you, Deborah, you're a darling. You have saved the situation. And now your father-in-law has gone and made it up."

"Oh has he? How wonderful! Hip, hip, hurrah!"

"What is the matter with you, Deborah? Just think! You're going to get married to a very nice young man, who will give you a comfortable home, and you will be able to do just as you please.... Any other girl would think herself extremely lucky to be in your position, especially if her father were poor and could not provide her with a dowry. Really, Deborah, I don't know why you treat your father-in-law the way you do, as if he were dirt. He's a very nice man indeed, I think. And I can prove it to you, Deborah. Guess what he's been telling me! He tells me that he has bought a pair of earrings costing no less than three hundred rubles. And they're going to be the bridegroom's wedding gift to you in Berlin. Isn't that wonderful?"

Deborah only smiled.

"Words are cheap, Deborah, but how can you doubt Reb Baruch Laib's affection for you when he does such extraordinary things. Honestly, I think you're a very fortunate girl. The Lord be praised!"

Deborah heaved a sigh.

For all his shortsightedness, Reb Avram Ber perceived that his daughter was sad and that her sadness was not to be dispelled by any glittering trinkets.

"Perhaps you'd feel better if you were to lie down?"

"Yes, I'm tired, ever so tired."

"All right, I'll ask Mother to keep you company. Isn't it strange that this compartment should be absolutely empty?"

Raizela joined her. After a little while they both fell asleep, and it was only when the train drew to a standstill in Berlin, at Alexanderplatz Station, about half past seven in the morning, that they opened their eyes. With her face deathly pale, her frock crushed and a mist before her eyes, Deborah swayed feebly as she rose to her feet. Through the window of the compartment she caught her first glimpse of the station – an immense place teeming with activity. With her mother she rejoined the others in the next-door compartment. Tertsa-Roisa was sitting up, wide awake.

"Good morning," she said. "Good morning, I hope you had a good night's rest. Oh, Deborah, just take a look at yourself! How rumpled you are! Dear me!"

Deborah obligingly took a look at herself and forced a smile.

Mingling with the hurrying throng in the station, yet distinct from this throng, were certain tall, clean-shaven Germans with proud mien and fat cigars and fat walking sticks, who held their heads high and their bodies erect – great hulking bodies such as were seldom to be seen in Warsaw. Firm as rocks in a troubled sea, unperturbed by all the hubbub and bustle around them, they marched forward with measured gait and their every movement had an air of deliberateness, of premeditation.

Reb Baruch Laib pulled the luggage off the racks. Reb Avram Ber did his best to help. Having negotiated his wife through the all-too-narrow doorway of the carriage, Reb Baruch Laib could now afford to pause and mop the perspiration off his shiny brow. The party waited, with the suitcases piled up at their feet.

A porter approached and, comparing Reb Avram Ber with Reb Baruch Laib, unhesitatingly selected the latter as the leader, to whom he offered his services in a very guttural and unintelligible German. His business-like trolley told its own tale.

"Do you mind telling him, Deborah, that we want to take a taxi," said Tertsa-Roisa, with an enquiring look at her husband. He nodded his approval, and Deborah acted as spokesman. She informed the impatient porter of their destination – The Kosher Hotel, Grenadierstrasse.

No sooner had he ascertained that it was in fact Grenadierstrasse they wanted and that all the other streets which he erroneously volunteered were unacceptable, he heaped the luggage on his green trolley and dashed off helter-skelter at such a pace that Tertsa-Roisa broke most of the fish bones in her corset in the chase that ensued. In vain they called on him to halt, in vain they shouted and hissed at him. Out of sheer desperation, Tertsa-Roisa somehow succeeded in keeping up with the rest, puffing and blowing and snorting.

It was a bright morning. Outside the station stood a long line of gleaming taxis. The porter raised his hand, and instantly the foremost cab drove up to the curb. The driver inclined his ear, and learning from the porter that his passengers were Polish Jews and whither they were bound, he rubbed his nose with a show of contempt. Reb Baruch Laib wondered how much the journey would cost, but the driver ignored him and meanwhile the porter stood waiting with outstretched palm. Reb Baruch Laib was thrown into confusion.

"What, two marks?" he gasped.

"*Jawohl!* Two marks! And you'd better look sharp! Time is money! *Verstanden?*" the porter snapped back at him with great severity.

"Daylight robbery, that's what it is! Still, it can't be helped. God willing, he'll spend the money on a doctor's bill. I wonder what sort of appetite this fellow has got," added Reb Baruch Laib, indicating the taxi driver, as the car moved off and he rebuttoned his back trouser pocket; his wife who sat opposite him, with Raizela and Deborah squeezed in on either side, just smiled.

Berlin was throbbing with life: the pulse beating in its veins had the regularity, the power of a vital, self-confident being.

"So this is Berlin! Well, it's good to be alive!" was the stranger's first impression on passing through the city that morning, all steeped as it was in sunshine. The streets were teeming. The cafes were besieged with workers, with impatient men and women at the bars and on the terraces, waiting to get their glass of beer. They gulped it down unceremoniously and hurried off to their work. Clanging and screeching on the rails, the crowded tram cars followed hard upon each other in endless processions. Early though the hour was, many private cars were to be seen winding their way furiously through the traffic. On the swarming pavements men and women were gabbling away at each other as fast as they could go. The city was bestirring itself with a will.

"Isn't it a magnificent sight?" cried Deborah, seemingly oblivious – for a breathless moment – to the fact that she was soon to be married. She felt she must share her joy. "Do have a look, Mamma!" She was oblivious, also, to the fact that soon all this human energy would be consumed by insatiable, smoky factories.

Raizela turned a critical eye on Berlin.

"I don't know how the people can stand it. The racket is absolutely maddening!" was her verdict.

Grenadierstrasse was certainly not so select as it might have been, but was nothing like the slums of Warsaw. In its own way, it was clean and fairly quiet. The Kosher Hotel was run by a Polish Jew, Herr Berger, or Reb Haim as he was more familiarly known to the hasidic Jews and rabbis who patronized his establishment. Herr Berger heard the taxi drive up. He hastened out to welcome his guests, whoever they might be. Opening the door of the cab and taking stock of its occupants, he gave vent to a joyous cry of "Peace unto you!" – a cry that was so jolly and friendly, withal respectful, one would have thought he had known these newcomers all his life. Then he paused and reflectively stroked his smooth white forehead, framed in a gleaming black skull-cap, as if he had forgotten something that he badly needed to remember.

Reb Avram Ber was the first to alight. Deborah followed and she helped her mother out. Then came the hardest task of all. Reb Baruch Laib summoned up all his ingenuity in extracting Tertsa-Roisa from the swaying cab.

"Will you please ask him what the fare is," Reb Baruch Laib panted at the hotel keeper.

"Right! You leave it to me, I'll square him!" Herr Berger exclaimed with a great air of authority, and simultaneously he flicked back the white starched cuff that had worked its way down his wrist – flicked it back smilingly, deftly, like a man who means to see that all things shall stay where they belong. He had it out with the driver, clinching the argument by pointing an accusing finger at the taximeter. The driver foamed with rage. His face, his ears and even the nape of his neck turned scarlet, and his eyes became bloodshot. At last his breath failed him, and wrathfully grunting "Dirty Jew!" he pocketed his due and made off in a cloud of smoke from the exhaust.

"Well, of all the dirty Germans!" said the hotel keeper, still smiling unctuously. "He tried to do one on me. *Me,* mind you! Anyone would think I was green, anyone would think I was a foreigner who couldn't read a taximeter. The miserable cheat, someone ought to give him a thick ear!"

Saying which, Herr Berger ceremoniously opened the door of the restaurant that formed part of his establishment. He posted himself in the doorway and with a flourish of the hand ushered his guests in. His boiled shirt gleamed proudly, the skirt of his coat – a cross between tails and a gabardine – fluttered bravely. He ordered a weedy lad of about seventeen to carry the luggage up.

"Go on, get a move on!" he said with an amused smile by way of encouragement.

Reb Baruch Laib beckoned to him confidentially and they held a whispered consultation. When their two heads parted, both faces wore a knowing expression. Herr Berger counted the party's strength on his fingers, then he asked them to follow him upstairs. The house echoed to Tertsa-Roisa's gasps:

"Phew! Ugh! Phew!"

Entering a large bright room on the first floor, with three windows – all of them wide-open and overlooking the Grenadierstrasse – the weary travelers settled down peacefully on the rather weary-looking upholstered chairs and sofa.

"You see, this is our best room. Look how bright and airy it is! It's a rest cure, that's what it is, believe me! Tell me, would you like to have some refreshments brought up? Or would you rather have a wash first?"

"Well, we haven't said our morning prayers yet," Reb Avram Ber spoke up for the first time.

"Haven't you really? Allow me to inform you then, that you couldn't have chosen a better time for your arrival, because we're just about to hold our morning service."

"Do you mean to tell me that you have sufficient Jews here to make up a full congregation?" Reb Avram Ber gasped in utter astonishment.

"Exactly," said Herr Berger. "In this hotel you will find everything you want. If it's a full congregation you're looking for – no need to look any further, here it is! And what a congregation! Believe me, when you see the type of guests I have staying in my hotel, you'll be surprised. Some of them are rabbis (God bless them!), and as for the rest, I have no reason to be ashamed of them either (God forbid!), not a bit!"

Reb Avram Ber rubbed his hands with deep satisfaction.

"Oh, God!" he rejoiced. "What a wonderful race Thy Jews are! One finds them everywhere, everywhere. And even in these foreign parts, there are Jews we can be proud of, upright and God-fearing!" he enthused over his new-found friends, friends whom he had not even met yet. The sight of a hasidic Jew like Reb Haim in the modern style of dress was very reassuring and reminded him of all that Reb Zalman had said about the bridegroom.

A gentile maid, blonde and rosy-cheeked, with a powerful bosom which was quite cramped within her tight bodice and which at every breath strained upwards as though eager to gain its freedom, conducted the womenfolk to the bathroom, where she initiated them in the use of the hot and cold water taps, and after having made certain that her services were no longer required, she went tripping down the stairs, whistling cheerfully.

Reb Avram Ber and Reb Baruch Laib took breakfast with Herr Berger's ten rabbis (God bless them! although ten was rather an exaggerated figure) and with the rest of the guests, of whom Herr Berger had no reason to be ashamed (God forbid!). They opened a bottle, drank to each other's health and treated each other to a great many benedictions. The new friends were promptly invited to attend the wedding, and the invitation was as promptly accepted by one and all. Before long it came to light that one of the rabbis, a skinny little old man with a straggly goatee, was one of Reb Avram Ber's long-lost, distant relations. And there was great and prolonged rejoicing.

Deborah felt quite carefree, even buoyant. Ever since she had set foot in Berlin, her constant gloom and despair had given way to utter calm. It was all very odd, but she had no particular wish to find out why – all that mattered to her was the fact that she had at last found peace of mind. She now had only one interest in life, and that was to discover who dwelt in that curious house across the road with the white, motionless, starched curtains. What sort of people were they, were they a large family or a small family, Jews or gentiles? She had had a wash and a change of clothes, and with her hair neatly combed, she stood at the window waiting patiently to catch a glimpse beyond those elegant curtains, as if the knowledge she hoped to glean thus was of vital importance to her, as if it were indeed the sole object of her visit. The maid was clearing away the breakfast things. Deborah was pleasantly aware of this. It was so good to be waited on, and to be free, utterly free! Now here she could stand without lifting a finger, and she could leave everything in the capable hands of the maid. It was charming, the maid was charming, and hopefully Deborah kept gazing out of the window.…

The non-arrival of the bridegroom was the cause of some anxiety and surprise. He was due to get in by the early morning train from Antwerp, but the family consoled themselves with the reflection that there might have been a delay en route. The only person who showed complete indifference was the bride! She was in a state of perfect apathy. If the house had suddenly come tumbling down, it would scarcely have disturbed her. Such complete calm, such wonderful serenity had never been hers before; she felt as if she had been born again, remembering nothing of the past and caring nothing for her future. Her in-laws, her parents, they all kept talking and brooding and wondering what had happened. Not so Deborah. She neither talked nor brooded, nor wondered: would he come, would he not come, what type of man was he, how was he going to impress her and how would she impress him? Not a thing did she worry about. Her head was altogether empty, devoid even of a stray thought.

Night came on. Last thing before going to bed they dispatched a telegram to Antwerp. Did that concern her? Surely, it had nothing to do with her!

On the following day, about nine o'clock in the morning, a smile blossomed forth on Tertsa-Roisa's face, such a great smile that her features could scarcely cope with it and they became all contorted.

"That's him! I can recognize his footsteps! It's him! He's coming!"

She made as if to run out to meet him, but was spared the pains. The door opened, and the maid admitted a tall plump young man with a smiling, self-satisfied, good-humored face framed in a circular, fiery-red beard; he had on an obviously new grey overcoat and held a new leather suitcase in his hand.

Deborah turned deathly pale.

The young man looked about him bashfully and quite bewildered. The sight of his mother struggling to rise from the sofa gave him his cue.

"Good morning, Mother!" He bent down and kissed her on the cheek. "How are you, Mother?"

"Thank God, I'm all right!" Tertsa-Roisa was beaming. "And how are you? This is your future mother-in-law."

The young man turned his head, with a rather furtive look in his eyes. His anxious gaze rested on Raizela. How pale and thin she was, as though she had just risen from a sickbed. He greeted her. He was not so sure that it was the proper thing for him to shake hands with her, as she was sure to be extremely pious. On this assumption he withheld his hand.

"And now I will introduce you to your bride."

Deborah made some sort of effort to smile.

The bridegroom blushed, so that even his circular beard seemed to turn from ginger to scarlet. A sunny smile settled on his face. He tried hard to articulate, but failed, and when finally he succeeded in mumbling something or other, no one took any notice anyway.

"What next?" he wondered, and then he had a brain wave. He decided to sit down on a chair that his mother had pulled up for him. The scene was heartrending. He had broken out into violent perspiration, and in his embarrassment he took refuge in the most sublime wisdom of all, the wisdom of silence.

"Hello, Berish, how are you?" His father saved the situation by arriving at a point where silence was becoming ridiculous, in fact impossible. Reb Baruch Laib's meaty old hand clasped the plump youthful hand of his son. "Have you seen the bride?" he enquired in a businesslike tone.

"How are you, Father?" the son hedged.

"Not so bad! *Well*?" Reb Baruch Laib was getting impatient.

"All right!" the young man gulped, his face turning an even deeper red than his beard.

"Ah, peace unto you! How are you?" Reb Avram Ber exclaimed at the threshold. He approached and shook the young man's hand so hard, he almost wrenched it off his wrist. "Well, well, we were getting very worried about you, but we'll forget all about that, now you're here. Have you said your morning prayers?"

"Yes, I said my prayers on the train."

Reb Baruch Laib smelled a rat; but he could do no more than glare at his son with a withering skeptical gleam in his crafty little eyes.

"Well then, we must be getting on with our own prayers," he said. "Look here, Tertsa-Roisa, tell them to lay the table in this room. We'll all have breakfast together. Are you coming Reb Avram Ber?"

"Why of course I am!"

No doubt it was Reb Baruch Laib's purpose to bring the bride and bridegroom together – he was anxious to break the ice, encourage them to exchange a few words; however that may be, at the breakfast table he made a proposal that they should all sally forth to Tietz's on a shopping expedition. Reb Avram Ber was left out of the party, as a matter of course, while Raizela excused herself on the plea that she was much too tired.

The weather was glorious. Berlin was radiant in the sunshine. The silks on display in the shop windows, catching the sun's brilliance on their folds, were like flowing molten gold, disturbing and dazzling to the eye. On the shady side of the street the costly fabrics showed their charms more demurely, flowing gently, coyly beckoning to passersby. The flagstones of the pavements sparkled as if studded with myriads of gleaming little diamonds. A leisurely throng filled the streets; the women kept stopping in front of the shop displays. The city bore a festive air now, quite different from the hurly-burly early yesterday morning. Loud, garish posters and commercial signs screamed their messages from the rooftops. All this evoked memories for Deborah of her first visit to Marszalkowski Street.

She had been paired with the young man; but she never said a word as she walked by his side. He too was silent. Confound it, if only he would leave off smiling in that sickly sweet little way of his! It was unthinkable that this young man was to be her husband. He did seem quite a decent fellow, but…but there was something dead about him. There was something dead about the way he walked, the way he smiled. Here her lips curled up in amusement: how he had come to life at the breakfast table, though, how energetic he had been with his knife and fork!…

Suddenly the living image of Simon arose before her, blotting out all else. There he was, majestic of presence, tall, with stooping shoulders. His face was radiant with intelligence, with a deeper intelligence than ever before. "Simon, don't you see that it's too late now, too late!" "*Why is it too late?*" "Because it is!" No, that was not the way he had spoken to her in reality. He had not tried to deter her from running away, but had goaded her on. "I congratulate you, Deborah!" that was what she could hear him say over and over again. Why, then, did he not cease tormenting her? What justification had he for haunting her thus? She was not fit for party work. She was no good at repartee. She was an utter fool. She was a wretched girl without a dowry!

Anyway, what on earth was her companion smiling at? Wasn't that fellow ever going to stop? Confound him! Really, Berlin was a most exciting city, it put Warsaw in the shade. There, he was at it again, smiling once more! Yet he did not look a fool. Actually, of course, there was no reason why he should look a fool!

"I beg your pardon?" her fiancé spoke up all at once, conquering his shyness. He knew full well that she had not said a word, but he hoped to entice her into doing so, and meanwhile he smiled patiently, good-naturedly. Deborah felt sick at heart. What the devil was he so pleased about?

"Deborah, will you please find out whether we're on the right track. Somehow I think we've lost our way," Reb Baruch Laib said, turning his big head.

Deborah stopped an elderly gentleman clad in a loosely fitting overcoat, every stitch of which looked typically German.

"*Königstrasse? Gewiss!*" he exclaimed in a very loud voice.

Deborah did not quite catch the gist of his staccato words, and after bearing left they turned to the right, only to come back where they had started. She inquired again. At last the name of Wertheimers stared at them in bold letters, and across the road was the house of Tietz. Within its portals there was an air of dignified calm. The interior opened up an immense perspective – a city within a city.

Reb Baruch Laib led the way from department to department, past interminable counters. At each stop, the display of colorful goods changed, yet retained a certain artificial symmetry and uniform beauty, like the patterns in a kaleidoscope. The variety of wares seemed inexhaustible.

Deborah's glance lingered for a fleeting instant on a pair of long white silken gloves. Her fiancé immediately bought them for her, together with a blue and white scarf which rather resembled the Zionist flag, and later on he presented her with an umbrella. Then he bought another umbrella, for himself, and a pair of brown kid gloves. It seemed very strange to her that a pious young man who wore a beard – and a ginger beard at that – should think of putting on elegant kid gloves that were obviously designed for a dashing dandy. Surely the people of Antwerp must be a queer, hybrid crowd!

Tertsa-Roisa made a number of purchases too. This was by no means her first visit to Tietz's; two or three years ago she had been there on a similar errand. The occasion then was the marriage of her eldest son who was living in Antwerp. This eldest son, unlike Berish, knew his fiancée, having been betrothed to her before he left Warsaw; but, like Berish, he was also wed at Herr Berger's Kosher Hotel. Tertsa-Roisa was therefore no stranger to this outlandish department store. All the same she could not for the life of her believe that the prices marked up were genuine and unalterable. And she lustily haggled over the lace neckerchief which was to be a present for her daughter in Antwerp, over the serviettes which were for her daughter-in-law, and again over the trinkets which were to delight the hearts of her grandchildren. The young shop assistant was about to lose her temper but, changing her mind, she pressed a push button instead, and a tall young man appeared clad in a long black frock coat and striped black trousers; his sleekly brushed head of black hair positively oozed brilliantine, his teeth were whiter than driven snow. Lightly touching the neckerchief, he smiled a gracious smile, bowed, and said in honeyed tones:

"Very sorry, Madam, but our prices are not subject to bargaining."

As though his words were law, Tertsa-Roisa opened her purse and paid the bill without any further ado.

They returned to the hotel with many neat little parcels; the smiling bridegroom was given charge of the two wrapped-up umbrellas, which he tucked under his arm. They all had dinner together. Deborah ate frugally, much to Reb Baruch Laib's disappointment.

"Why, if that's the way you eat, you'll soon be no better than a skeleton," he reprimanded her as gently as he could. Reb Avram Ber concurred, pointing out that eating was an essential function of living. Tertsa-Roisa argued that eating was merely a habit; if one lost the knack of eating, then one would never feel hungry, and anyone who did not eat could not expect to be strong and healthy. This statement was endorsed by all present (except the bridegroom). So Deborah ate her full portion, even though she felt she would choke.

The wedding ceremony took place on the morrow. The bride and bridegroom saw nothing of each other all day.

Again Deborah felt perfectly calm. She was as light-hearted as a child. Again she had not a care in the world. She had even left off caring who dwelt in the shuttered house across the road. But when evening was drawing in, and her mother told her to put on her wedding gown, she was overcome by a perfect frenzy of despair. All at once the horror of her situation became clear to her in a piercing agonizing light. And as if salvation lay that way, she began to plead desperately with her mother for a respite.

"Please, please, don't hurry me! And haven't I told you all along that I won't, I won't put on a ceremonial wedding gown?"

"Don't be childish, Deborah! You're just like a baby!" said Raizela.

"When I tell you to put on your wedding gown, do so. You know quite well that if this wedding had been celebrated at home you would have had to be dressed up in white all day long."

"Don't say white! Say black!" Deborah burst out.

Raizela clapped her hands over her ears.

Deborah stood praying at the wall facing east. A higgledy-piggledy train of memories, strange memories, went straggling through her brain. Old Hannah crossed her mind, and the kitten that Hannah had taken away when the family left Jelhitz. Did she see Joel before her now? Yes, but what was he doing in this faraway place? It was an apparition, but try as she might she could not get rid of it. His crafty old face obstinately refused to go away. "Congratulations, Deborah! Be a good girl and say your prayers!" It was Simon speaking.... Then Deborah recalled how Tertsa-Roisa had tried to bargain in broken German with the wide-eyed shop-girl who had so despairingly, so naively protested her innocence – *she* was not responsible for the prices charged, *she* was not to blame. Suddenly Deborah burst out laughing.

Raizela and Tertsa-Roisa looked up with startled faces.

"What on earth is the matter with you? Have you lost your reason? Don't you realize what a solemn prayer this is?" Raizela spoke as calmly as she could, concealing her exasperation, but it was preposterous for a bride to indulge in ribald laughter in the midst of her prayers. And there was no apparent cause for laughter: it was sheer madness!

Deborah heeded the rebuke. She stifled her mirth. She took three paces backwards, in accordance with the ritual, and then suddenly, against her own will, against her better judgment, she broke out into another uncontrollable fit of laughter. This time she laughed louder than ever, laughed hysterically. Raizela bit her tongue, deeply ashamed and angry.

Two hours later, beneath the nuptial canopy of red velvet upheld by four poles, beneath the night sky stretching far and wide over the courtyard of the hotel, Deborah stood trembling as with the ague; a crowd of onlookers – purring with self-content – all round her. Reb

Avram Ber himself officiated. Everybody, including the maidservant, assumed a solemn expression.

The man at her side was holding a ring in his hand. All bewildered, Deborah struggled in vain to remove the glove from her fingers. At last, in her confusion and forgetting that her wedding gown had detachable sleeves, she peeled the long glove, which the bridegroom had bought for her at Tietz's, violently off her arm, and in doing so ripped away the sleeve inside. She was left with a naked arm dangling for all to see and be ashamed of. The blood came rushing up into Reb Baruch Laib's head. His beefy face became inflamed, his tiny eyes kindled. But he held his peace. Deborah managed somehow to pull the glove back on to her arm again, and with the sleeve crumpled up in her hand ascended the stairs followed by the crowd.

Upstairs the tables were all spread for the banquet. The guests drank a toast to the newly-wed couple; congratulations and – where proper – kisses were generously exchanged.

Reb Baruch Laib, for reasons of his own, was burning with fury; but he exercised sufficient self-control not to explode prematurely. He was biding his time. The disgraceful incident of the naked arm had given him the pretext he wanted. And when the guests were all seated round the tables, and the first course was being served, he calculated that his moment had come.

"This wedding ceremony," he bawled, "has been the greatest humiliation of my life. To think that the wife I have chosen for my son, the woman who I fondly hoped would walk with my son in the ways of God, should dare wear a sleeveless wedding gown and make an exhibition of herself on this night of all nights. Just think of it! What a fool I have been to spend all this money on her, what a fool! Did *my* daughter wear a sleeveless gown on her wedding night? I should say not! It's no use arguing. I saw everything! Everything!"

And then Reb Baruch Laib let himself go. It was like a bolt from the blue, and there was complete chaos. The bridegroom felt so ashamed of himself and of his father that he would gladly have jumped into his grave and buried himself there and then. Tertsa-Roisa burst into tears. Deborah turned an inquiring look on the people around her, as if she were studying their faces. She did not seem to be greatly upset. Apparently she did not grasp what it was all about. Reb Avram Ber had not seen the naked arm and, therefore, refused to believe in it.

"I shall take my daughter away, and we shall leave at once!" he screamed at Reb Baruch Laib. "We're going home this very instant. The idea! Do you think I shall allow you to slander my poor child?"

Raizela bit her nails. She succeeded, but only by a supreme effort, in suppressing the tears that welled up within her. Her large grey eyes bore such a mournful expression, they shone with such grim despair, they might have been the symbol of eternal grief.

In the end Herr Berger's rabbis, and more particularly Herr Berger himself, brought about a reconciliation and peace. The party drank another toast, and blessings were exchanged all over again. Reb Avram Ber was radiant. What an occasion this was for rejoicing, the Lord be praised! A momentous occasion in a father's lifetime! (The recent unpleasantness was quite forgotten and forgiven, so far as he was concerned.) The company regaled themselves and made merry. The rabbis vied with each other in the telling of fascinating hasidic anecdotes. Reb Avram Ber was a good listener, but he was also a good raconteur, and he told some of the most breathtaking tales of all. Reb Baruch Laib contented himself with descriptions of life in Antwerp, not forgetting the wealthy diamond merchants. The bridegroom smiled knowingly, as if to confirm all that his father said. Raizela, at the lower end of the table, was rather flushed. Her eyes sparkled with festive gloom. Tertsa-Roisa kept shaking her head enthusiastically. She listened only to the words of her husband, and was simply flabbergasted by his pearls of wisdom. How did he manage to think of so many clever things? Her face was like a bowl of dripping, circular and shiny. Deborah was astonished to discover that she was not waiting at table, as usual, but was being waited upon. The hotel keeper's wife was dressed up to the nines. As each new course arrived she appeared on the scene like a joyous herald of good tidings.

The company ate and drank; the menfolk swayed happily from

their hips, left and right, as they sang hasidic songs. And from time to time they left their seats to dance round in a ring like children.

The bride felt numb. The heated atmosphere was stifling. It was sultry, terribly sultry. She felt out of place, she felt that she did not belong here, and did not know what to do with herself.

When they called on her to join in the ritual wedding dance, she tried to make some protest, but it passed unnoticed. She shrank back from the crowd that summoned her; yet she found herself whirling round with them in a ring – an enchanted circle of strangers to whom she was absurdly joined by the end of a stranger's pocket handkerchief. Round and round they went, until she was overcome with giddiness. And in the center of the ring stood Simon. He, too, was dancing, clapping his hands and mocking her.

"Congratulations, Deborah! On with the dance, on with the dance!"

She felt sick. She knew that if they did not release her this very instant she would fall into a dead faint. Perhaps the ordeal would have been less terrible if the hotel keeper's daughter, a slim, olive-cheeked girl of about her own age, had not come to the door to watch the spectacle in a stupor of amazement.

The next morning, when they clipped her curly hair to the roots, she offered no resistance. Her hair would grow again, in time. But the wig which they put on her head gave her an awkward feeling. Casting a shadow over her eyes, it lent emphasis to the deathly pallor of her face. Also the ring on her finger was uncomfortable, like something superfluous – and cold to the touch.... She said not a word, but meekly did all she was asked to do. Soon after breakfast the hotel keeper's daughter came running up the stairs with two belated telegrams.

"Please don't think me inquisitive, Madam, but...er...could you tell me, what is the name of that dance you all entered into after supper last night?"

"It was...the dance of the demons!"

"Beg your pardon? I didn't quite catch that."

"Even if I were to tell you, you wouldn't know. The dance is quite peculiar to Polish Jewry."

"Yes, but do tell me what it's called. I'm so interested, for it's the strangest dance I've ever seen. So beautiful, though; so fantastic!"

"It's a ritual dance," Deborah said, on the verge of tears.

"So it's a ritual ceremony? I see! Oh, how original, how beautiful!"

Deborah studied the girl's brown tresses. She felt like a clumsy old woman in the presence of this slim, vivacious, olive-cheeked girl, who was in fact two years older than herself. The girl went away satisfied with the information she had gleaned.

"*Madam!* She calls me *Madam!*" Deborah thought. She was alone now, and no one witnessed the outburst of pent-up anguish which brought a little solace to a heavily burdened heart.

A little later, when Deborah was dozing, completely exhausted, on a sofa in a tiny room divided off from the sitting-room by a plush curtain, she was suddenly roused by her mother's voice. The familiar tones had a new and hard ring in them, such as Deborah had never heard before.

"So now the cat is out of the bag!" Raizela was saying. "The mystery of Reb Baruch Laib's unprovoked and scandalous outburst last night – in the presence of strangers, mark you – is a mystery no longer. Oh, what a mean despicable creature that man is! And oh what a terrible mistake we have made, what a terrible mistake!..."

"Why, what's happened?" asked Reb Avram Ber.

"Everything has happened! I have had my eyes opened, but unfortunately too late, too late! We have given our daughter away to the wrong sort of people. That's what has happened! Do you remember that when we were on the train, Baruch Laib told us that he had spent three hundred rubles on a pair of earrings which were to be the bridegroom's wedding gift to Deborah?"

"Yes, that's right. I wonder why he hasn't given them to her yet. It's about time he did."

"I can tell you why," said Raizela. "It's because Baruch Laib is a liar and a scoundrel. That's the simple explanation. Early this morning I was lying on the sofa in that little room behind the curtain and quite unwittingly I overheard the old man enter into a dispute with the bridegroom. 'I refuse to have anything to do with it!' said the bridegroom. 'The "diamonds" in those earrings are fake, mere paste, and if you wish to give them to her yourself, you're welcome! But you can leave me out of this. Having made a promise, you should have kept it. If you knew you were running out of funds, then you shouldn't have made any such promise.' Next, I heard Tertsa-Roisa join in the argument. She begged her son to be reasonable and not to be a troublemaker. She assured him that in a few weeks' time, at the outside, Baruch Laib would get a pair of earrings with genuine diamonds in them, which would be a replica of the artificial pair and then he could quietly substitute the new for the old and no one would be any the wiser. That was Tertsa-Roisa's motherly advice to her son – *Be a scoundrel like your father!* But Berish flatly refused to be mixed up in this deceitful game. 'Supposing she were to find out,' he said, 'what then? Think how awful that would be!' 'So you won't give them to her, eh?' said Baruch Laib. 'All right, you needn't! I don't care. She won't even get dud ones now, she'll get nothing at all, see! Not a thing!' 'Is that what you had at the back of your mind when you started that disgusting scene at the banquet last night?' Berish inquired. Upon my word, you should have heard the language the old man used when Berish put that question to him point blank. 'Shut up, you miserable heathen, you low-down swine, shut up! Another word from you, and I'll wring your dirty neck! Speak when you're spoken to!' He bellowed away like an enraged bull, all because his son had put his finger on the sore spot. Berish had torn the mask away with a vengeance. You see, not content with having bamboozled us, pretending to us that he had paid three hundred rubles for so much worthless paste, Baruch Laib decided to extricate himself from an unsavory position by making a bullying attack on Deborah and by humiliating us in front of all those strangers. It was a put-up affair, to provide himself with a pretext for not honoring his promise."

Raizela heaved a deep sigh.

"You appreciate, of course," she resumed after a lengthy silence, "that it's not the actual earrings I'm concerned about?"

"Why, of course! As if the earrings mattered!"

Reb Avram Ber sighed gently. If he had not heard this strange story from Raizela's own lips he would never have believed it. Was it possible? Was Reb Baruch Laib really that kind of man? Even now he could not inure himself to the thought. But Raizela herself had told him so – Raizela herself! Reb Avram Ber sat crestfallen, as though lifeless, for a long time. Then he reached for his beard and began to tug it hard. Then he combed it with his fingers, stroked it, twirled it around his forefinger and finally he was biting it furiously.

"You understand, don't you," Raizela repeated, "that it's not the earrings I'm concerned about?"

"Of course I understand! Earrings!" Reb Avram Ber exclaimed with a world of contempt.

"There seems to be no privacy in this place at all," said Deborah, drawing the curtain. Raizela turned her large gloomy eyes upon her. "Mamma, I don't care. Don't say another word about it, please. You know I don't want the earrings in any case."

Raizela's gaze lingered upon her. Then she hung her head in silence.

Reb Baruch Laib and his wife were to accompany the newlyweds to Antwerp. They had their eldest married son and a married daughter living there, whom they had not seen for some years, and they were planning a family reunion. But Reb Avram Ber and Raizela were less fortunate. Not only could they not afford the fare to Antwerp, they had scarcely enough money left to cover their expenses back to Warsaw. Indeed, they had to leave for home that very same evening.

Raizela bade her daughter a subdued farewell. She planted a kiss on her forehead, opened her mouth as if to speak, but sucked her cheeks in between her teeth instead. Both mother and daughter were silent. They did not cry and had nothing to say to each other. They preserved a grim silence.

Reb Avram Ber said goodbye to Deborah in gentle fatherly tones. He kissed her upon the head. For some time he gazed heavenwards, apparently calling upon the Almighty, as he gave her his blessing.

She heard him murmur: "Oh Father, You are omnipotent, loving and merciful!" And then he climbed into the carriage of the waiting train.

Raizela put her head out of the window into the twilight of the station, bidding another silent farewell to her daughter, who stood surrounded by three strangers in a strange city, watching her parents leave for home. The engine uttered a long drawn-out piercing whistle. The train began to move. Reb Avram Ber and Raizela, with their faces glued to the window, saw their daughter dwindle rapidly, and then in a flash she was gone.

"Don't forget to remember me to all the folks at home, don't forget!" Tertsa-Roisa cried animatedly at a swiftly passing carriage and they returned to the hotel.

Chapter 14

On the journey to Antwerp Reb Baruch Laib went out of his way to create still further unpleasantness. The trouble this time was a book which Deborah had picked up from her mother (who had just finished with it), and to which she now turned eagerly to while the time away.

Before long she had become deeply absorbed in its pages – it was a Life of Moses Mendelssohn – and her heart bled as she followed the adventures of this poor suffering philosopher-hunchback. His indomitable struggle against his own physical infirmity and external antagonism aroused her deepest admiration. The account of how the authorities turned him back from all the gates of the city of Berlin filled her with profound pity for the bright-eyed cripple who, intellectually and spiritually, towered so high above the common clay that barred his way; and she was filled with hatred and contempt for the police who played such an abominable part in the drama. His ultimate triumph over untold opposition was like a personal victory of her own, and how she exulted! She was so carried away that her own life was forgotten. But Reb Baruch Laib took care that this forgetfulness should be short-lived.

"There can be no doubt about it now," he fumed. "She's a free-thinker! Look, she's reading the biography of that heretic Mendelssohn! Go on, have a look!" he urged his wife, pointing an accusing finger at the title page of the book which Deborah had laid aside for an instant.

Tertsa-Roisa duly inspected the title page (illiterate though she was, as her husband well knew), and she shook her head with an air of disapproval. She wondered what on earth could be wrong; but if Reb Baruch Laib was shocked, then that was sufficient reason for her to feel shocked, too. All the same, by means of timid gestures and obsequious smiles, she begged him to restrain his virtuous wrath and to preserve the peace.

The bridegroom was seething with rebellion. He, likewise, fixed a look of entreaty on his father; but there was something in his eye that boded evil. And with a pang of regret Reb Baruch Laib subsided.

Deborah ignored him. She quietly resumed her reading. Within her heart, though, all was tumult.

They steamed into Antwerp as the shadows of evening were gathering. The Central Station presented a picture of semi-darkness and utter desertion. The arrival of the express livened things up somewhat, but only somewhat. The streets, too, bore a dreary aspect – they were dark and desolate. The gleaming wet iron bars of the gateway to the zoo had a forbidding air, as if behind them lay a dark and wretched prison. A slight but penetrating drizzle, quite unlike a summer shower, settled tearfully on the windows of their taxicab.

The cab halted in Levrik Street, or "Boulevard de Levrik," as the wags of Antwerp humorously called it. The bridegroom in person knocked at the front door. He had to go on knocking for a long time, however, before he could make any impression on the din that was going on within. At long last the appearance of a drab greenish light in the vestibule showed that someone was coming. The door opened and the someone turned out to be a whole procession of people. It was headed by a tall woman in the early thirties, with a tremendous bosom and a flat blonde wig on her head; after her came a short, young, barrel-shaped woman, with a face as red as beetroot and with a piled-up black wig on her head; next, a tall, young man who was the image of the bridegroom except that he had a very much bigger beard; and, finally, a horde of children of all sizes and descriptions. They immediately fell on the newcomers' necks, shrieking and kissing and voicing apologies for having failed to come to the station. After a pause for breath they began embracing and kissing all over again. In the general confusion Reb Baruch Laib laid hands on the short young woman with the beetroot face and very nearly smothered her before he discovered that she was his daughter-in-law, and not his daughter, as he had at first imagined. He then made amends by brushing a kiss on to the face of his daughter, who was the tall woman with the big bosom and the blonde wig. His eldest son, the young man with the big ginger beard, whose wife had been the victim of Reb Baruch Laib's error, proposed that they should all go inside and get on with the kissing in the light, rather than hang about in the dark. This suggestion was adopted with alacrity, and in a twinkling the guests were deposited, luggage and all, in the residence of the taller and elder of the two women.

Here the air was clammy: it smote the nose with a tang of fungus and urine. The rickety wooden table was spread with an oilcloth which had so many holes and ink stains on it that it seemed to record the events of a long and crowded lifetime.... The curtains over the two windows were only partly torn, but dirty all over. The chairs creaked, and the baby of the family – a fine, chubby little boy between the age of one and two – was yelling in his cradle like a perfect demon: no doubt he was indignant at having been left out of the riotous welcome.

"So this is Antwerp! This is where the ship comes to port!" thought Deborah.

The big woman and the tubby woman both got busy with the tea things. The young man with the big ginger beard got a bottle of whiskey out of his father's suitcase. His mother, Tertsa-Roisa, handed him another bottle, saying:

"Will you open this, Lipa. It's sweet cognac for us women. There!"

They all gathered round with upraised glasses. Reb Baruch Laib and Lipa both proposed a toast to the future birth of a son. The womenfolk toasted the unborn son. Deborah was embarrassed, and her tongue failed her. The womenfolk exchanged a significant look, then they eyed the bridegroom and then they smiled. Deborah smiled, too, both vexed and amused.

After the oilcloth had been wiped dry they all got round the table. The young man with the big ginger beard engaged in earnest conversation with his father; he obviously had something very solemn and confidential to impart to him. And to lend emphasis to his remarks he kept plucking at his fine bushy beard. He had grown this beard for his father's especial benefit, just to convince the old boy that he, Lipa, was as pious as a rabbi, and that his, therefore, was a deserving case. Lipa knew that his father knew that man was made in the image of God, and that no good Jew would dream of interfering with God's will by trimming the growth on his chin. So this was Lipa's trump card, and he lost no opportunity of playing it. He gave the beard a tweak, and scowled. He gave the beard a tweak, and grinned. But just as he was about to lift up his chin and flourish it under his father's nose as a final demonstration of piety, the door opened and in walked the master of the house, a wiry man of about forty-five, with a really long beard that bristled with hairs black and grey.

He took stock of the whole situation at a glance. He evinced some astonishment, just for the sake of decency. He also betrayed delight, just for the sake of decency; but he did not overdo it. He went up to his father-in-law and said, "Peace unto you!" (but failed to notice the bridegroom). Then he twisted up his nose judiciously, like a connoisseur, and sniffed the air once or twice in a very suspicious way. Immediately, without the slightest hesitation, he strode across to the cradle where the baby was still howling like a creature possessed, and, again without hesitation, raised the quilt. A poisonous odor seeped over the room.

"Do you mind giving me your attention, my sweet! Will you step this way!" he said to his wife with grim sarcasm.

Meanwhile, the infant was kicking up his legs most violently, and all present instinctively reached for their noses and squeezed them tight for dear life.

However, the master of the house was soon mollified by his wife (the tall woman with the big bosom and blonde wig) when she beseeched his forgiveness. She had been terribly busy all evening, she said, and in any case she was sure the accident was of recent occurrence. He even condescended to help clean up the cradle, and every time she stooped over the sheets he gave her a friendly pinch in the fleshy part.

When it was all over the windows were opened at the top a wee bit. And in honor of the master of the house the beakers were filled again. This time the newly-wiped infant in the cradle was the toast: the hope was expressed that he would be a source of joy to his parents and to all the family. And with their noses still puckered up they all nibbled sweet honey cake.

Reb Baruch Laib, Tertsa-Roisa, the two stout young women and the young man with the flowing ginger beard called the bridegroom aside and they all went next door, apparently for a family consultation. Deborah remained with the master of the house and the crowd of children.

"I hope you have not been misled regarding your husband's ability to provide for you," said the master of the house, turning to Deborah with an ominous and malicious little smile.

Deborah's heart sank. It was the brutality, rather than the significance of his words that stunned and angered her. What kind of talk was this?

"Pray do not be so alarmed," her brother-in-law went on. "There's no need to despair. But it all depends on you."

Her uneasiness grew.

"The point I am trying to make is this: A clever woman can mold her husband like clay. If he is lazy, she will know how to make him industrious. A resolute wife can convert the worst of men into a model husband. I hope I have made myself clear. I imagine it would be superfluous for me to enter into details."

Indeed, thought Deborah, that would be quite superfluous. He had made himself abundantly clear. But she consoled herself with the reflection that this was obviously a case of personal animosity.

He gave her a stealthy glance to see how she had taken it. Deborah's gaze strayed round the room. It positively reeked of poverty and wretchedness. The light from the gas lamp flowed down in murky waves of a miserable greenish hue. The wallpaper was full of smears and in places was hanging from the walls in tatters. The floor was sticky underfoot, and the ceiling overhead was a smoky brown. In a corner by the door a fat-bellied spider was at work weaving a web for itself. She noticed a fly on a yellow fly paper, suspended from the ceiling, struggling furiously to escape the fate of scores of its fellows that had long since given up the struggle and lay dead in the sticky mess. But this one refused to yield, and in the end, by forfeiting a leg, it saved its life and the mutilated remains flew away with a horrible buzzing noise. What a foul thing to have in the home – a cemetery for flies! The sight of it, and many other things besides, made her feel sick at heart. The master of the house fitted in well enough with these surroundings. How dare he presume to give her counsels of wisdom? … All at once, darting another quick glance all round her, she quoted – almost involuntarily – an old Hebrew proverb:

"The wise man's wealth is his wisdom: he possesses no worldly riches."

She was herself taken aback at the suddenness with which this little-known saying had fallen from her lips. She wondered where she had picked it up. Then she remembered that her father used it occasionally in his rare tiffs with her mother.

The master of the house resented the imputation that he possessed no worldly riches. He knew, even if she did not, that at one time in his career, before he had divorced his first wife, he had been quite a wealthy man, and once a wealthy man always a wealthy man! As for his being a wise man, he took that for granted – after all, everybody else in the house did the same! He felt deeply offended, and flashed a look on Deborah that seemed to vow eternal enmity. Anxious to be rid of him Deborah began to play with the baby, who chuckled most delightfully.

The family consultation came to an end. It was agreed that they were to stay where they were for supper, Deborah was to spend the night with her sister-in-law (the short one with the very red face), and the menfolk were to put up in a hotel down the road.

Deborah's two sisters-in-law got busy. Lipa went out shopping. The master of the house, his face all wreathed in scowls, refused to take any interest in the proceedings. He even refused to give the family the benefit of his wisdom, and whenever he was approached for advice, he retorted that he would deem it a favor if they shut their traps and left him in peace.

When the tall woman with the blonde wig spread a tablecloth riddled with holes and full of ugly stains, Tertsa-Roisa was put to shame, and she motioned to her daughter-in-law to fetch another. The red-faced young woman hurried into the adjacent room, where she had her own little home, and soon returned in triumph with a starched snowy-white tablecloth that was a credit to her housewifery, whereupon the other woman turned her nose up, greatly piqued.

By this time Lipa had come back with a parcel of herrings and sausages, rolls and cakes, and bottles of beer. Reb Baruch Laib sat down at the head of the table. On his right was the bridegroom, and on his left the surly master of the house. Then came Lipa and the womenfolk. The children were ranged at the bottom of the table, all in a tangle like crushed sauerkraut. At first they sat quietly enough. Gradually, however, their bashfulness wore off and they began to enjoy themselves. They reached out with their smutty hands for the herrings and the sausages, and indeed any food within range; they picked up a roll, dropped it, and decided to have another instead; they stretched full length over the table in superhuman efforts to get at the cut cake. They licked their plates dry; they swallowed their food without chewing; they let their noses run recklessly.... Father and mother and all the family remonstrated and asked them where their manners were.

"Ugh! Don't you know any better than that?"

"Wipe your nose! Ugh!"

But the children took not the slightest notice and went their own sweet way. Even if they were to behave like angels they would still be preached at by their elders. So why worry? For some reason grown-ups always had a habit of saying, "Ugh! Don't you know any better than that?" They seemed to enjoy saying that sort of thing. But any child in his proper senses knew that it would never do to take such admonitions seriously. All the children here were eminently sensible, they looked very well after themselves indeed. All, that is, except the eldest boy; he fared badly. He had reached the mature age of twelve. And he could not very well degrade himself by acting the way the others did. Yet he was not considered a grown-up and was being left out in the cold. His eyes were glued on the dainties with fervent yearning, but he waited in vain for encouragement from his parents. He felt very sorry for himself, to the point of tears. At last he could stand it no longer, and with the fury of a rebel he began grabbing from this platter and that, like a hungry beast. The whole family were simply shocked beyond words. What! A big boy like that – it was terrible! Unbelievable! Without uttering a word in his own defense he began to take his little brothers and sisters to task, giving them first a pinch and then a dig in the ribs by way of emphasis. "Ugh!" he said. "Don't you know any better than that? I'm ashamed of you, that's what I am!"

At first the infant in the cradle seemed disposed to take an active part in the festivities. He crooned and chuckled to himself. Having finished his bottle and lying in clean sheets he was as pleased as pleased could be. But having no one to communicate with, except with his big toe, he finally fell asleep.

"What's the matter with those kids tonight?"

"Haim, d'you want me to rap you over the knuckles? Now, leave it alone! Put it down!"

"I'm only playing with it: I'm not going to eat it."

"Never mind, stop playing with it! Just put that apple back where you took it from!"

"I'm fed up! I don't know what to do! What shall I do?"

"What shall you do? Here, stick some snuff up your nose!"

"Yankela, sit up!"

"I'm sitting up!"

"No you're not! Do as you're told. Sit properly!"

"Ugh! Faigela, what's the matter with you, a big girl like you? Ought to be ashamed of yourself! Hurry, quick, wipe your nose!"

A profusion of handkerchiefs from Uncle Lipa and Auntie, and Grandma, and Dad; and even Mamma came dashing up with a pinafore. But too late. Faigela could not wait.

"If those impudent brats don't mend their ways they'll be sorry for it!" said the master of the house, glowering at Deborah the while. "Behave yourselves!"

For a while the children sat motionless, as though petrified, but they were only bracing themselves for a renewed and even more violent attack on the cut cake.

"You're not helping yourself. What can I offer you? I guess you don't think much of this Belgian sausage. It doesn't taste half as good as Polish sausage. But what else can you expect? Polish sausage is famous the world over," said Lipa, gallantly addressing Deborah, but gazing boldly across at his younger brother with a mocking smile, as if to say, "Now look, I'm going to get off with your bride. Stop me if you can, you dumb idiot!" The bridegroom lowered his eyes with an expression that seemed to say, "Go to hell!"

"No, not at all. The sausage is excellent," said Deborah, courteously defending the sausage without making any attempt to eat it.

Reb Baruch Laib was drinking hard, and so was the master of the house, who was now so absorbed in his bottle that he allowed the children to do just as they pleased. This was Lipa's finest moment for showing off his beard – and it was really a lovely beard, the sort of beard that would have done credit to a saint.

Each time he tossed off a drink he threw his head back and protruded his chin for his parents to rejoice in his hairy emblem of piety. If a beard like that was not going to make the old man fork out, then nothing would!

The bridegroom was all eagerness to communicate with his bride. He toyed with the idea of passing her an orange or a tot of cognac, he might even have spoken a few words to her, if only to spite his brother

Lipa, the insolent dog! But he could not get at her very well, she was too far down the table. It was most annoying. When brother Lipa had got married he had been seated next to his wife, Baila. Perhaps that was because they were cousins. No, that was not the explanation. The true explanation was that everybody had entered into a conspiracy against Deborah and himself. They were a mean lot!

At last the nuptial supper – the first of a series of seven ritual feasts – came to an end, in prayer. The children had all fallen asleep on their chairs and had long since been carried off to bed, one by one. It was past two in the morning. Deborah still sat with her head drooping with weariness. All the others had gone away, leaving her by herself. At last Tertsa-Roisa reappeared and conducted her into the bedroom next door. Here Lipa and his wife were sitting side by side at a tiny table. How Deborah wished she could tear off the bedcover and fling herself into the white sheets. It was an inviting bed, piled high with an inflated eiderdown and surmounted by a big puffed-up pillow trimmed with lace fringes and marked with an artistically embroidered monogram in red silk.

The young couple sat at the table, however, seemingly unaware of Deborah's presence. She noticed that Lipa held a plate in his hand and flourished a stewed prune in a silver spoon which he was trying to pop into his wife's mouth. It was all very curious!

"Oh, please leave me alone!" cried the fat young woman imploringly.

"Now go on, be a good little wifey and do as your hubby says. Prunes, you know, are good for you. There, down it goes!"

She protested coyly, pulling a wry face as if she were taking a bitter medicine, but Lipa was as firm as he was gentle. He insisted on her eating all the prunes, all of them, because her health demanded it.

"And now, sweetheart, I shall leave you and you can go to bed!"

He kissed her good night, and only on tearing his lips away did he discover that he had an audience. He became very confused and apologized, but Deborah had previously observed him peeping at her out of a corner of his eye. It was all very curious!

The fat young woman with the beetroot-red face gave her a smile and removed the bedcover.

"My husband is such a fool," she said in a plaintive voice, but with a gleeful smirk on her face. "He really is too good to me, the silly! He hangs round me all day, I simply can't shake him off. He's such a dear!"

Deborah very nearly tore her clothes off and flung herself into bed.

Tertsa-Roisa and Baila began to undress, unlacing their corsets at the back, undoing the clasps at the front, removing cotton wool padding from their hips and taking more pads off their buttocks, substantial though these were. Deborah gaped at them from under the bedclothes. What fanciful creatures these women were to enlarge their monumental backsides with cotton wool padding! The younger woman turned the light down to a faint glimmer.

Snuggling up against the pillow and curling herself up Deborah gazed out from the comfortable, wholesome bedclothes at the wall opposite. On this wall magnified shadows of the two women were prancing about. Shadowy ribbons were fluttering about fantastically. At last the shadows went to bed and all was quiet. The peacefulness of night was intoxicating after all the fuss and excitement. But Deborah was too exhausted to fall easily asleep. Incoherent thoughts went racing through her head until she felt giddy. She tried to rid herself of these meaningless thoughts by counting: one, two, three, and four, and five…but all to no avail. She kept a lonely vigil for a long time and then, in the early hours of the morning, she was roused from her sickening stupor by a whispered heart-to-heart talk between mother-in-law and daughter-in-law in the opposite bed.

"Are you asleep, Baila?"

"No."

"Why, what's wrong?"

"Nothing in particular. Can't get to sleep somehow."

"Well, how is it going?"

"I expect it in a couple of months' time."

"Yes, I know that. But how's Lipa treating you these days?"

"How's he treating me? Don't ask! Ever since I've got married it's been a cat and dog's life!"

"But surely he's changed now? He tells me he's a reformed character."

"He told you that, did he? Naturally! And I shouldn't be surprised if you believed him! I never noticed him saying anything to you."

"Well, you see, just before going to bed I had a little talk with him next door. I called him in specially. He was the first to break the news about your expecting a baby. There, you'll soon be a mother, and yet you keep on complaining that you can't get on with him. You mark my word, when baby comes Lipa will be a new man!"

"I hope so! All he does meanwhile is waste his time in Laibel's Cafe gambling at cards from morning till past midnight. And he forgets about me, I don't matter. I have all the housework to do, and do properly – look, you can see for yourself how tidy I keep my home, not like Rebecca does."

"Well, there's a reason for that. Rebecca has her hands full looking after the children, God bless 'em! You'll soon find out for yourself how difficult it is to keep house when you have a baby to look after."

"What about it? Don't I work as a dressmaker? Don't I have to slave from morning to night? Don't I have to dress up all the fine ladies in town, stand all their nagging in the bargain, as if I wasn't made of flesh and blood like them? Oh, how I hate them! I could murder them! I could murder them! I wish I were dead, God forbid, rather than have to go on leading such a poor, miserable existence!"

Deborah was both amused and scared. She heard a sound of muffled weeping.

"I hope she isn't awake."

"Of course not, you silly! She's fast asleep, that's what she is. Why, she was half asleep at the table! I wish I could sleep as soundly as she does. Old age is no joy," said Tertsa-Roisa, heaving a wistful sigh.

"Well, I can't say that I get any joy out of being young. For all the fun that I have out of it, I might as well be a widow weeping over Lipa's grave."

"Stop! Don't you dare speak like that about my son!" hissed Tertsa-Roisa in a sudden fury.

"Your dear little son! And I suppose I'm not a mother's child, am I? I'm an outcast!"

"Now, now, don't start crying again, don't cry!" said Tertsa-Roisa, instantly resuming her former coaxing tone. "After all, we're always ready to lend you a helping hand. What with the allowance you get from your father-in-law and what with the money you earn at your dressmaking, you should be able to make ends meet."

"Yes, but what's going to happen when baby comes? You've just admitted that's going to make all the difference. Will I still have to be the breadwinner?"

"Tut, tut, things aren't as black as you try to paint them," said Tertsa-Roisa, anxious to retrieve her previous indiscretion. "Please God, tomorrow I'll talk things over with your father-in-law. And I'll have something to say to Lipa as well. And, believe me, by the time your father-in-law has finished with Lipa, Lipa will be a new man. You mark my word! Anyway, when baby comes Lipa will become a good family man and he will settle down to work in earnest, because once he becomes a father everything will be different."

"I hope so! Although it sounds too good to be true. Anyway, what use are all these promises? Haven't I had enough of promises? At present I have to sit up night after night, sick and pregnant, all alone, like a dog on a chain. I sit up for hours on end, waiting for him, and when the feeling of sickness comes on, I have to go and fetch myself a glass of water, with no one to lift a finger for me or say a kind word to me. Not once has he dropped in of an evening to see how I'm getting on; not once in two years has he offered to take me out. If he had any decency in him he would ask me to go with him to the theater once in a while, but not him! No, not him!"

"Do you get Yiddish plays in Antwerp?"

"Of course we do. We have just had a marvelous company of strolling players come over from London. And do they make you laugh? They make you roar! People say there's one particular actor who sings such funny songs, that when you hear him you laugh till you get the bellyache. Lipa once brought home a sheaf of papers with all the songs written out, so as he could learn them by heart, and I hear nothing else these days but him singing the same songs over and over again. One of them goes like this:

'Anna's the girl who's fat and flighty,
Ever seen her wearing her naughty nightie?'

"Lipa's simply crazy about that actor. But have I ever been to see the play? Oh, no! I don't matter! I can stay at home like a dog on its chain. It's not worth living, this sort of life isn't, believe me!"

"What do you care about the theater? Rubbish! You should worry! I've lived all these years, thank God, without ever once having been to the theater, and I'm none the worse off for it, am I?"

"Things are different nowadays. It's a husband's duty to take his wife to the theater. No modern woman would stand for what I stand. It's a living death, that's what it is, God forgive me for saying so!" Again she wept – and wept bitterly.

Deborah listened, stupefied. She felt amused, yet rather sorry for her sister-in-law, and this compassion was intermingled with other vague emotions which brought the tears into her eyes; but she cried so softly, that the two women in the opposite bed continued their conversation undisturbed. The younger one complained and whimpered, the elder one tried to pooh-pooh it all. At last they both fell asleep. Deborah made some attempt to review all that she had overheard, but her head was light and no matter how hard she tried to concentrate, her thoughts kept scattering like so much smoke. They were strange thoughts, as strange and incoherent as the scraps in a beggar's bag. She fell asleep, and rose early with a headache.

"Hope you had a good night's rest?" Lipa greeted her with a broad, ambiguous smile.

His wife gave him an ugly look, then she turned with appealing eyes to her mother-in-law. There, that was the sort of man he was, nothing better than a brute! The more he showed himself in his true colors, the better she would like it. Let him get on with his little flirtation, by all means.

Deborah replied saying that she had slept very well. Again she noticed her husband staring across at Lipa with that unbrotherly look in his eyes that seemed to say, "Go to hell!" Much to her own surprise she was conscious of a keen sense of pleasure at finding herself the center of these little jealousies.

After breakfast she went out on a sightseeing tour of the city with her husband. It was a perfect morning, the air was fresh and pure as though cleansed by yesterday's rainfall. Deborah looked straight up into her husband's face. But for his trimmed beard, Berish was so much like Lipa, one could scarcely tell the two brothers apart. She recalled the conversation she had overheard in bed last night, and she brooded over her sister-in-law's plight, a plight that might very soon be her own. It was only natural that she should feel grave misgivings, even dread, and she strove hard to summon up such emotions, for they would have been far, far easier to endure than that dull little pain which afflicted her relentlessly, unremittingly, like a worm slowly eating its way into her heart. Would this young man walking by her side do as Lipa did – would he pop a sweetmeat into her mouth and then go away to gamble in a cafe, while she sat at home, the neglected wife? She was trying hard to think on these lines, but instead she found herself wondering whether the kitchen in her parents' home in Warsaw was in a mess, now that she was gone; and she found herself passing judgment on Antwerp as a repulsive and ghastly town from which she must flee – at once.

In parts the city was quite dead: one could quite safely go to sleep in the middle of the roadway, without any fear of being disturbed. The dwelling-houses were small, mainly two-storied, and they all stood spick and span like newly scoured pots and pans. The pavements were abnormally clean, too clean to be trodden on with comfort. It was like wearing new clothes. The gleaming window-panes solemnly reflected the silent streets. The motionless lace curtains traced patterns of dancing nude women and cherubs with fleshy little legs rather like the legs of her sister-in-law's baby. The luxurious blinds were of a quality unsurpassed by anything Deborah had ever seen in Warsaw or for that matter in Berlin.

They passed through thoroughfares wide and narrow, and much the same pattern unfolded itself repeatedly. Everywhere was the cleanliness of a newly washed corpse. In one of these residential streets, however, the solitude was shattered by the sudden arrival of a costermonger's little cart drawn by two large, workmanlike, fawn-colored dogs. On the threshold of each house a housewife appeared with a face as clean as her doorstep. The beefy costermonger favored the ladies with a sweet smile, and he addressed them with the courteousness of a diplomat. For their part the ladies smiled back at him as if they regarded him as their equal. And this was their strange greeting, which consisted of only a single word.

He: "*Madame!*"

She: "*Mynheer!*"

It was like a military salute. And their business transacted, the smiling ladies vanished at once behind their polished doors, as if the city were under a curfew.

Really, it was fortunate that a passing horse left its droppings behind in one of those soporific streets. But for that, one would never have seen the energetic little woman come bustling out of doors with a pail and shovel in her hand, nor would the excited little sparrows have flown down from the housetops. And the monotony would have been quite unrelieved.

All this while her husband made no attempt to make conversation: he was as dull and silent, as respectable and bright and shiny as the streets through which they were passing.

An elderly gentleman hailed her husband, "*Mynheer!*" She listened to their incomprehensible chatter in a tongue which sounded like a cross between German and Yiddish, and although at times she felt certain the phrases had a familiar ring about them, she was unable to follow the gist of it. Her husband paused to stroke his beard reflectively, and just as he was about to resume the conversation, the elderly gentleman politely raised his hat and with a knowing shake of his fleshless double chin, vanished down a side street.

Without offering any explanation her husband stopped and

suddenly brought one of the lifeless houses to life by rapping at a brightly varnished door with a gleaming brass knocker. The door opened cautiously, and a nose peeped out through the aperture. Behind the nose was a woman.

"*Mynheer!*" she said.

"Is the flat on the second floor to let?"

The woman opened the door another inch or two, and after subjecting Berish to a searching scrutiny she went on to study Deborah's new velvet costume.

"Can we see the flat?" asked Berish. Obviously it was still to let, hence the scrutiny.

The landlady gave the young couple another shrewd look before rousing herself from her reverie.

"Why, of course!"

She asked them into the vestibule and promised to be with them again in a moment, then vanished behind the broad, prosperous-looking door of her parlor. The linoleum underfoot was bright and slippery; the hat rack had a dazzling polish; and the pedestal bearing the aspidistra was positively brilliant. The lamp overhead was adorned with a large red shade, and on the walls hung massive framed portraits of old men wearing curly grey wigs on their heads and intricate white ruffles on the sleeves of their blue coats. They were a grim crowd. And beneath them hung many smaller portraits of stern-faced dogs that in some strange way seemed to bear a family resemblance to the men above. On the strip of blue carpet running the length of the vestibule a kitten was struggling playfully with a cotton wool sparrow. The woman returned.

"This way, please!"

They followed her up the stairs. It was an imposing staircase, with a blue carpet climbing up the varnished white steps. The brass carpet rods gleamed importantly. The little window on the landing above was draped with a small curtain of a dazzling white. A young knight on horseback smiled down at the strangers from his tiny frame on the wall. From one of the doors on the landing a young brunette emerged, in a very low-cut red gown, with many sparkling rings on her slender, swarthy fingers. She, too, smiled down at Deborah and her husband – a faint smile which broadened immensely as she exchanged a greeting with the landlady.

Next came a flight of bare, rough wooden stairs. The transition was at once sudden and saddening. The unexpected sound of thumping feet struck a discordant note. But the rooms on the top floor, for all their emptiness, were not uncheerful, being bright and lofty and airy. The wallpaper was cheap, but colorful and clean. And the ceilings, although by no means as ornate as in the lower part of the house, were still profusely molded. A refreshing draft was blowing in through the large, wide-open windows.

The rent was reasonable enough for a high class residential locality. Not that money mattered to a man like Berish, who had been promised a dowry by his father. So he decided to take the flat. Deborah told him that it was all the same to her: he was to do as he pleased. She confessed to having no opinion on the subject, which was perfectly true. The landlady interrogated her new tenants like a detective. Who were they, what were they, where did they come from, and why? It was only because they were such a nice-looking couple and would not bring any children into the house that she let them have the flat so cheaply.

"If I take kindly to people, I'm always willing to make sacrifices. I just happen to be made that way," she said, as she handed them their receipt, and so, with her good wishes to cheer them, and with the knowledge that they now had a home of their very own, they went on their way.

Berish was jubilant. What a glorious neighborhood! What a marvelous flat! And, best of all, what a long way from his relatives' place! What a pity, though, that his wife was so gloomy, so icy cold! Nothing, not even her new home, seemed to please her. Her mind seemed to be preoccupied with all manner of things, but apparently he was not one of those things. Now how could any normal brain contrive to be so busy? It was odd, but whenever he spoke to her she seemed to start and shudder a little, as though she were dreaming.

"Maybe it's partly my fault. I ought to be more of a man," he thought. She did, when spoken to, respond after a fashion. Yes, but even then there was something faraway about her. There she was at his side, yet she wasn't there. That was a very funny thing. Now, what could a fellow do to liven her up? If he had it in him to conquer his shyness he would certainly ask her outright what was the reason for her absent-mindedness. Maybe she was feeling tired or ill. She did not act that way out of spitefulness. No, it was not spite. "I suppose she'll start taking to me when she gets to know me better. At present we're almost complete strangers" – he sought consolation – "but I think that swine Lipa has found out the way things are between us, and he'll be crowing over me like the devil. Never mind, Lipa can go to hell!"

Whatever blemishes Levrik Street may have had, a state of torpor and deadness was not one of them. Its houses were no bigger than elsewhere, but they were certainly not clean to a fault. Nor was there anything melancholy about this busy little street. A great many men, young and old, were to be seen picturesquely clad in the flowing robes of Orthodox Polish and Galician Jewry. And each man wore a beard that was unique in character, whether short or long, red or black or grey. There were some beards that finished up in a sharp point, others that ended in fluff; beards that had only just been combed and beards that had never been combed at all. There was a great coming and going, endless bustle, in Levrik Street, and the little streets all round it. Men of all ages walked about gesticulating expressively in endless arguments.

Here, too, Jewish tradesmen were selling their wares from dog-drawn barrows, but the very dogs looked more human – they were more animated, they wore a more businesslike air and lent a touch of quaintness to the street scene.

Children were running wild and yelling at their play, just like children in Warsaw. One gang was chasing an elusive cat that looked as if it had been rubbed up the wrong way. The womenfolk were not shy of lingering on their doorsteps; in no way did they behave as if the city were under curfew. Shops there were in plenty, and of every description. Evidently the inhabitants of that part of the town needed something more substantial than purity of air and of flagstones to keep body and soul together. The Jewish womenfolk bargained vehemently with the Jewish tradesmen: they raised their voices and did not even trouble to smile sweetly. The stores were small, crowded, and scarcely a shop-window but displayed the sign "KOSHER." But even these signs were different one from the other; the letters ran irregularly, usually with one or two missing, rather like teeth in an old man's mouth.

The whole place was bubbling over with life. It brought back memories of Warsaw; but because realities are never so real and vivid as memories, Deborah's pangs of nostalgia were all the more poignant.

When Deborah and Berish got back, and Berish smilingly broke the news about the flat, his beetroot-faced sister-in-law puckered up her snub nose in disapproval, while his big-bosomed sister took him to task for having "run away" to so remote and unfriendly a neighborhood. The master of the house was still moping, so he disdained to make any comment. But Lipa, though he was not on speaking terms with his younger brother Berish, patted him on the shoulder with mock encouragement, crying:

"Well done, brother! You're not going to live in the Ghetto, like us paupers, are you? Of course you're not! A rich man like you!"

"Really, fancy going such a long way out when you might just as well have lived locally," said Tertsa-Roisa, likewise showing her displeasure.

"I can't see what all the fuss is about, Mother. The flat is ideal, the rent is reasonable, what more can you want?" Berish protested.

"Have you paid a deposit? You have, eh? Well, I suppose it can't be helped now."

"No, it can't be helped. He hates his own flesh and blood, he's an apostate, that's the trouble. Am I right?" said Reb Baruch Laib grimly, turning to Lipa for sympathy.

Lipa gleefully, proudly, stroked his flowing red beard.

"He's so refined, Father, that's the explanation. When I get that refined, I too, will desert the Ghetto!"

For seven nights running the family sat down to a ceremonial nuptial supper of sorts, and then at long last on the morning after the final banquet – Reb Baruch Laib and Tertsa-Roisa made ready to set out on the long journey homewards. They had finished packing their bags, which now lay stacked up on the floor of the living room, and Lipa had gone out to hail a taxi. But still Reb Baruch Laib showed no intention of handing over the promised dowry to the newly married couple. On the contrary, he seemed determined completely to ignore his obligations. Early in the morning he and Berish had locked themselves up in Lipa's room for a private quarrel, every word of which could be plainly heard throughout the house. Reb Baruch Laib roared like an angry beast:

"Don't pester me! Don't follow me about like a suspicious creditor! You needn't worry, I'll settle my accounts with you. I'll put paid to all my debts, believe me! What! You want me to furnish your home for you? You do, eh? You want a luxury home, is that it? It suits Lipa to share his home with Rebecca, but you – you swollen-headed fool! – you must needs go away to live in an expensive neighborhood like a man of independent means. Very well, then I must assume that you *are* a man of independent means. You know your own pocket best. But please, whatever you do, don't bother me!"

"Father, how many more times must I tell you that the rent for my flat isn't much higher than what Lipa is paying. Don't be unreasonable!" Here Berish paused, as if choking with rage. "Do you think anyone in his senses is going to live in a stinking hole like this when he has a reasonable chance of getting out? I want something clean and decent."

"D'you mean to tell me, you swine, that this isn't good enough for you? Why, believe me, your wife never had a better home or a better father than Baila."

"Don't mention them in the same breath!" said Berish scornfully.

Reb Baruch Laib very nearly burst a blood vessel. His tiny eyes became all bloodshot.

"Say that again, will you! Say that again! So I'm not to mention them in the same breath? So that's how things are!"

"Take it easy! Don't get excited! You know very well you're not on speaking terms with Baila's father, even though he happens to be your own brother. So why pretend? It's not for you to take his or even his daughter's part!"

"You impudent swine! Why, I'll give you the thrashing of your life! You apostate!"

Reb Baruch Laib was just beginning to let himself go; he was just beginning to indulge himself – for days now he had been itching and craving for a really big scene – when, much to his disgust, a neighbor looked in to bid him Godspeed. And when the exchange of courtesies was over, he found that his fury had abated. The craving was still there, but time was too short for him to work himself up again properly. Sorrowfully he realized that he would have to postpone his outburst until he got back to Warsaw. He would have it out with Reb Avram Ber and Raizela. And, by God, were they going to catch it!

Meanwhile, his wife was annoying him. She was getting on his nerves by her feeble efforts to act the peacemaker. If she did not desist he would – but no, he would not do a thing. The psychological moment had passed, and now there was nothing more to be said. He paced the clammy, malodorous floor in silence. Once or twice he stopped and growled, but went on again, backwards and forwards, as if to hasten the hour of departure.

However, at the last moment, when the taxi was waiting at the front door, he plunged his hand into his inner pocket and produced his wallet, which was still bulging with fat wads of banknotes. Lipa's mouth began to water, he licked his lips and held his breath. Reb Baruch Laib picked out three 100-franc notes, and stuffed them hurriedly into Deborah's hand.

"Be thrifty! Waste not, want not! Don't spend it all on furniture, as you will need some money to tide you over the next few weeks. I'm very short after all the expenses I've incurred over the wedding, and it'll be some time before I can let you have any more money. Well, goodbye, and God be with you! May God be your only support and may you never want help from anyone."

Tertsa-Roisa kissed Deborah goodbye, wished her happiness, and even shed a tear. The old woman had wept so copiously at this parting from her "children," that she was ready now to shed tears at the slightest provocation. The mistress of the house was unable to see her parents off because she could not leave the little one. Baila was feeling a little sick, so Deborah also stayed behind, and only the menfolk accompanied Reb Baruch Laib and Tertsa-Roisa to the Central Station.

"Any message for your mother?" asked Tertsa-Roisa, just as the taxi was about to move off.

"No!" Deborah answered, and she burst into tears like a lost child.

"Come, come! You mustn't carry on like that!" her mother-in-law chided her with a laugh. "You're not a baby now, you're a married woman!"

There was yet another indiscriminate shower of blessings. The womenfolk stood waving at the taxi as it moved down Levrik Street. They stood shrieking at the taxi as it gathered speed. The children all yelled in chorus, telling Grandma what presents they wanted her to bring when she came again to Antwerp. And then the taxi turned the corner: it vanished out of sight….

Deborah was unable to check her outburst. Every time she wiped her eyes, a new and mightier flow of tears came welling up. Disgraceful…a married woman…behaving like a baby…. She vented her feelings on the bank notes which she still clutched in her hand. She crumpled them up with all her strength. It gave her a thrill – a curious thrill of relief. She had not counted the money, but she realized that it could help her to accomplish the impossible: for instance, it could help her to run away. Already she was seriously considering how to escape, even though a few moments ago the very idea would have seemed utterly fantastic. A few moments ago she had felt that she was doomed for all time.

"If you're not careful, Deborah, you'll tear the notes to shreds," said Baila, greedily watching the convulsive movements of Deborah's fingers.

Deborah put the notes away in her handbag. Baila looked on with the intentness of a cat that has seen a mouse, and is crouching to pounce. And then, unexpectedly balked of her prey, an expression of surprise, weariness and self-pity settled on her face. How many notes did Deborah have? For aught she knew, there were only two or as many as ten. So strong was her curiosity, that in the end she finally decided to ask Deborah outright. She would put the question in an amicable, matter-of-fact way – that was the best approach. She hit on the right sort of careless phrase, and was just about to open her mouth when, unfortunately, Berish walked in.

"Come on, put your coat on and let's go out," he said to his wife, but with his eyes fixed suspiciously on his sister- in-law.

Baila left the room in a huff. Berish was soon back from the station; but where was her man Lipa? Her man Lipa had most assuredly gone out to spend the rest of the day with his boon companions. Such was life! A worthy woman like herself was treated worse than a dog, a silly little girl like Deborah had all the luck in the world. And thinking thus, Baila swallowed a pink pill that tasted terribly bitter – almost as bitter as her own feelings....

The sun had broken through the clouds and was shining brightly.

"Well, Deborah, everything's going to be all right," said Berish as soon as Baila was out of the way. "I had a word with Father at the station, and he explained everything. He told me he was rather short of money at the moment, and that's why he couldn't let us have our full dowry on the nail, but he'll let us have the balance later. After all, it's no use grousing: it only makes matters worse. Just a little confidence and everything will come right. Father did the same with Lipa's dowry – he paid it in installments."

Deborah made no reply, she was not interested. In her imagination she was visualizing herself at the railway booking office buying a ticket to Warsaw. And as soon as she was home again she would refund the money she had taken, which really belonged to her husband. That was reasonable and fair enough. Yes, but what folly, what madness had possessed her to do all she had done so far? Why had she run away from home in the first place? She had been blind not to foresee the crushing loneliness that lay in store for her when all her ties with the past were broken. Life here was meaningless: it had no content, it was empty, quite empty. How fascinating her life had been! Even her sufferings had not been bereft of a deep inner relish. Now she was face to face with nothingness. She was all alone with a stranger whose presence she could not endure. Why could she not endure him? That she did not know. She was in a foreign land among new-found relatives who filled her with loathing. And how they all hated her! Why did they hate her? That she did not know.…

Deborah took out the three banknotes and handed them over to her husband.

"What? He only gave you three hundred francs? Good heavens, he told me he'd given you five hundred! I hope he forks out soon, or we'll be in a jam. That's too bad! Still, I suppose the old man won't keep us waiting too long. I understand Lipa's going to get a tidy sum too. When he gets his, we'll get ours, I guess. Lipa keeps on the right side of Father by all manner of tricks. He pretends he's pious, grows a long beard, tells a pack of lies, cringes, and generally makes a fool of the old man. He's cunning is Lipa, but what a blockhead!"

Deborah laughed a malicious little laugh.

Her husband looked at her with covetous eyes. What a tempting little woman, and she was his own wife!

"Before we go any further, let's have something to eat," he said, and he took her to the cafeteria in Tietz's department stores, in the center of Antwerp. They lunched on sardine sandwiches, which he obtained from a slot machine built flush into the wall.

He was in a happy mood. His wife was a woman who went in for thinking. Well, what did she think of him now? Surely, thinker or no thinker, she could not help feeling astonishment and admiration at the way he conjured up sardine sandwiches out of a solid wall! He entertained her to another of his favorite tricks. He dropped a coin into a slot, and out popped two glasses of bright, frothy beer. Deborah declined the beer, so he brought her some coffee.

Berish was radiant with joy, his face was wreathed in smiles. He took his wife round the furniture shops, where everything was terribly expensive.

"Bah!" said Berish. "These people are barmy! All fancy prices!"

However, in the end the furniture dealers turned out to be perfectly sane, so he decided to buy no more than a couple of beds for the time being – beds being essential – and a table and a few chairs.

"As soon as we get the rest of the dowry, we'll complete the home in style!"

Deborah was much amused by the whole stupid business. She very nearly told him that for her part she was willing to forego the furniture, if only he would advance her a loan for her fare back to Warsaw. But she said no such thing. She merely told him that Reb Baruch Laib had warned her not to expect any more money for some time to come, as he was out of funds.

"Really? Well, he told me something different. What he said to me was, 'I'll send you the rest of your dowry as soon as I get back home.'"

"Well, he may do."

She flushed. Yes, she liked the beds. She liked everything. The shopkeeper rubbed his hands. He chose the furniture and fixed the prices to suit himself, and the bashful young couple accepted without demur. They were just the kind of customers he dreamt of in his dreams. And now they had come true!…

Chapter 15

They had settled down in their new home. They had already had letters from their parents in Warsaw bearing the new address.

The rooms they occupied on the second floor were large and airy and empty – all the more empty for being so large, dwarfing what little furniture there was. The floors were without any sort of covering. And the flight of stairs leading down to the first floor was as indecently bare as it had been when they first viewed the flat. Emptiness, vast and depressing, filled their new home.

All day long Berish reclined, fully dressed, on the bed. He usually lay face upwards, saying not a word. But there was no mistaking his enjoyment of life. It was a good life, this! It was fine for a man to get away from his relatives and live in a home of his own.

Deborah was puzzled to see him thus idling his time away. Did he not profess to be a diamond cutter? Then why was his diamond cutting machine always covered up in its blue dust sheets? The advice which her brother-in-law had tended to her on her first night in Antwerp would often recur to her now. She also recalled the pathetic conversation she had overheard in bed that night. But, strangely enough, these things never worried her. What did worry her was her husband's constant companionship. He was always with her, and she felt terribly uneasy in his presence. She felt as if a worm had eaten its way into her heart and was constantly sapping her strength away. Now she knew the meaning of the word "heartache." Not that she could have defined it, say, to a doctor. As a matter of fact, the physical pains at the heart, which had once caused her so much suffering, had stopped now. The new ache was not a real ache, yet it was more agonizing. The only relief she knew was when her husband went out. Then all her cares would be forgotten. Once, when she was all by herself, she even burst into song. But it was very seldom that he did go out and leave her by herself.

They had been living together for more than two months now. The money Reb Baruch Laib had left them was nearly all gone. The hope they had entertained of Reb Baruch Laib paying the rest of the dowry was completely gone. Lipa had sent a sneaking letter to his father, informing him that Berish had shaved off his beard, that Deborah was no longer wearing her wig. On the receipt of this startling news Reb Baruch Laib wrote the newly married couple a very long and very fierce letter, in which he heaped on them all the abuse and curses he could think of. He was especially angry with Deborah, whom he "excommunicated." It was her evil influence, he argued, that had led Berish into sinfulness; by himself he would never have done such a diabolical thing as to cut off his beard. He, Reb Baruch Laib, being a loving father, had gone to no end of expense to give to his son the daughter of a rabbi, as a shining example of godliness. But behold, instead of walking the ways of God, she was actually perverting and seducing the innocent boy, dragging him into the abyss. Would anybody have believed such a thing to be possible? If he, Reb Baruch Laib, had harbored the least suspicion, would he have exerted himself as he had done, all for the sake of marrying his son off to an indecent wench? And a consumptive wench at that! And so forth. And he finished up by assuring the newly married couple that they would never get any more money from him so long as they lived.

Some days after this letter had come she asked her husband how it was that he never did any work.

"Because there's no work to be done, my sweet, there's none to be had for love or money!" he said in reply, catching her round the waist and forcibly clasping her to his bosom.

Deborah tore herself from his embrace with dread and loathing. He was constantly filled with glee for no apparent reason, but surely this latest outburst was sheer craziness! Berish made as if to gather her up in his arms again. Why should he be a puny weakling, and act the shy youngster with his own wife? But he withdrew, of his own accord.

"You're just like a baby, and seem to be frightened of me, as if I were a stranger, a monster trying to assault you," he summoned up courage to administer a manly rebuke. He meant to break the ice once and for all. He hoped she would apologize, plead bashfulness – the sort of bashfulness that time alone would cure. He, himself, had been shy enough at first, but look at him now!... "I guess you're worrying about Father's letter, but you mustn't take seriously all he says. He'll fork out. He's only trying to put the fear of the Lord into us. He has that blustering way with him. But I never take his threats to heart."

"I'm not worrying. I'm not even interested."

Tut, tut! how extraordinarily shy she was! He ought to do something about it. He might take her to the theater. That would infuse a bit of life into her.

Deborah escaped into the kitchen to cook the dinner. But she could not shake him off. He followed her in. Making himself helpful as best he could, he grabbed hold of a pail and unwittingly splashed its contents all over the floor. If only he were less obliging, if only he would keep to himself!

"Tomorrow night we're going to the theater," he announced, gazing into her eyes.

"We can't afford to," she said, taking him into her confidence. "All we possess now is twenty francs." This, also, was by way of giving him a hint that it was high time he went out and found some work.

"Well, well, anyone would think we were broke!" he said merrily, and the hint passed him by.

The days wore on. He was unable to take her to the theater, but he still went on beaming with joy. The only thing that marred his bliss was her woebegone expression. All she seemed to do was worry, worry, worry!

"I bet she thinks I'm lazy and shy of work," a thought suddenly occurred to him. "I bet the in-laws have been at her, telling her a pack of lies about me. I'll soon find out."

"Deborah, you do understand, don't you? It's not my fault there's no work to be had for love or money. Father simply will *have* to help out, whether he likes it or not. I guess the family have been telling you the usual pack of lies about me. They even write sneaking letters to Father about me. They think it good business: the less money he sends me, they reckon, the more he'll have left over for them You see my point, don't you? If there's no work to be had I can't produce any from under my hat. Or can I?"

"Of course not!"

"Lipa's been unemployed for eighteen months now. It's only because Father sends him a weekly allowance that he's able to make ends meet. And he can thank his lucky stars that Baila works her fingers to the bone to keep him. He never earns a cent, never. As for my brother-in-law, although he's so mighty stuck up and thinks himself wonderfully clever, do you think he ever turns an honest penny? Not him! He's simply a great big windbag, a helpless nincompoop. If Father were to stop supporting him, he'd be out in the street with all his brats, starving, in no time. He just can't stand on his own two feet, that man! Father's constantly plying him with dire threats and 'final' remittances. And Father will do the same to us, don't worry!

"Do you know, Baila would be the happiest woman on earth if Lipa was as fond of her as I am of you. She's terribly jealous because she knows I spend all my time with you – not like Lipa, who's always out on the spree till the small hours gambling away whatever money his wife earns for him. I don't mind confessing, though, that if Baila were *my* wife I'd do just the same as Lipa, and worse. Not only would I leave her to fret her heart out till the small hours – I'd leave her for good."

Deborah listened with rapt attention.

So that's how things were. Her only support in life was to be none other than Reb Baruch Laib. Meanwhile in her sweet ignorance she had infuriated the very man to whom henceforth she must look for her bread and butter. She had discarded her wig, her husband had removed his beard. What a future! To be forever at the tender mercy of Reb Baruch Laib was, indeed, a delightful prospect. However, now she knew precisely where she stood. But, why on earth was her husband so remarkably cheerful? Did he not take his father's threats seriously? Maybe that was the explanation. Anyhow, it was no concern of hers. Whatever happened she could not go on living with this man who was supposed to be her husband. The best way out – and the most honorable – would be for her to confess her true feelings: when once he knew the reason for their uneasy conjugal relations he and she would part.

"It's strange," Berish resumed. "But the more callous Lipa is, the more Baila loves him. She's quite crazy about him. She nags him, curses him, and weeps, but all the same she can't resist giving him every cent of her earnings, knowing perfectly well that he'll only lose the money at cards. And look at you! You're such a baby! A sweet baby, but a very naughty one! Whenever I try to take you in my arms, you shove me away, as if I was trying to kill you. Let me be quite frank with you – I resent it. There, I'm being perfectly honest with you!"

Yes, thought Deborah, it was best to be perfectly frank and honest. For her part, she too must hold nothing back. She must tell him all about herself, the terrible mistake she had made. She was the chief culprit and deserved her punishment. She had abandoned herself, gloatingly, to an *idée fixe* that everybody, even her own mother, hated her and was anxious to be rid of her; a prey to this delusion, she had deliberately brought disaster upon herself, hoping thus to inflict pain on others – a fantastic imaginary act of revenge on imaginary persecutors … with what terrible results!

"I say, you are easily upset," he exclaimed. "Tut, tut!" Her eyes were brimming with tears and she hung her head, as though abashed by his rebuke.

"Listen to me," she said, after a prolonged and awkward silence. "And listen carefully. I am going to be perfectly candid with you. I hope you will understand … " and she told him her story, concluding with the avowal, "And the worst part about it is that I love him still, in spite of myself. That makes our situation – yours and mine – impossible. If I love *him*, I can't love you."

Her husband heard her out in silence, and the more he heard, the more he was fascinated by her. He was overwhelmed by such a passionate longing for her that he was willing to overlook any confession she might make.

She turned towards him to await his reply. She could see that her words had moved him, for his face wore a grim expression and he was biting his nails furiously. She did not exactly relish the prospect of returning to the parental roof. On the other hand, if he asked for a divorce, as he was bound to, she need not return to Warsaw. How would she live? Well, to begin with, she could pawn all her jewelry. All manner of speculations as to her uncertain future went flitting through her brain.

But no, he was not going to ask for a divorce. Indeed, he had not a word to say for himself. He seemed actually to have regained his composure. There, he was smiling again! He had taken her hand and was patting it, trying as best he could to comfort her. How extraordinary! What a strange fellow!

As time went on, all their jewelry found its way into the pawnshop. Only a few trinkets remained which would scarcely cover the price of a fourth-class ticket to Warsaw. Why did she not secretly dispose of them and go away while the going was good? Why not put an end to all this misery? As for the inevitable scandal, her parents would not eat her! Far better to face a scene, or even endure constant bickerings, than submit to this slow, relentless torture of the brain which could have only one unhappy ending – in the madhouse.

If only her husband were less angelic, how much easier her task would be! After hearing her unpalatable tale, instead of showing any self-pity, he had instead felt sorry for her. He had soothed her and said to her, "Never mind. Time heals all wounds. One day you will forget, and then, perhaps, you will learn to love me." And he had even promised her that until she said she loved him, he would not molest her. Sometimes, though, he forgot his promise and sought intimacy.

"Well, well, well. What's the use of looking for work when you know there's none to be had anyway," he would say at ever more frequent intervals as their plight grew more desperate.

Autumn came, then winter. Reb Baruch Laib for once in his lifetime proved as good as his word. He sent the "young sinners" not a cent. Berish began to search for work feverishly, but day after day he returned home with the same dismal tidings.

"Not a hope. There's an awful slump in the diamond trade, it's been like this for more than a year now. The whole town simply stinks of unemployment. What little work there is, is snatched up by the professional crawlers and cringers. They get down on their knees and lick the bosses' boots. I couldn't do that to save my life! It's the cadgers who get all the work, the others, like myself, hang around for hour after hour, only to be sent packing in the end – 'No More!'"

Their home was bare and empty. Their stomachs were empty. And even her head felt empty – quite empty, yet she had not the strength to hold it erect.

And then, with grotesque mockery, the landlady began to wax indignant because the new tenants had not carpeted the top flight of stairs. Every time Deborah left or entered the house she was accosted by the stern old matron.

"How is it that you take no pride in the house like the tenant on the first floor? And you only just married! Really, young woman, it's disgraceful!" And as her tone towards the young woman on the second floor grew daily more harsh and contemptuous, it became more honeyed towards the lady on the first floor.

Deborah would promise to buy a strip of carpet "one day next week or the week after, for certain." She invented all sorts of excuses; her favorite one was that she was looking for a pattern to match the rest of the staircase. But the landlady would not be fobbed off with idle pretexts.

"I know a shop where you can pick up a real bargain, just the thing you're looking for. I'll take you there myself! Now, that's more than I would do for anybody else, but you're really such a nice girl! I like doing favors for people I'm fond of. I'm just made that way! If you weren't so awfully negligent, I'd like you even better than the person on the first floor. I hate people who are stuck up and think themselves God Almighty! Now then, we'll take tomorrow afternoon off and trot along together."

No, unfortunately Deborah would be busy tomorrow. She appreciated the offer and would certainly avail herself of it some other day. And as she made her apologies, she thought: "If I had any money, you witch, I wouldn't spend it on a carpet, but on food. Can't you see I'm hungry?"

Thus the days went by; they turned into weeks and mounted up into months. Occasionally her husband found an odd job. With the proceeds he paid the rent, she settled the bill that she had run up at the grocer's, and then they were left penniless once again.

In none of her letters home did she as much as hint at the dire need she was in. What was the use, for her father was himself only a poor man who could scarcely support his own little home? Even if he had been able to help, she preferred to go hungry rather than beg. And she had no wish to bring sorrow on her mother – a frail little woman whose health was failing and who had never known much happiness at the best of times. Her mother was not wholly to blame for all that had happened. Looking back on the past, Deborah found that her father too was at fault, for had he not willingly given his consent to the match? But where did the final responsibility rest, if not with herself? She and she alone was the real culprit, for she could have averted the whole tragedy simply by saying "No!" If she must point an accusing finger, she must point it first at herself.

It was only by chance that Deborah discovered how profoundly her attitude had changed. One day she received a very long letter from her mother, in which Raizela beseeched her to write home more fully and more often. "Do not make me suffer, do not keep me in nervous suspense by stinting your correspondence with me. I am your mother and I want you to confide in me. Tell me the truth, tell me if you are happy. I am terribly uneasy about you. Do not make my life unbearable. Believe me, if I have done you an injury, I now have my punishment in full. Do not make things worse for me." Thus wrote Raizela – and Deborah found that her thrill of gratification was mingled with untold distress. She could never afterwards quite explain to herself what it was that impelled her to react the way she did, but there and then, without a moment's hesitation, she wrote back to say that she was completely mystified by her mother's letter, and there was certainly no justification for any remorse or uneasy forebodings. Thereafter all the letters that passed between Deborah and her parents were almost perfectly alike and almost perfectly meaningless.

"We were very glad to hear from you (her parents would write), and were indeed happy to learn that all is well with you, for which the Lord be praised. We too, thank God, are in good health. Pray God that we shall always have cause to rejoice in our mutual prosperity. With kind regards to your dear husband, etc."

And Deborah would write back in the same strain. Occasionally Raizela would renew her attempts to gain her daughter's confidence, but to no avail. There were times when Deborah yielded to the temptation of telling all. She would sit down and write endless letters; then, after filling many pages, she would stop to read what she had written, she would tear it all up and send off the usual postcard phrased in the usual way. Even when Deborah lay ill in bed, dispirited and hungry, she still insisted on telling her parents that she was enjoying good health, for which the Lord be praised, and so on and so forth.

So she became more and more estranged from her parents (although she still loved them in a new and aloof way), and she remained as much a stranger to her husband as when she had first set eyes upon him (although she was more and more conscious of his love for her). The iron entered into her blood. She learned to hate, to regard everybody with suspicion. All round her she saw enemies, masked and unmasked. Polite people were hypocrites. Rude people were deadly foes.

Whenever any of her husband's bachelor friends called in, she treated them so contemptuously that they withdrew quite crestfallen.

When her sister-in-law with the big bosom and the blonde wig once paid a courtesy visit, Deborah openly accused her of having come as a spy on Reb Baruch Laib's behalf, a charge of which the poor woman was quite innocent. If anyone tried to tell Deborah a lie, be it ever so harmless, she refused to let the falsehood pass unchallenged. Until very soon no visitor darkened her door.

When she had broken all bonds with the outside world, she found the loneliness almost intolerable. And still her husband aroused in her the selfsame loathing: his companionship tortured her. She could not endure his presence – for reasons beyond her understanding. And then came a time when her solitary confinement in the empty, poverty-stricken room played so badly on her nerves, that she would feel relieved to hear his footsteps coming up the stairs. But this feeling of relief was always short-lived.

She passed the day in idleness, not that there was anything for her to do. If only she could read! But no sooner did she set eyes on a book, than a cloud of specks, like a swarm of troublesome insects, began to dart about all over the printed page, and these hovering specks would make her quite dizzy. The empty room around her would sway drunkenly, and she would have to put the book aside.

And then a host of strange fancies would take possession of her mind. She could not shake them off, no matter how hard she tried.

For instance, it might occur to her that she was really born to be a housemaid and now at last she must answer her true calling. She must go out at once and do something about it. She knew all the time that it was an absurd idea. What chance did she stand of getting a job as a housemaid when she looked more dead than alive? She knew she must chase the thought out of her head. But no, it would not budge! It clung to her like a leech, sucking the strength out of her. "False pride is your undoing," a voice whispered, "and it is better to be humble than to starve. Now is the time to act!" "No," said another voice, "it's all nonsense!" And so the crazy battle surged back and forth in her tormented brain, ceasing only when she was exhausted and everything within her was numb.

Then the next day a different canker would prey on her mind. The more it festered the more she would struggle to remove it; but soon she would have to acknowledge defeat.

She would have to surrender herself to the one and only monstrous notion that nibbled and nibbled and nibbled until it gnawed through some barrier in her mind, and then a regular horde of similar thoughts, but each with a distinctive form of its own, went rampaging through her brain until everything was in a whirl. Then at last peace and quiet would descend on her.

But for her cowardice, she would have gone to see a doctor about it. That was indeed the only sensible thing to do. Yes, she would go tomorrow. But even as she formed this resolve, she knew she would not keep it, for there was one dread little word that she feared above all other words. Supposing the doctor were to utter that awesome word? Of course, in reality he would do nothing of the kind. And then she would be able to go home and laugh heartily at her own fears; she would at last be able to cure herself of this strange affliction. But she was too tired to go today. Tomorrow…

So the days and the weeks and the months wore on, and each day, each week, each month was like an eternity. Nothing ever happened that had not happened before, except that Deborah and her husband had to move twice at short notice. This was a merciful respite for Deborah, although no sooner had she become accustomed to her new surroundings, than she relapsed into her old mental habits. At their first flat they were all but thrown out.

"We're not accustomed to having paupers in the house," said the landlady scornfully, having finally convinced herself that the top flight of stairs would remain bare forever. She could see that all was not well with her second floor tenants, for Deborah was visibly shriveling up, getting more haggard every day.

They found rooms in a tumbledown two-storied building in a working-class district.

The landlady was a poor widow who ran a little baker's shop, and she had too many worries to care whether or not Deborah carpeted the top flight of stairs. For that matter her own part of the staircase was so shabby – the linoleum was all scrappy and worn out – that the bare rough boards above looked comparatively respectable. It was not snobbery that impelled her to give her penniless tenants notice to quit. It was sheer necessity. Her young married nephew and his children, who were on their way to America from Russia, had got stranded in Antwerp, and she could do no less than put them up until such time as they might be able to resume their travels. So Deborah and her husband had to go.

They went to the cheapest place they could find on the outskirts of the city. Their front window overlooked a military installation replete with barracks and underground fortifications. The little street they lived in was made up of a row of tiny, old-fashioned houses on the one side, and of a long wall with a big iron gateway on the other.

Deborah would sit at the window all day, her elbows resting on the sill, her chin cupped in her hands, and she watched the men at their drill. "One, two! One, two!" roared the sergeant-major, and the tiny uniformed figures marched off down the parade ground with machine-like precision; at a distance they looked like schoolboys who were only playing at soldiers. These military exercises were a great attraction to Deborah, and she never voluntarily left her point of vantage for an instant. She felt that she was a little girl again, and although she was not allowed to join in the games she had the pleasure of looking on.

Berish would be out all day. He had found himself a sweated job at twenty francs a week, a wage which enabled them to pay the rent and starve. She always felt very envious of the soldiers when the bugle sounded at meal times and bareheaded men carried across the parade ground huge cauldrons of soup that gave off a glorious steam. How it made her mouth water!

Their new landlady was a gentile – a short stocky woman with big hips and a neat coiffure, although her hair was so scanty on top that the parting down the middle looked more like a bald patch than anything else. She kept a small general store, and sold ham and bacon at cut-throat prices. Her shop was always crammed with customers – most of them soldiers off-duty – and of a Sunday there would be a regular struggle between those who wanted to get in and those who wanted to get out.

"Like moths around a candle," the neighbors would say with a knowing glance towards Georgette behind the counter. Georgette was the buxom young niece of the proprietress and according to local gossip she had not only conquered the army, but had broken the hearts of all the local shopkeepers. For them business was in the doldrums, and they were sick with jealousy. At one time they had even hatched a conspiracy to entice Georgette away and to poison Jacond, the aunt's dog, which was also a great favorite with the troops. One competitor, who was a widower, had even proposed marriage to Georgette, offering to put her behind a counter all of her own instead of having to work for a cross old aunt. He was sure she would yield to the temptation, especially as his own charms were irresistible. But man proposes and God disposes. Jacond was a wily dog, and all attempts at administering poison to him failed. As for Georgette, she would not dream of leaving her place, much less of marrying a widower.

Deborah was on the most amicable terms both with Jacond and Georgette. But Georgette never had a moment to spare the livelong day, and the old hag, her aunt, for some mysterious reason would never permit Jacond to pay any calls. Apparently she considered it beneath his dignity to do so. Whenever he did come upstairs, he had to steal his way up like a thief. Admittedly in the early days Deborah was rather scared of him. She would let him paw at her door and whimper away, until he took offense and stalked off in a sulk. But in time a tacit understanding sprang up between them. Their friendship began one day when he trotted in through the open door and set to fondly licking her heel. She did not shoo him off, although after he had gone she did brush down her leg at the spot where his fur had touched it. But by now both Deborah and Jacond had quite forgotten those early, aloof, diffident days, and they really were great pals. The moment he spied her on a Monday morning coming down the stairs with the rent book and the rent in her hand, he would lose his head completely. He would rush up to greet her, then dash backwards and forwards across the shop, wagging his tail furiously. He fussed over her, put his tongue out and licked her and kissed her and then, quite overcome with ecstasy, rubbed his fleshy muzzle on the floor in canine homage.

What she feared most had happened. Now if the landlady chose to do so, she could put them out on the street, and they might as well go and drown themselves in the Scheldt.

Poor Jacond was quite distraught. Deborah had failed to put in her customary appearance with the rent on the Monday. Meanwhile, he was under the stern eye of his mistress, who was determined that he should not slink upstairs. In the end, to make quite sure, she put him on the lead behind the counter, and for the second day running he was being held a prisoner there, for no good reason at all as far as he could see.

The situation had become truly desperate. Berish's employer, who was himself only an "outdoor worker," had been unable to get a single job from the diamond cutting factories during the past fortnight. There was a panic on the Bourse, and all business had practically come to a standstill – simply because an Austrian crown prince had been murdered in faraway Serbia.

"And yet people have the audacity to complain that there is no justice on this earth," Deborah mused aloud. "Here we are on the brink of war, all for the sake of Justice! How the conscience of the world is shocked when innocent blood is spilt, especially if that blood happens to be precious blue blood! Of course, ordinary red blood is cheap, inferior, and who cares if it is shed in interminable torments, drop by drop, day after day? I wonder if anyone would ever dream of stopping me in the street – 'You look hungry. Let me treat you to a meal!' Ha, ha!"

She laughed until the tears came into her eyes. What a fool she was, talking away to herself, and pretending to be a sort of Karl Marx in petticoats! Ridiculous!…

But seriously, if war was to break out, how would it all end? Might not things change for the better? After all, Simon himself had once prophesied as much during a heated debate: the next war, he declared, would be followed by a great social upheaval, there would be world-wide revolution, and then socialism would become universal – it would even spread to Mars.… She remembered his very words. He always theorized boldly and confidently, then threw in a witticism, which, far from detracting from his closely reasoned arguments, would lend them all the more weight.

Simon! Simon! Simon! Enough of Simon! There was only one thing she cared about now – to end her present mode of life and to return to her parents before it was too late, before she went mad. She must save her reason. But how was she to get to Warsaw when she could not even afford a loaf of bread?

War was inevitable now. That was what a soldier had told Georgette earlier in the day. And Deborah could see for herself that something big was brewing. For the past few days the barracks across the way had been throbbing with activity. Flashing bayonets and flashing brass buttons everywhere! From morning to night officers were busy drilling new recruits. "One, two! One, two!" they kept roaring without cease, so that the words were now constantly ringing in her ears, and the diminutive soldiers, herded together like sheep, kept rhythmically stamping their heavy boots, "One, two! One, two!" It was beyond her understanding. By what mysterious mechanism did the threat of war between far-off Austria and Serbia galvanize these Belgian barracks into a state of furious preparation? All she knew was that if Belgium did become involved in hostilities, then her fate would be sealed – she could never hope to return home. As if she had any hopes of doing so even now in peacetime!

Her husband came in, shuffling his feet: he had been tramping the streets all day.

"War has broken out between Austria and Serbia. Some people say that Belgium is going to get mixed up in it."

"Really?"

They went to bed. Her husband's face was horribly livid. It was none of her business. Neither he nor she had eaten a crumb for two whole days.

Daylight had come once more, and again she was at her seat by the window.

If only she had the strength to go out in the streets and lose herself in the crowd as her husband did. That would be fine! There was something else she wanted to do, but it had slipped her memory. Oh yes, she wanted to return to Warsaw and join her parents before all Europe was ablaze! Of course, that was it!

And then, even as she was thinking these hazy thoughts, a spasm of fear swept over her as she realized that her mind was wandering. This was her first taste of madness, sheer madness. She must pull herself together. How could she forget that she was penniless, that far from being able to set out on a long and costly journey, she could not even afford to buy herself a loaf of bread? How foolish of her to worry about the war, as if that could make any difference to her. She must remember always that there was only one thing she really wanted – food, food!

It was a shame though that she could not go along and see Meerel! Meerel was a kind soul and would surely have lent her the price of a ticket to Warsaw. Even if Meerel was to give her only a few coppers for a loaf of bread, that too would be splendid. Why not swallow her pride and try to buy some food on credit in the grocery shop down below? She ought to ask Georgette when the old woman was not about.

Meerel was such a lovable creature. Happy days! It would be wonderful if she and Meerel could go across the green meadows to the byre on the squire's estate. Meerel would give her a cup of milk straight from the cow – warm, creamy milk. And she would drink it up as eagerly as she had done in Jelhitz on those hot summer days when she was convalescing from a serious illness. Every morning, in the bright sunshine, she and Meerel would cross the meadows into the squire's estate. Oh, for those far-off days in Jelhitz! Was it very long ago? Yes, a long, long time ago!

She was only a child then of about eight. It would be good to know that Meerel was still managing the dairy on behalf of the squire, who was too aristocratic and too lazy to administer his own estate.

He was a handsome gentleman, was the squire, and so courteous. He always gave her a magnificent nosegay to take home. One day he seated her on his lap, and made her feel so very ashamed of herself, but he said he would not let her go until she kissed him. How he did love to tease her!

And then his brother arrived, a mere boy, who resided abroad. That was the only visit he ever paid to the family estate in all the years that she lived in Jelhitz. He was supposed to be a law student, although he did not look it. Meerel said that he was attending a German university. Ha, ha! How well she remembered him, as if it were only yesterday, with his freckled face and great wild eyes. He followed her about wherever she went. In honor of his visit the squire held a garden party to which he invited all his tenants. The whole of the festive scene came back to her – she could see it all now; but beyond Jelhitz, beyond the fields and the orchards of the squire's estate, she could also see the barracks and the Belgian soldiers marching up and down in formation on the parade ground. The squire ordered cartloads of planks to be brought from the forest, and this timber was laid out to form a sort of floor over a large meadow. Peasants were busy with huge sheets of canvas studded with brass rings, putting up marquees. The canvas was grey. Yes, of course it was grey! A few policemen were brought in from a neighboring town to keep order. Now the band was striking up a merry folk dance, fiddlers were fiddling and drummers were drumming. Among the many side shows was a Punch and Judy show. How the peasants guffawed to hear these rag dolls speak and quarrel, just like a real husband and wife, and when the husband began beating the wife, the crowd almost split their sides with laughing. What a great throng of peasants. They must have come in from all over the countryside.

Suddenly Deborah burst out laughing. Now, the squire's younger brother would admonish the crowd, saying "Stop pushing! Stop pushing!" So the crowd nicknamed him "Stoppush." Before long his real name was forgotten, but his visit to Jelhitz was remembered for many years. "If only Stoppush would come back again," the people would say with a sigh of yearning. "What fun we would have."

"And what a boon it would be for trade," the shopkeepers would remark, rubbing their hands in anticipation. Before her very eyes the dead past had come back, colorful and noisy. "Stoppush" tried to persuade her to accompany him into one of the marquees, so that he might show her what was going on inside; but she declined, for she was rather afraid of him. He then began to address her in German, as if he thought that by so doing he could more easily gain her confidence. At first she thought it was Yiddish.

"*Haben Sie nur kein' Angst, Krausköpfchen!*" he kept saying to her in a slow, deliberate way.

She started up from her reverie. The host of memories fled suddenly like ghosts at dawn, leaving her breathless with surprise, but the sweet ecstatic sensation lingered on, and her lips were twitching, smiling with delight.

What now? Now that the pangs of hunger were gone, what ailed her? Yesterday, she had been so hungry! No, thank God, she was not hungry anymore, not in the least. Only her head was aching more than ever.

She rose to her feet.

"Goodness, what's happened? I can barely stand on my legs. Why, I'm staggering! Hold on, hold on to the ledge! Good God, am I to become paralyzed? No, it must not be! I'll go downstairs into the shop and ask Georgette. If the old woman's there, I'll even ask *her.* Maybe Georgette is on her own today, and she'll let me have a loaf on the sly. But no, she won't, she won't do anything of the sort. She'll just say, 'Sorry!' as usual. 'I'm ever so sorry, but you know what the old woman's like, don't you? You remember the trouble I got into last time!' Poor Georgette, the trouble she got into last time! And there won't be another last time...."

The sun was still shining. Was it morning or afternoon? She glanced across at the barracks' clock. Dinner hour! The soldiers were filling up their mess tins at the steaming field kitchen. They seemed to have nothing to do all day except eat, and then eat again! Not that she could have touched any of their food. By now even her bodily weariness was gone. Her limbs had ceased aching. She would try and walk, to see how she got on. Yes, it was quite easy: the stiffness had gone out of her legs and she felt as light as a feather. As light as a feather and all empty inside. No trace of a headache now. What did annoy her was the buoyancy of her head, it would not keep straight, but swayed from side to side like a leaf in the breeze. That was a very strange thing....

Ah, here was her bed and she would lie down on it. Now that was better, much better!

She had not been resting for more than ten minutes when Georgette shouted up to her from the bottom of the staircase:

"Have you heard the latest? Germany has invaded us. It's war!"

Deborah heard her perfectly well, but she did not have the strength to shout back. What did she care, anyway? Still, supposing she had the money for a ticket, she would go back to her parents – at once. Before long, communications would be disrupted. The sergeant-major who walked out with Georgette every evening after shop hours had not shown up for quite a few days.... What had happened to him?

"What is the matter with me? Am I really going mad? Why am I obsessed with the impossible idea of getting back to Warsaw? This starvation is killing me...."

She lay perfectly still. Everything grew calm within her. There was not a thought in her head. She was devoid of all feeling. And then it was that a strange sense of bliss, beatific bliss, crept over her and took complete possession of her....

Suddenly she jumped out of bed. She feverishly assembled her whole wedding trousseau, with the long golden chain that had been put round her neck at her betrothal, as well as her husband's gold watch, throwing everything into one great heap. Her fingers were wonderfully deft and it was not long before she had done up all her spare chemises and underwear into another bundle. This she stuffed into the bright leather suitcase that her husband had held in his hand when she first set eyes on him in Berlin. She locked the door, leaving the key on top of the gas meter out on the landing. As she passed on her way through the shop, the landlady ignored her, but Jacond leapt up, straining at the leash, and he began to bark with such terrible fury that it seemed his tongue would drop out of his mouth. It was a long, lolling tongue, almost reaching the floor. No one could soothe the wretched dog. She kept drawing her cheeks in and out between her teeth. Out-of-doors a thousand suns were blazing over the city. The letter to her husband was finished. She hid it away under the pillow. Was there anything else needed doing before she left? No, nothing!

She took the suitcase and all that was in it straight to the municipal pawnbrokers. She was all atremble, her legs were sagging beneath her, her heart was beating violently as if, like Jacond, it was straining at the leash. The streets were busy with people hurrying home from work. She looked about her nervously. For all she knew she might run into her husband. So she began to fly along the pavements with the nimbleness of a child. She did not feel the impact of her feet on the flagstones – she was soaring onwards like a bird.

She was eager to get past the zoological gardens before closing time, when the wives of the wealthy diamond merchants would come trooping out into the streets. For this green and shady retreat was their habitual rendezvous in the summer. Too late! They were coming out now, all smiles, all jewels, all flesh. Some of them were so fat, they could scarcely waddle along. Nonetheless, they looked immensely pleased with themselves. Deborah gave them a hurried look, then turned her gaze on the younger women, those with the flashing eyes – eyes full of sensual greed, of unquenchable voluptuousness. As they tripped along they conversed with many a coquettish gesture and mannerism. They contrived to vary the curves of their warm, pulsating bosoms, without ever losing their graceful poise. They were not women, but goddesses, for each held lightning in her hands, and when, thoughtlessly, the goddess raised her slender fingers, a streak of summer lightning flashed forth upon the world from great and lustrous diamonds.... They minced along at their leisure, for – unlike herself – they were not running away. No, of course not, they were only going home to meet their perfumed husbands who had spent the day speculating and profit-making on the Bourse.

What was the matter with her? She must hurry. She had no time to stand and stare. She quickened her pace. Her hands fluttered excitedly. She scurried along like a frightened rabbit.

Thank heavens, here was the pawnbroker's shop and the door had closed behind her. She laid out her possessions on the counter, and gazed through the wire netting, which carved up the young assistant's face into a pattern of squares as he peered back at her.

"I don't know how much to ask, really I don't. Give me whatever you can, but please hurry!"

The young man's crisscross wire-netting wrinkles widened out as he bent his head forward, and he repeated in a friendly voice:

"How much?"

She pushed the bundle towards him, and he carefully examined all her gowns, then placed her golden chain on the scales.

"All right," she said, "I'll take 130 francs."

"Very well!" said the wrinkled young man, pushing a wad of bank notes towards her under the wire netting.

"Number two platform. The train that's just come in over there. See it? It's due to leave at seven past. Change at Brussels."

"Yes please, a single ticket to Berlin," said Deborah, almost in a voice of entreaty, and her left eyelid flickered uncontrollably as if she were winking at the clerk behind the grating in the brightly lit, square little booking office.

Thank heavens, the train had started and she was on it, with her suitcase upon her trembling knees, and with her buoyant head turned towards the window, through which she could see the flaming sun as it burst through the trees and enveloped the treetops, touched the ponds and the meadows with crimson fire, gilded the hillocks, the church spires, the peasant huts, the bogs, the fallen leaves.... And her spirits began to rise; the gloom that had weighed so heavily on her heart was dispelled, and life became like a song.

The train pulled up. Deborah was jerked forward. She got out on to the platform with all the other passengers. At a tiny canteen she bought herself a cup of coffee, two cakes and a small bag of acid drops. How delicious! What lovely cakes! And the flavor of the coffee surpassed anything she had ever tasted before.

Once more she was ensconced in a corner seat by the window. This was her favorite seat, the same as she had had on the outward journey a year ago. Only now everything was different. She was not traveling to Berlin to get married now – oh, no! – and she was so happy, so terribly happy. It was a boundless happiness such as she had never known before. Ah, the train was beginning to move. And all the newsboys and cigarette vendors were hurriedly jumping off on to the platform. The train was crowded to suffocation, but surely no one was as happy as herself. She, and she alone, was possessed of that wild spirit of abandon that lifted her high above mortal cares and mortal responsibilities, she alone was experiencing that frenzy of joyous escape, which made her oblivious of the past and even of the future. It gave her strength and courage. The wheels of the train were grinding on the rails, and each distinct grind carried her further away from that strange man whose company she found harder to endure than physical pain and hunger, that strange man whose presence was even more repugnant than the abominable atmosphere that brooded over the whole city of Antwerp. She was free, and had not a care in the world. She did not even care about herself. Hurrah! Absolutely free!

The lamps in the train were all lit up. A stout man opposite her shut the window and drew the dark green blind. Resting their heads on cushions, shawls or coats, or – for the lack of anything better – on the bare boards, the passengers all sat back and did their best to go to sleep. A weedy youth, who was rather like one of the soldiers she had often seen at the barracks in Antwerp, reopened the window. But the stout man next to him gave him a withering look, accompanied by a contemptuous smile – it was an ugly smile that made her shudder – and then, without a word, he closed the window again with a bang. All the other passengers looked on unconcerned.

Where was she? It was daylight again, and she was still sitting in the corner seat. But the train was at a standstill, and the engine ahead was spluttering wrathfully, like a man coughing his lungs up. Dense clouds of smoke went floating past the window. And then the train began to move again. The stout man with the ugly smile was gone and in his place sat a middle-aged German woman with a big black hat perched on her head, and she was eating some sandwiches out of a linen bag.

Deborah glanced out of the window. Wide open spaces, a far-spreading sky, here and there a crooked tree. Nearby a few children with sticks were chasing a cow. The cow was moving fast on her bandy legs, her udder swinging to and fro. There was a trace of a smile on the animal's comical face; indeed, she looked awfully stupid, even more so than the red and white cow which Meerel used to milk in the squire's byre. Deborah laughed aloud.

She stood up, smoothed her crumpled coat with her fingers, and then, studying her own reflection in a tiny mirror, muttered to herself, ironically, "You do look beautiful!" Well, well, it was about time she went into the restaurant car and had a snack. She was ravenous. In front of her stood a cup of steaming coffee and two rolls. It only whetted her appetite and she wanted more. But she must not have any more, or she would run short of cash. Never mind, she would have another cup of coffee. She simply could not resist the temptation.

The repast finished, she returned to her compartment. But her seat was occupied. The weedy youth who had got himself into trouble the night before had taken advantage of her absence and was comfortably installed in the corner by the window. As good fortune would have it, though, the German woman with the big black hat was about to get out, and so Deborah was able to go on gazing out of the window to her heart's content. It was a great comfort to have this little window – but not great enough to make her forget her hunger. Her stomach was nagging worse than ever. How was it that the weedy youth opposite showed no signs of hunger? He had not had a crumb to eat throughout the long journey and yet he seemed to be none the worse for it. He was bearing up very well.

She must do likewise. Though she could not forget that she was hungry she would stop worrying. She fixed her attention on a solitary peasant's hut in the middle of a field. Tied up to this hut was a dog – she could have sworn it was Jacond, she had never see two dogs so alike – and it was straining at its leash in a frenzy of despair and barking piteously. The poor dog was hungry! Now, what could that cozy little coil of smoke fluttering from the chimney pot mean other than that the womenfolk within were busy cooking dinner. It could mean nothing else. How delightful! Now great masses of clouds were creeping over the sky. The sky became all overcast and it dropped lower and lower, until it rested upon the rooftop of the peasant's hut. At last the train was on the move again. She began to count what was left of her money and wondered, could she afford another snack or would she be better advised to go without? She really ought to be ashamed of herself, because opposite her sat a mere boy who had not eaten a thing the whole time, yet he did not seem to care a bit. But just then, as if he had divined her thoughts and wished to confound her, the weedy youth produced a cut loaf of bread and a big piece of green cheese pitted with holes. He started to cut the cheese into slices.

"Would you care to share this with me, miss?" he said, offering her a sandwich.

She boiled over with rage. The impudence! And rising to her feet, she hurried off down the swaying corridor on her way to the restaurant car, leaving the weedy youth like a fool with the miserable sandwich still outstretched in his puny, charitable hand.

She spent two francs at the buffet, and still her throat was parched.

No matter how much coffee she drank she could not quench her thirst.

Where was she? The train had stopped. Oh yes, she must get out at this station. She found herself a seat on a platform bench and waited patiently. Hundreds upon hundreds of people were pouring out of this train and another train and they were all flocking to the exits. To pass the time away, she began to read in the lamplight the postcards which she had received from her parents ever since she had been married. There was a striking change of tone in the most recent ones: they were full of hints, obscure and ambiguous phrases. "Our Father in heaven is a merciful Father.... It is not for mortal man to question His wisdom.... We must take courage in His all-embracing love.... Grandfather is indisposed.... We may have to pay him a visit.... Circumstances may change...." Taken together, these postcards frightened her. No, no, she must ward off her terrible fears. She put the correspondence back into her handbag.

The express that would have borne her on to her destination if she had not run short of money, was steaming out of the station. The rain was coming down in torrents and beating down the smoke from the locomotive. A big cloud of smoke floated her way and made her cough. She got up from the bench and began walking up and down the platform with her suitcase in one hand and her hat in the other.

"Hello, curly!"

She found herself standing in the shadow of a burly man with a huge paunch and with a big, puffed-up, mauve-colored face – a railway official to judge by his shiny black raincoat and peaked cap.

"My dear, you're freezing. Come into my office for shelter," he said to her in German, pointing towards a tiny cabin at the end of the platform. "*Haben Sie nur kein' Angst, Krausköpfchen!* You'll be nice and comfy with me. I won't do you any harm, I'm no monster. I should hate to see a nice little girl like you freeze to death. Come on in! It's always terribly chilly at this time of night."

"No, I'm all right. Tell me, when does the next train for Warsaw get in?"

"D'you mean the fourth-class train? What, is my curly little gollywog traveling fourth-class, in a cattle-truck? Shame!" he cried, "Shame!" And his big breathing body seemed to grow bigger than ever.

A clock rang the hour. One! Two! Three! Four!... She moved towards the exit.

"Now, don't run away. Come into my office, and we'll look up the timetable. What? Surely you're not afraid of me? Tut, tut!" There was a wicked smile in his greedy little eyes.

She was terrified of him, and she crossed to another platform. Here she found two or three people to keep her company, but the wind was blowing the rain her way. She huddled up in a corner and waited for what seemed an eternity. Then there was the roar of a passing train. She rushed back, only to find herself once more under that same horrid shadow.

"Well, well, if it isn't my curly little gollywog! She's come back to me," said the fat, heavily breathing man, with that evil smirk in his tiny eyes; and loudly clearing his throat, he spat on the ground like a beast.

She felt terribly sick.... She felt the impact of his horrible little eyes as they pierced her clothing and caressed her naked body.

An inspector sauntered by. The puffed-up, mauve-faced official saluted with grotesque obsequiousness, and falling in with his superior, ambled off – the two of them, great hulking figures, both with hands clasped behind their backs.

A piercing whistle came rushing in from afar, growing louder and louder. Two gleaming red eyes approached in the darkness, growing bigger and bigger. There was a belching and sizzling of smoke, and into the station steamed the fourth-class train. She climbed up the steep steps, holding on for dear life to the rusty iron rail. She sat down near the door, at the end of a long wooden bench. It was a nightmare train, but strangely enough it answered in every detail to the mental picture she had formed of it whenever she had contemplated returning to Warsaw fourth-class. The carriage, which was not divided up into compartments, was in almost complete darkness. The air was foul and clammy. Everywhere on the floor children lay asleep on bundles done up in sackcloth. They snored laboriously through clogged little nostrils. Women sat wrapped up in huge dark shawls, as if it were midwinter.

"If only we could eat to the fill once in a while!" they moaned in chorus. "If something doesn't happen quickly, we shall starve to death."

"Yes," said a woman with a hoarse voice, who was hidden in the gloom, "that we shall. What we need is some capital to buy and sell, and make a little profit. Although that's not so easy as it sounds. Supposing you have the cash to buy poultry, well you have to pay through the nose, but when you go to market it doesn't fetch a decent price. That's the trouble."

"It isn't as if we were greedy and wanted a lot, is it now? I know there's precious little that I want! All I want is to marry off my eldest daughter and get her out of the way. And it won't be long before this one here is grown up either," said one of the women, pointing a withered finger at a little girl of about twelve, whose face was quite fleshless. The child sat chewing a piece of bread and her jawbones could be seen champing – like the jaws of a skeleton. "Look at her, she's bolting down her last piece of bread, and when that's finished she'll have to go hungry for hours and hours.... It'll serve you jolly well right!" The mother was a decrepit old hag – to all appearances she was over seventy, she was toothless, her skin was all shriveled up, her face was covered with hundreds of warts big and small.

"Shut up, you dirty Jews!" cried a tall burly fellow in an ill-fitting tweed coat. It was the sort of coat that the squire in Jelhitz used to wear. How, Deborah wondered, had he come by it? He sat puffing at a clay pipe. The fumes all but suffocated her. She moved over to the other end of the carriage, but everywhere the air was foul and clammy, everywhere was darkness, everywhere men and women lay groaning in their sleep. Those who were awake sat talking many foreign tongues.

At the frontier they all had to get out for the customs inspection. Hundreds of battered trunks were opened, hundreds of bundles were undone. A big-bellied woman, seemingly pregnant, was taken away for examination by a masculine-faced woman official whose features

Deborah had seen before. The pregnant woman pleaded and protested at the top of her voice. Deborah was not even troubled to open her suitcase. The customs officer simply waved her away, but began to rummage suspiciously in a soiled little bundle, whose owner broke into a shrill cackle.

"A fat lot he'll find in there! All my jewels, and I don't think!"

Was this really Warsaw? Yes it was Warsaw indeed! Here she was in the old familiar station; everything looked just the same as she had left it.

All she possessed now was a ruble and twenty kopecks. Should she walk home, or should she be reckless and take a droshky? She would certainly have danced for joy in the middle of the station for all to see, but her legs were failing her. They were very much enfeebled. Ah, there was the gilt-framed mirror hanging on the wall, and there the same right-angled sofa fitting so modestly into the corner!

"Hey, driver!"

The cabby whom she had hailed poked a weather-beaten face out of his oversized blue greatcoat, his hands emerged from his long sleeves. He touched up his horse with gusto, and away they sped past the station in the heart of the city. She lay back in the droshky.

All that she beheld was hers – the cabby, the horse, the droshky, Warsaw, they were all part of herself! The familiar streets reeled back dizzily as the droshky flew onwards. The streets were alive! The cobblestones were alive! Yonder were the treetops of the Saxon Gardens. They were alive! Krulewski Street had rather an outlandish air about it; but the girl who kept the soda fountain parlor happened to come to the door and she gave Deborah a smile of recognition. Deborah was about to return the greeting; however, the droshky was moving too fast for that. All the same Krulewski Street had now lost its outlandish air; the sudden appearance of that shop-girl imbued it with a friendly homely atmosphere.

"Warsaw! My dear own Warsaw! My very own! How I love you!"

"Whoa-back!"

"Why, we're here! Good heavens, I never realized it was such a short journey. I say, cabby, you certainly did it in record time!"

"Betcher life I did! Whatcher expect for yer twenty kopecks? Had yer money's worth, aintcher? Want me to take yer to Berlin, do yer?"

"Oh no, no, don't take me to Berlin! Please don't. Leave me where I am!" she felt like screaming.

The children playing in the gateway did not recognize her. Nor did the baker's wife, who sat on her usual chair in her usual corner of the gateway, selling bread rings out of a huge basket. She had a glass of tea in her hands, but she was not drinking. She was busy giving a piece of her mind to a man coated in flour from head to foot. Apparently he had kept her waiting a long time for the batch of hot bread rings which he was now pouring into her basket. He gave Deborah an amused wink and went his way. Deborah followed him across the courtyard, her feet buckling under her upon the tortuous cobbles. She began to climb the familiar staircase, littered with rubbish. Once or twice she slipped.

At last she had reached the doorway she knew so well, the varnished brown double doors. She knocked, and as she waited her heart slammed madly. No answer! Again no answer!

"After all, why should I knock? Surely I'm at home now! How silly of me."

She flung open the double doors.

"Oh!"

The rooms were all empty, quite empty. The windows were smeared with whitewash. On the floor stood a pail stained from top to bottom with paint of every hue, rainbow fashion, one layer of color merging into the next. There was a big heap of pink powder piled up near the sink. Reb Avram Ber's study was newly decorated, as was the bedroom. There was a crushed trilby hanging on the nail in the kitchen door, together with a pair of white overalls which had large holes near the pockets and were spattered all over with green and pink.

She stopped short, utterly dazed and panic-stricken. The shock was too much for her.

Where were her parents? Why had they not written to tell her that they were moving? What was the mystery? She stood stock still, as if petrified, powerless to move. She surveyed the bare walls, the newly-painted doors. The odor of fresh paint irritated her palate. Her tongue was trying to move in her half-open mouth; it was completely dry, as if someone had passed a hard cloth over it. What now? What was she to do with herself?

"Whom are you looking for, miss?"

"My parents used to live here. Have you any idea where they've gone to?"

"No, miss. I couldn't say!"

The decorator took his overalls off the door and began to put them on. She turned to go.

"Ask the landlord. He may know," he called out after her, buttoning up his red-and-green-stained overall trousers. "I don't know where you can get hold of him, though. I've been trying all morning to track him down, but he's blooming well vanished. I say, didn't the rabbi used to live in this here flat?"

"That's right. Don't you know where he's gone to?"

"No, haven't the faintest!"

She went downstairs, suitcase in hand. It was outrageous! Her parents had not even deemed it necessary to inform her of their change of address, and now, after such a long and weary journey, she found herself stranded. The disappointment was too great for her to bear. She was faint with hunger. Her legs were giving way. She was sinking, sinking fast. Soon she would fall headlong.

The baker's wife in the corner of the gateway recognized her.

"Heavens, is that you? Look what's become of you! Why, if it isn't our Deborah! How you've changed! What brings you here, now that your parents have moved from Warsaw? Didn't you know? Your flat's empty! It's to let. Good God, how ill you look! What's the matter with you, are you hungry? Nothing to be ashamed of, even if you are. Far better to admit it than to starve. Come and have a cup of tea with me!"

Deborah shook her head. She inquired after her father at the general stores, but the shopkeeper was not very helpful. He did believe that he knew Reb Avram Ber's new address – he had heard it mentioned – but he couldn't for the life of him remember it now. The landlord was out. Unfortunately he had been gone all morning, and several other people besides Deborah were searching high and low for him. At her wits' ends, she took refuge in the little restaurant at the corner of the street. Possibly the proprietor, who was a member of Reb Avram Ber's congregation, might know. He did not even recognize her.

"The rabbi's new address?" he grunted. "How the devil should I know!"

She ordered a bowl of soup. She could not afford to take any meat. Meat was not for people like herself who must consider dry bread a luxury.

The restaurateur set the bowl down with an angry bump, spilling part of its contents. He seemed to think her a pauper, and kept an eye on her, as if to encourage her to finish the soup quickly and then clear out. She lifted the spoon to her mouth, but she could not swallow. She felt that she was going to choke.

A young man strolled in and sat down opposite her.

"I beg your pardon, miss, I hope you won't think me inquisitive, but I should say that you're a stranger in these parts. Is this your first visit to Warsaw?"

"No, I live here."

"Do you really? That's funny, because you don't look like one of us, if you know what I mean. Not that that's anything to be ashamed of. Country folk are as good as us any day of the week. Well, well, and what do you think of the news? Terrible, isn't it? As if we never had enough to keep us worried, now there's this talk of war. War may break out any moment, they say. If it does, all communications will be disrupted and lots of people will be cut off from their homes. It's terrible! The first thing I did when I heard that trouble was brewing, was to pack my parents off to the village where they belong. You never know what funny things may happen in a big town like Warsaw. The papers say it all started because some prince or other was murdered. Have you seen this?" he said, pointing a tremulous forefinger at a crumpled news-sheet.

She was unable to read it, for the print was so greasy.

So it was to be war. Perhaps in the long run some good might come of it. The common people seemed to think war the greatest of all possible calamities. Were they right? Yes, of course they were! Only a madman, a killer, could think otherwise. When war came, humanity sank to the lowest depths of misery and wretchedness. Already the men in the barracks across the road were preparing for the slaughter.

"Deborah, pull yourself together! Stop talking to yourself. Deborah, are you all right? Deborah, look at me! Were you asleep?"

Deborah sat up in bed.

She looked all round her at the familiar room with the familiar window, through which the half-light of evening was now peering, and she rubbed her eyes in an effort to rouse herself from her stupor, to shake off the hallucination which was only now beginning to fade. She stared hard into the gathering darkness.

"Who's there?" she asked.

"It's me, Deborah. What's the matter with you? Have you had a nightmare? I say, Deborah, I met one of my old pals and he lent me two francs. We're going to have some supper."

Her husband struck a match and applied it to the gas mantle, but he forgot that the gas had run out days ago; the light instantly went out with a pop. He put a coin in the meter and relit the lamp. A flood of greenish light settled on the bed and filled the hollows of Deborah's livid face.

Her husband handed her a cup of tea in bed, together with a few slices of bread. Deborah tried to swallow a mouthful of bread, but it stuck in her throat.

"I say, Deborah, have you heard that war has been declared? We're in for it now!"

Deborah slowly sipped her tea in silence.

She was past caring.

Diamonds

ברילִיאַנטן

A novel
ראָמאַן

Translated by Heather Valencia

Introduction

Anita Norich

Esther Kreitman's second novel, *Brilyantn,* was published in London in 1944 and translated to English more than sixty years later, in 2010, by Heather Valencia. The novel focuses on the fortunes (and misfortunes) of a male protagonist, Gedaliah Berman, his family, and the vagaries of the diamond trade. *The Dance of the Demons* took its main character from Warsaw to Antwerp and ended as Germany invaded Belgium. *Diamonds* begins in Antwerp in 1913, moves on to London with the German invasion, and briefly returns to Antwerp at the end of World War I. En route, we encounter a range of characters and languages presented as hierarchies. The novel is unmistakably critical of such stratifications. Like Yiddish speakers everywhere, the characters are multilingual. Yiddish, Hebrew, Flemish, French, German, and English appear in the novel as people are driven from place to place by war and economics. German and English are the languages of business and are understood as having a higher status than Yiddish. The diamond trade is even more hierarchical, with polishers occupying the lowest rung, cutters (like Kreitman's husband) above them, followed by brokers and, finally, merchants, like Berman, at the pinnacle.

Similar hierarchies are seen in every social and economic sphere. The Jewish community offering social services to refugees discriminates between the rich and the poor. As a woman who is helping refugees condescendingly reminds them, "If you have much, you'll get much more. If you have little, you'll lose the little that you had before." (In the Yiddish text, this aphorism is given in transliterated German, underscoring the power "charity" and the speaker wield.) Informed by socialist sympathies and her translation of George Bernard Shaw's *The Intelligent Woman's Guide to Socialism and Capitalism,* Kreitman offers a condemnation of capitalism and the class structure it perpetuates. In the novel, diamonds serve as both a commodity and a metaphor for the inequities evident everywhere. Their symbolism is obvious: like the merchants who buy and sell them, diamonds are hard, with a polished surface but without intrinsic value. And the diamond trade is indifferent to the Black people who mine diamonds in foreign lands and to the poor who labor over them everywhere.

Kreitman's multi-dimensional characters are never simply rich or poor, malevolent or innocent, sinful or virtuous. As Yosef Hillel Levi wrote in his review of *Brilyantn,* Kreitman depicts individuals with all their *mayles un khesroynes* [virtues and defects]. The novel's political and social perspective is clear, but its characters are more nuanced even when they are rather unsympathetic individuals. The unfeeling rich are both criticized and humanized. The narrative perspective shifts among characters, exploring the complexity of each of their situations. Berman, who has and pursues wealth and considers himself superior to everyone, is also a loving son and a man nostalgic for the Eastern European Jewish life his family once led. His pampered son, Dovid, wears white spats that expose him as a dandy and a man incapable of productive labor, yet he seeks something meaningful to do with his life, something a later era would call "purpose." He fathers a child out of wedlock and leaves another man – a worker – to care for the mother and child. That woman, Gitele, deceives her husband, a poor socialist who eventually prospers and leaves his political commitments behind. Transgressions abound. Berman's daughter has a lover whose dissolute ways she finances. When she becomes pregnant, she seeks an abortion but cannot find a doctor willing to perform the procedure. Her parents arrange a marriage with an unappealing, much older man to avoid the scandal of an illegitimate child. Jewish women light candles on Friday night and then go to work. Although Kreitman's frankness about sexuality, abortion, and changing mores may appear controversial, these were inescapable topics in Yiddish literature of the period written by both men and women.

In *Diamonds* the struggle between generations, the rejection of the traditions of the past, has already happened and we are presented with its aftermath. There is no going back from the embrace of business instead of learning or the focus on individual greed and wealth instead of community or ritual. In his use of Yiddish and his religious observance, Berman's elderly, infirm father is a reminder of the past and is bewildered by his son's world. His Yiddish must yield to national languages. Yiddish is feminized as the language of the powerless, the aged, or women like Berman's wife who forgets to speak German in public. Yiddish is thus enshrined as *mameloshn* – the mother (and mother's) tongue – which also means that it is something the mature adult will grow out of and away from. Kreitman's rich Polish Yiddish prose belies this supposedly inevitable trajectory.

Kreitman is attentive to the physical environment and to history in this novel. Although men and women are subject to the same historical forces, they experience them differently. When, for example, men go to war in *Diamonds,* women go to work. There are no battle scenes in the novel, but the effects of war on individuals and families are inescapable. Kreitman is remarkably knowledgeable and detailed about the production and distribution of diamonds. She also offers vivid depictions of locales such as the Bourse in Antwerp and London, city streets, Hatton Garden, and Hyde Park Corner where the suffragette, Mrs. Pankhurst, makes an appearance. In this novel, as in almost everything Kreitman wrote, her main concerns are economic inequities and the plight of the poor.

All the characters in this novel are entirely fictitious.
Esther Kreitman

Chapter 1

None of Berman's people came to his office in Pelikaanstraat that day. There was no one clutching small paper parcels of diamonds and smiling ingratiatingly at the frosted glass door that led from the long, dark corridor into Berman's Holy of Holies. The office was shut.

In the homes of the diamond cutters the machines were silent, covered up like corpses. The women threw curtains or aprons over them, so that they didn't have to look at the cold, functional machines. At busy times, they sucked the lifeblood out of their husbands and sons, and at slack times they caused terrible tension in the household, when hunger and deprivation threatened.

Berman paced about agitatedly in his house, grumbling to himself. It was always the same. If there was some kind of holiday in the middle of the week, he would be overcome by a mood of black fury, which he was unable to shake off. Berman hated holidays, especially those Christian holidays, which had nothing to do with him. He was so used to his daily routine. In the early morning, Anneke, the maidservant, would bring in his viscous red medicine and, after taking it, he would lick his lips as if it had been a glass of fine wine. Then, having piously said his morning prayers, he would stretch himself up to his full height, crack his smooth, olive-skinned fingers and admire himself in the long polished mirror, which stood between the windows. He was indeed a fine figure of a man, with a well-combed, neatly parted beard, a thick silky moustache and intelligent piercing black eyes. Anneke would be waiting for him in the corridor, holding a brush, in order to remove the nonexistent fluff from his best black overcoat with its elegant velvet collar; he would take a last look in the mirror of the coat stand in the spacious hallway. He then stepped through the polished white front door, which Anneke held open for him, and walked to work.

It is the same routine every morning: as soon as he opens the door of the anteroom to his office, about two dozen yes men surround him, with inane smiles of false humility on their faces, grabbing the "good morning" out of each other's mouths, so that they can be the first to speak to Berman.

Berman knows that they all hate him like the plague but, nevertheless, he always gives the best work to those who manage the best smiles. "The poor can't afford to be proud," he says to himself. All the same, in his heart of hearts, he is annoyed with himself because, even though he doesn't like the Galician Jews, he always gives them his best diamonds. He tries to justify it to himself: "I hate paupers who put on airs!" He spits out the word "paupers," and starts poking around with his tweezers among the heaps of newly delivered diamonds, which look like small lumps of dried mud.

Berman carries on poking around until the men's hearts begin to sink and nervous blotches appear on their cheeks. Then he starts peering at the stones; he stares and stares, and if he doesn't find any blemish, if the stones have not been badly shaped by the cutter, he starts weighing them on his scales. Good, they haven't lost too much weight either. He pushes them to one side. Sometimes he makes one heap out of all the smaller piles. Sometimes he keeps the piles separate from each other, just as he keeps himself distant from the workers. Finally, he wraps up batches of rough diamonds in the little *brivkes,* or parcel papers. As a matter of course he warns the cutters to be careful the stones don't lose too much in the cutting. Then he holds out one parcel in the general direction of the crowd, who immediately rush forward like hens when the farmer scatters crumbs. Berman, however, doesn't let just anyone grab the package. His laughing black eyes flash, and he calls out: "Friedman!"

Little Friedman rushes up so fast that he almost lands on Berman's desk. The others stand there with outstretched hands. Eventually they are all crowding back down the narrow corridor, feeling that a weight has been lifted off their shoulders. "Thank God, got some work again!" they say with relief, although they know very well that tomorrow, and the day after, the whole procedure will be repeated. But it can't be helped and they are used to it.

Having got rid of the workers, Berman prepares himself to receive the brokers, whom he has sent out with his merchandise – his polished diamonds. He rubs his hands with pleasure. They appear one after the other. Berman greets them individually, with a special word for each one:

"Do sit down, Herr Rosenbaum! *Nu*, how are you, Herr Rosenbaum?" or: "Well, had any luck? No? What, still nothing? I beg you, Hatskelevitsh, don't play games with me. So? You really mean it? That's a fat lot of good to me!"

Berman enjoys hearing the brokers making flowery speeches, to persuade him to lower the price, so that it will be easier to sell the goods. He puts on a pensive air, his long nose gleaming and his black eyes smiling, and combs his beard with his fingers. The luckless brokers are swearing by their beards and sidelocks, by the lives of their wives and children, by God Himself, but Berman just cuts them off abruptly, saying there is no question of that at all, and calls Rosenbaum back in:

"Tell me, Herr Rosenbaum, you've already made some sales, haven't you? That's very good! And at a good price, you say? Excellent! That's what I like to hear. What?! Is *that* what you call a good price?"

"Listen, Herr Berman, if you're not happy with that, I'll take the goods back. They weren't all that keen to have them anyway."

Berman is taken aback, but he hides it with an ironic smile on his ruddy lips, speaking with an air of indifference:

"You're just making excuses, Herr Rosenbaum! With goods like mine I don't need, God forbid, to beg."

And he puts on his coat as a sign that he has to go to the Bourse immediately, and has no time to waste on nonsense. Rosenbaum accompanies him. He gesticulates all the way there, trying to persuade Berman that if he doesn't accept the price that has been offered, he will never be able to make such a good deal again.

"Huh!" replies Berman.

In the Bourse the noise and clamor are in full swing.

"Herr Berman, a parcel of blue-white?"

"I have some fine stones for you, Herr Berman, you've never seen the like of them. Fine goods, eh? I should have such luck!"

"Herr Berman!"

But Berman doesn't raise his eyes. Here, too, he sits poking with his tweezers. He is so absorbed in his work that you would imagine he would need at least twenty-six hours in every day, just to sort out his piles of diamonds.

This is Berman's normal routine. And now, out of the blue, a holiday! And a holiday like that, too! *Oy, oy!*

The Flemish people came out into the streets every year at this time to celebrate their annual *kermis* under the open sky. Every town and remote village kept this national holiday, but in Antwerp the festivities were greater than anywhere else. People from the nearby villages set out over the flat, sunny fields. Dressed in their best clothes, lighthearted groups poured along the highways and byways: over fragrant, mown grass in the bright sunlight, past golden sheaves of corn and stacks of still-damp hay. Old grandmothers were swaying along in little carts, their wrinkled faces bathed in sunshine, a smile in every wrinkle. The young people simply danced into town.

Hardly anyone, apart from old or sick people, stayed at home. And if a dilatory Antwerp housewife had not yet finished scrubbing the grey flagstones in front of her house, she hastily swept away the soapy water with her stiff brush and poured the last pails of water over them, at great speed, her wooden clogs paddling about in the wetness, like little boats, and tapping to the rhythm of her sweeping. Half an hour later, she was in the street, dressed up to celebrate the holiday.

Outside the cafes, on wicker chairs at green painted tables, stocky, red-faced Flemish men and women, both old and middle-aged, sat enjoying a glass of foaming beer. Infected by the gaiety of the young people, they joined in the singing of the popular Flemish song:

"*Oo-la-la!*
In het park van de nachtegaal

Ooooo-laaaa-laaaa!"

The girls' colored dresses dazzled the eye, and their ringing laughter delighted the ear. They threw bold, flirtatious glances and dimpled smiles, skillfully catching the eyes of the boys, and getting answering glances. The boys danced, played on mouth organs, strolled around among shiny automobiles, embracing and kissing different girls. Flags fluttered, ribbons streamed out, red, black and yellow.

Even the Bourse and the Diamond Club were closed, on account of the holiday. Rich Jewish diamond merchants had traveled abroad to the watering places. The middle classes had gone to Spa, and the minor traders and brokers, who traded in diamond powder and *bakvuils,* celebrated the Belgian holiday in Antwerp.

Berman was the only person who took no interest in the *kermis.* The singing in the street grated on his ears like the buzzing of an annoying fly. If he covered his ears with his hands, the muffled hum got on his nerves even more. He paced back and forth on the dark blue carpet of his dining room, which absorbed his footsteps and betrayed nothing. But his face spoke volumes. Every wrinkle told its story.

Suddenly, he stopped pacing about and surveyed the furnishings as if seeing them for the first time. The heavy silver pieces on the oak sideboard gleamed brightly at him. From the grandfather clock in the corner came a calm, regular ticking. The padded leather chairs stood solidly and at ease around the heavy table. A thin cobweb which, in such a spotless room, you would only notice on a very bright sunny day, stretched from the window to the mirror, which hung above the white marble mantelpiece. The room looked affluent, tranquil and harmonious.

"Huh! I've wasted my money on that no-good son of mine! It was pointless to let him study…thought he should get an education… should be able to do something that would stand him in good stead. And what's the result? Nothing! Why have I let these devils of sons grow up? I should have buried them at birth!" Berman had apparently forgotten that only *one* of his two sons, Dovid, was a "devil." "I thought I'd take him into the Bourse and make him a member. I'd introduce him to merchants; he'd start trading, work his way up, eventually make a rich marriage, and so forth. Isn't that what you'd expect? He's a good-looking, well-educated lad after all. And to marry into the Berman family is quite something! And with the big dowry he'd get, we could work as partners and expand the business. You can't entrust a fortune to a novice." Berman's face broke into a smile, and he spread his hands, as if to measure the exact area that the dowry would fill.

They would buy the largest parcels of diamonds, the very best merchandise. The biggest stones would fall into their hands. The most important merchants would regard it as an honor if Berman showed them a tiny parcel of blue-white. He wouldn't give the time of day to the small fry.

Suddenly, he realized that he was dreaming and gave himself a shake; his face darkened in anger and shame. Why on earth was he indulging in these fantasies?

"I'll tear him out, root and branch, the good-for-nothing! I'll chase him away like a dog. Away, out of my sight!"

The idea of chasing his son away soothed his nerves a little. He paced back and forth more calmly, concentrating on keeping the anger from rising up again inside him.

Chapter 2

A knock on the door roused Berman from his gloomy thoughts. He started straightening the chairs round the table, even though they were already straight. He smoothed down his square, silken skullcap, combed his beard with his fingers, and called out:

"Ah, it's you, Herr Shapiro! So pleased to see you!" he said, speaking elegant German, as he always did with business associates. He pulled out a heavy leather chair for his guest, and sat down at the top of the table.

"How are you, Herr Shapiro? Delighted to see you!"

Shapiro was a tubby little man with a black beard, trimmed into a neat, round shape. The whiteness of his plump face accentuated the blackness of the beard. He sat down, took out his spectacles, rubbed them with a piece of yellow chamois leather, held them up and examined them minutely, to see if they were properly clean. Then he set them on his nose with his podgy, white hand. His alert eyes took in everything in the room, and he quickly noticed that Berman was not in a good mood. "Aha! He's probably had another scene with that son of his. He thinks no one notices what's going on. Wait till I tell him the news, that'll really be the last straw!" He straightened his glasses and waited for Berman to begin.

"Well, how are things, Herr Shapiro?"

"Not bad, thank you. Thank God, one makes a living! And how are things with you, Herr Berman? Been doing good business?"

Berman looked sharply at Shapiro and gave a little sigh.

"No, unfortunately I've done no business at all! How can you do business when everyone has gone away? Damn these holidays!"

"You're absolutely right," agreed Shapiro, adding with a sly smile: "Have you heard the latest news, Herr Berman?"

"What latest news? No, I haven't heard any news at all."

"Oh, you haven't heard that Tsvaygnboym has made a match for his son?"

Berman trembled, and paled slightly. Shapiro looked at him over his glasses, enjoying his discomfort.

"*Azoy?* With Lieberman's daughter?" In his agitation Berman spoke Yiddish, instead of German.

"Yes indeed. And they *say* the bride is worth half a million francs. But I don't really believe that," said Shapiro consolingly.

Berman gave no answer, but he thought to himself that if Dovid were to appear at this moment, he would roast him alive. He started pulling at the fringes of the red plush tablecloth, then tapped on the table with his forefinger; but since the tablecloth muffled the sound, he started on the fringes again.

"So there you are!" continued Shapiro. "What a piece of luck for Tsvaygnboym. From now on he'll not have to worry about finding the money to buy diamonds. Heh, heh, heh!" And he gave a little laugh, which went right through Berman, grating on his ears, and jangling his nerves. He would have liked to have taken the roly-poly little man and thrown him down the stairs.

"Mind you, they say that the bride..." began Berman, about to remind Shapiro that Lieberman's daughter had a slight deformity. But Shapiro didn't let him finish.

"*Ach*, people say all sorts of things when they are envious. It's always the same!"

Berman knew that if this went on much longer he would make a fool of himself. To stifle his anger, which was now directed more against Shapiro than Dovid, he called his wife:

"Rosa, have some refreshments served."

His wife Rochl, who was only called Rosa in front of important visitors, took off her apron, turned down the gas in the oven, where half a side of veal was roasting, and came into the dining room, with flushed cheeks.

"The maid's gone out. These holidays are *such* a nuisance!" she said, excusing herself to Shapiro for bringing in the refreshments herself. Shapiro stood up like a gallant gentleman and made a peculiar bow:

"*Guten Tag,* Madame Berman!"

"*A gutn tog, a gut yor!*" answered Rochl, speaking simple Yiddish in her confusion. She sat down at the table with them and smoothed her wig, which had been specially coiffured for the holiday. She didn't know what to do next. Noticing that her husband was seething with suppressed rage, a situation very familiar to her, her heart began pounding. She prayed silently, begging God to spare her any embarrassment, by making Berman control his anger until Shapiro had left.

"Do take something, Herr Shapiro!"

"*Ach,* it *really* wasn't necessary. You shouldn't have gone to such trouble," said Shapiro, his darting eyes picking out the finest bunch of juicy, black grapes in the dish. He plucked at the grapes and told her the news about the engagement. Rochl blanched. She glanced at her husband and her heart sank. Shapiro's eyes glittered. He fixed his burning gaze on Berman, who sat rooted to the spot, staring into the distance. His thick, black eyebrows gave him the appearance of a wild man. He seemed transfixed, and with his large hand he pulled at the flesh of his own neck.

At last Shapiro got up to go.

"Well, don't forget, Herr Berman, I've got goods for you!"

This roused Berman from his stupor. He stood up, tried to smile, and asked Shapiro why he was in such a hurry, thinking all the time that it would serve him right, that Hungarian rogue, if he fell and broke his arms and legs on the way home.

His feelings of jealousy and rage at the news of the match, as well as shame at his weakness in letting Shapiro see his anguish, made Berman want to vent his frustration on someone. He looked round for Rochl, but she had gone downstairs with Shapiro and left the house. She went to the shop across the road to buy something she didn't need. When she realized that there was no way of avoiding the storm, she slipped softly back into the house. She peered through the keyhole of the dining room, her heart pounding. But her eyes lit up at what she saw; she could hardly believe her luck: Berman was sitting with his head on the table, both arms under his beard, snoring.

"Thank God for that!" she sighed with relief, and went into the kitchen. When she opened the heavy cast-iron door of the oven, a blast of heat reddened her face, and a delicious smell met her nostrils.

The meat had only started to burn on one side, and the rest was brown and juicy. "*Some* people get pleasure from their children," she thought, as she wiped the plates and prepared the dinner, remembering that her husband would probably wake up soon and, if not, she would have to waken him for his meal. "If only he hadn't had the mad idea that Dovid should marry that ugly creature! A handsome lad like my Dovidl, and her, a cripple, God forgive me for saying it! And now that Hungarian Don Juan, that Shapiro, comes along to add to my problems. He's not fussy whether they're old or young, and there are some old maids who would have him."

From the hall came the sound of singing:

"*Oo-la-la!*
In het park van de nachtegaal
Oooo-laaa-laaaaa!"

Their daughter Jeannette ran up the stairs three at a time.

"Oh my God, she'll waken her father." Rochl wanted him to carry on sleeping, but Jeannette's singing did, indeed, waken him. Berman stood up, gave a huge yawn, rubbed his right leg, which had got stiff during his nap, stretched, and came to the kitchen door, where he stood for a few moments, motionless. Then he came to, crossed the threshold, washed his hands and face, dried them on a white towel, and looked in the mirror over the sink. Rochl watched his every move and finally ventured to ask:

"Gedaliah, shall we eat?"

He didn't answer. That was the sign for the table to be laid.

"Jeannette darling, give me a hand, skip into the dining room, and set out the cutlery."

Jeannette made a face, but then she gave in, took a corner of her dress between her fingers and literally skipped into the dining room.

The clatter of dropped silverware and the sound of girlish laughter brought some life into the household. Jeannette came back into the kitchen, threw herself into the sagging armchair and carried on giggling. She had left the dropped cutlery on the dining room floor, and Rochl went and bent down with a sigh to pick it up.

The three of them sat at table, toying with their knives and forks. No one said a word. Jeannette knew that her father did not like anyone to talk at table. "No conversation at mealtimes," he always said. When they had finished, she went over to her father and took his head in her dainty hands. Berman trembled. The soft warmth of her young hands did him good. She kissed his beard, his moustache and his hairy cheeks.

"Promise you won't be cross, dearest Papa, if Mama comes with me to the Keyserlei? I'm going anyway, and it would be nice if she came too. You don't mind, do you? You should really come too, it's great fun. Even the pious Hasidim are out of doors today, winking at the girls. You should really come and see it."

"Listen to the girl! She doesn't know what she's talking about. Hasidim, winking at the girls? Fine sort of Hasidim!"

"What does she know? She thinks every man with a beard is a Hasid," said Rochl.

"Who are these Hasidim of yours, then?" asked Berman absent-mindedly.

"You see, Mama, I knew Papa would say yes. He's *such* a good Papa. *Dearest* Papa!" And Jeannette rewarded her father with a dazzling smile, just like she gave her young admirers.

"What do you say, Gedaliah, shall I go?"

"Oh well, I suppose even an old horse deserves a holiday!" That meant Rochl could go.

Jeannette flew down the stairs. Her mother, holding onto the banister, followed her more slowly. She stole a look in the mirror of the coat stand, and her heart beat faster as she thought, fleetingly, of the Hungarian Don Juan.

The youngest of her children, twelve-year-old Jacques, arrived just as they were leaving the house.

"Jacques, you can eat in the kitchen, do you understand? Don't go in to Papa, he's a bit on edge. And for goodness sake, don't make a noise. Do you hear?"

"All right, I hear you." Jacques leapt up the stairs, like a hare.

The Keyserlei was still buzzing with activity. You couldn't find an empty seat at a coffeehouse table for love nor money. The sun was scorching, and in the space of a couple of hours, women in low-cut dresses had red, sunburned chests. The air stank of roast pork, beer and baked potatoes. Oceans of beer had been poured down thirsty throats. Boys were singing bawdy songs and girls were throwing themselves into their arms. They danced on the pavements and in the middle of the street. The older people at the tables kept time to the music with empty beer glasses on tin trays, and, as they grew tipsy, they got daring enough to sing along, hoarsely:

"*Ooo-laaaa-laaa!*"

The Jewish women, all dressed up and wearing their best wigs, remained sober, but they joined in the fun with everyone else, laughing at the drunks. Jewish boys and girls walked openly, arm-in-arm, in front of all the rich women of Antwerp, not caring if they were gossiped about.

Rochl kept meeting acquaintances. "Well, what do you think of those *shnorrers,* forgive me for the expression! Those Tsvaygnboyms, and Lieberman's daughter. It's unheard of but such a piece of luck for them!" The women's words cast a shadow over Rochl's day. At the same time, she remembered that Dovid still hadn't appeared. Her main reason for coming out was the hope that she would meet him; otherwise, she told herself, she'd rather have gone to bed. It was now three or four days since they'd seen or heard anything of him, despite the fact that she had searched everywhere. God knows what had happened to him. And the atmosphere at home was worse than the fires of hell.

“Yes indeed, Frau Berman, better people than the Tsvaygnboyms wouldn’t be ashamed of such a stroke of luck!”

“Yes indeed,” sighed mothers of grown-up sons: “Well, may they only have good fortune!” They shook their heads with their newly coiffured wigs and, forgetting that they were walking in the crowded festive streets, had to scatter like hens when drunken lads, pushing their way through the crowds, elbowed and shoved them.

A filthy-looking boy grabbed Rochl round the waist. She nearly died of shock when he kissed her on the lips. “Pfui! Pfui!” She tried to spit out the taste of beer and pork, which the boy had left in her mouth. “Brrr!” Rochl shivered, and couldn’t understand why, just at that moment, the image of that Hungarian rogue, Shapiro, flashed into her mind.

Chapter 3

In Somersstraat, above a second-hand bicycle shop, a gentile woman in a blonde wig sat all day, scratching her bald head with a skewer, showering curses on the "idiots" on the second floor, a young Jewish couple, who came from the same Polish *shtetl* as the Bermans.

The two of them had come separately to Antwerp, and for very different reasons. The young man, Leybesh Bruckner, who back in the old country had been a brush-maker by trade, was a tall, healthy, brawny fellow, with straggly, fair hair like a gentile, and clear, greyish-blue eyes and a freckled face. Back in the *shtetl* the other Jews had not been very keen on him. No matter how affably he smiled at them, there was always someone who crossed the road in order to avoid him. They didn't answer his "Good morning" because they knew that the police had an eye on him. They didn't exactly know why. They did know, however, that it was simpler not to have anything to do with him.

"Did you hear that they arrested 'the prophet' yesterday?" other Jews would joke to each other: "he's a no-hoper, a real troublemaker."

"Of course I heard it," others would answer, adding sympathetically: "It's a shame for his mother. That poor widow, she stands all day on her swollen feet, burns her face at the oven, drags herself to the market to sell her biscuits, just so that her worthless lout of a son can eat his fill and use up her hard-earned groschen. I sometimes think old Meyer Aaron has it better than his wife, may she have long life!"

"*Ach!* He wasn't much better, may he forgive me for saying so. He let his wife slave away and all he did, so they say, was to sit reading worldly books. He made his son into a worker, and instead of studying the Talmud he only read the Bible with him. A fine son he made of him. What do you think?"

"And poor Feyge-Tsirl mourns that son of hers each time they take him to prison, as if he were dead. That's a mother for you."

"She suffers more than he does. He comes back hale and hearty; there's a devil in him."

"But all the same, our children should be protected from him," said the fathers and mothers, not realizing that their own children were already on the same path, for they were already Leybesh's disciples.

Reb Elyohu Kornhendler, the richest Jew in the *shtetl,* took the matter more seriously than anyone else. "Mark my words," he warned, pointing with his forefinger and making a fist of the other four: "It's a true saying that Satan doesn't only call at the other man's door. That scoundrel will spread his influence, God protect us! It's a mitzva, a good deed, to denounce him. Let them send him to Siberia, once and for all. If they don't, it'll affect us all. I'll denounce him myself. And if I speak to the police, it'll be to everyone's advantage – it'll be a mitzva!"

"As if Jews didn't have enough troubles," all the Jews in the *shtibl* agreed. Every one of them was glad that it was Reb Elyohu Kornhendler, and not he, who would be going to the police.

And certainly Reb Elyohu Kornhendler did carry out the task thoroughly, but it backfired on him. His own daughter, Gitele, a beautiful girl of marriageable age, also considered herself a bit of a socialist, even though she had not managed to plow her way through all of Karl Marx; she just couldn't make sense of him, even though she had a good brain. Nor could she get to grips with the various manifestos which she tried to read in bed at night; mostly she returned them to Leybesh unread. She was, however, a frequent visitor to Feyge-Tsirl's kitchen. She really loved its coziness, the free and easy relationship among the comrades, and the songs they sang while drinking glasses of weak tea. Every evening, they covered the kitchen window with a torn old quilt in order to muffle the sound of the discussions and singing. The boys and girls called each other "*du,*" and were just like one big family. Gitele particularly liked the way they shared books, cigarettes, food, and especially the warmth of their emotions. Though Feyge-Tsirl did not take part in their activities, she did not prevent them, but she often warned Gitele, the rich man's daughter, that it would be better for her not to come.

"It's not right for you," she would say. "These are poor people's children; let them do all these stupid things. But what are you doing here? If your father gets to know of it he'll be furious, and I'll be lucky to get out alive."

Gitele knew that this environment was not suitable for a Jewish girl of good family, and that in any case she was in danger of being caught, but what exactly was meant by "caught" she wasn't quite sure. One evening, however, she heard her father tell her mother during supper that the next day, with God's help, they would be rid of the scoundrel (she knew very well who that was), and only then did she realize that the whole business was actually dangerous. This attracted her even more to the kitchen, and she rushed out in the middle of supper, went to Leybesh and told him, word for word, what her father had said.

"Your father's a fool," joked Leybesh but nevertheless, the same evening he climbed out through the kitchen window and fled to Warsaw, and from there, to Antwerp.

Then a tragedy struck Gitele's family. Her mother suddenly became ill, and very soon was "snatched away" – as the old women who supplied her with chickens and fish put it. Gitele wandered round the elegant, empty rooms, which now seemed cold and lonely. She missed her mother very much. She began longing for the warmth of the evenings spent among her comrades in the poor little kitchen, and gradually she became convinced she was in love with Leybesh. Lying in bed at night, she would suddenly burst out crying for her dead mother, but she knew it was really Leybesh she was longing for. The cool silk of her thick feather quilt, and the fine, smooth linen of her sheets and pillows made her shiver. She felt the only place for her was that kitchen with its blackened, crumbling walls and the bright faces of the young comrades, for whom working towards a better life was a kind of religion. It filled them with enough warmth and love to melt stone. Karl Marx was their deity, and Leybesh, their simple, naive leader, was also a kind of God-like figure.

And the ironic name – "the prophet" – which the townsfolk had given him, became very dear to her. She felt it suited Leybesh. He never got any work as a brush-maker, nor was he temperamentally suited to that kind of work. He always went around empty-handed, and his eyes were full of spirituality, like those of a holy man.

Gitele's sufferings now increased. First, she missed her mother, who with her big apron and even bigger authoritative voice had filled all the rooms of the house with her presence. Now a cold wind blew through the elegant house, and Gitele could find no shelter from it. Second, Reb Elyohu Kornhendler decided that a Jew should not be without a wife. Evil temptations lurked round every corner, his house was empty, his daughter wandered around the rooms like a stranger, money disappeared far more rapidly than when his wife, God rest her soul, was alive, and at night in bed, he lay awake for hours on end. Strange thoughts went through his head that wouldn't be driven out, so that he couldn't sleep. So he went to see the *rebbe*, who told him he should get married again.

Gitele really hated her stepmother. She could not bear her taking her mother's place in the household, and every time she heard a butcher or fish seller calling her stepmother "Madame Kornhendler," Gitele put her hands over her ears. It broke her heart to see her father's new wife putting on her mother's jewelry. On her neck, the pearls looked to Gitele like scalding hot teardrops. Her father had even bought new trinkets for his wife, rings and bracelets, and he kept caressing her and flirting with her.

Gitele and her stepmother argued frequently. Once, after a particularly serious quarrel, Gitele decided to put an end to the situation. She simply couldn't stand any more. Her father felt the same. He listened to his new wife's complaints about Gitele. In a flood of words and tears she told him that his daughter begrudged her her position, and that she was saying things like, "Oh mother, why did you do it? Why did you let a stranger, an enemy, become the mistress in your house?"

"I'll go away," his new wife whimpered. "I'm scared of your dead wife. I don't want to stay here." As she spoke, gasping for breath, she shook her earrings, flashed the diamonds on her fat fingers, played with the pearls on her plump, white neck and sobbed: "Elyohu, I'm scared." And to heighten the effect, she started to take off her jewelry. Reb Elyohu Kornhendler was shocked and white with rage. He grabbed his wife by the arms:

"No!" he shouted hoarsely, "It's *your* jewelry, I gave it to you. You are to wear it in good health for the rest of your life."

He said quietly to his daughter: "If this doesn't please you, you are welcome to leave."

After weeping all night, Gitele decided to leave everything in her stepmother's hands and at dawn, when even the servants were still asleep, she got up and packed a satchel with her own pieces of jewelry: the necklaces, bracelets and rings which her father and mother and various aunts and uncles used to give her every birthday. She also took twenty rubles of her own money and set out for Antwerp, to join Leybesh.

Having been spoiled by her mother, Gitele went first to a fine hotel and enjoyed the good life, until she suddenly realized she had pawned almost all her jewelry. When she told Leybesh she hated the rich, and swore by her dead mother that she would never have anything more to do with her father and only felt close to Leybesh, he was dismayed. What on earth was he to do with her? He was almost starving. He did not have much faith in her hatred of the rich. But she was here and that was that. So he gave her his bed and slept on the floor. Gradually they bought one or two cheap pieces of furniture together, and before he knew it, they became lovers.

Chapter 4

Leybesh was now a diamond cutter, but he never had any work and spent whole days wandering about with nothing to do, just as he had in the *shtetl.* There was always something wrong with his work; sometimes he cut the stones in the wrong way, sometimes he cut away too much, and yet worse bunglers than he managed to keep their jobs. The bosses just did not take to Leybesh. They sensed that he was no friend of theirs. And he had another "virtue": he refused to curry favor, or give in, when the boss criticized him unjustly, and was determined to prove he was right. In the end the boss gave in to Leybesh, but at the same time gave him the news that unfortunately there was no work at the moment – perhaps another time. But the next time, the boss still didn't have any work for him. So Leybesh simply had to tighten his belt. It didn't bother him too much because he was used to it. A day with nothing to eat was quite normal and, indeed, he was really rather surprised on the odd occasion when he was able to fill his stomach and not feel the familiar gnawing pangs of hunger. It was only after Gitele arrived that he felt bad about these things.

When the Bermans learned that Reb Elyohu Kornhendler's daughter was in Antwerp, Berman began to enquire about her at the Bourse and at the Club. Rochl looked out for her in the Zoological Garden and the department stores, until one day she was absolutely delighted when she bumped into her on Pelikaanstraat.

"You look just like your mother!" she said.

"May she rest in peace," said Gitele.

Rochl was shocked to hear of her death. She asked Gitele all the details and invited her to their house.

And that was how Dovid Berman became a constant visitor at the Bruckners'. He gradually got used to the dark rooms, and a meal taken at the wobbly table with the worn oilcloth seemed like a banquet. At first the food had stuck in his throat, and he had chewed very gingerly, fearing that he was going to swallow something distasteful, but this soon changed. He stopped looking round all the time for a napkin when he realized that in Gitele's household such a thing did not exist. He saw that everything was in fact very clean, and it was only because the bits and pieces of second-hand furniture were old and worn, that everything looked so shabby. He gradually grew to love their poor home, and a warm feeling flooded over him as soon as he stepped across the threshold, a warmth which soothed him and filled him with contentment. So he kept coming.

For days at a time he would sit around their house, avidly following Gitele's every movement as she bustled about. He watched her as she rolled her sleeves above her elbows and started washing the clothes. This excited him. He found her thin, white, fragile-looking arms strangely attractive. Dovid had seen many half-naked women on the beaches in the summer or at winter balls, with smooth, white, plump, powdered arms, but none of these had attracted him like the trembling of the skin of Gitele's arms when she was at the sink. With her woman's intuition, Gitele soon sensed this, and started blushing coyly, and smiling with pleasure. Her heart began to dance. Sometimes she found herself singing as she worked, and her blonde plaits, the only inheritance left from her old home, became silkier and glossier. She started brushing her hair more often than usual, and the plaits swung forward over her narrow shoulders, almost covering her small breasts, which moved gently as she bent over the washing.

As this unspoken closeness developed between the two young people, Leybesh became more and more of a hindrance. Gitele no longer saw in him the deep-thinking person whose poverty had ennobled him in her eyes, increasing the mystery surrounding him.

Now she regarded him as nothing more than an irresponsible fool, a pauper and good-for-nothing, who could not even comprehend what a miserable state they were in. And it was into the arms of this man that she had flown!

Dovid came almost every day. Even though he was in a constant state of worry and agitation, and was bored to death with his life, he always managed to be clean-shaven and well turned out. He was always bareheaded, and dressed in a well-tailored suit, his gold pince-nez perched on his rather long nose. His face was smooth and of a dark complexion, his nails beautifully manicured. He wore gleaming white spats on his expensive shoes. His shirt was of the finest silk, with a wide black bow, like the Flemish actors wore. Moreover, he was an intellectual, a former student, and he possessed two season tickets, one for the Flemish opera and one for the French. Often, he carried a volume of Spinoza or Darwin around with him. And his eyes: deep, dark eyes which started smiling the moment they crossed Gitele's threshold. His sadness disappeared the moment he saw her. And Gitele's feelings overwhelmed her; she was helpless when he touched her. And so they became lovers, and she gave birth to a little girl.

Leybesh noticed that Gitele's face would light up and her eyes shine the moment Dovid came in, but this didn't surprise him. He said to himself that it was only natural, since they both came from affluent families and were both here in his poor dwelling by chance: the one from curiosity and a whim, the other because of indolence and bad luck. They recognized each other, for after all they were both of the same lineage! All the same, Leybesh did feel rather hurt, and he began to suspect that he himself was becoming fonder of Gitele than before. But he drove away these gloomy notions. In any case, he had no time for pointless thoughts like these, which occasionally creep into a person's head when he is feeling anxious.

He had already formed a "circle" in Antwerp. He was trying to set up a union, first of all getting together a library of socialist literature from Switzerland. It was easy to make propaganda here. No one bothered about it, and he already had a place where the comrades could meet. More than a year earlier, he had rented a room above a little synagogue. It still made him laugh when he remembered how he had got hold of this room. One Thursday evening he had been walking along Kievitstraat. As he was passing one house, he heard an old woman shrieking at the top of her voice. Beside her stood a man in a grimy, greenish frock coat with a darned collar and frayed cuffs, wearing a greasy skullcap on his head. He was waving a big red handkerchief in the air like a sword, and screeching even more loudly than the woman.

"I'm telling you once and for all: never on a Thursday!"

Leybesh was curious about this strange couple, and he tried to find out what was going on from someone in the crowd, but nobody gave him a proper answer. They just stood there, joking and laughing. Eventually someone enlightened him:

"You see, the poor old woman really has to work her guts out for a crust of bread. She says prayers for the whole town, poor soul, if someone pays her to do it. She isn't a *shnorrer* and she's grateful to God when she gets work and doesn't have to beg. She goes up to the room above the synagogue there, and prays as fervently as if she were praying for herself. When she has a good season, she works really hard and doesn't have to go begging round the houses – she doesn't *want* to live on charity. Sometimes, a mean woman who doesn't want to pay comes along and says her own prayers, but this doesn't worry her, even though it takes the bread out of her mouth. But she really has a hard time when nobody in the town is seriously ill and requiring her prayers. She has to live, so in that case she goes round the Jewish restaurants, trying to sell shoelaces or chocolate, and from time to time someone gives her some money out of charity. She isn't a bad woman."

"So why is she screaming? And what does the man want?" asked Leybesh, still puzzled.

"Well, recently he's got into the habit of locking up the synagogue on a Thursday and doesn't let the poor woman go up there. The rest of the week, he says, is all right, but not on a Thursday. It's a real shame," said Leybesh's informant, a pale, rather sickly looking woman, who spoke in a soft, emotional voice.

At last, the old woman buttoned up her grubby old overcoat, straightened her wig, which had gone askew, and, dragging her fat shapeless body, went wobbling off along the pavement, still cursing and sobbing. The crowd dispersed, and the old man wiped his sweating face with his dirty pocket handkerchief. Leybesh had an idea. He took the old man aside, and asked if *he* could have the little room on a Thursday.

At first, the man looked at him suspiciously, fingered his greasy whiskers and went into the courtyard to light a memorial candle in the synagogue. But when Leybesh fixed his serious eyes on him and said, "Sir, I mean business," the man looked at him again and said, "Not here: come into the synagogue!"

There Leybesh found out that the man had rented out this room to some young people who met there every Thursday; for what reason, the man didn't know. Leybesh offered two francs a week more, and so began his attempt to spread socialism in Antwerp.

Every Thursday, Leybesh dragged along a heavy suitcase full of literature, which he distributed among the few young men and women who gathered there, and on Friday he would cart the suitcase back home. In the little room, they chatted, smoked, debated, and even sometimes held a party for a male or female comrade, who had stopped in Antwerp, on their way to America.

Leybesh worked very hard. He didn't have an easy time of it, because most of the young people who came to Antwerp were young Hasidim who were fleeing to avoid being called up to the army, and knew that Antwerp was a town with many religious Jews. Leybesh realized that there was no point in trying to influence any of them. They had been old men from the day they were born, with rigid ideas which they had inherited from their fathers, grandfathers and great-grandfathers. After work, people like them would sit studying all evening in all kinds of little *shtiblekh*. They say you can't make bricks without straw, but Leybesh was an optimist, and didn't let himself be daunted. His friends joked that even if he had no friends at all, he would still form a union consisting of one.

So he tried to find a way of organizing the Jewish workers in Antwerp. He endeavored to make contact with the leaders of the non-Jewish union to discuss with them the degeneracy of the bosses and the oppression of the Jewish worker: every parasite persecuted and exploited him, crushed and humiliated him, maligned him as a fawning sycophant, and saw to it that he lost his body as well as his soul. Afterwards, when everything had been sucked out of him like a flower after a bee has visited it, the persecutor did not even give him what the bee gives the flower. No, the boss would then simply exchange him for a younger worker, very often the worker's own son. Leybesh tried to explain all this to the secretary of the union.

While he was speaking from the depths of his heart, depicting with great earnestness the life of the Jewish worker, the secretary was leaning back in his swivel chair, smoking a fine cigar, listening intently, smiling graciously behind his blond moustache. He didn't interrupt Leybesh, but let him carry on till he had said all he wanted to. When Leybesh had finished, the secretary gave him a cigar and told him in a very friendly tone that unfortunately it was not possible for him to admit a Jew to the union. Leybesh asked why not but, like a true diplomat, the secretary apologized, saying that unfortunately he was not able to divulge the reason. But Leybesh was not deterred. He thought that if he could just manage to express himself better to this idiotic secretary he would be able to show him that, of course, it was possible to admit Jews to the union. This was a civilized country, and it must be possible to get the better of asinine, self-satisfied secretaries. It was just a question of determination. So Leybesh decided to start learning Flemish properly, because without being fluent in the language of the country it was impossible to achieve anything. Very often, even while he was deep in thought about his work, an image floated into his mind, Leybesh didn't quite understand why, of Gitele and Dovid, together in his room, on the second floor.

Of all the Antwerp diamond merchants, Berman was the greatest expert in persecuting workers, especially Leybesh. He had no respect for manual workers, regarding them with even more contempt than he did the small-time diamond traders, who bustled around the exchange. The traders were, at least, trying to better themselves.

In the beginning, when Gitele had just arrived in Antwerp, and was still going around dressed in a manner that was appropriate for a daughter of Kornhendler's, with the necklaces, rings and brooches which so impressed Berman (even though all day he was up to his elbows in diamonds), he still had respect for her. But the moment he heard she was living with Leybesh, this changed to contempt. The prestige she had brought with her from the old country simply disappeared, like the sun behind a cloud. He soon stopped giving Leybesh any work, pretending that he wanted him to send Gitele.

"Send your wife to me. It's a shame that you should have to waste your time." And when Berman found that Leybesh did start sending his wife, and that she wasn't even embarrassed about it anymore, because the hunger was gnawing so strongly and she had to produce milk for the baby, he started looking for excuses. He got into a rage with her, regarding her as a *shnorrer*, completely ignoring the fact that she was a rich man's daughter.

"No, unfortunately, I have just allocated the last piece of work. What a shame, if you had only come an hour earlier." Berman always had an excuse, and not only did he not give her any work, but he poured salt in her wounds, by continually asking her about her father, how he was and what he had written to her.

"*Ach*, he was always my best friend."

Eventually Gitele was fed up with this game; her blood boiled and one day she slammed the door of Berman's office. From then on they became even poorer.

Leybesh took to going out a lot, and Gitele certainly did not grumble about this. No matter how late he came home, she didn't say a cross word to him, because Dovid had got into the habit of bringing supper with him, which they ate together. And after the meal, when Gitele began feeding the baby, Dovid was in seventh heaven.

He would have been happy to sit there for hours, watching the baby sucking, grabbing her mother's breast with her tiny hand, squeezing it so hard with her little fingers that Gitele had to bite her lip. He saw how the little mite held onto the breast with all her strength, as if she was afraid that it was going to be taken away again. The baby sucked greedily, the tiny veins standing out clearly on her temples as if someone had embroidered a blue lacy design there. Dovid was filled with joy when he saw Gitele's blue eyes smiling with motherly tenderness as she looked down at the baby, delighted that her milk had not dried up, and that she was still able to feed her. And Dovid began to regard these two creatures as his little family, and Leybesh as a rival or, at the very least, as an unwelcome guest who disturbed their intimate closeness in their warm little home.

Leybesh sensed the truth and yet didn't see the situation completely. Whenever Dovid had one of his quarrels with his father, it was Leybesh who suggested that he should stay with them until the storm blew over.

On one such occasion, the third night he had stayed at the Bruckners', just before the *kermis,* things came to a crisis for Dovid. "How is all this going to end?" he asked himself, but could not find an answer. There was no question of going back home. He had left, after such a serious quarrel that both his mother and Jeannette had been in tears. He only had the clothes he stood up in, and it was several days since he had had anything at all to eat. The few francs he had possessed had been used up; he had spent them on Gitele, convincing her that he had eaten during the day at a friend's house, and so forth. She saw through this but, seeing the pleading in his eyes, she realized that she should accept it, and not ask any questions. So she ate the food, although it stuck in her throat, and said nothing.

Now it was night. Dovid was lying on the shabby bed, unable to sleep. It was too hot and too bright; through the torn blind strips of light shone onto the floor, the table, and onto his bed. Apart from this, he could not help imagining that Gitele was whispering secrets to Leybesh in the bedroom.

And while he was lying there, listening, Leybesh, tall and broad shouldered, came into the kitchen in his underpants, with bare feet and tousled hair, and an unhealthy pallor on his face. He was walking on tiptoe, so as not to waken the guest. Dovid stirred and wanted to ask something, not really knowing what.

"Shhhh! Go to sleep! Sorry for disturbing you." Leybesh waved his hand and moved towards the gas stove.

"What is it?" asked Dovid.

"Nothing at all, really. But who was it who said it's hard to be a Jew? I say: it's hard to be a *father.*"

Leybesh lit the stove. Dovid saw a blue flame and heard the hissing of the gas. Leybesh was heating up a little water for the baby, who had a tummy ache. And it was Leybesh who was standing there, barefoot and half-naked, dealing with it.

Dovid was overcome by shame and started sweating. The baby began crying and he heard Gitele talking to her:

"Shhh! Shhh! Don't cry, my darling!"

A dull numbness came over Dovid. The shame he felt about his behavior towards his friend, whom he was betraying so despicably, overwhelmed him. He felt so mean and worthless that he wished the ground would open up and swallow him. One more minute, he thought, and he would spring out of bed and scream out loud into the night:

"Look at him standing there, the idiot, letting himself be made a fool of!"

He took refuge in spiteful cruelty. "But why does he not see what's going on? Why is he so blind? Why does he put up with it?"

"Go back to sleep. Don't worry about it," said Leybesh.

Dovid's anguished thoughts were screaming inside him and he was bathed in sweat: "It's hard to be a father, but even harder to be a filthy, treacherous, cowardly good-for-nothing." The child screamed even more loudly, and Dovid was filled with pity for the baby and a strange anger towards Gitele. She had no right to betray Leybesh in this way. When this flashed through his mind, he took fright at his own thoughts, and felt a terrible choking tightness inside.

Leybesh went back into the bedroom. Gitele comforted the baby and Dovid heard her talking to Leybesh. Dovid looked into his own soul and, covering himself with the patched quilt, he burst into tears like a child.

Chapter 5

At dawn, Dovid left the house, taking care not to wake anyone up. Like a thief, he very quietly stole down the steps from the narrow corridor and closed the door behind him, silently. His inner torments had left him exhausted; he was hungry, and had a bad headache, but his body felt light. Walking in the poor street in his elegant clothes, he looked like a drunken actor who had lost his way and wandered into this district from some nightclub or other.

The street was sunk in restful sleep. The shabby houses with their closed wooden shutters were already bathed in bright, pure, almost silvery sunlight. Behind the narrow, dirty shop windows, lay goods for sale in untidy heaps. Cats were dozing on doorsteps. Today there weren't any bins, full of refuse, beside the gutters. These were usually placed there by the housewives and shopkeepers, to be taken away by the dustmen. Their absence made the impoverished district look a little more festive.

The arrival of the milkman brought a bit of life into the sleepy street. His cart, decorated with gleaming brass and filled with milk cans, rattled merrily in the emptiness of the street. He stopped at every door, driving the cats from the doorsteps, leaving a can of milk and calling out his familiar "*Melkboer!*" He swiftly worked his way right down Somersstraat, hurrying because he wanted to be finished early so he could enjoy the holiday.

"*Dag menieër!*" said the milkman to Dovid, as if he had known him for years. "It looks as if we'll have a good *kermis,* don't you think? It's nice weather, eh, *menieër*?"

"Yes indeed, it looks like it." Dovid glanced up at the clear sky and hurried away from the street.

He started walking in the direction of Borgerhout. Some women were standing around. They had already scrubbed the pavement and the ground floors of their houses, cleaned the brass door knockers and poured enough pails of water to put out a fire. They also wanted to get finished early and enjoy the holiday. Dovid repeatedly raised his hat in response to the "*dag menieërs*" from unknown housewives.

"Hallo!" Someone was stretching out a soft warm hand to Dovid, who was delighted when he saw who it was.

"Jules! What are you doing in the street so early?"

"What do you mean? It's the *kermis* today!"

"So why are you in such a hurry?"

"Why are *you* in such a hurry?" retorted Jules Tsvaygnboym, immediately feeling a bit embarrassed by the familiar tone he was adopting. He was speaking to Dovid as if he were his equal, as if something had changed in their relationship, and this disturbed him.

"No, I really mean it," continued Jules. "Can one actually sleep on a day like this? Something draws you out of bed and into the streets. What a glorious day it is! Perhaps…" Jules was about to ask Dovid something, but hesitated. He pondered a little, glanced at Dovid, and seeing that the latter looked like a ghost, he ventured to make his suggestion: "Perhaps we could even celebrate the *kermis* together?"

Dovid had no intention of celebrating any kind of festival today, even though he did so every year. He framed his "no," but Jules was already walking along beside him, chatting, telling stories, and even infecting Dovid with his laughter. So they walked back into the town together.

The wagons from the villages had begun arriving, and the streets were already full of young people. The bright sunshine and the mixture of girlish laughter and good-humored oaths aroused in Dovid a genuine desire to celebrate the holiday. He forgot about the night and said: "Fine! Let's celebrate!" and Jules was delighted. "But first we must eat something," said Jules, thinking, as usual, of his stomach.

Dovid remembered that he hadn't a single centime to his name.

He, too, desperately needed to eat, but didn't want Jules to know about his predicament.

"What do you think, Dovid?" said Jules. "The thing is, I ate hardly any breakfast before I came out. I just grabbed whatever I could find. At home they're all sleeping like the dead," Jules chattered on. "And what about you, Dovid, have you already had breakfast?"

"No, actually, I haven't eaten a thing. But to tell you the truth, I haven't a single centime on me. I just came out for a walk and forgot to bring my wallet." Dovid blustered in his embarrassment.

"I'll pay, that doesn't matter at all."

"No, not at all, tomorrow I'll give you back what I owe you." And they went into a restaurant.

"Hey, over here, *garçon*," Jules called with cheerful assurance. It seemed to Dovid that Jules was addressing the waiter too arrogantly. He felt annoyed, as if he had been in the waiter's place.

The waiter, however, was not offended. Indeed, he appeared immediately, in response to the call, a short, fattish man with a flushed face, gleaming, fair hair and wearing a black frock coat, with a white napkin over his arm. He bowed and said: "*Menieër?*"

Jules looked at his watch: "Look, it's ten o'clock already, how time flies! It's no wonder I'm dying of hunger. Should we order sole?"

"Yes, that's fine," said Dovid, who was dying to see food on the table, no matter what it was.

The waiter came with two good portions of fish. After they had finished, Jules wiped his greasy lips and discussed with Dovid the fact that it was permitted to eat sole; it wasn't meat, so it was kosher. Dovid agreed that sole was kosher. Jules rubbed his cheeks and said casually:

"What do you think about my brother?"

"What are you talking about?"

"What do you mean? Have you not heard? Bernard has got engaged, and he's getting a hundred thousand francs, what's more, *and* a watch with diamonds the size of hazelnuts."

"I don't know anything about it," said Dovid, who knew only too well. Bernard's engagement had already caused him enough problems.

"Have you really heard nothing? Everyone is talking about it, I tell you. Diamonds the size of hazelnuts, that's not to be sneezed at! It's Lieberman's daughter he's engaged to."

"And what do you think about it?" asked Dovid.

"What should I think? If you make your bed, you have to lie on it; if he has consented, then I certainly wish him luck. With the greatest pleasure!" and Jules' corpulent body shook with mirth: "Ha-ha-ha! If you make your bed, you have to lie on it!"

Jules paid the bill, joking and laughing. Having drunk a fair number of glasses of beer so early in the morning, he was a little tipsy, and he took Dovid's arm as affectionately as if he were a girlfriend. They walked off towards the Sheldt in companionable silence.

The broad river sparkled merrily in the sunshine, dancing playfully around the little boats full of passengers, color, and singing. Everything was in constant movement. Passengers were disembarking and new ones embarking, to sail to Sint-Anneke. Workers, warmed by the sun and eager for the bright outdoors, the fresh air, the green trees and birdsong, stood in long queues waiting for a tiny space in one of the boats. They whiled away the time by singing folk songs, making jokes, and telling off their children. And the waves were swelling, flowing into each other, one swallowing another and then spitting them out again. Seagulls flew overhead with outspread wings, clamoring for food. The boats cut through the golden sunshine. Rays of sunshine flowed over the boats and the people with a warm caress, which raised their spirits.

From the distance, Sint-Anneke was a huge expanse of colorful movement. Girls were cavorting on the grassy meadow, and kissing and embracing their boyfriends. Their arms round each other, they were free to romance under the open sky, before the whole world, before the singing birds, which were flying from tree to tree and hopping from branch to branch. The birds were imitating the young people in the meadow, kissing each other, eating crumbs of bread from the outstretched hands of children, and generally enjoying the holiday. Men were kissing and cuddling their wives, as if for the first time. Little children were running around the meadow, getting under people's feet, and throwing themselves on their parents, giggling madly because they had caught Mummy and Daddy doing something naughty.

Dovid and Jules had just got off the boat, and before Dovid had time to turn round, he found himself being pulled down onto the damp grass by the shore. He stood up and tried to apologize to the blonde girl who was lying face down on the grass, giggling. But before he could say anything, the girl caught hold of his right leg and pulled him down to her, so that again he was lying on the grass beside her.

"God save us!" she shrieked and started shaking with laughter. Jules saw what was going on and flung his fat body down on the grass, almost crushing the friend of the girl, who was lying beside her. As if they had already arranged it, all four got up and went off for a walk in the field like old friends. They found nicknames for each other: Zhaneke, Maneke, anything which occurred to them, what did it matter? As long as they were having fun. Dovid threw himself into the holiday mood with savage fervor. He forgot all the problems which his father had heaped on him. He forgot that he didn't have a single centime in his pocket. He even forgot the searing pain he had felt the previous night, and all his anger.

When the sun began to set, the Sheldt was suffused with red, and the little waves looked like flames dancing on the water. Couples with children had begun gathering up their empty baskets, jugs, bottles and pots, which had held milk and food. The sky darkened, but it was still full of color: red, purple, rose-pink, copper, with streaks of dark blue. Tired children were carried on their fathers' shoulders. The young people were still singing lingering melodies with tired voices. Dovid, Jules and the two girls were already back in the town. Ravenously hungry, they went into a restaurant, sat down at a wet table littered with empty beer bottles and discarded cigarette ends stubbed out on plates, and waited for the exhausted waitress to come and serve them. She didn't come at once. Like a hunted animal she was running from table to table, and still couldn't satisfy anyone. Everyone was clamoring to be served, getting cross, complaining. Only these four had plenty of time. The girls shrieked with laughter at Jules' jokes, and Dovid hummed a song. When the waitress did finally appear, Jules ordered such a sumptuous supper that even he was satisfied.

They looked around the town and, not seeing any other Jews around, they started kissing and cuddling the girls and, after arranging to meet again, they set out for home. A delicious tiredness flooded through the limbs of the two sinners. "Are you drunk, Dovid?" laughed Jules, who could hardly stand upright.

The two friends wandered through the narrow streets of old Antwerp, where the poor people had come out into the street in honor of the holiday.

All year long, these dark, crooked streets are empty and desolate, and the silence tells dismal tales. In the taverns, girls sit all day long behind pieces of looped-back curtain, smoking cheap cigarettes, knitting, and keeping a lookout for possible clients. But if a sailor does happen to come past, he is usually penniless. His worn blue linen trousers, sunken cheeks and dull eyes bear witness to his poverty. His eyes light up briefly when he sees the girls, but they don't even interrupt their work for him. The sailor lowers his eyes and the girls realize he is ashamed. He can't even afford to come in and drink a glass of beer with them, which would give them a chance to escape, briefly, from their constant vigil behind the looped-back curtain. Sometimes a girl will take pity on one of these sailors but, mostly, she curses both him and his poverty.

In the evenings, things become more cheerful here. The curtains are drawn back and a greenish light pours out, illuminating the black uneven stones of the pavements which are so narrow that people can only walk one abreast. On Sundays, there is more going on during the daytime too. And if there is a holiday, especially the *kermis*, then there's a real celebration. The notices in the windows advertising "room to rent" are superfluous because there isn't a single inch of space to rent. The serving girls have their hands full. From all sides people try to attract them to their table: "Here, miss, over here!"

Today it had been especially lively. From early morning, the sun had shone brightly into the attics and cellars, not allowing anyone to sleep. The excursions to Sint-Anneke had begun earlier than usual, and people had poured from the narrow, crooked alleyways, which run into each other. Now, returned from Sint-Anneke, they all made for the taverns, crowding the streets, weaving around drunkenly, in a swirling mass of life; not like human beings with individual self-consciousness. The poor toiling dockworkers poured out into the street, like free citizens, to celebrate their annual *kermis.* Even the tiny patches of sky visible above the rooftops seemed prisoners, like themselves. Just as those people still looked dirty after they had taken a bath, so the sky here always looked dark, even on the clearest nights, even on this bright night of the *kermis.*

But was anyone looking at the sky? Old and young were dancing, kissing, embracing and weeping drunkenly. There were good-natured curses, people pushing each other off the pavements, joking, and neighing like horses. Women were trying to outdo the men and each other with jokes and quips, children were tripping people up and getting slaps, which they accepted philosophically and then carried on prancing around. Children with less stamina were falling asleep on doorsteps or in the middle of the street, running the danger of being trampled by their own drunken mothers. Some of the good-natured joking developed into bad feeling, and quarrels broke out; from time to time, a normally quiet respectable worker was led off to spend the night in the police cells, accompanied by drunken shouts, wails from his wife and curses for the policeman who took him. But after a while they forgot all about it and began singing a mixture of the bawdiest ditties and the most beautiful folk songs.

And so they celebrated the *kermis:* the poor man in his fashion and the better class of people in theirs. Both filled the pockets of the innkeepers and made the serving girls' lives a misery. The town stank of pork fat and all kinds of shellfish, eels, fried potatoes, malt vinegar and sweat.

Dovid made his way out of the drunken crowd. At least he had managed to forget the quarrels with his father and, humming a festive song, he went back to his father's house, threw himself into bed fully clothed and, a moment later, he was snoring like a real drunk.

Chapter 6

After Rochl had left with her daughter, Berman had a little nap with his head on the table, as he usually did. He woke up thinking that about ten minutes must have passed, only to find that he had been sitting there for hours. He felt strangely lonely. Stretching and yawning, he looked round the room. Not finding anyone to get angry with, he went into the kitchen to make himself a glass of tea. Despite the heat, a chill went through his body. It didn't feel like summer at all.

When he crossed the threshold and saw Jacques eating a large plateful of potatoes, he was really pleased.

"When did you come in?"

Jacques was startled. He put his hand on his heart and swore: "Papa, I promise you that I came in at lunchtime. That's the honest truth. You can ask Mama." With his spoonful of potato halfway to his mouth, Jacques kept on protesting: "I promise... honestly..."

"All right, all right, I believe you, you little rascal. Go on, eat!"

Jacques didn't need much persuasion. He had been running about all over the town and was ravenously hungry.

The gleaming copper kettle was singing comfortingly. Berman prepared his tea and turned off the gas. He took a glass down from the shelf, wiped it, held it at arm's length and looked at it against the light of the sunny window, just like he did with diamonds when he wanted to see their true brilliance. He poured himself a glass of tea. By this time, Jacques was eating his stewed fruit.

"Jacques, don't go out again. You'll come with me to the synagogue for the evening prayers, do you hear?"

Jacques nearly choked on his stewed fruit. Go to the synagogue on carnival day?! He had been gobbling down his potatoes while they were still burning hot, so that he could rush back out, and now this! He tried to protest, but Berman wouldn't listen. He took his tea into the dining room, leaving Jacques in despair in the kitchen. Jacques started writing with his finger on the windowpane, and thinking out arguments to use with his father:

"*Please*, Papa. May I never come back home again if you make me come to synagogue with you. All the other boys are outside today." But Berman felt that everyone had deserted him today and finding Jacques at home was some kind of miracle. He would not be moved by Jacques' pleading. The cold in Berman's bones had not been dissipated by the hot tea.

"Maybe, God forbid, Dovid has committed suicide." Berman shuddered, as this thought suddenly passed through his mind. "No! Not that! Not that!" a voice inside him kept repeating. He held the glass of tea in his hands, trying to warm himself a little. If Dovid came back now, this instant, he would not say anything bad to him. But this very thought brought his anger back again, and he sipped the tea and groaned as if he were in pain. Towards evening he went to the synagogue, taking Jacques with him.

In the synagogue there was certainly something to talk about today; the name of Tsvaygnboym was on everyone's lips.

Tall young men with thin red, blond or black beards, dressed in black or dark grey coats and striped trousers, some with a pince-nez on their thin noses, their hats pushed back on their heads, were crowding round Tsvaygnboym, nodding absent-mindedly, with greedy smiles on their lips, shaking his hand and wishing him *mazel tov.* What they all really wanted to ask him was that he should think of them when, God willing, he received the dowry. Some of them did actually ask, others bit back the words, putting it off till the next day. There were some men with broad beards, whose laughing eyes with their myriad creases and wrinkles only concealed their desperation. Their hats were twisted and so were their heads, from so much worrying over buying and selling diamonds, and managing to provide for *Shabbes.*

Even now, after such a stroke of luck, Tsvaygnboym's eyes had not lost their permanent worried expression. He saw that not a single shred of his beard would be left, and so he started plucking it himself, in order to save it from strangers' hands. But the Jews were resourceful, and since the beard was not available, buttons and lapels were also a possibility. One man almost plucked out his own beard, which was rather scrawny to begin with. He sucked his sunken cheeks into his toothless mouth, and pleaded with Tsvaygnboym with so much anguish in his forced smile that Tsvaygnboym's heart bled for him. He recognized the situation he himself had been in only the day before, and he made up his mind to help this man, if the engagement actually did take place and the dowry materialized.

"Do I need to tell you," the old man continued in an urgent tone, "that the value of diamonds is rising from minute to minute? I think you know this better than I. So I'm advising you, as a true friend, you should invest in diamonds now. Nowadays, when you buy a batch of stones, you've really got something in your hands. And you know that I, thank God, have access to the most important firms. They all know me and they daren't ignore me. They're well aware that I have numerous mouths to feed. *Ach! ach! ach!*" The man looked up at the ceiling, apparently seeking the One who could help, but seemed unwilling to do so: the Lord of the Universe.

"I won't, God forbid, forget anyone!" Tsvaygnboym reassured the crowd, just as you would try to placate a robber, so that he will spare your life.

When he saw Berman, he went to greet him.

In the town, Berman was regarded as an extremely wealthy man. Tsvaygnboym told him the news about the engagement, and invited him very respectfully to come to the signing of the contract.

"Good evening, Herr Tsvaygnboym!" said Berman with a smile on his face. "I have indeed heard the news. Well, let it be with *mazel*."

"He's already hobnobbing with the rich," muttered Tsvaygnboym's new friends, begrudging him this honor.

"Well, let him hobnob," interrupted one young man. "I wouldn't mind having the fifty or even twenty thousand, which he thinks he'll get, and won't." The young man was being moderate and taking eighty thousand francs off the promised amount of the dowry. "You know Lieberman's tricks. He did the same thing with his first daughter: promised a hundred thousand and actually gave ten. And, of course, the son-in-law was too ashamed to admit what an idiot he had been, and the fools in the Bourse believed he had got the dowry and were happy to give him credit. Well, anyway, at least it gave people something to talk about. And since he duped the first one, he's certainly going to do the same with this pauper. Lieberman will give him a hundred thousand plagues instead of francs."

"That's to say, he'll give him his daughter," laughed the young men.

"Believe me, that swarthy-looking man there," they said, pointing at Berman, "has more money in his breast pocket than Lieberman has in the world. He's all talk, is Lieberman. He really thinks you can fool everyone."

"Well, he's right too," a plump, clean-shaven man with a smiling, red face and round, black, owlish eyes, said gleefully.

Berman finished congratulating Tsvaygnboym, wished the bridegroom *mazel tov* as well, and stopped to chat with various people. He spoke little, but he heard a lot, and what he heard pleased him very much.

"Well! A hundred thousand, eh?! So that's how he does business, the rogue!"

And the smaller the dowry was reported to be, the more his anger against Dovid abated.

He accompanied Tsvaygnboym home. They chatted about business, and he asked casually about every detail of the dowry, and whether it had already been paid. He wasn't asking, God forbid, just out of nosiness, but purely as a friend. A hundred thousand francs, said Berman, is a good sum, and he looked Tsvaygnboym in the eye, dying for him to deny the amount. But Tsvaygnboym just agreed that it was a good sum.

"Thank the Lord, may His name be praised, I have nothing to grumble at, God forbid!" Tsvaygnboym continued, and Berman consoled himself with the thought that the man was a gullible fool, a real loser. You could persuade him that a bundle of straw was a plate of noodles.

When he got home, Berman's first question to Rochl was about Dovid. "Have you heard anything?" he asked anxiously. "God save and protect us, I hope nothing's happened!"

"He's back! I don't know where he's been, but when I came back I found him sleeping in his clothes. Poor boy, he looks absolutely exhausted. Gedaliah, please go easy on him, you've got to go easy on your own child."

Berman became impatient. He had been worried sick, and here she was going on at him, the stupid woman.

"Go easy on him? I'll go easy on him, all right!"

But supper was more cheerful than usual. Berman made a pretense of being in a good mood. In fact he was relieved that Dovid had not, God forbid, done anything to dishonor his name. In truth he had been really worried about him. It seemed that he wasn't destined to have joy of his son. Well, so be it. The Lord, may His Name be praised, would probably give him joy of the other two children. He stole a glance at Jeannette. "She's a wonderful girl, *ken eynore.* I must protect her like a precious diamond." But all the same, there was still something weighing on his heart, filling him with melancholy. He realized that during supper he had not yet given anyone an order, or lost his temper with anyone.

So he turned his attention to Jacques. "Jacques, go to bed." As usual, Jacques tried to bargain:

"Please, Papa, please, Mama, just a little while!"

But it was no use. After he had said the grace after the meal, Berman took Jacques by the ear, and personally took him off to the bedroom, which he shared with Dovid. Berman looked at Dovid's bed, wanting to reassure himself that Dovid really was back home. Rochl, feeling very tired, went into her bedroom, not even clearing up after the meal. Berman himself put away the prayer book which Jacques had left lying on the table. He took a religious book off the bookshelf, tried to read it, but the words wouldn't make sense.

"Hm! Even ten thousand francs is a fortune for that pauper! Ten thousand! Ten thousand! These words danced on the page. But he became uneasy once more. "But perhaps it actually *was* a hundred thousand? Who knows?" He had been slaving all his life to earn this much, he had had a rough time of it, and now a loser like this who couldn't hold a candle to him was to become his equal. Certainly Lieberman's daughter was no oil painting; to be honest, she was rather ugly. Apart from all this, Berman's father intended to pay them a visit. He said he wanted to see his grandchildren. Oh dear! What would he think of them?

Berman took a letter out of his pocket and read it over and over again. His father wrote that Berman's brother was, thank God, in perfect health, and he himself was feeling a lot better, so since the brother had taken over the shop after his mother's death, the well-off townsfolk had collected money for his journey and he intended, God willing, to come to Antwerp to visit his son. He had heard that Antwerp was, praise God, a Jewish city and that Gedaliah kept, thank God, a Jewish home. And he knew that Gedaliah would, with God's help, receive him with honor, because he had always been dutiful to his father. How well he had looked after him during the two years that he had lain in bed – it shouldn't happen to a Jew! So they would, God willing, see each other soon. And so on.

Berman put the letter away again and tried to read his book. But it was as if the events of the day were printed on the page, and the words would not hang together.

"Huh! Grandchildren! Such a loser... ten thousand!"

Berman realized that he was struggling to no avail, so he put the book back in its place, and recited *krishme,* pacing about the room as he prayed.

Chapter 7

The whole household was still asleep. Every day it was the same routine: as soon as he heard the milkman's cry and the muffled rattle of the can on the doorstep, he got dressed.

The maid was dozing on the iron bed in her little room. She rubbed her sticky eyes and hoped that a miracle might occur: that the master would sleep in because of the holiday the day before, and that she wouldn't hear the hated clatter of the wooden roller blind in the dining room being pulled up, announcing that she had to get up because he wanted a glass of *bavarke*, his favorite sweetened milk drink. She was dead tired after the celebrations and had a great desire to turn over to face the wall and carry on sleeping for hours.

But, just as he did every morning, Berman pulled up the roller blinds, intimating to Anneke that for *him* there had been no holiday yesterday. She gritted her strong white teeth and cursed under her breath: "*Godverdoeme!* God damn him!" Then she got out of bed, shivering with cold, though it was the middle of summer.

Berman went past her room, and out of the corner of his eye he caught a glimpse of her, barefoot, with her apron in one hand, while with the other she stifled a yawn, which was bursting out of her like a scream. He smiled and pretended not to see her standing there. Berman never had relationships with the maidservants, because afterwards they would prattle about it, which would not suit him at all; that's all one needed in Antwerp. He was not like Shapiro: all Antwerp gossiped about him, but it didn't bother him in the least. Shapiro had a bad reputation as a man of loose morals and, indeed, if he hadn't been such a good businessman that people needed his services, no right-thinking person would have stopped to speak to him in the street.

"Hmm, she's certainly not unattractive! A *shikse* but even so…" He smiled and went into the kitchen to perform the ritual washing of his hands.

Berman inspected the silver tray to see that all was as it should be: that the spoon was there and the glass of *bavarke* of the right consistency. With a nod he allowed Anneke to go. He was putting sugar in his drink when, without knowing why, he called Anneke back, looked at her, pondered as if he were trying to remember something, and then sent her away again.

"*Godverdoeme!*" muttered Anneke again, picking up the cat which was rubbing itself against her. She could have told the cat a lot of things, but instead she just kissed his little nose. She put him down, gave him a kick and said: "Scram!"

After breakfast Berman distributed some parcels of diamonds and received finished work, but there wasn't a great deal to do. The workshops had been at a standstill the day before, and because of the holiday the cutters had not yet finished the work. The polishers hadn't arrived either.

Berman went off to the Bourse, but no trading was going on there. In the big hall, with its massive gleaming pillars, there was hardly anyone to be seen. The few dealers around, who had not gone away, were unwrapping their parcels of diamonds. The stones caught Berman's eye with their flashing colors of white, red and blue. The dealers showed each other the bargains they had bought and then wrapped them up again. The Club was empty too and only the *Shenkl*, where the small traders dealt, was full of life. Bearded young men with worried expressions ran around like scalded cats, stopped at tables, showed each other tiny, rose-cut diamonds, about a hundred to the carat, or rough diamonds, which looked like little pieces of greyish washing soda. They weighed them on small scales, wrapped them up again, talked and gestured with their hands, and swore by their wives and children. They tried to make deals, found they couldn't get the price they wanted, closed their cases and ran to the next table.

An elderly man was sitting beside the window, poking with his tweezers at a large heap of *bakvuils*, which looked like loose tobacco, searching for little diamonds. He raised his red eyes and looked at Berman, smoothed his grey beard reflectively, as if he was trying to remember something. "Hmmm…" he said, "It's him! The black dog." Then he went on prodding around with his tweezers. Jules, his face red and shining as usual, was sitting directly opposite the old man. He was weighing grey diamond powder on a pair of scales, and wrapping it up in a paper packet, singing under his breath:

"On Sunday to Sint-Anneke I go,
Siiiint-Aaaa-ne-ke!"

A small, crooked young man with a melancholy look and nervous, watery eyes, stood beside him:

"If you please, hurry up a little, Herr Tsvaygnboym! It is almost lunchtime and I haven't managed to get anything done yet. I told you there wouldn't be enough diamond powder. I certainly wasn't trying to rob you. I've had to run back in the middle of my work, and now I'm wasting time for nothing," said the young man, justifiably upset.

But Jules, having seen Berman coming in, stopped singing and got up, taking the diamond powder with him. He stretched out his dimpled hand to Berman, and went as red as a beetroot. The young man with watery eyes just stood there, his hands raised in amazement and indignation: "Damn that bastard! Here I am, rushing around like a madman and desperate to get away. He could at least have given me the diamond powder *before* he went off to fawn around that black rogue." The poor creature was so agitated that he started coughing, and his dark face and little black beard seemed to shrink. It was almost midday, when the polishing machine would come to a standstill.

But the polisher need not have got so agitated, because Berman did not even give Jules his hand, but merely asked him hastily how his father was and then turned away arrogantly, while Jules stood there with his hand outstretched. Embarrassed, he returned to his table. A desire to prove that he really was the boss over the workers surged up in him, and he shouted at the polisher: "Just see that the stones turn out well! Do you hear me?!"

"Yes, yes," muttered the young man and hurried out of the room.

Berman looked around and saw that there was no one left to stop and chat to except the nobodies and paupers who were ten-a-penny. Nevertheless he answered the "good morning" greetings of the small dealers and brokers on his way out. He remembered that he had to go and see Shapiro; yesterday the Hungarian rogue had said he had some goods, so it was worth having a look.

"How dare he come to my house? The bastard, the scoundrel!" Shapiro's jibes of the day before had started to gnaw at Berman. His rage was rekindled when he remembered how Shapiro had deliberately riled him so that he had nearly had an apoplectic fit. He was tempted not to go to him, just to show him that he, Berman, was not someone to be treated lightly. But on the other hand, what else could he do? He had to go, for the sake of business. Shapiro had said, "I've got fine goods," and he was a man you couldn't trifle with. It would be better for him to go to Shapiro than for the latter to come to him, even though Shapiro was just a broker and he, Berman, a diamond merchant. Shapiro never had any difficulty in selling his goods. They were usually already sold before he actually had them in his hands. He had devilish cunning. He had access to the most prestigious firms and the finest stones, so that if you wanted to get hold of high-quality goods and make a profit, you couldn't afford to quarrel with Shapiro. He looked like a rogue but you could absolutely rely on his word. He never cheated, never "lost" any diamonds, or exchanged good stones for rubbish. He was honesty personified in his business dealings, and it was an honor to do business with him. No one could become a respected merchant without going through Shapiro.

Glancing at his gold watch, Berman saw it was too early to go to Shapiro's house, so he walked more slowly and took a detour round the side streets. It was better to be on the late side than too early.

He thought about Jules: "Huh! He's become a fine gentleman,

that impertinent so-and-so, just to add to my troubles. Hmm… I bet he just works with tiny stones, a thousand to the carat!" He smiled contemptuously, though it did irk him that Jules had held out his hand to him. "These *shnorrers* now think they're our equals. How can he be so presumptuous? Just because his older brother has made an advantageous match, he thinks he can become a successful dealer, and who knows, he might well succeed. *And* they're trying to drag the father out of the dirt as well." No one had been as sorely tried by God as he had, thought Berman, full of self-pity.

And so, bemoaning his fate, he arrived at Shapiro's house. Shapiro was sitting at a highly polished mahogany table covered with a thick sheet of beveled glass.

"Ah! Herr Berman!" Both their faces were beaming and they kept shaking hands as if they would never let go.

"Please, do sit down, Herr Berman!" Shapiro pulled out a chair for his guest, just as Berman had done the day before, and sat down at the head of the table. Berman saw his reflection in the mirror-like surface of the table and, looking up at the ceiling, noticed how fine it was. The chandelier was genuine crystal, the carpet beneath their feet was soft and thick, covering the whole of the floor. It was plain blue, without a single flower motif on it. And the walls were beautifully papered, the gold strips at the edges harmonizing so tastefully with the blue – magnificent!

"What this rogue has managed to achieve! He's just a broker, and I am the diamond merchant. How is it possible? There is so little furniture and yet it all looks so sumptuous!"

"Lenchen!" Shapiro called out to his wife.

Madame Shapiro emerged, as if she had been hiding, from behind a heavy, dark blue, velvet-covered door near the window. She greeted Berman, giving him her hand. She had dull round eyes, set far apart. A watery smile did not enliven her lethargic expression. Berman looked at her for a long time. "Hmm… I think she's even more repulsive than before," he thought to himself. In her well-cut skirt, heavy crepe de chine blouse and beautifully coiffured wig, all of which had obviously cost a great deal of money, she looked like a great lump of wood wrapped up in silk.

Madame Shapiro excused herself, went into the kitchen and came back, accompanied by a tall slender girl of about eighteen who wore a starched blue dress with a tiny tulle apron, with a white cap on her shining blonde hair. The girl carried a glass plate full of fruit and her dazzling smile and large, blue, childlike eyes contrasted favorably with Madame Shapiro's appearance.

"Don't wait to be invited, Herr Berman!" said Madame Shapiro, and Shapiro himself filled two glasses with sparkling liqueur from a fine cut-glass carafe. They clinked their glasses and emptied them.

"You can go now," said Shapiro, sending the girl back to the kitchen, devouring her with his eyes as if she had been honey cake. Berman could not understand how Madame Shapiro tolerated such a beautiful gentile maidservant, when she herself was so ugly. It was no secret in the town that Shapiro picked the servant girls, and that only after he had given his approval did his wife start to negotiate about wages and so forth; a few ducats more or less were not the deciding factor here. "My God, what a hypocrite!" thought Berman. "The way the rat calls her 'Lenchen' so affectionately, thinking he's deceiving everyone." Wiping his moustache, he said aloud, "Now, let's see what you've got for me."

From his breast pocket Shapiro took out and unwrapped a parcel of diamonds. They flashed red, blue, yellow, green. "What do you think of that? Fine goods, eh?"

The diamonds in Madame Shapiro's ears seemed to respond, lighting up in fiery colors as if they recognized old friends. The two men spoke for a long time, gesturing, one with his large brown hands, the other with his plump white ones, until at last they shook hands on the deal and started chatting about this and that: politics, the past.

Berman said goodbye to Shapiro, almost forgetting to give his hand to Madame Shapiro. But she pushed her bejeweled hand into his.

"*Auf Wiedersehen*, Herr Berman! Please give your wife my kind regards." Madame Shapiro's large, dull, black eyes, her nose, even her cheeks seemed to laugh and cry together when she spoke. Berman promised he would not forget, thinking that it was not surprising Shapiro was such a womanizer. Rochl suddenly came into his mind, dressed in her finest clothes, as she looked when she was going to a wedding or a bar mitzva. The image of her filled him with pleasure.

He wondered how old Madame Shapiro was. It was hard to assess. She could be anything between thirty and fifty. And Shapiro was still quite a young man. He must have married her for the dowry.

The women who gathered in the zoological garden on summer afternoons gossiped a great deal about the Shapiros and discussed Madame Shapiro's habit of sitting at her window for days at a time. She would gaze into the street to pass the time. She didn't come to the zoological garden because she was embarrassed; she knew very well that people realized the expensive clothes and jewelry which her husband draped round her did not signify deep love on his part, but rather his desire to make her into a living advertisement of his wealth. She had even heard the women denigrating her, and she wept not only with her eyes, but with her nose, cheeks, mouth, even the curls of her wig.

On the way home, Berman thought about the bargain he had just bought. In his mind he went through all the richest merchants in the Bourse to decide on the most suitable purchaser, but they had all gone away on holiday. Still, the stones wouldn't spoil. Thank God, that was a good purchase. Shapiro certainly was clever, damn him!

It suddenly occurred to Berman that once again he had not followed his doctor's orders to take a daily walk for his blood circulation. When you are always so busy, you forget all about your health! So not having anything particular to do until lunch, he set out on his walk for the first time in three months.

The streets and lanes of Zurenborg had all been swept clean. The brass knockers of the white and yellow doors were gleaming, and the windowpanes shone. Figures of women, children and angels danced on the lace curtains. But the streets were absolutely empty. Berman strode through all of Zurenborg until he came to Borgerhout. The pungent smell of fresh warm wax, which permanently hung over Borgerhout, poured out of the candle factory. Berman found it impossible to continue his walk here. He covered his nose with his hand and turned back into the city.

The afternoon activities had already begun. The department stores were full of women looking for bargains. Some had gone to the zoological garden for a cup of coffee and a gossip. The pavements were blocked by prams. They were pushed by women with cheerful faces and pointed red noses. Their white hands sparkled with diamonds. Little white bonnets decorated with Brussels lace and blue or pink ribbons were visible in the prams. The sleeping children, covered in silk and lace, were cuddling their dolls.

But there were also worn, grey-faced mothers pushing shabby prams with grubby children who were either sucking dirty pieces of rubber or sticking their hands into their mouths. These children had thin faces and sallow skin.

Berman pushed his way through the crowds. An elderly Jew was tottering along beside a plump middle-aged man who was clean-shaven and wore a light grey suit. The two were arguing. The old man saw Berman, raised his crumpled hat and greeted him. He was like Madame Shapiro, his eyes and cheeks seemed to be laughing and crying at the same time. The wrinkles round his eyes deepened as he spoke, his bluish lips became moist. In his efforts to gain the upper hand over the corpulent gentleman, he was working himself up into a frenzy. But the latter just kept smiling with an indifference which maddened the old man.

"You certainly won't regret it! Old Tsimerman always lets me have goods at a lower price than the others. I've already been lucky with him, and he knows that I am an experienced broker, not a crook!" said the old man eagerly.

"But I don't *need* small stones," said the merchant, making an impatient gesture. The old man's face fell.

In the middle of the street, pale young men with wispy beards and older men with long thick ones were riding on tricycles. Their sallow faces told sad tales. Their beards brushed the baskets full of fish, bread and meat, which these former diamond traders and other poor people were delivering to rich houses where parsimonious housewives lived, who were quite prepared to go into the shops, pick over the goods and haggle for ages. They were not prepared, however, to carry the purchases home themselves. The errand boys with long beards had to deliver the goods, while nostalgically remembering the time when they had arrived in Antwerp with their dowry in their pockets, full of hopes of becoming rich. But having no talent, they were soon fleeced in the Bourse or at the Club. And now this was how they made their livelihood. Some were in business for themselves and pushed flat carts with dogs harnessed to them, which they had bought in the *Vogelmarkt.* They had to push the carts to help the dogs pull the load, and they dragged themselves around the poor Jewish lanes which looked as crooked and exhausted as the peddlers themselves. They called out their miserable wares as if they were chanting from the Gemara.

It always amused Berman to see these hopeless cases with their dog carts. But he didn't, God forbid, laugh at them! For who can tell what tomorrow will bring.

Chapter 8

The table was neatly laid at the Bermans'. The silver cutlery gleamed and there were dishes with all kinds of *kugel* and delicious conserves. Siphons of soda water sparkled, and the red medicine which Berman took after meals was awaiting him. Anneke was still wandering about with a yellow duster in her hand, making a show of looking for dust, which was nowhere to be found in this venerable and luxurious dining room.

Dovid came down from his bedroom in his slippers and dressing gown. His hair was tousled and his face looked yellowish and puffy with sleep. Anneke grabbed her duster and made for the door, but Dovid called her back and pulled her to him. Blushing, Anneke broke free, then rushed to the door. Jeannette came down from her bedroom wrapped in a long blue silk dressing gown trimmed with white fur, and wearing high-heeled slippers. Her hair was wet and her dainty little ears were rosy. She ran to Dovid, sat down beside him on the wide velvet sofa and started kissing him like a lover.

"Oh, you're here, Dovid!" Then she prattled on: "Listen, Dovid, this week I read an amazing novel. You won't believe what happens in it! You'll go mad!"

"You certainly are mad!" said her mother, suddenly appearing at the door. "I can't imagine what she finds in those books. She doesn't even want to eat her breakfast!"

"Oh, Mama, if you could read you'd know what I mean. Dovid, you really must read it. It's extraordinary!"

"But you say that about every book you read."

"That's because they've all got something special about them. Oh! Dovid!" She hugged him hard.

"Aha, I see my sister has gone off her head!" Dovid retreated to the corner of the sofa.

"Look, Dovid, this is the way she danced!"

"The way *who* danced?"

"You'll see how the dance goes!"

Jeannette positioned herself in front of the mirror, lifted a corner of her dressing gown between her fingers and started dancing, slow and stately at first, then gradually building up to an ecstatic pitch, spinning round faster and faster, like a whirlwind. Suddenly she kicked off her slippers and raised one leg in the air, showing her blue silk underwear and her bare, brown legs. Dovid, reclining in the corner of the sofa, languidly followed her every movement, with the critical air of a connoisseur.

When Berman opened the door to the dining room, a flash of blue silk darted in front of his eyes, and he stopped dead. Jeannette was still dancing, spinning wildly then dancing with a more measured pace. She finally came to rest with both feet together, like a ballerina on the stopper of a perfume bottle. Berman just stood staring, rooted to the spot, hardly comprehending at first that this was his own daughter dancing. Jeannette was tired and sat down beside her brother on the sofa. When Dovid saw his father, however, he immediately stole off back to his bedroom.

"That's how she danced," Jeannette kept repeating, not noticing that Dovid was no longer there.

"Who danced?" asked Berman, puzzled.

"Oh, Papa dearest, I thought you were Dovid!"

"But *who* danced?"

"Oh, it was in my book. I have a French novel in which a girl dances because she's in love! You should read it."

"I can't be bothered with your foolishness! I don't know what you're talking about! Rochl, let's eat. I'm starving."

Rochl looked at Dovid's empty place and sighed: "Where will it all end?"

In the afternoon Jacques showed an elderly man into the Bermans' dining room, making use of the opportunity to slip out of the house. The old man was obviously expecting a cool reception. "I was just passing and said to myself: 'Well, surely they won't *eat* me.'"

Berman looked at him and replied with a cynical smile: "Well, I certainly have no intention of *eating* you – what a thought – ugh!"

Pretending not to notice the sarcasm, the old man approached the table.

"What is it you want?" Berman said quickly.

"Well…ehm…joking apart…" The old man took out his snuffbox. "Joking apart…" He tapped all four sides of his snuffbox to loosen the snuff. "As someone once said: 'There's no harm in trying,' so I thought, 'Well, perhaps,' after all, it was quite a dowry. But in fact, it really wasn't a suitable match for your son, was it? I realize that now."

"So what are you gabbling about then? One thing or the other: if it wasn't a match for us, why have you come to bother me now?"

"And what a joke! I thought to myself: she certainly is no spring chicken, but on the other hand – such a huge fortune! However, the moment I learned that the hundred thousand had shrunk to ten thousand, I took my hat out of the ring!"

"But didn't you have *two* different hats in the ring at the same time?"

"Who said that? God forbid!" said the man, with a start.

"I know you very well. As soon as you realized that I wasn't willing to sell my son to that old hag, not even for ten million francs, you went off to *them*. I'm very well aware that you were trying to play one of us off against the other. So what is it you want now?"

The old man pretended he didn't know what Berman was talking about. He sat down at the table, stuffed snuff up both nostrils, took a large red handkerchief out of the pocket of his long coat with the sheepskin collar which he wore both summer and winter, wiped his angular face, grasped his pointed, grey beard with both hands and sneezed loudly.

Berman moved away to the far end of the table; he had to sneeze as well.

"Listen, Herr Berman! You know very well that no one in Antwerp has ever got married without me. No one has ever slipped through my fingers, except perhaps where there's some question of being in love. But even then they have to come to me in the end."

"So what exactly is it you want from me? A kiss on the cheek? All right. Come closer and I'll give you a kiss." Berman laughed and stood up as a sign to the old man that he should leave. But the latter remained seated, until Berman simply said: "Reb Beynish, I have to go out. I simply don't have time for you just now."

Reb Beynish stood up, gave Berman his hand, and said: "Don't worry! Something suitable will come along, God willing. Then we'll have a drink of vodka together, that's for sure. Heh! heh! heh!" and off he went.

Reb Beynish was not lying. He made matches for all of Antwerp, and it was his habit to negotiate the same match with various families at once. Thus he almost always had success, because if it didn't please one family, then it did please a second one, a third, a fourth, a fifth. He had come to Antwerp as a young man, and hadn't let the grass grow under his feet: the very same evening he arrived he started matchmaking. Usually he snapped up young men from the hasidic *shtiblekh.* They had come from Poland or Russia in order to avoid military service. If one of these young men did not have any relatives in Antwerp, he usually had a letter from his *rebbe* to a Hasid who lived in the town. The young men from Galicia did tend to have relatives in Antwerp. Therefore Reb Beynish caught them in the street, in the synagogue, in the *shtibl* or at home. Among all the worshippers he was always the first to greet a newly arrived young man, ask him in great detail who he was, where he came from, what he did for a living and so on. Even if the young man was a silent type, or a slippery customer, or simply someone who did not like talking about himself, Reb Beynish always managed to prise everything out of him. It was impossible to hide anything from him, and when he had found out all he wanted to know, he started talking to the young man about making a match.

"You say you're not ready to get married? Always the same old tune! Heh! heh! heh! You're just teasing me, that's what you're doing. It's always the same! But never mind, you'll soon be ready, you'll soon be ready! After all, what are you going to achieve here? Nothing at all! You'll soon use up the few rubles you possess, and even if it's a few hundred rubles, does it make any difference? So, you'll learn to be a diamond cutter. Well, yes, that's a respectable trade," and Beynish tapped his bone snuff box to loosen the snuff. "A new livelihood. It may be a fine livelihood, but not for a Jew. Certainly if you were, God forbid, a *goy*, you could join the union, and you'd earn enough for your bread. Not just for bread, you could get drunk too on your wages, you could roll around in the dirt, heh! heh! But because you are, thank God, a Jew, and not *a goy*, God forbid, you'll have to work a good few years for nothing. In fact, why do I say 'for nothing'? You'll actually have to *pay* a few hundred rubles to be taught the trade. And do you think you'll be taught properly? Not on your life! *Half*-taught, that's what you'll be. And apart from that, they'll certainly not let *you* get your hands on a parcel of diamonds, because there are masses of cutters and polishers around who haven't a crust of bread to put in their mouths, and they're all running round after the bosses, trying to get hold of a couple of stones. If you don't kiss the boss, you know where, then, I'm sorry to say, you'll just be sent packing. What will you do then? I ask you, eh?" Then Reb Beynish took a pinch of snuff and held it between his fingers until the young man started sneezing:

"Atchoo! Atchoo!"

"Bless you! So you're sneezing at my honest words? May all Jews have the benefit of such sincere advice. I tell you, they're all cut-throats out there. They're just looking for a sucker who doesn't understand their tricks yet. And, at the end of your so-called training, you'll still have to pay off your machine, which'll be rusting in the corner. And even if you do get hold of a few stones, you'll make a mess of them.

For how could you know how to cut them? And then you certainly won't get any more. At home they'll get tired of supporting you and sending you money, because it's a real burden, do you understand me? When I see a young man like you in a synagogue or *shtibl,* it tears my heart out," sighed Beynish, making sure that the young man couldn't get a word in edgeways. He continued his monologue at breakneck speed, without pausing for breath. "If you follow my advice you will bless the day you met me. I've got a girl for you. She's not a girl, she's a jewel! And from a fine family! What am I talking about? From an *exceptionally prestigious* family! You will get a wonderful dowry and a furnished apartment. Your father-in-law will take you into the business and make a merchant or a broker of you – that's not bad either. We should all be as lucky as Shapiro who is better off than many of the great merchants! I tell you, if a broker has a good brain, then it's an excellent livelihood. You don't have to put your own money into it, but you certainly can take plenty out of it.

"What does a broker do, you ask? He mediates between diamond merchants. It's simple: you're a merchant and I'm a merchant. I have a parcel of diamonds I want to sell. The broker runs round the offices, the *Shenkl,* the Club, the Fortunia, and even the Bourse, until he catches a merchant – you, for example – and you just happen to need exactly the goods which he has for sale. You buy them, and the broker gets his percentage. Now what do you think, isn't that a good job? You don't have to invest anything in the business except your brains, and many brokers become rich. But, suddenly, on a normal working day, there is a huge commotion among the merchants. The town is buzzing with excitement. What's happened? Someone has lost diamonds again. So what does that mean? It means nothing at all. It means that the broker who was entrusted with some merchandise, has ostensibly "lost" it, or has been robbed. You know very well that it is just a trumped up tale, but what can you do, if he doesn't have it? Do you think he'll be put in jail? Or won't be able to show his face in the marketplace? You would be wrong. On the contrary, in a few weeks' time he'll be given even more merchandise than before.

Because those who aren't afraid to "lose" merchandise, also know how to sell very well and always get the true price, whereas those who never "lose" are considered to be mediocre, and no one wants to have any dealings with them. Apart from Shapiro, you don't know him yet, how could you? But everyone knows him. He is a rich man who, they say, never loses stones. And yet he goes round decked out in gold. He has his own way of doing things, they say, and no one knows what it is, but he is as rich as Croesus, and who was it who arranged his marriage? To whom does he owe everything? To me! And his wife, she's a really virtuous woman, a good soul!

"Follow my advice and you'll do well in the world. You'll have a home, a wife, a family, and you'll never be lonely. You'll never have to roam around. You can at least look at her! Someone once said, 'Looking is not marrying.' If she pleases you, then that's fine, and if she doesn't, well, we'll find another one who will please you."

Reb Beynish went on talking and talking, squeezing the young man against the wall in the corner of the synagogue, pressing against him with his heavy, bony body in the black coat with the sheepskin collar which he wears summer and winter, and didn't release him until the young man saw, whether he wanted to or not, the logic of Beynish's argument: that taking a look at her is not the same as marrying her. And the result is that for nine out of ten of them a match is arranged and he dances at their weddings in his black coat with the sheepskin collar, which smells of sweat, snuff and mold. Sometimes it happens that he doesn't succeed at the first attempt, in which case he goes to the young man's relatives and teaches them a little of his logic. He convinces them by all manner of veiled hints, even, if necessary, in a very rusty Flemish, that it would be greatly to *their* advantage if the young man got married and had a place of his own.

It happens very frequently that a young man passes through on the way to America. Even though he is only in Antwerp for a few days, Reb Beynish manages to catch him and arrange a marriage for him. Usually Beynish himself doesn't know who he means when he praises the prospective bride as "a jewel of a girl," because he has a long list of names inscribed in his notebook, which he can't possibly know by heart. His thick greasy little notebook is worth millions – who knows the total value of the dowries he carries around in his pocket? It's not until a young man agrees that taking a look does not amount to marriage that Beynish has recourse to his notebook.

Now, after his visit to Berman, Beynish was in a really bad mood: was this the way he deserved to be treated? "Is it possible? He simply threw me out! What a bastard!" Beynish just couldn't get over it. "I try to make a match on his behalf, to marry that good-for-nothing into a fine family, with a wonderful dowry, and not only does he not thank me for all the efforts I've made to no avail, but he gets into a rage with me. Well, all the same, it's not easy for him. God help a father who has such an empty vessel for a son, such a godless, dishonest wastrel. Berman will have to sort it out for himself."

With these thoughts Beynish made his way home, striding through the streets of Antwerp in his greasy coat. That afternoon he didn't even put his nose into the *shtibl* to see whether a new prospective bridegroom had turned up.

Chapter 9

When he arrived back from the synagogue, Berman was met by Rochl. She was wrapped in a dark shawl, her eyes red with weeping, and her wig uncombed.

"What's the matter?" asked Berman, shocked.

"Gedaliah, something terrible has happened! I told you that you should go easy on your children. Now what will people think of us? Antwerp will certainly have something to gossip about now. Our enemies were just waiting for this, may their tongues dry up!"

Berman stared at her, frowning with his heavy eyebrows. He did not understand what she was talking about, but he wondered where Rochl had suddenly found such a flow of oratory. Normally she couldn't string two words together.

"What's happened? Tell me now!"

Rochl sobbed loudly. "Dovid is going to be a simple manual worker! He is going to train as a diamond polisher. He says there's no point in trying to dissuade him. Oh my God, this is all I need!"

Berman burst out laughing.

"For God's sake, you almost gave me a heart attack. What I have to put up with from this fool and her son!"

He sat down at the head of the table, demanded his supper, and continued: "Don't worry, that lazy slob will never make it as a manual worker. Just let him try and he'll find out what it's like to have to earn your daily bread. My father didn't support me, so I had to learn the hard way. But Dovid's as likely to become a worker as I am to become a priest! What a thought! Dovid, a worker! He lies in his stinking bed till four in the afternoon, then he dresses himself up at my expense, parades around doing nothing for the rest of the day, and if you say a word, his answer is to run away from home, and his dear mama has to run around the town searching for him." Berman seemed to have already forgotten his own earlier anxiety about his son. "Bah, I know what he's up to. He's just trying to scare us."

But Dovid was very much in earnest. He had decided to put an end to his way of life once and for all. He was sick of the scenes with his father, and of lying in bed all day, simply in order to make the time pass. He had had enough of trailing aimlessly round the streets of Antwerp, feeling totally superfluous in society, a figure of ridicule to himself and everyone else.

And though his evenings with Gitele had been wonderful, had he not paid for them with his self-respect? Skulking around like a thief and a coward, not having the courage to say to Leybesh: "I love your wife and she loves me, and I am going to take her and the child – *my* child – to live with me." In fact he was worse than a coward, because he had no means of supporting her. He was a hopeless failure, that's what he was.

But it couldn't go on like this. If he couldn't trade in the Bourse, he had to find some other way of making a living. So he decided to learn a trade, which wasn't such a terrible thing. A worker is a human being too, after all. He'd be able to set up his own home, and even if it was very modest, he would be with Gitele and his child.

He went to tell Gitele of his decision, expecting her to be delighted. But instead, Gitele looked at him with a half-sad, half-ironic expression, made an impatient gesture and said dismissively: "Another of your great ideas."

Dovid had pictured her embracing and kissing him, weeping with joy and telling him that his honest, genuine love was more precious to her than jewels. She would promise that as soon as he was in a position to keep them, she would go and live openly with him as his wife. This would put an end to their ambiguous situation. Instead of that, she mocked him, declared that he wasn't fit to be a worker, and advised him against taking this step. "Listen, Dovid," she said, "manual work is the last thing you should do. It isn't for you, and you'll just get humiliated for no good reason. And in any case, what will you achieve? Let's say you do get work, you'll still remain a pauper for the rest of your life. You can see what the situation is in this house. Working for someone else is like working for the devil."

Just as Dovid had not anticipated that his mother would mourn him as if he had died, he had not expected Gitele to react like this. To hell with them all! Living like this was worse than anything. He was going mad. A man had to do something. So he approached Rosenkrantz, a well-known factory owner, and told him that he wanted to learn polishing. He said he wanted to become expert in all areas of the diamond business. The owner didn't really believe him, but asked no questions; if he wanted to learn the trade, let him get on with it.

When Dovid went into the factory, accompanied by the boss, fifty astonished workers turned to stare, their eyes popping out of their heads.

"Eh, what's Berman's brat doing here? And at nine o'clock in the morning?"

"He must have fallen out of bed!" muttered a fair-haired lad to an older, bald-headed man with a wrinkled face.

"Look, Rosenkrantz is demonstrating the scaif to him." The workers' curiosity increased. "Oh my God, perhaps his daddy's going to take over the workshop."

"Well, what's it matter? Do you think you'd get a worse deal?" said another, gesturing at the boss.

"You bet! Compared to *him*, ours is an angel."

"Oh yes, sure, an angel with wings!"

"A pure and saintly soul! If his saintliness migrated into a dog it would start frothing at the mouth!"

"Shhh! He's coming over with him."

The boss approached the man with the bald head. "Now, Berman, Kupershteyn will show you what's what, and if you apply yourself, you'll get good training in my workshop. Don't you agree,

Kupershteyn? Only good polishers go out of here, and if you've been trained with me, that's a recommendation in itself. Eh, Kupershteyn?" and he slapped Kupershteyn so heartily on the back that the latter nearly fell off his stool.

Kupershteyn's bald head became pink, and his eyes reddened. He muttered something inaudible, but the expression on his wrinkled face said, "Go to hell!"

Dovid sat down on one of the high stools, which were scuffed and blackened with age. The boss himself brought him an overall, and when Dovid put it on, he suddenly felt as if Rosenkrantz was somehow deliberately humiliating him. He was overcome by such a feeling of depression that it was all he could do not to burst into tears. When he looked at the overall it seemed as if it was responsible for the strange mess he was in, and that if he didn't have to wear this, it wouldn't be so demeaning to work in a workshop. He couldn't concentrate on anything the old man with the bad-tempered wrinkled face was telling him. All he was aware of was the bald head, which looked like a skull, and himself in a prison uniform. And why were they all craning their heads round and staring at him? What were they looking at?

He looked himself up and down and realized it was probably because he had forgotten to take off his white spats. One of the apprentices sniggered, others said "Shhh!" and Dovid felt keenly the absurdity of his situation. If only he hadn't put on that overall! His ears were burning, and he felt confused and embarrassed. He sat at the scaif, the wheel turned, and the whole workshop spun round with it.

The workers, in their dirty, often torn overalls followed the revolving wheels with their experienced eyes. They spun round faster than the layman's eye could see, and all Dovid saw was a circular blur of gleaming metal. On the wheels, diamonds of all sizes and colors were being polished: single cuts, small stones with only eight facets, as well as large, valuable full cuts with fifty-seven facets.

Kupershteyn was an old and trusted polisher, who never took the loupe away from his eye, nor his eye off the stone he was working on, in case it disappeared. Very large precious stones were entrusted to him, which he guarded with his life.

Dovid sat and watched. No one said a word to him, and Kupershteyn, his teacher, paid Dovid no attention at all. At last Dovid asked: "What should I do?"

"Just watch!" was the answer.

Dovid realized that all he was allowed to do was to look and look again. As soon as one facet was finished, the stone was taken off the disc, which then began flying round again at dizzying speed, like magic. A worker took the diamond off the dop, melted the lead on the little blue gas flame which, like the flames of hell, never went out, put the stone back on the dop and another facet was polished. The workers clustered round the scaif even though they didn't have a great deal to do. Looking was the most important activity. They all looked grubby, as if they worked in a coal mine instead of polishing diamonds to glitter on the necks, arms and breasts of leisured ladies and gentlemen. Even Dovid's hands were grimy and, under his beautifully manicured fingernails, a layer of dirt built up; this was the black diamond powder mixed with oil, which clung to the skin as soon as one went near it.

Old Kupershteyn took off his overall to go home for lunch, and Dovid saw with surprise that all the workers, as if at a given signal, got up, grabbed an overcoat or a scarf and eagerly made for the exit, as if they hadn't seen the outside world for years.

Dovid had felt so forlorn that he was positively delighted when the old man suddenly seemed a little friendlier, asking him whether he had brought his lunch with him. "No," said Dovid.

"I've brought mine!" shouted someone else.

"Hope it chokes you!" muttered the old man, and went out without even saying goodbye, leaving Dovid totally bewildered. "What a strange bunch," he thought. "Not an ounce of common courtesy."

The street seemed brighter than usual to him, and he felt as if everyone was staring at him. And, indeed, someone was walking behind him, discussing him at the top of his voice. "What do you think of that fool? I thought I'd die laughing. Imagine coming to the workshop in a pair of white spats!"

"He must be a bit touched, eh? Who is he anyway?"

"Who is he? Berman's son, of course!"

"*What?*"

"Yes, did you not realize?"

"What, is he short of money?"

"No, he's short of a brain!"

"Ha, ha, ha! Our boss is right when he says, "You can't have money *and* brains!"

"Ha, ha! Too right!"

The sweat broke out on Dovid's forehead and he was seized by a helpless rage towards the workers.

When Rochl saw him coming home for lunch with a grimy face, she clasped her hands to her stomach, like a goose flapping its wings when it sees something threatening. She begged him not to be offended, but asked him not to appear in this state in front of Anneke.

When Dovid looked in the full-length mirror, he was shocked at what he saw. He looked black, his hair was tousled and even though he hadn't done any real work yet, the strange exhaustion he felt showed in his eyes. He was tired out from just being at the workshop. He flung himself down on the big velvet sofa and Rochl brought in a basin of warm, scented water and a large white towel, after which she gave him his lunch.

"Dovid!" exclaimed Rochl, "For my sake, *please* don't persist in this."

"And what about the millions of workers who slave away their whole lives, in strenuous work like diamond polishing, and still they thank God that they have work, eh, Mama?" Dovid was really putting this question to himself.

"It's different for them, they're used to it. I myself…"

But she stopped herself just in time, realizing that it was better that Dovid should not know that she used to be a cook, and that she was the daughter of a carpenter. May her children not know about such a life, she murmured quietly, to God.

After a few days the work had become so unbearable to Dovid that he thought it would be better to go and break stones in a quarry, rather than work as a diamond polisher. He got along well enough with the bearded Jews in the workshop, with skullcaps on their pale brows, who would sing a hasidic melody while working with the stones. They were also there because they had no other choice, and Dovid felt that they understood what he was going through. So although they were amused by him, they behaved politely towards him, with the odd good-natured jibe. But it was the common young men whose fathers were tailors or cobblers, for whom it was an honor to work in a polishing workshop, who made Dovid's life a misery with their vulgar laughter over the incident with the spats, which they would not let him forget. They were so arrogant, and their language! The old man with the bald head who looked like a criminal would only speak to Dovid if he absolutely had to, and his stubborn silence got on Dovid's nerves. Above all, he couldn't bear feeling dozens of eyes on his back, knowing that they were full of contempt. This hurt him much more than the fact of having to stand around and watch the entire time. He felt like an absolute idiot, and the overall was the worst thing of all.

One morning, the boss came into the workshop elegantly dressed, his hair combed and his face flushed after his ample breakfast. He called the foreman to him and conferred with him for a long time, giving him orders, discussing the matter, then thinking about it, then giving more orders. After this he left to attend to his business affairs and didn't notice Dovid. In fact he had completely forgotten about him. He just noticed there was a trainee watching how it was done, which was fine. This really annoyed Dovid. The boss had not even come over to address a few words to him. And yet it was only a week ago that they had meet on the Keyserlei, greeted each other like equals, and although Rosenkrantz was considerably older than Dovid, he had been happy for Dovid to pay the bill, he had smoked a good few of Dovid's cigarettes, and now he didn't even know him. Dovid forgot that he was now only a simple worker, and felt tremendous resentment towards Rosenkrantz.

No, he wasn't going to carry on working there. He would show him, the bastard, that he, Dovid, could afford to stop if he wished. He would make fun of Rosenkrantz the next time he met him, he'd tell him that he was a fool to have thought that he, Dovid Berman, was really going to become a worker. His mother had been right.

"Look at the way he got himself all dressed up today. He just put on his best suit to provoke and humiliate me, and he deliberately raised his voice when he was lording it over the foreman. He was bellowing so that I would hear, and yet he refused to notice or recognize me."

Dovid was in such a fury that he suddenly pulled off the blue overall, threw it on the ground, and left the workshop without saying goodbye to anyone.

The next morning Rochl was so pleased when she saw Dovid was lying in bed without any intention of getting dressed to go to work, that she joyfully carried up his breakfast to him.

The men from the workshop stared in amazement when they saw Dovid sauntering around the streets in the middle of the working day.

"What, has he given up already?" they all asked, open-mouthed.

"Why are you asking me? Ask him." Dovid's mentor shook his bald head and took another stone off the disc.

"Well, what did you imagine?" said the foreman, a stout young man with a red beard. "Did you really think that Berman's son would sit here forever polishing stones with the likes of you? Did you think he had nothing better to do? He was just making fun of you, and you fools just let yourselves be taken in." He spoke with smug satisfaction and his eyes shone as if he had been dealt a hand with three aces in a card game in Hershl's Restaurant.

Each of the workers felt that Dovid had made a fool of him personally. They had believed he was serious and even been quite pleased he was working with them – when in fact that devil, that fawning cur, was just having a laugh at their expense.

"His father can afford to support his precious, aristocratic son. To hell with him! As for us, we're just the scum of the earth, we can't afford that luxury. Just imagine walking out of the workshop in the middle of the working day!"

"There's nothing you can do about it," a young disciple of Leybesh's said bitterly. "You have to cower here making sure that Rosenkrantz's diamonds don't, God forbid, run away, and that they end up looking magnificent, flashing and sparkling!" he continued, stirring up the workers and himself.

"Come on then, that's enough talking! Back to work!" interrupted the foreman.

They quietened down and the machines started up again, the wheels turning. The young Hasidim started humming their *rebbe's* melody. The monotonous routine of examining the stones, and the continual hissing of the hot tweezers as they were dipped into cold water to harden the lead carried on, just as it did every day.

Chapter 10

When Berman next went into the Bourse, he saw that the other merchants were giving him strange looks. There was suspicion in their sharp eyes, and they spoke to him in a less respectful tone than they had previously.

"Ha, that scoundrel has obviously kept his word and gone off to bring shame on my name!" thought Berman. It was clear that they had already heard that Dovid was training as a diamond polisher; there was no doubt of that.

Horowitz stretched out his hand to Berman with a familiar and friendly air, as if they were equals now. "Well, it seems that neither of us is a millionaire, eh? But don't worry, we'll manage somehow!" Horowitz and the other merchants would never have dared to speak to him in such a tone before. He was acutely aware of the way they looked at him.

"Well, well, Antwerp certainly hasn't been sleeping," he thought to himself. "They're already assuming that I am bankrupt." So was this the way Dovid had repaid his father's kindness in turning a blind eye when he came back from the carnival in such a state?

Muttering and grumbling to himself, Berman left the Bourse and went along Provinciestraat. Trintshe, the fishmonger, a large gentile woman, who almost filled the doorway of her shop, shouted a friendly greeting to him: "*Dag menieër!* Nice weather!" Berman looked up, suddenly filled with a feeling of warmth towards Shprintse, as the Jews called her. She greeted him as she did every morning, without funny looks, not knowing, presumably, that Dovid had become a worker.

Wanting to convince himself that he enjoyed the same respect as before, he went over to her and started examining the assortment of merchandise laid out on the large marble slab, unable to decide what he should buy. There were huge sole with white fins and even whiter bellies, little Dutch herring with silver scales and red eyes, fine broad bream with bloodshot eyes, speckled roach, mackerel with green backs and fat bellies, and a huge mound of little silvery fish, about a hundred to the kilo. Outside, on one side of the doorway, there was a big, square basin in which black eels squirmed around, and on the other side stood a barrel of salted Dutch herring and a barrel of pickled cucumber. Berman didn't fancy any of these.

A large salmon, which lay apart from the other fish, had attracted Berman's eye. Its stomach was slit open, and its dark silvery scales were stained with blood. To Berman, the salmon looked as aristocratic and haughty as he was, and he took pleasure in instructing Trintshe to wrap it up very carefully. She was surprised, for this was the first time that Berman had bought a salmon without asking if it was fresh and how much it cost, then offering half the price she had quoted him. She said nothing however but, as she always did, praised the fish as she was wrapping it up.

When she had the money in her hand, she drew his attention to a glass tank in which gleaming brown carp were swimming around with half of their scales floating in the greenish water. She asked him to be sure to tell his wife always to come early on Thursdays, because today she didn't have very many carp left.

Then the gentile woman, knowing that the next day was the Jewish Sabbath, wished him "*Gut Shabbes!*" in Yiddish.

Berman glanced at the carp. On a bench beside the tank was a dish full of pink shrimps. He looked at them crawling around, one on top of the other, in a slow-moving mass. He thought of the unspeakable things they devoured, which made them so vigorous. Berman turned away from the squirming creatures and couldn't help spitting in disgust. He was really spitting out the sour taste he still had in his mouth from the Bourse. He started for home with the fish under his arm, thinking malevolent thoughts about his son.

Among a row of Jewish dairies and grocers' and butchers' shops with prominent, but crumbling, dirty, kosher signs, one bright shop window displayed a skinned pig with a red, bleeding snout. It held a bunch of parsley in its mouth. On a white marble slab various chunks of horse meat were laid out. On both sides of the shop door hung about two dozen rabbits with their fur still on. The fat, ruddy-complexioned, clean-shaven butcher was standing at the door of his shop in a white coat, whistling cheerfully. He greeted Berman as though the latter had been his best customer, also telling him the news that it was nice weather today. Berman agreed wholeheartedly with this, and walked on with his fish under his arm.

"So that wastrel has got the better of me! He's playing games with me, while I have to pinch my cheeks to bring some color into them! I'll have to support that layabout for the rest of his life, feed and clothe him like a lord, while he spits in my face. That's all the thanks I will get for everything I've done for him."

When he got home, Berman threw the fish on the kitchen table and without even greeting Rochl, went into the dining room and sat down, tired and bad-tempered, to look through his private mail, which was waiting for him on the table. "All rubbish!" A young man has a new cutting machine, and since he hasn't been able to meet Berman in his office in Pelikaanstraat, and has had no reply to letters he has sent him, he is taking the liberty of writing to his home address. His letter is full of verses from the Bible and Talmud, and ends with *kol hatkhiles koshoys* – all beginnings are difficult.

"Just asking for favors! Just rubbish!"

When Rochl came into the room to ask what he wanted done with the salmon and whether he would like a glass of tea, he shouted at her, "Tell me, you! Where is your darling layabout son, eh? Don't shrug your shoulders; you know very well where he is working, eh?"

Berman's eyes glittered and seemed to be popping out of their sockets. Rochl shrank back in alarm, imagining that any minute now they would spring out and roll around the carpet.

"What do you mean, shrug my shoulders? Who says Dovid is working somewhere? He's still lying in bed!"

"Ha! Did he think better of it, then?" wondered Berman and edged open the door of Dovid's bedroom. Yes, there he was, lying on his back with rumpled hair and a thick book in his hands. He didn't notice his father peering in.

"So that's how it is? I wonder what happened. Did they mock him, or give him funny looks? I bet they're rejoicing at his failure. I wonder what went through his mind. A strange affair."

He turned on Rochl angrily. "Why are you standing there like an idiot? Get me a glass of tea!"

"Sons like him should be drowned at birth," muttered Berman, making the blessing over his glass of tea.

Chapter 11

That evening Berman didn't go to the synagogue, even though he should have said *Kaddish* for his mother. Instead he said the evening prayers at home. He lit the crystal chandelier, although it was still light outside.

When he had finished praying he lay down on the sofa and tried to take a nap, but he was too agitated. His thoughts raced around in confusion. People actually thought that *he*, Berman, the respected, well-established diamond dealer, was bankrupt? How many enemies he had! How delighted they were to think that he had gone to the wall! But who were his enemies? And who had gone to the wall? Dovid had not actually gone on to be a diamond polisher after all, even though he had made a show of threatening to do so. It was all that stupid woman's fault. As usual, Berman made Rochl the butt of his rage, even though he was not absolutely sure what exactly he was angry about.

A knock at the door interrupted his tangled thoughts. He sat up, and Anneke, not waiting for his "*Entrez!*" opened the door a crack, expecting him to tell her to bring in the tea. But Berman just rubbed his eyes and yawned.

While Anneke was wiping the glass for his tea, someone knocked at the front door, hammering like mad on the brass knocker, and Anneke ran to open it, her dishtowel still clutched in her hand. "*Godverdoeme*, what's the rush?" Anneke thought it was one of the errand boys with the long beards.

Instead of an errand boy, a Flemish porter stood there. He was dressed in a faded, dirty blue, torn linen uniform, and had a cap with a badge. He looked very fed up.

"Does *Menieër* Berman live here or not?"

"Yes, he does."

"That's his father!" The porter pointed at an old, bent Jew in a threadbare gabardine and muddy boots with a torn, velvet cap on his head. The porter carried two patched suitcases over the threshold and said something to the old man, from which he understood that he was to enter as well.

Anneke, not listening to the porter's words, saw a beggar standing there, one of the many hundreds who pestered her, and for whom she always had the same answer ready: "There's no one at home." She kept on repeating it, but when the old man didn't understand a word and just stood there smiling with half-closed eyes, she lost her temper:

"Can't I get rid of the likes of you? Look at the mud you're going to bring into the house. Can't you at least wipe your feet?" She addressed the old man disrespectfully by the familiar "*du*," pointing at the brown doormat.

"Why are you yelling at him?" interrupted the porter. "He's *Menieër* Berman's father."

Anneke laughed. "You're off your head!"

"Here, read this, and you'll see." And he handed her a scrap of paper. "A Jew at the station gave it to me. Hurry up, Miss, and tell *Menieër* Berman that he's got to pay me. The old man has no Belgian money."

Anneke hesitated, but finally knocked on Berman's door and announced quietly, in an almost guilty tone, that some old man had arrived.

"He says he's your father! I told him there's no one at home. But he's just standing there, and won't go away. And the porter says it's true." Anneke's face flushed fiery red.

Berman felt a surge of shame.

"Can it really be my father?" he thought. "Has he actually come?"

"You can go!" he said angrily to Anneke, as if it were her fault that he had not answered his father's letter and had not made sure that the old man arrived more appropriately dressed.

He went out into the hall, paid the porter, and ordered the maid to carry the cases into the room. A sudden strange feeling of warmth flooded over him, even though a few moments earlier the news of his father's arrival had upset him. He embraced the shabby, crumpled old man, kissing him over and over again.

"*Sholem aleichem,* Father! Welcome!"

"*Aleichem sholem, aleichem sholem,* my son!" The old man was trembling with emotion. He kissed his son on both cheeks, and murmured away to himself, praising the Lord of the Universe and blessing his son.

"Sit down, Father." Berman tried to make his father sit at the head of the table, but the old man protested: "God forbid! God forbid!"

His dim old eyes began to shine, and a gentle smile crept over his good-natured face, spreading into all the folds and wrinkles, into his broad, grey beard. The smile expressed the joy he felt that his son, by offering him the place at the head of the table, was fulfilling the commandment to honor his father. He looked round the room.

"What opulence, *ken eynore!*"

And his son wanted *him,* an old, sick man, to sit at the head of the table? And to think that he had agonized over the decision whether to come or not, especially as his son had not answered his letter. And yet it was obvious that his son was, thank God, an honorable Jew. He had, God be praised, a proper beard, just like his other son back home. "Oy! Have we not a good father in heaven! Not a hair of my son's head has been harmed, God forbid. Though he does look like a count, *ken eynore*!"

"Why don't you sit down, Father?" Berman had prepared another place of honor at the table for his father, opposite him.

His father wiped the seat with a trembling hand, wanting to protect it from his travel-stained coat. He sat down slowly, not quite knowing how to behave. Berman went into the kitchen and told the maid to make tea. She was not to bring it in, though, simply to knock on the door, and he would take it from her. After that she was free to go away if she wanted to. She wouldn't be needed any more that day.

Anneke skipped for joy with the tray in her hands, nearly spilling the tea, such a piece of luck didn't happen every day. "Strange folk, those Jews!" she thought in amazement.

The old man felt ashamed of his clothing. He simply hadn't expected such affluence. He looked so poor, and his son was dressed like a king. He should have changed. But then he remembered that he had changed, that this was in fact his best gabardine for *Shabbes*. It was a miracle that he had changed, but why did his best gabardine look so shabby? At home, he thought, it still looked like a perfectly decent garment.

Rochl came in with Jeannette. All day they had been looking round the department stores, searching for bargains for the approaching High Holidays.

"Oh, Papa! We've bought some material. It was a wonderful bargain! I found it, dear Papa." In her usual way she flung herself in jubilation on her father and started to kiss his bushy beard. Berman's father started back in amazement. Jeannette was chattering about their bargains and didn't even notice that there was someone else sitting at the table.

The old man was absolutely aghast. Could that be his granddaughter? The one his son praised so highly in his letters, calling her a sweet child, saying that he thought the world of her? That was impossible! You could see quite clearly that she was *not* a nice Jewish girl, although she was speaking Yiddish. But there were strange words mixed in with it, so that you could hardly understand what she was saying. Perhaps it was German she was speaking? But why was his son letting her kiss him in such an unrestrained way and what did she mean by "*goeie koop*" and "*charmant*"?

Jeannette did indeed pepper her Yiddish with Flemish and French and a good bit of German. Rochl was surprised that Anneke wasn't in the kitchen. She noticed the poor, dusty old man sitting there as if in a trance, and was astonished. Since she had known Berman, she could not remember him ever inviting anyone who looked like that to their table! Who on earth could it be? Berman was kissing his daughter, and some old *shnorrer* (God forgive her for saying it!) was sitting there, drinking tea.

Suddenly Jeannette sprang back with a squeal, as if she had been stung:

"Oh look, Papa, what's that?"

She was holding her hand on her heart to show what a fright she had got, and had called her grandfather "what."

"Jeannette, be quiet and stop playing your foolish tricks! Sit down and you will hear. And you, come here too," he ordered Rochl. "Do you know who this is?" Berman smiled with pleasure to think what a surprise his wife and daughter were about to have. The fact that his daughter had called his father "what" somehow made him feel closer to the old man.

The old man went red from the top of his head, which was hidden under his worn skullcap, to the tips of his toes.

"This is my father. Do you not recognize him, Rochl? And he's your grandfather, sweetheart, do you hear me? Your grandfather."

"You know, Father," he said, turning to the old man, "in this foreign country children grow up as savages!"

"Of course I recognize my father-in-law, may he remain in good health!" exclaimed Rochl. "How could I not recognize him? How are you, Father-in-law? It's a good few years since we last met." Rochl had forgotten that the last time they had met he had not yet become her father-in-law. "Shall I bring in something to eat, or would Father-in-law like to get washed first?" Then Rochl looked at Berman and reddened. Had she perhaps insulted his father by this question?

But Berman was quite happy, agreeing that he should go and have a wash. In any case they would have to change his clothes, he thought, so that at least Dovid and Jacques wouldn't see his father in garments like these.

"Certainly, that would be the correct thing to do," said the old man to his daughter-in-law, looking at his son with the helplessness of a small child. He got up with difficulty from his chair. Only now did Berman realize that his father was still half-paralyzed. He had difficulty walking and his right arm hung down uselessly. Berman was overwhelmed by pity and recollections of the sadness of the past, which plunged him into a melancholy mood. He took his father by the left arm, and led him to the bathroom, like a little child.

The old man had difficulty getting into the bathtub. Berman soaped and washed him, rubbing the soft sponge over the weary, old body. The old man groaned with pleasure: his own son was standing there in his shirtsleeves washing him, like a bathing attendant. That fine beard of his was dipping in the water and getting wet, and how dignified his son looked with his square, silk skullcap!

After the bath, Berman dressed his father in clean underwear and a black suit, which Rochl had found in his plentiful wardrobe. When he combed his father's beard, Berman almost started weeping, as his memories drew him back to the little Polish *shtetl* of his childhood, which now felt completely alien to him.

He brought his father back into the dining room.

"Do you remember, Gedaliah, how you used to comb my beard and give me water when I was in bed? Do you remember? That's why God, may His Name be praised, has granted you success, *ken eynore.* He will continue to multiply His blessings to you."

"Amen!" said Berman out loud.

"Amen," said the old man softly and earnestly.

Rochl had set the table with good things to eat, and she lit all the branches of the candelabrum. The silver and fine food looked even more attractive in the shining light. The festive atmosphere did not, however, delight Berman's heart as it was filled with a gnawing, bittersweet emotion. Strange thoughts came into his head which he could not drive away, and he felt that today he was not the same person as usual. His father realized that his arrival had awakened a great many memories in his son, and he knew that he was pleased to see him, for Berman kept passing him more and more things to eat, as did his daughter-in-law. He was seeing many of these foods for the first time, and some of them, he was sure, were forbidden to him. These tomatoes, for example, looked to him like some kind of fruit that wasn't kosher, and he was surprised to see his son eating them. He wanted to ask him about it, but couldn't bring himself to do so.

"Eat, Father!"

"Father-in-law, you should eat!" urged Rochl.

"It's good for you," insisted Berman encouragingly.

He himself ate only for appearance's sake.

Dovid came home. In the street he had already heard the news, and Berman was pleased that his son had come to greet his grandfather. "I'm really glad you've come, Dovid," said Berman, trying to bring the tension between them to an end. "Father, this is Dovid."

"*Sholem aleichem,* Grandfather," said Dovid, genuinely pleased to see the old man, to whom he took an immediate liking. "He seems to be a real, pious Jew," thought Dovid, looking eagerly at the food, for it was a long time since he had eaten at such a fine, festive table. He washed himself and recited aloud, "Lift up your hands in the sanctuary, and bless the Lord."

Jacques rushed into the dining room. "Papa, they say my grandfather has come!" He ran up to the table with such speed that he didn't even see the old man.

"Now, now, and what do you say to your grandfather?"

Jacques blushed. "*Sholem aleichem,* Grandfather."

"*Aleichem sholem, aleichem sholem,* my child," replied the old man, kissing Jacques on both his smooth olive-skinned cheeks, so that Jacques got his beard full in the face.

"Jeannette, this is no time to read. Put your book away and come to the table. That's it!"

"Lovely children, *ken eynore*! And you can see that they are Jewish children, praise be to God." The old man expressed his pleasure warmly.

"Well, what else would they be? Of course they are Jewish children!" said Berman, glancing swiftly at Dovid. "Hmm… of course they are real Jews."

After the meal the family talked until late into the night. They couldn't persuade the old man to go to bed and get some rest. Every time it was suggested, he made a dismissive gesture with his good hand, saying that he would be happy to sit all night long chatting with his children and grandchildren. All evening he kept looking round the room and giving thanks to the Lord of the universe. "Praise be to God, blessed be He, that He has allowed me to live to see this. Yes, may the Lord above be praised for His grace."

When they finally did go to bed, Berman couldn't get to sleep at all. He was remembering being a child in the tiny *shtetl.* He saw it in front of his eyes, clear and vivid. His mother, who had died just a few months earlier, had been a bitter, bad-tempered, and tearful woman. She had grumbled and groaned as she dragged herself round the cramped house, bemoaning her fate and bearing a grudge against her sick husband because he wouldn't take her advice and give up being a *shochet* in order to become a shopkeeper. Her father had given her a dowry of five hundred rubles, and anyone else would have opened a draper's shop in the market. But since he had to be a *shochet* of all things, as well as being a *mohel* and the leader of the prayers in the synagogue, he could at least have become a *shochet* in a big town like anyone else would have done. Instead, he had lived all his life in this godforsaken place where she and the children were dying of hunger. All he did was slaughter and father children. Slaughter? It was her and the children whom he slaughtered, not the animals! And where were the animals anyway? He thanked God when there was the occasional calf or sterile cow to slaughter. Even a hen appeared only rarely, unless someone was ill or giving birth in the *shtetl.* Ech! *Shtetl?* It was nothing but a village, a dump. And she was going to die here and her children as well and not a living soul would know or care. And he just refused to admit their troubles to anyone. Instead of screaming, "Help! We're dying of hunger," he just answered, "Thanks be to the Lord, may His Name be praised, for everything," if someone did actually once in a while ask him how things were.

And so she would go on, regurgitating the same words over and over again, thousands of times. The children knew this litany by heart and knew which sentence would come next. She never listened to her own grumbling. The children were really sorry for their poor sick father, who was being worn down by her constant complaining.

Now a dark period of his childhood assailed Berman. He remembered how one day his father felt pains in his right arm, and told his wife that he was frightened to carry on slaughtering in case, God forbid, he made a mistake and didn't slaughter the animal according to the Law. Then one morning he suddenly sat down on the edge of his bed, put his hand to his heart and burst out: "I feel ill!"

That morning had etched itself deeply on Berman's young mind. His mother had come running up with a bucket of water and poured it on the unconscious man, pinching him and emitting such strange cries that the whole *shtetl* came to see what the matter was. After this, his father did not leave his bed. Some men of the village laid him in bed and covered him with the heavy quilt, even though it was very hot outside. The rabbi came to visit him, and shook his head so that all the cream-colored lambs' tails on his hat bobbed around. He told the men that he had suspected for a long time that there was something wrong with the *shochet*'s right arm, because once, when the *shochet* had handed him the knife to inspect, the right hand seemed to have been shaking. Even then he should not have been carrying out the slaughtering.

"But may the Lord forgive him and grant him a complete and speedy recovery!" And the rabbi cast his rheumy eyes to the grimy ceiling. At that moment Berman was seized by such a hatred of the rabbi that he wished he would collapse on the spot, just like his father.

Then the rabbi said to his mother, without even turning to look at her, that their Father in Heaven would probably not forsake them, and Chaim Yoysef's wife should not lose her faith, and everything would be all right. He went away, leaving Berman's mother sobbing and weeping, and his father with a paralyzed arm.

Afterwards, however, the rabbi traveled round the forests and collected a hundred rubles from the forestry officials. This enabled

Berman's mother to open a little drapery shop. The *shtetl* employed a new *shochet*, but imposed a tax on him of ten percent for each cow and five percent for a calf to be paid to Berman's father. From then on Berman's mother was very busy: although no customers appeared, she sat all day in the shop, and the twelve-year-old Gedaliah had to look after his two little brothers and his one-year-old sister, who screamed all the time.

Berman's father lay in bed for eight years. His arm and one side were paralyzed. He would say that God, Blessed be His Name, had kept his left arm healthy for his tefillin. And so he lay, summer and winter, under the grubby quilt. His broad beard became grey and tangled. Beside his bed stood a little three-legged table, wobbling precariously, so that the various bottles, pillboxes and nonsensical cures, which women and even gentiles had supplied, and which were about as much use as cupping a corpse, were in constant danger of falling on the floor. As well as this, the children used to deposit bits of leftover stale bread there, and unwashed bowls, cups, and glasses stood on the table. Flies buzzed and crawled around, wandering freely and impudently over Berman's father's yellowed face. The old man put up with this until it became too much of a nuisance, when he tried to flap them away with his good hand.

He lay on his back with his beard over the quilt, studying a religious book. When food was brought to him, he dipped his hand in the clay dish of water, which stood on a stool beside his bed, said the blessing before food, and ate.

His wife had no time for him. Either she was busy in the shop with a customer, or she had gone to the neighboring *shtetl* to buy a few goods, and there was no one to give him his food, so he just buried his kind wrinkled face deeper into his book and forgot that he was hungry.

How clearly Berman could visualize his mother: her shriveled face, crisscrossed by hundreds of blackened wrinkles, looked like dark plowed up earth. She wore a threadbare satin bonnet on her head, its ragged lace framing her face. A few forlorn plums dangled there. The bare wires of their stems were visible, where grapes and all kinds of other decorations had once adorned it.

Berman shivered. Another dark morning from his past came to him, the worst moment of his childhood. This was the morning when he got up and went out into the street, and for the first time heard the children calling his mother "witch." They ran away and it seemed to him that even the adults had abandoned him.

He remembered how, despite the fact that his mother really did love his father, was faithful to him, and wept over his sad fate, she had moments where she couldn't help attacking him, scolding and cursing him. When this fit came over her, all she could do was to scream and shout. Her shrieking could be heard all over the *shtetl*; children and adults stopped at the window, and the children shouted through the window "*mekhasheyfa lo takhaye,* thou shall not suffer a witch to live." The adults got angry with the children but among themselves they said that "something" was screaming out of her, and that one fine day she might put an end to him, God forbid, with her shrieking and the evil spirit, which was staring out of her black eyes. Sometimes she would carry on screaming, cursing herself, her husband, her children, her customers and the young *shochet*'s wife who, in fact, was about ten years older than her, until she had no more strength left. Only then did she sit down on a chair, lean her head against its back, and go to sleep like a child.

After these scenes she would go round for several days in silence, not saying a word to anyone, not even to the children, and the house was so eerily, terrifyingly quiet that it was worse than when she was screaming.

It was the new *shochet*'s wife who had first called her a witch. She was a fat smiling woman with goiter. The people in the *shtetl* didn't hate her, but she hated them. She could not forgive them for taking ten percent of her husband's meager earnings for the previous slaughterer.

"My husband," she would complain, "creeps around in all weathers, in deep mud." And here she would put her hand up to her neck to show the depth of the mud he had to wade through. "He creeps about all the time, searching to see if there could possibly be an animal to slaughter somewhere or other. He never sleeps in the same place twice, and he gets dirty and miserable sleeping on planks in peasants' kitchens, just so that the countess there can prepare her *Shabbes*. Every Thursday morning, I haven't even had time to pour away the washing water, and there he is already, that brat, come for the money. And the impudence of it: he rushes in as if it were his own house, whining: 'Mother says you owe her half a ruble this week.' I owe her, indeed! She just puts the money into her business. She spies on me, so that she knows *exactly* what I owe her!"

Because of her terrible rage against the "countess" she spread it around that she was a witch. How well Berman remembered one particular summer night. They had sat all day in the hot, dusty shop, hoping in vain for customers. Not a single customer had as much as stuck her nose into the shop, even though it was a propitious time: the harvest was in, so that the farmers were not very busy and had got money from the sale of grain, vegetables, wagonloads of hay, and cows which had stopped giving milk and were being sold to save pasture. In groups of three and four the women wandered past the shop, all dressed up in hand-woven skirts, with flowery headscarves on their freshly-washed hair, and necklaces of red glass beads round their necks. They carried their new boots and walked on their bare, toil-toughened feet around the hot dusty village. Laughing and chatting they passed her and went into the shop directly opposite. All the shops were packed except hers, which was completely empty. Apart from all this, the sick man had had a bad day. He had been groaning all day long and, as if to spite her, the baby did not stop crying. About a dozen millstones lay on her chest, pressing and squeezing. She was so tense that she felt she would burst, her head ached and she was so depressed that she couldn't even scream.

So that evening, after putting the children to bed, she went out into the meadow and walked straight towards the river, without knowing why. She certainly wasn't thinking of suicide, in fact she had never heard of such a thing. She simply was drawn to the cool water, desperate to get away from her house, from her sick husband, from other people, and most of all from herself. She sat down on the riverbank, stared at the darkness, murmuring.

Just at that moment, the new *shochet* was coming home from a distant village, feeling very pleased with himself, with two rubles in one pocket and a nice portion of lungs and liver in the other. He saw the former *shochet*'s wife sitting by the river, deep in thought, holding her head with its patched bonnet in both her shriveled hands. She looked like a child who had fallen asleep by the river in the middle of its play. The *shochet* got a shock: a Jewish woman all alone at night by the river? He told his wife about it, and the next morning the *shtetl* was buzzing with the news that the former *shochet*'s wife was a witch, and that at night when everyone was asleep, she would go down to the river to cast her spells.

Women spat and wished bad dreams on her. The menfolk, however, were angry with them, calling the women "stupid cows." Some of them were even of the opinion that the new *shochet*'s wife's evil tongue should be silenced, and that to make amends for the sin of defaming the good name of a Jewish woman, she and her husband should pay an additional five percent slaughtering tax. They ordered their wives not to listen to these ridiculous stories. But despite their efforts, the nickname remained, and the children of the *shtetl* avoided the house. When they were sent on errands, they deliberately made a detour round various streets in order to avoid going past the shop, just like they used to do when they had to pass the hut of an old woman who lived at the edge of the town. When little Gedaliah appeared and wanted to play with the children, they scattered like hens.

Someone only had to say, "There he is!" for the crowd to flee. Humiliated, sad and bitter, the child would go back to his shabby house which smelt of mice, mold and medicaments.

For as long as the inhabitants could remember, Berman's father, Reb Chaim Yoysef, had been able to remove the spell of an evil eye from people. Everyone knew that if he pronounced the words to remove the evil eye, an affected person would recover on the spot.

Berman's mother used to fly into a rage if children came to have the evil eye removed, screaming at them that they shouldn't come bothering a sick man:

"It'll be the end of him! Every time he removes the spell, he's ill afterwards. It saps his strength."

But Reb Chaim Yoysef would gesture with his good hand, say, "It doesn't matter," ponder, and pronounce:

"Yes, it was the evil eye," or "No, it wasn't the evil eye."

Now that the children refused to go there, she missed them. If a child did come to have the evil eye removed, she was as delighted as if he had been a customer.

Twelve-year-old Gedaliah became a hermit. At this young age he had already begun to hate: first of all the new *shoḥet*'s wife, then the children and finally, people in general. So he sat at home, helped his mother, went on errands, and when the mess in the house became so bad that it literally wasn't possible to move, he would wash dishes, sweep out the room, put a basin of clean water at his father's bed, sit down by the bedside and slowly, dipping the comb in the water, comb out Chaim Yoysef's beard. The hairs which came out he laid, for his father's sake, between the pages of a sacred book. He did not love his mother very much, but he loved his father deeply.

"Father, when I am grown up I'll deal in all sorts of things and get very rich and when I have a lot of money, I'll give it all to you. You'll get well again and we'll move away from here to a big city. I'll get so rich that we'll be able to move to the biggest city in the world, to Warsaw, that's where we'll go!"

He was not telling his father stories simply to entertain him, but believed absolutely in what he said. His faith in the power he would have when he was older and his certainty that he would be rich were so strong that the chaos in the neglected house, the polluted air, full of the smell of the sick man's sweat, of dirt and medicaments, didn't have any effect on him. In his imagination he didn't live in this room but somewhere far, far away, in big cities and beautiful rich palaces. His dear, sick, half-dead father did not lie under a grubby quilt, but sat on a red velvet chair, like the rich man of the *shtetl*, reading a sacred book. But even then he saw his mother as she really was, in her torn bonnet, in her dusty little shop, and heard her screaming. He was unable to draw her into his fantasy world.

And that is how he pictured her now, in the darkness of the night, as he lay under his pure white sheets, in his richly decorated bedroom, where everything shone and glowed. The strips of light, coming in through the gaps in the curtains, fell on the blue, deep-pile carpet, and on his bed. All this brightness made his poor mother appear even more dark and dingy in his memory.

He remembered the morning when a large covered wagon drew up at their shop. It was lined with hay covered with a patched sheet. Pillows and a quilt were carried out. They, too, were patched but freshly laundered. Then some of the men of the *shtetl* carried out Berman's father and laid him in the wagon. They carried him slowly, as if they were scared he might break. The *shtetl* gathered round their house, as if for a funeral. The rabbi himself stood beside the wagon, shook the lambs' tails on his hat, gave his father some advice, which no one heard. A smile spread over his father's sallow face which Berman would never forget. His mother, sitting in the wagon, looked so tiny, huddled in her black coat with her black bonnet; she contrasted strangely with the white all round her. And so they took Berman's father off to the hospital in Warsaw. Berman recalled that he had been jealous of his mother, and even of his father, because they were going off to the big city.

Then his mother came back on her own, and they worked together in the shop. She felt a lot better from then on. The children and adults were sorry for them both and were friendly towards them.

"Poor thing! Without her husband. What a terrible thing!" The women sighed and started buying from them.

The sighs of pity made Berman resent the women even more. But worst of all he hated being a poor boy and he fantasized all the more about the things he would do when he was grown up.

His father was much better when he came back home. He didn't need to lie in bed all the time, but could sit in an armchair. Berman's little sister died of scarlet fever. His mother wept and wept and then stopped.

When Berman turned twenty he went to the nearby town, and with a small amount of money, which he had managed to save up, he bought a ticket for Antwerp. He paid no heed to his mother's reproaches that he was leaving her alone with his invalid father and the little children who were, in fact, no longer little children.

"Mother, there's no point in crying. It's time I started looking for a proper livelihood. And in any case I'll soon be called up to the army, so please, that's enough!"

He packed his good *Shabbes* gabardine and his tefillin bag and with these riches he set off one rainy evening and arrived in Antwerp.

As soon as he stepped over the threshold of the station restaurant, an old woman with a stupid face and a mouth full of gold teeth started to try to make a match for him. Berman said he wasn't interested, but the old woman wasn't put off by his reply. "You'll soon be interested," she said, speaking German to him. "When you see the bride you'll certainly be interested! And if you make enquiries about her, you'll find out that she is my own niece, and *then* you'll certainly be interested!" The old woman seemed to think that to be a niece of hers was a particular honor.

"Perhaps I can have a bowl of barley soup?" asked Berman, who was ravenously hungry.

"Of course, with the greatest of pleasure." The old woman opened a door and called: "Rosa, a plate of barley soup!"

Berman was astonished when he saw that the old woman's niece was none other than the daughter of Yankl Eli, the carpenter in his *shtetl.* His mother used to send him there as a little boy to collect wood shavings and bits of wood left over from the coffins which the carpenter was making. Yankl the carpenter's daughter, Rochl! She recognized him too. "What are you doing here?" she asked stiffly in German and blushed to the roots of her hair.

"And what are *you* doing here?" Berman spoke familiarly to her in homely Yiddish, not yet having absorbed any "foreign manners."

Berman had been attracted to Rochl for a long time, ever since they were children, in fact. He was always very ashamed to carry off the sack of wood shavings in front of her, as if, God forbid, he had been some peasant. But both his desire to see Rochl, as well as his love of sitting around in the coffins, daydreaming about leaving home, made him obey his mother and go for the wood shavings.

Rochl's father used to say to him that you shouldn't sit in a coffin, because it could bring about your death, but Berman didn't believe him: he knew that adults always like telling little boys that they "shouldn't do" things. So he used to answer that you couldn't die because of that, and carried on sitting there.

Rochl's father was a stout, good-natured man with a fleshy face which always looked tired from the hard work he did. His eyes were blue and childlike, his nose round and shiny, and he had a broad, thick, tobacco-colored beard which always had wood shavings sticking in it. He used to say, "you shouldn't…" and then just carried on planing his coffins, forgetting Berman's existence. Then Berman used to lure Rochl into the coffin too, and they would drive around in his "carriage."

When he was older and stopped coming for the wood shavings, he really longed to go back to their house, though he didn't realize what it was that attracted him to it. There wasn't really much to pine for, in fact. There was no furniture in the big square room apart from two beds, a table and a few chairs. On the long carpenter's table there was almost always a child's coffin, painted pale yellow, the lid decorated with a large brass or tin cross. On the grey floor, which was covered with heaps of sawdust, wood shavings, square bits of wood and little scraps of white and yellow tin, there were always adult coffins standing around; some were painted, some still unpainted, some adorned and some still bare. They told tales of measles, chickenpox and scarlet fever epidemics in the villages, of children with stomachs swollen from hunger, of somber funerals on dark wintry days, of black horses on the white snow, of the stifled weeping of peasant women and the lowered heads of their menfolk.

In this sea of curly wood shavings, Rochl's bad-tempered stepmother shuffled about, either grumbling and complaining under her breath about the houseful of girls who were idly lounging around, or actually quarrelling with them, so that the *shtetl* would gather to see the spectacle. Rochl's father, the carpenter, did not intervene between his wife and his daughters. On those occasions his plane would move faster and faster, working at breakneck speed, as if Death itself was driving him and demanding the coffin from him.

More than once Berman walked past the carpenter's house, hoping that by chance he might see Rochl coming out. But it didn't happen, because she had already gone off to live with her aunt in Antwerp. This aunt, who tried to marry her off to every boy who crossed the threshold of the restaurant, didn't dream she would have this piece of luck.

Berman did well. He soon learned all that was necessary, and became a broker. His sharp instinct for the business soon won him the trust of the diamond merchants, who recognized his ability. They sent him around with parcels of diamonds, and he soon learned to speak German, mixed with Flemish and Hebrew, like all the respected Antwerp merchants. He started making money. He loved Rochl, who was very beautiful, and because of her he always ate in the same restaurant, until one fine morning he took her away from her aunt's pots and pans, married her and set her up in her own kitchen, so that she should cook good meals, as only she could, for him, instead of for the general public.

After they were married Rochl proved to him how much she esteemed him for this, as she continued to do throughout their marriage.

Chapter 12

Berman got up late with a dull headache, and Anneke poured him a good warm bath. He got out of the bathtub feeling refreshed and put on his crimson satin dressing gown. It had black flowers and a broad silken girdle with two thick multicolored tassels, which swayed in time to his movements, giving dignity and rhythm to his gait.

His father was seated at the dining room table reading one of his sacred books. Berman smiled with satisfaction. Reb Chaim Yoysef was already quite a different person. Last night he had looked like an old beggar, but now, sitting there, he was a dignified old Jew. His velvet skullcap looked so homely on him, the yellowness had almost disappeared from his beard, and a gentle, childlike smile hovered on his wrinkled face. He was bent over his book, swaying backward and forward, like an obedient child who has been given a picture book to look at.

The old man realized someone was looking at him, and raised his eyes. The sight of his tall, broad-shouldered son in his satin dressing gown, with his long, neatly combed, black beard, in which a few silvery hairs gleamed, gave him a feeling of awe and respect. Here, he felt, stood a person of high status, and he even tried to stand up in order to greet him.

"Did you sleep well, Father? Have you already had some tea? Would you like to go to a *shtibl*?"

"Oh yes indeed, I certainly would!"

Berman took his father, who was a Gerer Hasid, to the *shtibl*. He wanted his father to have his own place there, and was anxious to show him that he was able to get that for him too. But in the *shtibl* Berman was not shown the same degree of respect as in his synagogue. Young and old addressed him with the familiar "*du*," as if they had been bosom friends all their lives. One man, wearing a grubby green frock coat, which reached to the very heels of his boots, poked his long snuff-stained nose right into Berman's face and, being deaf, bellowed into Berman's ear that he should pay for some vodka because the *shtibl* had a guest. He seemed to think that the guest was the *shtibl*'s, not Berman's. Everyone heard the remark and started demanding vodka.

Berman prayed, said *Kaddish* for his mother, paid for a generous amount of vodka and, following his father's wishes, left him in the *shtibl.*

"You know the way home, Father?"

"It's all right, don't worry, you can go, we'll show him the way."

After Berman left, the Hasidim started asking the guest where he came from and why he had come. They were really delighted that he was there. He had brought with him a flavor of the "*alte heym*" which they missed greatly.

Some old Jews sat and studied at a long, scratched wooden table spotted all over with wax instead of praying with the rest of the congregation. One of them was a thin, bloodless man with skin like faded parchment, a red translucent nose and a long scraggy beard. He recognized Chaim Yoysef. He placed a handkerchief full of holes on the open Gemara which he was studying and addressed him:

"Do you not remember me, Chaim Yoysef?" He immediately answered his own question: "I see you don't! I'm not surprised. It's been a good few years. Don't you remember? It was when the old man died, blessed be his memory."

"You mean the *Sfas Emes*?" asked Chaim Yoysef, addressing him by the formal "*ir.*"

"Who else would I mean? But why are you speaking to me so formally? You do seem to have completely forgotten me. Do you not remember Leybele Strotsker?" said the man, giving the name away himself.

"Ah!" exclaimed Reb Chaim Yoysef, greeting him warmly, and gazing with great respect at this man with the cadaverous head, which shook like a dry willow branch when he spoke. He smiled all the time, sometimes rather tearfully, like a child who has been hurt by something, and sometimes as if he were delighted that fate had chosen to cast *him* into this city of diamonds, where the Evil One can seduce anyone he likes, except him, Leybele Strotsker.

"Yes, now I remember you! Of course I do! Who could forget Reb Leybele Strotsker?" Reb Chaim Yoysef spoke with great respect to this skeletal figure dressed in rags. "Have you been living here for long?" He again spoke formally, absolutely unable to call his former friend "*du*."

"Ten years!"

"For ten years?" echoed Reb Chaim Yoysef, at a loss for words. He was full of amazement and pity that the great scholar and righteous man should be in such a state. "Ten years!" he repeated, as if the important thing was his having lived there for that length of time.

The next morning at breakfast, Reb Chaim Yoysef asked his son why the community allowed a great man like Reb Leybele Strotsker to live in that state. Berman told him Reb Leybele had a son in Antwerp who was a very rich man, but he was not pious, did not keep *Shabbes*, and his father refused to take a single penny from him. Indeed he would not accept help from anybody. At first this had caused the community great distress, but gradually they had got used to it and didn't bother about it anymore. And in fact the Hasidim suspected him of secretly being one of their rabbinical opponents, because it wasn't the way of the Hasidim to refuse charity. Berman smiled at this and carried on:

"After the death of the *Sfas Emes*, Reb Leybele stopped going to the *rebbe*'s court; it's no secret that he doesn't think much of the present one."

Reb Chaim Yoysef thought about this but his only reaction was to mutter into his beard: "Hmm! Hmm!" He didn't think much of the present one either.

Dovid came in, freshly washed and shaved, having got up early in honor of his grandfather. The old man smiled at his grandson, but looked at his clean-shaven chin, which still had a dark shadow because of the blackness of his hair. The old man was greatly displeased that his grandson had shaved his beard off, God preserve us! He was dying to ask his son how he could permit Dovid to do such a thing, but he didn't dare.

No, he didn't have Reb Leybele's strength of character.

Chapter 13

Berman saw Dovid once more lounging on the sofa in his silk dressing gown, yawning. But instead of telling him off, he regarded it as a miracle. Dovid would certainly never have gained entry to the Bourse had he carried on working as a diamond polisher. That thought horrified Berman. "The bastards would have refused to show me their best merchandise." Good friends would have pitied him, and his enemies would have rejoiced.

"Oh well, it could be worse. He could, God forbid, have married a *shikse.* When all's said and done, he's made his bed, so he'll have to lie on it. I can always give him food and clothing. Nevertheless, it hurts when a father has to watch his grown-up son lolling around and not doing anything. What will become of him? He'll end up being a *shnorrer.*" Berman knew the taste of poverty. But, as the saying goes: "You can lead a horse to water but you can't make him drink." He had given Dovid money, introduced him to the Bourse and shown him the ropes. And when the good-for-nothing made a mess of it all, he had tried, despite everything, to make an advantageous match for him. Marriage would have forced Dovid to work at diamond dealing. He would have got acquainted with the business and become a respectable family man. Berman felt he had done all he could as a father.

Mulling all this over as he changed to go to his office, he felt a sense of relief because at least he had a clear conscience. He gave Rochl money, instructing her not to give too much to Dovid, in case he was tempted to do something stupid: "Do you understand?

You're to see to it!" Rochl made it obvious she had no idea how to deal with the situation.

"You don't understand? What a genius!" Berman gave a condescending smile and walked out.

In the town they said this had been the worst summer for trade they could ever remember – business was completely dead.

For days at a time the diamond cleavers, cutters and polishers wandered around in their best clothes, which by now had turned into their everyday clothes, looking up into the empty sky as if they expected that some movement would come from there. Perhaps the obstinate diamond merchants from America, India and elsewhere would wake up from their aristocratic sleep, descend on Antwerp and put an end to the long fallow period, which was dragging as slowly as the seven days of mourning after a death. The machines all had their covers on, but the women sighed and dressed up in their best clothes to hide their poverty.

Shopkeepers had long since stopped selling on credit to ordinary people, and women didn't dare to go into the shops without money in their hands. Only the diamond merchants' wives were still buying on credit. The shopkeepers suppressed their rage against the rich women and vented it on the poor. And the rich women just kept on taking. The shopkeepers feared it would be dangerous to stop giving to them, since they would lose important customers as well as the money which they were owed. So instead they argued amongst themselves, quarreled with their wives and cursed each other and their own children. The errand boys with the long beards were weak with hunger, and the small diamond dealers simply could not hold out till a better season came. So they sold their diamonds at a loss. Brokers wandered round the streets with despair in their eyes, with empty pockets and empty hearts.

All this time Berman had kept on buying, and giving out work. He bought for cash and paid the workers their due. Other workers were jealous of Berman's people and were dying to get work from him, but Berman refused to act unscrupulously and change his workers. If a man worked for him, he should carry on doing so.

The anteroom of the office with the frosted glass door was crowded. About two dozen cutters and polishers were waiting with the parcels of stones they had brought, their hearts pounding and their faces expressing surprise and foreboding.

"What can have happened? He's never been as late coming to the office as this!"

"Perhaps he hasn't any work for us today and so he's taking his time! He won't miss the few francs at the end of the week. He'll have enough to pay his rent, that's for sure!"

"Rent? *Rent-shment!* Are you trying to tell us that's not his own house?"

"It could be his grave for all I care!"

"So why should he be bothered to come today if he doesn't want to? He's not going to lose any sleep over us!"

"Shhh, he's coming!"

"He's coming?!" they all exclaimed with one voice and then fell silent.

They needn't have worried. Berman told his secretary to hang up his coat, just as he did every day. He combed his beard with his fingers, straightened the square silk skullcap on his head, smoked a cigar, then puffed on his pipe. He sat down at his large mahogany desk with its green baize top which was covered with account books and papers. On one side of the desk stood a large gold-framed photograph of Jeannette in an old-fashioned crinoline. The skirt was a little on the short side and the wide, old-fashioned, pleated pantaloons edged with fine Brussels lace peeped out from underneath it. Her hair was smooth and her plaits were wound round her delicate little head. She had a gracious smile with just a touch of coquettishness. The photograph had been taken before she went to a masked ball in aid of the charity hospital, at which she took part in a dance entertainment with young amateurs from the rich Orthodox community. Berman looked at the photograph and beamed. Even his beard seemed to smile too.

"What a beauty she is, *ken eynore*!"

He instructed his secretary to open the correspondence, looked through it, and then told her which ones to answer and which to ignore. Then, at last, he remembered the people who had been waiting outside for hours, and he smiled. The scene in the corridor, though he witnessed it every day, never failed to amuse him. The way they all sprang about, competing to be the first to wish him "good morning!" If they had any sense they would concentrate on their work instead. Then they wouldn't make so many mistakes, he thought.

"Well, call them in!" he said.

He started re-reading a letter he had already read so that he did not have to look at the people while they were coming in. Finally he called out: "Friedman!"

When he had finished with the poor, long-suffering workers, he gave the secretary a multitude of tasks to perform before he returned, and went to the Bourse.

In the big, pillared hall the portly diamond merchants were strolling about. They would spy a fellow dealer, greet him, and stop to chat, giving the impression of not being there to do business, but just to ask each other how things were. At other times, when business was flourishing, the dealers would go round asking each other what was for sale. They would sit down at a table or, if it was business which had to be done in private, leave the Bourse and drop into a nearby restaurant for a glass of tea. Now, however, there was more talk than action. Berman sat down at a table where a ruddy-cheeked, heavily-built merchant was poking with his tweezers at a little heap of diamonds. His shiny nose looked so soft that a touch would squash it, and both his nose and his fat cheeks were crisscrossed by a network of little red veins. As he moved them around, the diamonds he had just purchased changed color from red to blue, white, fiery orange, translucent green, and back to blue. A huge diamond adorned the little finger of his podgy white hand, glittering along with the purchased stones.

As he peered through the loupe, this American dealer hummed an English song, the latest hit in the vaudeville theater. Berman took up one of the stranger's stones and looked at it, while the latter kept on poking around as if these were not costly diamonds but bits of glass he didn't care about.

"And when she smiiiled, my love," sang the dealer, enjoying both the song and the stones, which he had just bought for his firm in New York. They were a real bargain.

"Pity they're dark cape, don't you think?" asked Berman.

"Dark cape? How on earth can you call them dark cape?" retorted the American, addressing Berman by the familiar "*du*" as he did with everyone, young or old.

"Well what would *you* call them then?"

At this point the good-natured American began to lose his equanimity. His face turned even redder, so that it looked as if he had been scalded.

"It's none of your business. They're not for sale anyway!"

"What, are you going to pickle them?" Berman joked.

"They're already sold, you see."

"Well, they're yellow nonetheless." Berman paid no heed to the dealer's story that they were already sold. "Or are you trying to tell me they're blue-white?"

The American completely lost his temper: "I'd define them as silver cape. Anyway, they're not for sale. You mind your own business!"

"To hell with him!" said Berman to a merchant at a nearby table, where he stopped, even though he had no business to do there. "Yankee Doodle is raging. I think he'll burst a blood vessel!"

The other merchant laughed: "Yes, he doesn't look in very good shape!"

Berman sat down at a table by the window, which had just become free, took out a few parcels and started examining them. He put back some stones, and examined others again just for show.

"Hmm, these have turned out well."

Very soon some dealers and brokers had gathered round Berman's table.

"Top silver?" one of them suggested.

"Is that all you think of them?" countered Berman.

"They could be dark cape for all I care. I'm not buying today in any case."

Berman laughed. "If I had a parcel of blue-white you'd soon snap it up!"

"I've just seen some blue-white. Tsvaygnboym has some. He's got really fine goods. You know, that man's doing excellent business. They say he hasn't even got his hands on the dowry yet, and already everyone trusts him."

"I'm really pleased to hear it! I wish him well," said Berman, trying to smile, to the amusement of the other dealers. "He can pretend all he likes, but he's as jealous as hell," they said to each other.

A pale young man with a pointed nose and small, deep-set eyes burst into the room, looking as if he were about to faint. "Have you heard the news? The Dutch guilder has fallen!" he exclaimed.

"What?!" the dealers exclaimed. "How is that possible?!"

"Here you are! Look!" And he spread a Flemish newspaper out on the table and pointed at the page with his thin forefinger.

Then he raised both hands in the air and brushed the newspaper with them as if he was trying to wipe out the freshly printed news. Someone else brought in a paper.

"Look, here it is, read it! You see, the guilder has fallen; there's panic in the stock exchange!"

"And I have only guilders! Not a single franc." The young man was shaking and looked as if he were about to collapse; he had forgotten that speaking the truth in the Diamond Bourse was more dangerous than only having guilders.

Soon half the people in the Bourse were crowding round Berman's table, grabbing the afternoon paper, reading it, their heads lowered, their eyes devouring the tiny lines of print. Berman packed up his diamonds and smiled to himself. Out loud he said, "Others may be better looking, but I'm the clever one."

The crowd fell on Berman's words thirstily; all eyes were peering at him intently, anxiously waiting, as if the whole business depended on what he had to say about it; as if the guilder would rise or fall even further on Berman's say-so. Berman smiled wisely and said, "Last week I predicted that the guilder would fall."

The merchants all stood there, feeling that they had been made fools of.

"Is that all he has to say about it?"

Most of them went out into the street, where it was impossible to walk on the pavement. There were little knots of people everywhere: big dealers, little dealers, and even insignificant characters who had no guilders, no francs, no money of any kind, but who were also highly agitated. Flemish and Dutch merchants who were not normally seen in this street mingled with groups of Jewish merchants, talking frenetically, enquiring, consulting each other.

"Listen to what I say!" said Berman in a firm voice. Despite their disappointment at his earlier remarks, they all listened to him. "Let's stop getting so excited and let's not block the pavement, so that other people can get through." Berman had become public-spirited for a moment. "Let's stop trading for a day or two to see how things develop. It's possible this is just some kind of speculation and you are all getting into a state unnecessarily. We'll know in a couple of days. If the guilder really has fallen, then we'll just have to adapt. And if it is a case of speculation on the stock exchange, we'll get to know about it."

"That's right!" said some of the merchants of a calmer, more reflective disposition. Others were panicking and didn't want to go home. They just hung about the streets.

Berman, for his part, went home to eat. He had no guilders and did not see that there was anything to concern him. So he enjoyed his glass of tea with Rochl's home-baked biscuits.

The next day it turned out that the news in the paper was the invention of some cheap journalist or other who had no other news from Holland to fill the columns of the paper, so he invented this story to spice up the edition. The dealers were ashamed to look each other in the eyes. Why had it not occurred to them that a telephone call to Holland would have revealed the truth within a few minutes?

"What did I tell you?" said Berman triumphantly, as always. And as always, he congratulated himself on being a person of a calm, reflective disposition.

So once again he sat at a table, surrounded by dealers. People were apparently talking about everything and anything except business: they were discussing the city, or politics, making jokes and telling stories about mutual acquaintances. Then, as if it were just an afterthought, one of them would produce a parcel of stones. The rest would examine it. Someone else would take out a parcel. There would be a fiery flash, and then another pair of eyes would flash like the diamonds. A blue gleam, a trembling drop of water – and then there was a bargaining, a resolution, a shaking of hands and an exchange of "*mazel un brokhe!*"

And as Berman sat there peering through the loupe, concentrating hard on someone's stone, a woman in a black suit came into the Bourse. Her wide-brimmed hat was pulled down over her light blue eyes so that one saw little of her well-nourished, clear-skinned face. Her plump neck and the skin revealed by the deep décolleté of her crepe de chine blouse were white and attractively feminine.

She approached the table and the dealers started to pass remarks about her, some in a subtle fashion, while others, openly vulgar, made ambiguous jokes and shook with mirth. The woman ignored them. She took out a parcel from her large black handbag and handed it to Berman. He opened it and was taken with the fine sparkling stones, but immediately said that they were not for him. The woman said something, which only Berman heard; she leant over so close to him that he felt her warm breath. Everyone else strained to hear, but to no avail.

"Very well then," said Berman, "if you insist, please come up to my office."

This meant: "That's a different matter. I may be willing to buy stolen goods, but not here."

The woman shut her handbag, inclined her head and started leaving.

"Show us what you've got!" a dealer shouted after her. The others burst out laughing, though the dealer had meant it quite seriously and wanted to see her goods. But she pretended not to hear.

"What do you think of Gretchen? She's certainly putting on weight. We'll soon have to extend the walls of the Bourse."

"If we just knock down the pillars she'll get in all right," joked the dealers.

They continued to laugh, in their coarse, cynical fashion.

"She's a determined woman, and what a head she's got on her shoulders! They say that when her husband was alive, he sought her advice about business, and didn't make a move without her!"

Berman stood up, wandered about the Bourse for a while, exchanged a word here, a look there, and then he left and went straight back up to his office, nearby. The woman was already waiting for him. Berman sent his secretary off with a note to Rochl about his father's bed, even though he knew very well that Rochl couldn't read. She would have to wait till he got home to read the note to her. The secretary skipped gleefully down the stairs two steps at a time, thinking to herself, "I can take half an hour off!"

The woman brought her chair closer to the table.

"Herr Berman, you remember the blond *goy* who robbed the till and stole diamonds, and brought dishonor to the Bourse? You remember how poor Rosenbaum shot himself?"

"Yes indeed," said Berman, looking at her eagerly and enquiringly.

"The *goy* has been arrested, but the whereabouts of the goods are unknown, and the money has disappeared without a trace."

Berman pretended not to hear.

"How many stones to the carat?"

"To the carat? You mean how many carats to the stone! I'm talking about stones of five and eight carats, blue-white!"

"We'll soon see if that's true!"

"Very well, take a look."

Berman put his loupe to his eye and examined the stones, trying to hide the excitement he felt just looking at them.

"You've got black ones too?" He laid the stones on one side as if they didn't interest him at all.

"Black ones too, certainly."

The stones flashed black, red, green with a silver shimmer. Then red again. Berman gave an involuntary shiver. One seldom saw anything as good as that.

"He certainly knew what to steal, that damned *goy.*"

The woman was watching Berman's every move. She saw the impression the diamonds made on him. She knew this little game only too well.

The two of them haggled for a long time. The woman stood her ground and would not reduce the price by a centime. She knew that Berman would pay because he realized that he stood to earn a fortune. At last he said:

"Leave the goods here, and I will give you a definite decision in a few hours' time."

The woman counted the stones once more, gave Berman her soft white hand, inclined her head slightly and left. Her face was flushed as if she had drunk a large vodka, her eyes were shining and she had the sensuous beauty of a woman after making love, rather than doing business. She regarded the goods as sold. Berman would not be able to resist such a purchase.

Berman was rubbing his hands: Praise be to God! This was a wonderful piece of business. Then he remembered his father at home and gave a pious sigh.

"There'll have to be a trip to London. I can't keep this merchandise in my possession for very long," he thought. He decided that the next morning he would quiz the woman, who had suggested London, to find out exactly what the office in London was like. How did she know that the goods could be sold there? Had she herself sold stones there? And so on.... He wouldn't go to London himself; Shapiro could go instead. He was younger and more active than Berman, and why shouldn't he also profit from this? Berman was now feeling generous. He telephoned Shapiro at his office.

"Come here quickly, please! A very important matter!"

When his secretary came back, Berman told her she could go to the cinema. "There's nothing more to do today, but come early tomorrow morning. There'll be a lot of correspondence."

"Thank you, I certainly will."

This time the girl flew down the stairs three at a time, singing: "*Ooolala, in het park van de nachtegaal...*"

Shapiro, who never touched stolen goods or "lost" parcels, arrived at Berman's office. "That fellow will end up in prison one day, long beard and all. He's worried sick already, and yet he can't resist," he thought to himself and smiled when he saw the stones, which he immediately recognized. The woman had already shown them to him.

"Hmm...you know my principle, Herr Berman. Hmm...these goods are not for me."

Berman, confused and angered by Shapiro's response, was about to make a harsh riposte to him, but he swallowed it, even though it stuck in his throat. It was, after all, typical of Shapiro. He gave one of his sly smiles, which always made Berman nervous. This meant that he had already seen these stones and knew what kind of merchandise they were. So Berman just had to bite his tongue and be silent. Nevertheless, he was angry.

"You see how the bastards lose things! We'll have to be careful that they don't lose parcels of ours one day." He was just searching for things to say, just so that he didn't have to look at Shapiro's little smile.

Berman straightened up, but he felt a great tiredness in his aching limbs. It was always the same after he had struck a good bargain, but this time he felt as if someone had beaten him up instead.

"Damn it all, that Shapiro's just play-acting, striking a pose. He, Shapiro, wouldn't do such a thing, God forbid! What a thought! He, the respectable citizen. Bah! The cut-throat, more like... the... the...." Berman couldn't find the right words to describe Shapiro. His mind went blank. He grew angry with himself.

"What an idiot I am! Did I really have to phone *him*, that saintly character, that Hungarian rogue! I think he's just trying to pull a fast one."

"Listen to me, Herr Berman," said Shapiro, who could read Berman's thoughts, "I advise you as a good friend: don't get involved with that Gretchen. Don't jeopardize your good name through dubious deals like this. She even informed me of an office in London where I would be able to dispose of the goods. Ha ha! The way she called the thief 'the blond *goy*,' as if she herself were Jewish. You remember, Herr Berman, how poor old Rosenbaum, may his soul rest in peace, shot himself on account of those two bloody Germans?"

Berman's eyes had a glassy stare and he felt a shiver running through him. He was sitting hunched up with his hands tucked into the sleeves of his jacket, fighting a hard battle with himself. It was very, very difficult to relinquish diamonds like these. They danced before his eyes, filling the room, and flashing round the walls; their orange, white, red and yellow fire made his senses reel.

"Herr Berman, withstand this temptation and you will be grateful to me."

Berman gave a start: had he been asleep? How long had he been dozing? And Shapiro was still there? What was happening?

"You are right, Herr Shapiro!" Berman stretched and felt a sudden sense of relief, as if a heavy burden had rolled off his shoulders.

"That Gretchen will get what she deserves; mark my words, Herr Berman."

The two men carried on talking for a long time. After Shapiro had left, however, Berman looked at the diamonds again, and the temptation was just too strong....

Gretchen was sitting in a first class compartment, both hands buried in the sleeves of her loose traveling coat, thinking about her visit to the dirty office above a private pawnbroker's shop. The owner, a gentile with red hair, a pinched, red face and steely-grey eyes, was one of five partners. Gretchen had gone into the front shop by mistake, where the owner was standing behind the counter examining a pair of sheets, grey from frequent washing, which a tall gaunt woman in a patched velvet coat, with a man's cap on her head, was trying to pawn.

"Mr. Brown! On my word of honor, I only bought them a month ago," she assured him, seeing that he was not too keen. "Only a month ago," she insisted pleadingly, her watery blue eyes becoming even more despairing. And the curlers and hairpins in her thin, colorless hair bobbed about.

Mr. Brown laughed. He had a drunken look in his eyes, cracked jokes and roared with laughter, and the other ragged women with their strained, lined faces, who were standing waiting in a queue, roared with laughter too.

"Oh, isn't he a scream!" they all chuckled, showing their prominent front teeth, hoping thereby to find favor in Mr. Brown's eyes.

"But in which century was that?" laughed Mr. Brown, enjoying his new joke, and he flung the tall woman a few pennies across the counter.

The women started feeling their own packages, running their crooked, bony fingers over the bits and pieces of clothing they had brought in to be pawned, and their urge to laugh suddenly disappeared.

"Did you see what he gave her! He's gone mad!" they whispered to each other. "I won't be able to manage till Friday on that, it won't even be enough to provide dry bread, and the kids have such appetites!"

"It's the same with me. It's a disaster!"

Seeing Gretchen come into the shop, a thin man with a greenish face and cunning, grey eyes abandoned a package he was examining, and without saying a word came out from behind the counter, took Gretchen up to the first floor, showed her the door of the office and, still without speaking, went down the crumbling stairs again. It was here that Gretchen had disposed of the goods.

Chapter 14

When Jacques came home from school with his schoolbag on his shoulders, Berman told him to go to *cheder* immediately; he knew everything, and if Jacques tried to get out of it again, he would get what was coming to him that evening. And Berman told him that on no account should he forget to take his grandfather to the *shtibl.* Then he went off to take a nap.

Jacques set out with his grandfather. On the way he met some friends and when one of them whistled to him, Jacques changed direction and turned into Leeuwerikstraat, taking his grandfather into the wrong *shtibl* by mistake.

"There it is!" And Jacques disappeared like a streak of lightning. Before the old man had a chance to look round, Jacques was with his pals and Reb Chaim Yoysef had no one to speak to.

"Oh well, it is a holy place too," he thought. He took out his Gemara, found the page where he had stopped reading and sat down to study.

But the Jews all laid their pocket handkerchiefs on their books and started asking where he had come from, whom he was visiting and how long he was staying.

"Oh! Berman? Well, if you're visiting a son like that, then it certainly is a good thing to sit quietly studying. It is good to walk on foot beside a heavy wagon; don't you think so, Reb Itshe?"

"Yes indeed!" answered Reb Itshe, who was the *dayan,* the judge in the religious court. His rabbinical clothes hung too loosely on his small, bony frame. He went up very close to Reb Chaim Yoysef and peered at him with his little black eyes. Then, unable to think of anything else to say, he went back to his Gemara. One tall thin man, however, wouldn't let the *dayan* study. "Do you think he will be able to stay long at his son's house, eh, Reb Itshe?" he asked him.

Reb Itshe didn't reply but carried on rocking over his open book like a child.

"The reason I say that," carried on the man, who seemed to like the sound of his own voice, "is that when a good old-fashioned Jew from the old homeland comes over, and is not used to the customs here, it's really difficult, especially... well, anyway, may the Almighty stand by you."

"Well there certainly are things I don't approve of," admitted Reb Chaim Yoysef, who didn't understand what the speaker had meant by his "especially." "I mean, my son is, thank God, an observant Jew, but my grandson has removed his beard. It's very distasteful to me. Admittedly, my daughter-in-law says that he removes it with some kind of powder, and certainly that is permitted under the law. Indeed one reads that the sages were explicitly commanded to remove their beards in honor of every Jewish festival. But Jews in the Diaspora should not do it. That's the problem with being in a foreign country. At home, in Poland, a decent young man would never touch his beard, God forbid! But what can one do? And apart from that, they go around dressed like *goyim*. Even I am going around like that now."

"Oh well, if that's the worst thing that happens! He's just playing at being a *goy*. For our kind of people this isn't a real homeland," opined the previous speaker. "God be praised, my children are observant, thank God."

Reb Itshe smiled. "His sons have convinced him, the fool, that their beards don't grow!"

"What do you mean?" asked Reb Chaim Yoysef, bewildered.

Reb Itshe was about to explain, thought better of it, said nothing more and started swaying over his open Gemara again. When a woman came in to ask advice about a fowl, he folded down the page, closed the book, felt around in the intestines, licked the liver a few times, and pronounced that it was kosher. He was so delighted he was able to give this judgment and did not have to condemn it, that he did not go back to his studying, but listened to the conversation instead.

The loquacious man was still talking. "Hmm, from what you say, the law of the gentiles rules in your son's house! Thank God, I have better luck. My sons, God be praised, don't have any beards. At first I was really upset about it, but now, God be praised, I am really pleased. I see that the Almighty knows better than I what is for our good. For what if they had started shaving their beards, and then perhaps, God forbid, had completely left the right path? God preserve us, the things that can happen here!"

"What do you mean?" Old Reb Chaim Yoysef still didn't really understand, but the man didn't let him ponder long:

"You're surprised, eh? Well, you're not the only one. No one believes me. But my sons told me themselves."

Reb Chaim Yoysef, finally getting the point, gave a little smile and stuck his nose back into his Gemara.

"What a fool!" he thought, wanting to resume his study, but the other man would not let him do so.

"You know, if you had asked my advice before you set out, you wouldn't have come to Antwerp. It is Sodom and Gomorrah. Here, if you can't flatter, lie, swindle and steal, you can't make a living. Good Jews come here, poor creatures, and they think: 'Antwerp is a Jewish city, they deal in diamonds here, there'll certainly be no problem making a livelihood here.' They think they will get really rich and so they invest their few rubles, and who is it that gets rich? The absolute good-for-nothings! That's what this city's like!" He ended his diatribe with a heavy sigh.

"God forbid!" exclaimed Berman's father. "It's blasphemy to speak badly of a whole group of Jews. On the contrary, I have heard that there are many honest Jews, who honor the Torah and who sit here and study, just like at home. And after all, you know the saying: 'a people without bread is without Torah.' At home Jews can't get a livelihood, may it never happen to you, and they're in such a state that they can't even concentrate on looking at a sacred book."

"Is that what you've been told? Well, I can tell you a different story. You see that man who is just going out? That's Reb Mordecai Danziger. In the space of six months he lost about ten thousand rubles. And his wife, a woman from an illustrious family, had to take in shirts to sew. And now in their old age, when their children are grown up and have begun to support them, so that they could have expected to have a little peace and leisure, they have a new worry. Their children, God preserve us, have departed from the true path. I've heard that they even go to the opera on *Shabbes.*"

"What's 'opera'?"

"Oh, I don't know, it's a kind of thee-ay-ter. The son reads secular books and even non-Jewish books. He hasn't put his nose into a *shtibl* for years. It's even rumored that he doesn't bind on his tefillin. I'm sure that can't be true. But still, all the rest is shocking enough. And you'll meet many decent pious Jews here who are toiling away, trying to do business, running around the Diamond Club. A stranger, seeing them, would think that they are achieving something, but that's not so. They're running around the offices, wearing out their shoe leather and going home with nothing at all. And it's the same thing with the workers: more often than not they go away empty-handed. You see, it's all right for the *goyim.* If a gentile deals in diamonds, he is a rich man, because no poor gentile would think of going into business. But a Jew, as you well know, has no other choice, so he has to hold on by his fingernails. Take someone like Reb Leybele Poltaver, for example. A fine person, a great scholar, used to be a rich man in the old homeland, and what has happened to him? Ruined in an instant. Now his wife has opened a dairy business and she's not doing well at all. As I say, Sodom and Gomorrah." The man spoke with a mixture of anger and pity: he was sorry for those who had done badly, like himself. But he was also full of enmity towards those who had done well, no matter how honest they were. His motto was, if someone was doing well, he was probably a swindler.

Reb Itshe made a dismissive gesture, blew his nose loudly and said with irritation:

"That's absolute nonsense! I have lived in Antwerp for many years now and I know that there are good, pious Jews here, who keep the Law, and many real scholars of the Talmud, who are very rich men. So it's not just the good-for-nothings who get rich. The truth is that God helps the man who is destined to succeed. And if someone, sadly, is *not* destined to succeed, even if he's the cleverest swindler in the world, it will not help him one jot. It's the same in Antwerp as all over the world. If it is God's will, then honest men will make a livelihood, and if, sadly, it is not His will, then their lives, God preserve us, are bitter as death. But to give a bad name to a whole city? Probably there *are* some swindlers among us; that's very sad, and the whole community suffers because of them. If a Jew steals, then the gentiles say that *all* Jews are thieves – but for you, an honest Jew, to suggest such a thing? It's a terrible calumny, which harms us all!"

Reb Itshe had got really worked up, and his Adam's apple was moving up and down like a big plum in his scrawny throat. He could hardly breathe and his hair was sticking to his head with sweat.

"And apart from anything else, how can anyone rely on the word of a man who has convinced himself that his sons don't have beards?"

"Don't worry, I'm used to people saying things like that!" said the man, gesturing with his hand, which was shaking uncontrollably. An anguished smile appeared on his dark face, spreading into his unhappy eyes. "I've already said that no one will believe me."

Berman's father felt a great affinity with Reb Itshe and the warmth he felt towards him seemed to lift a weight off his heart.

Suddenly a new voice was heard: "Listen, everyone! This man is absolutely right. I'm not talking about his sons and their beards, that doesn't interest me." Everyone looked round. "Let him think that, if it gives him pleasure." It was Leybesh speaking. He was sitting in the *shtibl* waiting for the beadle to come with the key to the synagogue. "He's absolutely right. All rich men are thieves, because business itself is theft. Therefore the man who loses because he is not a good businessman – he's *not* a thief! And the one who succeeds – he *is*! It's quite simple: profit is theft, and the profiteer will do everything in the world to make a profit. He'll stop at nothing. Theft, murder, everything is kosher. And that's not just in Antwerp, but all over the world. And there's no difference between Jews, gentiles, mythical monsters, or whatever."

The three conversationalists looked round: "Ha? Who's that? Is it a madman or something?"

They didn't know Leybesh, were surprised by his intervention, and didn't understand what he was talking about. Where had he sprung from? What on earth was he getting at?

All three stared in amazement and huddled closer together as if to protect each other from this man who seemed like some kind of disturbing hallucination. And so they made up their quarrel.

In the evening rich Jews came into the *shtibl,* with fine beards and frock coats, some of them with longer jackets: a compromise between God and Europe. Many of them were dressed entirely in European clothes, with gold watches on thick chains dangling over rotund stomachs and diamond rings on their middle and little fingers. There were also Jews with dirty jackets and coats moldy with age, their beards poor and unkempt. Young men came in too, diamond cutters, polishers and cleavers, who had come to the *shtibl* after work to pray and study. Though these lads wore European clothes and straw hats, they looked even more unworldly and pale than yeshiva boys. They sat down at the long tables and waited round the open Gemara until their *rebbe,* a man with a rabbinical hat and an intelligent face, had finished chatting with some diamond dealers. They were talking about blue-white diamonds, about big and little stones, offering each other a pinch of snuff and being offered a cigar in return. After all this, the talmudic lesson which the *rebbe* gave them every evening could begin.

The worshippers went home. The young men at the long tables swayed piously over the open Gemara. The *rebbe* with the intelligent face stood swaying back and forth, intoning:

"And Rashi says...."

Chapter 15

Dovid had seen nothing of Gitele and the baby for over two months. He hung around Somersstraat, but she never appeared. Sometimes he got angry. He decided Gitele hadn't really loved him. She had just wanted to get her hands on his father's money, and when she saw that he wasn't likely to get any of it, she didn't need him anymore.

But what was he to do? He could find no peace, and pined for Gitele and his baby. He even missed Leybesh, at the same time both hating him and feeling shame for his own behavior towards him. In his imagination he saw the tall figure of Leybesh standing there barefoot and disheveled in the small dark kitchen, with that kind smile on his face, saying to him: "Go back to sleep. Don't worry about it," with such infinite goodness in his blue eyes. And he, Dovid, lying there in Leybesh's bed in that poor kitchen, enjoying Leybesh's hospitality. He felt like a worm.

No, he certainly couldn't go back there, and yet his longing grew stronger all the time, and he could find no solution. He sat for days on his parents' velvet sofa, unwashed and unkempt, in his blue satin dressing gown and slippers. He smoked constantly, filling the elegant dining room with thick smoke. He thought and thought but found no answer. If only he had some funds, he could make a new start in business.

After a long inner battle he at last suggested to his mother that she pawn her jewelry. It cost him a great deal to make himself ask her such a thing, but Rochl told him she only wore imitation jewelry made out of cut glass, the kind used for display purposes in jewelry exhibitions, and her real diamonds were in a safe in the Bourse. Dovid couldn't believe his ears. His mother didn't even have any real jewelry to wear! But he knew she would never tell him a lie, and he had to believe her.

There was no point in speaking to his father. Dovid had already lost ten thousand francs' worth of business, and knew that his father would not give him another chance, or another centime. So he sat on the sofa and counted the flowers on the carpet, though he already knew how many there were: every flower, every piece of silver on the sideboard, and every candle on the candelabrum. When it got too claustrophobic he went on one of the tedious walks he knew so well, or sat in the park trying to read, though he absorbed nothing at all. More often he just sat staring at the people around him. There was a young woman with a pram coming into the park. She asked Dovid if the place beside him on the bench was free, and sat down. A chubby little fair-haired girl about two years old sat in the pram, playing with a yellow velvet teddy bear. She was tormenting it, pulling its nose, poking its beady eyes with her forefinger, chatting to it, throwing it out of the pram and demanding that her mother pick it up again. The mother began to get impatient, and warned the little girl that she would not pick the teddy bear up again.

A dog ran up, stopped by the pram and looked up at the child with its black, moist eyes, its floppy ears quivering with excitement. It wagged its tail and barked at the teddy bear. The child bent out of the pram, nearly falling out, waved the bear in the dog's face and started chuckling. The child's laughter rang out like little silver bells. The dog shot off with the bear like an arrow from a bow, but brought it back. The woman chased the dog away and the child burst into tears.

Dovid's heart was aching. His longing for Gitele and their baby was so strong that he felt like embracing and kissing the woman, her little girl, and the dog – all at once. The woman stood up and went off into the park with her pram. Dovid got up too and walked off, not knowing where he was going.

He walked about the streets, not even bothering to look around.

Nothing had changed: the streets and people were the same as a year ago, or even ten years ago. Trintshe the fishmonger had the same broad smile on her greasy face as always. He tried to avoid Somersstraat but suddenly found himself there, right opposite Gitele's window.

The woman with the blonde wig sat knitting a vest, and greeted him with a mocking smile on her thin lips. Dovid sprang back as if he had been stung by a bee. He didn't answer her "*dag menieër,*" but turned angrily on his heel and walked on.

A horse harnessed to a high cart full of manure stopped with a whinny, shook its mane and started walking on again, its clumsy hooves fringed with dirty tufts of hair. Dovid stared after the man sitting on the box smoking a pipe and apparently dozing, and really envied him: a man doing a day's work.

He was already far from the Jewish district, and as he walked, he thought out the plan which he had been carrying around in his head for a few days. He was scared to put it into action, because he didn't want to act foolishly again and let people find out his situation.

He turned into Cogels-Oyslei, a beautiful wide street. The front gardens were all laid out differently from each other, with a variety of colorful flowers. He felt the street was like a poem, in which all the different individual words fused together in one melodious, harmonious rhythm.

The streetlamps were being lit. The lamplighter carried his long stick from lamppost to lamppost, even though the sun still shone on the flowerbeds. The man went down the street whistling a little melody, and the green gaslight mingled with the remnants of daylight, creating a bluish twilight. Here, thought Dovid, he could live with Gitele and their child, if he managed to make a success of his life… yes, he would put all his failures behind him! He had to try once again, or else he would go mad.

Suddenly he thought of his grandfather. *He* was really driving Dovid mad. "When you have to look at a corpse with a frozen smile on its dead face sitting there rocking back and forth all day long, is it any wonder that I have to leave the house?" Dovid thought to himself, with a sudden surge of rage.

He turned back into the town. An old school friend of Dovid's, with whom he used to play sometimes in their free time, lived on Pelikaanstraat, and Dovid went up the steps to his house. This friend was now a diamond cleaver with a very good reputation. The biggest and most expensive stones were given to him to split, and he did it really expertly.

Why was Dovid scared? His friend could only say no. But Dovid's heart was pounding in case he was making a fool of himself again. He threw open the door, not even pausing to knock, because he knew that if he hesitated for an instant, he would just run back down the steps.

His friend stared in amazement at Dovid. He was delighted to see him, but could hardly believe that Dovid Berman was actually paying *him* a visit. "Ahh! Who's this I see?" He stretched out a thin, freckled hand to him. "You are an unexpected guest. Do sit down. Please excuse the state of the place. When I'm working, I can't avoid it. It's a real pigsty!"

"No, no, don't worry, it doesn't matter at all: a productive mess is a good thing!" Dovid babbled in his embarrassment.

"And one's hands get pretty filthy too," continued the young man apologetically.

Dovid sat down on the chair, which his friend had wiped for him. The young man hovered around awkwardly for a moment or two, and then took up the diamond again, which looked like a piece of dirty washing soda, speaking to Dovid as he examined it: "If it didn't have so many imperfections it would be a real find!" He was about to cleave the rough diamond, but he had first to weigh up the possibilities: where and how to split it, in order to obtain the biggest and purest diamonds. "If one could find a pure stone of this size," he said, "which didn't need to be split, it would be worth a fortune."

"Really? Then diamond cleavers wouldn't be needed at all," said Dovid, encouraged to hear that such pure stones were very seldom found.

The young man brushed back his thick locks of red hair with his hand, straightened his skullcap, and explained to Dovid: "You see that little black speck? Like an island in the middle of water."

"You're right!" said Dovid, peering intently at the diamond.

"We have to get rid of that dirty little island so that only the pure water remains."

So saying, the diamond cleaver made a groove in the stone with another diamond, right on the black spot, after which he split the stone with one sharp blow.

"I'll have to split it further," he said. "What a shame! A giant like this and all we'll end up with are tiny little stones." The young man regretted this, even though the stone didn't belong to him.

Two other young lads worked there. They were cleaving small stones. They also looked, made a groove, gave a sharp blow. They glanced at the guest, obviously envious of him, and greatly impressed by his expensive clothing.

Dovid's friend talked to him, trying in a roundabout way to find out the reason for Dovid's unexpected visit. But Dovid sat there rooted to the spot, chatted about this and that and couldn't find an appropriate way to broach the subject he had come to discuss. He felt faint, and broke out in a sweat. How could he suddenly tell this former school friend about his problems? He and his friend had pursued totally different paths when they left school: the friend had started working and he, Dovid, the rich man's son, had gone to the high school to carry on studying. He remembered how envious his friend had been at that time, because he was more intelligent than Dovid, and really wanted to study; how could Dovid tell him that now, years later, he had come to beg him to teach him how to cleave diamonds? The friend would look at him as if he were mad. So Dovid was at a loss what to do. If only the two other lads hadn't been there, looking him up and down, from his head to his white spats, very obviously envying him and expressing their admiration to each other in a joking, ironic way. Dovid felt frustration welling up inside him.

Suddenly his friend looked at the fiery red window, illuminated by the evening sun. He stood up and said to the other two:

"Time to say *mayrev*! You probably haven't prayed yet either?" he asked Dovid.

"Eh? Prayed? Ehm … no … not yet."

"Then we'll pray together!"

The little room huddled into the approaching darkness. The window flamed even more brightly and particles of light from the setting sun made patches on the floor, but the corners of the room were engulfed in shadow.

When they had finished praying, the three workers tidied the room very quickly, and then all four went down the steps. Dovid walked along with his friend, and finally told him about his plan.

"But that's not for you! What on earth made you think of that? What an idea! And why would *you* need to do that?" His friend simply could not and would not understand him. "If one wants to be a merchant, does one have to learn the mechanics of diamond cleaving? No, of course not! That wouldn't occur to anyone else. If you're a merchant, you can deal in diamonds without all that. Did your father, for instance, learn how to be a cleaver? Take it from me, it's not necessary, so forget all about it. You'd pay a thousand francs for the apprenticeship, and waste several years of your life. If I had your money, I wouldn't sit up in that workshop for a single day. Even the smallest dealer has more chance than the best worker. I myself am starting to buy and sell in a modest way. I want to be done with this work. What an idea, a healthy man climbing into a sickbed!"

Dovid found no words to answer him.

"So that's no good either. I'm obviously a hopeless failure. I might as well go and jump in the Scheldt."

Chapter 16

The High Holidays were approaching, and Berman's mood became more somber. This period heralded the end of the summer and the coming of winter, which Berman dreaded because he always suffered terribly from bronchitis. Apart from this he always got rather depressed during this period. He greeted the High Holidays with a mixture of fear, respect, and joy, but the time leading up to them was very difficult for him. At night, all sorts of thoughts would race around in his head, preventing him sleeping. On nights like those, when everything was dark and silent, he would lie there, mulling over his life.

The stolen diamonds would often creep into his mind; they seemed to stick in his throat and choke him, until he felt such nausea that he wanted to wake Rochl and tell her the whole story. He would prove to her that actually he hadn't done anything wrong. Rochl was lying in the other bed, breathing rhythmically, and dreaming innocent dreams, not suspecting that Berman was lying awake for hours trying to justify his actions. But no matter how hard he tried, the Authority before which he was trying to justify himself kept rejecting his arguments, and pushing the same thoughts back into his head until Berman started sweating all over his body and burst out in a fit of coughing. Then Rochl would wake up and fetch a glass of orange juice for her husband. Before Berman had finished drinking it, she would be snoring gently again in the other bed.

If he had a night like this at any other time of the year, he would ask her to come into his bed and help him to get to sleep. But such a thing was not permissible so near the solemn festival.

So Berman just lay there wrestling with his conscience. After all, what should he have done? If he hadn't purchased them, someone else would have. Non-Jews might even have bought them. Would it have been better to let them fall into gentile hands? What would the gentile do with the money? Get a better dog, buy a new cross to adorn his church, or else go and get drunk. And in any case, did he, Berman, buy *only* dubious merchandise? No, every year he bought thousands of francs' worth of honest merchandise, and he always paid the full price for rough diamonds, according to all the regulations of the London syndicate. And apart from anything else: for whom did he provide a livelihood? For Jews. Didn't about a hundred Jews: dealers, brokers, polishers, cutters and cleavers, live off his business? *He* didn't give the work to gentiles, God forbid, like many Jewish merchants did, even though they had to pay a higher price. His principle was that one Jew had to help another, especially as Jews were cheaper anyway, and didn't bother with unions. Why was he tormenting himself? So he tried to drive away these troublesome thoughts, but they wouldn't leave him. He spat, turned his face to the wall, but still couldn't get to sleep.

Apart from all these other worries, he had now taken responsibility for his father; he had taken him out of poverty and wanted to keep him in a manner that was fitting, so that he too could benefit from all that God had bestowed on his son, and enjoy his old age. After all, we pray that God should preserve us into old age. Then Berman sighed deeply, as the thought of Dovid came into his mind. "Who can tell how children will treat one in one's old age?" he thought, and tears of self-pity welled up in his eyes. Immediately he felt much calmer; it was as if the tears had cleansed him from the sin of buying the stones and, at peace with himself once again, he fell asleep.

In the morning he got up refreshed, went to the Bourse and carried on with the usual wheeling and dealing, but the sleepless nights and the dark thoughts and the inner battles did not cease.

During the two days before Rosh HaShana, when other merchants were busy getting jewelry out of the safe and managing to do a last little bit of business before the festival, Berman was already sitting at home by the warm stove, looking at the New Year cards. No matter how warm it was outside, the stove was already lit in the Bermans' house. He was deciding who ought to receive a big gold card and who should get a smaller, silver card and who, finally, should only receive a white card decorated with a tiny purple flower.

This was a task which Berman enjoyed. He would choose the cards, smile, take a sip from his red glass of tea, and forget that night was coming on. He loved the unaccustomed leisure, and to enjoy it all the more, he would say to Rochl:

"And those idiots are even now pulling the jewels out of their safes."

Rochl sighed, but when Berman looked at her she put on a cheerful air, agreeing:

"Yes, what fools! In the synagogue, all packed together; what do they need their jewelry for?"

At the Bermans', everything had to be absolutely ready some time before Rosh HaShana. Since Berman had nothing much to do, he liked to take a walk around the streets of the Jewish district on the eve of the festival. He closed his office around midday, smiling at the workers as he paid out what he owed them, even expressing his gratitude. He wished them a happy and prosperous New Year, accepted with great pleasure the stream of good wishes from them, and set off on his walk.

He started out at the first stone arch of the long railway bridge, which divided Antwerp into two parts. One part had the atmosphere of the big city, with brightly lit streets, large, colorful shops and department stores, and garish advertisements in neon lights. There were theaters, cinemas, wide boulevards, cafes and everything which belongs in a big city. In the other part, where the Jewish district was situated, it was crowded, poor, and had a very intimate atmosphere. It was here that Berman took his walk, glancing first of all at the big railway station clock and checking the time with his own massive gold watch, which made him smile with satisfaction: "Accurate to the second!" It was a fine watch, which he had had for about twenty years.

He crossed Pelikaanstraat, and at once he was in the heart of the bustling Rosh HaShana preparations. Jews with somber faces were dragging cartloads of tasty foods and orchards of fruit round the streets.

"Fruits to greet the New Year, come and get them, ladies!" The vendors were yelling and the colors of the fruits shouted even more loudly. The shaggy dogs were exhausted; today they had run all over Antwerp pulling huge loads. The women were only making a show of haggling, as their minds were already on the joyful festival, and the spirit of Rosh HaShana was reflected in their faces.

In the dusty shop windows there were still mounds of plaited bread and poultry for sale. The hens, hanging upside down with their bluish skin, blackened blood and closed eyes, looked miserable, like blind people full of self-pity. The poor women who prodded these hens were hardly any less miserable, having had to wait till the very last moment to see if their husbands or sons would bring home some meager wages.

Because of customers like these, even the hairdressers had to work right up until the festival was about to begin. In the previous weeks they had already worked their fingers to the bone, fashioning all sorts of waves and curls and ringlets in the wigs of rich ladies. But even now, after weeks of hard work, these poor, tired fingers, which had been eagerly waiting for Rosh HaShana, were still not allowed to rest. They could be seen through the shop windows, listlessly curling the last bits of hair on the wooden heads, preparing the poor women's wigs.

When Berman saw all this, he felt an urge to raise his hands to heaven and give praise to God who had lifted him out of this wretched state of poverty. Then, once again, the thought of Dovid came into his head.

It was the eve of Rosh HaShana. Berman was dressed from head to toe in new clothes. He had even bought himself a splendid new prayer shawl with black stripes and long tasseled fringes. His new top hat was tall and shining. He was waiting for his father for whom he had also had new clothes made, despite Rochl's objection that he already had lots of good frock coats in his wardrobe which could easily have been shortened. No, his father had to have a fine new outfit. Berman had helped his father to dress, to ease his stiff old body into the new clothes. He was certain that the Almighty would repay him with interest for this good deed, and he felt a glow of satisfaction.

But the old man spoiled his pleasure slightly. It embarrassed him to wear a top hat, and he begged his son to let him wear his velvet skullcap as he always did. In the end, however, he gave in and put on the top hat, but for the first time since he had arrived in Antwerp he regretted having come to stay with his son. Nevertheless he forgave him, since he didn't want to bear him any grudge on Rosh HaShana.

Dovid's white spats shone whiter than ever. Both his grandfather and father blessed him, as if he had still been a little boy. It was the same every year. Rochl blushed as she made the blessing over the candles, and her glass jewelry sparkled. But there was a tear in her eye: she felt cheated and ashamed, as if she were betraying the candles at this holy festival, because their pure flame was being reflected in false diamonds.

Jacques couldn't prise himself away from the mirror. He was so pleased with himself in his new clothes that he couldn't wait to see the other boys in the synagogue and find out who had the finest outfit, though he already felt sure that he did. He stood admiring himself like a girl, until Jeannette pushed him away as if he were just some obstacle in her way. Wearing her grey fur coat, she filled the whole mirror. She put cream and rouge on her face, twirled in front of the mirror and twirled again. Everyone was waiting for her. They were in a hurry to get to the synagogue, but Jeannette wouldn't stop admiring herself in the mirror. Rochl put on her fur coat as well, even though the weather was still warm and humid.

All of Antwerp was going to synagogue. The little streets of the Jewish district were full of people. The great synagogue, where Berman worshipped, had a huge ornate interior. It seemed as if a special exhibition of diamonds, tie pins, cufflinks and rings was taking place.

The men had dressed up just as much as the women. In the women's section a huge sea of diamonds sparkled and flashed in the sunlight.

In the streets of the Jewish district, the sound of the shofar, the ram's horn blown on Rosh HaShana, still echoed around. During the following ten days of repentance, Jews prepared themselves for Yom Kippur, the awesome day of judgment in which their sins of the past year would be counted. They went around with lowered heads, piety written on their faces. During that period Berman went to the Bourse and his office, where he treated his workers with kindness.

As for Dovid, he slept even later than usual. The eve of Rosh HaShana, when he had let his father bless him, still lingered in his mind and rose up before his eyes, seeming to mock him. It was even more upsetting than usual. He spat, full of shame and disgust at himself: why had he not taken the silk prayer shawl with the blue stripes which his father had given him, wound it around his father's neck and strangled him? That would have put an end to it all! Dovid was horrified by his own thoughts. He got up and went out into the street. It was the day before Yom Kippur. As usual, Dovid tried to prevent himself going to Somersstraat, but found himself there in the end, thinking as always about Gitele, but finding no solution to his problems. Suddenly, there she was, coming towards him, dressed in a new coat and hat. She looked quite different, with fuller cheeks, clear skin, and shining happy eyes, which did not look so huge as they had when her face was thin and pinched. He had never seen her looking like this before. She smiled cheerfully at him and gave him her soft, warm hand. Dovid trembled: he wanted to hold her hand and never let go. He was scared that he would put his arms round her in the middle of Somersstraat and start kissing her passionately. But something stabbed at his heart.

"Why are you out in the street so early?" he stammered, looking at her with desire.

Gitele laughed. She realized that Dovid was jealous of her new clothes and her happy new appearance.

"Why are you laughing?" Dovid gave her an angry look, not

knowing himself why he felt annoyed. He didn't realize that he was upset to see that Gitele could dress herself smartly and look good without him.

"I see you're surprised, so I'll tell you what's happened. Leybesh is working for an employer, and he's earning. He already knows how to polish a stone perfectly."

Dovid felt the blood rushing to his head.

"How… how… I mean… where have you left the baby?"

Gitele laughed again, which made Dovid want to scream at the top of his voice: "*Stop* laughing; it gets on my nerves!" but instead he just repeated, "Where is the baby?"

"I've pawned her!" she answered, angry with him for looking at her accusingly, as if she were a bad mother who had neglected her child. And Dovid, who hadn't seen the baby for two months, had suddenly become her protector!

Dovid saw the ludicrous nature of his position and calmed down. Changing his tone, he asked:

"May I ask who he is working for?" as if it made any difference to him who Leybesh's employer was.

"For Rubin!"

"Do you mean Rubin the philosopher?"

"Yes, he comes up to my elegant residence; he has become a great pal of Leybesh's and gives him as much work as he wants. But I must get home because Leybesh has to go out and he won't have anywhere to leave the baby. I just came out to get some shopping. You know how Leybesh has a feast with his disciples every Yom Kippur. To tell you the truth, I'm not very keen on this…."

Dovid didn't wait to hear any more; he spun round on his heel and ran away like a scalded cat. Gitele wanted to say something else to calm him down, but he had already disappeared.

"So that's how it is, she has to run home to her beloved Leybesh." As if to torment himself deliberately, Dovid misinterpreted the sense of her words. "So, Leybesh is now the father of her child, and she leaves her with him, so that she can go and buy food for a Yom Kippur feast, even though she disapproves of it. Well!"

He strode home swiftly, his head feeling empty and dull. When he arrived he looked round the room, and was surprised to see everyone looking perfectly calm and busily occupied; it didn't occur to any of them that something terrible had happened. On the contrary, they were bustling around even more than usual. Mother was helping Anneke to pluck white hens in the kitchen, Jacques was absorbed in carving something with his penknife. Jeannette was reading, Anneke, her hands covered in blood, was plucking the birds and quietly singing a little song. It didn't seem to worry her that these hens, which were still warm, were the same ones she had heard half an hour earlier clucking and squawking, and that she had seen them lying dead on the cold stones of the slaughterhouse, bathed in their own blood – that same blood which was now all over her hands. She sang: "Her sweetheart is an idiot…" and kept sweeping up the feathers, which were fluttering all around the kitchen. When Dovid's mother saw him standing in the doorway staring as if he were in a trance, she called out to him: "Oh Dovid, I'm glad you're here. The cockerel has been lying tied up, poor creature, since this morning." She told him to take it and perform the atonement ceremony, so that she could have it slaughtered.

Dovid looked round and woke out of the state of paralysis which his jealousy, rage and sense of his own failure had inflicted on him. In his anguish he burst out into unnatural, spasmodic laughter, and his eyes filled with tears. Rochl was shocked: had her son suddenly gone mad?

Leybesh had been doing well recently. One of his previous disciples had a brother, Rubin, who was an adherent of the Haskala, the Jewish Enlightenment movement; he knew Hebrew but no Yiddish, he had a miniature picture of Dr. Herzl instead of a diamond in his gold signet ring, and he wore a soft black cap and gold pince-nez. He liked

Leybesh and hoped to make a Zionist of him, and so he gave him work. He often came up to Leybesh's place to try to convince him.

"I tell you, socialism is an abstract idea, and Marxism an abstract theory!" This was his favorite argument. "It's a fairy tale without a proper ending. Your best proof of this is the French Revolution. And another thing, what happened to the revolution of 1905, eh?"

But when Leybesh remained implacable, the boss took it philosophically and they remained good friends. He realized that Leybesh was an educated man with his own ideas. Eventually, he believed, Leybesh would realize that he had been misguided. But what about his own brother, Leybesh's disciple? How had *he* got involved with all this?

"You, with your bird brain, you want to save the world, do you?" Rubin reproached his brother. "You'd do better to sort out that tangle of wool inside your own head first!"

The young man took his brother's words to heart. In any case, he really hadn't understood a word of Leybesh's teachings. He used to fall asleep during the "sermons," and when he woke with a start he would see all the comrades smiling at him. The boys and girls would ask questions during a discussion and Leybesh would hear them out with great seriousness, making notes with a pencil on a scrap of paper, after which he would answer everyone's question in order. This young man was amazed at this and envied Leybesh and the comrades for being able to understand such things. He loved Leybesh for not making any difference between him and the other comrades, treating them all alike. But still, Karl Marx was too hard a nut for him to crack, and so he decided Rubin was right: one can be a good socialist even if one is not a wage slave. He took his brother's advice, got married and received a large dowry, then became a diamond merchant and did very well.

So Leybesh was working for this young man's brother. He would bring the completed work back to his employer and then sit chatting with him until late into the night, and the boss was so delighted that Leybesh almost always lost to him at chess, that he would sometimes stand him a bottle of wine. So this Yom Kippur, Leybesh was able to have a real banquet.

Outside, the sun was pouring down on a sea of top hats worn by Jews, rich and poor: the wealthy diamond merchants as well as the grocers, peddlers and even poorer people. Even the errand boys with the grey beards wore top hats today.

They were all going to synagogue, the women in fur coats, sweating within an inch of their lives, men with bellies on which dangled gold chains and watches as big as turnips, and others with worn-out frock coats and split top hats, together with their work-weary wives in their best clothes, hiding their poverty as best they could. The town streamed into the synagogue.

You would have thought that Antwerp ended here, and that the lively, vibrant city on the other side of the bridge had disappeared. It was as if the entire city were observing this awesome day. Only the trains clattered across the bridge in their normal everyday routine, puffing and whinnying out their long, echoing whistle which desecrated the solemnity of the day.

There was a merry atmosphere at Leybesh's. The two little rooms were packed with the male and female comrades, the "irreligious" girls were busy cooking and frying, and not allowing Gitele to do any of the work. They knew that Gitele did not approve of this business. She believed one could be non-religious and, indeed, she herself did not believe in anything, but nevertheless, cooking on Yom Kippur seemed to her to be overstepping the mark. The girls worked like mad to get everything done, singing revolutionary songs, catching a remark from a comrade in the other room, giving a riposte, laughing. And soon they were all sitting round the table.

Leybesh, taking a cigarette out of the large box which he had set out on the table for the guests, started heaping abuse on Antwerp and its Jews:

"You know what, comrades? In the old homeland I still had a grain of respect for the pious Jews. I could see their stupidity and prejudice, but nevertheless their absolute faith did sometimes move me. Faith has beauty! We believe that too because, after all, make no mistake: when we read Marx, although we have to agree that his mathematical calculations are absolutely correct, just like two times two equals four, and that although this decaying economic order is bound to collapse of its own accord, it's still our holy duty to *help* to hasten its destruction as much as we can; we mustn't wait until that decayed building does collapse and bury too many victims underneath, or let too many good human beings get TB from its damp, unhealthy walls.

"Nevertheless..." and Leybesh took a new cigarette, since the first one had burnt itself out in the corner of his mouth, "...nevertheless, we would have lost the courage to carry on if we had stopped having *faith* that a better tomorrow will come. Mathematical calculations alone wouldn't be enough to keep our disgust at so much nauseating hypocrisy and baseness alive, wouldn't keep us constantly *aware* of the filth through which we have to wade. Only faith holds us together. And that's why I say that I used to have a little spark of sympathy in my heart for the Jew who truly believed. Naturally I pitied him for his blindness, but I didn't despise him in the way I despise these ones here. When I see them going into the synagogue to repent, while at the same time they're sinning, even on their way there: carrying their jealousy, hatred, snobbery, vanity with them – in a word, everything that they'll soon be beating their diamond-encrusted hearts over – it makes me want to spit in their fat faces, so that they'd drown in that one huge gob of spittle!"

The comrades all agreed absolutely with Leybesh. Even Gitele was persuaded of the case he was making, and felt that she had never fully appreciated how clever he was.

"Where do the diamonds come from?" asked a girl who had just arrived in Antwerp from a *shtetl* in Poland.

Leybesh took another cigarette. He knew the history of diamonds better than many of the big dealers, who handled hundreds of thousands, even millions of francs' worth of diamonds every year. "Till the end of the nineteenth century they came from India, but now a great many of them come from South Africa. Diamonds were discovered in South Africa by chance. A child was playing with a little stone, and a certain Dr. Otterstone happened to see it and realized that this wasn't just any old stone, but a diamond. So they started digging, and now it's our black brothers who are digging out diamonds, making others rich and dying of hunger themselves. They work in dreadful conditions and when they finish after a grueling day's work, they are stripped naked and searched everywhere, even in their ears, to see whether they have, God forbid, hidden a stone to keep for themselves. They have the right to work for others, to be worked to the point of exhaustion, and illness, but they haven't the right to have enough to eat. And it doesn't seem to occur to anyone that this is an absurd injustice. No one bothers about poor white people, so is it likely that anyone will care about poor blacks?"

"Who owns all the diamonds after they're mined?" asked the same girl.

"An organization called the De Beers Company. They control all the main mines in South Africa, which are in Kimberley."

Gitele was amazed. This was the first time that she had heard Leybesh talking about diamonds, and he seemed to know all about them. She remembered that she had once asked Dovid, and he hadn't had a clue, despite the fact that *he* had gone to high school. And who knows what school Leybesh had attended? Dovid had said that his father didn't know anything about diamonds either. However he *did* know how to make money from them. When Gitele thought about this, her respect for Leybesh wavered slightly.

In the afternoon, Leybesh led the band of comrades to the House of the Inquisition, which for him was a sacred ritual every Yom Kippur. The grey fortress had stood in Antwerp for hundreds of years, from the time when Antwerp was just an insignificant township. The Jesuits later made the castle into the headquarters of the Inquisition, and it still stands there like a dirty stain on the city. The thick walls are as white as chalk in places, and as black as coal in others, or as black as the air inside its cellars. The narrow windows are black slits which seem encrusted with the dried blood of the tortured victims. Leybesh and his comrades made their way to this fortress.

When Leybesh opened the arched wrought iron door, and they bent their heads and went inside, a skinny little old man greeted them, smiling with his toothless mouth and his dim, blue eyes under their bushy eyebrows. He had a yellow pitted face, like old parchment, with a pointed trembling chin. He found some candles and, counting the visitors and the candles very carefully, gave each one a lit candle and said: "All right, quick march!" and laughed foolishly.

Led by Leybesh, they made their way, in procession, to the dark, narrow hole from which some steps led down to the cellars. It was so dark that they couldn't see each other, only the melancholy little flames twisting and turning like the sharp, dusty, grey steps, which seemed to have sad stories to tell. Trembling black silhouettes danced on the dark walls. The girl who had just come to Antwerp let out a scream and dropped her candle. Leybesh, expecting this, had been walking beside her the whole time. Now he took her arm and calmed her: "Don't be scared, comrade! There's nothing to be frightened of. If only people were as scared of the real evil in our world."

The girl appeared to calm down, and even managed a weak, tremulous smile.

Leybesh relit her candle, but she shuddered and categorically refused to hold it. She huddled up to Leybesh like a child and stared wide-eyed and terrified at the horrible instruments of cruelty which were now revealed. Leybesh explained them to her: "Look, that's how they broke people's fingers. And with those bits of rusty iron they broke people's arms. People whom they should have revered, people who were great free spirits!"

Leybesh showed her an innocent-looking machine which was standing in a corner.

"Human beings were locked into that and forced to stand motionless until they died. And that's the axe...."

"That's enough, comrade, please! I don't want to see any more! I can't bear it!"

Leybesh felt her violent trembling and decided not to show her any more. "All right, but I just want to show you one more thing. You see how the walls are covered in scratch marks, so that there is not a bit of empty space? If you come back another time to read them, you'll see that they date from hundreds of years back; they are dates, names, pleas, curses and prayers, which the torture victims scraped on the walls, as well as recent dates scratched by tourists. All of them read as a curse against the Jesuits who perpetrated such crimes, allegedly in the name of the true religion, torturing human beings to death in the eternal, holy battle for supremacy. This is the way they interpreted Jesus' teaching, that if a man strikes you on one cheek, you should turn the other one to him."

The girl listened, and every word that Leybesh said was a new Torah to her; she had never heard anyone talk about such things in her provincial *shtetl*. She had become more used to the darkness now.

When they got back up to the surface, the watchman was in the middle of his meal, munching with his toothless jaws and smiling in his good-natured but simple way. "Good day, *menieër*." He greeted them politely, remembering the generous tip Leybesh had given him the previous year.

Outside, opposite this House of the Inquisition, flowed the broad serene shining River Scheldt. They all gasped with relief and the girl from Poland positively squealed with joy: "Ohhh, how lovely!"

"Now comrades, let's go down to the river," said someone, and they all wandered slowly to the banks of the Scheldt.

The sun was just about to set, and here and there little patches of blood red, gold, silver and violet were reflected in the water. "I've never seen such a beautiful river," cried the girl with delight. This pleased Leybesh and he talked about the river with pride:

"I love the Scheldt because of its breadth – I love everything which is broad."

"Except women," joked one of the comrades.

Leybesh laughed heartily.

All along the Scheldt, almost at the very edge, lay boats of every size and color. A flag fluttered on each one, telling the world which country they came from. One large ship, which took up a huge berth, came from Hamburg. One boat stood out from the others in its luxury and its gleaming, pristine whiteness. Some of the crew were airing and cleaning the cabins. The doors of the first class cabins were open, and their mirrors, velvet furnishings and nickel plated fittings caught everyone's eye. The ship was empty because the passengers had gone into Antwerp to see all the essential tourist attractions.

"Perhaps some of them are in the Inquisition House," said someone.

"And some in the synagogues!" laughed Leybesh.

"*Lehavdil*, God forgive the comparison," said the provincial girl automatically and then blushed to the roots of her hair.

On the quay there was a long row of warehouses which received merchandise from all over the world. An elderly Flemish man in a pair of stiff shiny trousers and a torn, dirty, blue jacket was carrying a huge chest on his shoulders, almost collapsing under its weight. He had a thin, lined face covered with sweat, with a sharp nose and red, protruding eyes. It looked as if he could collapse at any minute and the heavy chest would fall on top of him and crush him to death. But the man was obviously used to the work and he deposited his heavy burden in its correct place, wiped away the sweat with a greasy rag, rolled himself a cigarette and started out again to collect another chest.

The skinny, stooped porters darted back and forth over the rails, their loaded green barrows making a deafening metallic clatter, which almost drowned out the din of the porters themselves, who were shouting to each other. The cranes continuously deposited one lot of merchandise and lifted another; it seemed as if the exchange of goods was going on all by itself.

The volume of merchandise was huge, and all this hullabaloo was going on as if it were a normal working day, even though many of the owners of the businesses had been spending the day in synagogues. The comrades walked almost the length of the Scheldt, and it was only when the sun had completely disappeared in the west and the tall electric lamps were lit, sprinkling the rippling water with fragments of gold, leaving other parts dark blue or black, and a galaxy of stars twinkled in the water, only then did the little band of comrades go back home.

The Jews had already gone home from the synagogue. Their souls were emptied of their sins and their faces were drained of blood. They had little packages under their arms containing their prayer books, prayer shawls, and smelling salts. They expressed their relief that the fast was at an end, that it was the evening after and not the evening before Yom Kippur. They all wished each other a good year; even the poorest of them shook hands then hurried home to break their fast.

Chapter 17

From the beginning of the month of Kheshvan fine rain fell incessantly. It dripped on everything with a monotonous rhythm, so that the city looked dull and shabby. Heavy clouds, like lumps of dirty cotton wool, covered the sky and the leaden mass seemed to press down on the earth. Instead of the usual winter cold, the damp crept over people's bodies like worms, penetrating their bones and choking their throats.

As a result, Berman's health was worse than usual that winter, and he constantly had to protect himself against chills. He paced around the brightly-lit, well-heated rooms of his house, wearing his red velvet dressing gown, reproaching the Almighty for punishing him with ill health while allowing all sorts of paupers, losers and other nonentities to wander round the streets, haggling and selling their wares. They went into restaurants with trays of chocolate, matches, cigarettes, buttons and socks. They went around half-naked in all weather, but it didn't seem to do them any harm. Even if they caught colds, they might cough a little but suffered no ill effects. Whereas the moment he, Berman, caught the slightest chill, the doctor insisted that he stay in the house, warning him that it could get very serious, because the bronchitis could weaken his heart. Who wouldn't be scared of that? So, poor Berman stayed at home, fretting. He would rather be out there earning money, and instead the office had been closed for over a month. That, of course, was not an insurmountable problem, because the workers came to his house to collect work from him, and he could sell from home as well, since his brokers knew where he lived. The real problem was buying new goods.

You had to be on the spot in order to buy. There were always plenty of people competing for a bargain. You had to look into the other merchant's eyes, and interpret a look or gesture of his which indicated that he had something to sell. Then you had to be astute, greet the other in a friendly fashion, ask after his health and his wife's health, ask him why he hadn't been around, take his arm as good friends do, and saunter out of the Bourse together for a cup of coffee in a back street somewhere. Only then would the real negotiations begin.

Instead, Berman was sitting at home. No one, he realized, was going to bring merchandise to his house. The diamond merchants were not working for the good of their souls and wouldn't think of coming to help a sick man; you'll only get food if you manage to get to the trough. He sighed and raged and stormed, and Rochl shrank from him, wishing she could transform herself into a cooking pot to avoid attracting his attention. He needed her constantly, however. One moment he was too warm in his quilted dressing gown, the next moment he was too cold in his velvet one. Then he had to take his medicine. Either the fire in the hearth was blazing too fiercely, or it was too low and needed stoking. One minute he was coughing and choking, then he was starving, or he was simply angry and had no one to vent his rage on, except Rochl. There was no point in her trying to hide or pretend she hadn't heard his call. The house became a living hell for her.

On top of all this, the old man had taken to his bed and stayed there all winter. At least he lay there quietly, and as long as he could put on his tefillin and pray, he needed nothing else. If someone gave him something to eat, he ate it, and if not, he didn't. But food was always available and Berman himself would come and bind on the tefillin for him. So the old man felt fine and wanted for nothing; that's what he said if one of the family happened to come in to see how he was getting on.

Dovid was at loose ends all winter. He listened to his father's tales of woe about the financial losses from the bronchitis, to his mother's timid little sighs, and to his sister bragging about her successes with all the charity dances she performed in aid of various schools and hospitals for the poor. He watched his grandfather's face becoming yellower and his fixed smile more and more like *rigor mortis.* Dovid did not know what to do with himself.

He told himself that his attitude towards Gitele was absurd and that he was doing her a great injustice. What had she done, apart from buy a few new clothes, improve her standard of living and in general look better, which any woman would do if she had the wherewithal? He knew he should root out the horrible rancor and suspicion he harbored against her, and not let them grow; otherwise they would poison his blood. But it was too late: the poison had already entered into him, so that day or night he could find no peace of mind and, gradually, he found himself turning against Gitele, and even against his own child.

Sometimes, however, when he was aimlessly walking round the streets in order to escape from the atmosphere at home, his feet would lead him to their house, and his longing would reawaken. Seeing their shadows through the curtains, he recognized Leybesh's tall silhouette with the tousled hair, saw Gitele's small form appearing and disappearing. He heard the faint sounds of the baby crying and someone singing to her. In those moments his longing to catch a glimpse of the child became unbearable. Using all his willpower, he would tear himself away. On those evenings Dovid did not go home, but found his way, not to his usual haunts, but to the cabarets, where he would drink the night away with Jules. In their new intimacy, Dovid didn't care who paid the bills.

His scandalous behavior was soon the talk of Antwerp. No one was particularly interested in Jules but Dovid was a juicy topic of conversation: everyone was keen to gossip about Berman's son. Rochl began hearing snippets and was devastated to realize that her son was at the center of scandal. Even worse, it was just at this point that the servant girl, Anneke, began to get yellowish blotches on her face. She often felt nauseous and had to run to the kitchen sink. Rochl realized very quickly that she was pregnant.

"What's this, Anneke?" she asked, pointing at Anneke's belly. Anneke flushed but immediately retorted: "Nothing!"

"What do you mean, 'nothing'?" persisted Rochl. Anneke burst into tears, then calmed down, blew her nose, wiped her eyes and told Rochl that she already had two other children and that the father had promised that this time he would marry her. "My dad says that if he doesn't, he's going to kill him."

Rochl was not unduly surprised. In her experience Anneke's situation was not uncommon among the Flemish people.

"And who looks after the children?" she asked.

"My mother, of course," replied Anneke, obviously surprised by the question. She carried on washing the dishes as if nothing had happened.

"My God, what a way to live, they breed like rabbits. God forgive me for the thought." Naturally Rochl dismissed her servant, but rumors were already circulating in the town.

"Is it true that Madame Berman has sent her servant girl away?"

"No! Really?"

"Well, are you surprised? With a son like that in the house?" the women whispered to each other, even though Anneke had never breathed a word of accusation against Dovid. She knew who the father of her child was and that he, a young man who worked in a coal mine in Charleroi, would not be able to keep her and she would have to carry on working, but she didn't mind that. Far worse than this was dealing with her father. When he came home drunk he beat not only her, but also her mother and the children. Anneke told people that when he was sober he was really good-natured, played with the children, kneeling down on the floor and letting them ride on him. "They can do whatever they want with me!" he would laugh.

He looked really comical, and he was tickled pink when his wife pretended to be angry with him, calling him "old fool." But it was a disaster when he got drunk. Then he would punch Anneke's mother in the stomach, and threaten to throw the children out of the window. Once he had actually almost done it, and who could tell whether he wouldn't really murder them all, some day?

"And you're no better than your mother!" he bawled at his daughter. "By the time she was twenty-two she had four children and no husband, and here's her daughter just about to have her third. You women deserve what's coming to you…" and, saying that, he spat in her mother's face.

Rochl went round for days with lowered head and a shawl round her shoulders, wiping her eyes and hiding so that Berman wouldn't see her crying. Eventually she decided to speak frankly to him:

"It makes it all the more painful when you think how much we have cherished our child, our Dovid."

"'Our child'? He's a worthless child! A loser, a lazy slob and an enemy to his own father! He's *your* child! It's a wonder you're not still suckling him!" Berman's bitter laughter brought on a fit of coughing, which started deep in his chest, mounted to a paroxysm and wouldn't stop. Rochl went and fetched his medicine. "Here you are. Take this."

One cold, bright, frosty day Berman got up early to get a breath of fresh air while the sun was still shining. Rochl handed him all the warm jackets he demanded, brushed the fluff off his overcoat, wrapped the woolen scarf round his neck and accompanied him to the door, glad he would be out of her way for a while. After he was gone she opened all the windows to let some air into the rooms and get rid of the smell of the medicines, exclaiming, with a great sense of freedom: "Ahhh! Thank God!"

The Bourse was more lively in winter than it was in summer, because the merchants were all back in town. The electric lights shone brightly. There was a warm, friendly atmosphere, and a homely, familiar din. It was as if the diamonds sparkled more colorfully than before, and the merchants were even more absorbed than usual in their trading. Berman concluded as much business with as many merchants as he could, and then went off to the Fortunia. Not knowing whether he would have another opportunity like this in the near future, he wanted to pack as much into the day as possible.

The long hall of the Fortunia was full of smoke, which mingled with the steam from the countless glasses of tea being sipped at the tables. The floor was damp and a layer of wet mud was spread through the center of the room, from the door right up to the counter at the other end. The merchants were sitting in groups around the small tables. Some were playing chess or dominoes, while others were exchanging jokes. About twenty people were crowded round one particular table, engaged in a serious game of cards. In the center of the room some young men were playing billiards. The white balls rolled swiftly and merrily around the green surface, and the players were so absorbed in the game that one would have thought they had come here purely to watch the white balls, and that there was nothing further from their minds than trading in diamonds.

One young man with a small black beard, a sharp nose and alert, attractive, black eyes (the kind which make girls fall hopelessly in love) stood watching with great interest to see who would win the game. Catching sight of Berman, he came over to him and stretched out both his fine, white, rather feminine hands to him: "Ah, how *are* you, Herr Berman? We haven't seen you here for *such* a long time. God willing, you're feeling better?"

"Yes indeed, much better, thank God! And how are you, Herr Tsvaygnboym?" Berman managed to call the young shrimp "Herr."

They sat down at a table and Berman, remembering that he was still not well, ordered a glass of warm milk. As he sipped it, he interrogated the young man like an investigating judge. He wanted to know how he was doing and how married life suited him. He was particularly interested in whether Tsvaygnboym was already finding his feet in the business, whether he intended to trade in rough diamonds like his father-in-law, or in polished stones, and whether perhaps he intended to go into manufacturing jewelry. Berman asked how much he had received as a dowry. He was *not* asking out of idle curiosity, God forbid, but because he felt a genuine friendship towards the young man, and was also a close friend of his father-in-law, as Tsvaygnboym knew. And that's why he asked.

But the young man gave nothing away, simply replying that he himself didn't yet know exactly what he intended. His father-in-law was doing well, thank God, and as for the dowry, he had nothing to do with all that, it was entirely between his father and father-in-law.

The more Berman asked, the less he found out, so eventually he took his leave of the young man and angrily went to sit at another table. These paupers, these Tsvaygnboyms, knew what was in their best interest; that was for sure. His idiot son on the other hand....

Merchants came to greet him from all sides, good friends who wanted to know how Berman was, expressing their pleasure that he was back in business, and trying to sell him parcels of diamonds. Berman greeted and responded to each one, had a look here, a sniff there, peered through the loupe, poked around with the tweezers, and took out some parcels of his own. He opened up one and shook it to make the diamonds glitter. They sparkled like dewdrops in the sunshine when they are shaken off a leaf.

Berman did good business both here and in the Bourse, and around three o'clock he wrapped his scarf round his neck, buttoned up his long overcoat to the neck, and went home while it was still daylight. He didn't have many days as good as that for the remainder of the winter.

Chapter 18

Winter gave way to spring; then the sun became hotter and spring turned into summer. Berman was back in the Bourse doing good business, always being the first to spot fine merchandise. He was constantly in the company of clever young men in well-cut suits who wore large diamond rings on their middle and little fingers; both he and the young men glittered like cats' eyes on dark March nights.

His office on Pelikaanstraat was open and once more the workers smiled at the frosted glass door of his Holy of Holies. The normal routine was resumed. In fact, Berman was doing better than before, and was just beginning to recoup the losses he had suffered during the winter, when as luck would have it, some prince or other in Serbia had to go and get himself assassinated. Because of this prince, whose accursed name Berman had never heard before, a wretched war broke out and put a stop to everything! Business ground to a halt, the Bourse was empty, and all anybody talked about was the war.

"It's a serious matter, you know, an Austrian prince! Austria isn't going to take that lying down, why should they?"

"I knew straight away that Austria wouldn't take that lying down! You can't play games with Austria!"

Berman couldn't have cared less whether Austria was going to take this lying down or not. All he was concerned about was that his business was being ruined. No one was buying or selling. No one knew what to do and everyone was scared to buy, for it was obvious that the value of the goods was going to fall. Who would be interested in buying diamonds when war was raging? Some merchants thought the opposite: that this was the very time they should be preparing diamonds for sale. That would be a prudent move, they argued, because in wartime the supply of rough diamonds from Africa was going to dry up, and when rough stones were in short supply, the price would rise, and anyone who had polished diamonds to sell would make a pile of money.

So they talked and talked, expressing their opinions and giving advice to all and sundry, but no one really knew what the best course of action was. No foreign merchants came, and those who were already in Antwerp rushed to get home as soon as possible, especially the Americans, who were the best buyers. Work stopped and trade came to a standstill; it was an absolute catastrophe.

Once again Berman wandered around his house in a state of agitation. The machines in the diamond cutters' houses were again standing as still as corpses, covered over with a bit of curtain or an apron, their inactivity seeming to mock their masters, the workers, robbing them of their livelihood and sucking their lifeblood. But the workers could do nothing about it. *Their* greatest worry wasn't whether or not they should buy diamonds, but whether or not the baker was going to allow them to buy a loaf of bread on credit. They hoped, even though it was obvious that no one would sell bread on credit in wartime.

So even before the actual outbreak of war, people were going around in a dark and troubled state of mind. As soon as they read the first rumors in the newspapers about the imminence of war, they started taking everything they possessed to the pawnbroker.

The streets were full of people. Crowds were everywhere. All the inhabitants of Leeuwerikstraat had come out of their houses and were milling around in the street. They were gesticulating, shaking their beards, airing their own theories and dismissing the ideas of others. Galician Jews were giving strategic advice to the Austrians and Germans, and putting paid to the enemy with a wave of the hand or a frown. This annoyed the Russian and Polish Jews, who started shouting and bawling: "In God's name, whoever heard of such a thing!

These enemies of the state are allowed to stand in the middle of the street, peeping out from under their black hats and giving 'advice' to the Germans."

At this the Galician Jews, with an air of intellectual superiority, pushed their hats back on their heads so that their foreheads were uncovered and their sidelocks emerged from behind their ears. They plucked at their own and other people's beards, lapels and buttons with their white hands. In squeaky effeminate voices they tried to vanquish the enemy, waging war in the middle of Leeuwerikstraat with the Russian and Polish Jews. So the Russian, Polish and even Lithuanian Jews forgot for a moment that they were all supposed to hate each other like the plague and made a united front to drive back the impudent Galicians. They mocked the Galician "heroes" who were rejoicing prematurely and boasting of German superiority.

Even Hasidim, who went to the court of the same *rebbe,* and normally ate the remnants at the same *rebbe's* table and trembled together at the door of his study, divided into two camps and waged war on each other day and night in their synagogues and prayer houses. In the end, the beefy Russian Jews refused to have any dealings at all with Jews from the enemy camp. If a Galician "arse-licker" happened to be holding a newspaper which was just off the press, so that you could still smell the ink, a Russian Jew would ostentatiously reread his old newspaper (which in any case was usually only about two hours old), ignoring the new one, in order not to come into any kind of contact with the "enemy."

Women didn't even get round to combing their wigs because they were so busy helping their menfolk in the war against "the swinish Russian" or the "accursed German." Mixed marriages were a terrible problem; if a Galician woman had a Russian husband, or vice versa, she would suffer double pain, on account of both her husband and her country. Even children were drawn into the battles.

This wasn't just happening in Leeuwerikstraat. All of Antwerp had taken to the streets. This year the Flemish people couldn't celebrate their annual carnival, but nevertheless the sun was shining, generously flooding over everything and pouring out heaps of gold, as if war had never been heard of. The broad pavements on the Keyserlei were packed. The uniforms of officers and soldiers created splashes of color, and their wearers drank and flirted with women. Countless flags fluttered majestically from windows and balconies, shouting out the national colors wherever you turned. It was a sea of yellow, red and black. The newspaper boys shouted out the latest news.

Flemish and Jewish housewives hurried round the shops in order to provide themselves with foodstuffs for the "four-week war." The diamond cleavers, cutters and polishers wandered around dressed in their best clothes and stood in front of the Bourse talking politics, trying to guess how long the war would last. It was only from their faces that one could tell the merchants from the workers. And the sun carried on pouring out her festive light, soothing and warming everyone and shining on friends and enemies, bosses and workers, adults and children. She did not care one bit that human beings were going mad with worry, that workers had put on their festive clothes to hide their far from festive spirits. It was a matter of complete indifference to her that the merchants could not decide whether or not to buy diamonds. She even shone on the silent machines.

Berman alone stayed at home.

"Four weeks!" he said, jabbing with his finger at his Flemish newspaper, though he wasn't very competent in the language. "*They* think they know that it'll last for four weeks. Huh! If you get into a war, who can tell when it will end!"

The streets got more and more crowded, with groups of people talking everywhere. At last even Berman, anxious to hear what they were saying in the Bourse, went out into the street. He stopped and listened to one of the groups which had congregated there.

"Fools!" he thought, turning away from them. "Squabbling about their countries, these paupers, one defending Efroim-Yossel's kingdom, the other the czar's, idiots that they are! They'll see, Franz Josef and Nicholas II will soon give them a means of earning their livelihood..."

"What do you think of this terrible business?" A young man addressed Berman. He had yellow, parchment-like skin, short, crooked legs and wore a cotton jacket, green with age, which was mended here and there with white thread. He stretched out a clammy hand to Berman.

Berman snatched his hand away impatiently, leaving the young man's hand suspended in midair, and consoled him with a mocking, disdainful smile: "You have nothing to worry about. *You're* hardly likely to be sent to the front line."

It was Berman's smile more than his words which upset the young man; he tweaked the left side of his spectacles where the lens was cracked, and saw two Bermans. He glared angrily at them both and retorted:

"You can never tell who will survive and who will not." Berman, unnerved, stepped back.

"Damn him, that rat; that pathetic, consumptive weakling, opening his trap and spilling out such rubbish! He's already coughed up most of his lungs and yet he's worrying about the war! Let him go to hell!"

Berman went away, shaken by the young man's doom-laden words. The latter was, on the other hand, very pleased with himself that he had managed to unnerve Berman. "I really gave him something to think about," he thought as he wandered off, his greenish jacket and the uppers of his worn boots shining in the sunlight.

Berman looked after him, and sent one final curse after him: "I hope he dies like a dog!"

It had been a strange day. Still not completely recovered from this exchange, he walked on, in an agitated frame of mind, to the Bourse. On the way he was stopped by another young man of about thirty years of age, who held out a large angular, rather grubby hand to him and asked the same question:

"What do you think of this terrible business?"

Berman was suddenly scared. He felt as if the other young man's hand lay in his and those doom-laden words, "You can never tell who will survive and who will not," were haunting him. He snatched his hand away as if he didn't know this young man who, not noticing Berman's strange reactions, continued speaking: "I've just come from the Bourse. It's a catastrophe, an absolute tragedy. They say that the Germans are just across the border, and today or tomorrow they'll be here, damn them to hell! What do you feel about it, Herr Berman?"

Berman felt as if all the spineless characters were swooping on him today, and he wanted to shout out: "What are you trembling for, you fool?" but, since it was one of his brokers standing there, he swallowed the harsh words, finding it difficult to hide his own fear.

"What am I saying?" continued the young man. "Who *wouldn't* be worried about it? And to make matters worse, my wife's expecting. We're already eating into our savings."

These last words especially made an impact on Berman. When you start living off your capital it flows away like water, as he well knew. He was about to tell the young man that he agreed with him, but the latter didn't let him get a word in edgewise. He was constantly touching a deep furrow in his left cheek. It was surrounded by little lines and puckered skin, and his left eye, which looked like a glass eye, was sunk deep in its socket above his cheekbone.

"Do you see this?" he said, pointing to his disfigurement without any embarrassment. "Do you see it? It cost me a fortune in money and pain. I risked my life so that I wouldn't have to go and serve in the czarist army. A Jew, I said to myself, should not serve the czar. Instead of respect, all you get is humiliation. You have to do the hardest and dirtiest work, they beat you, stuff pork into your mouth whether you want to eat it or not, and mock you. These fools, these dunderheads, who haven't as much brains in their entire bodies as the stupidest Jew has in his little finger, mock you. My brother served in the Russian army, and that was enough for me. When I came to Antwerp I saw it was different here and that if you serve here it's just for ten months and apart from that, you're a citizen, and they treat you like a human being among equals. Why did I start telling you all this? Oh yes, I wanted to say that I'm not scared on my own behalf, because they'll not send me to the front line, my Russian experience has already seen to that, but nevertheless it is a terrible tragedy. Do you know what it feels like to start eating into your savings? I tell you, it's a really terrible thing."

When Berman arrived home, the door was locked and there was not a living soul in the house to open it for him. For the first time in his life he had forgotten to take his keys with him.

"Damn them all!" he said. "Those fools and idiots! What are they thinking of? Hell and damnation!"

Cursing and swearing he went off again, and wandered into a park for perhaps the first time in his life. He sat down on a bench, leaning on his walking stick like an old man, and basked in the warm sun. He suddenly felt utterly alone, as if he had been driven away from his own home. "Hmm, eating into your savings, a terrible thing!" he thought, remembering the young man's words.

The park was flooded with light, and fine white threads were floating in the air and attaching themselves to the trees. Spiders spun their square, finely woven webs between the bushes. The grass was dry and burned brown by the sun which had been blazing for weeks. Flocks of birds were whirling around in the air, twittering as if they knew there was some kind of danger hanging over their heads. Here and there, soldiers and their girls were walking arm-in-arm, holding on to each other full of longing, whispering secret words of love, pensive and anxious, and then parting. Apart from them the park was empty and forlorn.

Berman went back home to see if anyone had returned. Rochl came to meet him with a cheerful expression on her face:

"Gedaliah, we have visitors!"

"Visitors? Who?"

"Gitele and her husband!"

"Oh, for God's sake!" muttered Berman crossly as he exchanged his hat for his silk skullcap. "Could they not have found a better time to come paying social calls?"

But he entered the dining room with a broad smile.

"Whom do I see here? A guest! Welcome!" He didn't see

Leybesh until the latter stretched out his hand. "Oh, I didn't notice. You're there too. Well, sit down!" The expression on Berman's face reminded Leybesh of the days when Berman told him to sit and wait, only to give him the news that he didn't have any work for him that day.

"I knew that I'd find them eventually," said Rochl, very pleased with herself. "I was just walking along the street, looking for Dovid. I was thinking that it isn't a good idea for a healthy young man like him to attract too much attention just at the moment. And then, whom do I see, but Gitele! And all this time, that naughty girl hasn't even come to see how we're getting on. It must be a year and a half since we've seen each other – fine *landslayt* you are!"

She carried on chattering: "And what do you think of the baby? She's already a proper little lady, *ken eynore*! Rochl lifted her out of the shabby pram which stood in the corridor and brought her in to show Berman. She was a skinny, sleepy little creature dressed in a worn woolen dress and her knickers were damp.

Gitele was sweating with embarrassment, which Rochl didn't notice at all. She pressed a biscuit into the child's hand and carried on chatting to her: "We're quite a young lady now, mmm?"

The child had a very serious air. She took her grubby finger, which very frequently had to make do in place of food, out of her mouth. Her dark, melancholy eyes looked large in her tiny face and told of hunger. Rochl took her hand with the biscuit in it and guided it to the child's mouth, but she started to cry.

"Shh! Shhh! Oh, I see you've really been spoiled, mmm? Now shhh! Sweetheart!"

Leybesh took the child, who calmed down in his arms and started nibbling the biscuit.

The maid brought in tea, and Gitele nearly died of shame when she saw that the maid was better dressed than she was.

"What a pity the children aren't here, especially Dovid. He'd be so pleased to see you. If he knew you were here, he'd come running back immediately." Rochl carried on talking, not dreaming that every word she said about Dovid pierced Gitele's heart and made her burn with shame.

"What do you think of the terrible business?" said Gitele, trying to deflect Rochl from this topic. She glanced at Leybesh and felt furious with him: "For God's sake, I wish he would stop eating. He just carries on munching and munching. It's *really* embarrassing," she thought.

As if Leybesh had read her thoughts, he nonchalantly took another pear from the dish and started peeling it. He ate it with relish, all the while counting the silvery beads on Rochl's blue silk dress and thinking that she fitted perfectly into the ambience of this bright, cheerful dining room.

Gitele moved nearer to the table, trying to hide herself behind it, not knowing where to look and wishing she could disappear. Rochl kept on talking, and every word was directed at her. The silver on the sideboard, like its owners, exuded affluence and respectability, just like the silver on the sideboard in her father's house, and it seemed to Gitele that it was looking down on her, smiling scornfully as if to say: "What's going on here, in *our* dining room?"

"Yes, it's a terrible thing!" Berman finally replied to Gitele, after deliberating and drumming with his forefinger on the tablecloth for a long time. Gitele, meantime, had forgotten what she had asked him. "Yes indeed, it certainly is. Human beings are always searching for something new. They get tired of the eternal struggle for a crust of bread. If they *do* have a livelihood, even if they are rich and have sampled all the delights of the world, they become jaded, feel bored and empty, and sometimes even long for a little hardship to spice up their lives. The way horseradish makes meat tastier and the juicier the meat, the more horseradish one craves. And so you prepare a huge pot of horseradish so that your eyes are stinging from it. And when you've tried the bitterness, you don't want to admit it's too sharp, and so you avert your face and wipe your eyes and smile at your companions at the table and urge them to sample it too. You assure them that it is good for them, and they persuade others, because they don't want to admit it's too sharp. Instead they just bite their lips until they bleed.

That's war. Do you understand what I'm saying?" And Berman stirred his tea reflectively. He had forgotten his worry about eating into his capital, because he felt so pleased with his own oratory.

Glancing at Gitele he saw that she understood very well what he was talking about. "A fine young woman!" he thought. "What a shame she has thrown herself away!"

Leybesh gulped his tea, bit into some honey cake and thought that for once Berman was talking almost like a human being. And it was many years since he had eaten such good honey cake.

When Leybesh and Gitele were leaving they met Dovid on the doorstep. Gitele was covered with confusion. Her shoulders trembled and her face turned as white as chalk, then fiery red. Her desire to see Dovid had made her put up very little resistance to Rochl who, she presumed, had invited them in to bring some life into the house during this trying time. Why in God's name could she not have taken control of the situation? She felt humiliated, and lowered her eyes but glanced surreptitiously at Dovid. She could not help wanting to see what effect her presence was having on him, and to get an impression of how well he was managing without her. Instead of feeling reproachful, her eyes suddenly filled with fear when she looked at him. Dovid was bent over like an old man and his face was a waxy yellow.

She wanted to ask him what had happened, but she couldn't speak. Dovid broke the silence.

"I have just signed up for the army," he blurted out.

"What?!"

"What have you done, Dovid?" said Leybesh, equally horrified.

"It's the best solution," said Dovid hastily and disappeared quickly into the house. He went straight up to his own room and locked the door, speaking to nobody. "She did go pale all the same," he thought. "Perhaps that means that there's still a spark of something there. But this is the best solution." He felt very, very tired.

Leybesh eventually broke the awkward silence between himself and Gitele: "If it wasn't an imperialist war, I would sign up too! I really can't understand why Dovid feels he has to take part in this mess.

Someone who is living in such luxury, why does he have to quarrel with that fine father of his? As far as I can see, Dovid doesn't have any kind of ideals, so what's preventing him from following in his father's footsteps and living like all the other parasites? Perhaps it's true that he is not suited to business, but that doesn't mean he has to throw himself into this conflagration. It's a real shame for his mother, who obviously really loves him. She's a nice woman and it will kill her. I just wish my boss's only son would do the same; all these stinking bourgeois should taste hardship for once!" Leybesh went on in this way to Gitele. She wasn't listening to a single word and gave Leybesh a look filled with so much hatred that he didn't open his mouth again.

Leybesh's boss had realized that he had no influence on Leybesh. He was getting nowhere in trying to make a Zionist out of him. Leybesh would carry on believing that Karl Marx's teachings were the only truth. Furthermore, he finally realized that Leybesh was the better chess player, but that he didn't take it seriously, and always let the boss win. This made the boss wild. He considered himself to be a great intellectual. He knew the exact dates of Moses Mendelssohn's birth and death, all about his friendship with Lessing, and why and when the Jews of Holland had persecuted and finally excommunicated Baruch Spinoza from their community. He knew when the Zionist movement began, and could recount the history of the Lovers of Zion movement. He was a man who carried Herzl's picture in his signet ring instead of a diamond and this nobody – *his* library was worth more money than Leybesh had ever seen – this *good-for-nothing* was trying to make a fool of him? Leybesh obviously thought that he was some kind of simple ignoramus, just a diamond merchant whose sole aim was to make money, while *he*, Leybesh, had studied Karl Marx. Who was this Marx anyway and what importance did he have after all? Thus Leybesh's boss had a quarrel with Karl Marx and stopped giving work to Leybesh. Then in the Bourse, the Fortunia, the Club, or even in the *Shenkl*, whenever the subject of socialism came up, which it did almost every day, he casually mentioned that a plague had come to Antwerp and its name was Bruckner, a man who led pious young people astray, led our sons and daughters off the straight and narrow with a new Torah, Karl Marx's Torah.

"It will all end with our children forsaking Judaism, mark my words." He wagged the finger on which he carried Herzl's picture instead of a diamond.

The merchants took him seriously and from then on didn't give Leybesh a single diamond to polish.

After Leybesh and Gitele had left, Berman lost his temper with Rochl. He raged and stormed at her:

"I just want to know, you stupid fool; who asked you to invite that devil into my house? That's the last thing I need, for people to find out about it! One good-for-nothing attracts another; God damn you, you stupid cow!"

Dovid heard his father's shouting from his room, but he felt total indifference. What did he care about Leybesh now? He couldn't even summon up any real pity for his mother.

Chapter 19

Once again, Berman got up the next morning with a headache. He had slept badly and had been plagued by bad dreams. He had been beating up the tubercular young man with the doom-laden words, and had started shouting out in his sleep. Rochl had just got to sleep at that point, and she jumped out of bed in fright. She woke him up and pulled away his hand which was clutching his own chest.

"What's the matter, Gedaliah? Why are you shouting?"

Berman stared at her with a frightened look as if he didn't recognize her, rubbed his eyes, and as his dream gradually came back to him, he spat:

"Damn him, I hope he dies like a dog!"

He got dressed and went into the kitchen, pulled up the wooden shutters with their familiar clatter, and asked for his drink of warm sweet milk. Putting on his prayer shawl and tefillin, he got ready to say the morning prayers.

Rochl's heart was heavy and she felt weak. She could not stop thinking about Gitele and her baby.

"How dreadful! What awful poverty! That poor little mite; suffering from hunger, so early in her little life. If Gitele's mother came back from the grave and saw how her daughter was living, she would die all over again. That father of hers is a pig!" Rochl was shocked by her own words, which she had shouted out loud.

At breakfast, as Berman was putting sugar in his coffee, Dovid began twisting and turning in his chair, not taking his eyes off his mother while he sipped his coffee. He opened and closed his mouth once or twice, wanting to say something but not knowing where to start. How would his mother react? He knew very well what she would do: she would tear off her wig and sob. That's what he feared. He couldn't stand tears.

His own eyes were moist, and he tried to speak but couldn't find the words. His tongue stuck to the roof of his mouth. Berman noticed his discomfiture.

"He needs money again, the wretch!" He'd give him a plague instead of money; that was for sure. If you eat into your capital, it flows away like water....

In the middle of these gloomy thoughts, he heard, or perhaps he imagined, Dovid calling him "Papa" like he used to do when he was a little boy. Yes, Dovid was talking to him, but Berman couldn't understand what he was saying. Why was he repeating: "Papa, Papa ... ?"

Finally Dovid blurted out: "I've joined the army!"

Was it nighttime? Was Berman still dreaming?

"*What* did you say?"

"I said that I've signed up for the army."

"Are you mad? Is this some kind of silly joke?"

"I am not mad and it isn't a joke. I have to report for duty tomorrow."

Berman's eyes looked as if their pupils were going to burst out, leaving two black holes in the middle of the whites, which were bloodshot from his sleepless night.

Rochl did not tear off her wig, nor did she sob. She simply said, "I don't feel well," then slid off her chair and lay on the soft blue carpet, like a corpse. Father and son worked together for the first time in years, lifting up the unconscious woman, putting some brandy to her lips and rubbing her with vinegar. When she came to, they carried her into the bedroom and put her to bed.

Jeannette stood there shrieking in her silk nightdress. The servant girl brought a hot water bottle. Jacques was the only one who didn't lose his head, but ran to get the doctor. Rochl suddenly remembered what had happened and started weeping uncontrollably.

"Dovid, what have I done to deserve this? What do you want of me that I haven't given you?"

Deeply concerned, old Chaim Yoysef had come into her bedroom and tried to comfort her.

"Don't weep, daughter, with God's help we'll find a solution. We won't let Dovid fall into the hands of the *goyim*. With God's help!"

Berman sat on a pink basket chair with his head in his hands. He looked as if he were in mourning. Dovid was sitting on his mother's bed, wiping the tears from her eyes and stroking her cheeks as if she were a child.

"Don't worry, Mother. We have to defend the country. Someone has to go!" He tried in vain to convince her that the step he had taken was right.

Chapter 20

In the city, the scent of war was in the air.

German and Austrian citizens were ordered to leave the city within twenty-four hours, but this edict didn't apply to many gentiles, apart from a few rich hotel owners, and it was the Jews, as always, who packed their bags and left. Yesterday's confident German and Austrian patriots now took all their worldly possessions, their tearful wives and bewildered, sleepy children, and crept to the railway station, with bowed heads. The streets in the Jewish district were empty and abandoned, with lowered blinds and locked doors. In among them, like the living in a graveyard, the odd Russian or Polish Jewish family remained.

At the Bermans' the atmosphere was frighteningly still. For days at a time the shutters remained open, and Berman sat reading prayer books. Jeannette, who couldn't stand the gloomy atmosphere at home, went to stay with a friend. She couldn't bear to watch her mother endlessly wandering about the house, hunched up and wrapped in a shawl, wringing her hands and weeping as if she were bereaved.

Flemish families, on the other hand, were different. When their sons had to say goodbye to their parents, relatives, dogs and cats, the family accepted the situation as if it were the most natural thing in the world. Some fathers even envied their sons, regretting that they themselves were unable to go and defend the fatherland, but then they had a fatherland to defend.

"Ah, we'd teach them a lesson, those damned Germans!" muttered old men into their grey whiskers.

In front of the door of a shabby house stood a group of men puffing clouds of smoke from their clay pipes, talking agitatedly, with excited smiles and with rage in their voices. Now and then they spat into their leathery palms and looked at their hands.

"We're not scared of *them*! There's no such thing as a small, helpless nation!" exclaimed a fair-haired young man, slapping his thigh with his iron fist, his eyes gleaming with an unnatural brightness.

"We'll show them," spat out a toothless old Flemish man, wearing a pair of brown striped velvet trousers. "I don't know what to do with myself," he went on angrily. For the last few days his life had been turned upside down. For over forty years he had set out every morning with his wagonload of clay, smoking his pipe and serenely contemplating his big Belgian horse with its bushy mane and large hooves clip-clopping along. It knew the way, when to stop and when to carry on. Now the man was hanging about with nothing to do, while the horse stood in its stable eating him out of house and home, and not even earning its keep.

"They're never satisfied, those damned Germans, and they think we are all afraid of them," said someone else.

"Afraid? *Godverdoeme!* Who's afraid of them. Do you see this hand? It's itching to get at them," said the fair-haired young man, scratching his palm. Everyone laughed.

"There's no such thing as a small, helpless nation," repeated another. "If a nation is determined, ha! … if a nation is ready to go through fire and water to defend its land … !"

"To protect our homes," cried a woman and burst into tears.

"We'll show him, that bastard of a kaiser!" The flaxen-haired young man went on, showing his white teeth as he grimaced. "We'll give them '*Deutschland über alles!*'"

"It should be '*Deutschland unter alles,*'" shouted a few voices and everybody laughed again.

"Long live King Albert!" exclaimed someone, and everyone joined in: "Long live King Albert!"

"Do you see these arms of mine?" A small man with a straw-colored moustache pushed up his right shirtsleeve, revealing an arm with a mass of thick, greenish veins.

"I'll put bullets into those Germans just like I hammer the nails into shoes. If they'd only let me, they'd find there's no such thing as 'too old'," shouted another voice in the crowd. "Who wouldn't give his last drop of blood for our country? Who wouldn't leave everything, even his wife and child and all his possessions? I ask you."

"Don't forget to mention the cow and the calf, you couldn't take them into battle either," laughed a passing milkman who continued on his way with his little cart full of brass-trimmed milk cans. "All for the fatherland!" His words resonated against the big milk churn, leaving an echo behind him.

"You see, he thinks I'm right," said the shoemaker, not realizing that the milkman had spoken with an ironic smile on his face, and he became even more passionate: "Long live Belgium!"

"Long live Belgium!" they all shouted.

"Belgium and our King!" the shoemaker went on with wild excitement.

"*Godverdoeme!* Are you all off your heads? What are you getting so worked up about?" A fat, red-faced shopkeeper appeared on the doorstep of his fine butcher's shop. He wiped his hands clean of the pork fat which was dripping off them, fixed the crowd with his burning eyes and laughed bitterly. "Our lives and all our possessions are in danger and they are whooping with joy!"

"Aha! He's afraid for his possessions," said the shoemaker, glaring angrily at him. "*That's* the problem with *him!*"

"Oh, they've all gone mad!" the shopkeeper muttered and went back into his shop.

The milkman's wife, whom the shopkeeper had just served, came out of the shop with a full basket of goods, which she had just purchased to help to see her through the "four-week war." She stopped and listened to their conversation.

"You should stop talking when you don't know what you're talking about," she said. "They're clever and powerful. What are we compared to them? We're just worms. They'll squash us underfoot." From the way she took the part of the Germans, it seemed as if she had forgotten that she was Belgian, that her husband was a naturalized Belgian and that she had Belgian children. "You're going to pit your strength against Germany, are you? What a joke!" she said, and went off.

"She's German, you know, and so's her husband! You're all just sheep, not soldiers at all! What great heroes you are!" mocked a woman, sparks flying from her eyes. "You should have torn her apart like a herring, that's what you should have done! She's a traitor!"

The people looked at each other. "God damn it! We should have broken her bones!"

"We should have done her in," said the shoemaker, hoarse with savage rage and burning with desire to do just that.

The merchants came into the Bourse, had a little look, a little sniff around, and went away, for there was nothing to do, and the emptiness of the place drove them home again. The deserted *Shenkl* was worse than the Bourse. There were no black hats, no small-scale dealers with red cheeks and white, feminine hands, weighing their insignificant "goods" adeptly on little scales. They were no longer poking skillfully into piles of diamond waste with their tiny tweezers, tying up their little finds beautifully and shaking diamond powder into white paper parcels with tissue paper lining.

They had been disdained when they had been there but they were missed now they were gone. If they had been there now it wouldn't have seemed so deserted, and the atmosphere in the *Shenkl* wouldn't have been so dismal for those who came in: there would, at least, have been something going on. The Russian and Polish Jews had been sorry for those other Jews when they had seen them leaving with their wives and children, with hanging heads and stifled weeping, leaving the homes which, by working hard, they had managed to make into cozy nests. Jews who remained had tears in their eyes; at that time they didn't think about the fact that these people came from enemy countries; they saw Jews being driven out, not knowing where they would end up. They felt great sympathy for their plight.

Berman went to the *Shenkl* just to have a look. Even though he knew that no business was going on, he wandered around from one place to another, just to get out of the house. He felt bad at home and even worse when he was out. He was scared of meeting people; he felt that they were pointing the finger at him and judging him: "What kind of father is he? He's driven his own son away into the arms of death."

He didn't know what to do with himself, and sat down at a table where some Jews were carrying on a military campaign on a scruffy chessboard, trying to capture strategic positions from each other. This made Berman really cross:

"You're just like children! Is that all you can think about?"

The others were surprised and embarrassed, and Berman didn't know what had come over him.

"What? Is the war over already, that you're *not* thinking about it?" laughed one of the men. "I hope the real war is over so soon!"

"It will be, it will be!" someone else reassured him. "A war like this can't last for long, certainly no more than four weeks."

"I think so too," put in a young man. "If it does, the world will come to an end. You can't play games with a war like that. Am I not right, Reb Elye?" He turned to a self-important man who had been giving advice on strategy, deferring to him as if he were a great expert in matters of warfare.

"God forbid!" pronounced Reb Elye after a moment's deliberation. "Stuff and nonsense! It won't even last four weeks, I promise you that!"

The Germans, however, paid no attention to Reb Elye's promise, and drew ever nearer to the city.

Among the Belgian aircraft which had been buzzing in everyone's ears for days, more and more enemy planes began to appear, flying wildly around Antwerp's peaceful sky. Quite unexpectedly, in the middle of the day, people had to leave everything and creep into the cellars. It was even worse, though, when they had to crawl out of their warm beds in the middle of the night.

One night Berman wasn't feeling well. He had finished reciting the evening prayers, had gone to bed early, and had only just fallen asleep. He was in the middle of a vivid dream when suddenly the alarm sounded, and everyone had to go into the cellar. Berman stood there in a state of shock, holding his trousers. He looked around as if he were a stranger in his own house, then shuddered suddenly and raced downstairs. He had time to see a dark mass of people in the corridor, who had been out in the street when the alarm sounded and had knocked on every door they had passed. They were standing in his corridor like lost sheep, and seeing Berman rushing past with slippers on his bare feet and his trousers in his hand, they all darted after him. Rochl was wailing:

"Where will my son hide?"

The people in the cellar tried to console her:

"Believe me, there are forests there where you can escape from the shooting. And if, God forbid, it's not possible to escape, then hiding is not going to do any good. And anyway, do you think you're the only mother? Even if he hadn't signed up, he'd have had to go now in any case. They're all going: gentiles, Jews, young and old. You're not the only one to be affected by the war, Madame Berman."

"Great sorrows bring their own consolation," said someone else comfortingly.

Berman was sitting on a cushion in the corner of the cellar. His nose was pinched and pallid, and he had put his fingers in his ears so that he would not hear the rumbling of the "destroyers" above the rooftops.

Suddenly the house shook, and they all thought they were going to be buried in the dark cellar full of spiders' webs, in which the only light was a tiny flame from a paraffin lamp which the servant girl had placed in the furthest corner so that it would not shine out too brightly. The light flickered and the shadows on the walls started madly fluttering and dancing about, filling the people with horror. An old woman kept going "Ssshhhh!" even though nobody had said a word. Then, crash! A house collapsed nearby. Berman sprang up, then slumped back down again.

Afterwards, when with great difficulty they had helped old Reb

Chaim Yoysef back up the steps, and laid him on a bench in the kitchen to sleep, Berman calmed down again, but the old woman absolutely refused to go back home. She sat down beside the big stove, warmed her frozen hands, and kept on going "Ssshhhh!"

This drove Berman mad. "Go home! Do what I say: go home!" he shouted in a very ungentlemanly fashion at the confused old woman.

"Go home and recite a psalm or two!" joked Jacques, for whom the business of creeping into the cellar was great fun.

The alarms became more frequent and the visits to the cellar tedious. People's fear, however, increased and their mood became more depressed. The rich diamond merchants had gradually left the town, locking their doors behind them and taking with them as many assets as they were allowed. Some had gone to Amsterdam and others to England. It was mainly the poor people and shopkeepers who were left. It was not so easy for the latter to take their merchandise with them, and so they stood for days at a time at their shop doors, not even unpacking their bundles of woolen undershirts, towels and underclothes. They stared at the sky and soon were able to recognize an enemy airplane at first sight, whereupon they locked up their shops and were the first to get into the cellars.

Most of the houses had closed shutters. The highly polished doors of elegant houses were locked. The city emptied as the panic intensified. Life got more monotonous, and those who were left became ever more dispirited. Berman alone made no move to go. He was existing on pills and all sorts of medicines, and a proliferation of white hairs had invaded his beard. He slept badly, fearing death, starting at every noise, constantly sleeping in his clothes. There were long periods when he could not take a bath in case an air raid started; all this exasperated him, but he stayed nevertheless.

"There's no other way, one has to just sit it out! Building up a home and a business is difficult, destroying it all is easy," said Berman to himself. And his great fear of death and love of life could not outweigh his determination to hold on to everything he had achieved with so much effort.

Rochl had no desire to leave either. It seemed to her that here in Antwerp she was nearer her son, and if she went away she would be abandoning him and subjecting him to even greater dangers.

But early one morning, when the Bermans had just got to sleep after a night during which their beds had been shaking and seemed to be lifting off the floor, a policeman knocked on the door of the bedroom where they all now slept together, mumbled something indistinctly and hurried off down the stairs again. The policeman was overworked that morning. Like a Jewish beadle going round to waken everyone in the *shtetl* to come and recite the prayers of penitence, the policeman proceeded from house to house, hurriedly ordering the sleepy people to leave the town.

Berman rubbed his eyes, not having understood a word. Had someone denounced him about the business of the little "bargains" he had purchased, or was the policeman really a spy? In wartime anything was possible. His normally dark complexion had turned a waxy color, and his eyes were red-rimmed from lack of sleep.

"*What* did he say?"

Rochl didn't know either. Her teeth were chattering with fear.

"Perhaps we've been robbed?" suggested Jeannette.

Berman's face lit up. He actually prayed to God that there would be such a simple explanation. But soon a neighbor knocked on their door.

"Hurry, Herr Berman, don't waste a moment!"

Berman looked out of the window and saw people fleeing to the railway station. They were streaming from all directions, carrying packs and babies and leading older children by the hand. The Bermans swiftly packed a few necessities and by the time they were ready to leave, the town was abandoned. There was a throng of people at the railway station.

The city stood empty and deserted, as if in mourning, veiled in smoke and gloom. Occasionally the sky was lit up by rockets, flaring up and then sinking back into the smoky darkness.

Because of the old man, the Bermans made slow progress along the streets, and it seemed to them that they would never reach the station. Suddenly the thunder of exploding cannon lifted people off their feet and Berman's father had to quicken his pace to keep up with everyone else.

They managed to get onto the last train, which took a whole night to get from Antwerp to Holland. The peasants left the villages on foot. The city was already cut off. Berman and his family were the last to squeeze into a carriage, where the people were packed in like sardines, standing, sitting or lying on top of one another. The closed, black curtains created an oppressive muffled silence which caught in the throat and depressed the spirit. Even children did not cry. They looked around and like the grownups, they forced themselves not to burst into tears.

Chapter 21

Dawn was the color of blood. Early morning sunshine flooded the cottages in the little villages, shining on blue and white checked tablecloths, crockery, and healthy, early-rising Dutch peasants. Their breakfast of freshly baked bread, delicious yellow butter, real Dutch cheese and steaming jugs of cocoa was laid out on the long tables, calling temptingly to them.

The sun illuminated the dark carriages with the same generous silvery light, stealing in through the cracks, caressing and warming the crumpled travelers. It stroked the children's faces, creeping into their dimples and making them smile, even conjuring up a spark in Berman's black eyes. It didn't spare the glass of the carriage windows and the black curtains, which had been drawn back; the sunlight made both look even grubbier.

Berman stood at the door of the carriage. The train was now traveling at normal speed, and he saw brown, white and dappled cows and grey sheep lying on harvested fields. Horses with glossy coats were grazing on the fresh grass and the farmers in their wide linen trousers, wooden, snub-nosed clogs and wide straw hats were already working in the fields, bringing in the abundant grain harvest. They looked at the trains, which streamed endlessly past on their journey from Belgium, packed with people who the day before had been affluent citizens and were now paupers.

Peasant women were going out into the fields. They wore deep-brimmed bonnets on their freshly-washed hair, and pleated skirts of woven linen with close-fitting bodices which revealed the fine lines of sturdy female limbs and firm, full breasts straining against the stiff fabric. Many had children with them, whom they would suckle and lay to sleep in hammocks or even in the fragrant grass. All were going to spend the day in healthy, productive work under a free and peaceful sky. The sun shone down on the scene, warming both the fields and the people.

Some had been in the fields since very early in the morning, digging potatoes. The spades gleamed as they came out of the black earth, catching the sunlight, before burying themselves again. Others were making hay and stacking it, or cutting the ripe corn. The women laid the corn to dry on the bare, newly harvested fields. The golden sun poured out its abundant warmth, drying the crops and blessing the peaceful, harmonious labor. Everywhere on the train's route, windmills reminded the exhausted refugees that they were in Holland, a free country which always maintained its neutrality.

Berman breathed deeply through the open windows of the carriage, drawing in as much of the early morning air as he could. He almost felt happy, until he remembered his possessions in Antwerp, and then the fields disappeared and the sky became cloudy and overcast, shrouded in deep gloom.

The train stopped in Rotterdam. The disheveled passengers, their faces yellow and exhausted after a night cramped up in the stuffy carriages, woke up, yawned loudly and tried unsuccessfully to find space to stretch their stiff, painful limbs. Some attempted to stand up and get out of the carriages, but could not get past the solid wall of bodies. An old man, still half asleep, didn't know where he was and, rubbing his sticky eyes, he cried out:

"Is this another pogrom? Jews, let's bar the doors!"

His wife and a few neighbors managed with great difficulty to calm him down. He stared at all the people, not recognizing them, and unwilling to believe that it was "nothing at all," that they had fled because of the war. Eventually he remembered, rubbed his eyes again, shut his toothless mouth and fell silent.

"What a life! Wars, pogroms..." someone else started to

philosophize. Gradually people managed to get out of the train, and on the platforms there were scenes of confusion, as people's luggage got mixed up and they shouted and argued. But soon representatives of the Jewish charity organizations arrived. The very sight of these officials with their civilized appearance: placid, well-dressed and well-groomed, reassured the bewildered fugitives a little. They were packed into buses and driven off to some unknown destination.

Then they got off the buses and were placed at tables, where numbers were stuck on their luggage. The men were shown where they could go and pray. Berman was not happy with the arrangements. How could he sit and eat with people like *that* at one long bare wooden table?

"Why on earth did you have to wait until the last minute? I *told* you this was going to happen," complained Jeannette. "You see what kind of people these are? Paupers and *shnorrers,* the lot of them. No one like us at all!"

Berman didn't answer her. "That'll do as a breakfast for them, but not for me," he said, pushing the plate of bread and butter away.

A young lady in white overalls with a string of real pearls round her neck and a polite smile on her thin red lips came up to Berman, putting on a more dazzling smile which revealed her small white teeth. She could see by his fine, well-groomed beard he must be a "better class of person." She started apologizing:

"You must excuse us! We have had so many people to deal with quite unexpectedly. It has been absolutely impossible! But I shall report it." The young lady, a voluntary worker who herself came from an affluent family, understood the situation and reported it to the secretary, a fair-haired young man wearing spectacles with thick, brightly polished lenses. He told her to serve the Bermans separately: "We'll see. Perhaps he is a better sort of person, or perhaps he's just one of that kind that we know very well…"

"He *is* a better class of person. You can see that by his smart clothing."

Some of the refugees were discussing their new situation. Others sat silently. Poor people, who had been longing to leave Antwerp but hadn't been able to afford the fare, were loudly lamenting the fine houses they had left behind and describing how they had been impoverished by the war. Those who really had wealth and possessions entered into their fantasy and started believing what they were telling them.

"And you know what?" boasted an old Jew who had made his living by selling a little chocolate round the restaurants, "for my business alone I wouldn't take a thousand francs."

"That's because nobody would give you a thousand francs for it!" joked someone else.

"And I suppose you are a millionaire yourself?"

"Well, I'm not boasting."

"Because you haven't anything to boast about." Everyone laughed.

Berman wandered round the streets of Rotterdam on his own, angry with the world. If only they had been set down in Amsterdam, he could have gone into the Bourse and had a look to see what was going on. "Everything is going to the dogs!" he thought, forgetting that if he wished, he *could* go to Amsterdam and have a look at things. "When you are living off your capital you might as well go and bury yourself alive. When you eat into your savings, they just trickle away like water." These words kept running through his mind, and suddenly his childhood home flashed before him; he remembered all the ugliness which went with poverty. He saw himself as if he had been his father, lying helplessly in bed under the grubby coverlet, and the rabbi swaying over him with the lambs' tails bobbing around on his shabby hat.

He was roused from his reverie by a lot of shouting, and felt immensely relieved that for the moment he was still the affluent Gedaliah Berman who had fled the danger of the war.

The shouting came from a group of people standing at the edge of a canal, talking loudly and agitatedly, and evidently angry with a small boy who was standing there. Berman approached them.

The boy had been playing with some of his friends at the water's edge, sailing paper boats and trying to catch fish. Suddenly he lost his balance and was floundering around in the water. He surfaced, grabbed hold of the rope of a barge which was moored at the edge, lost his grip and was about to go under again.

A fisherman with a ruddy complexion, who was carrying his catch of shellfish and frogs, handed the sack to someone, jumped into a boat and fished out the young rascal. He brought him back to the bank to a storm of applause from the onlookers. He sat the boy down on a stone, dripping wet, and spoke sternly to all the boys:

"I'm going to keep him sitting in my house for a whole day! And I'll let the lot of you drown if you don't get away from the edge of the canal! One day there'll be a real accident!"

"Where's the policeman?" wondered the onlookers, getting themselves worked up in sympathy with the fisherman. "Oh, he'll arrive when he's not needed any more. *Godverdoeme!*" said the fisherman crossly, drawing on his clay pipe and exhaling clouds of smoke through his nose.

In the end he wrapped the little boy in his own sheepskin jacket and, with his bag over one arm and carrying the child in the other, he took him home.

Berman stopped and, in his broken Flemish, asked someone what was going on. A fair-skinned Dutch lad with a long shiny nose, wearing wooden clogs, told him that a little boy had drowned.

"*Almost* drowned, you mean!" a voice from the crowd corrected him. Berman went on his way. "What a stupid lot they are," he thought "not even knowing exactly what happened. But this town – nothing but water wherever you turn. It's a wonder they don't all drown. The town's a river – nothing but water and refugees. Whoever heard of *goyim* wasting their time wandering about with nothing to do, staring all day into the water? Of course, for all the lazy fools from Antwerp, this is the high life. The war's a blessing in disguise for them. They've got enough to eat, so they're just strolling around with their hands in their pockets, as if the world belonged to them. If they had left everything behind, as I had to, the results of years of toil, it wouldn't be such a joyful holiday for them!" Thus Berman, who seemed to have forgotten that he himself was also just "strolling around," vented his spleen on the people who filled the streets of Rotterdam. In reality, they were full of the quiet desperation of people who have nothing left to lose.

He stopped by a stall and bought a herring fillet, ate it, licked his lips, and went back to the lodgings. He lay down on the mattress which now served as his bed, and tried to make up his mind which option would be better, to go to Amsterdam or to England. How on earth could one make that decision? Who could tell which would be the better choice?

One morning the fair-haired young man polished his spectacles with particular thoroughness, positioned them very carefully on his fleshy nose, assumed an extremely serious expression and came into the big hall where the refugees were sitting round the tables, drinking cocoa from dented tin mugs. He tried to speak in a deep voice, but it came out with a squeak, which spoiled the whole effect.

"Nobody is to leave the building today!" he announced and without further explanation he retreated into his office again. The refugees were anxious to question him about this, but they couldn't get to him. He had put the chain on the door and wouldn't let anyone in.

So they had no choice but to sit around playing chess and trying to guess where they were going to be taken. Some guessed it would be London; others thought that they would all be spread around Holland. But no one knew and, as their feelings of bewilderment grew, they started fighting over a knight or a pawn, taking out their uneasiness and anger on each other. Berman was most displeased with the situation: that a young ruffian should order *him* to sit and wait, without giving him any explanation! How dare a scabby boy be so insolent to *him*, Berman? So he stood up, combed his beard with his fingers and knocked on the door of the office.

When the young man saw through the window that it was Berman, he came out:

"*Mein Herr?*"

"I should like to ask," said Berman, also speaking German, "the reason for this."

"Oh certainly, sir, of course," answered the young man respectfully: "I have received an instruction that this evening all the Jewish refugees are to travel on to London."

"So! *Danke!*"

Berman was pleased that they were going to London. Fate seemed to have made the right decision, and he felt quite satisfied. He had managed to bring some fine goods with him and had no doubt that he would be able to do business there.

"What? So we're actually going to London? Why didn't he tell us?"

"Why should he tell *you*?" laughed Berman.

The people made angry objections to the young man, when he came out into the hall that evening with a thick cigar between his fat red lips to announce that they were leaving in an hour:

"But they say that we'll soon be able to go back home. How long can the war last? So what's the point in dragging us all the way to London?"

"Ask the Germans that, not me!" he answered, and left the room. The refugees got into a terrible state of agitation.

"Who would have expected this catastrophe?!"

"They've really sold us down the river."

"We're sitting here like cats in a sack. We're not little children, after all!"

"They think they can do just what they like with us!"

The refugees raged and stormed, but nevertheless stayed where they were and didn't try to leave the building. Jews who used to push little carts, sell knick-knacks in restaurants, or slave away in shops which didn't even provide a livelihood, were jubilant, but even so, they joined in the protests volubly, not wanting to advertise their poverty by remaining silent. The young people, who were always keen to travel, were more delighted than anyone.

During the night they were led away like sheep. Women were weeping for the homes they were leaving behind, even though they had already left them by coming to Holland.

The ship was dark, and the bunks, which were stacked on top of each other, were just hard planks of grey wood. The only lighting consisted of a few dim lamps. The people sat or lay silently with their mouths pressed firmly shut, in an attempt to control their nausea. Now and then someone couldn't cope and vomited all over the person underneath. A few girls got together and started singing, joking, making fun of the older people who were groaning and moaning and vomiting, all in an attempt to make themselves look brave. But in the middle of it, they too were overcome and threw up.

The voyage lasted through the night. Berman, suffering from terrible stomach cramps, lay there clutching his belly, with a wet cloth wrapped round his head, inhaling from a bottle of smelling salts.

Berman's father whispered softly. Rochl was weeping with muffled sobs. She was imagining heaps of slaughtered corpses without arms and legs, and among them was Dovid, lying in a pool of blood and mud, dead on the field of battle, with no one to cover his wounds or to bury him. And *she* was traveling away from him, far away to England, leaving him lying there dead. The more she tried to drive away these terrible thoughts and shocking images, the more they crept into her mind, assuming ever more dreadful forms, and England seemed to her a million miles distant from her son; the greater the distance between him and her, the greater the danger for him. She sobbed loudly.

Meanwhile, Berman was preoccupied with his own problems. The stomachache and nausea prevented him from getting to sleep. He didn't want to sleep in any case, because he wanted to keep his eye on the merchandise he had brought with him.

And so the ship slowly made its way through the rough, black sea; the sky was cloudy and a cold rain was falling, in contrast to the warm, bright weather in Holland.

Chapter 22

The Bermans stood slightly apart from the other refugees, their suitcases at their feet, in the strange, huge railway station.

Berman was carrying a large silk umbrella which he had bought in Rotterdam, having heard that it rains all the time in London. He was feeling extremely impatient. What a dreadful noise! What chaos! There were people milling around everywhere, and the cries of the newspaper boys nearly drove him mad. Names of racehorses and the latest headlines about the war were echoing from one end of the station to the other. Berman tried to stop up his ears, but the cries managed to penetrate, deafening him:

"All the winners! All the winners!"

"German airplane brought down!"

"Eight people burnt to death!"

"Murder case verdict! Murderer sentenced to death!"

The refugees all stood in the enormous railway station listening to these strange foreign words echoing in their ears with a dull, rattling sound, like beans being thrown on a metal surface. The terrible tumult and the huge size of the place angered Berman, and he was indignant that he was being kept waiting for such a long time. As usual he took his frustration out on Rochl.

"This isn't a railway station, it's a madhouse," he grumbled ill-temperedly to her.

Tall phlegmatic Englishmen constantly entered and left the station. They wore grey coats and mildly surprised, tight-lipped expressions on their clean-shaven faces. They glanced surreptitiously at the refugees as if they were a collection of small-town relatives who had come to attend the wedding of some rich London cousin who had been too busy to come and collect them, or had simply forgotten all about them.

Two Englishwomen walked past. They wore sporty grey suits and their neatly coiffured heads were crowned by broad-brimmed felt hats. Their mannish shoes, gloves and suitcases were all of good quality brown leather. As they passed they shook their heads and quietly expressed their sympathy with Berman, who stood apart from everyone else:

"Poor man. Isn't it a shame!"

"He looks like a gentleman."

"Yes, indeed," agreed the other.

"He looks different from the rest."

"Yes, indeed," agreed the other.

"So this is London!" said Berman loudly with a grimace, as if he had understood what they were saying.

"He seems to be a fine chap," said the older woman, glancing at Berman with her steely grey eyes.

"Yes, indeed," agreed the other.

They both walked off, the mother with her grey bun, the daughter with her blonde one.

At last some Jews arrived to meet the refugees. They appeared to be well-nourished, and wore gold watches dangling over their stomachs and Star of David tiepins in their cravats. They were all carrying umbrellas. A tall young man, the under-secretary of an institution, wrinkled his sharp crooked nose and muttered something to himself. His keen eyes darted around. The secretary with the flaxen hair from Rotterdam stepped forward to meet him, and smiles, sweet as honey, beamed from both their faces. Two hands, one white and plump, the other brown and lean, pressed each other heartily, holding on as if they never wanted to let go.

The London under-secretary twitched his nose and called out to the crowd in general:

"Follow me!"

The refugees looked at each other: "What does he mean?"

"What does he mean? He means we should follow him!"

"How can we be his followers if he's not dead yet!" joked some witty individual, but all the refugees felt despondent and nobody was in the mood to laugh. They followed meekly after the London "cousins" who had remembered to collect them after all.

Outside the station, buses were waiting for them. Once again the refugees were packed in together, some sitting, some standing, being driven off again to an unknown destination.

By standing apart from all the others, Berman managed to achieve what he desired from the under-secretary: respect. The latter reserved two benches in the bus especially for the Berman family, made sure that they were not squashed, and quizzed the Rotterdam secretary about Berman.

"Who is that man over there?" he asked, pointing at Berman's broad back.

"Oh, that man? He is a better class of person." With this he had divulged all the information he had about Berman to his London colleague.

The refugees were taken to the Eastern Hotel. This was an old Jewish institution, whose very walls seemed impregnated with the troubles of Jewish immigrants and saturated with Jewish tears. Its dismal redbrick walls rose up from its massive grubby foundations; it was blackened by the dust of many arid summers and the smoky black fogs of many winters.

No one could say who was more amazed at the new type of immigrants who had just arrived, the ancient walls of the hotel or the hotel porter. They were not so dirty, dejected and exhausted as the thousands and thousands who had stayed there on previous occasions. These immigrants were dressed more respectably and what they saw with their astonished eyes caused sardonic smiles, rather than tears, to steal across their faces.

"Is *this* our place of refuge?" these immigrants seemed to be thinking, smiling dismissively, like people who know their prison sentence will only last for one day.

Soon the London assistant secretary began to go up and down the benches at a leisurely pace taking down people's names, occupations and Antwerp addresses.

"A polisher? All right!"

"What kind of cutter, ladies' or gentlemen's?"

"What do you mean?"

"Well, are you a cutter of women's or men's clothes?"

"We're not *tailors'* cutters! We're diamond cutters!" The Antwerp workers regarded his assumption as blasphemy against their craft, and gave him contemptuous smiles and condescending looks.

The assistant secretary, however, was not impressed by their mention of diamonds, and he called out in a loud voice:

"Be seated round the tables."

His loud harsh voice, his piercing eyes and the solemn, almost fierce expression on his face intimidated the refugees so much that they began to look more like those other immigrants with whom the secretary normally dealt.

Berman alone was completely unabashed. When the secretary came up to him, Berman didn't wait to be interrogated, but instead started to interrogate the secretary.

"Tell me, my good man," he said, smiling sarcastically, "for what reason are you wandering around with *two* pencils?"

The secretary, who was not accustomed to being questioned, looked at Berman's face and was so taken aback that he lost his power of speech, just when he was supposed to be noting all Berman's personal details in his little book!

"I…I…ehm…I wanted to ask, I mean…" he stuttered: "Eh, what is your name please? You understand, I must give it to the authorities, I mean…."

"Oh, I see, that is what you wish to do! Excellent! And of course for that reason you need *two* pencils. I understand perfectly: the one behind your ear is the reserve pencil. Well, my name is…" Berman finally decided to stop teasing the young man.

Once they had got rid of this self-important official, the Jews felt more at ease and some lively discussion got under way.

"What do you think of this welcome?! You know, those Germans wouldn't have eaten us, believe me," asserted an Austrian Jew who had Russian papers. "They're actually fine people."

"Well, just go back to your 'fine people' then!" retorted a woman from Odessa who had a deep mannish voice. "Even when I was still in my mother's womb I hated those pigs of Germans. All my life I've managed to avoid having anything to do with them. When I came across them in Berlin, on my way to Antwerp, I nearly died. Such stiff, pompous brutes, with murderous eyes: that's your 'fine people' for you. You can see what a fine mess they have made of a great country like Belgium, where people are accustomed to live and let live."

"Well in my view they *are* fine people and they'll be here before you know where you are, I can assure you of that!" blustered the Austrian Jew.

"Bite your tongue off for saying such a thing! We should denounce him; he's obviously a German sympathizer." Everyone was now in a rage and it looked as if a new war was about to break out between the Galician Jew and the rest of the refugees.

A small woman wearing a stiff white apron like a nurse, with a dark lively face and a large black bun on top of her head, waved a bundle of keys and, with her nose in the air, called out imperiously:

"Sit down at the tables and be quiet!"

The young man, who had returned to the room, repeated it after her like a good mimic.

"Sshhh! Quieten down!" the woman repeated. No one paid much attention to the man, but the little woman looked like someone who was used to her orders being obeyed.

The people all sat down, but there still wasn't complete silence. Here and there someone spoke, a young man whistled, a girl quietly imitated the "nurse," and everyone laughed. The woman saw that she was dealing here with a quite different type of immigrant; she pursed her lips and fell silent.

Berman had no intention of staying there. He planned to go out to Hatton Garden to have a look around. However, there was no harm in waiting for a couple of days. For one thing it was better that the merchants in Hatton Garden shouldn't get to know that he had been one of the last to flee Antwerp, together with all these paupers. And apart from that, he had heard that rich diamond merchants were not kept here, but provided with proper accommodation and paid subsistence money.

And so it turned out. The organization found out who was who, and divided the refugees into two groups: the common people were sent to the Palmolive Hotel, where they were provided with the basic necessities, and the "better-class" refugees were sent to the Central Hotel.

Chapter 23

The Palmolive Hotel was packed with refugees. Every time a new family was sent there, the tiny area which the inhabitants called their accommodation became even smaller. The folds of the flowered curtains on metal rods which closed off the living areas were bunched closer together, and everyone became uneasy. "We soon won't have any space to sit down at all!" they complained.

It was exclusively workers who were living there. The men went out to work every morning. Diamond cutters and polishers learnt within a couple of weeks to be tailors' pressers or to operate sewing machines. Their meager wages contributed to the costs of living in the hotel. And their wages were indeed meager. The bosses didn't pay much, because they believed that the refugees were getting their subsistence free, and so they exploited them. Someone whose abilities qualified him to earn two pounds a week was paid less than one pound. No matter how efficiently and quickly they did the work, the bosses insisted that they weren't yet properly trained and still had to learn the trade.

The refugees got used to working hard for very little money, and to living behind curtains instead of walls. If you took the curtain away, they were totally exposed to a hostile world. However, a good number of new English citizens did emerge from behind the flowery curtains, and the Anglo-Jewish charity workers who looked after the refugees were honored with the role of *sandek,* holding baby boys during circumcision ceremonies. They paid for this honor with presents for the babies, who were greatly loved and cherished, especially in a time of war. The parents very quickly realized that because of the children, they themselves were treated with more respect, and they applied themselves diligently to fulfilling this objective!

Everything settled down and their lives were going reasonably smoothly, apart from the problems caused by a few revolutionary "troublemakers," as the members of the committee called those who voiced the justified objection that they were having to contribute to their living costs, while the rich diamond merchants, who earned nuggets of gold, were living like lords in the Central Hotel, and not paying a penny. Why did Mr. Brown stand at the exit every morning stopping every worker and making him inscribe his name in a list, so that he would not be able to get out of paying a shilling or two of his earnings? Why, on the other hand, did no one control the movements of the diamond merchants at the Central Hotel? It was simply because they did not need to go out until about eleven o'clock and at that time no one, it was assumed, goes to work.

Because of those "revolutionaries," animosity flared up in the hotel. No matter how much Mr. Seltzer, a naturalized Englishman who wore a big, shiny top hat even on weekdays, tried to reason with them, arguing that all people are not equal and cannot expect to live in the same way, he was unable to convince them or to quell the jealousy, which was increasing all the time between the two camps, the Central Hotel and the Palmolive Hotel. Every time a refugee went to visit friends or relatives in the Central Hotel, he would come back with stories that made people's eyes pop out.

"My cousin lives there. You should see the rooms, the furniture, the mirrors, the marble walls, the porter at the entrance!"

Hearing descriptions like this, people's imaginations started to run away with them and they fantasized and painted such pictures for themselves that they were eaten up with desire, these "common people," and tears of frustration came into their eyes. It got to the point that if someone had a relative in the Central Hotel, he would bask in the reflected glory and refuse to come out from behind his curtains, not wanting to mix with the *hoi polloi.*

But the members of the committee found a way of dealing with the revolutionaries. They gave a stern warning, threatening that they would evict them and take no further responsibility, leaving them without any support. So the revolutionaries quietened down and suffered in silence.

One young man, who was a member of the committee, was able to pour oil on troubled waters and repair the damage which had been caused to relations between the committee and the refugees. This Mr. Greenberg, who was in his early thirties, devoted his time – and he had a great deal of time to spare – to the inhabitants of the Palmolive Hotel. He knew everyone by name, knew their history and their aspirations, their problems and joys, and he treated them very well. He remembered all the children's birthdays and always gave them little presents. The children adored him, as did the women. He would appear in the yard with a friendly smile and a shiny top hat perched on his pomaded hair. He wore an English suit of good quality and dazzling white spats over expensive shoes. He only had to wave a yellow chamois leather glove and the children would run from all the corners of the hotel and swarm round him, like bees round a honey pot. They spoke English to him, learning the language before the adults had time to turn round. The children knew this would make a good impression on Mr. Greenberg, so they really made an effort. Mr. Greenberg took his time and waited till the clamor had died down before he said casually, to no one in particular: "Whose birthday is it today?"

It was apparently *everybody's* birthday, but they couldn't pull the wool over Mr. Greenberg's eyes, and he had a good look round and was able to see who was lying and who was telling the truth. He put a beautifully manicured finger to his nose, assumed a stern expression and warned them: "I don't want to hear any lies! Anyone who tells lies won't get any sweets for three months. And in any case, I *know* who it is," he went on, taking a psychological approach. "Come here, Miss Blum!" He picked out one little girl and gave her a bar of Nestle's chocolate. "It's *your* birthday, isn't it?"

The children realized that he really did know, so they stopped lying to him and began pestering their mothers: "Mama, when's my birthday, when's my birthday?"

The mothers scolded and smacked them but couldn't put them off, so they made up the dates of their birthdays and grumbled to each other: "This is impossible! He's really spoiling our children!" But though they went through the motions of complaining, in fact they idolized him so much that their husbands began to be jealous.

The situation in the Central Hotel was very different. When they had started looking for another place to accommodate the increasing numbers of refugees pouring in from Holland, it transpired that it was impossible to find anywhere suitable, apart from this elegant hotel, which had formerly belonged to an elderly German Jew. The owner had left England because of the war, and the government allocated this hotel to the refugees. The rich English Jews took on the work and in the course of a few weeks they had created an institution which was a model of philanthropic effort. They could hold their heads up high before the English government, which was providing for the Christian refugees.

The refugees who were being accommodated were impressed by their surroundings:

"Have you seen the dining room? Amazing! Mirrors and marble everywhere!"

"Yes, but it's not costing them anything! They just took it over from that German."

"Serves the old *yekke* right! Ha, ha, ha!"

"We'll live like kaisers here!"

"What a shame that Kaiser Wilhelm can't be here!"

"Yes, he'd really have had a great time!" one young refugee quipped.

"'Rejoice, oh young man, in thy youth!' What naiveté!" retorted the Galician Jew with the Russian papers, who was enraged at their jibes. "Just you wait, he *will* be coming here, Kaiser Wilhelm, *and* Franz Josef, he'll be here too, you'll see! The war's not over yet!"

Everyone started shouting:

"Throw him out!"

"Let's denounce him!"

"Yes, that would be a mitzva."

"Just leave him be, he'll betray himself out of his own mouth, the fool! He won't be able to keep his mouth shut."

"Go on then, do it, am I stopping you? Denounce me if you like! You can all go to hell – I've got papers, ha, ha, ha!"

An elderly man was beside himself with rage: "I'll go and denounce him myself!"

"No, Reb Mordecai, don't soil your mouth! He's not worth it! These Galician patriots; Kaiser Efroim-Yossel's their *rebbe.*"

"Well, at least we've got proper leaders. Who are your *rebbes*? Those bloody Russians! Just wait; you'll all be subjects of Franz Josef in the end!"

There was a tremendous tumult:

"He's insulting Jews. He's an atheist! Throw him out!"

Thus it almost came to a punch-up on the very first day those fortunate refugees spent in the Central Hotel. But the feud between the Galician and the Russian Jews soon abated. They couldn't get enough of admiring the opulence and luxury of the place, the gleaming mirrors, the marble and the crystal chandeliers. The next morning however, some of the older men were tut-tutting discontentedly. They had to sleep under fustian blankets and almost froze to death. Despite the magnificence of the marble, it certainly did not keep them warm.

Soon there was something in the air which was impossible to define and yet was enough to overshadow the mirrors and marble and make the refugees forget that there were such things in the hotel. It began to have the smell of an institution. This odor rose up from the cellars and penetrated as far as the sixth floor, right into the bedrooms. Apart from this, the women were unwilling to be confined in the kitchen all day, peeling potatoes and washing dishes. So tensions started emerging between the providers and those provided for.

Despite all this, the people in this hotel were, on the whole, fairly well-off. They had separate bedrooms, and larger families were allocated two or even three rooms. The children were cared for by an English nurse with a scrubbed face and flat, straw-colored hair. She wore a large white starched respectable cap and a light blue pleated dress with a stiff round white collar which cut into her neck and gave her a double chin. She went round distributing portions of rice pudding, milk and other good things, which made the adults' mouths water. But this righteous nurse tried to make the adults understand that she had her orders: it was only for the children.

She absolutely could not comprehend that some people could not speak English, and that the women, who were trying to persuade her to give them a little of the food for themselves, simply did not understand what she was saying to them. The women, on the other hand, couldn't understand how this nurse, who had such a naive look in her eyes, could possibly differentiate between one word and the next, since she gabbled all the words in one breath, and they all sounded the same in any case. And yet these Anglo-Jewish philanthropists understood her very well. They shared jokes with her when she was talking with them, and she laughed with them, obviously very pleased with herself.

"It seems as if this English is a real language after all!" said the women to each other.

Once she started shouting, put on her straw hat and seemed to be about to leave forever. The women were shocked, but one of the female voluntary helpers talked her round, and in the end she started smiling again, said it was "all right" and was soon busy at the serving table, baffling the women with her strange chattering.

Even stranger than this nurse was the "old maid" with the large, horsey teeth, a hat permanently on her head and huge spectacles on her nose, who was employed down in the cellar, entrusted with distributing bundles of clothes to the refugees.

When the women, who till recently had been the mistresses of affluent households, heard that clothes were being distributed, they descended on the cellar like locusts. The old maid, poor thing, had a really hard time of it, and she scolded the uncivilized women who were besieging her, desperate to get their hands on a few underclothes, or a pair of shoes, or a winter coat, or all of those things. But she was loath to give away such expensive clothes which, ten or fifteen years ago, had been worn by real ladies, women of the highest rank in society. It vexed her that common people, refugees at that, should wear these things, so she could not bring herself to do her duty even though these clothes had not cost her anything. Thus the cellar became another battleground.

"Can't you see, Miss Jacobs," said a woman pleadingly to the old maid: "I've been waiting for hours and you're letting people in who have just this minute come down, and giving them the best things, just because they are dressed in fur coats. They don't even need the clothes; they'll not catch cold in any case. But I'm going round in my summer jacket, and I'm freezing!"

"And I suffer from rheumatics. This damp cellar is making me ill," complained an elderly woman, her teeth chattering. "Because they're wearing diamond rings you give them the best clothes as well, and us poor people get nothing," she said, justifiably upset.

"That's just it, if you don't have any luck, it would be better not have been born," another woman mused.

"I had to leave all my good clothes behind," explained someone, thinking this might help her.

But the old maid knew who had actually left possessions behind and who had had nothing to leave. Sometimes she simply lost patience and gave so many things to the first person who came in that the recipient could hardly carry the load. This was not any kind of solution either.

"God forgive me for saying so, but the *shnorrers* have all the luck! She won't give anything to me, though I've asked her six times. You have to be able to whine and plead, and I just can't do that!" said a skinny old woman, sucking in her sallow cheeks and chewing her blue lips, which were split and dried up.

"Well, what have you lost by it?" retorted a fat woman with a wobbling, wrinkled, double chin and grey whiskers.

While they were arguing among themselves, a lady came out of the room which was the goal of all their aspirations; she was dressed in a beautiful fur coat and carried under her arm a neat parcel wrapped in brown paper. The parcel was tied with a new piece of string, as if it had been bought in a shop.

"Just look how she's packed it up for her! I won't tell you where I'd like to pack all of them up and send them," exploded another woman, cursing all the women in fur coats.

"Why are you in awe of them?" protested the old woman with the grey whiskers. "Tell them straight, the wealthy *shnorrers,* that they should be ashamed of themselves, coming down here in their fancy coats and flashing those diamonds, scrounging and still thinking they're better than us."

"Don't you realize, they've actually come to make a contribution!" laughed a young man who was coming out of the room.

"Eh? What are you doing here? Why were you not queuing for men's clothes?" asked the women in surprise.

"My wife is ill and I came to get a coat for her. You obviously could have done with my assistance too."

"God bless him, he's right," gushed the old woman with the whiskers. "The man certainly has brains."

"Oho, he's certainly courageous!" laughed the women, and the muffled echo of their laughter reverberated through the cold, damp corridor of the dark cellar.

The old woman finally lost her temper, decided to act and simply knocked on the door of the room. The old maid came out and peered around in the darkness, blinking her red eyes.

"Who had the temerity to…?"

"I did," said the old woman, looking her straight in the eye.

"Listen, my good woman, I must serve these ladies first. They've been waiting far too long as it is."

"That's a lie! We've been waiting much longer! You're giving *them* all the best things, and spending time wrapping them up in brown paper. *We* will…"

The old maid was frightened. After all, she was on her own and there was an entire mob of them. And she couldn't rely on the stupid boy who helped her to pack up the parcels. He would just stand there staring with his bovine eyes and by the time he grasped what he had to do, they would have beaten her up. She started hurriedly making excuses:

"It's not my fault, I'm only following orders. And you know the saying, 'If you have much, you'll get much more. If you have little, you'll lose the little that you had before.'"

"Yes, but why should it be like that?" protested the women, unwilling to accept this idea.

But the spinster had fled back into her room, taking with her one of those who was to get much more.

Scenes like these were an everyday occurrence in the hotel, and people got used to them. The only person who could not get accustomed to such upsets was Frau Zederbaum, the lady president of the Committee, a tall, thin woman with a decidedly Jewish nose, wide-open blue eyes that made her look naive, and a lugubrious expression.

She wore a prickly black straw hat which nearly hid her long angular face. Frau Zederbaum, who had originally come from Galicia, and had married a naturalized Englishman, was a millionairess, but the only luxury she permitted herself was an expensive black ostrich feather which she wore both winter and summer. She did many charitable works and was very active in all the philanthropic institutions.

A knocking on the table which made the walls tremble announced to the refugees that Madame Zederbaum had arrived and was about to preach a sermon to the effect that she had yet again discovered some heinous crime which had been committed in the hotel. She inevitably chose to give these homilies just when the refugees were sitting at the tables having their lunch. She would stand on a little square of red velvet which acted as a sort of podium, separating her from the "poor people." She would speak as follows, her attempt to speak Yiddish coming out as slightly garbled German:

"*Mein geehrte Damen un Herren!* I am really sorry to disturb you in the middle of your lunch, but I can no longer keep silent about the following matter. Once again I have actually found a dirty milk pan simply thrown away in the corridor. All the inquiries made by our respected supervisor have not succeeded in identifying once and for all who is so shamelessly discarding cooking utensils, just because they have got burnt. It is absolutely shocking! Therefore, ladies and gentlemen, we are forced to hold all the inhabitants of the hotel responsible and penalize everyone. We shall have to cease giving out milk and also coal for the bedroom fires, so that there will be no possibility of milk pans being burned."

To reinforce the impact of her words, Madame Zederbaum produced the pan, wrapped in newspaper, which the supervisor, who had presided over this lecture, ceremoniously handed her. She unwrapped it and held it up, so that everyone could see it.

The refugees sat with their spoons halfway to their mouths, apparently listening with great seriousness, and trying with all their might not to burst into gales of laughter. The long skinny lady left her podium and went walking about the tables as if nothing had happened, enquiring about the meal: "I'm sure your lunch is delicious?"

Jacques left his table and followed her, imitating her walk, and asked in a quiet, refined voice: "I'm sure your lunch is disgusting?"

The people burst out laughing and Madame Zederbaum shook her black feather, and nervously left without saying another word. The refugees, after their moment of mirth, sat there in gloomy silence. She had ruined their appetites. The truth was that this enforced idleness had made the women so lazy that they couldn't be bothered to wash a single pot.

Madame Zederbaum wouldn't have interfered in such matters if it hadn't been that the "potato king" – so the women maintained – had needlessly shoved the dirty pans, which were already the talk of the Central Hotel, under her nose.

This potato king had a thick, flaming red beard and a neatly trimmed and pomaded moustache, and his nose was as round as the King Edward potatoes which he peeled from morning to night. He really worked hard, the king, and the three deep furrows on his low forehead became even deeper and wider as he worked.

His wife, the queen, looked so like her husband that if it hadn't been for the fact that she wore women's clothes, no one could have told them apart. She also had a little red beard, smaller than his, naturally.

This couple had come from Belgium with all the other refugees. No one knew why they had been picked to help in the kitchen, peeling the potatoes which were cooked every day. Nor did anyone know who had crowned them with their royal titles. The refugees liked the nicknames, which certainly suited the couple very well. However, what happened? After he had inherited his kingdom, the kitchen, the king began to act like a despot: stern and uncontrollable, never asking for or listening to advice from anyone. A veritable Nicholas the Third.

The other refugees rebelled, and every lunchtime, a new Civil War broke out. They suspected the potato king of not putting all the available meat and potatoes into the soup, so that the soup was thin and didn't satisfy their hunger. So they demanded double helpings. The king did not deign to answer them. He did give out double helpings, but only to certain people who had found favor in the king's eyes, namely, the rich people. No lunchtime passed, therefore, without screaming and shouting, but it was like talking to the wall.

In the end, someone would pluck up enough courage to go to the office and put the matter in the hands of the authorities, the philanthropists, so that they should judge it. The "tattletale," as the ladies and gentlemen of the institution called him, would, however, come out of the office looking crestfallen, and after these episodes the king would reign even more despotically than before. When the people saw that they were not going to have any effect on the king, they began to squabble among themselves and take their anger out on each other.

Berman did not like the hotel at all. The mirrors and marble did not excite him in the least. He wrinkled his nose and declared to all and sundry that this was no place for him.

Madame Zederbaum made a gesture with her delicate white hand, as if to say: "*Ach*, you'll soon get used to it!"

But when she saw that her promise to put more furniture in his rooms on the first floor, to install an easy chair on the balcony, and even a gas stove in the bedroom, hardly impressed him at all, she realized that she was dealing here with a better class of person, which impressed her considerably.

"*Ach* so, Herr Berman, we shall see what we can do. I shall raise the topic at the next meeting and you will find you can rely on me. You will in all probability get a private flat."

Berman decided to humor her and stay for a few more days. "He is a very nice man," she said to Mr. Green, her assistant. "Yes, one can see that straight away," agreed Mr. Green.

The potato king had already heard of Berman when they were both still in Antwerp. With a doglike instinct he sensed that Madame Zederbaum thought highly of Berman, and he immediately allocated him a double helping.

One morning when Berman came down to lunch there was a great turmoil going on. A woman about fifty-years-old was making a fuss, shouting at a thin woman some twenty years younger, who had squeezed herself in at the head of the long table where the cream of the Antwerp Jews sat. These were stout men with long beards, fat stomachs and even fatter wives. The young woman, who had a child on her knee, was weeping and, at the same time, trying ineffectually to dry her eyes with a rather grubby pocket handkerchief.

The older woman's bosom was heaving under her silk blouse, diamond earrings dangled from her bluish, elongated ear lobes, the whiskers on her chin were trembling, and her thick lips were purple with rage and flecked with spittle.

"The insolence of it! Scrawny little fool! She has the cheek to think she is my equal! Thank God everyone else from Antwerp knows who I am! How dare she come and sit at this table, the *shnorrer.* No sooner is a little bit of soup doled out than she sticks out her dirty hands and grabs it. She doesn't even know that anyone who grabs gets their fingers smacked, the skinny little idiot!"

The young woman was sobbing, not understanding why the woman was shouting at her. She tried to ask the people at the table what she had done wrong, but she was so upset that she could hardly speak. Some of them thought it was funny and just laughed at her, others were asking the indignant woman to stop shouting; everyone else was busy with their own concerns, and no one answered her.

Berman looked at the older woman and recognized her as the wife of a rich merchant with whom he did business. He glanced at the young woman. "What on earth is a woman like her doing at this table?" he thought, and then he realized, with horror, that it was Gitele. He asked someone else what had happened, and found out immediately, for *he* had no difficulty in getting an answer, that a second helping of soup had been set out for this woman. Gitele, who hadn't yet had any, had assumed it was for her, and had put her hand out. This had made the other woman apoplectic, and she had started screeching at Gitele.

To make matters worse, the potato king came out of the kitchen and started bellowing at Gitele:

"Shut up, will you! You'd think someone was murdering you. Stop scrubbing at your eyes. The committee doesn't like scenes like this. If you carry on like this Madame Zederbaum will come in and when she sees what trouble you're causing she'll send you to the Palmolive, where you'll have something to cry about!"

Berman was very tempted to tell the potato king that Gitele was in fact the daughter of a rich man in Poland, but he decided that it was better to know nothing and not to get mixed up in the whole business. He gestured to Rochl, who understood what he meant and also said nothing. But she refused the double helping which she was offered, and old Reb Chaim Yoysef sank his head so low that his beard touched the table. He sighed heavily and almost choked on the bread which he had softened by putting it in his soup. He said quietly to Rochl, whose eyes were brimming with tears: "This is what we've come to, daughter."

Not only did the potato king have his favorites, but the people themselves had formed cliques. As if by magic, each table was occupied exclusively by people of the same type. At one table sat people who filled their day – before, during and after the meals – with discussion of higher matters. Shakespeare was never absent from this table for one moment, and Bernard Shaw, Ibsen, Heine, Goethe, Homer, Rembrandt and Michelangelo all occupied places of honor there. The intellectuals at this table were experts in everything: sculpture, music, literature. And, of course, they discussed all these matters in loud voices.

The rest of the eaters, even the bearded men at the top table, and their wives with the silk blouses, began to listen in to these conversations, not understanding a word but with a feeling of respect for the people at that table.

The potato king inclined his hairy ear to them and listened intently to find out what those snotty-nosed intellectuals were jabbering about. Hearing them constantly pronouncing names which he had never heard of, neither in Antwerp, nor in London, nor even in Galicia, he started to ask around and when he found out that it was books they were discussing, he shook his big head and asked:

"So why do people discuss books? Books are for reading! Not for messing up your brain. *Ach*, what fools!" He decided on the spot that *they* would certainly not get double helpings.

"A crowd of lazy good-for-nothings, that's all they are!" he said to his wife, but nevertheless he put their food in front of them without banging it down on the table.

He sat Gitele at that table, and she became even more dejected. When the group saw a young woman with a child at their table, they completely ignored her. So she looked for another table and sat down at one with poor women whose husbands, even here, were going out to work in order to be able to contribute something towards the bill. These women helped in the kitchen with the washing up – they couldn't afford to throw away dirty saucepans. They sat all day in the women's room, sewing pillowcases and sheets for the hotel bedrooms. At this table everyone welcomed Gitele's child, petting her, and telling Gitele stories about what lovely homes they came from; although their husbands were simple workers, they had kept nice kitchens with steel fittings, sideboards, and even gramophones.

Here Gitele felt at home, and yet, not really at home.

Chapter 24

One morning Berman dressed himself like a bridegroom in his smartest clothes in order to make his first visit to Hatton Garden. He paid particular attention to his beard, plucking out all the grey hairs which had appeared during the last few months, after which he combed, brushed and smoothed it, and divided it neatly into two halves. Then he put on his best frock coat with the silk lapels and a deep cut in the back, his fine, woolen overcoat with its velvet collar, his brown leather gloves, and took the black silk umbrella which he had bought in Rotterdam. Altogether, he looked like a Jewish banker.

In a leisurely fashion, he came down the broad, marble stairs of the hotel and walked along the wide corridor. He paused on the long mat, which lay in a recessed oblong of concrete at the entrance. He was greeted by Mr. Green:

"Good morning, Mr. Berman! Going out in weather like this?"

"When needs must," said Berman, with a stern smile, and went out into the street.

The streets were shrouded in thick black fog and even though it was not raining, Berman's face was soon damp. The sky was not visible; the grey layer which hung so low that it seemed as if any minute your head would touch it, did not look like sky at all. The wet tarmac gleamed black and cold.

"Brrr!" Despite his thick warm clothes, a cold shiver went right through Berman, into his very bones. He hesitated near the broad door of the hotel. Should he carry on or not? To go back would be bad luck, but he was afraid of going on.

The tall buildings of the city and the dense traffic on the streets were both enveloped in the thick blackness. The streetlamps looked like the tiny flames of penny candles suspended here and there in the fog. The muffled clatter of heavy goods carts, the jangling of trams, and the warning shouts of conductors and carters rang out dully through the thick air. The traffic was a dense mass, stretching all along the street; it stirred, moved on, and then was immediately tangled up again. The pedestrians on the pavements kept close to the walls.

Berman spread out his arms like black wings in an attempt to avoid bumping into other people. After walking along for a few yards he was completely disoriented. At the edge of the pavement some workers were mending sewage pipes. The paving stones, which had been removed, were heaped at the edge of the road. The long trench was marked out by little red lamps, and big torches swinging in the fog illuminated a small stretch of the road. An old man sat in a little wooden hut, warming himself at a brazier. The coals glowed in the midst of the fog. The workers stood around leaning on their spades, smoking pipes and chatting about the weather, as if it were something new. A few of them were surreptitiously warming themselves at the brazier. The foreman, who should have been seeing to it that the workers weren't slacking, was chatting and laughing with them. The trench could wait. But finally one of them felt that it wasn't right, and they really should get on with some work, so he jumped into the trench and started shoveling out earth. The others carried on chatting, but didn't stand in his way: "If you want to work, you're welcome to get on with it!"

For a good while Berman crept gingerly along the walls of the buildings, feeling his way in the gloom until he came to the corner, where several streets met. A tall policeman raised his white-gloved hand, which looked dirty in the fog. A mass of pedestrians seemed to emerge from nowhere, and suddenly rushed across the road.

Berman jumped on a tram, which was dripping with moisture inside. The green light could hardly penetrate the bluish steam in the air. The passengers and the benches both looked damp, and wet dirty tram tickets were lying about the black slimy floor. Berman could hardly breathe.

The conductor called out his familiar, "Tickets, please!" and told each and every passenger the news that the fog was terrible. The passengers admitted that he was right: "Terrible!"

At last, Berman reached his destination.

A grubby square building with unpainted walls, blackened slates, a window splashed with mud to more than half its height, and a crumbling, dirty, wet "kosher" sign: this cafe served as the Bourse. Berman couldn't believe his eyes:

"Is that all it is?" Why had he bothered to dress up smartly? However, soon he saw that the whole of Antwerp was here. All the merchants were known to him. They had exchanged their Antwerp frock coats for English clothes, but business was just as lively as in the Bourse in Antwerp. They were sitting round long tables covered with black oilcloth, poking around in little heaps of diamonds as they had done at home. As usual, the colors of the diamonds were flashing and changing: blue, red, green, gold, brilliant white. They glowed and burned, fascinating the eye, but the merchants hardly even looked at the spectacle. They were examining the diamonds for fractures, and feeling completely at home, as if they had been born and bred here.

For a moment Berman was disconcerted, feeling that he looked like a clown, out of place in these clothes. Oh well, it was easy enough to change his frock coat for English clothing, and if this was where he was to try and earn a franc or two from now on, then so be it, as long as it was possible to do business.

The London merchants were drinking tea with milk, which looked like coffee. They spoke English with a Yiddish word here and there, and as well as diamonds, they showed each other gold, platinum and strings of pearls. Minor dealers and brokers who did not have entry to the Antwerp Bourse mingled here with the important merchants.

"They've done well for themselves," thought Berman. He resented the fact that the war had brought them advancement.

At a table by the window sat a young man, poking among big mounds of diamonds rather than small heaps. "Is this what Hatton Garden's like? Hmm!" said Berman to himself.

"He's doing great business, that youngster," said a merchant, joining Berman at the table where he had sat down.

"Long may he continue!"

"He's still wet behind the ears, and yet they say he's extremely rich. Do you know him?" asked the merchant.

"Who doesn't know him? He's Lieberman's older son-in-law, Kuper."

"Oh, I see, now I understand. He comes, I believe, from Antwerp."

"He comes from Antwerp, he comes from London; he's here, there and everywhere. He grows! They say that he's even going to overtake his father-in-law. Yes indeed!" said Berman, sighing, and looking over at the young man.

An elderly man with yellowish eyes came and stood by Berman's table, coughed, put his hand to his hollow chest and asked Berman if he had a few carats, for he had a customer. But before Berman had time to reply the old man went off again as if he had just asked for the sake of asking and didn't have a customer for the "few carats" at all.

"He's not interested after all, then! How do you like my customers?" laughed Berman.

The merchant waved his hand dismissively:

"*Ach!* He's not worth bothering about. There are a lot of people like him, just trying to persuade themselves that they're doing business. And look over there," he continued, "at the way those little brokers are swarming round Kuper like flies, and he gives them goods; he really is a good-natured young fellow, I must say."

"Hmm, well, goodness like that would make a dog rabid!" laughed Berman.

The young man was shaking his head, tossing back his thick fair hair, which kept falling over his red face. He glanced around with his blue eyes before poking around again with his tweezers, pretending not to see the crowd of eagerly peering brokers who were swallowing up his heaps of diamonds with their greedy eyes.

"I got notink!" He thought by speaking in broken English he could drive them away, but the brokers pretended not to hear him.

"Herr Kuper, I give you my word, I have a customer waiting. I desperately need a few carats."

"Is that my fault? There are other merchants sitting here – why don't you go over to *him*?" he said, pointing at Berman and laughing.

"Some hope! He'd rather kick the bucket than help someone to earn an honest penny."

The waitress brought a glass of coffee and put it on the table. The young man pulled her to him and pinched her, whereupon the girl tore herself away with an expletive and hurried off to another table.

"Well," continued Kuper, "tell me, do you think I can't conduct my own business? I don't need any brokers!"

"Already he's doing without brokers!" said the other brokers with sad resignation.

"You can rely on him, he knows what he's doing, he's a clever one," opined a middle-aged broker, pulling at his pointed beard and winking at the young man as if to say, "Those idiots don't understand you, but *I* do!"

"Here you are then!" said Kuper suddenly, distributing parcels of diamonds. "But see that you get the full price for them. And that's all the goods I'm giving out today. Diamonds are rising in value just now, so I'm losing money on every bit of goods I dispose of."

The brokers weren't listening anymore, but were all going out into the thick fog. They started scribbling in their notebooks at the door and then rushed off to the various merchants' offices.

"In Antwerp, the Bourse shuts at three o'clock during the winter," Berman told the London merchant.

"Very nice!" laughed the merchant. "If we only operated during daylight hours here, we'd do no diamond trade at all; it's always night in London!"

The waitress brought two glasses of tea with lemon and Berman sipped his, never taking his eyes off Kuper.

A Galician Jew with a venerable grey beard came over. He was an ex-broker who had never had any success and now constantly hung around Hatton Garden.

"Listen, Herr Berman. I tell you, it's absolute stupidity, the way they are holding onto their diamonds. It's wartime after all, who's going to buy diamonds, eh? Who's thinking about diamonds at the moment? They have persuaded themselves that diamonds are rising in value and they're holding onto them. Take my advice and get rid of all the goods you have. Later you'll be glad you listened to me. Those idiots are going to lose their shirts!"

Berman laughed.

"If I had his money, I'd go mad," continued the old man, pointing to Kuper. "He's just a baby, and yet he thinks he knows it all and won't listen to a single word of advice from an older person."

"Well, carry on! What's stopping you from giving him some of your good advice?" said Berman, teasing. He stood up and went over to Kuper, with the old man following him.

"How are you, Herr Kuper. Doing a lot of business, are you?"

"So-so."

"You've brought the goods?"

"Yes and no."

"What do you mean by that?"

"I mean that I really have no desire to sell them. Diamonds are rising in value!"

"Stuff and nonsense! Don't let yourself get taken in by this madness which has suddenly infected them all. They're all going to come a cropper. Who's going to be interested in diamonds in wartime?" retorted Berman, making use of the old man's argument.

Kuper shot him a poisonous look and did not answer.

"So, have you got them or not?"

"I have them, but I'll only sell them according to our agreement, as I told you. And there's another thing."

"What's that?"

"I want Reb Mordecai to earn something too. You know what I mean."

The old man's yellowed cheeks glowed with pleasure: was he actually going to earn some money that day after all?

Berman acted as if he hadn't heard. Kuper took a parcel from his breast pocket and shook out about a dozen stones onto the black oilcloth. Their flashing colors lit up the room as if the sun had suddenly come out.

"Are they clean?" asked Berman, just for something to say, trying to hide the impression the stones made on him.

Kuper did not answer.

Berman had already seen the goods the day before at Kuper's house, where he had examined every stone. Nevertheless, he put the loupe to his eye and started peering at them again. Without a word he took out his checkbook and wrote Kuper a check.

"That won't do!" said Kuper angrily, giving him back the check. Berman frowned, worrying that Kuper might change his mind and the whole deal would fall through. He was a moody young man. Berman started tugging at his own beard and stopped when it started hurting.

"Why have you put them back in your pocket? I've given you the amount you asked for! Why are you not shaking hands on the deal with the usual '*mazel un brokhe?*'"

"I already told you yesterday, and today once again that I want five pounds for Reb Mordecai."

Berman growled like a lion in pain. If it hadn't been that diamonds were indeed rising in value every day, he'd have taught that insolent young devil a lesson. But what could he do? He didn't see stones of this quality every day and he couldn't possibly let them slip through his fingers.

"The devil knows where he gets hold of these goods! The best diamonds seem to fall into his hands. And he supports a gang of brokers that he needs like a hole in the head. He throws money right and left, and yet he's as rich as Croesus. It's always the same, God helps the rogues."

Reb Mordecai had started to lose hope. "That black dog Berman has never helped anyone to earn a franc. Nothing's going to come of this. If he bought them, I might get something. I can't understand why Kuper is haggling with him. I'd be happy with three pounds, or even two would come in very handy," thought the old man, gradually lowering his expectations.

But nothing swayed Kuper: neither Berman's objection that he was buying the goods directly from Kuper and couldn't see what Reb Mordecai had to do with it, since he had played absolutely no role in the transaction, nor the old man's silent prayer that Kuper should become more tractable.

"I'm not moving an inch from our agreement." Kuper started examining a heap of rough diamonds and smiled with double satisfaction. It gave him great pleasure to have Berman pleading with him. But he was even more delighted that the waitress kept hovering round his table, and each time, when he gave her a pinch, she complained that he didn't behave like a gentleman. He paid no attention to Berman, who finally wrote out another check and handed it to Kuper. The latter saw that Berman would have liked to stuff the check down his throat, and this filled him with glee.

"Here you are, Reb Mordecai, five pounds for you." He handed the old man five crisp green banknotes and Reb Mordecai couldn't believe his eyes.

"Well, Kuper, you certainly are an accomplished merchant, there's no denying that," said Berman, complimenting Kuper so that the latter should not think that he had impoverished him. But he couldn't bear to look at Reb Mordecai's trembling hand.

"You see, Reb Mordecai? That's the way to get blood out of a stone!" said Kuper, laughing.

"For this you should be rewarded with blessings and success wherever life may lead you!" exclaimed the old man, trembling with emotion.

Berman shook the diamonds out again, put the loupe to his eye, even though this was totally unnecessary, and turned them over and over. Each stone gleamed and sparkled with changing colors in the electric light. Berman gazed into their brightness. Like a loving mother looking into the eyes of her only child, and rejoicing in their purity, he peered into the diamonds for the hundredth time, reveling in his stones and finding it difficult to pack them away from view. He moved them around with the tweezers, though these diamonds were big enough to hold without them. He could hardly prevent himself laughing aloud with delight.

"Wonderful goods!"

He would soon squash Kuper, without any difficulty! That one was more interested in girls than business. To sell goods of this quality at this time, when diamonds were appreciating in value? Even though he had his father-in-law behind him, he was nothing but a rotten charlatan, not a real merchant. Berman took malicious pleasure in these thoughts, avenging himself for the injury and humiliation that Kuper had caused him. He ordered a steak.

The delicious aroma of the brown gravy whetted his appetite. Berman tucked his beard into the big white napkin and, dipping his bread in the meaty juices and the sharp horseradish, wallowed in the pleasure of it.

"Ah, who's this? Whom do I see here?" It was Shapiro. He sat down beside Berman like an old friend, shaking his hand over and over again. Berman was pleased as well.

"Have you been in England long?" asked Berman.

"Yes indeed, I came as soon as war broke out."

"So what's new? Are you doing good business?"

"What else should I be doing, writing the texts for mezuzas? And you?"

"So-so! This is the first time I have been to Hatton Garden, so how could I have managed to do business yet? I see that everyone dresses like an Englishman here," said Berman, looking at Shapiro's new suit.

"When in Rome ..." Shapiro was pleased that Berman had noticed his new clothing.

Another man came and sat down with them. "Ah, Herr Mandelboym!" said Shapiro. "Don't speak German here; it's better not to."

Mandelboym took off his hat, and the white skin of his bald head gleamed. His ears stuck out and he had glittering deep-set eyes, white fleshy cheeks and thick red lips. He looked more like a piglet than a human being.

Berman concentrated on his steak and pretended not to notice Mandelboym, whom he had always considered to be an obnoxious person.

"So how are you, Herr Berman?" asked Mandelboym, ignoring Berman's obvious dislike of him. It really didn't matter much to him whether people liked him or not.

"And you?" asked Berman, not raising his eyes from his plate.

"I'm *alright*," replied Mandelboym who was already mixing English in with his Yiddish speech, "except that you can't get anything decent to eat here. I like to eat noodles at lunchtime, and you'd think I'd be able to get them with *my* money, wouldn't you? If I can't have noodles, then my *dinner's* not my *dinner*. The meat isn't meat and the fish isn't fish. 'You'll just have to eat something else,' says that snooty waitress – I hope the worms devour her! If I hadn't had to meet a merchant here, I certainly wouldn't have stuck my nose into this dung heap!" Having worked himself up into a rage, Mandelboym put his hat back on his head and went away again without even saying goodbye.

"Let him go to hell," laughed Berman. "Him and his dinners!"

"*And* you and your non-existent business deals!" said Kuper, who had suddenly appeared at their table. He had been ready to go home when he was seized by a desire to bait Berman once more. Shapiro gave a little laugh, and Kuper said goodbye to Berman and left.

"We should go too," said Berman, seeing the dense dark grey swirls of fog seeping in through every crack. When Shapiro opened the door, a thick black mass enveloped them, making their eyes smart and their noses sting. They went out into the street and the cold cut right through them. They linked arms like an old married couple and, shivering, they went off into the darkness to find a taxi.

Chapter 25

Gitele lay on the iron bed in the small "servant's" room on the sixth floor of the hotel for days on end, tormenting herself.

Why did Dovid go away without even saying goodbye to her or to their child, on a journey from which he might very well not come back? What had she done to deserve this? She kept asking herself the same questions and could not find any reason for what had happened between them. Had he simply wanted to free himself of her? Perhaps he didn't love her any more. But in her heart she knew he did, so why had he done this?

As she went over it in her mind, she could still feel his every touch and caress, and saw him looking at her with infinite love in his dark eyes. She felt such warmth flooding over her that she could hardly breathe. At the same time she was deeply troubled. Why had she let him do whatever he wanted with her?

Gitele was filled with both shame and yearning. She felt burning hot. She knew that if Dovid came back now, she would not hesitate. She would go with him and make love to him. She would *want* everything to happen all over again.

What about Leybesh? What did she care about *him*? She hated Leybesh for the way he sometimes laughed at Dovid. Leybesh, she thought, was just a socialist without a heart. If only Dovid would come back, or at least write her a letter.

When she lay awake at night, feeling cold under the regulation brown fustian coverlet, the image of Dovid always appeared before her. They had been alone together in the shabby little room in Somersstraat and Dovid had lifted her up in his arms as if she had been a little child. She hadn't had the strength to resist, and why should she try to deny it? She had not wanted to resist. She blushed as she remembered. She felt his fingers gently exploring her body. She had tried to speak, but Dovid had whispered, "Don't say anything Gitele, hush my darling!" and he had covered her mouth with his sensuous lips, kissing her over and over again until she almost suffocated.

And now – not even a letter. She pressed her face into the hard pillow and wept with a mixture of shame and happiness at these memories.

There was the sound of crying from the little green cot: "Mama! Mama!"

She wanted to ask Leybesh to go and see what the child wanted, but seeing his bed still made up and empty, she shivered and got out of bed. The little girl was screaming:

"Papa! I want Papa to come home!"

Gitele gave her a drink, rocked the cot and sang her a lullaby, trembling with cold and emotion. She saw the child's dark eyes, Dovid's eyes, gradually closing, veiled by lashes which seemed thicker when she slept. She looked at her for a while and realized that when she grew up she would look just like Dovid's sister; she would be a beauty like Jeannette.

The little one was fast asleep again.

Gitele was tired and cold and couldn't see Dovid clearly any more. She tried to carry on reliving her memories, but now he appeared as if in a mist; she could see the child, but not Dovid. She thought about the way Leybesh often peered intently at his little daughter, and each time after doing so, he didn't come home for several days. Gitele didn't fall asleep until dawn.

When she started up out of this uneasy sleep, the first thing she noticed was that Leybesh's bed was still empty and hadn't been slept in. The child sat up, laughing merrily, threw off the few bits of bedclothes and called for her Papa to come and lift her up. Then she burst into tears: "Where is Papa?" She started stamping her little feet and howling: "I want Leybesh to come home!" Then, tickled at hearing herself call her Papa "Leybesh," she started giggling.

Leybesh was hardly ever in the hotel, because he was really busy. He knew all the London contacts. In fact, however, the London socialists weren't particularly taken with Leybesh – there were far more important big shots than him in London, and Leybesh's considerable knowledge of Karl Marx's Das Kapital didn't impress them very much at all.

He was soon sidelined and never given any important work to do. The way he flaunted his knowledge made them want to push him out. Any time he tried to make a point during a discussion, the chairman either didn't see Leybesh's raised hand, or else he tore up the note which Leybesh had sent over to him, and it was always some insignificant young lad who was given the floor, but never Leybesh.

So Leybesh gradually distanced himself from the work of these circles. Nevertheless, he was itching to do something. He tried, but failed, to create a circle of his own. Other comrades who also bore a grudge against the clique were keen to break with it and go with Leybesh, but somehow they never did.

Meanwhile, letters had started arriving at the hotel, all with the same contents: workers were required. Minor employers came in person to recruit them. Because of the war there was a great deal of work and a shortage of hands. These small-time tailors, shoemakers and cap makers who previously had existed on private work, using only their wives and children, now needed thirty or forty employees. Khaki uniforms, shoes, shirts and caps had to be made for the soldiers who were getting ready to go to the front. The employers had contracts with the government, but were unable to deliver the work on time. They were scratching their heads, unable to solve the problem.

Leybesh was the first to go off to work. He was as excited as a small child: for the first time in his life he was in demand and his work was needed. Soon, however, his joy abated when he began to think about the fact that he was now participating in the "imperialist" war.

He observed the girls with their hair cut short, broad leather straps over their slim shoulders, wearing high laced boots and short skirts, adjusting men's caps on their charming little heads and calling out with a triumphant gleam in their eyes: "Tickets, please!" They carried out the work as efficiently as if they had been used to it all their lives. This upset Leybesh. If only girls like these all over the world would devote their boundless energy to a different cause! If only they would open their bright eyes to the task of getting rid of the governments which were the cause of this pointless bloodbath, what a magnificent ideal they would be helping to realize. It annoyed him that they got such satisfaction from this work. Such bright eyes, and yet they were so blind!

But what about Leybesh himself? Wasn't he going into the workshop to press uniform trousers? Who knew whether some Dovid somewhere or other would die wearing a pair of trousers which had been carefully pressed by him? How many mothers, Jewish and gentile, were dying a little every day in their anguish over their sons on the battlefield?

But the world took no notice at all of Leybesh's ideas. Everywhere, in the ammunition factories, on the trams and buses, even on the railways, women were working. More and more they were replacing the men who had gone to the front. They had forgotten that women were supposed to be delicate, and to pamper themselves. It wasn't only girls, but middle-aged women too who cut off their hair, put helmets on their womanly heads, donned blue uniforms, white gloves and clumsy, masculine shoes. Their weather-beaten faces took on a masculine appearance as they did guard duty or directed the traffic as efficiently as male police officers did. They were doing their duty for king and country with energy and amazing patience. Even the Soho pickpockets and "corner boys" of Aldgate began to have respect for these forceful females. They stopped making suggestive remarks and laughing in the faces of the helmeted policewomen.

The women liked the work. They suddenly discovered that they were a force in the country, a force which would later have to be reckoned with, and they had no desire just to sit in workshops sewing trousers. Jewish girls discovered that there was a great demand for office workers. One can learn shorthand and typing in six months, so even the poorest of mothers saved their last ha'pennies, and didn't send the girls into workshops when they left school at the age of fourteen; instead of making sweatshop workers out of them, they aspired to make them into office "ladies," working with their brains instead of their hands.

The workers were in clover: the employers treated them like kings. When the Jewish owners of tailoring workshops came to recruit workers among the refugees, they found that this trade had been unheard of in Antwerp. There you could get all sorts of occupations: diamond cutters, polishers and cleavers, unimportant merchants and brokers, market traders, street traders, beggars – everything in the world except tailors and cap makers. But the Jewish employers were undaunted:

"We'll teach you! You'll see, it's not a bad business at all! Just come, it'll be all right! *Anyone* can be a presser! Even a baby can do it. Anyone can learn to operate a sewing machine. In a week's time you'll become expert machinists!"

To the girls they said:

"Even if the trousers are not absolutely perfect, does that mean the soldiers won't be able to wear them when they're lying in the trenches? Just come and work for me. It'll be all right!"

Leybesh was the first to volunteer. On the first Thursday the boss said to him:

"Why should you go back to the hotel? It's such a *schlep*! A little bit of food is neither here nor there for me; if I'm providing for ten, there's enough for eleven. Do they really give you good fresh food there? I see that you are a fine young man." The boss offered Leybesh a small room of his own, and Leybesh eagerly seized this opportunity. He wanted to put as much distance as possible between himself and the hotel, Gitele and the child.

That evening Leybesh put away his iron exactly at the moment when it was time to stop work, but the thin, dark-eyed young man who was in charge of him showed no sign of intending to stop. Furthermore, the boss was plucking his beard and asking beseechingly, with such pleading in his eyes, that they should do overtime.

"I don't work on *Shabbes*," he explained to Leybesh. "So the time is short and I have to deliver early."

Leybesh hesitated. He was against working overtime on principle, and the mitzva which he would be doing thereby, helping the boss to keep *Shabbes*, did not accord with his philosophy either. But the boss seemed to be such a decent man that he couldn't refuse him, and he carried on working until far into the night.

Jack, Leybesh's instructor, banged his iron down, emitting clouds of cigarette smoke through his nostrils at the same time. He was angry with Leybesh for not paying attention and making a mess of the trousers. Either he damped them too much or he ironed them completely dry.

The boss pretended not to hear, and hummed a hasidic melody to stay awake. He told his oldest daughter Katy to go to bed. But Katy refused the privilege and insisted on working on with the men, glancing at Leybesh all the time she was sewing.

At long last they draped the work over the chairs and went to bed. In the morning, when Leybesh got up and dressed himself, still half-asleep, the boss was already standing with a candle in his hand knocking gently on one of the doors at the front of the house:

"Children, time to get up!" he called softly, in a slightly guilty tone. "It's getting on for seven o'clock."

"Aa-ll ri-i-ight!" From the other side of the door came a drowsy voice, accompanied by a loud yawn.

"Good morning! Why are you up so early?" The boss's wife, carrying a jug of milk, greeted Leybesh with a friendly air. "Did you ever hear anything so stupid? It's not six o'clock yet and he's waking the household. Strangers want to sleep a bit longer, but he won't let them. As if the children don't know his trick! They'll not get up for another hour anyway, so what does he carry on like this for? He's mad, that's all there is to it!" she exclaimed, crossly.

"What does a woman know about it?" the boss retorted. "I simply can't get it into her head that if I tell the truth, the children will turn over and at seven o'clock I'll have to go and wake them all over again! They'll say: 'It's cold, it's foggy, it's dark, let us sleep!'"

"Let us sleep, let us sleep!" said his wife imitating her husband and turning a kipper over in the pan.

"Would you like some breakfast?" she asked Leybesh, turning over another kipper.

Leybesh did indeed want something to eat, but the smell of the kippers took away his appetite.

"Well, certainly, I'll drink a glass of coffee if you have it and perhaps a roll."

"Why won't you have a kipper? They're nice! I should be so lucky as to eat them all the time! *My* kippers don't stink the house up, like the neighbor's. I swear the king himself could eat in my house!"

Soon a noise was heard in the corridor, the door opened and several girls tumbled in, one after the other.

"Hello! Not kippers *again*?" exclaimed a girl of about twenty, apparently the youngest.

"All right, Sadie dear, tomorrow I'll make something else."

"Tomorrow you'll cook bloaters for a change!" Sadie laughed, showing a mouthful of little white teeth, pointed like a puppy's.

When she noticed Leybesh she quietened down and sat down at the table. The other girls wandered about the room, looking for something, combing their hair and powdering their noses. Jack came in with his hair standing on end, wearing slippers, with his braces hanging down over his trousers and his shirt unbuttoned, revealing his thick black chest hair.

"Good morning, Sadie!" he said, embracing the youngest daughter, who pushed him away with both hands, squealing with delight and scolding him at the same time:

"Go away, you dirty dog!"

The boy was about to start again, but he saw Leybesh and stopped.

When they had finished eating, the girls drank their tea standing up, shouted goodbye to the world in general, and hurriedly went off to catch the crowded bus or tram to get to their offices.

When they had all left, the old woman sat down to enjoy the peace and quiet. "Ah, thank God for that!" she sighed with relief.

Mr. Marks, the boss, put out the lamp and the room was shrouded in darkness. Letting out a screech, his wife got up and lit the gas again. Wisps of fog tinged with a melancholy greenish color drifted round the room. Mr. Marks combed his sparse beard and the few grey hairs which sprouted from the crown of his head, put on his prayer shawl and phylacteries, and started to pray.

The old woman laid the table, put out a pickled herring, a pickled cucumber and a brown loaf. Leybesh's mouth watered and he took a piece of herring.

"Ah, a real Jew from the old homeland!" said the boss with approval. Seeing Jack going out to get a packet of cigarettes, he continued, "Look at that savage, Jack! He won't even deign to try a piece of herring. And what these children eat isn't to my taste at all. I wouldn't take a hundred kippers for a piece of pickled cucumber."

"Well, we've got to put up with them, we've no choice!" sighed his wife: "Since they're the providers, they're the bosses, can't you see that?"

Mr. Marks frowned in embarrassment. He didn't want Leybesh to know that until a few weeks ago he had been living off his children. He made no further comment on that, however.

"This war's a miracle for us!" said the old woman, looking at her husband with disdain.

On Friday evening, Mr. Marks invited Leybesh to go to the synagogue with him and Leybesh accepted because he had nowhere else to go. Mr. Marks was delighted.

"Oh, it's wonderful to meet a real Jew from the old homeland! That Jack would never come to synagogue with me. He'd sell all the prayer houses in the world for a game of football!"

Mr. Marks put on a shirt front and cuffs made of paper, found his top hat and off they went.

The synagogue was brightly illuminated by electric lights, and before the Holy Ark hung a velvet curtain embroidered with real gold thread, which the president of the ladies' group had made herself. On the *bima* which looked like the stage of a theater, stood the cantor, a fat red-faced man in a black frock coat with a starched white shirt-front. His round shiny collar looked like a raw bagel which has been simmering and is just about to be popped into the oven. Surrounded by his helpers he gave a speech to welcome the *Shabbes.*

The men of the congregation, who all turned their heads to greet the newcomers, looked more like blocks of wood, than normal Jews.

"Hello, Mr. Marks!"

"Good *Shabbes*, good *Shabbes*," replied Mr. Marks, smiling with satisfaction, and glancing at Leybesh as if to say, "Now do you see who I am? Though I'm not well-off, they honor me here in the synagogue as if I was the finest master tailor."

"And who is the young man?" asked a stout man wearing a big gold Star of David on a thick chain. Not waiting for an answer, he went on, "Aha, Mr. Marks, I understand. Mazel tov, I congratulate you!" and to Leybesh he said, "You're all right with Mr. Marks, young man. He is our Torah reader, you know, and not everybody can do that. Well, I certainly couldn't! Ha, ha, ha!" He laughed merrily at his own shortcomings.

Mr. Marks opened his mouth to say something, but changed his mind: they obviously thought…but why not, it did no harm to let them think….

"That's our president. He's very wealthy, you know!" said Mr. Marks to Leybesh, basking in the reflected glory of the president's affluence. "He has about twenty workshops. He used to be a simple tailor, and he can still show his workers how to make a first-class coat."

Going home from the synagogue, Leybesh was amazed at what he saw. Through the windows of crooked, impoverished little houses, *Shabbes* peeked out with an embarrassed air. In the back rooms of the tiny workshops two or even four brass candlesticks stood on tables laid for the evening meal. The flames flickered shyly, watching as the same hands, which an hour ago had covered the women's eyes while they were saying the blessing for the candles, flew over the army trousers and tunics, working away skillfully, making buttonholes, sewing on buttons, pulling out basting threads. The men were sitting at the machines sewing together chalked pieces of garments, and pressers were lifting their irons, spitting on them to test the heat, then banging them down on the finished clothes, so that the flames of the *Shabbes* candles jumped and trembled, throwing shadows on the grubby walls.

In one such room sat an old woman with a tiny dark-skinned face, all lines and wrinkles, wearing a black wig. She was playing with a child. She pretended to touch the candle flame with her thin fingers and then touched the child's neck with them, each time saying, "tickle, tickle!" The child laughed heartily, trying to imitate the old woman. She was obviously trying to entertain her grandchild so that the parents could carry on working. The Jews coming home from the synagogue looked in at the work going on in the workshops and were interested to find out how many employees their various acquaintances had working for them. Unlike Leybesh, who stared in amazement, they were not at all surprised at this activity.

"Why have the women lit candles?" he asked. "Are they religious?"

"Ha, ha! You're just like all the new immigrants! You think it's shocking to work on *Shabbes* with the candles lit? That's the way it is here! Did you see that old woman? When she came from Poland two years ago, she was so shocked that she wanted to run back home. She wept the whole time because people worked on *Shabbes,* and she wouldn't eat at her daughter's house, but now, as you see, she's got used to it all. You'll soon learn, Mr. Bruckner, that in London it's very, very difficult to keep *Shabbes*!" concluded Mr. Marks with a feeling of superiority.

After they had eaten, Mrs. Marks shook out a pile of monkey nuts from a paper bag, put out a dish of oranges, bananas and grapes, and went up to bed, tired out. Mr. Marks told Leybesh that he would have to go out again because the association of Jews from his *shtetl* met every Friday evening to study a portion of *Eyn Yankev.* "And a member can't be an ignorant peasant," he said as he left.

Chapter 26

Berman was prospering. Not only had he been allocated an excellent flat and an allowance, but he was doing good business in Hatton Garden. His time was taken up with buying diamonds. He didn't concern himself with selling, relying on his brokers for that. There were always people keen to buy Berman's goods, because he was a genius at nosing out and snapping up the special bargains. Before other merchants realized that they were selling something for which there would be many eager buyers, Berman saw it in the twinkling of an eye. He would appear, make faces, wrinkle up his nose and ask offhandedly what the price was. Then he would burst out laughing and try to persuade the merchant that he couldn't be serious and was simply having a little joke.

And although the other merchants were also very astute, Berman managed to get the best goods at a low price. He always paid cash, and although the merchants realized that he only bought at knockdown prices, the temptation of his pounds sterling was too strong. They also knew that they had no need to lie awake at night worrying in case he went bankrupt, so they were happy to do business with him. It was also well known that Berman was willing to purchase goods that other merchants didn't want to have lying on their hands, and so it was to their advantage to stay in contact with him.

It was the same with the cutters and polishers he employed. He demanded first class work, but paid rock bottom wages, absolutely sucking the workers dry: no cutter or polisher could make a living by working for Berman, unless he was prepared to work fifteen hours a day. Nevertheless the workers, as in the Antwerp days, fought to be taken on by him, for the simple reason that there was no slack time with Berman, and he did not sack his workers. If a worker was good enough to satisfy Berman, he had a job for life. He never had anything to do with gentile workers. He did not like their way of doing things nor their way of thinking; they couldn't make any decisions for themselves, but with every trivial issue they ran to consult the secretary of the union and never made a move without his say-so. And when that official made a pronouncement, the employers would burst with frustration as the gentile workers demanded their rights! (The handful of Jews in the union were no better, however.) For these reasons Berman avoided gentile workers like the plague. It was a mystery to him why so many Jewish workers were unemployed and desperate for a bit of work, and yet Jewish workshop owners were taking on gentiles. As a Jew, Berman felt that he had a duty above all to help other Jews to earn their living. No, he decided, God would not punish him for this.

Now that he did not produce his own cut and polished diamonds, he had time to nose around, so he had bought plenty of goods for himself. Occasionally, the thought that perhaps the value of diamonds would indeed fall crept into his mind to torment him. He banished this niggling worry with the same decisiveness that he had shown in relation to many different issues where he had not shared the general opinion, but had turned out to be right in the end.

Berman had made one significant change in his life: he had begun to live more modestly, without his customary luxury. He left the three rooms of their flat as the committee had furnished them, without adding to or altering them. And because he had so much free time, and having time hanging heavy on his hands was torture to Berman, he began involving himself in household matters and checked up on every penny which Rochl spent.

Rochl was frequently ill and Berman, undaunted, did the cooking himself. The doctor said she had a weak heart, so she should not work and, especially, should not worry. So Berman bought himself a white smock and demonstrated that his cooking skills were just as good as his ability to trade in diamonds. After all, more than once, he had chopped up fish for his mother when she was busy in her shop. He knew exactly how much pepper, salt, sugar, and bitter almonds one should add. Fish, he had explained to Rochl, should be cooked for three hours, slowly, with not too much water and, most important, uncovered.

On Thursdays he prepared the chicken: he made it kosher and scalded it, examining it with the same attention he devoted to his diamonds, making sure that not a single feather was left on it. He scraped the fish as well, feeling it all over with his hands to make sure that every single scale had been removed. He cut off the head and laid it in a deep bowl so that it couldn't jump out, letting the blood spill. If the head did start to jerk about in its own blood until all the life went out of it, or jumped out onto the floor and lay there dead, then he groaned over the little bit of blood in the same way that he groaned when he thought he had made a bad purchase in the Bourse.

When Jeannette saw the dead fish's head on the floor, she started shrieking, her eyes almost popping out of their sockets: "Papa, I'm going to die! Please don't touch it!"

Jacques, however, liked their new way of life. He had great fun chopping up orange boxes for firewood, and was thrilled to see his father busy in the kitchen, his white smock stained with blood. "Papa, you look just like a *shochet*!" Jeannette objected to this, saying: "Wrong again: he looks like a surgeon."

Berman got the same pleasure out of preparing for *Shabbes* as he had formerly from handing out parcels of diamonds in his office on Pelikaanstraat. Rochl, on the other hand, found it absolutely impossible to follow the doctor's advice not to worry, and of course she wasn't short of things to get agitated about. When she received a card from Dovid, with half the text blocked out by the censor, she got into a state, not believing Dovid's assurances that everything was all right. She wondered what the censor had obliterated. If the post was delayed, she also worried. Then she remembered that she was supposed not to worry, and this worried her all the more.

Furthermore, Jeannette had started behaving in a wholly improper fashion. Rochl was frightened that similar problems to those they had had with Dovid were starting all over again. Jeannette was growing up, and for days on end she didn't come home. Rochl was terrified that Berman would find out. She found the situation very worrying. Jeannette was a beautiful young girl, and she had a willful and tempestuous nature. Rochl was also uneasy about taking the responsibility of concealing Jeannette's behavior from Berman, even though her father-in-law had warned her against telling him anything:

"You know that he has a hot temper. With God's help everything will turn out all right. If you forbid her to go out, then she'll be even more determined. It's better to leave her alone. *I* never reined in my children and yet, thank God, they all turned out to be decent people. Take Gedaliah: is he not an honest Jew? Well, he has a bit of a blazing temper, but that's just his nature." With these words the old man tried to comfort his daughter-in-law, but he sighed nevertheless.

Rochl followed her father-in-law's advice and didn't say anything to Berman.

Often there were concerts in the Central Hotel, to which artistes gave their services free; some of them had considerable talent, some none at all – the organizers were not very choosy. Jeannette alone was chosen from amongst the refugees. This was such a huge surprise and honor for her that it almost turned her pretty head.

She bought a pair of wide trousers in striped green velvet, started to smoke cigarettes in a long amber cigarette holder, and wandered round the three rooms of their flat with her long hair loose and flowing over her shoulders, wearing dangling earrings in her dainty little ears and about a dozen bracelets on her arms. She spoke to no one, but spent her time dancing and rehearsing her part. Her behavior shocked Rochl.

"Perhaps, God forbid, she has gone mad?" she suggested fearfully to her father-in-law.

At one of these concerts Jeannette made the acquaintance of a young man, a violinist and writer, and fell head-over-heels in love with him. Even though he was the son of a rich factory owner, her lover never had a penny to his name. Before becoming an artist he had worked as a commercial traveler for his father, an Englishman and a Conservative, driving around all day in a big black automobile, supplying mineral water and other drinks to smart restaurants. At one point, however, he met a writer, a cunning person who, having discovered that the young man had literary talent, accepted a good lunch as payment for this insight, smoked the young man's cigarettes, drove around with him in his father's automobile to all the London nightclubs in order to gather material for the young commercial traveler, and the latter began to write.

When he had finished his first novel, the "new talent" abandoned the automobile in the big wet yard of his father's soft drinks factory and walked out of his job, leaving behind a huge pile of unsorted accounts, and went off to the literary cafe by the Thames. He sat down, stretched out his legs languidly in bohemian fashion and waited there for the writer who had "discovered" him.

This cafe stood in a lane where baked clay jugs were sold, from which "various pharaohs and kings had drunk mulled wine thousands of years ago." In every other shop window all manner of Egyptian, Roman and Greek gods were for sale. Chinese gods smiled down, revealing huge stomachs with protuberant navels; strings of beads, all of them hundreds of years old, were hanging there, and all sorts of other things lay in a chaotic jumble: stags, elephants, cats and dragons. There was a Madonna holding up the carved folds of her gown, a naked baby Jesus on her arm, and her round, maternal breasts exposed to view. She looked down on her son, a world of warm and holy love in her eyes. And beside her was the Messiah himself, already crucified this time, with congealed blood on his hands and feet. Wealthy factory owners ordered "classical masterpieces" in this lane, which were carved or painted in an attic studio and ready within a week. Artists strolled around in flannel trousers, with sandals on their bare feet, and wild, tousled hair.

The artists' cafe completed the scene. Jeannette's lover, the ex-commercial traveler, introduced her to it, and she became a frequent visitor and a close friend of the owner: a young woman with sallow cheeks, big, blue-grey eyes and messily painted lips. She wore a hundredweight of beads round her neck and long dangling earrings swung about and brushed her cheeks as she served the customers. Her black satin dress had a deep décolleté, revealing her naked back, the cleft between her breasts, and various red scratch marks on her freezing body.

This woman was great friends with all the scribblers and failed artists who would sit there for days on end without buying anything, filling the cafe with smoke, literary trash, envy, scornful, malicious jibes and decadent behavior. Jeannette got to know this motley group very well, and talked to them in various languages: a little English, a soupçon of French, and a smattering of German. The artists were not absolutely sure what to think of her. The men were all keen to give her a kiss. The old maids who also frequented the cafe, however, hated Jeannette like the plague. They constantly carried their yellowing rejected manuscripts around with them, enveloping themselves in blue smoke, shooting out sparks of hatred and refusing to accept her as one of them. Whenever she tried to speak to them, they fixed her with a frozen gaze and a cold smile which revealed their large front teeth.

Ronald, Jeannette's lover, with a salesman's instinct for ingratiating himself, soon fitted into the cafe society. He had a pleasant smile, was as elastic and malleable as a snake, and above all, the little bit of education he possessed stood him in good stead. He was soon the best of friends with this group of artists, even the few respected writers and theater directors among them. He did not, however, have the slightest spark of talent. The novel he had written soon became a joke among the trashy writers and a tribulation for the real writers whom he had already bored to death with it. He had begun to realize that he had no ability and wanted to go back to the factory, but his father was implacable. He was not prepared to forgive Ronald for not joining up like his brothers and proving himself to be a good Englishman. He could have excelled as a soldier and brought honor to his parents. The two crimes together had put Ronald beyond the pale as far as his father was concerned. He wouldn't let his son over his threshold and refused to speak to him. Thus Ronald had no choice but to loiter round stage doors or sit for days on end in the cafe borrowing small sums of money from people, until at last he found a new means of making a living.... Girls began to fall in love with him, one after the other.

Now he hung around with Jeannette who, as a result, soon got into financial straits and started racking her brain to think how to get some money out of her father. This created a new problem for Rochl: she had to prevent Berman finding out about his daughter's way of life, and had to silence Jeannette, so that she didn't blurt it out to him. So against her will, she gave her money. And Jeannette's financial needs increased from day to day: Ronald had to have good evening meals, theater tickets and cigarettes. Rochl wept and counted out the money.

The couple strolled around the elegant Oxford Street and Piccadilly, mixing with the leisured rich, with strange tall ladies and gentlemen who led little curly-haired dogs on leads, with Belgian and French refugees who had nothing to do with their time, with officers and soldiers who were waiting to be sent to the front and were passing the time by dallying with women of dubious reputation.

Ronald kept nodding to passersby and then relating to Jeannette what important people they were:

"The man with the beard is the greatest living English sculptor. That one with the lady beside him is a Lord. And that man with the long hair and the velvet jacket is the famous writer, Pinkerton."

Jeannette was thrilled. She had become infatuated with Ronald and plundered her mother mercilessly.

She particularly liked walking along Oxford Street. She couldn't get enough of staring at the expensive shops, attracted by the satin evening dresses with long trains, white fur cloaks, hats, shoes, socks, gloves and various elegant trinkets which decorated the huge, shiny shop windows. She adored these sumptuous clothes and longed to take them home. She wanted to stroke them and put them on. But she didn't even have enough money to buy a new hat. Ronald took it all.

In the beginning, Ronald's mother had sent him an occasional check, but he simply took them without thanking her and asked for more as if it were his right. So she stopped sending him money and instead tried to persuade her husband that it was wrong to drive out one's own child. She argued that they might still be proud of him in some other way. If he became a writer, for instance, they would have as much honor from that as from the sons who were officers at the front.

Her heart ached. One day while she was arranging the flowers in the salon, she thought of Ronald. "Who knows if he even has enough money to buy himself his Sunday dinner?" she sighed. That afternoon, when she and her husband were sitting in their comfortable easy chairs beside the glowing fire, she tried to persuade him to take his son back into the business. Her husband laid the Bible down on his knees, took off his spectacles, looked at her with a hard-hearted expression in his clear eyes, moved his pipe into the corner of his mouth and muttered hoarsely between his clenched teeth:

"Never!"

The old lady sighed, and they both started looking at the Bible again, until the old man leaned his grey head back in his armchair and started snoring. Ronald's mother got up, touched her husband's shoulder and suggested in a mild voice: "Would you like to lie on your bed for a while, dear?"

That was the end of her attempt to intervene on behalf of her son, and it was Rochl who had to pay the price for her failure.

Chapter 27

The mood at the Bermans' was gloomy and subdued. In the evenings they sat around with nothing to do except keep warm round the black iron grate. Jacques and the old man went to bed early, Jacques because he was told to, and his grandfather because he was exhausted, though when he got to bed, he couldn't sleep. Only Berman and Rochl stayed up, she with her hands folded in her lap and he with a religious book on his knees, looking like a doddering old man. His heart was heavy. They were waiting and hoping that for once Jeannette would come back home from the dancing. Both were terrified of what this gallivanting was leading to, but neither admitted this to the other. The experience with Dovid had taught Berman that it was better to stay silent.

Did this mean one had to stay silent even if one's heart was breaking? Yes, it did! So he carried on looking at the book, even though he was taking in nothing at all. The door was the focal point, to which his head turned at every little noise: the door and the clock.

Days and weeks and even months passed like this. Sometimes Berman couldn't take it anymore and would lose control and start shouting. Then Jeannette would come running in, rush over to her father and put her hand over his mouth, kiss his beard and talk to him as if to a child:

"Is my little Papa cross then? Papa, dearest, *feh*, that's *naughty*!" Then she would kiss her mother:

"Poor little Mama! Is Papa a naughty boy then?"

Her silly antics made Berman want to laugh, but this feeling lasted only a moment or two, and then his laughter died on his lips. Somehow his daughter was different, her teasing and joking not as spontaneous as it had been in the Antwerp days. She looked more serious and older, a lot older. This ritual, of embracing and kissing, seemed somehow like a performance, as if she were pretending to be impetuous and carefree. He was sure she was hiding something, and he became very perturbed. He didn't smile and stroke his beard with delight as he used to do when his daughter kissed him. Rochl was almost demented with worry: "A young girl like that...."

One night when he was lying in bed, Berman decided that he couldn't let things go on this way. Perhaps, indeed, he *had* been too strict with Dovid and had driven him away. Perhaps, if only he had... but he couldn't bear to think about that. However, because of that mistake, was he to allow a young girl to wander around all night in a city like London? Perhaps by being too soft he was doing her more harm than he had Dovid: "A young girl like that...."

One day he followed her. In Bloomsbury, opposite the British Museum, he saw her kissing and cuddling with a fair-haired young man, obviously a gentile. Lying in bed that night he didn't shout at Rochl. For the first time in his life he discussed his fears with her and both of them desperately tried to find some way of separating her from this man. Finally Berman had an idea:

"Do you know what has just occurred to me? We'll get her married, that's what we'll do!" he said to Rochl, delighted with this solution. "You know Rubin?"

"You mean the old bachelor?"

"He's not as old as all that! Furthermore he's just inherited about fifty thousand pounds, and he already has a huge fortune of his own."

"Oh no, he's a really peculiar old man. He has no intention of getting married, and in any case, do you think for one minute that Jeannette would meekly accept him? If someone tried to suggest such a match to her, she'd scratch his eyes out! What an idea!"

"You never know. I'm telling you, Jeannette is perfectly able to appreciate the advantages of having a rich husband. We can at least try."

Rochl burst into tears. "How can we do that to her, in all conscience? She's just a child and he's old enough to be her grandfather!"

"What are you talking about, you stupid woman! Is the *goy* a better match then?"

"Please, Gedaliah, don't rub salt into my wounds. I agree that she mustn't see that man anymore, but we can make a better match for a girl like Jeannette, even if we have to give a few thousand francs for a dowry. She doesn't have to take an old dodderer like him! Is she an old maid, is she ugly? You know very well that she's a beauty."

"I know that, but we will try to persuade her to take Rubin. What do you know about it anyway?"

When Jeannette found out from her grandfather that her parents knew whom she was going around with, she actually felt relieved. She had already been trying to find ways of getting rid of her lover. Her feelings had changed towards him and now she really loathed him. Apart from the fact that he was always sponging off her, he had recently started flirting with other girls who came into the cafe and would leave her sitting alone like a stray dog. Whenever she couldn't give him as much money as he demanded, he shouted at her like a cruel husband. He was vindictive and spiteful. Sometimes he secretly pinched her flesh to hurt her. And he was always threatening to go and make a scene at her parents' house. He didn't really intend to do this at all, but Jeannette believed him, and so she stayed with him, did what he wanted, and felt more and more trapped.

When her father spoke to her of the proposed match, therefore, he was amazed to find that she fell on his neck and sobbed so that he had to comfort her. She swore that she would never see Ronald again:

"You'll see, Papa, I'll stay at home every evening and never leave the house."

Encouraged by this, Berman got in touch with the matchmaker. One Thursday evening in the middle of the bustle of *Shabbes* preparations, when pots full of different foods were cooking on every flame and a comforting red glow shone through every crack in the stove, there was a knock on the door. Berman hastily threw off his white smock, smoothed his beard and called out: "Come in!"

By the time the matchmaker had crept down the few steps which led from the ground floor to their basement flat, Berman was sitting in the wooden chair at the head of the table, reading a religious book and wearing his elegant silk skullcap, which gave him a calm, dignified air.

"Good evening, Herr Berman! What a dark, dismal night. You could, God forbid, get murdered in the street! And these stupid houses have stairs everywhere. They may not have any sense, these English, but they've certainly got stairs. What strange people they are!" grumbled the matchmaker, finding fault with both the houses and the climate.

Berman drew up a chair for him at the table, but he preferred to sit beside the fire.

"Aahhh! It's nice and warm here in your house. In mine, you freeze; no matter how much coal you pour on the fire, the heat just escapes into the street. This is delightful!" Steam rose off the old man into the warm room. His beard and whiskers were wet and he wiped them with the palm of his stiff old hand and sighed with pleasure.

"So, what have you to tell me, Reb Beynish?"

"Nothing much. He won't hear a word of it. I've already suggested lots of matches for him, but it's like talking to the wall. Do you know what he answered me when I asked him, 'And what about the commandment to be fruitful and multiply?' That he's wiser than the Lord of the Universe!"

But the next day the matchmaker came hurrying back as fast as his old legs would carry him, and even before he got round to unbuttoning his overcoat in order to warm himself at the fire, he blurted out with great satisfaction: "I've managed to persuade him to view the bride!"

"Hmmm! *Managed* to persuade him, eh? I don't believe a word of it! I would be willing to bet that he's so excited about the prospect of seeing her that he won't be able to sleep tonight!"

"Well...perhaps, what does it matter? The main thing is that on

Sunday, God willing, he will go to Bournemouth. I've told him that your wife and daughter are staying there for the sake of your wife's health. That's what you wanted, isn't it?"

"Yes, yes, and…?"

"And, nothing! They'll have a look at each other! Neither of them knows what the other is doing in Bournemouth, and so if they like each other, well, it'll all end happily, heh, heh, heh!" The old man took a pinch of snuff from his bone snuffbox, sneezed, tapped the box to shake down the snuff, and offered it to Berman, who refused it politely. Old Reb Chaim Yoysef however, who was sitting there silently, stretched out his healthy hand for a pinch of snuff.

"Here you are, enjoy it in good health!"

"Atchoo, atchoo! Very fine snuff!"

"So the crux of the matter is," said Berman to Rochl, "that you and Jeannette will go to Bournemouth."

"And what about *Shabbes*? Has someone prepared it, then?" asked Rochl.

"What a fool! You can take fish and meat with you. They're very expensive there. Listen, Rochl, you'll have to make sure that Jeannette behaves properly and doesn't make faces or do anything silly. This fellow thinks a lot of himself, and certainly he has got something to boast about."

"Oh, my God!" Rochl laughed and sighed all at once.

Jacques, who had been listening to this, suddenly blurted out: "Well, he's such a youngster, time's on his side, isn't it?" Berman looked at him and was about to shout at him for interrupting when adults were talking, but the mockery in Jacques' intelligent black eyes and the bitterness and hatred in his smile took him aback. He was embarrassed in front of his younger son. He noticed that on Jacques' upper lip there was the trace of a moustache, which intimated that he wasn't a child anymore and had the right to interrupt when adults were talking. Berman had a premonition that Jacques' growing up was going to cause yet more problems for him.

Jeannette was sitting in the spacious, comfortable lounge of the hotel. She was leaning back in the deep plush sofa, stealthily smoking a cigarette, and from time to time surreptitiously glancing at the door and blowing out columns of smoke. She had rouged her full lips, which looked like two sweet, moist ripe cherries. Her hair swept down so smoothly from its center parting that not a single hair escaped to tumble down over her rounded forehead.

A cheerful bright fire burned in the hearth, the yellow and blue flames licked the coal, leaping and crackling merrily. The lights were reflected in a large gilded mirror above the mantelpiece, which cast bright splashes onto the dark carpet, creating a festive atmosphere in the luxurious room. Velvet and silk cushions were scattered around on all the sofas and armchairs, and even in the corners of the room, and heavy curtains were drawn over the broad windows. Outside, the noise of the sea could be heard. It was a cold day, and the hotel lounge seemed cozy and intimate by contrast.

Rochl appeared at the door of the room with an old man of about sixty, or so he looked to Jeannette. She swiftly stubbed her cigarette out in the ashtray, trying to guess who the man could be. Then she realized. "It's *him*, that old dotard!"

She wanted to burst out laughing: was *this* going to be her husband? "Oh God, whoever has money can get whatever he wants!" she thought.

Her hand went cold when he touched it, but she managed to say, "How do you do, Herr Rubin?"

"Not bad, but what do you think of the weather outside? It eats into your very bones!"

Jeannette invited him to sit down, pulling out a chair for him, but, as the matchmaker had in their house, Rubin sat down right beside the fire, warming his dried-up hands. He "aahhed" in satisfaction, in a cracked, old man's voice. Then, remembering that he had to act young, he broke into a friendly smile.

Jeannette laughed: "Are you cold, Herr Rubin?" He bit his lip and blamed the weather: "It's cold outside!" he repeated.

Not being able to burst into tears here, Jeannette just laughed to herself.

That morning she had walked to the poor part of the town and found a doctor's surgery. In the waiting room, the leather seats of the chairs were shiny and torn, and on a round table lay a pile of old magazines. The waiting room was empty, apart from a young woman wearing a tucked-up skirt, a thin woman who looked as if she was depressed. A boy sat beside her, of about twelve years, who had a red nose, greyish skin and the eyes of an old man. His hair was cut very short, almost shaved, except for a tuft of fair hair at the front.

Another patient came in: a small woman in black with a screaming child in a ramshackle pram. The child looked round the room fearfully and stopped crying, managing to control himself like a grownup.

The door of the doctor's consulting room opened and Jeannette was aware of a red face, a white coat and a strip of greenish light. The doctor ushered Jeannette in. After he had interviewed her he asked her to go behind a screen and he admitted the woman with the twelve-year-old boy. "Yes, my lad?" he said to the boy, who looked at his mother. "He's coughing, Doctor," she said, "and he has a sharp pain in his left side."

"Well, get undressed, but be quick, for a doctor is a very busy man, my lad!"

The boy tried to get undressed, fumbling clumsily, and the doctor repeated, "Yes indeed, Mrs. Brown, nowadays a doctor is a very busy man," for the benefit of the smart lady in the fur coat, by whose visit he felt honored.

"Oh yes, I realize that," agreed Mrs. Brown, nodding her head.

He put the stethoscope to the boy's chest, making him repeat "ninety-nine" again and again. The little boy stood half-naked, holding his trousers in his grubby hands, looking timidly at his mother and the doctor and trembling with cold. The doctor went into an anteroom and came back with a bottle of brown chicory water.

"Give him this three times a day, and come back in a few days' time!"

He took two shillings from her and came to examine Jeannette.

"There's nothing wrong with you, Madam, you're pregnant; that's all."

Jeannette's legs gave way and the doctor caught her in his arms.

"Sit down, Madam! Why are you so shocked?"

"I don't want to have a child! Suppose I wanted to get rid of it... I mean..." stammered Jeannette.

"No! I don't do that sort of thing. It's a criminal offense, Madam!"

Jeannette felt faint and everything went black before her eyes. The doctor laid her on the couch and gave her some drops. When she came to herself she started sobbing so violently that the doctor became anxious. But there were patients waiting, so he left her resting behind the screen and went back into his consulting room to carry out his duties.

Later he came back and put the stethoscope to her chest. "Better?" he asked.

Jeannette was still sobbing.

"Listen, Madam, that's not going to solve anything. You must see that he marries you!" said the doctor, who realized what the situation was. "Are you from these parts?"

"No!" sobbed Jeannette. She paid the doctor, who stroked her soft fur coat as he accompanied her out of his consulting room.

When Jeannette came back to the hotel, Rochl didn't know what to do with her daughter, who sat all day on the sofa in the corner of the room lost in thought, refusing to eat anything. Jeannette knew she had to control herself, which she did, like an older and more experienced person, like her father when he was negotiating over diamonds. Then she started laughing, and couldn't stop.

"Do you still feel cold, Herr Rubin?"

"When I look at you, I feel warm!" said Rubin, rubbing his hands together, feeling pleased that he had managed to transform himself so cleverly from a frozen old man warming his cold bones at the fire, into a prospective bridegroom talking amorously to his fiancée.

"In that case I must come nearer, so that you can have a good look at me."

She stood up and, smoothing down the dress over her stomach as if she were brushing off crumbs, she came over to the fire and sat down beside Rubin. The bridegroom smiled with delight.

Jeannette was looking even more beautiful than usual that day. She had smoothed cream into her olive-skinned face, and had combed, stroked and caressed her hair as if it too had been weeping. In the light of the standard lamp with its green shade, she looked extraordinarily beautiful. Her anxiety gave her a serious expression and seemed to reveal more delicate traits in her young face.

"She's not just beautiful, she is clever as well," decided Rubin.

A tall waitress with a white cap on her fair hair announced that dinner was served. Rubin called her back and demanded she wipe off the chair again before he sat down, even though there wasn't a speck of dust to be seen on its gleaming surface. Jeannette herself tucked the napkin into Rubin's collar as if he were a child.

"You know, Fraulein Berman, the napkin is poking into my neck a little," he said coyly, like a flirtatious young man, in order to get Jeannette to come over to him again. She stood beside him once more and adjusted the napkin, touching his scrawny neck with her soft warm hand. Rubin started sweating with embarrassment and pleasure.

"*Ay*, what a girl! She's certainly worth getting married for!"

Having finished the grapefruit, which was bitter and tasteless, Rubin ate the main course, liver and onions, with great enjoyment and felt on top of the world. Through his thin cheeks one could see every little bit of bread being chewed, and his Adam's apple jumped around in his throat. His napkin kept falling from his collar, and now it lay on his knees. He never took his eyes off Jeannette. He felt his tired old blood coursing round in his veins, bathing him in a pleasurable warm glow. He observed how Jeannette held her knife and fork in her long, beautifully manicured fingers, and how elegantly she ate. "She's a real lady too," he thought.

It occurred to him that she was bound to laugh her head off at him and mock him mercilessly when she found out why he was here. But she was smiling at him so warmly, so charmingly, and yet there was an earnestness about her; he thought that she really must be in love with him. He glanced at himself in the mirror opposite: "Hmm! Why not?"

He saw his long face and fine white hair. He looked intelligent, which was not surprising: hadn't he read a great many books? What a lot of reading he did in the course of one of his sleepless nights! And of course that was visible in his face.

"My word, the little lady certainly has good taste. She knows what she wants!" And gradually he became more and more confident of his success.

When Berman arrived in Bournemouth in the middle of the week and began sounding out his daughter, he couldn't believe his own ears: "Rochl, it's going to be all right! Go and talk to her, strike while the iron's hot. He is certainly keen enough!"

Rochl wiped away a tear. "Gedaliah, think for a moment! She's just a child. He could be her grandfather!"

"What a heartless creature," she thought. "He's thanking God that his daughter did not lose her temper and make a huge scene as he had expected. That's all he's interested in." And she carried on bargaining with him.

Berman lost his temper. "Look, stop playing stupid tricks, trying to get round me by making eyes at me. Just go and talk sense to her, if you have any yourself, that is. If you don't, then she can just go off and marry the *goy*, do you hear? This fellow is an extremely wealthy man. So stop whining, you stupid cow!"

Rochl's legs were trembling. A young girl like her... Berman was a brute. He was just using this *goy* as an excuse! Jeannette wasn't even seeing him, she had been sitting all day at home, and *he* was using this as an excuse to sell off his own child.

Rochl felt a strange pain in her heart. Somehow today Berman's brutal language had really stung her, even though she had got used to it over the years; apart from when they were in bed, she never heard a kind word from him. But somehow today it really hurt her.

"You go and talk to her yourself! Then it'll be your fault if she starts making a scene in a strange place! If you want to sell her, go and sell her yourself. What do you want of me?" Because they were in a strange place, Rochl actually dared to stand up to him.

Chapter 28

"So what shall I tell him?" Rochl asked her daughter again, hoping that perhaps she might think better of her decision. Jeannette looked at her mother, longing to pour out her heart to her, tell her the truth and ask her advice. She could see that her mother was dismayed and grieving that her daughter was going to marry the old man. Jeannette thought for a long time, but still could not summon up the courage, and instead shouted in hysterical anger: "What are you standing there for? I have *told* you I'm going to marry him. I like him! I like him! I like him, and if you don't like it you can go to hell!" She started laughing like a madwoman: "Tell him that I find him attractive and I want him! Do you hear me?"

Rochl was horrified. She was sure that her daughter had lost her mind and she started to cry.

"Well, what's the news?" Berman was pacing back and forth on the soft carpet of the neighboring room, waiting. He had heard his daughter laughing and his wife weeping, and had even peered through the keyhole, but had only taken in disjointed fragments of conversation.

"I think she has gone mad. I tell you, she's ill, she doesn't know what she's saying. She says she wants him, that she's yearning for him. Or perhaps, like you, she really believes she *has* to sell herself to that old carcass," said Rochl, turning her rage on the fiancé.

"Is that so? Well, it looks as if I did know what was right for her after all! I always said that, with God's help, I would be proud of her!"

"Proud of her!" Rochl turned away from him. "Well, it's all the same to me now. My heart's broken in any case. This is just the last straw."

Berman went in to see his daughter.

"Mazel tov to you Jeannette, my dear daughter!"

He embraced her, pressing her in his big strong arms like a lover, kissing her on the cheeks and forehead.

"You don't know how happy you're going to be. You will be the richest woman in Antwerp when, God willing, we return home after the war. And in London there aren't many husbands with hundreds of thousands of pounds in their pockets either!"

Jeannette wept all night, and then stopped. Gradually she began to convince herself that it was a good match after all. Nevertheless she kept running from one doctor to another, getting the same answer everywhere she went:

"That's a criminal offense, Madam!"

So she started trying to find some way to speed up the wedding, not realizing that her father, afraid she might change her mind, was doing this in any case.

At the engagement party, Jeannette sat at the head of the table, wearing a black silk dress which shimmered in the electric light. Her fiancé looked really festive in his new suit, with neatly combed white hair, polished pince-nez and elegantly manicured fingernails. The skin of his face had a brownish tinge, the tiny blue veins on his temples were pulsating and his rather elongated nostrils quivered. He sat beside Jeannette, wallowing in delight.

A girl like this, fresh and innocent, this was what he had been waiting for all the time. Those idiots of matchmakers just hadn't understood what he meant when he said that he didn't want to get married because he didn't trust modern girls. They thought he was just making excuses. But *this* one was different! Such a sweet child; just weaned off her mother's milk, a young sapling, slender and graceful, a new Queen Esther. Yes, it really had been worth waiting. There was only one thing which spoiled his pleasure: he was angry with his prospective father-in-law.

Every time the large diamonds on Jeannette's long fingers and the brooch in her décolleté flashed, he felt a new surge of anger. Berman had insisted on selling the stones to him, and had demanded a ridiculous price, as if he, Rubin, had been a simple schoolmaster and not a diamond merchant himself. But what could he do, when Berman fastened onto him like a leech? *Oy*, what a sum he had had to pay for these diamonds! Oh well, he consoled himself, it was too bad, but for a girl like that anything was worth it. That father-in-law of his was a bastard, but never mind! And to console himself all the more, he kept running his cold, dry fingers over Jeannette's bare back. Jeannette shuddered.

The matchmaker was also there. In honor of his great triumph he had, for once, taken off his overcoat with its sheepskin collar, and was sitting at the table in a greasy greenish frock coat with two worn buttons over the split in the back.

Rochl had dressed herself up. She smoothed down her best *Shabbes* wig and smiled at the bridegroom as bashfully as if she had been the bride, while Berman sat stroking his silky beard, trying not to see how the old rogue never took his hand off Jeannette's back for one moment, and how his daughter vainly kept trying to move away.

The hotel owner helped to bring in the supper. She was a small pale woman with a little snub nose and light grey widely-spaced eyes. A piece of sticking plaster covered a spot which had appeared on her forehead, but despite this she was an attractive woman. She never took her eyes off the bridegroom, thinking that this was the kind of match she herself would have liked to make.

The matchmaker looked her over thoroughly, knowing that she was a widow.

"Hmm … not a bad-looking woman! We'll have to do something for her." Today Reb Beynish was confident that whatever match he undertook to negotiate would have a successful outcome.

Shapiro sat opposite the bridal couple. He was sighing with envy – look what money could achieve! *He* had sold himself to an ugly bitch for money, and here was a father selling his lovely daughter – such a beautiful young girl being wasted on an old blackguard like that!

Madame Shapiro envied the bride. In her view, a woman should always take a husband who was a lot older than herself. "Certainly, today's young women have sense," thought Madame Shapiro wistfully.

"It's agreed, then. The wedding, God willing, will be at the beginning of the month of Adar. So let's drink another toast!" Berman raised his glass above his head. "*L'chaim*! To the bride and groom! *L'chaim*!"

Everyone in Hatton Garden knew about the engagement. When Berman went in the next day, dozens of hands stretched out to congratulate the lucky father, whose business was now doubly secure.

"Mazel tov! May the marriage be successful!"

"That kind of luck doesn't happen often!" confirmed all the merchants.

"Who would have thought that Rubin would get married!" the fathers of grown-up daughters said enviously to each other.

"I hear that Rubin has been unusually generous?" said Kuper, coming to greet Berman with a smile and a mazel tov. "Those diamonds must have been a nice surprise, eh?"

Berman stared at him: "What do you mean?"

"Oh, nothing at all. The setter showed them to me, that's all. After all, no one would give a bungler stones of *that* quality to set, so they want people to know about it."

"Indeed? So he is showing *my* stones all over the place? Nice to know! Those workers have nothing better to do than gossip!" said Berman, thereby betraying what Kuper knew already, namely that he had sold his own diamonds to the bridegroom.

Old Reb Mordecai sat down at Berman's table. "Mazel tov to you, Herr Berman! May God bless this union! God willing, you should have joy of your only daughter!"

Berman smiled, thinking: "He probably thinks I'll take out my purse and hand him a fiver, the old ruffian."

When Rubin came to Hatton Garden a few days later, the same

ritual repeated itself; outstretched hands, mazel tovs, hidden smiles and unspoken jests.

Rubin glowed. Let them burst with jealousy. Some merchants who were much younger than he had ended up with wives who were already bloated, faded old women, and here was he, Rubin, with a lovely young girl.

The wives of the diamond merchants were making more extravagant preparations for the wedding than the bride's mother. Each one wanted to outdo the others, and they all spent days going round the expensive shops in the West End.

Meanwhile, the war was raging. Young, middle-aged and even elderly men, among them many Jews, were besieging the recruiting offices to volunteer "for King and Country." Columns of uniformed recruits marched through the streets, their thin legs wrapped in khaki puttees. Their army boots were new and shiny, and their eyes shone with a mysterious glow – the anticipation of victory. They were fresh-faced and happy, as if they were going to a ball, and as they marched, their hob-nailed boots ringing rhythmically on the road, they merrily sang: "It's a long way to Tipperary...."

Both gentile and Jewish women and girls on the pavements stared at the soldiers with admiration and curiosity. Elderly women turned their failing eyes heavenwards and piously asked for blessings on them, their thin lips murmuring prayers that God should protect the "boys." Girls blew kisses to them, which the soldiers caught with their hands, and returned in the same way. Then their song rang out even more loudly: "... it's a long wa-a-y to g-o-o-o..."

The sky had now cleared a little, revealing patches of blue here and there among the masses of heavy clouds. On windy days, wide tracts of sky appeared... and the soldiers carried on marching.

Rochl and her daughter had samples cut from different silks, velvets and laces, and Berman inspected everything and gave his verdict. Not relying on the women's judgment, he accompanied them when they went to buy furs. The amount of money he was spending did not concern him at all. "She must have a dowry which is fitting for Berman's only daughter!"

Jeannette tried on the clothes, twirled in front of the mirror and was absolutely delighted with herself. Her passion about clothes made her forget her situation, her fiancé and everything else. She floated around among silk and satin, raised her arms and spread them out as if she were about to fly off, making the silk shimmer, when suddenly she felt a sharp pain in her side. For the first time she felt nauseous, retched, and started vomiting. Her eyes were bulging and streaming with tears. The dress was stained.

"Jeannette, what's the matter with you? God forbid you should be ill!"

"I'm. . . ." Before Jeannette was able to reply, she had to be sick again.

By the time she arrived home she looked green and gaunt, as if she had lost pounds during those few moments. A thought crept into Rochl's mind, but she tried to banish it: "*Feh*! How can I suspect such a thing! Since Dovid's been away there have been ill winds blowing round our home. I must stop this: just thinking dark thoughts can bring on bad luck."

But nevertheless she sensed misfortune creeping closer, like a venomous snake. "*Feh, feh!*" However much she tried to banish the thoughts from her tormented mind, the heaviness lay on her heart. Without exactly knowing why, she suddenly began to feel relieved that her daughter was getting married, even if it was to old Rubin.

The wedding day arrived. The large room was brightly illuminated by electric lights shaded by yellow bowls, which hung from the ceiling. The light was gently diffused over white tablecloths, glowing silverware and vases of flowers, which stood all along the tables. It lingered on the powdered faces of the women, and on their bare arms, breasts and shoulders, making these boldly exposed bodies look very white. The light awakened the glittering fire in diamond earrings, bracelets, brooches and necklaces, and made white shirtfronts and bow ties appear more dazzling. The tailcoats and silk skullcaps on the men's heads appeared even darker by contrast.

Jeannette and her bridegroom stood in the wide doorway welcoming guests, smiling at them, kissing them, smiling again, kissing again.

Then the guests sat down to the meal. Jeannette sat there tightly corseted and pressed her lips together so that she would not be sick.

Afterwards the couples went into the ballroom and danced, whirling to the music. Burly men pressed their fat fingers into even fatter female backs, young men had their arms round the waists of slender girls. Then suddenly, before she had time to reach the anteroom, the bride vomited violently in the middle of the dance floor. The music stopped and the couples stood rooted to the spot, as if turned to stone, with arms around waists and hands on backs.

This frozen silence lasted for a moment, then noise and confusion broke out. Rochl was wringing her hands and the bridegroom turned as white as a sheet. His right leg started trembling like it belonged to a very old man. People were fetching water, vinegar, lemonade and chairs. Rochl felt she was about to collapse, which would cause yet another scene. Her previous suspicions had now turned to certainty and only her dread of the imminent scandal enabled her to stay on her feet.

Berman alone did not lose his head. Looking pale, he came in from the dining room where he and some other pious Jews, who were not joining in the dancing, had been sitting at the tables, conversing. With his new black frock coat, dazzling white shirtfront and elegant long beard, he was an imposing figure. He advanced with measured tread towards the chair where the bride sat.

The room went deathly still.

"I told you," he said, addressing Rochl, "that she shouldn't be allowed to fast! You know this always happens! But she is a stubborn lass," he finished in a fatherly tone, stroking his daughter's head and the white tulle of her veil. "Oh well," he carried on, addressing his wife: "it is her wedding day after all and because she really *wanted* to fast, the mitzva will be all the greater." He even managed to smile.

The women stopped staring and even the bride smiled, strengthened by her father's reassurance. His words freed her from the fear that people would suspect. She threw back her veil, powdered her face again, and the rest of the wedding passed off smoothly.

Though Berman was now fairly certain what the situation was, he started grilling Rochl as if she had been the bride, insisting that she should find out the whole truth from Jeannette.

Rochl protested. Perhaps Jeannette was simply unwell. How could she voice such a suspicion to her daughter? Jeannette would bite her head off. But Rochl's fears were unfounded, for instead of biting her head off, Jeannette put her arms round Rochl's neck and in floods of tears she begged her mother to help her and tell her what she should do.

When Rochl got back home from Jeannette's she crept into her bed with all her clothes on and wept until she had no more tears left.

Berman came in from Hatton Garden that evening with his pockets full of cards of congratulations and his heart full of apprehension – as if he were weighed down by stone instead of his diamonds. What would happen if his suspicion turned out to be true? He would have a grandchild from a *goy*. And how far gone was she? What would his son-in-law say? What would the world say? He still hoped that Rochl would meet him with a beaming smile and scold him for his suspicions: this time he'd be happy to be the fool.

However, seeing Rochl lying in bed still wearing her clothes, not even having taken off her coat, he shuddered and woke his wife.

Rochl opened her eyes wide and stared at her husband for a moment or two as if she didn't recognize him, then started rubbing her red eyes.

"Now come on then! Out with it! Come on! Tell me!"

Rochl carried on rubbing her eyes. One of her cheeks was as red as fire, the other creased and pale as death. During the last couple of hours, all that she had suffered over the years had appeared in her face. She had, all at once, turned into an old woman.

"No! No!" yelled Berman. "So I'm to have no pleasure from my disgusting brats! Whenever there's a celebration in other families, they laugh with joy. In this household, we weep. They should both have perished in your womb. *You* should have perished before I met you. Let her be struck down on the spot. She and her bastard should die a horrible death, right now, this very day! And I hope that Dovid doesn't come back. It would be for the best if a bullet finished him off over there!" Berman broke down and sobbed like a woman.

Rochl's eyes were dull, lifeless and unseeing; everything had grown dark. All she heard was Berman's torrent of curses against his own children – against Dovid. She listened to his sobbing.

Jeannette carried on seeking a solution to her problem, but all the doctors gave her the same answer:

"It's a criminal offense!"

She tried to bring up the topic delicately in conversation with other young wives, expressing the opinion that it was better not to have a baby too soon after getting married, that one should have the chance of having a good time with one's husband first, because apart from anything else, Jeannette asserted, having a baby really ruined one's figure.

The women all agreed with Jeannette and gave her lots of advice. She tried everything, but nothing worked. A piece of iron would have melted, but still the baby lay contentedly in Jeannette's womb, as if these efforts didn't concern it at all. Time was marching on and it began to look as if she would give birth six months after getting married.

She tried to talk to her mother, who just looked at her in a way that made her flesh creep.

Quite unexpectedly, however, her maid Mary saved her mistress, Jeannette's parents, and her husband from a great misfortune. Jeannette had occasion to tell her that she was not doing her work well. She said it in a kindly fashion, because her own situation made her more considerate of her maid's weaknesses. The maid promised that in two or three weeks she would be able to work like a horse, and that her present lethargy was because she had just had treatment in a clinic.

"What's wrong with you?" asked Jeannette.

"*Now* there's nothing at all wrong with me," sighed Mary and, kneeling on the floor with a scrubbing brush in one hand and a piece of carbolic soap in the other, she told her mistress that her "young man" had left her to join the army when she was three months gone. "He had nothing to eat, the poor devil, so he had to join up but I was left in that state – so what could I do? I had to get rid of it," the girl explained, and a tear dropped into the soapy water.

Jeannette's eyes lit up. "And have you actually done it?"

"I had to!"

"Who does that, Mary? Tell me, my dear!" Jeannette went into one of her affectionate moods and started kissing her maid as she used to kiss her father's beard.

Mary thought her mistress had gone mad.

"Mary, I'll give you two pounds if you let me have the person's address!" insisted Jeannette.

"Madam, it's illegal, I can't!"

"Mary, I'll never mention it to a living soul, I swear! Come on, give it to me!" and she pressed two pounds into the maid's hand. Mary, trembling, gave her the address.

"I wouldn't have done it," she carried on, trying to justify her actions, "if my mother could have looked after the child, but my father has joined the army too, he just left my mother with all the children and went off, and she has to go out washing floors. So what else could I do?"

Jeannette went there with her maid. The "clinic" consisted of a middle-aged woman with a wrinkled face, thin grey hair and a strange, unpleasant glint in her eyes. At first the woman, frightened off by Jeannette's fur coat, wouldn't hear of it and couldn't remember having met Mary. "I don't do such things!" she protested. But Jeannette offered a fee that the woman could not refuse, and it was arranged that she would come to Jeannette's house.

When Rubin came home that evening, his young wife was lying in bed. The doctor whom the old woman had brought with her explained to Rubin that his patient had fainted. Now the danger was past but she must rest, and on no account get out of bed yet. Rubin was bewildered; "A child like her, being so ill?" he thought. He ordered a car and rushed off to tell his parents-in-law about Jeannette's illness. Berman glanced at Rochl and started to say, "May she…" He was about to burst out with an oath again, but managed to stop himself and accompanied his son-in-law to visit his sick daughter.

Jeannette looked gaunt and exhausted. Her maid, Mary, was attending to her. She put the florins and half-crowns which her mistress had given her into her bosom, and kept silent.

Jeannette smiled weakly at her parents and husband.

"Well, at least the problem's solved, that's the main thing," growled Berman when they got back home. "But that slut isn't my daughter anymore. I don't want to have anything more to do with her. That… that…" He trembled. He was full of conflicting emotions.

Rochl could not cut herself off from her daughter, and as any mother would, she went every day to look after her during the period of her recovery. She wandered round the luxurious rooms of Jeannette's house, spitting to drive out the evil eye and weeping incessantly.

Jeannette smiled weakly but affably at her husband. She let him kiss her endlessly and did not even wipe her lips with her hand afterwards. She was as sweet and nice to him as she had been just after their wedding, with the difference that then she had used her charms to keep the old fellow in a state of perpetual excitement, whereas now she didn't allow him into her bed. She had the excellent excuse that the doctor had forbidden it.

Rubin, believing her, groaned with disappointed resignation. He had waited for so many years for a wife, and now, when he had tasted such bliss, he was again deprived of it. He hoped that she would get better, and in the meantime he consoled himself with the fact that he had a home and a faithful, loving wife. Rubin had always been a quiet man, who had never talked about himself, but he suddenly became loquacious and bored everyone with endless accounts of Jeannette's merits.

"Let me tell you, after waiting so long, I've found a wonderful woman! Do you know how much she loves me? I come home and find my wife in bed, looking so ill that I nearly faint from shock myself. When I say to her: 'You silly, little woman, why did you not send for me? I would have rushed home immediately,' she just smiles like a little child, with such affection in her eyes that your heart would melt, and says so lovingly, 'sweetheart, I didn't want to frighten you.' I'm her 'sweetheart'! Even though she's an only daughter she doesn't have a crumb of egotism in her nature. You don't find that nowadays. Most women today run around all day nibbling sweets, stuffing themselves and flirting. Even though they are as healthy as horses, they're constantly mollycoddling themselves and running to doctors. And there's my wife lying ill in bed, and she doesn't even send for her husband because she doesn't want to frighten him. Such an innocent child – she knows nothing of all those womanly wiles, she just knows that it's a wife's duty to look after her husband the way our mothers used to do."

Chapter 29

Leybesh had long since stopped working for Mr. Marks, the "Torah reader," and had gone to work in a large workshop in the West End. He was a proper presser now, not just an under-presser. The firm was flourishing. The electric motors and two long rows of sewing machines in the long bare hall were humming and vibrating all day. The girls' crooked, pricked fingers flew and the needles flashed as they sewed khaki trousers for the soldiers. The foreman drove them on.

"Hurry up, faster! it doesn't matter if you miss a stitch. The main thing is: get a move on! The trousers don't have to be perfect. They're only for lying in the trenches with – as long as we get them done!"

The girls worked their fingers to the bone and sang all kinds of sentimental and bawdy war songs to fight their exhaustion and to drown out the clattering of the machines, the dull thumps of the heavy irons, and the hissing steam spreading round the room. So the needles flew over the work and the girls told stories about their flirtations with soldiers standing by the walls of buildings and lying on the grass in Hyde Park. They laughed and joked about it openly, without any feelings of shame or embarrassment, as if they wanted to experience life now, and felt they had a right to, because their fiancés might well die on the battlefield and they would die as old maids. Those who were children now would grow up and get married but they, the girls sewing the trousers, in which their own fiancés might die, would be left all alone.

So they sang and laughed and kept throwing more pairs of trousers onto the huge heap of finished work which lay on the floor in the middle of the room, waiting to be ironed. Beside them was stacked another pile of already pressed trousers, which Leybesh and his comrades added to all the time. The foreman would come and inspect them, giving his verdict: "All right, these'll do for fighting in. Faster now, come on!"

As they worked and sang and laughed, the machines clattered and the irons thumped and the girls' voices mingled with the general din:

"I want some lo-o-o-o-ve just right now...."

Leybesh worked all week and in the evenings he went to English language classes. He was the best student in the class, and the teacher was very pleased with him. As soon as the teacher saw him coming into the cold green room with high, barred windows, his lips drew back into a smile which showed his teeth.

"Good evening, Mr. Bruckner. You're early again this evening!"

Leybesh was pleased and embarrassed all at once, like a schoolboy: "Well, I've got nothing much else to do so I just came here." Leybesh sat down at one of the long empty tables.

The teacher started organizing the books and exercise books, but there was still no one there apart from Leybesh. Eventually a few refugees trickled in, all older people, as the young people had better things to do in the evenings. The room remained almost empty and the lamps burned brightly under their green tin shades, making the room look like a hospital.

The lesson began. It really was very simple: how could anyone not grasp it?

"I remember, I remember,
The house where I was born...."

Even so, they just couldn't manage to learn it by heart. Someone would start and say the first few words, but couldn't continue. Just as he nearly had it, the words flew away like a bird when you're about to catch it. Leybesh was the only one in the class who could soon speak English. He was very well informed about politics. He read all the English papers with the help of a dictionary. If people in the hotel were arguing about politics, they would look round for Leybesh: "It's a shame Mr. Bruckner isn't here! He would soon tell you that I'm right!" Each person was certain that Leybesh would assure him that he, and not the other person, was right.

But Mr. Bruckner was never there. He was working, studying, thinking. Recently he had been thinking a great deal.

Whenever he had a little free time, he would walk round the streets, and cover every inch of Hyde Park. He really loved this vast unkempt park in the most affluent district of London. It lay there like a slovenly housekeeper, with all its possessions scattered around. The benches were all over the place and the deck chairs were not in rows like in other parks, but spread around in a higgledy-piggledy fashion. The trees also grew where they pleased, popping up here and there, all over the place. There was a huge grassy area which lay empty under a cold grey sky in the winter days, and in summer was covered with people, young men and girls, who rolled around wantonly on the grass, free to do as they liked, as if they were in their own bedrooms. Their ringing laughter could be heard all around.

On Sundays Leybesh felt he was at a fair. Early in the morning he walked like a leisured gentleman in Rotten Row. On the long stretch of well-trodden earth rode ladies and gentlemen in black close-fitting riding coats, with stiff hats on their aristocratic heads, and shiny, elegant boots on their feet. Both the ladies and gentlemen wore riding breeches, so that it was difficult to tell the difference between them. They rode along in the fresh early morning air on glossy horses with small hooves, dainty, intelligent faces and eyes which seemed to sparkle with laughter. Some galloped, while some walked slowly alongside each other, the riders chatting and laughing. Their laughter was so melodious, merry and carefree, that you would have thought there was no war on at all.

Leybesh stared and stared at them, then he spat in disgust and walked off to the "madhouse" at Hyde Park Corner. Listening to the speakers, he didn't *entirely* agree with the entrenched pacifist standing on a soapbox, bawling his head off. The man was trying to make such important points that he wanted everyone to hear them. He tried to drown out the neighboring speakers who were standing less than three feet away from him. He was sweating, the veins in his temples and long skinny neck stood out as thick as rope, and his wrinkled skin was brick red. But he had a calm expression on his face, and he even smiled at the dissenting shouts from members of the public. He seized the moment when the listeners were quiet, and continued:

"Don't you see the stupidity of it? You'll join up, you'll be crippled, you'll be flayed like a carcass, or you'll die. Your children will be orphans, your wives widows, or perhaps even the mistresses of those for whom you have sacrificed yourselves. It is an imperialist war. The capitalists are fighting each other; what they steal from us every day, they are now trying to pinch from each other. And they send *us*, the victims of their theft, into the battlefield to fight their wars for them. They convince us that it's 'for King and Country,' and even if it were, what has all that to do with us? Whose 'country' is it? Not ours, at any rate. Do we get a great deal from the country? All we have is the right to work our fingers to the bone and to starve. And if we can't get any work, then they just let us die like dogs. They take the cream. They send their children to university – they should send the brats off to the battlefields and let *them* get butchered. What can they do to you, if you refuse to go? The worst they can do is put you in jail. Well, I ask you, is it not better to sit out the war in prison, and then come home to your wives and children as healthy men, and be able to start your lives again? What have you got to lose?"

Voices in the crowd shouted:

"Get him off! He's a traitor! He's betraying his own country! He's a spy! Arrest him: he wants the kaiser to win the war. String him up!"

"Comrades!" shouted Leybesh suddenly, "Friends! Just one word! A single word!"

The din was deafening but someone shouted:

"Let him speak! Let's hear what he has to say!"

It was impossible to say how or why it happened, but suddenly everything went so quiet you could hear a pin drop, and Leybesh started speaking:

"Friends! Everyone is shouting the same thing: defend your own country! Certainly we have to defend ourselves. We should remember though, that the world belongs to those who toil, those who build it. Only those people and nobody else have the right to enjoy the fruits of their labor."

Clapping was heard. The pacifist shouted, "Down with the warmongers!"

"Go to Rotten Row," continued Leybesh, "and you'll see healthy young men galloping around on horses, flirting with girls, breathing in the fresh air in order to sharpen their appetite for all the good food which someone else prepares for them."

The policeman on duty was listening with a quiet smile. It didn't cross his mind to put a stop to any of the speakers. Let them talk, what did it matter? The English policeman had broad shoulders.

Beside the skinny pacifist was another Englishman, a tall, hefty, fresh-faced man with ruddy cheeks, standing on a tiny wobbly platform. He spoke in a relaxed manner, with a clear voice. From time to time he wiped his face with a clean handkerchief and smiled with sparkling blue eyes. He preached nationalism, arguing that it was the sacred duty of every Englishman worthy of the name to join the army and defend his homeland:

"It is your sacred duty to fight to the last man for your king and your country," he said, warming to his topic, "if you want to be worthy of bearing the name of Englishman. Think of Lord Nelson!" He looked round triumphantly with a smile, which seemed to say, "Can anyone claim that I am not correct?"

Again there was clapping and shouts of "hear, hear!" and of "down with him!"

The pacifist urged one of his supporters to cause a bit of a riot to drown out his opponent.

Slightly further off, a young Indian doctor was speaking. He had white even teeth and large laughing black eyes, whose whites looked dazzling in his dark face. He maintained that it was the duty of all good Indians to make use of this moment of opportunity and fight heroically for India's liberation.

A bit further on a young Jew with a gold pince-nez on his fat white nose was talking, more with his hands than with his mouth, which had thick crimson girlish lips. He was explaining how important it was for the Jewish people to have their own Jewish legion.

A priest with a shiny round collar was saying that in a time of war, people should go to church more often. There was a nun with a dark wrinkled face in a black habit and veil, and someone with a long grey beard, whose thesis was that he was a member of the ten lost tribes, and that, although he was not a Jew, he was really a Jew. "We," he insisted, "are the only true Jews." Taking his sparse beard, which reached his waist, in both his skinny hands, he swore that this was true.

Mrs. Pankhurst was also speaking, surrounded by hundreds of women and a few men. She stood there, speaking with great feeling:

"We will not rest, we will not stay silent, we will speak and agitate, never letting the matter rest and never resting ourselves, until they give equality to us women. Did you see how our dear friend threw herself in front of horses and was trampled to death in order to draw attention to our cause? We are prepared to bring many, many more sacrifices in order to liberate women, and we *will* liberate them!"

Voices were heard:

"Hear, hear!!"

"Good old Mrs. Pankhurst!!!"

Chapter 30

It was the winter before the Armistice. The city was shrouded in fog all winter long. The sky was hardly ever visible. When it occasionally did manage to free itself from the fog, it looked like a heavy sheet of iron which was just about to fall on the city and its people, destroying both.

Berman had already bought a great deal of goods. He had decided he was not going to buy anything, apart from rare bargains, and he was not going to sell, but rather wait and see. He was not worried about how much the market in diamonds was going to fall; he did not fear for *his* goods. But it was prudent to live frugally nevertheless.

He was content in his warm house, which seemed even cozier because of the bad weather outside. Since he didn't have anything else to do, he sought useful occupations for himself. He put on his white smock and busied himself during the evenings, cooking the next day's midday meal. From his gentile neighbor on the first floor he even learned how to mend shoes. He bought himself the necessary tools and set to work. When there weren't any shoes to mend he tried to read a religious book, but somehow he did not have the taste for it anymore. In Antwerp, when the children were still at home, when people were always coming and going and he had a thousand different business matters to attend to, he had really enjoyed reading holy texts, because it had calmed him down.

Now things were too calm. It was so quiet that one could hear the buzzing of a fly. The moment he started looking at a book, the sizzling sounds in the black iron stove gradually faded, his head sank down and his snoring could be heard throughout the house. Often, the only thing which interrupted his delightful nap, when he rested his head on the table, was the sound of a whistle and the cry: "Take cover!"

Berman knew this whistle well, and he would rub his eyes, focus his startled gaze and, a moment later, he would be sitting in his usual corner of the cellar, with both hands tucked into the wide sleeves of his warm dressing gown, his broad skullcap on his head; his nose looked pinched and livid, and his eyes stared blankly, like those of a dead fish. Then the danger was past, the enemy had been driven away. They could again mount the few steps from the cellar to the bedroom. But Berman would carry on sitting there with a bewildered air, fear in his dark eyes, and aching all over his body as if someone had broken his bones. Rochl would rouse him:

"Gedaliah, it's over, thank God!"

Then he would drag himself up the steps and sit on his bed. With his fringed undergarment draped over his stomach he would recite *krishme,* saying earnestly, "threescore valiant men … of the valiant of Israel." Then he would go to sleep.

And so it went on throughout that long winter. The only things Berman still got a little pleasure from were earning a little bit of money on a weekday – once in a blue moon – and taking an occasional walk up Whitechapel Road on a Sunday afternoon. On these Sundays, Rochl had to put on her expensive black fur coat with the big brown skunk collar, a broad border at the hem, and deep cuffs round her wrists. This coat really engulfed her now. Her face had become pinched and grey. She wore a pair of white leather gloves which were now too big for her thin hands. When she completed the outfit with a broad-brimmed hat on top of her wig, Rochl herself was hardly visible at all.

Berman, in his expensive black overcoat with its beaver collar and lapels, and his elegant beard, looked like a king as he strolled among the Jewish men and women who had come out into this wide street for a Sunday afternoon walk. All the burly, corpulent men in their good winter coats somehow seemed ordinary and workaday in comparison with Berman. His coat was neatly buttoned, while theirs flapped open. From their fat stomachs hung thick chains with dangling gold coins or Stars of David, diamond pins glittered in their cravats, and large gold signet rings adorned their stumpy fingers. And yet they lacked the true stamp of affluence. Somehow they all looked like paupers who had come up in the world and wanted to show off their fortune. Their wives, with their double chins and black fur coats which were also trimmed with skunk fur wobbled along on their fat legs wearing high-heeled shoes which pinched their feet. They held their gloves in their hands to show off the thick rings on their fingers, which were coarsened from too much peeling of potatoes and frying of fish. They, too, looked like jumped-up servant girls in comparison with the shriveled little figure of Rochl.

Gradually, the Bermans became a focus of interest for the regular Sunday afternoon promenaders of Whitechapel. People couldn't fathom what sort of people they were and they decided that he must have been a rabbi from St. Petersburg, and began to give him the title of "Rabbi."

"Look, there's the rabbi," the wives would say, pressing up against their husbands in order to make way for the Bermans.

Berman didn't realize that they were talking about him, and he just walked on with Rochl to visit a niece of hers, a restaurant owner, whom Berman had come across here in London. The niece received them with a broad smile on her greasy face. She felt great delight and pride that Berman was visiting her, and served them portions of hot salt beef with pickled cucumber, positively beaming with pleasure: "Eat it in good health!" she said.

She had a waiter bring large chunks of apple cake and clear red tea in sparkling glasses. Whenever she managed to find a free moment, she came over to have a chat, asking if they wanted anything more to eat, begging them to have just a little bit more for her sake.

The diners at the other tables kept looking over and trying to guess who the two people at the private table were. Rochl's niece didn't leave them in suspense for too long. "They're my uncle and aunt. He's extremely wealthy, you know, very, very rich!"

"Is it true that he's a rabbi?" the customers asked.

"He was before the war," she answered without hesitation, transforming Berman into a rabbi so that she would get even more reflected glory as payment for the free meal she had served to them.

Berman didn't stay long in the niece's restaurant. The latter protested: "Why are you in such a hurry, auntie? Let uncle stay for a little while." But Berman was in a hurry to get home. "We don't want to make ourselves cheap!" And if the niece insisted, he had a good excuse: he had to get back because of his father, even though, in fact, he had taken his father in to a neighbor, a man who would have given away everything he owned for a game of cards. Every Sunday he sent his wife and children out somewhere and a crowd of his friends came in; they all rolled up their sleeves and started playing okey or sixty-six. They were so absorbed in their game that they completely forgot old Chaim Yoysef, who sat by the stove reading a prayer book or dozing.

Rochl longed to stay on in the cheerful, brightly lit restaurant, watching the people coming and going. It helped her to forget her problems for a while. But Berman was in a hurry. He always had to go home just when things were getting really lively in Whitechapel, just when the young people began to erupt out of the narrow lanes. From the dark crooked little houses, which seemed in danger of collapsing and burying the Jewish poor under the earth, young men and girls appeared, all dressed up, noisy, buzzing like bees, making the streets echo with merry laughter, and dazzling the eye with bright clothes and cheap make-up.

Berman turned up his nose at them. He detested their long ball gowns which swept along Whitechapel Road, and their too-tight jackets, which they wore in order to look slimmer. With his expertise he could judge the quality of their silver fox furs. Nor could he stand the young men with tight shirt cuffs, patent leather shoes, yellow suede gloves and thick, rolled umbrellas à la the Prince of Wales.

"They think they're fooling everyone!" he said to Rochl. "Have you ever gone into the little lanes where they live? There's hardly room for a person to walk along them. It's really disgusting, the way they're parading through the streets, showing off in front of the *goyim* at a time like this!" Berman seemed to have forgotten that he and his wife were also parading around, all dressed up.

Rochl, however, really liked the hubbub of the street. The shops, too, were all open, with light pouring out of their windows. The dainty shoes in the big shoe shops were so nicely arranged that they seemed to be calling out to the people: "Come in, try us on!" There were furniture shops with bedrooms, dining rooms and salons fit for a king.

Red and green satin and silk cascaded down amid the furniture, as beautifully draped as in the most elegant West End shops. The charming wax figures in the clothes shops were dressed in expensive ball gowns, furs, or flowery silk frocks, which reminded Rochl of summer and of lovely flowerbeds. There were fine men's shirts, ties and gloves. And, equally elegant, was the waxen young man with slick black hair in a dark red silk dressing gown, sitting in a relaxed posture in the shop window. His carefree, sophisticated smile attracted the customers.

Looking at him, Rochl forgot everything for a while; even Berman looked at him in amazement:

"Who buys all these expensive things? After all, the alleyways around here are simply packed with poor people, Jews and non-Jews alike."

The smartly dressed Jewish men and women had managed to make a little money because of the war, and with the few shillings they had earned through working like slaves all day and half the night, they bought some bits and pieces of jewelry, to have something set aside "for a rainy day." And in the meantime they dressed up in this finery, put on their rings, wore their brooches on the décolleté of their old dresses, and pushed their way along the crowded pavement. On the opposite side, the pavement was deserted and forlorn, and the few shops there were so huddled together that one could hardly distinguish one from another. The most prominent position on that side of the street was taken up by a large black church built in the Gothic style, with a spire which stretched up into the sky. It seemed to have a kind of fearful mystery about it. The building was adorned by all sorts of lacy tracery, where flocks of skinny pigeons had made their nests. It cast long spreading shadows which swallowed up the surrounding area into its blackness.

Even tramps avoided that side of the street. They were to be seen shuffling through the crowd: a pair of inflamed eyes, a swollen scabby mouth, tufts of matted hair surrounding a black, crumpled rag, which was the face, and old newspapers, secured by dirty string, wrapped round their loins. They only stopped to pick up a cigarette end or a bit of crumpled paper, in case there was something inside it. If they found nothing, they carried on along the brightly lit pavement to claim a place under a bridge somewhere to lay the bundle of newspapers which was their bedding and prepare for the night. Among the well-dressed people they looked like heaps of dirt which the road sweeper had swept together and then left lying there.

Berman looked at them, and it occurred to him that Dovid would look like them in his old age, if he couldn't provide for him, or find a solution to his problems. God willing, he *would* provide for him. As soon as Dovid came home, he would take him into the business and try his best to make a man of him. He would provide for him in his will. If only he came home safely, he would, with God's help, make him into a respectable person. Dovid could still become a diamond merchant.

This thought gave him such a warm feeling in his heart that he suddenly felt full of kindness towards humanity, which led him to sing the praises of Rochl's niece:

"A fine woman!" he said, and Rochl was thrilled to hear him praising one of her family, for once.

Chapter 31

Winter was drawing to a close. The square patch of sunlight on the floor of Rochl's kitchen got bigger every day, and the shadows in the corners ever smaller. The black range was cold. It was not needed during the warm weather leading up to Passover.

Just like the range, Rochl's face looked darker as the days got brighter. She was not needed either, and so she wandered aimlessly round the flat. She felt that Passover didn't really have anything to do with her, and apart from her aged father-in-law, she had no one to talk to. Her husband was taken up with his business dealings again, and when he came home in the evenings, she didn't dare to mention Dovid's name. Dovid was the only subject that interested her now.

If she went to call on her daughter, the cheerful atmosphere there irritated her. Jeannette dressed her maid in a black satin dress and the daintiest cambric apron a servant ever wore. She had the finest muslin collar and cuffs and the most beautiful cap to be found in all of London. Every afternoon, the moment she finished her work, the maid dressed up and manicured her fingernails. These were Jeannette's wishes.

Jeannette had bought herself a little curly-haired dog just like those belonging to the heroines in her French novels, and she wandered around all day in dressing gowns of silk, satin and velvet, embroidered with dogs, monkeys, opium-smoking Chinamen, Arabian women with flasks of wine balanced on their heads, and French dancers.

She was the best of friends with her maid, so that the latter almost forgot she was a servant. The mistress and the maid exchanged all sorts of confidences. They laughed and joked together and played with the little dog. Sometimes, however, in the middle of some game or other, Jeannette would suddenly have a fit of madness and start screaming at her in such a rage that the maid soaked the kitchen with her tears. But just as suddenly Jeannette would call her back and make up with her, blaming it on her nerves, and they would be good friends again.

Rochl seldom went to her daughter's house, but when she did, she would observe all this and she felt that Jeannette was even wilder than she had been before. She didn't feel at ease here, but she didn't feel at ease in her own house either. She preferred, however, to be in her own kitchen with her old, crippled father-in-law.

But her daughter would prevent her leaving, swearing she *did* usually get dressed and it was only that day that she was going around all day in her dressing gown. She begged her mother to sit down and even sent the maid out to buy something nice for her to eat. Rochl saw her reflection in all the mirrors at once, looking more dead than alive, and it seemed impossible to her that she would ever have the strength to walk back to her home.

"Oh, Mama, you look awful, you're wearing yourself out," Jeannette greeted her each time with what she thought was an appropriate remark.

"I don't need to wear myself out; they've done it for me already. The doctor says that it's nothing, that I have a weak heart, and that's all, he says. But I have a feeling I won't last very long. If only my death could save my son, I'd die happy!" She cried hot tears of pity for Dovid and for herself.

When Jeannette scolded her mother, telling her to drive away these melancholy thoughts, Rochl sobbed all the more, just managing to get out the words, which Jeannette already knew by heart:

"I hope I'll be proved a liar! But I tell you, my heart's giving me warning signals!"

When her son-in-law took her home after finishing his supper, she begged him not to try to console her, because that made her even more agitated. So they walked in complete silence along the quiet streets of North London. Their every step echoed on the empty pavements. The houses were just as silent, all the windows covered with expensive curtains and heavy shutters. The different scents of spring rose from the front gardens. Green spikes of tulips appeared in the flowerbeds, trees were full of sap and new life, ready to burst into blossom at any moment. Some already had plump buds and little bright green leaves, as tiny as match heads.

This scent of resurgent life irritated Rochl. It was as if she begrudged the trees their rebirth, and she started to walk more quickly, wanting to get back to her house with the black range and the crippled father-in-law. The chirping of the birds grated on her and she pulled her hat down over her ears and turned up her collar, trying to shut out the birdsong.

"Are you cold, Mother-in-law?"

"No, no!" the mother-in-law (who was considerably younger than her son-in-law) answered agitatedly.

On the first floor, above the Bermans, lived a family who had experienced the same tragedy as many other families had. Their son had gone off to the front, hale and hearty, and all that came home was a package of clothes, a couple of medals and an accolade from the Ministry of War, which stated that he had fought as a hero and died as a hero. From that moment, every time there was a knock at the door, Rochl thought it was the postman with a black-edged envelope. It didn't help when her family reassured her, telling her a thousand times that more soldiers came home safely than were killed, that, like everything else in the world, it was just a matter of luck: that if it was your destiny to enjoy a long life, you would come back, even from the Other World, and if not, then you would, God forbid, fall sick and die anyway.

Rochl listened to what they said, agreed, and did actually realize that because it had happened to the family upstairs didn't mean that it would happen to them. She spat to ward off the evil eye, and tried to drive out the bad thoughts, but they kept on gnawing and boring away at her. The stone she felt lying on her heart wouldn't budge.

Berman prepared the Passover meal by himself. He ordered matzos, chose the fowl at the butcher's, ordered wine and all sorts of other drinks. He cleaned the house, making sure it was kosher for Passover. He went around in the evenings dressed in his white smock, boiling and frying food, and showing Rochl all the good things he had bought for the festival; he wanted her to feel the hens, and he examined the eggs with one eye shut to check their purity, with just as much interest as he checked the purity of his diamonds.

Rochl wouldn't touch or test anything, but nodded in agreement to everything, wishing he would leave her in peace.

When Passover arrived, the long table in the front room was covered with a white starched tablecloth for the first Seder. There were three bouquets of flowers which Jeannette had got her maid to deliver. All the silver was spread out on the table, and a decanter of glowing wine surrounded by golden goblets stood on a golden tray, with some dusty bottles of wine from the Land of Israel beside them. In the open grate a fire burned brightly, giving out a lovely intimate warmth and a feeling of comfortable affluence. All the lights were lit and shone brightly. Tall candles were burning in the silver candlesticks, making the atmosphere festive.

Berman sat at the top of the table wearing a white robe and a white skullcap with silver embroidery, and opposite him sat his old father, similarly attired. They looked like two kings. Berman's daughter and son-in-law also sat at the table.

Rochl was wearing a festive dress, but she looked downcast. Jacques sat at his father's right side, ready to ask the Four Questions. Suddenly, there was a soft knock at the door and the neighbor from upstairs came in, dressed in mourning, with a thick crepe veil over her hat, covering her face. She carried a basket in one black-gloved hand and in the other she held a letter. The woman lifted the veil slightly from her pale face, and was about to say something, but before she was able to get out a single word, Rochl stood up, made a grab for the letter with her outstretched hand, but couldn't get quite near enough to take it. She gave a sob and screamed: "God help me, it's my son!" then said softly "I'm not well." Then she swayed and fell to the floor like a stone.

There was great confusion. Everyone started shouting, pulling her, pouring brandy between her clenched teeth. They pinched her and tried to coax her back to life. The neighbor's husband and children, all in black, came running down from the floor above.

Forgetting that he was a cripple, old Reb Chaim Yoysef rushed towards his daughter-in-law, stumbled, and pulled down the tablecloth. Dishes clattered everywhere with a silvery ringing sound. The wine splashed out of the gold goblets. The tablecloth caught fire and lay blazing on the floor beside the dead woman.

The shouting and wailing rose heavenwards. Jeannette's maid brought a pot of water from the kitchen and tried to put out the fire. Jacques was the only one who had the presence of mind to call the doctor, who lived nearby.

The doctor was bewildered at the strange scene which met his eyes: two Jews dressed all in white, a family in black, gold and silver dishes lying about the floor, and a dead body lying in a pool of water and wine, with fire burning round it. The living, who themselves looked like corpses, were coaxing her or wringing their hands. A small woman dressed in black was standing in a corner, staring with glazed eyes at one spot.

All the doctor could do was to certify that Rochl was dead, and that the probable cause of death was a heart attack.

For the duration of the festival the house was full of good friends. Jeannette kept horrifying the already traumatized family with fainting fits. Reb Chaim Yoysef went to bed and lay there like a lump of clay, not moving a muscle. He had become completely paralyzed, though he could still speak. He had forgotten that the doctor had pronounced her dead, and kept asking "Well, how is she? How's Rochl?"

"Better!" they grunted at him and turned away.

"Better? God be praised!" The sight of the old man's yellow, wrinkled face, and the dead smile in his dull eyes, frightened them. It seemed as if death itself was smiling at them.

It was some time after the funeral that Berman came across the letter which the woman had been given by the postman as she was coming in from the street. It hadn't occurred to him till then that this letter had caused his wife's death and his father's complete paralysis. Now he turned the envelope over and over, looking at his name on it. A shudder went through his body when he opened it. The letter began in German:

Sehr geehrter Herr Berman,

Please inform me immediately of your price per carat. If you agree to the price I have offered, the parcel is as good as sold. If not, I should like to know your price. Please reply immediately. My best wishes to your wife, and I wish you a kosher and happy Passover.

Hochachtungsvoll,
Julius Shapiro

Chapter 32

After the war Berman went home to Antwerp. It was the middle of summer, and the city looked completely different: wider and brighter. The sky seemed higher than in London, higher than he remembered it in Antwerp before the war.

The city smelt of clay, lime, brick and concrete, and almost all the houses were covered with scaffolding. Workers in white overalls spattered with paint and lime were plastering, painting and cleaning everywhere. Some were throwing bricks up onto the scaffolding, which were skillfully caught by the workers above. There was the sound of shouting up from below and down from above. A new life was being constructed.

Berman opened up his house. It smelt like a tomb, and the darkness filled him with terror. He opened shutters, windows and doors – it was a ruin, not a home. The carpets were trampled down, torn, full of cigarette burns, their colors obliterated. The plush sofas and chairs were scattered around, sagging, threadbare, with wires and stuffing sticking out of them. The table was scratched and the piano was ruined. Wallpaper was peeling from the walls, which were covered with greenish mold. The tiles in the kitchen were brown and filthy, and some had fallen off. The crockery was broken and everywhere there was dust, dust and more dust. Dust and cobwebs, in which fat flies were caught. The spiders had tirelessly spun themselves new webs.

"Papa, I don't like it here, I'm scared," said Jacques. He now looked like a young man, yet he spoke to his father like a child: "Ugh!"

Berman rented a house. He soon calmed down, corresponded

with lawyers, kept writing and running around, moving heaven and earth, until he was awarded a handsome sum in compensation, after which he began to renovate his home.

When the renovation work was finished, Jeannette came over from London. When she saw the new, white-painted house, she exclaimed:

"Papa, don't dare to buy one single piece of furniture without me! Nowadays you can get modern furniture which is totally different from the old rubbish. You won't know what to buy. Do you hear me, Papa? You must rely entirely on my judgment!"

Dovid came home. He had aged. His jet black hair was streaked with white and his face was lined like an old man's, which gave him an earnest, dignified appearance. He did not move into his father's house, but went to Brussels. In Austria, where he had been a prisoner of war, he had learned a trade. He had become an electrician. He had written the same answer to all Gitele's letters:

"I will provide for the child, but it's all over between us."

One Sunday morning Jacques came to see Dovid and begged him to let him come and stay with him.

"I can't stay there. I have to get away. It's horrible in that house. Everything is new. That madwoman has bought the most expensive stuff. She's off her head! She has forgotten Mama already, as if it was just a bad dream. And she keeps on kissing him all the time."

"Who?"

"Our father."

"You can stay here with pleasure, Jacques. You can stay right now; you don't have to go back home." Dovid was pleased Jacques had come because he was finding the loneliness difficult to bear.

Dovid made tea and asked Jacques to relate once again exactly how it all had happened, how their mother had died. Jacques told him everything, not just how she died, but what her life had been like since Dovid had left. And so the brothers remembered their dead mother, whom they had deeply loved and respected. The eyes of both filled with tears, and they vowed not to have anything to do with their father or his money.

Berman was alone in the house. He had no one to speak to. He stared at the furniture, the elegant wallpaper, the mirrors, which showed him that he was an old man with a white beard. He felt he really didn't belong in these surroundings.

Everything was so new and so different. Not only his house but the city was new, shining and cared for. Even the Jewish district was fresh and new, with no sign of its original dark appearance. But all this newness annoyed Berman. He could not stand it.

When he went into the Fortunia he found even that had been changed. They had installed some kind of strange machines. All day young merchants threw coins into them, and colored balls started whirling round. The merchants stood shoulder to shoulder around these machines, as if they had all gone mad, peering with stupid, staring eyes to see where the mighty ball would land, as if this were their only aim in life.

All this drove him back home. He sat down and the image of Rochl floated in front of his eyes. Ah, she had really looked after him. She had treated him like a kaiser. And now?

"*Oy!* It's horrible being alone. My sons don't want to know me, my daughter's in London living with that old man. How will it all end?"

He was filled with self-pity and Reb Beynish, the matchmaker, with his sheepskin collar came into his mind. Yes, thank God, he, Berman, was still a vigorous man, and Gitele was really a rather fine woman. It was as easy as spitting nowadays to get a divorce from a husband in Russia. So he sat down and wrote a letter to Reb Beynish, which he intended to send to him in London. He felt a lot more cheerful. Gitele would certainly be delighted, suddenly to come into wealth like his!

Having posted his letter, he paced around in his elegant, modern dining room, and a little smile stole across his face and got tangled up in his grey whiskers. Yes, he thought, with God's help he would start a new life.

He was full of satisfaction at this prospect, and then it came into his mind that he had to…no, he didn't *have* to, but nevertheless tomorrow morning he *would*, God willing, send for the monumental sculptor and order tombstones for Rochl and for his father. Yes, God willing, he would do that before his wedding. And another thing: he would overlook the fact that Dovid had fallen out with him. He would send for him and Jacques and give both of them money to start up in business. They should also have a good life.

The little smile hiding among his whiskers broadened, spread into his eyes and came to rest in his beard. The smile became a burst of joyful laughter, and a feeling of happiness came over him. Delighted with himself and his plans, he started looking among his father's things, which they had sent him from the "home of rest" for old people in London. It occurred to him that it was possible that his father, despite his illness, had managed to write a will of some sort. He wanted to carry out his father's wishes to the letter. And indeed he found a note.

It was a crumpled little piece of paper. The handwriting zigzagged and the letters were shaky, some big and clumsy and others tiny and round, just like his father's handwriting had been when he was still in good health. Peering at the piece of paper, Berman made a great effort to read it. The more he looked, the more his face darkened, and his eyes became larger and more melancholy:

"I ask you to respect my last wish. In God's name, do not put up a tombstone for me. I rue the day when I came to live with you. I do not want a tombstone bought with your money. Chaim Yoysef ben Rivke."

All night, Berman paced up and down his luxurious modern dining room, back and forth, back and forth. He didn't even think about going to bed. He didn't think at all. The crumpled piece of paper lay on the polished table, staring at his every step. Only at daybreak did he collapse, exhausted, into the deep plush armchair and fall asleep. When he awoke in the morning the letter was still lying there, grubby and crumpled as before. He looked at it. It seemed to him not like a piece of paper, but like a dirty tattered life lying spread out before him. It drove him out of the house. He grabbed his hat, put it on his grey head, and went out into the streets and lanes of Antwerp.

The piece of paper didn't take its eyes off him.

Glossary

Chapter 1

"In het park van de nachtegaal": A slightly risqué popular Flemish *kermis* song of the time, referring to the Nachtegaalenpark to the south of the city, which would then have been on the edge of the city and is now in a residential district of Antwerp.

Spa: A popular resort to the southeast of Antwerp.

Chapter 2

The Keyserlei: De Keyser lei (named after a 19th century painter, Nicaise De Keyser) is a busy street in the commercial centre of the city.

The pious Hassidim: The populist movement known as Hassidism, to which Esther Kreitman's father belonged, arose in Eastern Europe in the middle of the eighteenth century. Its adherents, the Hassidim, grouped themselves round a *rebbe* or charismatic religious leader. Hassidism placed great emphasis on personal, ecstatic communication with God through prayer, music, and dance.

Shnorrers: A Yiddish word for a scrounger, commonly used in English too.

Chapter 3

Shtetl: The word describes the small towns in Poland and Russia where communities of Jews lived.

Talmud: A collection of Jewish writings which make up the basis of Jewish religious law, consisting of early scriptural interpretations (*Mishnah*) and the later commentaries on them (*Gemara*).

Reb Elyohu Kornhendler: "Reb" is the Yiddish term for "Mr".

Shtibl (plural: *shtiblekh*)*:* A small Hassidic prayer house. The term is commonly used by Jews in English also.

The boys and girls called each other "du": *Du* is the familiar form of address in Yiddish. Normally the formal *ir* would be used by adults until they knew each other very well. Freethinking groups like this would always use the familiar *du* as a matter of principle.

Chapter 4

To light a memorial candle: Jews light a memorial or *yortsayt'* candle every year on the anniversary of the death of a close relative.

Chapter 5

Melkboer (Flemish): Milkman; *Dag menieër* (Flemish): "Good day, sir."

Borgerhout: Until the 1980s Borgerhout was a separate municipality to the east of Antwerp, near the old Jewish diamond district. Now it is a district of the city in which many Jews still live today.

Kosher: Ritually pure according to certain religious laws, suitable for consumption by Jews.

Sint-Anneke: At that time the village of Sint-Anneke on the left bank of the River Scheldt, with its seafood restaurants, spa, and beach was a popular destination for tourist excursions. Now a dormitory town for Antwerp.

Chapter 6

Mazel tov, mazel: Good fortune. Both terms used when congratulating someone and wishing someone good luck.

Shabbes: The Jewish Sabbath, the day of rest which begins at sundown on Friday evening and ends at sundown on Saturday evening. Traditionally Jews light candles and eat a special meal with wine on Friday evening. The extra expense was often a problem for poorer families.

Ken eynore: (From Hebrew: *ayin hora*), literally "no evil eye". Said to ward off bad luck, especially when making some optimistic assertion or praising someone.

Krishme: The prayer beginning "Hear, oh Israel, the Lord our God, the Lord is One," which is said in the morning and evening, and before retiring for the night.

Chapter 7

Shikse: Rather derogatory term for a non-Jewish girl or woman.

Bar mitzva: The ceremony which represents the entering of the thirteen-year-old boy into religious responsibility. At his *bar mitzva* the boy is called up to read from the Torah (the Pentateuch, the first five books of the Hebrew Bible), in the synagogue, and a celebration follows.

Zurenborg: A smart district on the eastern side of Antwerp, near Borgerhout.

Vogelmarkt: A large market in the centre of the city, where all sorts of things can be bought, including birds, dogs, and other animals.

Gemara: A collection of commentaries on the Talmud (see note for chapter 3). The term *Gemara* is often used to refer to the whole Talmud.

Chapter 8

Kugel: A dish made with noodles or potatoes.

Goy (pl. goyim): A non-Jewish male.

Chapter 9

Loupe: The magnifying glass through which diamonds are examined.

Chapter 10

Shprintse: A Jewish female name.

Chapter 11

Kaddish: The mourners' prayer, said at a funeral and on the anniversary of someone's death.

Goeie koop (Flemish): A great bargain; *charmant* (French): charming.

"Lift up your hands….": Psalm 134, verse 2.

Shochet: A ritual slaughterer, who kills animals according to Jewish Law to ensure that they are *kosher,* suitable for consumption.

Mohel: The man licensed to perform the circumcision of Jewish males.

Tefillin: Phylacteries. Small leather boxes containing biblical verses on pieces of parchment. The phylacteries are bound onto the forehead and left arm by leather straps during morning prayers.

"*Thou shaft not suffer a witch to live*": Exodus 22:18.

Chapter 12

A Gerer Hassid: The various groups of Hassidim are known by the name of the place from which their *rebbe* originated. The Gerer Hassidim originated in the town of Ger, in central Poland.

Sfas Emes (literally "language of truth"): this was the name given to Yehuda Leyb Rottenberg, the second *rebbe* of the Gerer Hassidim, who reigned from 1870–1904.

Chapter 14

Cheder (literally "room"): A Jewish school for young boys, teaching Hebrew language and Jewish religion, which was usually held in the teacher's house.

Torah: The Pentateuch, the first five books of the Hebrew Bible.

Yeshiva boys: Yeshivas are institutes for the study of the Talmud attended by pious young men, known in Yiddish as "*yeshiva bokherim*" (yeshiva boys). They studied long hours and were usually poor and undernourished.

Rashi: Rabbi Solomon ben Isaac (1040–1105), one of the most important commentators on the Bible. ("Rashi" is an acronym of the first letters of the Yiddish version of his name: Rabbi Shloyme Yitskhaki.)

Chapter 15

Cogels-Oyslei: An elegant street in Antwerp with beautiful art nouveau architecture.

Mayrev: The evening prayer.

Chapter 16

High Holidays: The ten-day period encompassing the two most important Jewish religious festivals, Rosh HaShana (the New

Year) and Yom Kippur (the Day of Atonement), which falls in the autumn.

Feast … every Yom Kippur: Yom Kippur is a strict day of fasting, where neither food nor liquid may be consumed, from sunset on the eve of Yom Kippur until sunset the following day. Jewish secularist and socialist movements sometimes demonstratively ate during that period to register their rejection of the religious practices.

… to pluck white hens in the kitchen: They are making the preparations for the meal which will end the Yom Kippur fast.

The atonement ceremony: An old rite in which a live cockerel is swung round the head before being slaughtered, and the words are recited: "This is my substitute, this is my vicarious offering, this is my atonement. This cock will go to its death, but I shall have a long and pleasant life of peace." This rite was rejected by scholars of Jewish law as early as the thirteenth century, and is seldom practised nowadays, except in some ultra-Orthodox communities.

This grey fortress: This is the Castle Steen on the eastern bank of the River Scheldt. Built sometime after 900 C.E., it is one of the oldest fortresses in Europe and functioned as a prison for several centuries The artist Pieter Paul Rubens lived in the castle during his old age, and it is now home to the Scheepvaartmuseum (Belgian National Maritime Museum).

Lehavdil (literally: to divide one thing from another): This is said by pious Jews when a sacred and a profane thing are mentioned in one sentence, or immediately after each other. The girl is embarrassed that her traditional religious upbringing has slipped out in this way in the presence of her new secular comrades.

Chapter 17

Kheshvan: The eighth month of the Jewish year, falling in October/November.

Chapter 18

Galician Jews: The province of Galicia was part of the Austro-Hungarian Empire. Traditionally, there was enmity or at least rivalry between the Galician and Polish Jews, as there was between the Russian, Polish, and Lithuanian Jews (see below in the next paragraph). Now, in addition to this, as subjects of the Austrian Emperor and the Russian Tsar respectively, the Galician and Russian/Polish/Lithuanian Jews found themselves on different sides in the conflict.

Efroim Yossel's kingdom: the speaker is referring ironically to Kaiser Franz Josef of Austria through a comic Yiddishised version of his name.

Landslayt: People who come from the same area or *shtetl* in Eastern Europe.

Chapter 23

Tailors' pressers: Those who ironed the clothing in its various stages of manufacture.

Yecke: Term commonly used by Jews for German Jews (sometimes thought to be derived from German: "Jacke," a jacket, because the assimilated German Jews wore short jackets in contrast to the Eastern European caftan).

"Rejoice, oh young man, in thy youth!": Ecclesiastes 11:9.

Nicholas the Third: The then Tsar, the repressive Nicholas II, was particularly feared and hated by his Jewish subjects.

Chapter 24

The café: The Diamond Bourse in Hatton Garden did not open till 1940. Until then business was conducted in the street or at Mrs Cohen's café in Greville Street. (I am indebted to Carole Timms for this information. HV)

Mezuzas: Small boxes containing a small piece of parchment with biblical verses, which Jews attach to the doorposts of their dwellings.

Chapter 25

Ha'pennies (halfpennies): A very small coin in the old British currency pre-1971. There were 480 halfpennies to the pound sterling.

Bloaters for a change: Kippers and bloaters are in fact both smoked herring, prepared in slightly different ways.

Bima: The platform in the synagogue from which the Torah is read.
Eyn Yankev: "The Fountain of Jacob," a popular religious book from the 16th century.

Chapter 28

Adar: The twelfth month of the Jewish year, falling in February or March.
L'chaim! (Hebrew): "To Life!" Words used in a toast.
Florins and half-crowns: British currency before 1971, the equivalent of ten pence and twelve and a half pence respectively in modern British currency.

Chapter 29

I remember, I remember...: A popular poem by Thomas Hood (1799-1845).
The "madhouse" at Hyde Park Corner: At Speakers' Corner on the edge of Hyde Park, anyone who wishes can speak on any issue, so that there is usually a cacophony, as speakers on themes from the conventional to the bizarre compete for the audience.
... we will liberate them: The struggle for women's suffrage in Britain was led by Emmeline Pankhurst and her daughter Christabel. The suffragette martyr who is mentioned here was Emily Wilding Davison who deliberately stepped in front of a horse owned by the king, shouting "Votes for women" at the Derby race of June 4th, 1913, in the presence of the Royal Family and the elite of society.

Chapter 30

Take cover!: In 1915, there were German Zeppelin raids over London and in 1917 bombing raids using aircraft. Both types of air raid caused casualties.
Threescore valiant men: This is part of a verse from the Song of Songs (3:7), which reads: "Behold his bed, which is Solomon's; threescore valiant men are about it, of the valiant of Israel."
Okey, sixty-six: Okey is played with coloured tiles, *sixty-six* is a card game. Both were popular with Eastern European Jews.

Chapter 31

Matzos: Crackers made from unleavened flour which are eaten instead of bread during the eight days of Passover.

Kosher for Passover: Religious Jews clean their homes thoroughly before Passover in order to make sure that no leavened bread or food with yeast in it remains in the house.

Examined the eggs… to check their purity: An egg which has even a speck of blood in it is not kosher.

The first Seder: The first of two ceremonial meals on the first two evenings of the Passover, during which the story of the exodus of the Children of Israel from Egypt is retold.

Four Questions: Near the beginning of the Passover Seder the youngest child present asks four questions about the festival of Passover, each beginning with: "Why is this night different from all other nights?"

Chapter 32

A husband in Russia: From this we can infer that Leybesh, like many enthusiastic young socialists, went to the emerging Soviet Union at the end of the First World War, or that he joined the Russian army, like Avrom Kreitman, under the 1917 agreement (see introduction).

Chaim Yoysef ben Rivke: "Chaim Yoysef, son of Rivke," the traditional form of Jewish names, emphasising the matrilineal descent.

Blitz and Other Stories

ייִחוס: דערציילונגען און סקיצן

Translated by Dorothee van Tendeloo

Contents

Introduction

Anita Norich

Esther Kreiman's 1949 collection of Yiddish short stories is entitled *Yikhus*, after the title of one of its fourteen stories. *Yikhus* means lineage, pedigree, legacy. It announces the importance of the past, signaling pride in one's descent from learned ancestors. In this collection, however, the term is best understood as ironic, pointing to the ongoing battle between learning and the modern prestige bestowed by money. Dorothee van Tendeloo's translation of these stories takes its title from another of Kreitman's stories, "Blitz." It changes the order of Kreitman's collection separating it into "Shtetl Stories" and "London Stories." In both locations, the characters are beset by war, poverty, and alienation.

Kreitman's most well-known story, "The New World," appears first in this collection (though not in the Yiddish collection, where it appears second). It may remind the English reader of Laurence Sterne's *Tristram Shandy*; like that novel, it presents the emotions, thoughts, and expectations of a child in utero. Perhaps this is

Kreitman's way of underscoring the need to imagine the lives of those whose voices are ignored or not heard: women, the poor, refugees, immigrants. These are the protagonists of almost all the stories in *Blitz*.

As always, Kreitman is critical of the rich and those who take advantage of others. In "Becoming a Tramp" the consumptive character has no job or home, and his wife is forced to sleep with her landlord in lieu of paying rent. The dead metaphor "it's a dog's life" or "he's gone to the dogs" becomes literal in "Dogs," where it is clear that animals are treated better than the poor. Kreitman's major themes are best summed up by a paragraph near the end of the story (and of the English story collection): "Young Jewish men who only yesterday were reading prayer books and who today are petit bourgeois, wealthy women who belong to all kinds of clubs and societies, had all come to try their luck [at the dog races].... They had all come to the dogs." And, not surprisingly, the poor man who bets everything he has, loses it all.

Kreitman is very critical of those who reject Judaism or retain only meaningless vestiges of its rituals. In "Breaking the Fast," for example, ritually observant Jews are mocked by other Jews; one Jewish character observes Yom Kippur by eschewing bacon and eggs for breakfast and eats (unkosher) chicken instead. In "Too Late," Mrs. Segal – "English through and through" – lights Sabbath candles but it is a pointless gesture. In "Jewish Nobility," [*Yikhes*] a father wishes to marry his daughter to a scholar in order to buy the *yikhes* his family lacks but learns that *yikhes,* like happiness, cannot be bought. The eponymous Jim remembers that he is a Jew only when he marries a Christian girl and then wonders who or what he is. The plight of Yiddish among assimilated Jews is another concern in several of these stories. One character must sell his Yiddish books to support his family ("She Is Not Blind"). "Two libraries" contrasts the library full of English books with the Jewish library where there are no Yiddish books.

In one of her most graphic stories, Kreitman describes the Blitz that she knew only too well. "Death is lurking everywhere" says the narrator of "Blitz," who compares Nazi airplanes to the Jewish myth about "spiders who once brought fire to the Temple." Just as spiders destroyed the Holy Temple in Jerusalem, bombs now threaten to destroy London and its inhabitants. Readers may be left wondering about all the other destructions invoked by this image. But Kreitman's stories also invoke images of what has not been destroyed: Yiddish, Jewish law, lore, and people.

The Shtetl Stories

The New World

די נײַע וועלט

I first felt unhappy while lying in my mother's belly. It was so hot! I twisted around, curled up and pretended not to be there. That's how it was for me.

Then, five months later, when I started to feel stirrings of life, it really got to me. I was bored stiff by the whole affair! I was truly fed up. Most of all, I was tired of lying in the dark all the time and I protested. But who could hear me? Crying was no good. So one day, after coming to the conclusion that my tears were useless, I began to look for other ways to free myself.

I wanted only one thing – to get out.

After some considerable thought, I realized that the best thing for me to do was to start fighting with my mother. So I began throwing myself around, stamping with rage, often poking her in the ribs: nothing could stop me, but it was all to no avail. The only result was that I got myself a bad name so that, for instance, whenever I got tired of lying on one side, and would turn over, to be a little more comfortable, they would start grumbling. Well, to cut a long story short, I did not get anywhere. I had to lie there the whole nine months – all the way to the end!

So, I comforted myself, as I did not have any choice. I would have to get used to coming out later. When, eventually, they let me out into God's world, I would already know how to behave.

I had no doubts that I would be an important guest. There were several reasons. First of all, I would often hear my mother talking to some woman or other, who later turned out to be my grandmother.

"It hurts a little, but I hardly feel it," my mother said repeatedly. "I am so happy. Oh, I used to be so afraid of being barren. Do you believe me? Two years after the wedding, and there was still nothing to show for it. Minke, the barren, was also convinced that she would give birth one day. So I thought, why should I be any luckier than her?"

"Well, praise be! With God's help it will all come to pass in good time; and the evil eye, God forbid, will not interfere," was the standard answer of my grandmother.

From such conversations, I gathered that I would be a welcome guest.

I knew that here in the other world, where I lived as a soul, whenever an important person was about to enter, everybody prepared to receive him with pomp and ceremony. First of all, an enormous brightness would spread itself throughout the heavens. Angels would be flying in to welcome him: merry, resplendent, and cloaked in bright sunlight. He would be surrounded by celebrating cherubs who radiated such holy joy that the person could only regret he had not died earlier. It is therefore no surprise that I, an important, long-awaited guest, expected to be born in a big, bright house where the sunlight would be streaming through the open windows.

I was looking forward to being greeted every morning by a multitude of birds singing me their song. Moreover, I was to be born on the first of Adar – a month of joy in the Hebrew calendar. "When Adar begins, people rejoice."

But here it comes – my first disappointment.

My mother is lying in a tiny room, an alcove. The bedroom is draped with dark curtains which keep out even the smallest ray of light. The little window has been tightly shut so that, God forbid, no fresh air can creep in. One must not catch a cold. The birds are, apparently, not very keen on barred light and closed windows, so they have gone elsewhere to look for a better, freer place in which to sing. In the meantime, there is not much happiness to speak of, since I have turned out to be a girl, and everybody in the room is disappointed, even my mother.

In short, there is no happiness at all. I am already almost half an hour old, but apart from a few slaps from some woman as I came into the world, no one looks at me. I feel so alone!

My grandmother comes in and smiles at my mother. She seems overjoyed – probably because her daughter has come through her ordeal all right. There is not so much as a glance in my direction.

"*Mazel tov* to you, my daughter, that you may live!"

"*Mazel tov,* that one may live with good fortune!"

My mother smiles too, but not at me.

"I would have been happier if it had been a boy," says my mother. My grandmother winks roguishly and comforts her. "It doesn't matter, there will be boys too."

I find it hard to believe all the things that are being said. What was I born for, if all this joy had nothing to do with me! I am already sick of it all. Oh, how I want to go back to the other world!

Suddenly I feel a strange chill all over my body and my thoughts are swept aside. I feel myself clasped between two big, fleshy hands, which lift me up in the air. I am shaking all over. Maybe – a frightening thought occurs to me – maybe they are going to put me back in for another few months? Brrr! The very idea makes me shiver.

But then something makes my head swim and everything is spinning round me. I am completely soaked, tiny as I am! Am I in a river? But no, a river is cool and pleasant, whereas I feel slightly scalded. But that doesn't bother me as much as my fear of what those two big clumsy hands are going to do with me. I am completely in their power.

Thank God! I have been taken out of the water. They carry me back into the alcove, all dried and dressed. Then I am passed around the room, everybody takes a look at me, says a few words. Finally, I am put back to bed. My mother puts some kind of sweet liquid thing in my mouth; I am really hungry for what the world has to offer.

My mother looks at me with kind, soft eyes, and it warms my heart.

A sweet fatigue comes over me and soon I am lost in a happy dream… but my happiness doesn't last long. I have been brutally woken up by somebody screaming. I open my eyes and look around. Where does it come from? Who is screaming? It is my mother!

People are crowding around.

"What happened? Why did you scream?"

My mother gestures, tries to point at something. Her lips trembling, she wants to say something and can't. She sinks back onto the pillow, almost fainting.

Realizing that they won't get anything out of my mother, they start looking everywhere – in the closet, under the bed, in the bed.

All of a sudden there is the sound of the nurse yelling. With a strange shrieking voice, she shouts repeatedly: "Cats! Help! Cats!"

People exchange glances, not understanding what she is saying. What does she mean? Apart from the word "cats" they can't get anything out of her either, she is so upset.

My grandmother is clearly shaken by this unexpected drama. But she pulls herself together, takes a good look around in the bed and laughing, as if to hide her own fears, she calls out, "*Mazel tov,* the cat had kittens, a good sign!"

Apparently, this is not a good sign. People are uneasy. They murmur.

"On the same day… in the same bed with cats?"

"People are born the same way as cats."

They have managed to calm my mother down. Once again, nobody has eyes for me. My mother falls asleep. And with that, the first day has come to an end. I am, thank God, one day old, and I have already gone through quite a lot.

The third day following my birth is the Sabbath. Some big, red-faced gentile woman has put me in the bath this time. I am not so afraid anymore because I already know what is happening.

I am lying in bed with my mother. She looks at me with even greater tenderness than yesterday. I open my eyes, wanting to have another look at the new world. I am already used to the darkness. Suddenly it becomes even darker than before.

A group of women have come in, taking over the alcove. I look at them. They say something, make hand gestures, take me in their arms, pass me around like a precious object. They smile at my mother and me. In the meantime, my grandmother has come in with a tray full of cakes and liqueurs.

The women make her plead, pretending not to want to taste any of the treats – the preserves, the cherry brandy, berry juice and honey wine – but eventually, when my grandmother doesn't give in, they open their little beaks and are willing to eat something for her sake.

Men also stick their heads into the women's alcove. They talk, their faces contorted from frowning, with their hands waving in the air and their beards trembling with excitement. They are almost having convulsions.

This time it is my father who manages to convince them, not my grandmother. I am given the name of one of his relatives, Sarah Rivke.

Now they need a wet nurse. My mother is weak and pale, with such transparent, blue-veined, narrow hands, that she can hardly lift me. As a middle-class woman, she is unable to breast-feed me. I am the opposite: a strong healthy girl, a little guzzler. I never stop crying; all I want to do is eat.

My grandmother says that she will not give me to a gentile wet nurse, if she can help it. She cannot find a Jewish one. The pharmacist claims that if I get used to powdered milk, it will be better than my mother's milk. I, however, make it clear that I don't want to get used to powdered milk, and I throw up all the time.

It is all rather difficult! My grandmother is upset. My mother even more so. But my father comforts them by saying that surely the Lord will help them. And He does.

One of our neighbors has remembered that she knows this wet nurse, and she has brought her to us. She is called Reyzl. Her voice is that of a soldier, and she has two red eyes, which scare me. She will not come to our house; she has six children of her own. But she has no choice.

Everything is arranged. She receives a deposit.

Reyzl lifts me out of the cradle. She takes out a big, white breast, which looks like a piece of risen dough, and gives it to me to suck, to see if I like it. Well, what can I tell you? I almost drown with pleasure. I sense the taste of a good wet nurse.

Reyzl looks from one to the other happily.

"Well, what do you have to say?"

My mother and grandmother glance at each other furtively and keep silent.

Now I have the good fortune to be living with Reyzl. Not that she really needs anyone else around – they are living in a room the size of a large cupboard. When Reyzl brings me home, her husband comes to welcome me, carrying their smallest child in his arms with the other five heirs swarming around him. He looks extremely pleased with my arrival.

"Now, what do you say to that, eh?" beams Reyzl. "Ten zlotys a week, upon my word as an honest Jewish woman! Plus old clothes and shoes. On top of that they will give all their repair work just to you from now on! Do you hear me, Beyrish?"

Beyrish remains silent. He has turned away so that his breadwinner will not see his delight.

"She is more of a man than I am, I swear. She earns a zloty faster," he thinks to himself. But he pulls himself together immediately. "Where are we going to put the cradle?" They think about it for a long time.

Then Reyzl's husband, who is a master at rearranging all the things in his tiny home, hits his wrinkled, low forehead with his hard hand and calls out cheerfully: "Reyzl, I've got it! Under the table!"

To cut a long story short, I am shoved under the table in my little cradle.

My eyes wide open, I stare in amazement at the table's filthy under-side, which is covered all over with spider webs, and I think with sadness, "This is the new world I have tumbled into? And this is its heaven?"

I weep bitter tears.

A Silk Gabardine

אַטלעסענע קאַפּאָטע

The Gliskers had lived in the village for a very long time. Yidel Glisker had inherited a shop, which supplied all the needs both of the village and the surrounding countryside. He ran it single-handedly. He was a tall, broad-shouldered Jew, more than capable of looking after himself. The peasants held him in the highest esteem.

He would not allow his wife to help him in the shop, except for those times when he had to leave the village to buy new stock.

"A Jewish woman," Yidel claimed, "is responsible for the home and the children. That's best for everyone."

Rochel, his wife, did not agree. But she knew only too well that if Yidel said no, it meant no, and she preferred not to argue. So she set up her own business, a dairy farm.

Yidel let her get on with it. As long as she did not interfere in his affairs, he raised no objections. On the contrary, he was pleased because it gave the womenfolk something to do. He even went so far as to help her pick a few head of cattle. He paid the farmers and went drinking with them afterwards to celebrate striking the bargain.

Rochel was as good at business as Yidel. Like her husband, she refused to depend on anyone else. She did everything – she milked the cows, heated the basins of sour milk, lifted the heavy stones onto the cheeses and churned the butter. She even sewed the cheese bags herself.

The only thing her daughters did was to tend the cows grazing in the meadows as they sought the longest and lushest grass. When the cows returned in the evening, their udders were ready to burst. Rochel would then squat with a sense of deep satisfaction on the three-legged milking stool. She pulled the brownish pink teats with her strong fingers until the udders started to become longer. She would then quickly move her stool and the pail to relieve the next cow.

The cows licked her hands with their moist tongues. It was their way of thanking her.

The warm milk in the pails and the smell of manure in the shed made Rochel feel strong. At moments like these, she felt able to move mountains.

As for her daughters, who always spent the whole summer in the open air, caressed by the warm sunlight, they grew up tall and slender, like the pine trees in the neighboring forest.

Visiting Jews from the surrounding villages, who drove up in their rickety little carts drawn by emaciated horses to buy milk and butter and the enormous cheeses, could not help noticing all this. These Jews dared not venture near Rochel's shed out of fear of being thrown in the air by a cow and they were angered at seeing the Glisker girls grow up doing the kind of work non-Jewish girls did. It wasn't done! And Yidel himself was wholly engrossed in business and Rochel looked more like a sturdy peasant than a Jewish woman.

So, whenever Rochel refused to lower the price of the milk or cheese, they were quick to remind Yidel that their way of life was highly improper.

"What will become of your children, may they have long and happy lives. How come that a Jew like yourself, Reb Yidel, allows his daughters to grow up in the fields? What are they, *shikses*? You can't have it both ways. You will never be able to make a match! What is all this? It is completely unheard of for a fine Jew like yourself, Reb Yidel, to have his Jewish children looking after cattle, especially your children, Reb Yidel!"

Yidel could not have cared less. The only effect their words had on him was that he felt like grabbing his wife's customers by their scrawny necks and giving them a good shake, so that they would never again feel the desire to poke their noses into other people's affairs.

He knew perfectly well they did not mean a word they said. They were angry because his wife refused to give her goods away at half price, while they themselves had no qualms whatsoever about charging the poor women in the *shtetl*, the little town where most of the Jews lived, twice as much for a pint of milk or a few ounces of butter. That was the reason they said those things. They were envious of his prosperity, may no harm come to him. And so Yidel paid them no heed.

But then something happened. One evening he chanced upon his eldest daughter Royze locked in an embrace with a non-Jewish lad, lying out in the open fields. They lay there just like animals. It was a forbidden liaison; it couldn't be allowed!

After this encounter, Yidel no longer ridiculed the small-minded Jews and their endless comments. On the contrary, he listened to them attentively, pondering and brooding over every word they said. And towards the end of summer, instead of preparing themselves to drive into the nearby town for the High Holidays as mere visitors, the Gliskers sold their secluded cottage. They loaded all their merchandise onto spacious carts, and roped the cattle up behind them. They packed themselves off to the *shtetl* for good.

After they had settled on the other side of the forest, Yidel gradually remembered all the stories he had once been told about village Jews; how their children would mingle with non-Jewish boys and girls, get a bit too friendly with them, and bring shame upon their parents.

As he was having these thoughts, his heart went out to the respectable town Jews who were his new neighbors. For the first time he felt some real affinity with them. He looked at them in a way which was very different from before, when these same people had come to his place to buy wood from him. He even regarded his wife's old customers differently. He noticed how some of them sat in the small synagogue every evening and studied what, he did not know. He soon found out, through the *shammes*, the rabbi's assistant, that one of them, the fellow with the scrawny neck, was well ahead of the others, and was working hard – on a chapter of the Mishna.

Yidel would peep furtively over their shoulders, and to his dismay he found that not only did he not understand a single word, he could not even read the script. A strange new desire took hold of him. He wanted to have access to the hidden mysteries of these yellowish well-thumbed pages of the Talmud. An idea struck him. He would hire a tutor. He would pay him whatever he asked and more, but on one condition only: not a single soul was to know about it. On no account did he want to be thought of as a peasant.

People in the town knew that Yidel was a man of means. On the very first Sabbath following his arrival, he was called up during the synagogue service, a special honor. The *shammes* assigned him a place among the most dignified members of the community.

Life in the *shtetl* suited Yidel. His business flourished. He had found himself a teacher and he made good progress in his studies. There was one thing that really upset him, though. He was the only one at the front of the synagogue wearing a worsted gabardine. With his great height and huge back, which concealed half a dozen other worshippers, he looked inappropriately dressed in that woolen coat. There he was, in the easternmost section of the synagogue, surrounded by silk and satin. He felt completely out of place.

On the face of it, it seemed simple enough. He could certainly afford a new coat, praise be to God. All he had to do was order a few yards of silk and send for Fishel, the tailor, and that would be that.

As it turned out, Yidel, the man for whom nothing in the world was too difficult, was unable to get himself a silk gabardine.

So, every Sabbath, after the service had ended, Yidel would pace up and down the front aisle of the synagogue nervously, unsure where to put his big clumsy feet. Softly he repeated in a wistful singsong voice, half to himself, half to the people around him who were all clad in silk and satin:

"*Gut Shabbes! Oy, Gut Shabbes, Gut Shabbes,* May you have a good Sabbath!"

On one occasion Yidel's eccentric behavior brought a smile to the face of one of his fellow worshippers. The man muttered something into his distinguished beard and snorted out an incomprehensible comment, hinting at the vulgarity of Yidel's conduct; the way he circled the small synagogue, his work-worn hands folded behind him, a spotted red handkerchief clutched between his massive fingers.

One boy of about thirteen, Simcha, the Talmud master's youngest son, was quicker than the grown-ups to understand what this fine Jew, Reb Mordechai, was getting at with that delicate twitch of his nose. And so Simcha started pacing up and down as well, his own skinny body hiding behind Yidel's broad shoulders, and with a roguish smile he chanted softly:

"*Gut Shabbes! Gut Shabbes!* Soon we will enjoy the traditional *Shabbes* meal, *grobe kishke* and a *cholent* stew!"

Yidel folded up his prayer shawl and handed it over to the *shammes.* As soon as he had left the synagogue, everybody burst out laughing; nevertheless they reprimanded Simcha: "Shame on you, little rascal! Making fun of a Jew, on *Shabbes* no less!"

Little did they know that Simcha was Yidel's tutor, and that once a week he went over to Yidel to help him read a chapter of the Torah, for which Yidel paid him two zlotys. Every Sabbath afternoon, Simcha would make his way secretly through a fresh layer of blue-white snow. It required some effort to get to the house, which was located at the far end of the *shtetl.* It stood there submerged either in snow and sunlight or in snow and mud, depending on what day it was, eagerly awaiting the guest.

Every Sabbath he would find Yidel upright in bed, looking wide awake and rested. He bossed his middle daughter Fayge around in a fatherly fashion.

"I say, Faytshe, hand me a glass of water, will you. And make sure it is cr-r-rystal clear-r – I don't want any wor-rms in it!"

His emphasis on these words invariably tickled Simcha. They conjured up two images: one, the flashing crystal shine of running water; the other, a stagnant pool full of wriggling worms. When Fayge appeared again with a glass of ordinary water, he felt cheated by father and daughter alike, and spitefully he imitated Yidel under his breath, rolling his tongue: "I say, Faytshe, cr-r-rystal clear-r-r, and no wor-rms!"

But Yidel was blissfully unaware of Simcha's clowning; the peacefulness of the Sabbath had taken hold of him completely. The boy watched him drinking and scrutinizing the glass after every sip, to make sure there were no worms. When Yidel had finished his glass, he put it on the floor. He wiped a few glistening drops which had settled in his beard with the edge of the bed sheet and only then would he become aware of Simcha's presence.

"Ah, Simchale, *Gut Shabbes!*" He was always pleased to see him. Cheerfully he would call to his wife: "Rochel, time to get up! He's here already!"

On the opposite side of the room there was another carved bed, an exact replica of Yidel's, and Rochel lay there fully dressed, her feet resting on a three-legged milking stool. She was very nearly as tall as Yidel, and almost as sturdily built. She was wearing a white linen blouse and a red checked skirt. With a red and yellow kerchief tied around her head and a string of scarlet beads around her neck, she certainly looked like one of the peasant women who came to the *shtetl* on Sundays.

Yidel's words made her stir in her sleep, and she turned around in the bed. The little stool started moving with her. It tumbled slowly towards the edge of the bed, only just clinging to the heels of her shoes, until it finally landed on the floor with a big thump. This really woke her up. Struggling to balance her large body, she sat upright and smiled respectfully at the young scholar: "Ah, Reb Simchale!"

"*Gut Shabbes!*" Simcha tried with all his might not to look at her. Still, from the corner of his eye he could make out that the red headscarf had slid down somewhat, revealing her hair; real, shining, black hair with a wide, pale parting in the middle – something he had never seen with any of the other Jewish women in the *shtetl.* Simcha was shocked. It was the same almost every Sabbath; but she never seemed to notice that anyone could see her real hair.

And it was not only little Simcha who wondered. The whole *shtetl* was mystified. Nobody understood the Gliskers; they were clearly Jews, pious Jews even, but at the same time they were different from everybody else. No other Jews behaved the way they did.

It was completely unheard of: Jews who were healthier than gentiles; it was unnatural to have daughters as tall as trees, large-breasted giants with enormous shoulders and brightly sparkling eyes. It was simply too much! The mother was just as tall, just as strong, and fit, and her eyes were shining just as brightly as those of her daughters. The amount of work these women took on was incredible!

After they had settled in the *shtetl*, Rochel had taken charge of Yidel's business. Week in, week out she stood behind her counter selling a seemingly endless supply of herrings. The peasants did not want to buy anywhere else. It was all "Rochele this" and "Rochele that." It was hard to say why they all liked her so much, except maybe – may God not punish me for these words – for the fact that she looked like one of them. Oh dear! Rochel herself did not pay much attention to her customers, except when a peasant wife crushed the herring while looking for roe or when some old crone tried to slip a fish into her bosom. She weighed the merchandise on the green scales. She lifted the large bags of salt with such ease one would have thought they contained feathers instead of heavy crystals. She even rolled big barrels of petrol and oil over the greasy, black shop floor, as swiftly as if they were empty, and if one of them got stuck behind a loose floorboard, she simply lifted the barrel over her shoulder and that was that!

Since everybody preferred to buy from Rochel, the other tradeswomen might as well have closed up shop. They sat there idly, with nothing to do the whole day but wallow in their misery. The floors of their shops dried out; the herring in their barrels turned soft; the rest of their stock went putrid and their herring barrels rusted. The salt shrank in their bags. Even the oil barrels seemed to dry out. With each passing day, the envy and bitterness of the shopkeepers grew greater.

The Gliskers, for their part, kept getting richer. Their shop was bursting with merchandise. There was not one single empty shelf. Sabbath meals at Yidel's home became ever grander, and the naps afterwards longer. The fruit and sweets with which they treated Simcha were more delicious than ever before.

Rochel got up and smoothed out the blanket. She then went out to freshen herself up after her rest.

Yidel had stumbled out of bed in the meantime. He put on his clothes and followed his wife into the other room. Devoyre, the youngest of the girls, who was twelve but had the looks of a twenty-year-old, arranged her father's bedding. She made it just as smooth as her mother would have done. Yidel stretched himself out, and removed a few small feathers which had crept into his beard while he'd been asleep. He rolled them into tiny balls and shot them across the room. He smiled at Simcha. They both took a seat at the table.

"I say, Simcha, how many yards of silk do you reckon I'd need for a new gabardine? Hmmm, what do you think?" he asked the boy as if he were a tailor.

Simcha glanced at Yidel as though to measure him. It struck him that the man might easily need thirty yards.

"Well, I should say about fifteen," Simcha blurted out, and he blushed fiercely.

Yidel did not reply. He already regretted having asked the question; he felt ill at ease, as if he had made a fool of himself. He quickly got up and walked to the bookcase, where he took out a *Chumash* containing the five books of Moses, bound in calf with large golden lettering on the embossed spine. Turning to the weekly Torah portion, he respectfully carried the open book to the table as if it were of great importance.

Yidel sat at the head of the table with Simcha at his right side and Devoyre opposite him. Her elbows planted firmly on the table and her fists embedded in her fleshy cheeks, she did not take her eyes off Simcha for a moment.

Simcha pretended not to notice her presence. His thin forefinger began to flow along the printed lines.

"'*Vayaitseh Yakov mibeer Sheba*,' which means – And Jacob went out from Beersheba, '*Vayelich Charana*,' and went towards Charan."

The meaning of the sentence was simple enough, thought Yidel. Jacob had left Beersheba, just as he, Yidel, had moved away from Bojonitz. But what he could not manage to figure out was the meaning of the individual words. He was too ashamed to ask. He got more and more confused as he blundered his way through, much to the dismay of his young teacher, who tried to make him understand each word. Tirelessly Simcha explained everything, over and over again, like a born teacher.

Yidel bore it patiently. He kept trying until he finally got it. His face beamed. Simcha was so delighted that he forgot his earlier reserve and looked at the girl triumphantly.

Devoyre's large grey eyes stared back at him, not understanding why these two were so happy all of a sudden. She was mystified as to why her father, who was such an important man, would allow a little boy to teach him a lesson.

In the meantime, Rochel had come in with a large tray of sweetmeats. Even though Simcha was sitting with his back to it, he could feel its presence, and it spurred him on. His thin forefinger danced across the page now:

"And Jacob went out from Beersheba …"

"Well, well!" Yidel rubbed his hands contentedly. "It's time to have a bite," he said, and he placed the bookmark back on the page. Rochel carried the book, with great reverence, to the bed where she placed it carefully on the green blanket, as if it were a weak, sickly child. Then she started to hand out the sweetmeats.

"Eat, Simchale! Don't be ashamed! As it is written in the *Ethics of the Fathers*… Uh…" Yidel was lost for words. "Hmmm? What does it say there again?" Yidel wrinkled his forehead as if he expected to find the answer there.

Simcha quickly helped him out: "Where there is no food there is no Torah."

"Exactly." Yidel remembered the phrase now, and he offered Simcha a poppy seed cake: "Eat, and I hope you'll enjoy it!" Yidel radiated contentment as he himself dug into the delicacies his wife was offering.

"Reb Simchale should eat more," Rochel said while she placed an enormous piece of strudel in front of him. "Please, you must have some of these as well," she added, pushing a plate with almond biscuits in his direction and pouring tea at the same time.

That winter Yidel would go straight after his Sabbath lesson to the synagogue with Simcha. Rather, he would go first and Simcha would follow a few moments later, on his own, as if he had nothing to do with Yidel. Darkness came early in those months; there was hardly enough time for Rochel to stumble through the prayers she had to recite at the close of the Sabbath.

When Yidel returned from the evening service, he found the fire already glowing. A gigantic iron kettle with potato peelings for the animals was boiling in the kitchen. Next to it stood another pot, not much smaller, with potatoes for the family. The red bubbling mass of beetroot soup filled the house with its sour smell.

Rochel hastily mixed the food for the chickens, which flew impatiently down from their shelves behind the beds. They circled around her like angry devils. It did not take long for a cackle to erupt among the birds, picking madly at the food and at each other, stealing bits out of each other's beaks, although there was easily enough for all of them. At times, the battle became so fierce that some even lost a few feathers, but when Rochel scolded them, they immediately started to eat more quietly, as if they realized that their mistress was right.

The livestock in the stall were getting impatient too. Especially Rochel's favorite. All her cows were good looking, but this one was supreme, a real beauty! Rochel had raised her single-handedly. She had bought her as a small calf and raised her like a princess. The cow was brown with white shining patches, which gave her extra charm. Her udders were also different from the other cows'; not miserable flabby things, but healthy udders, bursting with thick, creamy milk. It took all of Rochel's strength to milk her!

Those Saturday nights were more than even Rochel could cope with, and she had to ask her daughter for help: "Feyge, add some wood to the fire! The potato skins aren't boiling! Feyge, you are crushing her udder. Not like that, Feyge, you silly girl!"

But Feyge was hardly ever there on Saturday evening. She usually slipped away right after they had finished the stew and she did not come back until long after Havdala. Things were even worse when Yidel took it into his head to drive to town overnight to replenish his stocks. Then Rochel not only had to deal with the chickens and the cows, but she also had to prepare a meal for Yidel before he went off on his trip, and she did not know which mouth to feed first.

At such moments, Rochel would get flustered and she would no longer be able to remember the name of objects or people. Everything became "thingamy" – the cow, the horse, the chickens, her husband, her daughters. They were all referred to by one single name: "thingamy."

"Yidel, have you already given thingamy to the thingamy?" What she meant was: "Yidel, have you already given hay to the horse?"

"Yidel, don't forget to take the thingamy!" In other words, "Yidel, don't forget to take the piece of paper!"

"Thingamy, the thingamies will get thingamied!" This was Rochel's way of saying: "Feyge, the potatoes will get boiled to pieces!" It was one of Rochel's weaknesses to think that, as soon as she had put on a pot of potatoes, they were already overdone.

Yidel studied long and hard with the help of Simcha, until one day the local matchmaker, who knew everybody's secrets, decided the time had come to match Yidel with Reb Isaac, the Talmud master. And so, in due course a marriage was arranged between Royze, Yidel's eldest daughter, and Menasseh, who was Simcha's sixteen-year-old brother.

As soon as Royze was betrothed, Rochel had to stop ordering her around. It so happened that Yidel had decided that his daughter was in fact a delicate creature, and she had to be spared. No more rough jobs for Royze he warned his wife. Besides, as a future daughter-in-law of the Talmud master, she'd have plenty of dainty work to keep her busy!

And so Royze sat whole days tracing monograms on pillowcases for herself and for her husband-to-be. (Needless to say it was Yidel who provided everything for both parties.) She crocheted, for herself and for her future father-in-law, matza bags for the unleavened bread that they would eat on Passover. She sewed covers for the challah, the braided bread for the Sabbath, and embroidered a *tallis* bag for her betrothed's prayer shawl. She toiled over endless quantities of linen and even made an apron for her future mother-in-law. Royze labored and Yidel paid, since Reb Isaac, the Talmud master, was a most learned man, a most particular man, a most irascible man and ... a hopelessly penniless one.

It had not been easy to convince Royze she was now a fragile flower, because she loved to be hale and hearty, as indeed she was. There was nothing she liked more than hard work. Except maybe the long Sabbath afternoons and the ensuing Saturday evenings, when she should have been at home helping her mother, but hardly ever was, since it was so hard to tear herself apart from her village sweetheart. She detested doing needlework and pricking her fingers. She hated having to dress up like a doll and walk carefully around the house. She hated behaving like a lady. What she hated most of all was Menasseh, her future husband. But gradually she got used to the idea (or so it seemed). She admitted that she was a different person now, and there was no way her mother could order her around anymore.

Rochel had no choice but to work like a dog – especially during the long winter evenings following the Sabbath. In summer, when the days were longer, Sabbath lasted the whole day, thankfully. Then she just had to wait for Yidel to come home and make Havdala. She would recite the *Shema* for the last time in the day – and hop into bed! In summer there were no potato peelings to be cooked after Sabbath, no chickens to be fed. The cows were satisfied; the meadows were there for them to graze on just as they pleased. The chickens happily scraped around outside the whole day, laying their eggs amidst the wooden boards. Rochel hardly saw them. Yidel would stay in at night and life was good.

Yidel also preferred the Sabbaths in summer, although he did not mind the other ones as much as his wife. His affairs had prospered exceedingly in his new home. His stock of timber had multiplied, so that it took up more and more space behind the spacious wooden cottage. The cows now had to graze in fields much further away from the house because of it.

In summer, Yidel did not accompany Simcha to the synagogue because the evening prayers were taking place much later. But Yidel could not renounce the pleasures of the Sabbath.

He decided to send Simcha home and stroll around amidst his piles of timber, while measuring them with his eye.

He knew it was forbidden to measure on the Sabbath. Therefore he measured only with his eye, which gave him great satisfaction. Soon there would not be a single empty patch of grass left. The cows were hidden from view already! The piles of wood had almost driven the animals into the lake. It was not a bad thing, thought Yidel, since the grass was lusher over there. But why was it forbidden to count? The question kept nagging at him. He felt a sudden urge to count the various kinds of wood he had in stock: pine, alder, and birch. The desire was so strong that he quickly clasped both hands behind his back and walked in the direction of the cows in order not to give in to the temptation. Without knowing it, the cows had saved him from a sin.

He noticed that the grass was indeed good next to the lake. The cows were begging to be relieved, though. The Sabbath dragged on, and Yidel felt pity for the cows and their bursting udders. There was nothing he could do, and he walked back to the wood. That wood was worth a fortune, may no harm come to it, he thought as he squeezed himself between the piles.

Yidel loved the wood. What he liked about it was its smell. Especially on a hot day, when the resin became soft and trickled along the trunks like honey. The fragrance was so delicious that he was tempted to scrape it off the tree.

Yidel was only human. Although he tried very hard not to, he occasionally touched one of the cows, or counted a few pieces of wood. And who knows, maybe that was allowed after all?

On the one hand, he would like to ask the rabbi's advice. On the other hand, however, he could just tell what his reaction would be. The rabbi would be shocked: How could a Jew not know something so basic, that one was not allowed to count wood on the Sabbath? Counting by mouth, that was forbidden too! And using only your eyes, yes, that too was a sin of course! That's what the rabbi would say. He might smile in a friendly fashion at him, but deep in his heart he would mock him for such a foolish question. Even a child would know the answer, and the rabbi would regard him as a peasant.

Yidel sighed deeply and turned around to the path that led to the synagogue. The chickens followed him, as if they recognized him. Yidel hated it. He chased them away with the yellow and red handkerchief: "Shoo! Shoo!"

He looked around and saw they were still there: "Shoo! Shoo!"

He hated looking like a peasant. And, of course, just at that moment, Borechl Keppel showed up. They bumped into each other almost every week, since Borechl liked to go for a summer walk through Yidel's wood, to inhale the sweet fragrance of the pine resin and to look at the clear blue sky.

"*Gut Shabbes*, Reb Yidel," Borechl said, and a small hairy hand appeared out of a paper cuff. Dark glistening eyes smiled at Yidel. Borechl had a smallish head. His moist black hair hung onto the paper collar around his neck. It was hard to distinguish the beard from the hair on his neck.

"*Gut Shabbes! Gut Shabbes!*" Yidel grabbed Borechl's shriveled little hand with his own enormous fist, in which it disappeared completely, and he gave it a friendly shake, which made Borechl jump into the air.

"Aaaaahh! How are you doing, Reb Yidel?" Borechl tried to extricate his crushed fingers from Yidel's iron clasp.

"Fine, praise be to the Almighty!"

"When will the marriage, God willing, take place, Reb Yidel?"

"Why do you ask?" The question surprised Yidel.

"Just like that, for no special reason! A good friend is interested in these matters."

"Nothing has been agreed yet, but I reckon it's going to be on the *Shabbes* after the fast of Av, God willing," Yidel replied, and both men walked to the synagogue to attend the evening prayers.

Together they strode along the meadow, which was patchy and dry where the piles of wood had left their mark. Furthermore, in many places, the grass had been ripped out by its roots. The earth seemed to be wounded.

Yidel's shadow was gliding across the grass like a giant. Borechl noticed how insignificant his own shadow looked as it danced alongside that of Yidel, pursuing the mighty figure moving through the empty landscape.

He did not even reach Yidel's shoulders.

Borechl tumbled down the ladder of his own self-esteem when he realized how tiny he looked next to Yidel. Desperately he tried to make himself taller, by walking on his toes. He did not stop talking for a minute, gesticulating wildly with his small hands, so that his alter ego on the grass made odd, grand gestures, and he sweated.

Thus they had walked almost every Sabbath together to the evening service. And every week Yidel was perturbed because he did not dare to ask Borechl about the issue of counting wood on the Sabbath. It would have answered his question once and for all, but he did not have the courage. And every week Borechl was depressed because of his own pathetic size.

That day Yidel was distressed about something else as well. When they passed the synagogue alley, he had heard the women, who met every Sabbath for a chat on the bench in front of Chane-Rochel's house, gossiping about him and his family.

"So, I am asking you, does a Jew look like that? If he was really a Jew, would he live the way he does? Jews aren't supposed to be so lucky. And then I'm not even talking about 'them'! Have you ever seen Jewish daughters as healthy as *shikses*? Or a *yidene* who kisses her cows? May hair grow on the palm of my hand if they are Jews!" Chane-Rochel exclaimed, as if this was definitive proof that the Gliskers were not in fact Jews, but converted peasants.

The sun was still high in the sky when Borechl and Yidel entered the synagogue that day.

"*Gut Shabbes,* Reb Yidel!" The rabbi himself came up to him.

The little synagogue was steeped in sunlight. Golden motes of sunlight were pouring in through the closed window, dancing on the *bime,* the raised platform from where the prayers were said, and ending with a glitter of splendor on the menora. The sight filled Yidel's heart with joy, and all his earlier worries disappeared instantly, like clouds melting in a sudden burst of hot sunshine.

"*Gut Shabbes! Gut Shabbes! Gut Shabbes! Gut Shabbes!*" Yidel burst out in endless greetings. He was overjoyed by the honor bestowed on him by no less a person than the rabbi, and by the sight of the sunshine resting on the menora which he himself had recently donated. A piece of solid silver, it stood there on the *bime.* No wonder the golden sunlight was attracted by it, he thought.

Thus Yidel lived surrounded by riches and honor. Everything he touched became a success. Even his lessons with Simcha started to pay off, and every Sabbath Simcha was a little more satisfied with him.

The moment had come. Yidel's large front room was bare of all furniture except for long wooden benches lining the walls. A large paraffin lamp hung from the center of the ceiling. Smaller lamps, which looked like Chinese lanterns, had been suspended across the freshly whitewashed room. The walls were draped with colorful paper ribbons, plain and curled, coiled or crimped – a dazzling mixture of green, red, yellow and orange! The floor was strewn with fine, light-colored sand.

Rochel was not wearing her usual red headscarf, but a black shiny wig, which had been combed up high. It was fastened at the side by a white silk bow, such as she normally wore on Rosh HaShana.

Yidel was clad in a new silk gabardine. In honor of his daughter's marriage to the son of the Talmud master, he had finally made the transition to silk. His old woolen coat had been discarded for good. The sheen of the material looked magnificent on his imposing body and was only matched by the glow of his rosy peasant cheeks. Linking himself to such a fine young man with a fine family had given him the strength to assert himself, and indeed, the new coat suited him well. It rested comfortably on his broad shoulders and it exuded an air of joy – honestly, it was as if the silk gabardine itself was rejoicing.

Rochel was helping a hired woman to arrange the cake on the trays, as well as the other delicacies. Today she called everything by its proper name; not once did she revert to "thingamy." Feyge and Devoyre were dressed in yellow embroidered dresses trimmed with endless frills and they had white ribbons in their hair.

The bride, all dressed in white, sat on an upholstered armchair, her feet resting on a little stool.

The guests were beginning to arrive. First were the village maidens, their faces reddened by hard washing, bodies tightly laced in starched fabric, in the company of their pious mothers who smelled of honey and vinegar.

The musicians were about to start playing: Gimpel with his fiddle, Hersh-Layb with his bass and Dovidl with his flute.

The bridegroom would arrive any minute. He would be accompanied by the most notable young men of the *shtetl* and by fellow students from his faraway yeshiva, the rabbinical academy. Simcha would walk in their midst, since he was over thirteen and considered a man now.

Yidel was so happy he could not stand still. He kept walking in and out of the rooms. He paused for a moment in front of the laden tables. He turned the paraffin lamp full on again, to reassure himself that the wick was not smoking. Then he took out his handkerchief to wipe the place of honor, where the bridegroom would soon be seated. Finally, he went into the women's room, to have another look at the bride.

What was going on? The bride sat squirming on her chair like a worm and she softly groaned into her white veil. Nobody had noticed anything, it seemed. The women showered her with kisses and blessings, they suffocated her with their embraces, drowning her pitiful, muffled moans. The girls kissed her too and wished her well, but they were more interested in the white frock, the long veil over her head, the elegant little shoes on her feet. They did not see how the bride's face was distorted in agony, changing rapidly from deathly pale to green. And now the orchestra had started up, accompanied by loud shouts:

"*Mazel tov*! Congratulations! Here comes the bridegroom! Play us a merry tune! Here comes the bridegroom!"

Women were clapping their hands:

"Here he comes! Here he comes! He has arrived!"

"May happiness be theirs their whole lives long!"

Yidel left Royze writhing on her armchair and hastened forward to meet the bridegroom, who had only just crossed the threshold. He was a pale, skinny young man, not much taller than his younger brother Simcha, and with exactly the same pointed nose. He stood in the corridor, surrounded by a cluster of young men who were all wrapped in silk, just like himself. Music filled the house.

Royze was bent double. She saw through the open door how her future husband was led through the hall. A wisp of a man, just like a doll, she thought, a silk doll.

She was seized by pity and rage at the same time. An insane urge to laugh welled up inside her. But a pain deep within her belly overwhelmed all other feelings. She wailed out loud. The women instantly surrounded her. A great uproar broke out. The bride kicked her feet in agony. She was crying like a little girl. Chane-Rochel started weeping too. Rochel kept asking for a "thingamy," completely forgetting there was no such thing as a doctor in the *shtetl.* The bridegroom, scared to death, was quickly hustled into another room. The other young men stared at him, grinning stupidly, not knowing what to say.

Somebody ordered the musicians to play as loudly as they could.

The wife of the Talmud master was so distressed that suddenly, while absent-mindedly pulling at a lock of hair, she tugged her wig off. Bald-headed, she stood there amidst the bewildered guests.

The only person who did not lose his head was Yidel. As he watched his daughter, a terrible suspicion entered his mind, so terrible that he would have been glad to see the accursed house crash down on him, his family, and all the damned guests as well.

The rabbi suggested that the bride be put to bed, to treat her with compresses and to proceed with the ceremony at her bedside. By doing so, the bride would, with God's help, soon recover.

At that moment, the Talmud master started to scream.

Yidel did not listen to the rabbi, nor to the Talmud master. Instead, still wearing his silk gabardine, he stormed into the stable, brought out two strong black horses, hitched them up, wrapped his daughter in a white eiderdown which he had grabbed from the bridal bed and carried her outside like a child. He bundled her into the cart and before Rochel had the chance to realize what he was doing and jump in with him, Yidel had climbed up on to the seat. He cracked his whip and was off in the direction of the forest.

A deadly silence filled the house. All eyes were on the cart and its strange load. Yidel, his silken back gleaming in the twilight, whipped the horses as if he were possessed. For a short while, the cart was shrouded in a cloud of dust, and then it was gone. The forest stood motionless in the distance as it always did.

The forest was inhabited by dark forces. Nobody in the *shtetl* doubted this. In summer witches skimmed over treetops on their brooms and in winter they appeared in the guise of wild wolves.

Strange stories were told about that forest. But none as strange as the news Yidel brought with him, after a mere half hour's stay there.

A whirlwind of dust announced the return of Yidel's cart. Immediately, the racket in the house died down and it was replaced by an expectant hush. Evil tongues were silenced by this sudden development.

Royze was sitting in front next to her father. Her cheeks had regained their color. She got out of the cart by herself, without any help.

"The wedding is off!" Yidel said unceremoniously to Reb Isaac.

The tumult caused by these four words was such that no one afterwards remembered quite what had happened. One thing everybody was agreed on, though: the forest clearly had a hand in this. The dark forces had whispered in Yidel's ear, and there was no doubt that they were behind the horrible sin which he had committed on his daughter's very wedding day.

The only one who could have told them what had taken place in the forest, was Yidel himself. Only he knew about the tree on which he had meant to hang himself; that is, before he learned from Royze that his terrible suspicion had been unfounded. But he did not say a word to anyone. When she heard him breaking down in tears and laughter at the same time, Rochel was convinced her husband had lost his mind.

That same night, after Yidel had finally managed to get rid of the last guests, he locked the front door. Then he threw off his silk gabardine and put his old woolen self back on again. The family ate their supper out of simple clay bowls, just like in the old days before they moved into the *shtetl.*

And to this day Yidel's silk gabardine lies forgotten in the attic, on top of a pile of useless junk. Every day, at dusk, it briefly catches a beam of coppery sunlight. It lies there wrapped up and motionless, underneath a layer of golden dust, like the relic of a long-lost dream.

Reb Meyerl
ר׳ מאירל

That evening Reb Meyerl came home upset. The rabbinical courtroom was cloaked in somber shadows. A lamp, standing on the large brown table, cast its light on holy books and manuscripts. They lay there, as usual, waiting for him to have something to eat and to start studying.

But Reb Meyerl was completely oblivious to the world around him. He had simply forgotten that today was Monday and that, as an observant Jew, he had been fasting the whole day. He was unaware of himself sitting there with both hands in the pockets of his heavy fur coat, staring aimlessly into the dark. He had not even heard Menasseh, his assistant, ask him three times whether he could bring in supper. Eventually Menasseh had sent for the rabbi's wife.

Reb Meyerl stood up and took off his fur coat. A puddle of water had formed on the floor near him, coming from the ice clinging to his shoes. Only now did he take off the high fur cap he had been wearing and replace it with a velvet yarmulke, his usual skullcap. Then he sat down in a carved wooden chair at the head of the table, and started to study and write.

It was so quiet in the room that one could clearly hear the scratching of the pen with which Reb Meyerl wrote down his thoughts. He wrote something down, crossed it out, wrote something else, and crossed that out as well. He was not getting anywhere. He got up and stretched himself to his full height. He almost reached the ceiling. He took down a book from the shelves.

The walls were covered with religious books – all kinds of books, precious old first editions, bound in rough leather with broad spines worn thin from piety – talmudic tracts, works of the prophets and all the holy writings he could muster. He had everything in several copies. Some of them belonged to his father-in-law, with whom he lived even though he was rabbi of the *shtetl*; some he had received as wedding gifts. Next to the thickly bound volumes stood all sorts of smaller books by contemporary rabbis and other Jewish scholars, who had written new interpretations of the Law. Like little children, these books huddled close to the good and serious adults, who seemed so solid and wise.

He was looking for something, checking it and checking it again, but he could not find the passage that would give him real insight into the problem that was troubling him. It was impossible to solve it that day. Finally he placed his handkerchief on the book, folded a sheet in his manuscript and began to pace up and down the courtroom. His shadow followed him around, one moment spreading itself onto the walls, the next stretching out to the size of a giant on the floor, only to become strangely fat and squat a moment later.

The lamp on the table did not spread any light onto the rest of the room, which was covered in darkness. In the end, he sat down again at the head of the table. He thrust his big brown hands into his sleeves and gave up.

He realized that the evening was now lost, and that he would not learn anything that day, let alone succeed in writing any of it down. His deep, dark eyes were shining. His cheeks, which had looked crimson earlier on when he was on his way home from the synagogue in the clear, frosty night, now seemed dull brown, almost yellow. Wrinkles covered his high young forehead, as if he were an old man.

His wife had been standing next to the table for quite a while. Only then did he notice her.

If not for the wide pleated dress and the silk jacket trimmed with a mass of black velvet, and the yellow silk headscarf, which was bound tightly around her small shaven head, one could have mistaken her for a twelve-year-old girl; she seemed so young and small, even in these old-fashioned clothes.

"You will make yourself ill. You haven't eaten anything yet. You seem to have forgotten that you have fasted the whole day." She spoke quietly and respectfully, very unlike the way in which a wife normally speaks to her husband.

"Maybe you can go and wash now?" she asked him softly, so softly that he could hardly hear. But he did get up.

"*Nu, nu,* all right then," Reb Meyerl said without even looking in her direction. She handed him a letter. While he opened it, she kept standing there for a while, waiting for him to tell her what the letter was about. But Reb Meyerl had already forgotten she was in the room. He was reading the letter, and the more he read, the more astonished he became. Apparently, the city of Pilsk wanted to appoint him as their rabbi. The letter was signed by a delegate of the synagogue council and by a number of Jewish community members.

He had read the letter once, and then twice, and he still did not understand what it meant. He knew that Pilsk was an old city, renowned for its great rabbis. Was it possible? Could it be true that the dignitaries of Pilsk wanted to receive him in their midst, to follow in the footsteps of the great rabbi, who had made the whole world tremble with his rulings? He wasn't even thirty years old! And what a coincidence that the letter should reach him tonight, when only a minute ago he had said to himself in despair that he would be glad to leave his *shtetl,* Molits, if only he could find a post elsewhere. It was simply incredible! If he had not been an opponent of the mystically inclined hasidic Jews he would have thought it was a miracle. But it had to be Providence. There was no doubt about it. It could not have happened just like that, for no good reason, that the letter had arrived precisely this evening, on the very same day that the well-off members of his community had caused him so much trouble.

He read the letter once more and in spite of himself, a bright smile began to soften his noble features. The wrinkles disappeared from his forehead. His dark brown eyes sparkled with warmth and beauty. They looked so full of depth and wisdom; Chanele, his wife, had never seen him like this before. It was as if he had been touched by the Divine Presence. She did not understand why her husband was so happy. Especially on a day like this when, according to Menasseh, the rabbi had every reason to be sad.

Menasseh turned on the main light. Immediately the courtroom felt warm and cheerful. The parchment lampshade looked old and grey now. It did not seem to give any light. Menasseh switched it off and removed it from the table. The shadows had vanished.

Menasseh struggled in with the copper basin, together with a heavy, copper jug, and the rabbi started to wash. The water in the basin glistened like silver and seemed boiling hot.

His wife came back into the room with a servant girl behind her carrying the food. Menasseh took the tray from her at the door, and Chanele placed everything on the table with great care. A cloud of steam rose from the silver dishes, and soon a wonderful smell pervaded the whole room. But Reb Meyerl barely touched his food. He made one blessing after another and hardly ate a thing. Then he recited the final blessing and Menasseh cleared the table.

Reb Meyerl tried once again to work on his manuscript and to consult various books, but he failed to make any sense of it. It was impossible to study. His cheeks had a dark red color again. He felt guilty towards the Jews of Molits, the rich as well as the poor ones. After all, he had grown up in this *shtetl.* It seemed to him that he had sinned against them today. While drinking his tea after supper, he remembered how he had smiled with pleasure at the letter, which he read over and over again. He looked at the shiny, scalding hot samovar, and noticed how it stood there, comfortable and cheerful, humming its familiar tune for him, Reb Meyerl, as it had done for many generations before, in this wealthy, venerable home. It suddenly dawned on him that the samovar took up too important a place: it was standing in the center of the table, amidst his books and papers, and he told Menasseh to move the samovar to a corner.

Menasseh could not believe his ears. This was the first time he had heard the rabbi speak in such a critical way about his beloved samovar, which stood by him during every need and difficulty, but he did what the rabbi asked him to do. "He is putting everything off this evening, even his studies. He is in a dream," Menasseh said to himself. "Hmmm, evil spirits are getting a hold over him today."

Reb Meyerl was starting to feel hot. He simply did not know what to do. But then he had an idea: he would write to the dignitaries of Pilsk, offer them his apologies and stay in Molits. Yes! That's how he would atone for his sins.

He started to write straightaway. In order to formulate his own reply correctly, he read what the letter had to say one more time. Suddenly he noticed a few tiny lines that were added in the corner. He had not seen these before due to his earlier excitement: "And so, if the frost is not too bad, we will arrive, God willing, in Molits tomorrow late afternoon or early evening."

That put the whole affair in a completely different light. Now he had no choice but to receive them. It also meant that the matter had been somewhat taken out of his hands.

He kept torturing himself with all kinds of thoughts. Eventually a bright idea brought him some comfort: he would simply take a step back and leave everything to Providence.

The last thing he did was to send Menasseh to one of the council delegates of Molits with a note informing him about the contents of the letter, including the fact that the group from Pilsk was expected to come with a formal invitation. He also expressed the wish to see the delegate the following day, God willing, in order to discuss the matter with him further.

What he had not specified in his note was when exactly the delegate should come. He had done this on purpose; it was part of his resolution to rid himself of all responsibility. Providence was to make sure everything would turn out well. He would wait and see. If the official from Molits arrived before the delegation from Pilsk, then he would stay. If he did not turn up the following day, then that would be a sign that he had to go and become rabbi of Pilsk.

He started to feel somewhat lighter. It was as if Providence had taken a heavy weight off his shoulders. After all, can a human being know God's ways? Providence would run its course.

After reading the evening prayers, he went to bed early, so that he would be able to get up to recite the midnight prayers. He was so calm now that he fell asleep in less than five minutes.

It was the middle of winter, and the snow had been lying for weeks like a massive blanket, held in place by the frost. Not a single snowflake was moving. Only those who had to, ventured out on the street. Nevertheless, that afternoon the synagogue was bursting with people. The wealthy Jews had gathered there, as well as Jews who prayed alone at home most of the time and who normally only came on the Sabbath.

They all wanted to hear the latest news; they wanted to find out what the outcome of the whole affair would be. Would their rabbi, who was still only in his twenties (whom they remembered being carried into *cheder* for children's Hebrew classes, as if it were yesterday), stay on in Molits, or would the Jews from Pilsk take him away from them?

The *shtetl* was in a spin.

Come on! It was all so trivial. All the rabbi had done, long may he live, was make an effort on behalf of the poor. He had suggested that rich members of the Molits community should pay twice as much tax this winter because of the harsh weather conditions. The money would then be used to deliver a bundle of wood to those who needed it, some cooked food as well, and they would be able to donate shoes to poor boys learning Torah. What if he had scolded the wealthy a little? They deserved it! Respectable Jews! Did they really think that God had created the world for them, and them alone? As the workers discussed this, deep in their hearts they were secretly enjoying the scandal. At the same time they dreaded one possible outcome:

that the poor Jews of Molits would not receive any help and that they would lose, God forbid, the rabbi, their dear rabbi, the young genius of Molits. After all, yesterday that fat pig had told the rabbi that it was his job to give his opinion on religious matters, and not to interfere in community affairs. He had added that the council members would take care of that, as the rabbi was too young and had no understanding of worldly affairs. So what if the rabbi really stepped down! He definitely didn't need the few rubles they paid him every week. He gave these away to the poor anyway. He even added some of his own and he received more money from his father-in-law for charity than from anybody else. So who knows, they said, especially now that these people from Pilsk had suddenly appeared.

The council representative was angry with the rabbi that he hadn't sent a letter to Pilsk immediately, saying that he would turn down their offer. Nevertheless, he had called a meeting of the members of the Molits community (the "respectable" members only, of course). There had been a lot of talking and shouting, and still they were unable to reach an agreement: should they go to the rabbi and persuade him not to leave, or should they wait and see what he had in mind?

Some members thought it was best to go and dissuade him, and to offer their apologies. But the more affluent members, who were held in the highest esteem, did not agree. They said it was never a good thing to try and persuade anyone by begging. "If we beg him to stay, we will only make matters worse! He will drive us mad afterwards," said one of them, a complete idiot, who had a great deal of influence because he gave large amounts of money to ease the needs of the community.

The whole situation created such a stir in the *shtetl*, it was as if it were a matter of life and death.

The one who made the biggest fuss was the rabbi's mother-in-law, Khaye Devoyre. "You will never convince me to send the child away!" she told her husband. Khaye Devoyre still referred to the rabbi's wife as "the child" because she was their only daughter and rather small at that. "I will not send the child away to a strange city. She was born here, and this is where she will stay until she's a hundred and twenty! Do you understand? And it is high time you had a wash. The food is getting as cold as ice," she said angrily.

Reb Avrom Aaron slowly washed his hands and dried them with the large, white towel. He said a blessing before the meal and smiled at his grandchild, who was sitting on his wife's lap, all the while expecting another scolding from her, Khaye Devoyre, because he had dared to suggest that there was a possibility of her Chanele leaving Molits.

But Khaye Devoyre's thoughts were elsewhere. She was busy serving the food and keeping an eye on the "little one," meaning Chanele, and making sure that, God forbid, she did not drop the baby; and so she had already forgotten the whole business. Admittedly, when Menasseh had told her the news earlier it had made her nervous, but now, at the table, the whole affair seemed a long way away. It was like a dream: while you were having the dream, or when you had just woken up, it all felt incredibly real but a few moments later, when you started doing other things, you just forgot about it.

Molits had not forgotten, though. Far from it. The whole *shtetl* had fallen prey to the tortuous dilemma.

How was it possible? Their rabbi! The pride of Molits! The great scholar! The great saint! Who did they think they were, these strange Jews from another city, to come and take him away!

"Molits will not allow this to happen!" These were the first words uttered at all the meetings and discussions. Everybody blamed everyone else. Although it was the middle of the week, Jewish workers had put on their Sabbath clothes to come to the synagogue and listen, maybe throw in a word or two themselves. Even the women were concerned that the rabbi, may he have a long life, should stay in Molits.

Pious, wealthy Jewish women were so agitated that their diamond earrings trembled. They pinched the beads on their hats nervously and twisted the fringes of their silken headscarves. They huddled in their fur coats, as if to derive comfort from them, while they were listening to every word the men had to say.

After considerable discussion the Molits community agreed that they would approach the rabbi later that afternoon. They would offer their apologies and ask him to stay. This had been a bitter pill to swallow for the council members, because as far as they were concerned the rabbi was just a child, while they were the respected elders of Molits.

Reb Meyerl had not set foot in the synagogue the whole day. He had prayed alone. He had also fasted again and it was only now, close to evening, that he had eaten a little. He had just finished reciting his prayers, and was about to start studying, when the door of the courtroom opened. Three Jews came in, dressed in heavy fur coats with raised collars and swathed in scarves. Their heads were covered in the most enormous caps to prevent their ears freezing in the bitter cold.

Reb Meyerl got up when he noticed the visitors. Walking towards them he stretched out his large brown hands and bade them welcome. He told them to get rid of their coats, and he called for Menasseh to take their dripping clothes away. While he offered them a seat, he also asked Menasseh to bring in the samovar. By sheer force of habit, the assistant placed the samovar in the middle of the table.

The Jews were hugging hot glasses with their frozen hands. As they sipped the tea, they almost groaned with enjoyment: "Ahhh, what a pleasure! So lovely and warm!"

Reb Meyerl glanced sideways at the wall and he realized that in a few moments his destiny would be determined. Would he really become the rabbi of Pilsk? Pilsk was a city, compared to Molits. On the other hand, he didn't feel like exchanging his small *shtetl* and his dear Jews – those simple, pious, sincere Jews of his. But the clock kept on ticking. The heavy yellow weights were swinging quietly back and forth. The hands, especially the big one, were moving. And so the time had come.

At that exact moment a group of the most respectable members of the Molits community arrived at the rabbi's house (that is, at the house of his father-in-law, Avrom Aaron). Most of them were still standing at the door, while some had already entered the hallway.

They were a few steps away from the rabbinical courtroom when they noticed the rabbi. He looked pale and taller even than usual, his eyes penetrating and serious. They saw how he got up from his chair, unaware of their presence, and they could see him glance at the clock and mumble to himself:

"They didn't come."

And turning around to the Jews from Pilsk he said something with a voice so soft and serious it almost sounded like a prayer.

"*Mazel tov,* Rabbi of Pilsk!" the Jews from Pilsk were positively beaming.

Only now did Reb Meyerl notice the dignitaries from his own town. But it was too late. He could not take his words back anymore.

And all this because the Molits delegation had arrived five minutes too late, they had spent so long agonizing. Feeling remorseful about the relief he had felt earlier, he knew he had to atone for his sin; but against his own will, there was a joyful tremor deep in his heart, even at that moment.

"Well, this is the way it was meant to be," his father-in-law called out.

"Apparently, Providence has decided in this way," Reb Meyerl replied softly, as he sat there lost in thought.

"Goodnight, Rabbi," the group from Molits said quietly as they prepared to leave. But the head of the worthies from Pilsk was in such high spirits that he invited them to make a toast together. The locals, on the other hand, were keen to leave as quickly as possible. But then their leader, the fat one who was already standing at the door, paused a moment and walked back to the table. He offered the rabbi his hand, mumbled something that nobody understood and then quickly added out loud: "May you be successful, Rabbi!" The others repeated the words after him and then they left the bright warm courtroom, which had seemed so *heymish,* homely and comfortable.

Menasseh brought the vodka and they all made a toast. After that, the Jews from Pilsk immediately felt at home. They agreed that they would return to Pilsk that same week, together with their new rabbi.

After they had made all the preparations and the rabbi's wife was ready, they would come and collect her as well.

"So, has it turned out the way you wanted or not?" Avrom Aaron asked his son-in-law, slightly worried.

"God forbid! The way Providence wanted." Reb Meyerl felt a gnawing sense of nostalgia, as if he had already been away for years – from his home, from the *shtetl* where he had grown up, married and become rabbi.

This feeling of nostalgia would stay with him for the rest of his life. Within a few years he became a person of great renown. The invitations to become rabbi elsewhere kept pouring in from the biggest cities, because by then he was no longer the rabbi from Molits, but the *Gaon* of Pilsk. But Reb Meyerl was simply not interested in going anywhere else. One sin was enough.

"It is absolutely extraordinary how much Reb Meyerl cares for Pilsk," people from elsewhere remarked. They could not understand the reason and they were envious of the city.

"Do you have a cemetery there?" he would ask when people became ever more persuasive.

"What kind of a question is that? Of course we have a cemetery," these respectable Jews answered with a big smile.

"We have one in Pilsk as well!" Reb Meyerl smiled back at them, and that was the end of it.

Shloyme
שלמה׳קע

If it was up to Shloyme he would not lift a finger from one end of the year to the next.

Even begging is too much for him. He would rather go hungry, dreaming away the day, nestling on other people's doorsteps, as free as the air. His skinny feet are covered in dried mud. They look as if they have been kneaded from clay. He has a small pale face on which you can hardly see his little nose for the dirt around it.

The eleven-year-old causes a lot of trouble to the women in the *shtetl.* They know they will never be able to turn him into a "good" boy.

"Sholemke, if I catch you one more time on the steps next to my shop, I will tear you to pieces, that's what I'll do! Beat it! Get out of here! Do you hear me?" The shopkeepers chase him away like a dog. Shloyme never even looks at them but stays exactly where he is, pulling his coat over his red frozen ears.

But when hunger starts to gnaw at him, he gets up, shakes off the dust and goes off in search of food.

"Can you give me a piece of bread? Can you give me a pie?"

"Be off with you! Go away! There is no bread here! You aren't ill! You can work! What kind of charity would it be to give you anything? To help raise a thief, hmmm! What will become of you?" Though they felt a little guilty, the women only offered a few crumbs of comfort. "What a shame to go around begging like an orphan. God forbid!"

"Can you give me a piece of bread? Can you leave me a few…"

"Get out, I said! Or otherwise I'll throw this bucketful of slops over your head!"

But Shloyme knows the routine already: he won't budge. When they try to give him stale bread, he refuses it. He only has to give them one look, one flash of those big burning eyes that stare out at them from his dirty little face, and he can break their resolve. They don't understand why but they all give him something in the end: a baked roll, a piece of fresh bread, a cracker, depending on what's been baking on the day. Instead of thanking them, Shloyme gives them an impish smile, and off he goes.

"Go to hell, you big fat cows!" he shouts at them while his sharp little teeth break pieces off their tasty crackers.

"Sholemke, do you want to earn a few groschen, Sholemke?"

"I don't want to earn anything!"

"Sholemke, a *mitsve,* a good deed – and money with it!"

"I don't give a damn about *mitsves*!"

"And money, Shloyme, what about money?"

"I don't want anything!"

"To hell with you! Just try begging here again!" The women are seething with rage.

Shloyme does not answer. Instead, he whistles so loudly that he almost chases away the wintry clouds. Then he just skips away.

"It's a sin that such a creature is allowed to grow up in a Jewish community. It's a *khilul hashem,* a blasphemy against God," the wife of the synagogue warden says, proud to show off her Hebrew.

"Shloyme, I will turn you inside out and chop you up, if you don't stop giving us a bad name. You scum! Woe to your mother who brought you into this world!" Every Friday evening his father, Hershl the idiot, creates such a racket that their shabby little house shakes to its very foundations.

Shloyme's big eyes stare at his feet and he says nothing. He knows his father is right. He also knows that his father will get up, take off his belt and start roaring at him. He will stretch himself out so that it seems as if he is supporting the whole ceiling. He will shrug his shoulders and shake his broad square beard. Eventually, he will put his belt back around his patched-up trousers, loosen his fists and throw himself back upon the straw mattress with such force that the bed creaks under his weight.

Afterwards he will call him, Shloyme, and ask him to take off his heavy boots and undo the bandages that are wrapped around his aching feet. The room will soon be filled by a powerful smell of sweat, and Shloyme will bring in a bowl of warm water of his own accord. His father will then soak his feet and groan with pleasure: "Ah-ah-ah-oy!"

Shloyme's sister, Shoshe, will arrive looking smart, wearing a clean pinafore dress, her hair done up like a landowner's wife. She will be wearing two golden earrings which she has received as an engagement gift from her fiancé. She will conjure up a piece of cooked chicken out of her pinafore, as well as two pieces of fish and a small shining plaited loaf of challah for the Sabbath.

Shloyme's mother will not want to accept it. Shoshe will swear by her betrothed that his mother knows about it. In the end, Shloyme's mother will take the food with a big sigh and Shloyme will be happy. His mother will spread out two torn towels on the small table instead of a cloth. She will then go back to the little black oven to finish preparing the watery potato soup. She will carefully put two tiny candles in the small clay candlesticks, which he has made for her. It won't be long before she starts telling him off:

"Your father is a saint. You should be glad that he hasn't broken all your bones yet! How many times do we have to tell you not to go begging?"

She will show him her hands: "Look at these hands. Who do you think they are working for if not for you? Does your father have to come home on Friday, broken from a week's hard work, to be shamed on the Sabbath by that thief Khetskel in the synagogue? To be shown up in public! To be told in front of everyone that he should stop sending his son out to beg! You could work in Khetskel's butcher's shop, for heaven's sake. But no, begging is easier!

"So we are making you beg? And what about Shoshe? Aren't you putting her to shame as well? She is about to get married and I tremble when I imagine what could happen to her engagement because of you."

Shloyme thinks to himself. "Why don't you give me enough to eat then? And Shoshe the golden bride – she doesn't care for me one little bit. And Khetskel? May he rot in hell! He kicks me like a dog for no reason at all." His eyes burn like torches but he does not say a word. He looks at his mother with pity and clenches his small fists, thinking of Khetskel, of Shoshe, and of a way to escape.

"Your father won't go to the synagogue at all today; that's for sure."

Shloyme is startled out of his thoughts. It is only now that he hears the heavy snoring that fills the room.

"Oh, don't worry about it," says Shloyme.

"Come on, go and wash. It's Friday night, the start of the Sabbath. Take a look at yourself!"

"Tomorrow, Mother, tomorrow I will wash myself in the lake. The water is already warm, just as warm as in the middle of summer."

"Tomorrow you will take a bath! On the Sabbath?" his mother exclaims in horror. Then she sighs.

Hershl moves around on his mattress. The small bed creaks. He rubs his eyes and looks at the room around him for a while like a total stranger.

"Have you already 'cursed' the Sabbath candles?" he jokes, and scratches his beard with satisfaction.

He gets out of bed, wraps a bag around his bare swollen feet, takes a seat at the head of the table and starts to make the blessing over the wine to observe the start of the Sabbath. He forgets that he has not said either his afternoon or evening prayers.

The cheap fat is trickling down the clay candlesticks; the candles have nearly burnt out. The little flames are quivering. The shadows on the dirty walls are dancing madly.

"What else do we have? There is only one challah here."

Shloyme pulls a roll out of one of his pockets and places it next to the challah.

Hershl gets up and towers over him menacingly:

"May the earth swallow you up, you little thief."

"Father, I swear by all that is holy that the synagogue caretaker gave that roll to me for polishing the menoras. He couldn't do it himself because he was ill."

His father believes him.

He begins: "It was the sixth day; heaven and earth were finished." He pulls the bag tighter around his feet, cuts the small challah into pieces and hands them around. He does not touch the roll. Shloyme's mother gives his father a piece of the fish. She divides the other piece in two. She spoons out the boiling potato soup and adds small crumbs of chicken to it. She hardly takes any of it for herself. Shloyme is happily sucking his dirty fingers as well as the chicken bones.

That's how it is all year long, but not on the days leading up to Passover. Just before Passover, Shloyme will do anything. He is on his feet from morning to night. The women know this and they happily abuse it:

"Sholemke, will you come and help me make the dishes kosher?"

"Sure!"

"Sholemke, please carry this basket home for me, will you?"

"No problem!"

"Sholemke, you little *mamzer*, can you help me pluck the chickens this week?"

"Absolutely!"

He even gives Khetskel a hand.

He does not have to beg. The women give him bread, almond cakes, biscuits, pastries – all the things they have not allowed themselves for the whole year and kept aside for a special occasion. And now they have to get rid of all traces of leavened dough. They also give him old rags and leftovers of vegetables. Shloyme sells everything for cash. He is very pleased with himself.

Their little house is sparkling clean. It looks lovely now. A white cotton bundle is hanging down from the low ceiling in the center of the room, full of freshly baked matzos. Shloyme does not allow himself as much as a glance in their direction, for fear of making them dirty just by looking at them. But he does occasionally check the barrel in the corner in which big chunks of beetroot are left to pickle. When he sees everything is fine, he is satisfied and closes the lid.

He does not see his mother and father at all. He is much too busy to miss them.

And then the eve of Passover arrives. His parents have prepared everything. The clay candlesticks have been made festive with red crepe paper. A new cloth is lying on the table. Special foods are laid out for the Seder, the Passover service and meal remembering Jewish slavery and redemption in Egypt. The matzos almost take one's breath away with their freshness. There are at least six pieces of fish, decorated with carrot slices presented appetizingly on a long dish. The rich redness of the wine glistens inside a slightly chipped carafe. Small portions of *kharoset,* a sweet dish of chopped fruits and nuts ground up into a paste with wine, are arranged on plates. The hard-boiled eggs have been peeled. They are shining and there is a hint of blue around each yolk. Even the salt water looks appetizing. Large candles are burning in the candlesticks today.

Shloyme looks at everything with rare respect. He does not dare to touch a thing. He is waiting for that special moment, the beginning of the Seder he loves so much that he would give up half his life for it. He is sitting there on his polished crate. His father looks like a king on his white cushion at the head of the table, his mother opposite him. The light of the polished candlesticks burnishes everybody with a golden glow. Shloyme is dressed in a new suit. His cheeks are glowing and his big eyes are burning. His heart is full of joy.

"Ah, *Pesach*!" he almost cries out loud in sheer delight. He is sure that he knows every word of the four questions by heart. And just at that moment his father nods at him and Shloyme begins:

"*Ma nishtana ha'layla ha'zeh?* Why is this night different from all other nights … ?"

Jewish Nobility

ייִחוס

Even though he had never mentioned it to anyone, everyone in the *shtetl* knew that Hershel was saving up so that one day he would be able to marry his daughter to a scholar.

Everybody knew that he regretted being a tailor, and that deep in his heart he resented the fact that his mother, who was no longer alive, had encouraged him to become a craftsman.

Hershel's father had been a scholar, a God-fearing man, and as poor as Job. Being someone who never had any luck, he had held out great hopes for his son.

"Hershel," he would say, "sit down and study. You are a clever boy. You just have to want it. And if you want it enough, with God's help, you will become a rabbi." But fate had decided otherwise.

Hershel's mother was descended from a family of simple, ignorant Jews. Immediately after her husband's death, she decided that Hershel had to be taught a trade, and she had taken him to a tailor. This had been particularly painful for Hershel as he was already studying at the yeshiva. He had even taught himself Russian to increase his chances at the rabbinical examination and to help him find a position afterwards. He never wanted to suffer as his unfortunate father had done.

When he was twenty years old, instead of warming a bench in the yeshiva, Hershel was slaving away at a sewing machine. Day in, day out, he tacked and sewed and pressed, and before he knew it, he had become the best tailor in Zhelechits.

"He may have a head for the Talmud," people in the *shtetl* said, "but his talents certainly don't end there!"

Hershel put on a brave face. Although it disturbed him to be an artisan, doing his job gave him satisfaction, as it allowed him to provide for his mother and the other children now that their father was dead. And if, at times, his heart was assailed by a deep longing for a rabbinical throne instead of his humble wooden workbench, he would comfort himself with the thought that Yonatan HaSandlar had been a craftsman too – a cobbler.

His daily outfit was not that of a tailor, but of a Hasid. On the Sabbath he always wore a silk gabardine and a small velvet hat. He prayed at the front of the synagogue, among the other Hasidim of the *shtetl*, and he often went to the rabbi's home as an honored guest for the closing meal of the day. He prepared himself to do that which his own father had done years ago, namely to make sure that the boys would grow up to be fine Jews, and that the girls would get fine husbands. For Hershel, "fine" meant having an aptitude for religious learning.

Hershel knew that his boys were good at learning and the rabbi would confirm this every time Hershel sent them to him to be tested.

"Reb Hershel, your children are good, thank God! They can and want to learn, thank God!"

These conversations with the rabbi always raised Hershel's spirits, and he would forget any resentment that he might otherwise feel. He then worked with renewed energy and great enjoyment, softly humming a hasidic melody. At such moments, he was convinced that everything was meant to be this way. It was Providence that had made his mother force him to become a tailor. Just imagine: if he had been poor, God forbid, he would not have the money to pay a teacher for the boys. He would not be able to provide a dowry for their sisters, and they would be obliged, God forbid, to marry simple, uneducated Jews.

Thinking along these lines, his mood improved even more and he started singing out loud. His two journeymen joined in. A jubilant atmosphere soon filled the whole house. The shopkeepers, standing idly in their doorways, waiting for customers who did not come, heard the joyful sounds and they could not hide their jealousy.

"He's a lucky Jew, that Hershel," they sighed.

Binyomen the tailor was his greatest enemy. The other people in the town called Binyomen "the wanderer" because he had to travel increasingly far afield to beat Hershel at finding customers among the farmers. Nobody ever heard him sing. He had no reason to. He barely scraped a living. All his children had left; the girls worked as servants in Warsaw and both his sons had joined the military. He had a cold and lonely heart. He blamed Hershel for taking away his source of income. It was all Hershel's fault, because he was so much better at his trade than he was, in spite of the fact that Binyomen was descended from a long line of tailors.

"It's the evil eye," Binyomen muttered to himself.

Even though Hershel worked very hard, he and his family lived frugally. They ate black bread with herring for breakfast and gruel for supper. On weekdays there was not even a slice of meat on their plates. On the Sabbath Khaye-Beyle, Hershel's wife, sometimes bought a cow's head or foot, and occasionally a piece of lung or liver, but only for her husband and for the boys. She, her daughters and the workers could no longer remember the taste of meat.

Hershel stood bent over the long workbench near the window for the whole day, and often part of the night as well. He was very careful at drawing the outlines of the patterns. The piece of chalk in his hand glided confidently over the material, whether it was the coarse cloth of a peasant garment or a piece of shiny silk, which would end up around the shoulders of a local landowner or a hasidic Jew. Whoever they were, they were all anxious to have their clothes made by Hershel.

He would take a long time before actually cutting the fabric. When he finally sat down at the sewing machine, he worked with such fervor that his two assistants, who had been quietly stitching away until then – they had no reason to hurry – became infected by his enthusiasm. Hershel's machine rattled so excitedly that they unconsciously increased their speed, as if they too needed to save money for their future sons-in-law.

Opposite them, next to the other window, stood Sarah, Hershel's eldest daughter. Just like her father, she measured and drew patterns, the piece of chalk sliding over the silk and woolen fabric. She sewed for the "finest ladies" in the town. Among her clientele there was the wife of a rich man, who did not patronize any of the other seamstresses in Zhelechits, but who had most of her clothes made in Warsaw.

One day the *shtetl* had a surprise visit. It had been a fine summer's day. Everyone had been basking in the sunlight. The air was saturated with the fragrance of acacia trees and the smell of the ripe fruit emanating from the nearby orchards. The birds had been singing cheerfully, a bit like Hershel himself on days when the rabbi praised his sons for their intelligence. That day the entire *shtetl* witnessed how the wife of a wealthy landowner had arrived at Hershel's house. Not even Warsaw was good enough for this woman; she normally had her wardrobe made in Paris. She had taken Sarah with her, in order to have her measurements taken in the privacy of her mansion, after which she had ordered a whole series of light summer frocks that she would wear during her stay at a spa abroad.

Sarah was very slender, so people mockingly called her "Hershel's model." Sarah could not have cared less. She knew they said it out of jealousy. People held a grudge against her because she had such high-class customers, and because she and her father had managed to put aside so much money for her dowry, that one day she might marry a rabbi and become a *rebbetsin.* When she thought about this, her big black eyes would suddenly light up. They shone with pride and contentment and she too began to sing.

Sarah's moral conduct was as strict as that of her father. She did not make friends with any of the common girls in the *shtetl.* This meant she had no friends at all, since the daughters of the well-off Jews snubbed her for being a seamstress and the daughter of a tailor.

Her younger sister, Toybe, helped her with the needlework, and like Sarah, she often did not get any fresh air for days on end. However, unlike Sarah, her behavior was not impeccable. She was only seventeen, but she was already involved in an illicit love affair with someone who was not exactly a rabbi either!

Her lover was an apprentice with his older brother, Leybish, the baker. Leybish had managed to get a contract to supply bread to the army base right next to Zhelechits. As if that was not good enough, he also ran his own food shop. He was indeed a rich man. If Leybish had not been an ignoramus, Hershel could have been quite pleased with such a match. After all, Nechemia, Toybe's beloved, did not need any dowry so it could have been perfect.

But Hershel was not looking for a match for Toybe. He was completely unaware of her burning desire to get married. He did not even know that his daughter was in love.

Toybe was tall and slim. She had a pair of glittering black eyes, just like her older sister, and long dark hair. While she was at work, the curls danced merrily around her smiling face – how could Hershel have guessed that this had anything to do with love? She had always been a naughty child who could never sit still.

Another thing that had never occurred to Hershel, nor to Sarah for that matter, was to pay Toybe for her work.

"She's a real blessing, that girl, may no harm come to her," Hershel thought from time to time when he saw her working hard at her sewing machine, or when he noticed how expertly she added the finishing touches to a piece of work. All that fire she had within her seemed to flow into her needle and into the numerous songs that Nechemia had taught her.

Khaye-Beyle worked like a dog. All year she stood at the hot stove, rattling the enormous skillets in which she fried never-ending piles of onions. She could be seen running around the market to buy food, always on the lookout for bargains. Or else she busied herself with the laundry, in the courtyard during the summer and indoors in winter. She never took a rest, other than at the times when she had to sit down anyway to fold or repair clothes.

This was how things were during the week, but the Sabbath was different. On the Sabbath Hershel went to bed after lunch for a nice long nap. He fell asleep in no time, buried deep under a heavy eiderdown regardless of the season. Thus he killed two birds with one stone: he built up strength for a whole week, and he performed a commandment by observing the Sabbath as a day of rest.

Sarah would usually sit on a stool, which she had taken out on the street, and read a chapter of the Tanakh or other holy writings. Afterwards she too would relax on the sofa bed in the alcove where Toybe and she both slept, and read innocent romantic novels.

The boys spent the afternoon with the teacher.

For Khaye-Beyle Saturday afternoon was the time to have a chat with her neighbors. She felt at ease among these simple women, who were her friends. They would all sit down together on the threshold of Gedalya's grocery store. Khaye-Beyle would tell them how hard it was for her to make ends meet and how she did not even come near a piece of lung or liver the whole week long.

"Not that I'm asking for a piece of meat during the week, God forbid. May I not be punished for saying this, but really, I'm sick and tired of food that tastes like gruel. I feel sick if I just smell it!"

The women would wink at each other and say to her that she only had herself to blame. If she was clever, she would know how to speak to Hershel and get him to open his wallet. There would be enough for her to have not only meat but even *tsimes*, stews of vegetables or fruits, during the week.

It hurt when they talked to her like this, but she liked their company too much to go home. She was incapable of taking a nap like her husband, or dutifully reading a book like her eldest daughter. So she pretended not to hear their spiteful remarks, for she enjoyed catching up on the latest gossip and picking up all the news she had missed because she had been too busy during the week.

Toybe's Saturday afternoons were not spent in studying Torah or with the neighbors. Nechemia would be waiting for her in the nearby forest, in Leybish the baker's orchard, or simply in the open fields.

Nechemia was tall, even taller than Toybe and just as slender. He had blond hair and clever blue eyes. Despite their light color his eyes had such a penetrating expression that Toybe felt scorched by his mere gaze. Recently he had begun to kiss her as well. Toybe knew they shouldn't do this and that it was a terrible sin, but what could she do when his burning lips almost suffocated her? And why deny it? She too was possessed by a feverish desire. She did not really want him "to stop it," as she kept pleading with him while pressing her body even closer to his.

Both of them were healthy and young, and very much in love with one another. If it had been up to them, they would have married then and there – on the Sabbath.

In the meantime, Hershel was sound asleep. He was busy building up his strength for the week ahead, and doing what every good Jew was supposed to be doing on the Sabbath: rest. Even in his wildest dreams he could not have known about this; his youngest daughter lying with Nechemia in a field, where no Jew would normally go. None of the other boys and girls, who slipped away in secret after lunch, ever strayed that far. It was very close to the next village, where only non-Jews lived. Toybe and Nechemia would lie in the field, or else in a remote corner of the forest, under a fragrant pine tree, or in Leybish the baker's orchard. They lay there in each other's arms, kissing one another, like *goyim.*

Nechemia's father was a butcher. He was a tall man with a broad bony face. He had a thatch of blond hair, which was going grey, on top of which was perched a small cloth hat. His long hair hung down from underneath the hat on both sides of his face and merged with his beard, covering most of his neck. Day in, day out, he wore a pair of boots covered in blood and mud, the legs of his trousers tucked deep inside them, and a shiny apron, which had bloodstains on it.

Nechemia's mother was the exact opposite. She was small and thin, and her dresses were invariably spotless and neatly ironed. On her head she wore a cap adorned with little ribbons. It stood precisely in the middle of her head, so that one could see her thick red hair peeping out from all sides. Unlike all the other women in the *shtetl*, she was not in the habit of shaving it off.

She liked to sit on the threshold of her son Leybish's shop to observe how the business prospered, may no harm come to it. But often she was chased away by her daughter-in-law, who scolded her for being in the customers' way. Then she would remove herself and sit down in the street, on a small wooden stool, which she had filched from the bakery, unbeknownst to her daughter-in-law.

As she was sitting near her son's shop, she was never short of women to chat with. Word went round in Zhelechits, that it was because of her, Pinchas' wife, that the shop sold so much. There was nobody else in the *shtetl* with whom one could have such a pleasant chat, as with her. Most of the time her daughter was there too, a girl almost as tall as her father and with the same fiery red hair as her mother. She loved to talk with the other women as much as or even more than her mother did. In fact, she already looked like those women, even though she was not yet married.

Leybish and Nechemia were ashamed of their mother as well as their sister. Leybish had adopted a way of life which was suitable for a wealthy man. He gave generously to charity. One Sabbath, when he had been honored with a Torah reading, he gave a large donation to the synagogue, for the poor. After that, he was treated as one of the most respected members of the community and he did not hold back his money. He gave with a sense of gratitude for his own prosperity. Although he was not in the least bit learned, the people in the little town did not regard him as a simple Jew. Moreover, his wife was refined. Her father had been the owner of a small kvass factory, and he had known a thing or two about the Talmud as well. What was more, his wife had black hair, which greatly impressed Leybish who was descended from a family of redheads. Nevertheless, even though it irritated him, he never reproached his mother for sitting on his doorstep the whole day long.

Leybish also felt he had nothing to be ashamed of as far as Nechemia was concerned. The boy was following in his footsteps.

It also pleased Leybish that Nechemia had chosen a girl who would make an honorable addition to the family.

But then, suddenly, everything changed.

Pinchas' wife no longer sat in the doorway of her son's store. Misfortune had struck the family of Pinchas the butcher. It was his middle son, Mendel.

In the past, more than one mother with grown-up daughters had wished to have him as a son-in-law. "What a treasure, that boy is," they would say.

"He's a real fixer! Who do you think arranged that contract for Pinchas to deliver meat to the military? Of course, it was him! It's because of Mendele that his father's business does so well. He is another Leybish in the making."

He had been the star of the family. His mother doted on him, more than on any of her other children: "There is no one like my Mendele." She never stopped singing his praises to the other women in the community. He was a great help to his father, tirelessly combing the villages as he tried to find the best oxen and bulls for the army. He always managed to haggle and get the price down as well. All his father had to do was slaughter the animals, and Mendel often gave him a hand there too. He did most of the delivery work as well.

"Father," he would say, "you just stay here on the wagon to make sure that nobody steals anything, and I'll take care of the rest! You only have to sit here like an emperor on your throne and guard the meat. Are you listening to me, Father? Mendele will do the rest. Trust me. I'm better at this than those crooks. Ha! Ha! Ha!"

The last thing this golden boy needed was for a *shikse*, a non-Jewish girl, to fall in love with him. However, that is exactly what happened. It was more than falling in love. She became obsessed with him. She followed him around everywhere and used all the tricks she had in her power to charm him. It did not take her long to convince him that he was in love with her as well. And because of this *shikse* with her round pockmarked face, he had left the *shtetl* and converted.

He had ruined the life of his parents and brought misery upon his brothers.

The "house" of Pinchas the butcher sank into despair. Pinchas himself turned grey overnight. He stopped eating. He could hardly speak. He turned into a mere shadow of his former self. As soon as the seven days of mourning for Mendel were over, he closed his shop. From then on he just wandered around the *shtetl* with his long unkempt hair and beard. He no longer combed them, and he did not allow anyone else to touch them either. He had an air of melancholy and the little boys in the *shtetl* started calling him "crazy Pinchas." He never uttered a single word to anyone, so people began to avoid him.

Pinchas' wife had become smaller, even more shriveled than before. There was nothing left of her.

Her red hair turned completely grey. Her little cap was dirty all the time. Her dress stuck to her body. She sat alone at home the whole day and never stopped crying. Mendel's sister had gone to live with a relative in Warsaw. She never came home anymore. The sight of her parents' disgrace was too much for her. The house was no longer a house but a grave, she said. And she was right.

Leybish did not show his distress, though his heart was full of bitterness. Nechemia said that his brother deserved to be killed.

What Nechemia didn't know, of course, was that his brother was close to killing himself. Mendel racked his brain day and night, about how he could get out of this new milieu he found himself in. Already on the day of his marriage, when he was about to enter the church, the whole thing suddenly seemed hateful to him. As soon as he heard the unintelligible chanting and smelled the incense, as soon as he saw the priest in his white robes, an awful memory came back to him from his childhood. He could not help thinking about all the Maundy Thursdays when the Jews of his *shtetl* had been terrorized with fear. This was the same priest who used to walk slowly around their marketplace, dressed in the same white robes with the same large cross on his chest, accompanied by white-clad girls, who carried around a statue of a baby and his mother in their arms while chanting just as they did now for his wedding. He also remembered how once, during the High Holidays, he and some other children had been left at a neighbor's house, while their parents were in the synagogue. Suddenly he had heard people screaming outside. He left the house to see what was happening and saw the streets filled with peasants. They were wielding hatchets and iron bars. Just at that moment their parents had come running in, their faces twisted with fear. They had quickly grabbed their children, locked all the doors and windows, and sat down in complete silence. That night the *shtetl* burned.

He had been very young at the time. He had forgotten all about it until the moment he stood in front of the altar with his bride, when those awful images came back with great intensity. He felt a sudden urge to spit in the faces of those around him. He wanted to run back to his mother and father, and never in his life be a non-Jew again. But it was too late. A sense of fear took hold of him, just like when he was a little boy. He saw them right in front of him, hatchets and bars in their hands. He heard wild screams all around him. Everything had become just like that day long ago. For a moment he thought the church was on fire.

Although his father-in-law was not a poor man, and even owned a bit of land, the family lived simply, like wretched peasants.

Mendel, who by now was called Matchek, had to eat from the same bowl as his wife's younger brother and sister, as well as her drunken father. His breath stank of alcohol and tobacco all the time, and "Matchek" was disgusted by the way everybody dug into the same bowl. It made him gnash his teeth in anger. The food stuck in his throat. He also could not stand the smell of pork, which filled the whole cottage when his wife was frying onions. He knew that she always cut bits off the large brown piece of smoked pork meat, which hung constantly on a hook next to the oven. There were worms creeping out of it, long white worms.

Whenever they had a fight – which happened quite often – she would yell at him, "You filthy Jew!"

His own family did not know anything about all this. They had erased him from their memory and never mentioned his name.

Old Pinchas no longer thought about anything these days. His mind had gone completely blank. But his tiny wife, who had also aged enormously, had not forgotten her son entirely. Every time she remembered how they had torn their clothes as a sign of mourning for their "dead" son, she started crying all over again. The fact that she still loved him made her feel guilty, as if her feelings were sinful. She never stopped having dreams about him, mostly sad ones, but once in a while a happy one too.

Sometimes he appeared in her dreams as a small child still, sometimes as a tall, handsome young man towering over her. She even dreamt about him coming back home, throwing himself in her arms and weeping: "Oh Mother, I don't want to go back to those *goyim*, Mother don't make me go back! Mother!"

On such nights she would call out loud in her sleep: "Don't go away, Mendele, don't go! Stay here! Stay! Stay!" Or else she would scream: "Why are you mourning for him? He is alive!" Waking up confused and with a heavy heart, she would ask whether he had left again. Then she remembered everything and realized it had only been a dream. Tears streamed down her face.

It happened in the middle of the day as well. She would suddenly remember that awful mourning scene and she muttered to herself: "I wish they had killed me too, my child." Her own words terrified her.

In the meantime, Toybe and Nechemia grew more and more impatient. Even though they enjoyed their Sabbaths together, it was no longer enough for them. They longed for each other and wanted to be together all the time. They felt it was time to get married.

All the things they could not get enough of in the past – the long romantic walks among the fragrant pine trees, the twittering of the birds, the hunts for fallen pine cones, the playful wrestling in the grass and the mouthfuls of juicy black cherries from Leybish's orchard – seemed less than exciting to them now. However, they did not have the slightest idea how to make their wish come true.

They knew very well that Hershel would never agree to this match.

For a long time they racked their brains. It caused them sleepless nights. They thought long and hard, and all they came up with was to get married secretly without Hershel's knowledge.

In Hershel's home, they had been obliged to tighten their belts even further recently, now that it had been decided that Sarah was going to get married. Her future husband was a diligent student, a descendent of a long line of scholars.

It was early morning. The *shtetl* was still covered by a light film of dew. Thin trails of mist slowly glided through the streets. The sun was about to break through and it would not be long until the glistening drops had evaporated. The little leaning cottages huddled close together in their sleep. At this hour of the day, they seemed even smaller than usual. Somewhere shutters were opened. There was a rattling sound of an iron grille being removed from a shop window. Jews were already coming back from the first prayers in the synagogue, with their prayer shawls and phylacteries under one arm, when one could hear muffled noises coming from the narrow river, which ran just behind the *shtetl.* A couple of small black boats were tied up to the shore. They had come from Zakrotchin. A few women, future in-laws of Sarah, climbed out of the boats, eager to inspect the bride.

They had left the future bridegroom behind in the yeshiva where he studied. His mother, a Cossack of a woman, ran a small struggling shop with leather goods in Zakrotchin. She was quick to whisper a secret into everybody's ear, while urging them not to pass it on, especially not to Hershel. The secret concerned her noble background.

"Oh," she complained, "it is so painful. If only my husband, may his memory be blessed, were still alive, we would have never given our consent to a match with a tailor. Hershel knows this. He knew my husband very well. Everybody knew my husband. But what can I say? I am just a poor widow."

The women of the *shtetl* listened patiently to this conceited relative whose tiny head was adorned with a gigantic satin hat. They noticed how her double chin quivered nervously, how she kept fingering the decorations on her hat, and they were all "deeply sympathetic" to her suffering.

After Hershel had agreed to provide the couple with full board and lodging, in what had been the alcove where the girls slept, and a considerable dowry on top of that, the woman decided that Sarah was a very nice girl indeed, and that settled the matter.

Hershel was delighted. Such a pedigree and such a fine person; it was more than he had hoped for. Hershel knew the young man from the time when he himself had studied at the yeshiva in Radzimin. "Yes, I worked so hard for it, and now I've got what I wanted, blessed be His name. It has all been worth it. Praise to the Lord above!" Hershel almost spoke the words out loud.

The marriage was to take place in six weeks' time. Hershel was keen to get hold of the bridegroom as soon as possible. The boy's mother agreed, even though she made it clear to Hershel that she was not in any great hurry. Though deep inside she knew very well that she could not have supported her son for very much longer.

In Hershel's home everybody worked incessantly on the preparations for the wedding. Hershel sewed from early in the morning till late at night, whether for the bridegroom or himself, the little boys, or for the Jews of the *shtetl* who all seemed to have waited for this one occasion to order a new silk gabardine.

Sarah was simply drowning in work. She was responsible for her own outfit in addition to all the clothes she had to make for her mother, her sisters and all the women of the *shtetl.*

Toybe labored hard and suffered deep inside. She became paler every day. She would shed tears on the wedding dress, leaving marks on the precious fabric.

The bridegroom came down on a Sabbath. He was tall and pale, with black curly hair and side curls, and a pair of dark blue eyes. He had girlishly red lips and small, white hands. His beard was black and short.

Sarah fell in love with him immediately.

The whole house revolved around Sarah. Nobody even looked at

Toybe anymore. Recently Sarah had started treating her differently, as if she felt superior to her younger sister.

Toybe began to hate her sister and her father. Despite all her efforts to help Sarah with the preparations for the wedding, she had never received a word of gratitude. On the contrary, Sarah ordered her around as if she was some kind of apprentice girl.

Toybe suffered in silence. Only on the Sabbath did she pour her heart out to Nechemia. Then she expressed all the bitterness which she had bottled up during the week.

Nechemia, who had never liked all that hasidic mystical nonsense in the first place, now developed an even greater hatred for Hershel than he had felt for his converted brother.

It was the end of summer. For weeks on end the *shtetl* was held captive by the warm sunlight. The sun shone so fiercely, you had to hold a hand above your eyes in order to see the little houses, which were shimmering in the heat. There was not a single white cloud in the sky, which looked like a magnificent blue canvas stretched out high above the *shtetl.*

The pine trees in the nearby woods spread the pungent fragrance of the warm resin. Some cornfields had already been cut, others still lay there, brown and ripe. Here and there one could see neatly tied-up sheaves, ready to be taken into the barns. Because of the heat everything had become ripe much earlier than usual that year. The low fruit trees were almost bending down under their heavy load. Even winter fruits were ready to be picked.

On one of those days, many of Sarah's relatives descended on the *shtetl.* Her future mother-in-law had kept a close watch on the guest list. Only people of a certain status had been invited.

They had all arranged to stay with family or friends in the *shtetl.* Since Zhelechits was only a short distance from Zakrotchin people generally knew each other well. All the furniture and sewing equipment had been taken out of Hershel's home. The journeymen were sent home, so they would not be in the way.

The largest room was now full of long tables and benches, which the family had borrowed from the synagogue and neighbors. Some were newly-made for the occasion by Moshe the carpenter.

New white cloths covered the tables, resplendent with all kinds of delicacies: cakes and spirits, various strudels and honey biscuits. There were long rows of plates with chopped fish. At the head of the table stood a large dish with two carps' heads, one for the bridegroom and one for the rabbi. A delicious smell wafted from a freshly baked, gigantic challah. In the alcove, the bridal bed was waiting, made up with new, dazzlingly white linen.

Gedalya, the grocer in whose house Hershel lived, had offered his largest room for the women and girls to dance in, and a smaller one for them to get changed in. The latter also served as an extra guest bedroom for some of the women.

Hershel had invited the most respectable members of the community, and they had all come. Hershel would have nothing to do with the craftsmen and other ordinary folk that day.

It was almost evening. The bride and groom were on their way back from the synagogue courtyard where the marriage ceremony had taken place. A sea of colored lights welcomed the newlywed couple back home.

Nearly all the men were dressed in silk gabardines, with fur-edged hats or little velvet ones on their heads. The young women wore skillfully styled wigs and dresses made of satin and velvet. Young girls and children even joined in the dancing of "*Aheym fun der khupe*, Coming home from the wedding." Blue, white and red ribbons bounced around the room. There were smiling faces everywhere. The green and violet sequins on the women's dresses and jackets glittered as they whirled around the room. The silk on the men's shoulders gave off a veritable sheen.

Sarah's eyes were filled with tears of happiness. She looked tiny, almost like a twelve-year-old girl, in her white outfit. Her thick black hair, which would be shaved off the next day, seemed even darker from behind her white veil. Her little brown hand now had two rings on it: a diamond ring – which Hershel had given her when the engagement contract had been signed, while pretending that it was a present from the groom's mother – and a gleaming gold wedding ring. She could not stop looking at it. She was overjoyed.

Hershel's little boys, Haim and Yosele, were dressed in brand-new silk gabardines and little satin hats. Their faces were red with excitement. They did not move from the bridegroom's side for a single moment.

The family of Leybish the baker also celebrated a wedding today. The best room in the house had been prepared, the flowery curtains washed and ironed.

Leybish's wife loved the sight of fresh flowers. For this special occasion, she filled the room with vases. As if to apologize for decorating the room in such a non-Jewish fashion, she had unearthed a wall hanging she had embroidered years ago, before she was married, and hung it in a prominent position, where it would be clearly visible to the bride and groom, the rabbi and the other guests.

The tapestry depicted various scenes: the Jews on their way out of Egypt, angels ascending and descending Jacob's ladder, Joseph in Pharaoh's palace explaining the dream with the seven fat and the seven lean cows, and in the middle of all of this a flock of white sheep could be seen grazing in a green field. The embroidery covered half a wall and it told whoever looked at it that Leybish's wife was a good Jewish woman, despite the fact that she loved flowers.

The long table in the center of the room was full of fine wines and liqueurs, cake and spirits, and all kinds of exquisite fruits from Leybish's own orchard.

The floorboards were so white it seemed as if they had been sanded, rather than just scrubbed.

The wine in the glass carafes sparkled in the bright light of the paraffin lamp, which brought out the silver gleam of the knives and forks on the table. Cups and glasses, normally kept aside for Passover, had been made kosher; they were now acceptable for a meal which contained bread.

Leybish and Nechemia were both dressed in long black coats with a white flower in the left lapel. Leybish had learned about this fashion as a guest at a wedding in the "German synagogue" in Warsaw, in the days that he worked there as a baker's apprentice.

Dressed identically, the two brothers resembled each other so closely that it was hard to tell which one of them was the bridegroom, except for the fact that Leybish had a short yellow beard, while Nechemia, who was several years younger, was clean-shaven.

The rabbi was seated at the head of the table. He was one of those modern rabbis. Leybish had brought him in from Warsaw, where he was struggling hard to provide an income for his wife and a horde of little children, may no harm come to them. Unlike other rabbis, this one spent most of his time performing secret marriages and divorce settlements. If, at times, the demand was low for his presence at such ceremonies, he resorted to sewing aprons. This was a craft he had mastered during his time in America, from where he had returned after an economic crisis there.

The rabbi had a broad fiery red beard and a pair of thick fleshy lips.

He possessed a mouth full of strong white teeth and his face was round and plump. His eyes were the most amazing amber color. He was not a lucky man. Whenever he tried something new, it soon turned into a disaster. In the end he understood he was never going to be more than a simple rabbi on a poor street in Warsaw.

Now he sat there at the head of the table, waiting impatiently for the bride. On the very evening of Sarah's wedding, when she was dressed up anyway, Toybe had to slip away from among the women and the girls in Hershel's house, and go to another celebration, that of her own wedding.

For the first time in his life, Nechemia had been biting his nails. He paced up and down the decorated room, asking himself for the thousandth time: "Will she come, or will she lose courage at the last moment?"

Toybe arrived with a workaday coat flung over her wedding dress. As soon as she came in there was a burst of applause. The family showered Toybe with kisses. Men and women kissed each other as well. Toybe was beside herself with joy.

Before she knew what was going on, they had erected the *chuppa*, the wedding canopy. The required minyan of ten men, for the service, seemed to have appeared out of nowhere. And there was Nechemia, already repeating a formula which the rabbi said out loud while Nechemia put the ring around her finger. A golden ring just like the one Sarah had. Kisses were exchanged again. Then it was time to enjoy the wedding meal.

Of course, Leybish would have liked to have invited more distinguished guests, especially on this occasion, when his son was marrying into such a noble family. Just imagine, a match with Reb Hershel! But it so happened that they had been obliged to organize the whole affair in secret. Even his guests had only been informed at the last moment about the true reason for the celebration. All he had said to them beforehand was that they would not regret it. None of these men had known that apart from himself, nine other Jews had also been invited.

The whole ceremony had taken place so fast, that even now, after the *chuppa* ceremony, these guests could hardly believe what had happened. But when Leybish invited them to sit down at the table, like close relatives, they were quick to do so. They tucked into the various dishes. The meal was delicious; the men had never tasted anything like it. One plate after another disappeared down their throats, washed down with generous helpings of wine. Leybish already felt sorry that he had put his best fare on the table for them.

"We should have just sent them home with a few extra guilders, these beggars," Leybish said to his wife, who had never liked the idea in the first place. She had not opposed it, however, since she did not want to upset her husband. She had also felt humiliated by the whole conversion story of her brother-in-law, and she hoped that bringing Toybe, a daughter of Hershel, into their family, would restore some of their lost honor.

Old Pinchas sat at the head of the table, next to the newlywed couple and the rabbi. As usual, he did not utter a single word. He did not touch the food or the drink either. Despite his new suit, which Leybish had ordered for him for the wedding, he looked just as wretched as always, with his hair and beard unkempt.

The groom's mother was in no better state. By now she had shrunk so much that she hardly reached the table. Just like her husband she looked miserable in her new outfit. What was left of her hair had turned completely white. It was just visible from underneath the delicate silken kerchief, which Nechemia had bought for her on the occasion of his wedding.

Toybe sat next to her husband, quiet and pale. Although the room was hot, she kept on shivering. The rabbi tried to cheer her up with anecdotes from the secret marriages he performed in Warsaw: "You should see how happy they are, these brides, they are beside themselves with joy!"

Toybe was crying.

Nechemia held her hand in his, trying to warm it with the heat of his own hand. He implored her to calm down, not to look so frightened. He kept filling up her glass, most of which he drank himself. Her lips barely touched the glass.

Suddenly she started crying even louder. She sounded just like a small child.

Velvel Shtok, the peddler, stood up to his full height, and he gave such a hard bang on the table that it shook everything on it. He was dead drunk. He called out:

"No wonder the bride is crying! Just imagine, her father did not want to come to the wedding, the wedding of his own daughter. And why? Because the family isn't good enough for him. To hell with that bastard! Hasidic Jews are invited by him, but not us – ordinary, simple Jews. He is ashamed of us, that little tailor!" In his drunken outburst, Velvel poured out all the bitterness he had always felt towards the hasidic Jews of the *shtetl.*

"Ah, what a great fellow you are! You are much better than all of us put together! Let's drink another toast to you, Leybish!" he cried out. He wanted to put his arm around Leybish, but he missed and landed on a bottle of wine. Amazed he stared at his fingers, which were full of blood and broken glass.

His speech had caused a stir. Leybish fled to the kitchen to find his wife and told her it was time to put an end to the meal.

"If we don't stop them now, we will never be able to get rid of them," he hissed.

The guests had no intention of leaving, though. There was no end to the drinking and cursing. They all got drunker and drunker.

"And you, Leybish, are you better than those hasidic idiots? Would you have asked us to your daughter's wedding?" they stammered. By now they were just talking nonsense.

Some of them fell asleep at the table. These poor wretched creatures were not used to good food and drink, and it knocked them out. They sat there, heads hanging down, and snored. Some of them still smacked their lips in their sleep, others talked out loud.

At that moment, Binyomen the tailor walked in. He had come to Toybe's wedding of his own accord. Nobody knew how he had found out about it. Leybish received him like a guest. He honored him with a toast and invited him to the table.

But Binyomen did not want to take a seat. He had a drink, congratulated the newlywed couple and the relatives, and with a telling smile on his wrinkled face, left and went straight to Sarah's wedding.

The lights in the silver candlesticks had almost burned up by now. The rabbi was still talking about the speech the groom had given earlier. He praised him to the skies. "Reb Hershel, your son-in-law is a learned man, blessed be His name," the rabbi finally concluded.

The guests stood up. They were slightly tipsy from all the toasts and they were ready now for a bit of dancing. The women from the groom's side wiped their eyes, nearly choking with emotion. The groom's mother could barely restrain herself; she almost cried out loud from sheer exultation.

Khaye-Beyle watched them without saying a word. Deep down she could not stand the groom's mother and her hasidic tricks.

Suddenly the door opened and Binyomen the tailor entered, looking gloomy and angry as always.

When Hershel noticed him, his heart skipped a beat. "He must be up to something," he thought, but what? Hershel stood up and walked over to him. When he stood very close to Binyomen, he asked him why he had come. Immediately, he felt sorry for what he had said. Today he wanted to be kind to everyone, even to his enemies, since God had granted him every reason to be proud and grateful.

"What I mean is, I'm happy to see you," he quickly added. "Let me pour you a glass of wine and together we will drink to my daughter's wedding."

"No need to bother," Binyomen answered with a smile. "I have already drunk a toast to the wedding of your younger daughter today. I should be so lucky! What a handsome couple they are, Pinchas the butcher's son and your daughter! As if God had ordained it. Apparently, you didn't want to come to Toybe's wedding. The family of Pinchas the butcher is not good enough for you, it seems. So I went. It would be a sin to put a Jewish daughter to shame, wouldn't it, Reb Hershel? Now I'm here to wish you *mazel tov.* You have a lot of *mazel,* good fortune indeed, Reb Hershel, may no harm come to you. You have saved all that money to get one son-in-law, and now you've got two!"

Hershel looked at him, bemused. He thought that Binyomen had lost his mind. What was he talking about? Toybe, a wedding? He was sure that he had seen Toybe dancing with the girls only a moment ago. He had seen it with his own eyes. The man had obviously gone completely mad.

"*Mazel tov! Mazel tov!* Congratulations! Congratulations! Dance Hasidim, dance!" Binyomen shrieked at the Jews in their silk gabardines and their fur-trimmed hats. They had formed a circle in the meantime and they were about to start a hasidic dance.

"Dance! Reb Hershel deserves a double *mazel tov.* He has become the relative of Pinchas the butcher. Reb Hershel has become twice as noble today!"

The London Stories*

* In addition to italicized Yiddish and Hebrew words, we have italicized Kreitman's use of transliterated English words and phrases found in the original Yiddish stories.

Jim
דזשים

Jim gradually emerged through the fog. With long, thin, work-worn hands stretched out in front of him he felt his way carefully down a porter's alley before arriving at the main street.

There, among the long line of lorries, cars and trams, which passed by on the wet asphalt, his tiny lamp started flickering as if it would give up the ghost at any moment. His face, which was almost as dark as the damp black tarpaulin that protected the merchandise on his cart, had a pallid look and a sickly red glow around the pronounced cheekbones and hollow cheeks. The tip of his sharp thin nose looked strangely pale. His half-open mouth revealed a couple of crooked yellow teeth. Sharp black bristles covered his chin. He spat into a dirty rag and was reassured when he saw there was no blood. He continued to dream about having a home of his own. It was his dearest wish. It kept him going, and gave him the strength he needed to do his job.

He was indeed a lucky Jim! Every week he took home thirty-five shillings. His income was not dependent on the seasons, like that of so many other workers in London. His boss was pleased with him. It sometimes happened that when he had worked particularly hard, his boss would show his appreciation by giving him a hearty slap on his narrow shoulders. Then Jim would grin and reveal a row of yellow teeth, by way of a smile. It made him feel so good, this friendly slap, that he failed to notice the hollow sound it made. Nor did he notice that he felt no pain. His eyes would simply get moist and shine like those of a grateful dog. He was happy because he had work and he no longer had to go all around London looking for factory work as he had done in the past.

He would never forget those times, like when his mother gave him sixpence with a trembling hand, telling him he had to eat, even though she knew all too well that he had to pay for so many other things with the money.

"If your father, blessed be his memory, were still alive, things wouldn't look so bleak," his mother had said, wiping away a tear.

"I am lucky!" Jim exclaimed and stopped his daydreaming. He was so excited he could not stop coughing. His cough sounded dry. He clasped his chest with one hand and held the other in front of his mouth. What a relief, no blood clots, not even a single drop!

A gleaming black Daimler indicated it had to park. Jim immediately moved his cart closer to the pavement. The car rolled softly into the parking space with an air of absolute disdain. It was as if it expected the whole of London to doff its hat.

The chauffeur got out of the car. He was wearing a brown uniform with shining golden buttons and a pair of fur-trimmed leather gloves. He softly hummed a song, *"My darling, it isn't right to sit alone in the park on a moonlit night,"* as he walked into a shop.

Jim stood beside the gutter with his cart, crammed with boxes, and decided to have a rest.

"He's a lucky fellow," Jim said to himself. He was jealous of the chauffeur. But he did not think much of the lady in the grey fur coat in the car. She looked like a dry old stick.

The chauffeur's gloved hands turned the steering wheel, and the car slid away with a self-satisfied purr, leaving behind the acrid smell of petrol and a mother-of-pearl shine on the wet road.

Jim smoked a cigarette. The lady in the car was still on his mind. He compared her to his girl in the box factory, and smiled to himself – what a difference! He looked at the cart and checked that the tarpaulin was still in place. He tightened the rope and harnessed himself to the cart. Navigating the traffic with care, he gradually got into the middle lane again.

He turned off at the street by the shoe factory where he had to make a delivery of a load of boxes. He pulled the bell next to the entrance. A small boy with short hair came running down and opened the door.

Brushing aside a lock of hair, he rubbed his face and greeted Jim like an old friend: "*Hello* Jim, you could have whistled! What did you ring the bell for, you idiot!"

"*Go away, shrimp.*" He was irritated by the boy's cheek and thought how nice it would be to be able to whistle. He twisted his mouth in a comical way, and it was hard to tell at that moment if he was laughing or crying.

The boy wanted to carry the boxes upstairs, but Jim would not let him.

"*Go away, you dog.*" That was the last thing he needed. The little imp might damage the boxes or make them dirty.

The cart was empty. Jim threw the tarpaulin and the rope inside. He smoked a cigarette which somebody had given him. Then he harnessed himself in again. He was happy that the job was done.

In the box factory, the girl who always made tea was already making her rounds, even though the bell had not yet rung. She crept silently, like a cat, between the piles of paper and the boards, trying not to trip over the wires, which were everywhere. Now and then, she looked furtively in the direction of the supervisor, who pretended not to notice her. She drank the tea, for which everybody, except for her, had to pay thruppence a week.

When Jim came upstairs, the long tables looked deserted; half-finished boxes were strewn all over the place, a pair of scissors were still stuck to a sheet of paper, a brush was left in a pot of glue. It seemed as if everything had been turned to stone by a magician's touch and the people round the tables had simply vanished.

In the break, the girls had a bite to eat, drank a *cup of tea,* and laughed at each other's stories. Some went out to powder their noses or put on some lipstick. The tea girl put all her makeup on again. She even took the trouble to brush her thin, mouse-colored hair.

Jim looked around. All the crates were occupied, so he sat down on the steps leading into the office. He wiped the sweat from his brow and tried to get rid of some of the mud. He was waiting for his girl to bring him tea. He was so thirsty that his throat was itching.

"Hello, Jim!"

Jim looked up at the green metal lampshade on which a big fly was buzzing around, playing in the dust.

"Hello!"

She stood in front of him smiling, her face and lips made up in garish colors. Her cropped hair looked as if it had just been brushed. Her dress was short. It was well above her knees. She was holding a steaming cup of tea.

Jim thought about the lady in the Daimler and blushed. He shivered for a moment, afraid that she might guess his thoughts. He decided that his girl was very pretty indeed and that he would marry her one day. He would not listen to the doctor's advice. How could living alone and depressed, like a dog, be healthier than having a mate and a home? He thought about his savings, and he smiled with satisfaction. He had set aside every penny for this. Then he remembered that she was waiting with the tea. He hastily took the cup from her and almost scalded himself. The girl burst out laughing. She touched his moist, curly hair affectionately. As soon as she had sat down next to him on the steps, she started to tell him off: "Jim, just take a look at yourself! All the girls see you looking like this!"

Jim was ashamed of himself. He felt as if a needle was stuck between his ribs, sharp and pointed. It was such an odd sensation. When he talked to her, he always had the same feeling. She was so loyal. She always made sure he got hot tea even when he came in a little late. She had even brought a mug for him from home. He did not understand what she saw in him. He knew only too well when he walked past a mirror what he looked like! He would certainly try to keep himself a bit tidier, if only for her sake, he thought.

"You know, when you sweat, the dirt gets everywhere, and your clothes slip down," he justified himself. He wanted to say something more but was interrupted by the sound of the bell.

The girls had a last quick look in the small mirrors of their handbags before they walked back to their workplaces.

Jim took the large broom and started sweeping the floor. He put the rubbish into bags. Soon sweat was pouring down his face again. From time to time, he looked at the girls and then carried on sweeping.

At the end of the day, he wiped his sweaty face with his girlfriend's apron, which she always left on the table, ready for the next day. Then he took her to the tram. There was a lot of pushing and jostling when it arrived. He had to use all his strength to help her get on. He felt more dead than alive as he walked to his lodgings.

He unwrapped the *chips* he had bought on the way home and poured vinegar over them. Then he went to the little cooker and put the kettle on for tea. He had his supper. Every bit of bread and every piece of potato was visible through his scrawny cheeks. He slurped his tea as he leafed through the paper (this was his only luxury; it cost him a penny every night, and tuppence on Sundays). He checked the number of *accidents* that day, read the latest football news, and looked at the pictures. Then he started reading an article about the royal family, about the duchess who was about to go into labor… but his eyes were already closing. He put the paper aside, went to bed and fell asleep immediately.

It was Sunday. On Sundays, Jim always dressed up in a plum-colored suit. The trousers were so wide on him that they flapped around his skinny legs like petticoats. He put on a green and gold check tie, which he had bought at Woolworth's on his girlfriend's advice. He had lunch in a restaurant and afterwards he read an episode of an Edgar Wallace detective story, as well as the rest of the paper. In the evening they went to the *pictures* together, and while they were standing in the long queue for cheap tickets, they ate most of the sweets they had brought to eat during the film.

That Sunday evening Jim was finally persuaded. He was sitting next to his girl watching the screen, his arm around her waist. When the star on the screen was embraced by her lover, she looked so passionate and seductive that it took Jim's breath away. And there he was with a warm, sweet creature in his arms.… He proposed to her that very moment. They wouldn't postpone it, he said, they would get married as soon as the law permitted. And he kept his word.

The big day came and Jim had put on his best suit for the occasion. When he was about to put his signature on the wedding documents, his thin hand suddenly trembled: he remembered he was a Jew. He even saw the two flickering lights of the candles in front of him that his grandmother used to bless every Friday night. He saw his father – blessed be his memory, as his mother would say – and the pen slipped from his hand.

On Monday, they went back to work. The girls had put some money together to buy a cake. Even the boss came down to have a piece. He did not say anything about them taking half an hour for their tea break in honor of the young couple.

Jim scarcely took any part in the celebration. He replied automatically to all the words of congratulations. He kept hearing a voice in his head, saying, "Jew," "*goy,*" "Jew," "*goy.*" He did not know himself what he was anymore. He kept himself aloof, as if the party had nothing to do with him.

Breaking the Fast

אָפּגעפּאַסט זיך

Old Borenstein came home from the slaughterhouse utterly exhausted. He had been wiping his knife all day long, sliding it past his thumbnail and over the plucked necks of the chickens. The boys had not given him any breathing space. They kept on at him all the time:

"*Come on,* Reb Borenstein, *come on, hurry up!*"

He had hardly emptied one crate of birds before they shoved another one in his direction. His fingers were smeared with blood. He barely had the strength to keep pushing the chicken heads through the holes in the table next to him. His white coat had turned bright red. His rolled-up sleeves were encrusted with blood. Small beads of condensation ran down the low dividing walls. The boys were happily smothered in feathers. Mr. Borenstein's face was covered in perspiration. The shrieks of the chickens were driving him mad. And as if that were not enough, there was the racket of the market outside, in the *Lane.*

The women had descended on the *Lane* like locusts, looking for bargains. But the chicken sellers were not in the mood to give anything away that day. After all, it was Yom Kippur, the Day of Atonement, when everyone was preparing for the fast, and it was only once a year! They chased the women away and would not allow them to pick their own birds. The saleswomen made such a row, you would think they themselves were being slaughtered, and if a particularly stubborn Jewish woman insisted on checking out one of the birds for herself, she could expect a slap on her wrist.

The commotion went on until late into the night. The special prayer books for Yom Kippur were selling fast.

"Come and buy, Jews! Buy here, it's dirt cheap, Jews! *Grapes*! Don't forget to fast! Yom Kippur candles! Parsley! Jews! Jews!"

Old Borenstein was completely deaf by then, but the stalls outside were still buzzing with excitement. The chickens looked almost green in the strange flickering light of the lamps, as they shone on the intestines, gizzards and livers. Dark shadows were playing on the flustered faces of the saleswomen, giving them a ghostly look.

The blood. The voices. The heavy work. It had all been too much for him. When he came home, he could still hear the screams echoing in his quiet room. He immediately got undressed. He could not stop yawning while he said his evening prayers. Then he went to bed.

But he was too tired to sleep. He started thinking about Yom Kippur the year before, how he had come home even more tired than now – so tired that he had thrown himself on the bed still dressed in his bloodstained clothes.

He had woken up late that day, he remembered. He had only just managed to find a *minyan*, a quorum of ten men, also latecomers, with whom to say prayers. When he came back the flat had already been beautifully arranged for the occasion. Everything had looked so festive. His wife had made several tasty dishes from the chicken. He hadn't wanted to stop eating. Then night fell; they finished their meal. The table had been covered with a sparkling white cloth. In the high silver candlesticks four small blue flames were leaping towards the ceiling. A light flickered in the middle of the table, in a thick glass candle-holder covered with greasy fingerprints.

She had been alive. She was standing over the candles and with both hands covering her face she had softly poured out her heart to God in heaven. He had prepared himself to go out, wrapping up his prayer shawl and the prayer book for the High Holy day. He had waited for her to finish blessing the candles, so that they could go to the synagogue together that evening for *Kol Nidre,* the first service of Yom Kippur.

Now he was twisting and turning in bed like a werewolf. It was no good to be alone. No good. No good at all!

After a sleepless night he got up late. Again, he barely managed to find a *minyan.* On his way out to the prayers, he heard the *landlady* from downstairs chattering to her cat.

She was giving the cat a kiss right on its mouth. At the same time he heard a man laughing like an idiot.

It was his neighbor on the second floor. He spent whole days downstairs because he did not get along with his wife. She used to work in a factory, and all she had ever done was roam the streets with the other factory girls. There were two things she enjoyed – going to the cinema and powdering her nose. She did not care much about religion. Although she was a Christian, she never went to church. She even cleaned the rooms on Sundays. He, on the other hand, was the son of a Christian mother and a Jewish father. He was very pious, a devout gentile and he went to church every week. He observed all the Protestant laws as strictly as possible. He had even joined the Salvation Army in an attempt to atone for the sin of having a Jewish father. Whenever his wife shouted at him, he would find refuge downstairs with his friend, the *landlady.*

His wife was always nagging him about spending too much money on things she considered ridiculous, such as a hat with a stiff brim, embroidered with gold letters, which was part of his Salvation Army uniform. Yesterday he had been even more extravagant. He had bought himself a blue coat with epaulettes like a general. He had spent a fortune, and so now he sat downstairs with Mrs. Stone.

She understood him, Mrs. Stone. She was a plump Jewish woman with long grey curly hair. She had a fleshy wrinkled neck and a hard face the color of wine. Though her eyes bulged slightly, they still had a twinkle in them which was unusually lively for a seventy-year-old.

Over the years she had had many different *tenants* there, but none was as nice as Mr. Davies.

She had lived in the house for over forty years. She had buried her husband there, as well as her old father, and at least two dozen cats. Now there was nothing left for her to do but look after herself and the cat, and therefore Mr. Davies was a most welcome visitor. She could tell him all her problems, how she simply couldn't stand that butcher on the second floor, for instance. Recently, another disaster had struck, the way they were making a complete mess of her wonderful neighborhood. She complained: "*Isn't it a crime, Mr. Davies? Have you seen what they are doing!*"

Mr. Davies understood her very well. They were sitting in a long, dark room, in wicker armchairs with faded cushions. Opposite him there was a framed picture of two dogs and a cat hanging on the wall. Next to it there was another picture of Mrs. Stone's parents, and then there was a large portrait of Mrs. Stone herself.

Mr. Davies blinked his Jewish eyes as he softly stroked the cat's rough, black fur. He was a willing contributor to Mrs. Stone's lamentations. He told her how on a beautiful summer day, when the sun was hovering like a piece of old gold over the large front gardens and beautiful flowers, he had seen a group of tanned and muscled non-Jews arrive in their neighborhood. They had come to demolish perfectly elegant white stucco houses and their fine brass door knockers. Bang! Bang! Bang!

Polished doors and windows had fallen. Old, well-built houses, like hers, had been destroyed. They had erected a white fence around the site, and in less than a year they had replaced the houses with a whole row of shiny brick-red tenement buildings. Instead of nannies in their smart blue cloaks, the only thing you could see now was the children being let out on a leather leash, like dogs. There was nowhere for them to let off steam. They had to spend their whole time inside the tenement buildings.

"*I wish 'he' would move there!*" she waved her plump old hand in the general direction of the second floor. "The whole of September he has been making *noise* with that ram's horn of his: 'Tra-traaaa, tkuk-koooo.'" As she imitated old Borenstein, she grew even redder in the face, thoroughly enjoying her own joke. It reminded her of another one of his misdeeds.

"Do you remember," she asked Mr. Davies, "the infernal racket they made, when his wife died? It was a *disgrace*!"

Earlier that morning, Mrs. Stone had treated herself to roast chicken, instead of her usual breakfast of *bacon and eggs*, to celebrate Yom Kippur. She had bought the chicken in a non-kosher shop. Now Fred Davies was going to drive her to the liberal synagogue. She was all dressed up with long dangling earrings. She carried an English version of the prayer book with her in a small leather suitcase.

When she came home, there was a card waiting on her doormat, wishing her a "Happy New Year." It was from the Davies family. She was so touched, she could not stop looking at the card, at the purple flowers and the golden embroidered *Shana Tova* New Year greeting which she could not read as she did not understand Hebrew. Instead she read the English inscription, which brought tears to her eyes.

Old Borenstein came home in the evening, tired after a whole day of fasting and praying and blowing the ram's horn. He had carried back his prayer shawl, his slippers and the Yom Kippur drops which he had sprinkled on his handkerchief to help him keep alert during the service. He walked up the dark stairs very slowly. He lit two candles. He could see the dark blue night sky through the windows and could hear people walking by downstairs, Jews who were coming back from the synagogue, wishing each other all the best for the coming year.

Mrs. Stone downstairs and Mr. Borenstein upstairs. Both of them were sitting on their own, breaking the fast…

Becoming a Tramp

געוואָרן אַ טרעמפּ

Bill rolled his sleeves down. His long, stick-like arms were covered in thick green veins. He beat the flecks of flour off his old jacket until it became dark again.

For the past eight years, he had had to change jobs many times and not out of choice. If it had been up to him, he would have liked to stay in his current position for the last few years he had left. But, of course, nobody ever asked him what he wanted. It was always the same: just as he was getting used to a place, to the job and the people, there would be a hitch – and he would be asked to leave.

This time he was working in a bakery. They were good people. He earned two pounds and ten shillings a week. They always paid him on time, and he was never bullied.

The baker's wife, a buxom Jewish woman with a wide parting in her thin grey hair and a round smiling face, treated him like a son. Every morning before he went home after a long night's work, she would put a paper bag full of bagels in his hands: "So, Bill, today at least you'll have a nice, Jewish *breakfast*," she would beam with pleasure, and all the warts on her flabby cheeks and chin would smile in unison.

The baker himself was a short Jew with a floury beard, who never stopped threatening his workers that he would send them home, all of them, saying that he didn't need any "union shmunion" people in his bakery. In spite of that, most of them had worked for him for at least ten or fifteen years. So it was a real shame that he had to give Bill the sack.

One day, one of the workers, a tall boy with broad shoulders who had started work at the age of fourteen when he left school, and who was already a father, imitated the baker:

"I don't need any 'union shmunion' people! This is a bakery, not a union!" he said with an angry voice, while trying to appear shorter than he was. Everybody had been in stitches and Bill felt at home.

Today, the boys each slipped a shilling into his hand and looked at him sadly.

"What do you think you're going to do, Bill?" one of them asked. Bill turned around in surprise. Ever since he had started working there, nobody had called him by his name, except for the baker's wife. When he had arrived in the bakery six months earlier, the boys had taken one look at him and decided to call him a *shlemiel,* he was such a wretched, simple creature.

The skin on Bill's finely etched cheekbones was dark and thin. The lines on his low forehead appeared to have been drawn by a knife dipped in black ink. Dirt filled the nails on his long bony fingers. His eyes were bloodshot and watery. Then there were Bill's clothes – the jacket he wore each and every day was shapeless and threadbare. It had got so thin in places you could see his bones. The jacket made his elongated body look even skinnier. He looked like a dead tramp that still had a smile on his face. It was a brooding smile.

The baker paid Bill an extra week's wages, and said apologetically to his wife, "What can I do, when the customers stay away? They are disgusted by him!"

His wife wrapped up a small piece of bread in the meantime, and added a few biscuits that had gone soft: "Here, Bill, for the children!"

Bill had left the shop quickly. It was full of light and sunshine. Everything in it exuded an air of plenty. The baker's wife followed him with her eyes and shook her head: "If only he would have kept himself a bit cleaner…"

"Don't talk nonsense!" the baker said, as he arranged the cakes on a tray. He then told his wife why Bill did not keep himself "a bit cleaner."

"You know, he's got tuberculosis, and his wife won't let him into the house. He doesn't even have a place to shave. Did you see his chin? It's so sharp and bristly. Just like a black pig.

"He insisted on fighting in the war, our hero. Well, he's paid a heavy price. And who is going to help him? Poor sod. Who is going to employ a man whose lungs have been shot to pieces? *They* won't, for sure! He can still get a job with one of us for a few weeks. But with them? It is a fact, Bill offered to mow the lawn of the lady with the big garden, and she just slammed the door in his face. She wouldn't even talk to him. Apparently, she said to her servant – the one with the blue dress who wears a stiff white cap on her grey hair – that his mouth 'was as empty as a grave' and she was disgusted he was so dirty."

The baker's wife, who had been tut-tutting as her husband spoke, rejoined: "That's how they are. They don't know anything about compassion. For them, if you have money, you're lucky. If you don't, you can start digging your own grave."

"It was Mrs. Levy, that lady's neighbor, who convinced me at the time to give him a job in the bakery. She said she knew him. 'He is an honest fellow and he deserves a chance,' she told me. That's why I took him on. But I can't lose customers because of him, can I?"

Bill did not have any desire to go home. He knew the look his wife would give him. It would make him feel hot and cold at the same time. He would start coughing up blood, and then there would be nothing else to do but slink away again. So he walked to a nearby park.

It was a sunny day. The array of well-kept flowerbeds made for a dazzling colorful display and there was a lovely fresh smell in the air.

Children were screaming and laughing as they rolled on the grass. Dogs frolicked around and barked loudly with pleasure. Couples were lying in each other's arms, forgetting that they might be needed at work. Loving each other on the grass meant they would not get any money at the end of the week.

"There is no work," they said to each other, "but there is sunshine! And when do we get any sun here?" They decided to live for the moment.

On a separate piece of freshly cut grass a group of about ten elderly men were bowling. They stood there slightly bent, with serious faces, their grey eyes transfixed. They followed the black balls with intense curiosity as they rolled smoothly over the grass.

Their wives were sitting on two wooden benches nearby – shriveled old women in dark clothes with pious faces and big hats on their grey heads. They looked at the game. Some of them were knitting waistcoats.

The Jewish women were sitting a bit further on. They were having a chat about cooking and baking, and Jewish troubles. They were also amused to see how seriously the old people took their game.

"That's a clever game they're playing there, isn't it?" they said, shaking their heads in a mocking fashion.

"Absolutely. Just imagine a Jew going bowling!"

Bill sat there a couple of hours, watching the black balls on the green grass. From time to time, he really got involved in the play, wondering whether the ball would hit the target or not. Finally, he went home.

His four boys were sitting in the kitchen, on a clean rug, which was torn in places. They were busy building a "palace," They even had a pennant, stuck between the wooden blocks. All four of them had the same granite grey eyes and they looked well-fed with healthy red cheeks.

When they saw their father, they were very pleased, not so much because of him, but because now they had a chance to show him what a fine palace they had built.

"You see, Daddy," the middle one said ecstatically, "that's what Mr. Brown has bought for us. He says that he will buy us a real palace if we don't cry when Mummy goes away."

Bill smiled sourly.

"So, he's a good man, is he, that Mr. Brown?" he asked his eldest, who was eight years old. With a cheerful "yes" on the tip of his tongue, the little one suddenly saw how his father was looking at him. The words stuck in his throat and he stopped talking. Without understanding why, he frantically started to pile up the blocks higher and higher. Then, with a sudden gesture, he destroyed the whole edifice. The wooden blocks shot out in all directions – and the word "yes" lingered on in the air.

"Where is your mother?" Bill asked the children angrily.

They did not answer.

"Where is your mother?" he coughed.

"Mummy has said that I should say that I don't know," the four-year-old said. The oldest boy giggled. He shut up immediately and started collecting the wooden blocks from the floor.

"Mummy has gone away with Mr. Brown. He said that if she didn't go with him she would have to pay the rent again," the oldest boy said softly, as if telling his father a secret.

"You won't tell her that I've told you, will you?" the little one asked, wanting reassurance.

"Not tell her!" Bill muttered under his breath.

"Not Mr. Brown either!" the six-year-old called out abruptly. He was a plump boy with blond hair and a snotty nose, his little hands full of the blocks he was picking up from the floor. "Otherwise he will not buy the palace," he said, explaining the logic to Bill.

Bill left. He went back into the park. He took a seat on a bench next to a lake. A blue-winged duck was swimming in the water, followed by a dozen yellow ducklings.

Bill threw the soggy biscuits in the water. The duck swam straight at them, together with all her ducklings. He watched how greedily they nibbled away at the biscuits.

A shabby old man with an overgrown grey beard, long tousled hair and a pair of worn-out shoes which revealed all ten naked swollen toes on his cracked feet, sat himself down with a heavy sigh.

"Hello, Bill! Are we having another holiday?"

Bill looked straight through the old man. His thoughts were very far away.

"She was once a really decent woman, I can tell you," he said to himself while he stared fixedly ahead.

"What do you mean?" The old man looked at Bill with sickly, bulging eyes; he thought Bill had been talking to him.

"He has taken her away from me for the rent and the children's food."

The old man had no clue what he was talking about.

Night fell. It was not long before they heard the sound of a bell and the voice of the park keeper calling, "Everybody out!" Bill, who was still holding a small piece of bread, left the park together with the old man to look for a place to spend the night.

They settled down on the stone steps of a tobacco factory. They shared the bread the baker's wife had given Bill and the old man's rags.

Bill had become a tramp.

Too Late

צו שפּעט

The Segals are preparing themselves for a big party in their home. They are expecting a very important guest from abroad.

All the lights are burning in the enormous, crystal chandelier. Even the little lamps on the embossed wallpaper, normally merely decorative, have been switched on today, throwing their long shadows on the walls opposite and onto the deep yellow Persian rug. The long room is bathed in a sea of light. The crystal vases and bowls on the sideboard are caught in a sparkling dance of green, red, yellow, and white. The colors leap up like flames, chasing each other and bouncing off the oval mirror opposite.

The heavy, shining mahogany table has been pulled out to its full length. Fine pieces of silver are displayed in a glass case near the table. In a picture above the mantelpiece, Shirley, the eldest daughter, observes everything with a smile on her face. It looks as if she could step out of the picture at any moment and take a seat at the long table, while the frame would remain there, empty and forlorn, above the marble mantelpiece. The parquet floor surrounding the carpet gleams like a mirror. It has been polished to the point of danger.

A love scene between Greek gods is unfolding on the small carpet in front of the mantelpiece. Shirley looks down on them with some amusement, but without the slightest intention of leaving her frame.

The cook is sweating. She has been standing on her swollen feet since early that morning, and she is still not ready. She keeps on cooking and frying, roasting and baking: there is chopped fish and fried fish, chicken soup and roasted duck, meat loaf and rolled veal, cake and all kinds of *puddings*, *apple pie*, and strudel – a combination of Jewish home cooking and authentic English dishes. She has even thought of making *Yorkshire pudding*.

Mrs. Segal has become English through and through. She knows that it is correct to say, "*I haven't done it*," rather than, "*I didn't done it*." She laughs at *foreigners*, and keeps herself to herself. She even has a little dog, which she takes out on a leash when she goes to buy fish and chicken and expensive fruit, which is later brought to her door by poor Jewish or, as is more often the case, non-Jewish delivery boys.

With true Jewish pride she always gives the *goyim* a larger tip, so as not to make antisemites out of them.

And of course, she keeps up Jewish traditions. She lights the candles every Friday night and places them carefully in the front room. She turns on all the lights in the room and never closes the heavy, plush curtains. She is not ashamed – on the contrary, she is proud to be Jewish. She derives great pleasure from watching the *goyim* stand there gawping outside her windows. She loves to see the look of amazement on their faces when they notice the large luxurious room where the heavy silver Sabbath candlesticks spread an air of festiveness.

The imminent arrival of a visitor is causing a great stir in the household, not least of all because there are three daughters in this house, and the guest is a cousin of theirs. They also know that he is no ordinary young man. He has a university degree. In fact, he has just become a doctor. The brother-in-law of Mrs. Segal, her sister's husband, has written to them to say that his son has not simply graduated, oh no, he has received the highest distinction. His professor has advised him strongly not to let himself be led astray, which happens to so many young doctors: on no account should he open a "shop"; he has to continue his studies and become an eye specialist. Therefore, he asks them, the Segals, to help his son make his dreams come true.

Mrs. Segal does not really understand what he means by the word "shop." What she does know, however, is that her brother-in-law is a learned Jew, not like her Jack, and even though he is very poor, he has encouraged all his children to study. Apart from his son, who will arrive any minute now, he also has two girls who go to good schools, which she in fact pays for. She knows that if it were not for her generosity, they would just die of hunger.

Mr. Segal paces back and forth in the large room in eager anticipation of his guest. In order to make time pass more quickly, he stands still every once in a while next to his daughters, who are sitting on the sofa and in the large armchairs. The girls are petite and slim. They are wearing short dresses that are pulled up far above their knees, revealing fine legs in real silk stockings.

The small dog follows every step its master makes, and it pauses whenever he does. It snorts through its little black nose with happiness because everybody is there in the room and he is there with them.

Mr. Segal takes in everything in the room and, to his own surprise, he realizes for the first time how pretty his daughters are.

He takes a look in the mirror, and he sees that he himself is still looking good and young for his age. When he peeks at his wife, he wonders how it is possible that he has not noticed how much weight she has put on. Her bosom has become enormous. Her hips are large, her shoulders broad. There are grey streaks in her hair.

It seems to him as if all this has happened overnight. They have lived together for thirty years now and he has never noticed any changes. She always looked the same, he thought. Only now does he remember his wife's constant complaining: that she is getting too fat, that after every childbirth her *varicose veins* are getting worse and her feet more swollen, practically bursting out of her shoes.

Is she, this woman with the three double chins, with the bright chubby face and the tiny deep-set eyes – is she the same Hannah, the girl with the long face, full of character and the sharp protruding chin? Is she the one with the big blue eyes, the girl he had to fight a battle to win? His girl, who blames him each and every day that he cheated her. She thought that he was an intellectual in that *shtetl* of his, but soon after fleeing to London together, it turned out he was nothing more than an ordinary tailor.

"Ha, ha, ha!" he laughs, "was she really worth fighting for?"

His wife scrutinizes him with her piggy eyes. She does not have any idea what he is thinking about.

"Did you say something, Jack?"

"No. Nothing! *It's all right.*"

He looks at their wedding picture, which stands on a small table in the corner, and then at himself again. He has to admit that he has changed quite a bit himself as well. He takes off the square *yarmulke,* which he has worn the whole day, revealing a gleaming, white patch. All that is left from the fine thatch of brown hair in the picture is a silver rim. It disturbs him to discover that he is already grey too, or rather, that he is even greyer than she is. And the longish, slightly bent nose has become a lot fleshier, thicker and rounder. He turns away from the mirror and puts the *yarmulke* back on his head.

"None of us is getting any younger."

He looks at his hairy wrist with the broad leather band. His watch tells him that it is half past five.

"It's getting late. He has to be taken to the synagogue," he says to his eldest daughter, who is leaning close to the radio, listening to a symphony.

"*I suppose they will soon be here.*" She does her best to sound casual. She does not want her father to know that she is at all interested in seeing her cousin, whom everybody in this room already considers – without speaking about it and without the boy's consent – the future son-in-law.

The grey car, which was sent to the station an hour ago to pick him up, arrives with a roaring noise.

The trees in the small front garden, their branches cut into a round shape, enjoy the golden light of dusk. The brightly colored chrysanthemums look more beautiful than ever in the last rays of the setting sun. Just like the owner of the house, the sun seems to refuse to admit that it is past its prime.

All three daughters move simultaneously towards the bay window, careful to keep behind the tulle curtains. They do not want the guest to know how curious they are.

Mr. Segal himself adjusts his *yarmulke* and he walks outside in a light-hearted fashion to welcome his wife's nephew.

Mrs. Segal remains in the doorway. She is standing there, her face beaming, holding her plump arms wide open, ready to swallow him up in her embrace, tall as he is, and to cover him with kisses.

It has been thirty years since she left her home. In a flash she sees her *shtetl*, and herself as a young girl, her whole family waiting for her, also with wide-open arms. A tear rolls down her right cheek.

A man jumps deftly out of the car. It's Harry, the Segals' only son: blond, portly, dressed in a bright suit and white shoes. He stands next to the door of the car, smiling, waiting for his cousin to come out. When he sees the little dog, he picks it up and starts talking to it.

Emerging from the car behind him is a rather gloomy man, about thirty years old, who is wearing a crumpled grey suit and a pair of worn shoes. He looks extremely worried. His dark brown eyes have a hungry glint.

The girls exclaim in unison: "Oooh!" They return to their armchairs and make themselves comfortable. They really could not care less what they look like.

In the meantime, Mr. Segal takes the young man by the arm and introduces him with great ceremony to his aunt.

Mrs. Segal has turned pale; she has completely forgotten that she has to kiss her nephew. When she remembers, she just kisses his forehead. Her dream has been shattered. Her entire past has been erased in one single moment.

Mr. Segal almost stumbles over his wife as he tries to get past her, holding his guest by the hand. She just stands there on the doorstep, paralyzed. He has no idea what is wrong with her.

He introduces the guest to his eldest daughter. All three girls jump up at once. Extending their slender hands, they ask politely, "*How do you do?*" They try very hard not to burst out laughing when this man in his shabby shoes takes the hand of each one of them, brings it to his lips and kisses the long red fingernails. He then answers back softly and with quiet confidence: "*How do you do?*" He sounds like a born Englishman. They stare at him in amazement:

"Huh! What's this?"

The servant girl, who is wearing a bright blue blouse and a black satin skirt in honor of the guest, brings in tea.

With great dexterity the young man holds the fine porcelain cup in one hand, the plate in the other. He even calls it "*a cup of tea.*" He does not seem at all uncomfortable. He enjoys the delicacies he is being offered from all sides. If anything, he is the one who is smiling sarcastically, at the girls' lack of sophistication.

Later on, Harry shows him the bathroom. A white stove burns pleasantly in there and a shiny black bathtub, almost filled to the rim, is waiting for him invitingly. But when he catches sight of himself in the full-length mirror, he starts feeling less sure of himself.

Next to the little rubber mat right beside the bath there is a real carpet, a black one, with a bunch of yellow tulips woven artfully into the pattern. They almost look real in the soft glow of the dying sunlight.

Mr. Segal tactfully brings in a fresh set of underwear and socks, a suit and a pair of shoes. He begs his nephew to try on the clothes, since he gathers that something must have happened to his luggage along the way.

The young man turns red and starts stuttering: "Eh, yes … I mean …"

But Mr. Segal interrupts his nephew's search for an excuse.

"*Please, hurry up.* We have to go to the synagogue quite soon." He walks out of the bathroom, relieved to leave his nephew there.

The young man looks bemused: "Synagogue Jews, really? Oh yes," he now remembers the *yarmulke* his uncle is wearing. "What a curious country!"

The clothes fit him perfectly. Mr. Segal has sewn the garments himself by guessing the measurements of his nephew with the help of a picture. Mr. Segal has always had an eye for these things. He still loves to sit down amidst the workers in his factory and show his master tailor how to do a particularly difficult piece of work.

He places a shiny top hat on his round head. He is wearing a black dress-coat and a pair of pressed pinstripe trousers. A pair of brown leather gloves complete his outfit. He puts the small dark-red *tallis* bag, where he keeps his prayer shawl, under his arm, and Mr. Segal is ready to go. Harry has replaced his white shoes with brown ones. His soft grey hat askew, he is playing with the dog again. When Mrs. Segal has finished blessing the candles, they all go to the synagogue.

The synagogue is suffused with light. The chandeliers send glittering rays down from the ceiling.

Jews are coming to meet him. Almost all of them are corpulent men with big bellies, top hats and smiles on their faces. They greet him and want to know how life is in "the old country." Some used to know his father. One of them, the heaviest of them all, with the biggest diamond pin in the broadest tie, says he remembers him from there; they used to go to *cheder* together. He tells him that when he was about to start at the academy, his parents had taken him to London.

"And here we are!" He is clearly very pleased with himself.

The guest does not believe his eyes: this large Jew, with his ostentatious tiepin, who looks more like a pig farmer than anything else, was the neighbor's ten-year-old son? Wasn't he the one all the other boys made fun of, because he was always going around in torn trousers that had become too small for him? But this man looks fifteen years older than him! And yet, when he takes a good look at him, he does indeed see similarities. Yes, it's him.

"I've heard that you have become a doctor. You always were clever. I was never any good at Hebrew. *But I don't really care, believe me!*" The man has lapsed into English, forgetting that he is talking to a newcomer. "After all, I've got twelve butcher shops now," he says proudly.

"*I am very pleased to hear that,*" the "newcomer" answers him, in perfect English.

"What? So you don't come from the old country then?" A cloud of disappointment spreads over their round faces.

"I most certainly do," the guest comforts them. "People study English there as well, you know."

"They study there better than anywhere else," Mr. Segal says with satisfaction, and Harry laughs, then says in English: "*I think he'll give you all a lesson in English, ha-ha-ha!*"

They start praying. Harry sways above his prayer book and looks up. He counts the red and blue panes in the tall windows of the synagogue. The building used to be a church, which the Jews have bought and rebuilt.

Back at home, Mr. Segal says the blessing over the wine; he muddles up all the words. It does not matter to him because on this special occasion he feels like doing it by heart. His nephew has to bite his lips not to laugh.

The food is spectacular, though. Never in his life has he eaten dishes such as these; they look irresistible. The young man hesitates: he has no idea what one is supposed to do with the mountain of plates and endless rows of knives, forks and spoons. But he watches his cousins closely. He imitates every movement of his uncle who turns out to be an expert, and thus he manages not to make a single gaffe.

The girls hardly ever see their cousin. His days are spent elsewhere and in the evening he sits at his desk, red-eyed and surrounded by heavy books. He has no time for them.

The girls are rarely at home anyway. They play tennis all day long, they swim or they go off to Bournemouth. Sometimes they stroll in the West End and look at the shop windows. In winter they go to *charity* concerts. At night they are out dancing. In fact, they just don't care about their cousin and his affairs, especially now that he seems to be getting more and more involved in that eye research of his. Even the clothes, handmade by their father, look baggy on him, and his eyes are getting redder every day from studying at night.

Mr. and Mrs. Segal are becoming nervous. They are afraid that their daughters will go off with other men and leave their cousin to his own devices. The parents would much rather have him, a relative, as their son-in-law, especially now that he is about to start his own practice in Harley Street and become a *specialist.*

"Listen to me, you have to ask him how much longer he's going to study." Every night Mrs. Segal nags her husband while both of them are lying awake in bed. "He could be a specialist already. But he doesn't know you are ready to help him set up the business. The other day you had the perfect opportunity. You know, when he was saying that specialists nowadays have machines at home with which they can see what's going on in their patients' eyes. It would have been so easy, if only you were not such a *fool,* to tell him then and there that you will arrange for him to have such a machine. Then you would have had a nice talk and you could have told him that it's time to start thinking about marriage."

"What are you going on about? They're not even engaged, and you are talking about marriage already!"

"*Nu,* so, then we'll make an engagement!"

The couple quarrel deep into the night until they finally come to an agreement. The engagement will be announced on Sunday.

"*Well, I wish you luck!*" Mrs. Segal kisses her eldest daughter, Shirley, early the following morning. The girl is sitting in her pajamas at the *dressing table* in her smart bedroom and puts a green cream on her face.

"*Why?*" There is a look of amazement in Shirley's streaming eyes, in which she has put drops a moment ago to make them shine.

"*Daddy* has agreed that Sunday will be the day of your engagement to Dennis and we will rent an apartment for him on Harley Street. Enough with the studying! He should know how to do the tricks of his trade by now! Your sisters will start looking for husbands and you will become an old spinster, if we have to wait for him. He thinks to be a specialist, he has to get old first."

"And nobody has asked me anything? *I have nothing to say, or what?*" Shirley, who has a beatific smile on her face, caresses her mother's cheek affectionately. Suddenly she jumps up, grabs her mother by the waist, and dances around the room with her. Mrs. Segal is huffing and puffing; she can barely follow the slim girl. Eventually she manages to free herself and she drops heavily on the silk blanket on the unmade bed.

"Do you love him?"

"Love him? *Well, I don't know. But,* you know, Mother, *they'll go mad* with jealousy when they find out that my fiancé is a specialist in Harley Street."

"*Of course, darling!* It's good that you understand. I've always known that you are a *practical girl!*"

Mr. and Mrs. Segal are sitting opposite their nephew feeling rather flustered, almost ashamed, as if they are about to commit a sin. They summon up their courage and start talking about their decision. They tell him that it is time for him to *settle.* The younger girls will not wait endlessly for Shirley, and they as parents don't want to bring shame on Shirley by allowing her sisters to get married before her, and so on and so on.

The young man's face darkens. He too has got something similar to say. He has prepared himself carefully. He has rehearsed every word many times. It's difficult, but he doesn't have a choice.

He has a girl. She is very sweet. He would do anything for her. She loves him too. She'd give her life for him. He feels that the time is right for them. His uncle has a good heart. So does his aunt. They will understand. They were young once. He even knows, his mother has told the story many times, that her sister brought shame on everybody by falling in love with a tailor and running away with him. Of all the people in the world, his aunt must know how it feels: to be apart from the person one cares about most in the whole world, and not to be able to bring her over because of a few lousy pounds.

They will surely help him. He hasn't done anything wrong, apart from being a fool, a naughty little boy. He should have talked to them earlier, that's true. But, at least he knows now that very soon he will be able to pay them back, bit by bit, for everything they have done for him. When he has a *flat*, he will be able to live lawfully together with his wife. They must be pleased about that. And how wonderful it will be for him, and for his girl especially, not to have to live with this terrible yearning any longer.

"You impudent rascal!" Mrs. Segal bangs on the table. She tries to hold back the tears with all her might, but she can't. She weeps like a little girl.

"What will Shirley say?" she sobs.

Shirley laughs as she wipes away the tears from her mother's face. She keeps telling her that she wouldn't have wanted him anyway. She never really liked him in the first place. He's such a bore.

"*She can have him!*" she calls out cheerfully, and she walks upstairs to her room, hiding her own tears.

Two Libraries

ביבליאָטעקן

Light pours into the library's large anteroom with its green shiny walls. Thick smooth columns support the finely vaulted ceiling. The red and white tiled floor is cold and clean, except for a small puddle of muddy water by the door. A long bench is crammed with the old and the young – elderly men and women who have sat down for a moment to pause for breath, and small children waiting for their parents who have gone in to pick up books. Above the bench, warning notices sternly caution the public:

Smoking Is Strictly Forbidden.

No Spitting. Offenders Will Be Prosecuted.

A pillory stands right next to the window, a permanent reminder! An inscription is carved in this instrument of torture, with an explanation for the viewer about past forms of punishment. Back in olden days, when mankind was not yet civilized, the sinners would have been wedged onto the pillory, in the middle of the marketplace, so upright citizens could come and do good deeds by throwing rotten eggs and rubbish at them. The really pious would throw stones as well. Most often, the sinner died of shame and anguish.

It is Friday evening. The anteroom is bustling with people walking in and out. One would expect to find the young girls and boys, who are coming in to exchange books, in dance halls or cinemas, rather than in here. Yet they take two, three books at a time! Some of the boys are dressed in short trousers, revealing bare knees. All kinds of hikers and cyclists are walking in, accompanied by girls with broad mannish shoes and hair cut short, like a boy. One also sees many young Jewish faces. Old gentile women are entering with large Victorian hats towering over their pointed faces. The husbands have watery eyes and small bony faces, an extinguished pipe in their toothless mouths.

Little schoolboys are dashing in with red cheeks and mischievous eyes, followed by fresh young girls in high-heeled shoes. Housewives, baskets in hand, are hurrying in after them. Even pregnant women come here to have a good read.

Inside, in the big hall with the overfilled shelves, there is a big rush on Edgar Wallace. Old women take out Mrs. Henry Wood – you can shed a pleasurable tear over *East Lynne*. The hikers, cyclists, and girls with short hair try a book in translation once in a while. People make their way through the library like a dense forest, not knowing where it begins or where it will end.

Lithe girls with manicured nails and painted lips bring in yet more piles of books. Their weight almost crushes them. It looks as if these lovely slim bodies might snap in two at any moment and the heavy books will all end up on the floor of the library, uncovered, ashamed of their nakedness. But the girls are used to doing their job. They place the books where they belong with great care and the next moment they are whirling through the long shiny hall again, ready to pick up a new load.

The girls at the entrance and exit doors also have their hands full. Books need to be stamped, dates have to be filled in, and baskets, which are not allowed in the library, have to be taken from their owners, ostensibly out of respect for the printed word, but possibly also for another reason.

The whole place is brimming with life!

The Jewish library is an entirely different world.

The counter stands in a long hall as a dividing line between the reading room and the lending library.

Elderly Jews come here, not so much to borrow books, but to have a nap or a chat, to meet up with an acquaintance, to have a look at the papers. The girl at the counter does not have much to do. So she sits and knits the whole day. Knits and yawns. Yawns and knits. Jews tell stories in here, they talk about the torture chambers in Germany compared to which the pillory is a toy. They say that Jews are tormented in concentration camps, in old and more modern ways. They talk and sigh. Then they switch to Poland and tell each other stories about the plight of the Polish Jews. "What a miracle he has not invaded England. Thank God!" They start discussing antisemitism in general. In the end the yawns of the girl behind the counter become catching and people think it must be time to go home.

The hall gradually empties.

The small gentleman with the black eyes, dressed in a shabby fur coat, a briefcase under his arm, has gone through almost all the foreign papers. He has also had a look at the literary magazine. He pulls a miserable face. An old man, a chicken plucker on the *Lane*, has finished reading the gripping feuilletons in the daily paper. He flicks through a magazine, mumbles something to himself about it being incomprehensible, and leaves. A Hebrew teacher, who is almost collapsing under his own excessive weight, has read out all of his poems to a suffering, hungry writer. The teacher is still basking in the beauty of his own creativity, when he realizes that his only listeners are the walls. In the meantime, the writer has managed to borrow a shilling from someone and has sneaked out to get something to eat. The teacher is so angry that he soon leaves as well.

The girl at the counter has become lazy because she does not have enough to do. Sometimes she does not even bother to put away the few books that have come in.

Her only break comes in the form of a bookseller who, as a sideline, supplies her with excellent Yiddish books that could be a great success among the non-Jews too, if only they could read them. By some miracle, he manages to sell her a few books.

The librarian herself is no expert in these matters. She does not really know any Yiddish, so she purchases the best Yiddish literature along with sentimental novels. She has up to two or three times as many of the latter. If she likes the cover, she buys the book. The library is not short on funding in any case.

But when the bookseller has left as well, and her hands are sore from too much knitting, she suddenly becomes upset. She shouts at the few remaining souls that sit dreaming at their tables, their heads resting on their elbows:

"Be quiet!"

They wake up, rubbing the sleep out of their eyes. They look around at each other in the gloom... and start talking.

She is Not Blind

זי איז נישט בלינד

The small house stands on its own, completely isolated. The houses on either side have been reduced to high piles of burned crumbling bricks, broken, rickety furniture, and the charred remains of enormous black beams. All kinds of tools and appliances are lying around amidst endless mountains of broken glass. Inside the house, destruction weaves its silent web, just like the cobwebs appearing between the flowers and the grasses, which have sprung up wild and free among the ruins.

No one has had the courage to tear the finely woven labor of thousands of drunken spiders. No one has dared to pick the high, violet-colored flowers, which might have adorned a table or a sideboard in a poor man's house. No one even comes near them.

The house itself has subsided somewhat. In the window, different creams, soaps, powders, and perfume bottles are on display. Two mannequins made out of wax stand at either end. One is blond and wide-eyed, with a white, almost transparent neck. Her big blue eyes have black curled eyelashes and the eyelids are covered with glittering blue shadow. Her golden hair is glossy and her nose small and haughty. The long curls are tumbling down her comely shoulders, falling onto the small, pale, half-naked breasts. The other one is dark, with a mass of black shiny hair, which is held up high in a bun by a large comb set with glittering stones. Her pitch-black eyes are incandescent and suggest rich exuberant laughter. Her dark breasts, full and pert, are half covered with red satin. Various brochures are lying at their feet, full of advice about what you should do to look as gorgeous as the two wax beauties. Beads surround them – red, blue, white, amber – every color and shape. There are brooches, parasols, and even cigarettes. Everything is covered with a film of dust.

The display window is so low that it hardly stands out above the pavement. You have to bend down very low in order to enter.

Inside, the owner is dressed in a dazzling white coat, just like a doctor. The trousers that stick out from under his coat have the smoothest of creases. His brown leather shoes shine, the satin shirt is an immaculate white, and his broad red tie hangs in a perfect knot. The blond rim around his pinkish bald pate has a veritable gleam to it. He looks pleased with himself and the world.

He is bending over a large man who lies in a high reclining chair with soap all over his face and a white napkin tied around his neck, as if he were a small child being fed by his mother. The proprietor, Berl Melzer, feeds him all kinds of stories, which he has invented especially for him, or he talks about politics.

Mr. Melzer is flanked by young men dressed in white jackets like waiters, who tower above the clients that are sitting down all over the place. Some of them have been soaped and are ready to be shaved by the boys in the short white jackets. Others are being cut in a whirlwind of dancing scissors and smoothing combs while the boys eagerly tell their stories, stories about anything and everything. They could even teach the women upstairs a lesson or two.

The customers often know more about what's going on than the boys can tell them. They were also at the dog races, or the horse racing, or at the football match, and it is quite impossible to tell them anything new.

Many of the clients are sitting on the long worn-out plush bench opposite the high chairs. They look at their reflections in the mirrors that are covered in soap specks, and wait patiently for the proprietor.

They all want to be seen just by him, although he has so much work to do that they often wait in vain. But if a customer manages to get a seat next to the chair where Mr. Melzer is already busy washing or powdering someone, then he can sneak into the chair while it is still warm, and then he too has the privilege of being cut or shaved by the boss.

The stories that he tells them are very colorful indeed, and all of them are made up from what he observes.

"*He is a jolly clever man, that Mr. Melzer,*" the customers say. "When he tells you a *story,* you think that you have seen it all with your very own eyes. Sometimes it even seems as if what he tells you has happened to you."

He is well known all over the city, and all the Jews come to him for a haircut, even those living in rich neighborhoods, where they have to look elegant in order to fit in with their smart surroundings. They would rather go a day without a shave or a week without a haircut, just to be able to go to Mr. Melzer himself and pick up a *story.* His name is celebrated, not only in his own town but in many others as well.

One day a man arrives, a writer with a bundle of books which he has printed himself and which the poor fellow now has to carry around to sell. He knows the best place for him is in this small, half-sunken house with the two dusty beauties in the less than spotless display window. And indeed, the welcome he receives is almost too much for him. The wet handshake of the boss is soft and warm – as warm as the look in his kind, smiling eyes.

All the anger and frustration caused by the lack of recognition, by people not wanting to believe that he is the greatest writer of his generation, that it should be allowed that a great man like him has to haul himself around to sell his own work, disappears. It is blown away like a cloud in the wind, and he feels a warm stream running through his body.

"How are you doing, comrade?" The writer calls Melzer comrade instead of Mister, because he knows that Melzer comes from a family of socialists, fine people.

"Please, come in. My niece, Perele, will receive you in a moment, I am terribly busy!"

Inside, in the room which is not very big, everything is clean and pleasant. A fire is blazing in the open fireplace, even though it is summer, and it spreads a sweet, peaceful warmth over the faces of the people, and over the glowing furniture. The flames can be seen dancing in the mirror opposite and in the gleam of the radio cabinet.

Mr. Melzer leaves the guest behind in the room, and he rushes back to finish a client.

Inside, Perele is busy working. She is dressed in a white coat as well. Her small face is surrounded by black hair, and she has a pair of sparkling coal-black eyes. Her complexion is dark, her lips are red and full. She tends to pout while she is talking, and occasionally reveals a mouthful of sharp white teeth like a puppy's. The girl does not stand still for a second. She does not simply walk around the house, she runs. She does not have a moment to spare. But that does not mean she is not ready to drop everything instantly and she treats the people her uncle brings in every now and again with the greatest respect.

Before the guest has had time to count to three, a white, neatly pressed tablecloth has already appeared on the table, as well as a silver samovar with boiling hot tea, a little jug of milk, and a pot of sugar. Tasty, thinly cut sandwiches are being piled high on a big porcelain dish and a freshly baked cake is placed upside down on a tray. Everything is beautifully laid out with great taste. Perele even places the flowers from the radio cabinet on the table in honor of the guest. She pours tea and smiles at him so warmly and charmingly that immediately he feels at home. He would love to stay there the rest of his life, being waited on by "comrade" Melzer's niece; simply sitting there, endlessly watching the little one, looking at the colorful perfumed flowers and the red, yellow and green flames dancing around in the fireplace.

"Please, just help yourself. The sandwiches are made with kosher sausages, the other ones don't have meat in them," she says, just in case the guest is vegetarian. She has thought of everything.

"Please, my uncle will be angry if you don't eat."

The guest does not need any encouragement, rather the opposite. And, while she is talking like that to the guest, she floats in the direction of her uncle. She moves her full warm lips so close to him, one could think she is about to kiss him. What am I talking about! She is just whispering in his ear that it is time for him to eat something. She begs him to take a break and have a *cup of tea.* People can wait, even with soap on their face. She does not care.

Her uncle revels in her sweet words, but he is not coming, not yet. How can he? He is too busy! Apart from that, he does not mind if his niece comes in again to ask him a second time. He does not mind feeling her warm lips close to his burning ear once again. He knows that if he doesn't leave his customer – the man's mouth and ears wide open in eager anticipation of the rest of the story – to go inside, she will get angry with him; her brilliant black eyes will grow even darker and rounder, *sweeter than wine.* Only then will he go inside for a while, sit himself down at the table and take a sip of his tea. He will have a quick chat with the guest and pop back to work with his mouth chock-full of the biscuits that Perele will have tempted him with.

All of a sudden the guest feels a shiver running down his spine: a ghostly figure comes shuffling out of nowhere with her hands stretched out in front of her as if trying to feel her way. It seems as if she does not trust her own steps, as if she does not recognize the room. She walks as if this is the first time in her whole life she has set foot on the floorboards which, although covered, hide a deep abyss underneath the fine carpet – and there is no way back.

Looking at the apparition, he notices that her heavy dark eyelids are lowered, and he is unable to see her eyes. He can make out her round shape and dark features. Her hair has been cut short. She has a fringe, which covers her forehead completely, all the way down to her thick black eyebrows. Her nose is small, too small for her face. Her blue swollen lips are dribbling.

She shuffles on regardless, all the time tapping the air around her with her small, sweaty, swollen hands. She mumbles something to herself. It looks as if she is smiling at the same time. He starts to feel uncomfortable. His lips are trembling. He wants to say something but he can't. The figure passes him and disappears.

Suddenly there is a bang. Perele looks up with an angry flicker in her eyes, her little mouth is twisted. "One day she is going to kill herself. We tell her not to crawl around, to stay in one place, but no, she has to behave like a ghost and scare my poor uncle to death. As if he isn't hurt enough already."

Melzer rushes in from his salon with a fearful look on his face. He glances at Perele and sees that her eyes are full of tears. Then he remembers the guest and his face turns red in shame, as if he has been caught in some obscene act. It does not last longer than a second. He runs into the kitchen where he tries to pick up his wife who is lying paralyzed on the stone floor. She is as heavy as a corpse. Eventually he leads her back into the room like a small child. He props her up on an old armchair covered with half a dozen shabby cushions, and he pleads with her.

"I beg you, Feygele, don't try to do anything. Everything is being done for you, isn't it? You know that you are weak."

"I am not weak!" The little woman hisses and bites her lips. One can hear in these four words a whole world of protest against her husband, against her niece, against life, against God himself. She is just sitting there as if she were dead. It is hard to know whether she has hurt herself or not. It seems as if she is almost smiling. Yes, indeed, she is smiling. An air of mute happiness surrounds her.

The door of the salon opens and a tall slender woman walks in. She has an abundance of golden hair and she is dressed in an elegant grey suit. Pinned to the left lapel is a golden monogram, together with a small bunch of fresh flowers. Her low-cut blouse, which is made of blue taffeta silk, shows off real pearls around her wrinkled neck. Her slender yellowish white hands, with long red fingernails, are laden with diamond rings. She is wearing a ring of dark silver so big that it covers half of her middle finger. Around her wrists are several bracelets, one of which is covered in precious stones. The large brooch crowning her décolleté is full of different animals, birds and dragons, their snouts and wings sprinkled with tiny diamonds.

"Hello, Mr. Melzer!" she calls out cheerfully.

"Hello, Madam Zesha, how are you? Did you have a good time?"

"Is it possible to have a good time without you?" she smiles roguishly and winks at him.

The customers are all looking at her. They practically devour her with their eyes. One of them even gives her a light tap when she passes by. She lifts her lovely golden head and walks slowly into the room:

"Oh Perele, my darling, I want a cup of tea! I am simply dying for a cup of tea, and I am hungry too."

Perele goes into the kitchen to fetch tea for the woman who is her aunt on her mother's side.

"Sit down, don't lift a finger!" she says, while stretching out both hands to her niece. "I will make myself a cup of tea. You have done enough, my sweetheart. They will suck the strength out of your bones, you little fool!" All the while, she is examining her long nails, and it is obvious she has no intention of making her own tea. Suddenly she notices the guest.

"Oh, I do beg your pardon! I just didn't see you. I am very pleased to meet you," she says, stretching out a long wrinkled hand, and she then goes into the kitchen to wash her hands. She notices the broken crockery on the polished counter. Some of it is still lying on the stone floor.

"Oy, she's such a pain in the neck! She has scared the wits out of everyone again. She really is too much!" she starts ranting, as if she and not the sick woman were the lady of the house, and she has been terribly embarrassed by the other's behavior. She comes in again with one hand on her low-necked blouse and, while taking a bite from a piece of cake, her eyes wander approvingly over the table, which is covered in delicacies.

"What do you think of my niece?" she asks the guest.

"A fine child, extremely fine."

"Oh, if only you knew. If her mother were still alive. My God! The child was born for the piano, not the sink. The education she was given; the fine schools, and the piano teacher. If only you knew.... Her piano teacher was one of the greatest German professors. He said that this child would take the world by storm one day with her talent, and now she has to serve that!" She points her finger at the sick woman. "I ask you, can you tell me why such a thing is alive? She has no children. My sister had to die, but this one here is alive. No children, no eyes, no body, no life! Every once in a while she gives you the creeps! When she falls down, you think to yourself, right, that's it, it's over. But no!"

The short dark woman is sucking both cheeks inside her mouth. Suddenly she looks gaunt, as if she has holes in her face. She is picking at the flesh of her swollen little hands, and she smiles her dead smile.

After she has finished eating and being coquettish with the guest, Madam Zesha goes upstairs to lie down for a while. In the meantime Perele cooks lunch, which is eaten only in the evening here, and she lays the table. Melzer comes in and throws off his coat. He tidies his hair with a comb, which Perele passes him. Everybody takes a seat at the table.

Melzer sits at the head of the table, with Perele on his right, and Madam Zesha on his left. The guest has been given a seat next to her, and then at the very far end of the table sits the lady of the house.

The sick woman takes a small mirror out of her pocket and tidies her hair. She places both hands on the table like someone who has nothing to do.

"What have you brought with you today, comrade?" Melzer asks the writer.

"I have only recently published one of my best books. Mr. Melzer, I can assure you, this time I have surpassed myself. Do you remember my last book? Do you remember the wonderful depictions of people, animals, nature, everything? But still, it wasn't as good as this one. This is an absolute masterpiece, I swear. No Yiddish writer has ever written such an important book. I count on you, Mr. Melzer, a long life to you. I know what a fine person you are. And a colleague at that."

"Me? A colleague? I am not a writer, am I?"

"Who is saying that? Of course you are a writer. One can tell from that letter that was published in the local paper that you have great talent. I was simply bowled over by it. So what do you think, would you be able to sell a lot of my books to your customers?"

"I will do everything I can. I am sure I can sell at least a dozen."

The writer gets up, takes a book out of his bag and hands it over to his host. Melzer takes a good look at the subtitle, which takes up a considerable amount of space, and smiles contentedly. He puts his coat back on and is already standing on the doorstep when he promises that he will write down a list of names of prominent local Jews – and quietly slips a few bank notes into his guest's hand.

In the evening Melzer turns the sign on the glass door saying *Closed* to the street. As it is a summer evening, he takes a chair outside and sits down in front of the door to read a little. He is not able to read for long. Neighbors come from all over the street to have a chat with him. They want to know his opinion on this, that and the other. They are looking deep into his eyes, waiting to hear what he will say. Melzer has an answer for everyone.

Perele and her aunt have gone for a walk. Perele wants to talk to her, but her aunt is doing most of the talking.

"You are a silly little girl, broken shards outlast whole pots. Besides, what do you like about him? He is an old man, after all. I am sure he is in his fifties."

"But aunt, who told you I have such a thing in mind? My uncle loves me as if I were his own child."

"Oh, for heaven's sake, don't make a fool of yourself. I've got eyes in my head – thank God. When one has been married three times, one knows something about these matters! Let him give you some money, then you can leave for America. Your brother there wouldn't make you work like a servant. You should play the piano, that's what you should do. That is your profession, not cooking."

"But who will look after my uncle?"

"And who will look after you, when you are an old maid?"

"Aunt, I can't allow you to…"

"*Nu,* then I will say it without your permission. And where is the house he was supposed to buy in your name?"

"I don't need a house."

"You don't need it?"

"My God, I am losing my mind," the girl cries out as she is clasping her head with both hands. She trembles, tears glistening through her long black eyelashes. One by one they trickle down her dark cheeks, leaving lines in the powder on her face.

Upon their arrival back home they find Melzer lying asleep with his head on the table. He is resting on a piece of paper, a list with names. His sick wife, who sits next to him, is stroking him. She looks so soft and sweet, as if she were a baby being fed at her mother's breast.

As soon as the sick woman hears that "*they*" are back, she sneaks out like a thief and goes back to her usual seat in the corner. And all the time she is smiling her endless smile.

"Perele, stay here. Don't walk away, sit down. Yes, you're a good girl!" Madame Zesha says, as she comes downstairs dressed in a sumptuous nightgown, the satin shoulders embroidered with flowers, and a pair of red satin slippers on her feet. As usual, she is clutching an enormous handbag, in which she keeps the entire fortune of her three rich husbands who are all dead.

The writer has also returned. He apologizes for having stayed away so long. He tells Melzer that when he does ever manage to sell a book, the purchasers expect him to sit and listen to their life stories. They all assure him that they themselves would have written novels, if only they had the patience.

"*Nu,* well, what can you do? They've no need to ask any questions," the writer sighs deeply and sits down at the table.

"Perele, take a seat, I will make tea," Madam Zesha says, but pulls her own chair a bit closer to the table. So close even that both Melzer and the writer can smell all her perfumes and the different creams she is wearing.

Finally, everyone goes to bed.

Melzer leads his wife into their bedroom. He lies down on his back and stares at the ceiling. Unlike other nights, he is not reading. He is thinking. He tries to recapture something of the dream he had earlier that day during his afternoon nap on the table. His sick wife is lying next to him, the heavy eyelids covering her dull eyes. She does not move. The body simply lies as heavy and cold as a lump of earth. As if she were dead.

Suddenly she hears her husband's voice.

"Are you asleep, Feygele?"

"No, why?" she asks full of surprise, because she has been lying awake next to him all night for years. Awake and silent, while he reads without ever asking her anything. He never utters as much as a word. As if she were merely part of the bed, a piece of wood. And now this!

The woman feels a sudden stir of life inside. This is the first time since the Blitz she has felt like this. It makes her weep. She is crying warm, silent tears. They are streaming down her cheeks: she is like a plant which has lain dormant for a long time; its roots are deep inside the earth. They still have some life left in them. She is a flower that wilted because of a long drought, but which suddenly feels the first drops of pleasant warm summer rain. It starts to show signs of life. So warming are the four words he has spoken to her, that they revive her cold, half-dead body. Her breasts, her belly, her knees that always feel frozen, now start to warm up slowly. It is as if her brain itself has become light and clear. She feels young again, and playful, almost mischievous. Yes, mischievous. She remembers love with the man who has become such a distant stranger, albeit so near, who just says, "time to go to bed, Feygele," or "don't be foolish," or "don't wander around all the rooms, so people believe that you can actually see," or "don't annoy Perele with your smile." Now he is being as sweet as he used to be years ago. He even turns around to face her. He wipes away her tears and says, "Try to sleep, Feygele."

But she does not sleep. She lies awake, and remembers herself at home with her parents. Her father is cross with her because she is singing. Girls should not sing, according to him. Her mother is shouting at her: "Feygele, walk normally. Why do you dance around as if you are crazy?" They pretend to be angry but deep down they adore her. She once heard her mother say to her father: "Don't worry, we will manage to find a *shidduch*, a match for Feygele even without a dowry. She is a real beauty, may no harm come to her."

At the time it had made her laugh. She knew that she did not need any *shidduch*. She was in love with Berl and she wanted to marry him.

And she looked at the house opposite, the house of the barber-surgeon. There, on the first floor, Berl was standing in his shiny white coat. He was smoking a cigarette and he exhaled so skillfully through his nostrils that the smoke spiraled upwards, as if by magic. Then he blew the smoke over the balcony in the direction where she was sitting with her little sister in her arms. Her fiery eyes flashed a smile back at him. "Black diamonds" – that is what Berl used to call her eyes during their secret meetings. She recalls how her mother would not allow her to stand on the balcony: "What are you standing there for like a *golem*, like a lump of clay? It is not your child, so why be afraid to drop it, right?... The girl is mad as a hatter, she has left the broom in the middle of the room only to sit here and stare at nothing... get inside, do you hear me?"

She remembers how Berl once sent her a little note through the apprentice boy. Her mother, who was bending over the cradle in the alcove to feed the baby, came running to the door, but in her haste she had forgotten to button up her blouse. One of her breasts was just hanging there, naked. She just about managed to see the boy off. Feygele laughed so hard. Oh, how funny her mother looked that day. And the boy had whistled all the way downstairs.

"What did he want? Tell me!" her mother shouted at her.

"He wanted to know when the afternoon prayers start today. It is the anniversary of the death of the barber-surgeon."

"Oh really? You see, there is nothing stronger than a Jewish soul," her mother said, and walked back to the child that was screaming for attention. Feygele can still hear her screaming.

She thinks about Perele, how she took her out of Germany. Feygele wanted to be a mother and a father to her. And now she is thinking about her brother. He used to play tricks on her whenever he could, just like her father. And now there is his daughter. "She thinks that I don't know what she is up to. From the moment she arrived here she has put me to one side, telling me that I am blind. She has taken over everything. They have even convinced the doctor that I am blind. I can see well enough to watch my enemies' downfall. I can see things now, and there is not that much light. How can I be blind?" Suddenly she turns around to face her husband and she touches his shoulder.

Melzer sits up immediately. He thinks his wife is ill.

"Hah? What's the matter?" he says while rubbing his eyes.

"Nothing. Nothing at all. But I wanted to ask you what it was you were talking about this afternoon in your sleep. You kept saying, 'Feygele,' 'Perele,' 'Feygele,' 'Perele.' What were you dreaming about?"

"I wasn't dreaming about anything. I wasn't dreaming at all," Melzer says half with anger, half with kindness. He turns over.

She is beyond tears. She feels how her body is filling up with lead again, how it becomes heavy, dead almost. She is lying there next to her husband like a piece of risen dough. He is sleeping peacefully. She is only able to fall asleep just before the dawn.

On the Sabbath, Melzer invites the writer to his place. After the meal, Madam Zesha and Perele make themselves smart. In the meantime, Melzer takes a nap at the table and afterwards he helps his wife get into her Sabbath clothes. The sick woman powders her face blindly, and some of it falls on her black coat and on her shoes. She checks her appearance in a little mirror. They set out on a bus tour in honor of their guest.

The bus sways and jolts along and finally they end up somewhere south of the city. There the fields are vast and green, cut into symmetrical lines. On both sides of the fields there are rows of little white houses with red tiles on the roof and delightful little front gardens. There is music and sunshine everywhere. Girls and boys are playing tennis on a patch of grass, and every time the ball rolls out of sight, they burst into laughter. Youngsters are galloping by on horseback. They are all wearing fine costumes and brightly shining boots. If it were not for the occasional sight of neatly coiffed hair on a feminine shoulder, it would be impossible to tell the boys from the girls.

"Why don't you buy a house here? You work hard the whole week. You could really relax here during the weekends, and even on weekday evenings," the writer observes. Melzer sighs: "Because my wife doesn't want it."

"She doesn't want it? But it would help her illness too."

"*Nu,* you can see for yourself, can't you? She wants to be with me day and night. She is afraid of being alone. She feels good there amongst the ruins, she says."

"Alone? But why can't she stay with your niece? She's a good girl. A kind girl. And Madam Zesha, she's cheerful, no?"

"She is about to go away. She has only been here for a couple of months. And my niece shouldn't live alone with my wife. It's not right to condemn a young girl to a life with a sick person."

"It's a shame," the writer sighs. "If you had a house here, you could organize a literary evening for me here."

"I would do it with pleasure."

The bus comes to a halt. Madam Zesha takes the writer by the arm. Perele walks on the other side of him. They are happily chattering away, all three of them, and they quickly forget about Melzer, who has to lead his small, heavy wife.

She walks with little, stumbling steps, like a child that is learning to walk. It is tiring for him to try and move so slowly. He forces himself to walk with the same small steps, but nevertheless he is going too fast. It is suffocating for him. He feels hot and heavy. He starts to sweat, and he wipes his forehead constantly. He feels envious of the three people in front of him who can walk as freely and as quickly as they want. His wife, nearly blind and paralyzed, leans heavily on his tired arm. She drags him down with her towards the ground.

Clocks

זייגערס

Mrs. Jacobson stood there again that evening, just as she always did. She was all ready to go out, with a brown suitcase in one hand, and a blue and white striped woolen blanket in the other. She was pleading with her daughter, who was about twenty years old, with a small, turned-up nose and bright amber-colored eyes – intelligent, smiling eyes – to come along and spend the night in the shelter:

"Come with me. Stop torturing me like this. Long live Hitler! You're such a stubborn girl! It will be a miracle if I get a night's sleep. Why do you have to be so obstinate?"

"Mother, I'm not going to drag myself in and out of shelters as long as I have a *room* and a bed to sleep in. I have told you a thousand times already. "*Goodnight*, Mother, and *good luck*!"

Mrs. Jacobson bit her lip and went out, mumbling a prayer to God, may He protect her child, her bad child, and may He forgive her for causing her mother such heartache.

"She's such a silly girl! She doesn't understand!" She tried to explain to the Almighty that her daughter Bella was a good girl deep down, and that He should protect her and make sure that no harm came to her. She walked out through the garden gate lost in thought.

The small front garden was ablaze with colors and bursting with birdsong. The bright flowers of late summer were talking to each other intimately in their own wordless language. They stood there idly, bathed in the golden light of the setting sun, no longer of use to any living creature. Nobody looked at them or smelled their wonderful fragrance. The small trees, which had once been pruned, and tamed by metal wire, now grew wild, and they wondered why nobody took care of them anymore. Not even Bella.

The alleyway exuded an air of Yom Kippur – beautiful, sad and eerily quiet.

Mrs. Jacobson shuffled along the empty pavement with her luggage in both hands, sighing wearily.

A neighbor rushed past her like a whirlwind, shouting over his shoulder, "*All the best!*" and before she knew it, he had disappeared. He was running to secure a place in an underground station, otherwise he might end up having to spend the whole night standing up.

Mrs. Jacobson, deep in thought, did not answer him straightaway. When she realized what had happened, she started running after him. Just as on Yom Kippur she could not afford to offend anyone.

"*All the best!*" she called out desperately, in the silence of the evening.

Bella was lying in her narrow child's bed. She listened to the roaring Nazi airplanes and to the dull, faraway explosions and gunfire, which became increasingly clear as the planes came nearer. She heard the whistling sound of the bombs, which by now were coming down almost onto her own roof. As they fell, some of them wept like little children, others howled like mad dogs. She could see the flames through the window, rising up to the sky. Then another fire exploded in the blazing sky with such force it was as if somebody had poured a barrel of petrol onto a burning building. It lit up her girlish bedroom and the bed she was lying in. A strange feeling of excitement took hold of her. She pulled the silk blanket closer to her face, and watched the spectacle with both fear and curiosity. She even fell asleep for a moment. When she woke up again, she was surprised at herself: "Hmm…oh dear…to fall asleep at a moment like this!"

It was almost morning when the sirens finally sounded the *all clear.* There was nothing she wanted more than to turn around and sleep for half a day, but the office was waiting. So she got up about an hour and a half later, and exactly at the same time as every other day, at eight o'clock precisely, she was already half dressed downstairs in the *morning room.* As usual, she first gave the cat a bowl of milk. Then she put the kettle on, and started doing her exercises.

"One! Two! Feet together! Don't bend the knees! Hands on your hips! One! Two!" the lady on the radio called out energetically. Music followed. The kettle hummed cheerfully on the gas stove.

Bella spluttered as she threw cold water onto her face. She quickly brushed her amber hair. She was still finishing her *cup of tea,* as she walked to the door, wearing her coat and carrying a small handbag.

"Are you off already?"

She saw her mother, dressed in what seemed to be a dozen coats and carrying her luggage with both hands.

"A fine night we've had. Hitler should be so lucky! God forbid, I didn't sleep a wink! But who cares?"

Bella smiled.

"*Goodbye,* Mother, it's late," she said, and she stretched out her small pale hand with the long red fingernails to check the time. Bella wanted to give her mother a kiss, but all she could see of her mother's face were two bloodshot eyes. The rest was wrapped up. So she planted a kiss on the blue woolen scarf which she had knitted for her mother so that she could protect herself against the drafts down in the underground, and left the house.

The front garden was veiled in bright silver sunlight that morning. The flowers warmed themselves in the sunshine and the last drops of dew were disappearing rapidly. Bella picked a flower and put it in her lapel. A small drop quivered on one of the leaves for a second, and then vanished.

Together with the flower, Bella had picked up a pointed piece of grey metal. It had sharp edges and was still warm. She put it away in her elegant handbag, so that she could show it to her colleagues at the office.

"It will be a souvenir," she thought, and hurried to the bus stop.

The earth lay there like a corpse prepared for an autopsy, its innards wet and glistening. Sewage pipes were sticking out everywhere, like intestines falling out of an open belly.

The trolley bus had to wind its way through endless side streets because all the main roads had been closed off and lined with signs saying, "Danger! No Through Traffic!" Finally, Bella reached her destination.

"Good morning! Do you recognize the place where our building used to be?" Her boss greeted her with a broad smile. He rubbed his hands contentedly and his face beamed with happiness.

"It happened five minutes after I left. I had been staying late, last night, to sort out some bills. God has been very good to me! Do you know how many people got killed here?"

Bella looked up. Suddenly she started shaking so violently that her boss only just managed to keep her on her feet, helping her with his big, strong hands.

And there it was, in the ruined street, among the piles of bricks, earth, bent metal joists and glass, and the smoke and smoldering fires which the firemen had not yet managed to extinguish: the high-pitched, regular ticking of their office clock. It was still hanging on the one remaining wall, which was covered in black smoke. It ticked monotonously, vibrating slightly, like the only soul left living in a cemetery.

"Tick-tock! Tick-tock!"

Bella looked again at the dark wall. There was such horror in her eyes when she stared at the clock, that it frightened her boss. On the way home, the melancholy drawn-out wail of the sirens sounded again.

The bus stopped. Bella had not intended to go into any shelter, but suddenly, without knowing how she got there, she found herself in the basement of a church, together with the other passengers from the bus.

Gloomy old women sat on low benches, boxes and stones, with quivering, toothless mouths, their dead eyes smiling in a mechanical fashion. They were busy knitting socks and gloves for the *boys* with their thin, black-veined hands.

The air downstairs in the cellar was grey and foggy. It smelled of mold and the chill of graves.

Wardens dressed in blue aprons with silver buttons helped the older children down the stairs. All the children were crying. The emergency lights which gave out a dark and cheerless glow, spread more shadow than light. The women just kept on knitting.

"Why are you looking at me like that?" one of the women asked Bella.

Her voice startled Bella; she thought that the clock had suddenly started talking to her. She began swaying with such force that the old lady could barely prevent her from falling down.

"Sit down," she panted heavily, and offered Bella a seat next to her on a gravestone.

Bella looked around. Only then did she realize that the place was full of gravestones: some were large and impressive, others low and humble; there were smooth stones and carved ones; there were really tiny stones on children's graves, and old green stones covered in moss. She shivered. It seemed to her as if these women, with their yellow crumpled faces and sad smiles in their lackluster eyes, their toothless mouths trembling constantly, were in fact the corpses who had come out of their graves, and who were now sitting on their own gravestones, quietly knitting socks and gloves for death itself. She started to make her way towards the door.

"What are you afraid of?" The old woman kept on talking to Bella. "You are in the right place. If anything happens, you don't even need to have a funeral," she joked. "We sit here all night long, and often part of the day as well," she babbled on. "The air is not good in here, but at least it's safer than outside." The old woman spoke reassuringly, as she made herself comfortable again on the gravestone. Her dull eyes still smiled their dead smile.

Bella came out onto the street. Outside, one could hear the

explosions and the muted gunfire. She breathed freely, eagerly drawing the fresh cool air into her lungs. She walked home.

The front garden was brimming with life again. The golden light of the afternoon flowed freely; the flowers looked magnificent. She opened the door. The house had never been so dear to her as at that moment.

Suddenly she noticed the clock on the mantelpiece. Their homely old clock. Her mother, luggage in hand, stood next to it. She was ready to go to the shelter, even earlier than usual.

"Wait, Mother, I'm coming with you. Wait, wait, wait! I'm afraid of... of the clocks." Bella did not see one clock, but hundreds of them all around her. They stood there, not on the mantelpiece, where a bright fire was spreading an intimate feeling of warmth and coziness, but on gravestones. The gravestones were old and green, overgrown with moss, and they were saying something to each other, mumbling in their own secret language.

"Wait, Mother, wait! Wait!"

Mrs. Jacobson, her bloodshot eyes wide open, did not understand what her daughter was saying. But she quietly praised the Almighty for giving her daughter the wisdom, at last, to see that it was better to go and sleep in the shelter... after all.

Blitz
בליץ

A drawn-out wail, heavy and melancholy. The announcement coming from the siren sounded like a song of lamentation.

The people living round the docks did not even have enough time to be frightened.

"It came down suddenly. It seemed to fall straight from heaven," the East Enders would say afterwards.

The heavens had expanded over the city, as wide and clear as if they were hovering somewhere over the Orient, and not over wet, misty London, bathing eternally in soot, smoke, and darkness. Its inhabitants were pale and withdrawn, haunted by the dampness that pervaded everything.

It was September and the sun poured its cruel heat over the black city, covering the grime that had been gathering for years, in the little alleyways, on the identical, flat-faced houses.

The rays of the sun were fierce and penetrating. They crept into the wrinkles of poor people's skin, revealing the dark pores, the tiniest hairs on a chin or mole, and the blue lips of old and middle-aged gentile women who had just come outside with their baskets and purses, their wages fresh in their hands, ready to go and buy meat for the Sunday roast.

It was the afternoon of the Jewish Sabbath. The gentile women, and those Jewish women who worked on Saturdays, were all in a hurry. They were on their hands and knees, busy scrubbing lime onto the doorsteps of the narrow house entrances. Copper door knockers were being polished until they shone as brilliantly as the sun whose rays were caught in them.

Canaries could be seen hopping around in their cages in low broad windows with checkered wooden panes. These had lost their wooden appearance a long time ago and now looked more like old corroded tin, peeling and crumbling everywhere.

Satisfied, filled with the warmth of the bright sun, the birds were singing cheerfully, oblivious of the war taking over the world.

Cats were sitting nearby, looking with wondering eyes at the frenzied cleaning, as if they were about to ask the women what the point was of washing doorsteps and polishing knockers at a time of war, when there were so many more urgent things to be done.

The Jewish women who had already rested were sitting outside the small houses. They discussed the war: the sons who were in the army, and those who would be called up soon to help to protect England, and to save the world from that crazy brute.

Mothers sighed and assured each other that with God's help he would die a violent death, that Hitler.

The men were in shirtsleeves because of the heat. They sat rocking on low kitchen stools while telling their neighbors it was a sin to talk like that: "The more one swears at him, the stronger he gets!" – adding curses of their own. "May he die in torment!"

"So what? Heaven and earth have sworn that the world will not come to an end," the old Bible scholar Abrams threw in, as he closed his copy of the *Eyn Yankev.*

And tall Simon, a Jewish boxer, made a fist. "We will show him," he said, and he squeezed his hand so tightly that you saw his five white knuckles, which looked as if they could kill a man with one blow.

"Of course not. The world will not come to an end," Jews comforted themselves, and the sun melted the creases on their Sabbath faces into a smile. Its light crept inside the narrowest of houses, through half-open doors of homes that looked like black crates.

"A wonderful world, if only we were allowed to enjoy it," the mothers said as they tried to wipe away stubborn tears, which reappeared as soon as they had dried up.

Little girls raced past them on the cobblestones, small whirlwinds of silk and satin, jumping over ropes, flaunting flowing locks of hair. Their mothers had tried to outdo each other, skillfully creating snake-like curls.

The sun made its way into every little corner. It slid down behind a clothes hanger, and onto the peeling furniture in a house basking in its Sabbath mood. In a shop, the light crept over a few green apples, a shriveled bunch of parsley, a couple of wrinkled tomatoes, and a head of garlic. Carefully it threaded the blue lines of a silk *tallis,* weaving itself into the prayer shawl's string of tassels. It warmed and lit up the gold leaf on all kinds of holy books and women's prayer books in a neighborhood bookstore. Then it disappeared discreetly into the background, so as not to trouble the gramophone records, *Brivele der Mamen* and *Rozhinkes mit Mandlen,* and the Haggadas for Pesach, which had all been cleared away out of respect for the approaching High Holidays, and which were now lying peacefully under a layer of dust.

Boys and girls were getting ready to go out and leave the hot narrow streets, which smelt of rotting fruit, scorched trousers – from being in the tailors' workshops – horse dung and stables. They had their minds set on a part of London where the streets were not all tangled up and cut off by the Commercial Road. They were longing for a part of the city where the streets were broad, beautiful and spacious. Even in these days, the windows were covered with brown strips of paper all the time, and grey sandbags were piled up around magnificent buildings, hiding half of the display windows.

Youngsters looked as neat as a new pin. Girls combed their hair until it was shining and smooth, their fingernails polished to perfection. The boys seemed to have been bathing themselves in brilliantine.

The creases in their trousers were as sharp as knives. None of them seemed troubled by the fact that soon they would be leaving for the front. Quite the reverse; they would rather go today than tomorrow!

"Oy, how we will hit them!" The young men could hardly wait to give the enemy a hell of a time. Their Jewish hearts were burning with the desire to beat the Nazis. But, in the meantime, until they would be called up, life was there to be lived.

"Oy-oy-ooooooy," wails the siren, imploring the young not to go. It is dangerous and even before its sound has died away, one can hear explosions, together with the roar of hundreds of airplanes. They are like birds of prey, filling the sky with their flashing steel. "Bang-boom!" and the little black houses are blown in all directions, like shards of coal under a miner's hammer. Suffocating black smoke is carried this way from burning buildings in the docks.

Long rows of houses are on fire in no time at all. Flames dance in a pandemonium behind every window. They stick out fiery licking tongues and look like devils – strangely beautiful, even. The flames come in many different shades of green, red, yellow, orange – a feast of color, as if to make fun of humanity and signify its ruin. The food supplies for the coming winter are all on fire. The food had been brought over by brave seamen. They risked their lives to take care of this country, which has not provided for itself with ripe cornfields, nor with its own bread, like other nations have done.

The barges lie burning on the Thames, like low mountains on fire. It seems as if the river itself will soon be on fire. The Thames and the sky: both seas of blood.

In the alleyways, men and women flee in all directions, dragging with them their own and other people's children. Some of the children are crying, others are struck dumb with terror. They try to save themselves, but they cannot find a way out. Death is lurking everywhere. Glass is falling, it is raining bricks, the roofs come crashing down, whole houses are collapsing – all at once. Human beings are buried alive; men, women and children.

Their cries and the groans of the wounded are drowned out by the shouts of people standing outside their front doors who do not want to leave their ruined homes. Recklessly, they grapple with the fire, wanting to remove the debris with their bare hands, the molten lumps of earth and the bent iron beams glowing from the heat. In an attempt to drag out the people who are still alive, they only succeed in burying themselves.

The lamenting around the ruins becomes increasingly bitter, when people find the bodies of their own mothers and fathers, their own children and neighbors.

"Where is God?" asks the wife of old Abrams and she looks up at the brightly lit sky.

But a bomb blast hurls her away. She lies there motionless, clutching her wig tightly in one hand. She does not ask any more questions.

Tall Simon has been working tirelessly. He has pulled body after body out from under the rubble, handing them over to the emergency workers. Crippled bodies, covered in blood, some of them dead. Now, all of a sudden, he loses his mind. The relentless neighing of the horses in their locked-up stables in the docklands is too much for him. He abandons everything, and walks away, treading on the living and the dead.

Then he throws himself into the fire and rips open the stable doors. A numb panic surrounds the horses as they leap out.

They gallop wildly off into the narrow streets, trampling everything underfoot. Within seconds, they are like running torches, fleeing the suffocating smoke. They collapse in mid-flight, stretching out as if in silent protest, with their hooves raised to the blazing sky.

Night was falling. The sun was going down, enflamed and glowing red. The heavens were left to bleed. Two fires lit up the sky: one in the east and one in the west.

The Nazi airplanes were still there. Just like the spiders who once brought fire to the Temple, they flew in more and more bombs to drop on the Jewish alleyways, where nothing was left to destroy.

Dogs

הינט

Tom turned the few coins between his bony fingers and stared at them with hard grey eyes. He had no idea what to do next. He had only one thought in his head. His conscience was troubling him. He knew perfectly well that what his wife said was true – he never had any luck with the dogs. He had already pawned his winter coat, as well as the linen. All that was left were a couple of swaddling clothes for the baby. He had not paid the rent for the last three weeks. The landlord had given him notice that day, warning that if he did not pay up, he would be thrown out on the street, together with his wife and child, even though it was the middle of winter.

"Do as I say. Don't go! You'll see, you will lose again! My heart's heavy and I know what that means. You know my heart can always tell what's going to happen! Every time I tell you not to go, you lose!" Mrs. Dickson said as she studied her husband's steely expression to see if he was listening to a word that she said. She stood next to a rusty tin tub rubbing the baby's clothes between her thin fingers. The washing stayed dirty because there had been no money to buy soap.

"Do what I say. Take him this week's money and tell him that we'll pay the rest off, one shilling a week. He'll say yes, I know he will."

Tom did not answer her. He saw how the child was gnawing a crust of bread. The saliva was running out of his little mouth. He had started biting the big toe on his left foot from sheer hunger. His face was pale, the small eyes were red and swollen. The foot pointing up in the air looked green, bony and crooked.

He became angry with the infant.

"Stop biting your toe," he snapped, while hastily pulling it out of the baby's mouth. Now he started crying; teardrops were running down the wan cheeks and into his little blue mouth.

Tom got even angrier.

He stood up. He looked through the dirty windowpanes and saw the big clock above the public house, the White Elephant. It was already very late.

"Come along if you want to. It won't make any difference now. This time I'm going to win – you'll see. Listen, I'm going to go anyway. If you come with me, it'll cost one shilling more, but that way you'll see the result there and then. You'll save yourself from lying here miserable, all alone. Come on, it'll do you good!"

He had already brought out her faded coat. It had once been brown. She would not know what color to call it now. She was ashamed to wear it, even to go to the dogs. The child was dressed in old rags that had become too small, and Tom no longer had an overcoat.

But what was she going to do otherwise on such a long dreary evening? Besides – if he won and she was not with him – he might end up in the White Elephant to celebrate his winnings with his mates and then she would still be left with nothing.

She combed her thin hair, wrapped up the baby and set out to try her luck.

"Those people are all crazy! They would give their lives for the dogs. Just look at what is going on there!" Mrs. Dickson marveled, as if she was witnessing the spectacle for the very first time.

Tom had forgotten the cold. He did not feel the water coming in through the holes in his shoes, soaking his feet. He had bought two tickets and he radiated happiness.

"I have placed our bet on Black Albert, he's a sure thing! I know we'll be lucky today."

"I doubt it," Mrs. Dickson thought to herself. She sighed. Nevertheless, she was drawn into what was happening around her.

Her heart was beating fast. What was she going to do if he lost again?

"He won't," she thought resolutely, pushing away her gloomy thoughts. Now that she was here she would pray to God and beg Him to send them the winner. For once, only today. "No, no, no! He can't lose. He won't lose today. Of course he'll win." She was trying to fend off the terrible thoughts, which were forcing themselves on her.

She looked around. The crowd was getting more and more excited. They only had one thought in their heads – the dogs. Twenty thousand people had come there to watch this canine spectacle.

Electric lamps throw a dim, dark shine on a round patch of grass cut very short, creating the illusion of a green lake. A circular strip of grass runs around the "water." It is ablaze with light. On it stands a white, freshly painted pen, which looks like a doll's house from a distance.

The arena is beautiful.

People with money are seated comfortably on a separate balcony, similar to boxes in a theater. The whole place is lit in a festive manner. The lights are twinkling. Dozens of lamps are dazzling people's eyes. A large building resembling a factory is taking in flashy cars and the rich punters. The darkness outside absorbs the buses, which have taken the poor to the dog track as if guided by their blood and tears.

The "water" and the strip of grass around it creates a division between the rich visitors and the rest. On one side an entry ticket costs five shillings, on the other only one.

The one-shillingers are pouring in from all over London. The buses that are pulling up are packed with human flesh, with human sweat and human folly. And it is not only the buses, but trolley cars as well that are bursting with people. London is going to the dogs!

Red-faced bookies keep close to their stands, trading happiness for just a few shillings, offering red sheets of paper with the names of all the dogs.

The crowds descend on them like bees on honey.

The bookies are raving, their faces growing ever redder. Their eagerness to attract ever more customers gives them strength.

Their loud cries can be heard everywhere.

"Two to one, four to one!"

There is the blare of trumpets. The masses stop swarming around like insects. Some people sit down, others remain standing. All eyes are focused on the arena. All hearts are pounding with anticipation.

Six men dressed in white coats, like doctors, are leading out six slender, good-looking dogs. They are wearing little jackets so that they will not catch colds, God forbid! They are paraded around the stadium. The dogs have a haughty bearing; they do not deign to look at their mostly disheveled fans, many of whom are wearing torn trousers. Few have overcoats. They shiver with cold.

The dogs are led into the pen. A stuffed white hare is brought out onto the circular strip of grass. The hare runs on electricity. You can hear a racket from inside the pen. The dogs are howling with excitement. Their barking gets mixed in with the buzz of the tense crowd. Suddenly the lights go out. Silence.

The door from the pen is lifted. The hare shoots out – followed by the half-crazed dogs.

The crowd goes wild with excitement. People are screaming at the top of their voices.

"Go on, Mick! Good old Mick! Go on! Beat them!"

"Go on Black Albert! Run! Show them! Go on! Go on! Go on!"

The hare disappears. One dog has reached the finish. Dead silence. Disappointed faces. Downcast expressions. Only a few people are walking up the stairs. They approach the bookies to claim their winnings, their faces glowing. The others stay exactly where they are. They look like losers.

The bookies look satisfied. They go about their business with renewed energy. Tom feels in his pockets.

He decides to try one more time. He has to try to win back all the money he's lost. The bookies have their hands full.

Smartly turned-out gentlemen, stiff hats on their greased heads and spotless white gloves on their kosher hands, signal to the other side who has won.

After just fifteen minutes fresh dogs are brought in. The whole ritual is repeated seven or eight times more, and then the last race is over.

The crowd disperses. Mrs. Dickson, the child in her arms, the color drained from her face, is crying bitterly.

"How am I going to buy milk for the baby? How are we going to pay the rent this week?" she snivels. Tom's eyes are bloodshot. He is shivering in his thin jacket. His hands are deep inside his pockets. He gives his wife threatening looks, warning her to keep quiet, not to make things worse with her moaning.

Young Jewish men who only yesterday were reading prayer books and who today are petit bourgeois, wealthy women who belong to all kinds of clubs and societies, had all come to try their luck. And so had the *goyim*, rich, drunk or in a festive mood. They had all come to the dogs.

"*They* will not be thrown out of their homes," Mrs. Dickson groans.

"Shut up, I said!" Tom's eyes have a murderous glow. The bustle remains undiminished and it is even worse outside. Little boys dart about in the streets, delivering their news about the triumph of some dog or other.

"All the winners! Read all about it!" The words resound all over London. The newspapers are selling like hot cakes. In the general commotion nobody notices her quiet moaning. Tom has nothing to be afraid of anymore.

Additional Writings

Contents

Essays

Appendix

Introduction

Anita Norich

The following works are divided into several sections. The first – Newly Translated Short Stories – contains short stories originally published in the periodical press between 1934 and 1955. "The Wanderer's Path" appeared posthumously to mark Kreitman's *yortsayt* [anniversary of death]. The other stories were published before *Yikhus;* it is not clear why they were not included in that collection. Set in London, Paris, or Warsaw, these narratives wrestle with many of the themes found throughout Kreitman's writing: economic injustice, the brutality of war, the plight of Yiddish writers, the effects of antisemitism, and the hypocrisy of those who purport to be charitable. Kreitman also offers a sharp critique of those who, in seeking to assimilate, abandon Jewish ethics and learning.

In addition to two short stories recently translated by Vivi Lachs (that appeared as this volume was going to press), readers will find variant translations of two of Kreitman's stories. Alongside *Blitz*'s translation of "The New World," there are versions by Barbara Harshav and Joshua Fogel. Similarly, Maurice Carr's "The Relic" and Ellen Cassedy's "A Satin Coat" are included in addition to *Blitz's* "A Silk Gaba rdine." Because translation is always an act of interpretation, these alternative versions invite readers to consider how different eras, contexts, and artistic choices shape the reading experience. Rather than seeking a "definitive" text, these variants are meant to spark curiosity about Kreitman's original Yiddish and to encourage readers to delve more deeply into the world her writing evokes.

Following these stories are two essays by Kreitman reflecting on the rebirth of Yiddish culture in Paris after the Second World War. Mourning the six million murdered Jews and the devastation endured by writers, artists and activists, Kreitman marvels not only at the reemergence of Yiddish culture, but also at the quality of the work being produced. Especially struck by the artists' ability to transcend political divisions, she offers these essays as a call for the unity so powerfully embodied by the Parisian Yiddish community.

Although Kreitman left no diary or memoir, her brief "Autobiographical Notes" – prepared for a planned lexicon of London's Yiddish activists – present a glimpse into how she wanted to be remembered. She cites her contributions as a writer and situates herself within her "rabbinic and literary family."

Appendix

Kreitman's son, Maurice Carr, expanded on his mother's story in a moving Yiddish obituary, "Kaddish for My Mother," and her granddaughter, Hazel Carr, remembers "Buba Esther" as a daunting, rather frightening figure. Maurice Carr, insistent that his mother was misunderstood, portrayed her lovingly as a woman of formidable intelligence, deep social conscience, and a profound emotional sensibility – qualities that, in a post-Holocaust world, left her "all but destroyed." What some labeled madness or depression, Carr described as a "tremendously rare sensitivity." These intimate family memories offer a counter-narrative to the traditional critiques that have pathologized Kreitman.

Like so many Yiddish writers, Kreitman faced barriers to publication and recognition. The letters from Stefan Zweig and George Bernard Shaw underscore her desire for a wider readership and remind us that her novels and stories belong firmly within the broader context of European literatures.

Newly Translated Short Stories

Translated by Anita Norich

The Hungry Ones

די הונגעריקע

[*Belgishe bleter,* vol. 3, no. 2, Feb. 1937]
[Edited version of "*Di hunger-marshirer,*" (The Hungry Marchers), *Dos fraye vort,* March 9, 1934]

The day was in tears. Timidly, the sun hid behind dark clouds. It knew that it didn't shine for the poor, so it was afraid to tease them. Suddenly, it was pitch black. The clouds creeping across the sky resembled a group of half-paralyzed cripples. The sky was so low, it looked like it would fall down at any second and destroy everything and everyone in its wake.

An ugly, cold, unyielding rain dripped, freezing the emaciated marchers. Their worn, thin raincoats – many full of holes – were no protection against the rain. It clung to them, making even clearer their limbs and pointy shoulders. Their filthy knapsacks swung on their narrow backs or dragged them down.

Sallow twenty- and thirty-year old people with drawn, wrinkled faces appeared. Here and there could be seen a healthy face, with color in its cheeks. And then, again, pale, drawn faces telling of long-endured hunger and the kind of pain that ages people.

It was difficult to walk in their torn, soaked shoes and blistered, purulent feet. For hours, they trudged through the pouring rain in rows that stretched through rich Oxford Street to the sad, well-known Hyde Park. Hyde Park, the "home" for all the homeless, for worn-out streetwalkers and those unemployed who no longer had even a few pennies to pay for a night's lodging.

Surrounded by policemen as if they were criminals, they plodded past rich, luxurious buildings that rose up proudly and securely in their Sunday rest.

Hundreds of wax ladies in store windows, dressed in fantastically rich dresses and furs, seemed to tease the poor women who had marched all the way from Scotland in order to display their own attire to London.

"Look, Mama, how beautiful!" said a young child with an old face who had marched with her mother all the way from Shoreditch. She dragged her mother by the hem of her red, drenched raincoat. "Look how beautiful it is," said the child, pointing to a wax figure in a sky-blue flowery silk dress. It revealed a pair of well-formed shoulders, a thin white throat, a charming bare back and, behind the dress's train that lay folded over red velvet, a pair of silver dancing shoes peered out.

But when her mother didn't turn around, the child's striking brown eyes stared at the mannequin as she chewed a piece of damp bread.

Another child, carried in his mother's arms, kept looking around with a pair of frightened, startled eyes and, like a grownup, kept himself from crying. The child attracted everyone's attention with his frighteningly pale appearance.

"What a shame," said the women looking on. One, a tall woman in a grey fur coat, sorrowfully expressed her opinion of the poor woman who was almost falling to the ground from weariness.

"She should be ashamed of herself for taking along a sick child!" she said to her husband, a tall, clean-shaven Englishman who held a large open umbrella protecting him and his wife from the rain.

"Ignorance!" he said disapprovingly.

The couple quickly disappeared into the mass of male and female workers who had arrived in the thousands despite the heavy rain. Meanwhile, the marchers streamed from all sides. At the main entrance, a man in a sandwich board welcomed them, saying:

"Tremble, you unbelievers. God will take His revenge on you!"

The marchers remained calm, quiet. Their eyes looked nearly extinguished, but still there remained a spark that could flicker once again.

The police were not interfering.

The local unemployed Londoners were less weary than those who had come from afar. They brought a bit of life to the scene.

People called out:

"Down with the new bill!"

Singing the "Internationale," the people dispersed throughout the large park. The marchers sat on the soaked ground, their wet rucksacks beneath them. They tried to eat their damp, unappealing sandwiches.

On the platform appeared both prominent and unfamiliar speakers. Strong and heartfelt words were spoken. Thousands upon thousands of sympathetic ears listened attentively and with fellow-feeling. Evening fell quickly. Many of the people had already slipped into the neighboring cafes. The lucky ones made themselves comfortable in cushioned chairs, ate heartily and let themselves be served by young waitresses in brown dresses and lemon-colored aprons.

Having rested and listened with great appreciation to the speeches of the leaders, the walk was now different. Once again, rows formed. The "Internationale" rang out more loudly, the shouting was more lively. Once again, the cadence of thousands of feet could be heard as they went back to their temporary "homes." Among the marchers were some young people in green shirts and flannel pants with green berets on their heads. They carried a flag that asked:

"Why are the Greenshirts marching?"*

People shrugged their shoulders. They didn't understand. What were those Greenshirts doing here?

"But that's what we're asking too!" said the Greenshirts, laughing.

The park was empty and huge. Even the Indian with his colorful,

---

* The Greenshirts were members of the political Social Credit Party of Great Britain and Northern Ireland.

strange clothes who stood on a soapbox and called out the names of horses for no apparent reason, even he was getting ready to go home.

Darkness descended on the park. Those unfortunate people who had been rejected by life began to arrive with their baggage. They unpacked their things and got ready for a cozy night of sleeping in the wet park.

Nightfall
נאַכט פֿאַלט צו

[*Dos fraye vort*, London: Oct. 19, 1934
and *Oventblat*, Lublin, July 28, 1939]

The Thames flows, partly lit by single lanterns or triple octagonal ones that look like bouquets. The lights enfold the water, as lovely as antique gold.

Enormous dark barges are already lying along the shore. Their contents are covered with heavy, filthy canvas. Lazily, they seem to doze, as one does at dusk. From afar, a flame approaches, a whistle is heard, a boat wanders by. Because where there's water, there should be a boat.

Grubby children hang over the low, stone fence, delighted with the golden water. No one comes to look for the emaciated children with their twig-like greenish legs. No one comes to wash them, feed them, and put them to bed. Other children, well-looked after, are already in their clean beds crying that it's too early to go to sleep.

A bit further off, huge government buildings stretch to the sky, arrogant and secure. Wooden planks wind around Parliament House looking like bandages. They are being removed. Parliament House will emerge in winter even more demanding than ever as it plans the political future of other lands and, at the same time, quietly takes care of itself.

Big Ben looks around with undisguised curiosity, his great round face gazing at everything to see what's happening nearby and far away. He sees frightened mothers come by, bowing to the massive Tomb of the Unknown Warrior, their shaking hands laying down flowers, blue lips murmuring, and wiping away a tear from blurry eyes with small, white handkerchiefs.

He sees honorable, respectable Englishmen take off their hats as they pass by. The Unknown Warrior observes the respect he is given and all the wreaths laid at his feet, but he seems to have lain down here, in this seat of government, in order to irritate and mock those who had a hand in his untimely death. Now people are taking off their hats and bringing flowers.

"Thanks! Thanks a lot! Don't make wars and don't bring me flowers. Don't send your own children to their deaths and don't wipe away your tears!" That's what the memorial seems to be saying, and Big Ben is moved to ring its bells.

"One! Two! Three! Four! Five! Six...."

A bit further off stands stony Nurse Cavell looking looking toward Trafalgar Square. She's tall, proud, happy, reverently celebrating her fate; she had the enormous honor of dying at the hands of the enemy during a just war. A war to end all wars.

She watches her sisters – pious "*laydees*" – bringing little sacks that look like the bags men use to carry their tefillin. The women take out handfuls of crumbs and toss them all over the square for the flocks of blue pigeons that come flying from the four corners of London to greet the good-hearted, compassionate old maids and rich widows.

The idle old ladies read the quotation on Nurse Cavell's monument as they shake their wattles piously and melt with pride: "Patriotism is not enough. I must have no hatred or bitterness for anyone."

They don't look at the loudmouth "whistlers" who gather to snatch a seat on a bench or a step. These people come with flat, scabby, tired feet and emaciated, filthy bodies, knotted wiry hair, faces so pockmarked they look like graters, grimacing and swollen blue lips. You can't see more than the whites of their eyes. They wear rags made of sacks or even old newspapers to guard against the freezing, rainy nights.

The "*laydees*" go home happily, with a clear conscience.

"Husband, I've done a good deed once again."

But they're not entirely pleased. They complain about orderliness.

"It's a terrible shame," says one lady, grimacing. And everyone says amen.

They're disappointed that such carcasses are allowed in such a fine area.

A small, dried-up woman lies on a bench, her legs stretched in front of her like two wooden beams, and looks at the girls in their strange clothes, blood-red cracked lips, young bodies and old faces. Their thick powder can't hide their pockmarked skin.

The girls stroll up and down the square, flaunt their cigarette smoke, and wait for customers. But no customers appear.

The pious women shake their heads and turn away so they won't have to look. But they're furious at the woman whose legs are like wooden beams.

"Such an old woman!"

The woman looks at them with her half-blind eyes and sighs. She remembers former times.

When the pigeons are sated and there's not a crumb left, and the women go home unhappy because it's still too early to get into their cool, honorable beds, an older man, dressed quite well, comes to the square. But his deep-set, melancholy eyes reveal that he is a newcomer. Only recently has he come to sleep outdoors.

"Sit!" And the woman moves her stick-like legs. "Isn't it warmer here than near the Thames? Like this...." She instructs him how to arrange himself. She's sharing her bench.

"Warmer!" he says, cuddling up to the nearly lifeless old woman. Anything is better than feeling lonely.

A Spoiled Holiday

אַ פֿאַרשטערטער יום-טוב

[*Dos fraye vort*, Dec. 28, 1934]

Christmas was only two days away. Mrs. Rubin decided she just had to host a Christmas party this year. Since God had helped them acquire their own small factory and they were no longer toiling away for others, she'd have a celebration, especially since she'd done all the work to get to this point.

Mr. Rubin was an educated man who had once studied in Germany. If he had been able to get his high school diploma, he would have gone on to the university. He and his friends knew this and thought of him as a sacrificial lamb.

"What a pity!" his friends say, shaking their heads. "If not for that misfortune, a man like him wouldn't have to do this kind of work. What did he do to deserve this?"

"What a pity! He sat for the exams twice and they didn't pass him!" lament the Hebrew teacher's wife and Mrs. Davis, who doesn't understand where he had been sitting and to where he should have gone on. But she doesn't ask. She understands it certainly wasn't jail.

Mrs. Rubin worked hard. She was almost done making all the toys and she was sweating, her long red fingers flying, and trying to make "him" go faster.

"Hurry up, *it'th* getting late!" She had a lisp and couldn't pronounce the letter s.

There was a doll that needed some more color on its cheeks. An elephant's nose had become loose. A yellow stuffed bear was missing an ear. There was lots to do.

Mr. Rubin's right foot shook nervously. The shiny patches on his knees shook. He tried to fix the elephant but couldn't.

His wife glanced at him impatiently. Her looks made the elephant's nose become even looser. Mr. Rubin couldn't figure out what to do. His drawn face became more earnest, his yellow eyes even more melancholy. His thin, black hair fell in strips that left bald spots on his head. His mustache drooped.

Meanwhile, Mrs. Rubin packed all the wild beasts into a box, grabbed the elephant, fixed it in a flash, and gave the box to the boy waiting for the merchandise.

"Be careful. Don't bend *thith* box!"

The boy whistled softly, said "*oh yeah*" even more softly, and loudly assured her that it would be "*okay*." He went down the stairs happily whistling and singing, glad that his three months of running from shop to shop was ending with this delivery and the long-awaited Christmas holiday was coming.

Mrs. Rubin walked away from the long worktable, spoke to her only employee – who looked like someone had artfully put a wrinkled black disk on a stick and dressed it in rags in order to lead it around the foggy London streets.

"*I vith yu a meri krithmath, Jim,*" she said, and hurried downstairs.

Mr. Rubin examined the two-shilling coins in his hand, making sure there was no half-crown among them. He gave Jim his wages and shook his hand, pressing Jim's thin hand with his own. Jim's watery eyes shone with delight.

"Thank you, sir. Thank you. Merry Christmas to you."

It was cold and foggy in the large square kitchen. Mr. Rubin sat down at the table, waiting for something to eat. But other than a mountain of unwashed dishes and the gnawed head of a herring, there was nothing to be had.

He waited eagerly for his wife to get busy in the kitchen. He wanted to hear the teakettle boiling as his wife washed a herring and boiled eggs while he chewed on a piece of bread and cheerfully watched all those good things being prepared. He rubbed his hands together in happy anticipation. But no! She wasn't doing any of that. Instead, she put a large iron pot of water on the stove and poured flour into a clay bowl sitting on a narrow table. Instead of washing a herring, she washed raisins, cut up dried fruit, poured spices. A strong aroma spread through the kitchen, tickling the nose. She took a new wooden spoon and stirred everything vigorously.

"*Lithen,* Rubin! We're having a party *thuch ath* you've never seen in your life!"

Mr. Rubin nearly fainted. He stood up, his leg shaking even more nervously than before. All the colors on his spotted pants – red, green, yellow – shook too. He said, "*Partee! Shmartee!* It'd be better if you gave me something to eat!"

"What? You think you have the right to talk? Did you help me even a little bit? I could have made the pudding two *dayth* ago if I hadn't been working *tho* hard. Who *knowth* if it won't be too raw to eat now!"

Mr. Rubin was worried. Did this mean she wouldn't prepare supper tonight? He grimaced like someone in mourning. There was nothing to eat in the cupboard and it was already almost eight o'clock. Maybe being especially nice would help.

"Well, Sara," he said in a pitiful voice. "Can I get a bite? I'm fainting from hunger."

Sara softened. She was hungry too.

"You know what? Come *thtir* the pot and I'll run to the *thtore*."

Mr. Rubin took the wooden spoon in his hairy hand and began to stir. Soon, he grew tired of it, but when he heard his wife's footsteps, he started stirring vigorously.

After they ate, she gave the pot one more stir. She was exhausted. The pudding needed to cook all night, so she put a very small flame under the pot and went to bed.

In the morning, Mr. Rubin was the first one in the kitchen. He paled. The pot was completely cold because he had forgotten to put a shilling in the gas meter last night. She had warned him to do that before she went shopping. After a few minutes of drumming on the table with his bony fingers, an idea occurred to him. He turned the flame up high. When the water in the pot boiled, he lowered the flame as if nothing at all had happened.

It's six o'clock on Christmas day. The parlor is decorated. Golden streamers glitter down from the ceiling. The curtains are white and starched. The chandelier in the middle of the ceiling burns brightly. Coals glow in the fireplace, emitting a joyful warmth. There's a large bouquet of paper flowers on the table.

The doorbell rings.

"Rubin, someone's at the door!"

"So open it. Go ahead. Open!"

"Ah! What guests!" says Mr. Rubin, holding out a dry hand. "Sit, Mr. Cohen!"

Mr. Cohen makes himself comfortable near the fireplace, crosses his legs, wipes his red face and neck. He and his wife look like they're covered in brick-red flowing wallpaper. He puts his pipe in a corner of his mouth and immediately launches into a conversation about politics.

Rubin agrees with Mr. Cohen. He doesn't want to argue with him. He knows Mr. Cohen is an ardent Conservative and hates the left just as ardently. On top of that, he's a very poor man so Mr. Rubin takes pity on him. In any case, he's too lazy to think about politics and so he just agrees.

"Yes, you're right, of course. The Socialists are worthless! Totally worthless!"

Mrs. Cohen folds her pale arms over her stomach. She is wearing a sleeveless dress that looks like it contains a whole butcher shop. Her black eyes lie buried in her white cheeks. She smiles and tries to look like she's listening.

Mrs. Rubin's grey eyes smile sarcastically.

The doorbell rings again. The Hebrew teacher and his wife arrive. He has a red, full face, always smiling, a large hairy nose. He makes a fuss of sitting down. His wife is small, greenish and, of course, she too has a hairy nose.

The Hebrew teacher talks a lot. The celebration begins. People are warming their hands, groaning with pleasure. And then Mrs. Davis, the widow, enters.

"Hello! Look who's here!" she says, particularly glad to see the Hebrew teacher. He brings over a chair for her. "Sit here, near me, Mrs. Davis!"

She sits there. She's tall, big, wearing a red satin dress, long red earrings, and a long string of big red beads.

"Oh, it's nice and warm here!"

The small woman – the Hebrew teacher's wife – smiles and looks like a person who's laughing through tears.

"I knew that once you came, the party would really begin."

The widow appears to be looking at the bookcase.

"Whenever I come here, the bookcase has grown. When I go past Shoreditch, I always see Mr. Rubin standing at a stall, choosing books. Tell me, what is in such fat books? When does anyone have time to read them all? Men do seem to like fat things!" she says, laughing at her own witticism.

"Oh, you're mistaken. I don't buy anything in Shoreditch," Rubin objects, refusing to admit that he pays a penny, sometimes two or three, for his fat books with their thick, golden spines into which he never looks.

The table is set. The women cut up herring. Then they serve the pudding. Things are even merrier.

"Mama," says the Rubins' six-year-old son. "It's true there's a Father Christmas, right? Jackie says there isn't one. Jackie says Mama and not Father Christmas put up the stocking."

"It's wrong to say such things to a Jewish child," the Hebrew teacher says, like a true pedagogue.

Mrs. Rubin is insulted.

"No one needs to teach *uth* what to do. We know how to *raith* our child. I *altho* bought him a *thtocking* for Hanukka and told him the

Jewith God brought it for him. We're not *goyim*," says Mrs. Rubin, glancing over at the bookcase.

"Alright. Enough. What's the difference?" says Mr. Rubin, interrupting them and pouring a glass of wine for the teacher.

The widow tells jokes that make the teacher forget the disagreement. Meanwhile, they gobble up the pudding.

They hear yelling and laughter from the Christian family on the first floor. A gramophone is playing and couples are dancing.

The Rubins' apartment grows quiet when they take out cards.

"Listen to what I did," Rubin says, suddenly talkative.

They all look at one another, winking. They know what he's about to tell them. Whenever he drinks a glass of wine, his tongue loosens and he tells the same two stories. The widow yawns.

"Oh my, it was so funny! There was a man reading the Gemara. It was quiet and dark in the study house, lit only by a small candle that had dripped on the table. There were dark shadows on the wall. I crawled under the table and suddenly the man sprang up! Ha! Ha! Ha! Someone had grabbed his feet and was holding them tight."

"What should we play?"

"No, you need to hear the other one."

They are all silent. Resigned!

"Listen! This is a funny story told by a Hasid. His rebbe was once traveling with some of his followers. It was a Friday. Suddenly, late in the afternoon, the horse dropped dead just when it was getting close to sunset. What should they do? They can't travel on the Sabbath! The Hasidim were at a loss.

"Then the rebbe asked, 'Do any of you have a herring?' His Hasidim looked at one another. Why does he want a herring all of a sudden? What good would a herring do now? 'Yes,' said someone. 'I have a herring.' 'Harness up!' ordered the rebbe.

"His Hasidim didn't know what to do. But it's the rebbe's order! And what do you say to this? Precisely when it was time to light the Sabbath candles, they got to the shtetl!"

'What are you talking about?' cried a skeptic listening to the Hasid's story. 'Are you trying to convince me that a herring brought a wagonload of Hasidim and their rebbe to the shtetl?'

"'Well, see for yourself!' said the Hasid calmly. 'Here they are!'"

Rubin is laughing so hard, he's crying.

"Ha! Ha! Ha! That's good, isn't it?"

When they finish playing, they start arguing about where to spend the next day, Boxing Day. Everyone invites the group home, all the while hoping they'll go somewhere else.

The Rubins get ready for bed.

In the middle of the night, four telephones ring in four doctors' homes begging the doctors – whose holiday it was – to have pity and come save them. People in four homes in different neighborhoods in London are doubled over in pain because of an insufficiently stirred and cooked Jewish Christmas pudding.

Blood, Drop by Drop

צו ביסלעך מיט בלוט

[*Dos fraye vort*, February 22, 1935]

Sticky, slimy, rancid air, like the odor of rotten corpses and dead fish. A bed right next to the "window" with a bunch of rags thrown on it instead of bedclothes. A large black oven in the middle of the room taking up the "best" spot. The little window – half sunken into the ground, frozen shut with dirty frost, its cracks stuffed with bits of blackened, dirty cotton wool hiding rather than letting in light. In this dark Warsaw basement lived a Yiddish writer named Dembe with his wife and six-month-old daughter.

His neighbors were angry with the writer. Dembe was a tall, thin young man with a long, bony face that was as black as the oven in his apartment. The distressed, ragged women cursed him. They blamed everything that went wrong on him.

When things were good, people would keep to themselves and look for any work that would earn even crumbs. But they didn't earn. When everyone's head was full of the daily bustle of a poor Warsaw courtyard, they forgot all about him. But, if a child became ill, a woman had a difficult labor, a "tree" – God forbid – left the world before its time, then the neighbors remembered the couple in the basement and blamed her even more than him.

"A man is one thing, you see! But if a Jewish daughter – and from a hasidic household to boot – believes in free love, lives with a man she's not married to, it's no wonder that so many sorrows descend on the courtyard, so many misfortunes fall on Jewish heads!"

"We hear they're both spitting blood!" people said, relishing the couple's misfortune. "The hell with them! It's just a pity for the little one born of sin."

The sinning mother began to see blood soon after her child's birth. She had been coughing for a long time.

When she met Dembe, he had just recently begun to write. He came to Warsaw from a village, bringing a pair of healthy red cheeks, a bundle of hopes, and a bag of deeply-felt flowing poems only he had seen. With a wonderful rhythm and even more wonderful Yiddish, he sang of fields and woods. His poems emanated with the aroma of corn fields, clear skies, cottage, and barn.

His happiness, goodness, innocence, and cleverness quickly brought him friends who were also young writers. In his bachelor home each of them had read their poems, praising and criticizing one another. They argued and quickly made up, laughing at one another but also offering friendly encouragements. Dembe was in his element, especially when the most important Warsaw journal began to publish his poems.

"Now, Dembe, you've got the stamp of approval," said a tall, broad-shouldered young man whom everyone called the "man from Chelm," although he actually came from White Russia. Everyone agreed that if he could write as well as he could reason, he'd be a genius.

"Do you really think so?" asked Dembe, wanting to hear the "stamp of approval" one more time. What an expression!

"I'm telling you so! How did I come to be well known?" answered the "Chelemer" – who was not yet "stamped" but was delighted with the one poem he had once managed to squeeze into a journal that "stamped."

Dembe's luck kept growing. He published five poems in quick succession. But Dembe was naive. Once, his editor read to him one of his own poems even though he wasn't a poet, as he himself said. He read every stanza and, after each one, he'd stop and look at

Dembe as if to ask: "Aha, what do you say to that? That's how to write, isn't it?"

But he couldn't catch Dembe's eye. Dembe hid behind his shut eyelids and was silent. Since then, according to Dembe, many waters had flown under that bridge. The four years during which he had lived with his young bride felt like forty years. He no longer wrote poems. But since he couldn't leave it alone, he had taken to writing novels, stories, criticism, articles, and more. Everything was lying in wait. Not a single line was printed. Editors couldn't find the tiniest bit of room for any of it. And if there's no room, there's nothing you can do.

Some of his friends stopped writing entirely. Some escaped their narrow confines and became "names." Dembe became consumptive. He caught it from his own troubles and also from his wife with the coal-black, sparkling eyes who was spitting her lungs out behind the counter in a confectionery store on Franciszkańska Street, earning six gulden a week.

Dembe cleaned the cellar apartment, cooked dinner – when it was possible to save a few groshen – did the laundry, rocked the baby, and wrote on both sides of the pages in his notebook.

Once in a while, when he came into the Literary Association, writers were careful not to speak to him – no matter how much their hearts bled for him. What can you do? They had to protect their own reputations. It was, they knew, always worth it to speak with someone greater than they. And that was difficult, because someone greater also sought someone greater. So Dembe wandered around a bit through the long room with the tapestried walls, looked into its four corners, disparaging it all. Colleagues drank tea, chatted, played chess. But if no one was looking at him, he'd go into the dark reading room, glance at the foreign newspapers, and go home depressed.

Once, an important Yiddish writer came, so great that he needn't be afraid of anyone. His reputation exceeded everyone else's. And the Chelemer, who now worked in several newspapers, earned money, and trembled to say even a word to Dembe, couldn't stand seeing Dembe's situation. One dark evening, he went into Dembe's hovel and said, "Go, Dembe! He'll let you. Go, show him my card." And the Chelemer wrote down a few words.

In the morning, Dembe went. It was a cold, clear day. His hands and feet shook. His black cheeks turned deep red. He spit out a chunk of blood, folded his filthy handkerchief into his pocket and went in.

The writer was sitting on a comfortable chair near a table. In the room, the white tiled oven laughed at a square strip of sun falling on a polished floor. All was bright, clean, and warm.

On the table stood a glass of clear reddish tea. The writer extended a large, soft, and warm hand to Dembe and invited him to sit. He read the crowded lines of two poems Dembe had once written. Dembe saw the writer become serious, scanning the paper with lowered eyelids.

"You really can write!" he said, handing back the poems.

Dembe stood up.

"Sit, Comrade Dembe. We'll drink a glass of tea together." He said Dembe's name as if they were old friends.

Dembe was bathed in sweat.

"Give this letter to the editor. Be well and write many more poems like this," said the writer, pressing Dembe's cold, moist hand.

Journals and newspapers took him in after that. Everything he had written was "sweetened," regardless of the fact that Dembe was skilled in poetics.

The writers were thrilled with it all. They weren't lacking in topics; they didn't need to break their heads. Everyone was talking about Dembe:

"What did Dembe mean with such and such comparison?" "When did Dembe write this particular poem?" Yes, they knew: in 19.… "Dembe is going to Katsherufke tomorrow." "Dembe came back from Katsherufke." "Dembe ate." "Dembe yawned." Dembe this and Dembe that. Ears were ringing!

The previous Dembe was forgotten like a bad dream. Dembe was reborn.

But Dembe and his wife couldn't forget the former Dembes because they were both still spitting blood, drop by drop.

Doctors

דאָקטוירים

[*Belgishe bleter,* November 1936]

Bent over the machine, Mrs. Shulman has only one thought: her work has a purpose. Quite a purpose!

The workers in the factory can't stop marveling at this woman who, year in and year out, works hard but shows no sign of her labors.

Girls who work alongside her get married, become mothers, grow into plump ladies. The factory's owner has a heart attack and dies. His son is a young dandy who spends summer days taking his father's car without permission and running around with girls. His winter evenings are spent at dog races or dances. He's self-assured and too genteel to do any work. By the time his father dies, he has his own household and a fat belly. And, still, Mrs. Shulman doesn't look a day older.

She has been working on the heavy treadle sewing machine for ten years. Long hours working in the factory during the day and at home at night and, still, she hasn't changed a bit. Her eyes are just as black and shiny as when she first shyly crossed the threshold of the factory. Her face is just as fresh, her hair as thick, brown, and curly without a single grey hair. And her hands are soft and white.

Everyone in the factory marvels at her beauty. More than one presser has tried to start up with her; more than one machinist working alongside her has – as if accidentally – tried to trip her up.

The young men simply can't leave her alone.

"Such a *zaftig* young woman! What a body! No man has anyone like her. If she wants to be so pious, why does she dress like that, damn it?" The young men know their complaints are justified.

"He must have been some idiot, that husband of hers, to leave a golden woman like that," says a broad-shouldered presser licking his thick lips.

"I can't look at her!" says a tall, thin young man smoking a cigarette and sending sparks flying from his machine.

"Getting anywhere with her is like talking to the wall. If you approach her, you might as well ask the heavens to open up. Have you ever seen her *boychik*? He's all dolled up like some artist's son. You know?" says the young man, winking impishly. The others laugh.

Mrs. Shulman knows she is disliked in the factory, but she doesn't much care. After all, she's only working temporarily, until she can quit, so why should it bother her?

Even after leaving the filthy factory reeking of dust, mice droppings, and pants burned by the irons, even after squeezing her way out of the packed tramway and the noisy street, she can still hear the day's tumult in her small apartment.

After scoffing down her meager supper, she starts arguing with the "*boychik*," urging him to eat another egg and drink another glass of milk. When the child does as she asks and also shows her the good grades he earned that day in school, she looks first at the child and then the notebook. And she grows a year younger.

"No evil eye," she says, using an expression in which she doesn't believe. And then she cuts material to sew a dress for a rich woman who will wear it to a bar mitzva.

As she cuts the black satin pinned on a sewing pattern spread out on the table, she sings quietly.

"From far and wide, we hear

"Bright days are near!"

As she sings, she looks at the boy soaping his well-built chest with a fragrant piece of pink soap in his plump hand, a hand that seems more suited to a grown man.

He rubs the washcloth over his chest and repeats a sentence in Latin. Then he plays with the soap bubbles. The colors intrigue him. He doesn't want to take his hands out of the water.

"Alfie, hurry up! Alfie, eat up. You'll be late for school tomorrow," says Mrs. Shulman, hurrying him along.

But Alfie knows his mother doesn't really want him to go to sleep. He knows they don't see one another all day long, and she's happy to have him stay as long as possible. He knows that as soon as he goes to bed, she will be sad in the gloomy apartment. He also knows how much she likes to look at his well-formed body, his muscular arms, his moist, curly hair.

And Alfie likes how much his mother likes it all, so he plays games with the soap bubbles, twirls them in the basin, chases their varied colors: green, purple, gold, red. Then he pretends to be doing gymnastics. He makes two fists, puts them under his mother's chin as if he were a boxer. She laughs loudly.

"I'm serious, Alfie!"

In the end, Alfie finally goes to bed, and Mrs. Shulman begins to work on the black satin dress and Alfie's future.

She sees everything clearly. He's won a scholarship. The teacher says there's no question he'll get a degree. After only five years he'll be – a doctor! Then her mission will be completed.

"Is this a child? He's gold, not a child! May all your troubles fall on my head, not yours," Mrs. Shulman says aloud and her eyes tear up with joy and the shiny material slides around on her white, soft fingers.

It's a pleasure to work for such a child. She's not working for nothing. She's working for a goal.

Suddenly she sees her husband standing before her, alive. She pushes him away. What does she care about him? If he's really alive why should she care? And if he's not, her thoughts won't bring him back.

It's so satisfying to work, she thinks, pushing away all thoughts of her husband who once left to join the People's Convention and disappeared after that.

Patience! Then she'll be able to spit at the factory and at the women who need dresses for bar mitzvas.

***

Years go by. Alfie has his degree and is ready to begin his internship with a doctor in London. And, just then, there is an economic crisis. Bad times begin. Mrs. Shulman's employer goes bankrupt, moves to an elegant neighborhood, and closes the factory. She can't find another *dzshab*. If there are any jobs to be had, they're looking for young girls who can be paid low wages and work long hours.

Alfie, Mrs. Shulman's dream, sits all day long in the squares of London. Her meager savings are soon gone. There isn't enough left to buy him a suit, so he always goes around in a pair of grey flannel pants and a shabby jacket, the kind worn by young students in hospitals. In this outfit, he wears out the heels of his shoes and the doors of offices. But he receives the same answer everywhere:

"We need a young man with experience!"

Alfie, the Latin and physics expert, sits in the squares and tries to avoid his mother. Lately, he's become terribly angry. He yells at her at the slightest word. And if she pretends to ignore it, wanting to protect him, he yells even louder.

In the course of one year, Mrs. Shulman has become an old woman. Her hair is now a salt-and-pepper color.

Not surprisingly, Alfie avoids her. A child can't bear to hear only sighing. What a goal he's achieved!

Every inch of Mrs. Shulman cries as she bends under the weight of day-to-day living. One year of worrying has achieved what ten years of hard work couldn't.

Doctors!

At the Place de la République

אויפֿן פּלאַס דע לאַ רעפּובליק

A Sketch

[*Loshn un lebn*, July 1946]

Near a large display window full of heavy machines stood a three-year-old girl looking intently at the large iron things. Amazed at the sight, she put her little brown hand on the window, moving her index finger around, and murmuring to herself. Near her, on the same sidewalk, shuffled an old woman in a black, patched dress and a black shawl folded three times, its edges reaching the hem of her dress. On her head, she wore a strange-looking bonnet decorated with bits of tulle and black beads. Her dark face was furrowed through her sunken cheeks and around her chin and cloudy eyes. Wrinkles, wrinkles, and more wrinkles. In one hand she held a huge bouquet of flowers. In the other, a small, long loaf of some kind of bread.

She touched the child's back with the bread and said something. The child held on to the old woman's dress, constantly turning her head toward the shop window, and said something aloud.

The old woman wasn't listening. She kept her eyes on the ground and looked at the bread with great reverence.

The statue in the Place de la République stood tall, proud, lofty, confident, with an olive branch in her upraised, muscular hand. Like a patient mother, she looked around the square that seemed like a city within a city.

The statue saw the old woman and the child disappear in one of the gaps that looked like open doors leading to streets and alleys. Thousands of people passed through them every day, going to and from the Place de la République. There were people of every appearance and language, all sorts of colors and voices.

The old woman left the child playing in the courtyard and, sighing and panting, she crept up five flights of grey steps. In the courtyard, a brown-skinned young man in a pair of soiled, stiff pants, naked to the waist, was fixing a broken bicycle and whistling a tune. In a battered cage a greenish canary hopped around as if trying to sing along but was unable to utter a peep. Four large metal garbage cans in the yard reeked. Five stories of open windows, looking like dark holes, breathed in the stench of the garbage cans and never even thought that things should be different. The high walls of the stony yard looked like they had been decrepit from the moment they were built.

The old woman screeched something in a piercing voice. The young man put the bicycle aside. The brown girl stopped arguing with the canary. She straightened her dress like a grown-up, and they both went upstairs.

Quickly, the old woman tore pieces of bread and gave them to her son and grandchild. She added a few potatoes. Meanwhile, she soaked some bread in water.

The father and child finished eating quickly, but the meager food left them hungry. The toothless old woman gummed her food. Then she put some of the bread she had soaked into a metal cup in one hand and, in the other, the bouquet of flowers whose falling leaves she trimmed. She crept down the flights of grey steps, gave the soaked bread to the canary in its cage, and urged it to eat.

Outside, hundreds of people sat around tables, their shirt sleeves rolled up, some entirely without sleeves. They spoke loudly about politics, some complained that it was already late in the summer and there was no sign the season was about to begin. Others told jokes, laughed, smoked cigarettes, and drank wine. The cafes – almost all of them in a row right next to one another – looked like they all belonged to the same owner. The tables were so crowded with wine, beer, and coffee glasses that it was difficult to tell them apart.

Crowds of people were on the sidewalks, strolling, laughing, singing, chatting. Couples clasped one another tightly, kissing in the middle of the street, free as could be. Delighted. Chinese merchants kept bringing their bargains for sale: toys, bracelets, brooches. Their broad faces smiled sadly, baring teeth in mouths even wider than their broad nostrils. They were annoying in their insistence that people buy something, whether they needed it or not. One of them left and two would appear in his place. They all wanted the same thing: to sell. They all wanted to eat. Everyone was sick of these merchants' unwillingness to leave them alone. It made people furious.

An old man was carrying several paper bags with roasted nuts. He couldn't understand why people refused to buy such tasty things. Turks with red fezzes on their narrow heads, eyes gleaming, flitted from place to place and pled with people to at least look at their colorful carpets and the animals embroidered on shawls. But everyone was too used to them to pay any attention. A gaunt young man stood next to the gutter, took out a violin and played dolefully. The violin told such sad stories it was unnecessary for the man to say anything. People began to pay attention. A tear appeared in someone's eye. But then someone else came: an old man with a gramophone playing an old, sad song. People closed their wallets and neither the young man nor the old one got anything. A third person began to play. And then a fourth.

A thin, tattered man skipped from table to table in a torn fedora that looked like it belonged on a scarecrow. His nose was pointy, red, and constantly dripping. His small eyes darted around, gleaming madly. The toothless hole in his wrinkled, sunken cheeks smiled crazily. He wasn't waiting for anything. He didn't stop in the hopes of getting something. He just flew from table to table and disappeared. And then came the old woman with a bouquet of flowers in one hand and the brown girl in the other.

"Buy, good people, buy. The child wants to eat and doesn't have a mother. Buy fresh, fragrant flowers," she cried with her toothless mouth. She was frightened when she saw a small red leaf fall on the wet table. A drop of blood appeared, and the old woman's cloudy eyes filled with tears.

The tall buildings were indifferent, going about their daily affairs. The Hotel Modern took in as many rich guests as possible and exchanged moneys.

The flower-sellers sat on their high stools selling fresh, blooming flowers. They were the old woman's competition. Newspaper kiosks spread the news. Jewish girls wearing short, white stockings on their brown legs, brown berets on their shorn heads, short petticoats, and knitted jackets had no money, no papers, and no work permits. They strolled around with young men wearing shabby raincoats despite the hot summer day.

Night fell. Lights appeared on stores and hotels. The neon signs sparkled. Poor writers and artists, who had not a franc between them, came from Montparnasse to spend some time "here," instead of there. The Place de la République grew more crowded and louder until far into the night. Cars flew by. The cafes were lively. The statue, branch in hand, grew darker. The old woman dragged herself home with her wilted bouquet of flowers.

"May everything wilt like these flowers," she cursed.

"Not everything," said the child, clasping something in her soft little hand.

"Do you see what the *monsieur* with the beard gave me?" she said, showing a franc. "Do you see?!"

The old woman hung her head in shame and was silent.

The Wanderer's Path
דער וואַנדערוועג

[*Loshn un Lebn*, June-July 1955]*

"Every man, woman, and child – all Jews – must report to the prefecture today at two o'clock. They must bring their identity documents containing date and place of birth, full name, address, etc."

Among the thousands of Jews – men, women, and children – ordered to appear were two Jewish women who lived together. One had a baby, the other was an older woman. They took their coats, examined their clothes to make sure the yellow Jewish star was clearly visible and tightly sewn and, trembling, walked to the prefecture. The order meant that some of them – the healthy ones – would be chosen for work.

Sitting on the long bench waiting for their turn, Khaytshe, the older woman, stood up and, with a slightly raised eyebrow, signaled to the young mother to follow her. Behind the backs of people giving their names to the official at the desk, Khaytshe slowly inched her way toward the exit with those who had been chosen. She hoped the guards would think she had already gone through the line and belonged to the group who would soon be sent to work. The guards ignored her. Success! And she imagined herself once again free. But

* This never-before published story is printed here on the occasion of the writer's first *yahrtzeit*, the anniversary of her death.

for how long? She was alone, but she didn't know about the mother who had remained with her child.

Khaytshe didn't go home. She was tall, pale, blonde. She took her large, black leather handbag under her arm, used it to cover her yellow star, and went to one of her friend's neighbors. The neighbor took her to the coal cellar, hid her under all the scraps of material she could find, and anxiously went to make something to eat.

Khaytshe had a thought: very early, when everyone in the house was still asleep, she crept quietly up the stairs, took a jug she found in the cellar, and went out to the street. She wanted to look like she belonged, a person simply going to buy milk. Not like a Jew.

Jug in hand, blonde, clothes not particularly clean because of the rags under which she had lain, she drew no attention to herself.

Slowly, she made her way out of town. After a day of wandering as if in a dream, she found herself under a bright blue sky, a free, bold sky lying as if it were at home, gazing down and listening to the cows, horses, and sheep chewing the damp grass. Like the sky, they wore no yellow stars, held no jugs in the hopes of protecting themselves from a dreadful death.

Khaytshe wandered further. Suddenly, she saw a small brick red house in a thick grove of trees. It looked like someone was cooking dinner for the household. Khaytshe's knees began to shake. Suddenly, she felt human again and very, very hungry. As if she had just awakened, she saw herself wandering aimlessly and now standing like a statue, jar in hand, placed there in order to be ridiculed. She threw away the jug, straightened her stiff fingers, and approached the door. She knocked. An old woman opened and, without even asking what she wanted, brought her into the house, told her to sit, and handed her a glass of milk.

"What do you want, my child?" she asked sympathetically.

"I'm a Jew, and I'm looking for protection. I want to live!" Her stiffness disappeared. She began to weep.

"Don't cry," the old woman entreated. "My son will soon be home. He works nearby. If he agrees, we'll keep you here as though you were a member of the family. The house is his, not mine. I take care of his children. They have no mother."

Only now did Khaytshe notice three frightened children. There was a boy of about seven and two little girls who had been playing and were now huddled together, frightened and staring at Khaytshe.

Khaytshe drank the milk in one gulp and looked around. On the wall opposite her she saw a picture of the Mona Lisa and another of three small, white kittens wearing red bows around their necks. They had such mild eyes. As if there were no Gestapo in the world. She saw no crosses.

The door soon opened and a tall man about thirty-five years old came in holding a cane. He tapped the cane as he came closer to the table. He sat down.

"Well, what's new? Were the children good? Where are they?"

"Here they are," said his mother pointing as if she were speaking to a man who could see.

"They're so quiet. What's the matter? Come here. Don't you want to give your Papa a kiss?"

The children didn't move. They just looked at one another.

"What's happened, Mama? The silence frightens me."

"Nothing, my son. There's no need to be frightened. The children are fine. I'm preparing supper for them. But we have a guest."

"A guest?"

"Yes, a young Jewish woman is seeking protection here. What should we do? The danger is great. What should we do, my son?" the old woman said, her voice full of fear, and pity in her watery eyes. "Tell me. I'll do whatever you say. Your life and your children's lives are so dear to me. I don't care about myself."

"What do you mean? She'll stay with us. Give her Janet's clothes. She'll help out in the house. And you, Mama, will be sick for a while. Do you understand?..."

The old woman went over to her son, took his head in her hands, bent it down, and kissed him.

"May Holy Jesus and Mary protect us along with this unfortunate woman!" She wept, her tears streaming over her son's face.

"Stop it, Mama. No more foolishness. You know I don't like it. Just prepare the food and let's eat."

"Come closer to the table," he said to the young woman. "Tell me your name and what you look like, Mademoiselle."

"I look like an Aryan. Not at all like a Jew."

"It's true," agreed the old woman. She's fair, blonde, tall but, alas, pale. You look more like a Jew than she does. So do I."

"Good. That's very good. You'll stay with us and nothing bad will happen to you. I'll show the Boche!" he said, raising his fist as if he were fighting the Germans.

After eating, the old woman gave Khaytshe her son's bed, and he made a bed for himself elsewhere.

Khaytshe was exhausted from her long days of fasting, the constant fear that the Gestapo would knock on her door, and worry about what had happened to her elderly father. He was a learned man, a scholar who worked for YIVO, the Yiddish Research Institute. He had been deported a few weeks ago and she had heard nothing from him since. She hadn't even been able to leave her apartment to ask about him. She was worn out from waiting day after day for the one hour when she was allowed to go out and buy something to eat only to be told, "You're too late, Mademoiselle. Everything's been sold." And then she would weakly creep back home with empty hands and continue to fast.

She fell asleep immediately.

Slowly, the neighbors got used to the fact that Pierre had quietly married the pretty, blonde girl who said she loved him deeply and loved the children as though they were her own. And she loved the old woman, took care of her, and wouldn't let her do any heavy work. The house was clean, as were the children. They blossomed. Never in her life had the old woman had so much rest and care. And Pierre? What could one say about Pierre? He worked and sang. Everyone could see that he was in love.

Khaytshe grew accustomed to the home that had saved her from death. She worked in the kitchen, in the small field where she sowed and reaped, and took care of the flowers around the house. She washed and ironed, picked the cherries, apples, and pears that fell in the nearby orchard and made them into preserves for the children. But she didn't sing.

Her light eyes showed her great sorrow. They showed that she was Jewish, that her learned father was a Jew well-known and respected throughout Paris and that he had been beaten and bloodied and packed into a wagon taking him God knows where. Maybe straight to the ovens to burn him alive. Khaytshe's eyes also showed her sorrow over the young mother and child, the friend who had not followed her out of the prefecture. She had probably been too afraid her child might cry and endanger all three of them. She had remained sitting, waiting her turn.

Years passed. Terrifying years. Every good person, every free spirit, every intellectual, or simply an ordinary person with a soul wasted away in concentration camps. And most of all, the Jews. It was enough for Jews to have committed the sin of being born for them to be thrown into German hands and to have those hands burn them, turn the marrow of their bones into soap for German women, their skin into lampshades with which to decorate German homes or purses for German whores to carry to parties or the opera to marvel at the arts. All this while Jewish children, men, women, grandfathers and grandmothers burned in ovens.

Like everything else in the world, the six years of war finally came to an end. The world was "liberated." Khaytshe and her blind husband went to Paris to see if they could find out anything about her father.

"In the ovens," she was told.

"Khaytshe, leave that *goy*. Khaytshe, it's a disgrace to your father's memory. Go to the Land of Israel. That's where you'll heal!" people said, knowing she was once a member of the Zionist movement, Poale Tziyon.

But Khaytshe didn't want to listen or remember. "I love him!" she insisted. "He's not really a *goy*. He doesn't believe in anything. Neither do I. So how is he different from me?"

Once, Khaytshe and her blind husband were with some of her friends who had survived and returned. They drank tea. There was wine. Her husband drank rather more than was good for him, and he began to talk a lot.

"I don't know why, but I don't like the Jews," he said drunkenly.

They all looked at one another. Khaytshe blushed so deeply it seemed her skin would burst. It was the first time she had heard her husband speak like that.

"How can you say such a thing? Your wife is Jewish. You convinced her to marry you!"

"Oh, my wife is different! If all the Jews were like my wife, I'd like them too."

"That's what all the *goyim* say," mumbled Khaytshe, wounded. And she moved her chair to the furthest corner.

Once he had sobered up, she brought him home. She made his bed without saying a word. When he fell asleep, she quietly left the small home she had grown to love. With tears in her eyes, she returned to Paris and her friends.

Previously Published Short Stories

The Question

די שאלה

A Humorous Tale

[*Di post*, 1928]

Translated by Vivi Lachs

Rabbi Borukhl, the town rabbi, sat wrapped in his prayer shawl and phylacteries, with his skullcap a little askew. The *tefillin* box on his scholarly forehead gazed down proudly.

Rabbi Borukhl stroked his long black beard interwoven with silver strands. His keen brown eyes perused a religious tome lying on the table as he prepared to start his prayers.

The door opened, and a small, thin, elderly woman entered, draped in a tattered shawl.

"Good morning, rabbi."

Rabbi Borukhl lifted his eyes from the book.

"Holy rabbi, I have a question."

"So," said Rabbi Borukhl and gestured with his hand, as if to say "ask."

"A question, God help me! Everything happens to me. Well, who else would it happen to if not to a pauper? Not to wealthy Chave Leah; she has, thank God, someone looking after her. Well, never mind!"

"What's the question?" the rabbi asked.

"The question? What should it be? It's nothing, just a tiny thing. If it had happened to a wealthy woman, it wouldn't be a big deal, but then it wouldn't happen to a wealthy woman. I'm telling you, all the hard and bitter things only happen to the poor. I wouldn't wish it on you, it should only happen to scoundrels. God in heaven, have I got a cough! It shouldn't be such a big deal. I mean, what pauper doesn't have a bit of a cough? But I just can't sleep with it. I've done everything I possibly can to get rid of it, but nothing works. I can't go to the doctor because – that is, I can go, but, God damn him, he won't see me unless I pay him in advance, like it's my fault I still can't pay the debt I owe him for my late husband, may he rest in peace.

People ask me why I don't go to the clinic. Oh, my goodness! If they were in my shoes, they'd know what it's like going to the clinic! They don't listen to you there, so when I start telling them the details of what and when and how, the only thing they say to you is 'be quick' and 'make it snappy.' If you want to say something particular about your cough, because who knows more about your cough than the person who has it, he tells me that if I don't spit it out in just a few words, he'll tell the nurse to throw me out. I hope he gets ninety-nine fevers thrown at him, dear God! So, what can I do? I drink milk. Fine, I have to drink milk; I hope Laybl the milkman has as much trouble earning his crust of bread as I have getting a drop of milk out of him.

He gets all high and mighty! He said that it isn't worth him selling me just a half a pint of milk. You hear that? It wouldn't be worth it at all. It would cost him his grandmother's inheritance if she'd left him one. Who doesn't remember when that scoundrel Laybl slept in Berish's barn, thanking God that Berish let him deliver the milk for just a crust of bread? He used to bring me a half pint of milk a day because then my husband, may he rest in peace, was still alive! But those were different times. Now he acts like he doesn't know me anymore. I hope he forgets how to feed himself as well, merciful God in heaven!"

Rabbi Borukhl kept his kind, gentle eyes lowered and waited for the woman to finish asking her question. He didn't want to interrupt her. He sighed quietly for the poor Jewish soul who was pouring out her heart.

"In short, I had such a night, I wouldn't wish it on my worst enemy: endless coughing, sounding like I was chopping wood the whole night long. I barely survived until dawn, when I dragged myself out of bed to heat up my little bit of milk. I picked up a piece of kindling, but it was wet through. I started to make a fire but, no bloody use, it wouldn't burn. I blew on the fire but began to choke with my cough, God have pity on me. Blow blow blow, and the bit of milk was cold as ice. If I'd had decent shoes, it wouldn't have been so bad, but how does a pauper get decent shoes, how? I went to a neighbor to ask her to lend me a piece of dry wood, but it was pouring with rain and my shoes were torn to pieces. Rabbi, you should live long, just look at these shoes I go around in."

And saying this, Genendl Dvoshe took off a shoe to show the rabbi, and sand dropped onto the rabbi's table. The rabbi saw what was happening, but it was already too late, the sand was on the table, and Genendl Dvoshe was back standing in her two shoes.

The rabbi became impatient, but Genendl Dvoshe was apparently reaching the point of her story. She told the rabbi that while she was blowing on the fire to make it burn stronger, the milk, which was slowly warming up, boiled over onto a pot used for meat dishes and unfortunately soaked the little bit of Sabbath cholent.*

Rabbi Borukhl ruled that after twenty-four hours she could kosher the pot, and Genendl Dvoshe went home happy.

* Cholent: traditional stew with meat, beans, and potatoes. Cooked on a Friday before the Sabbath eve and kept warm to eat on the Sabbath day (Saturday).

The Dowry

דער נאַדן

A London Tale

[*Di idishe shtime*, 1951
(reprinted from an unknown earlier source, probably 1930s)]

Translated by Vivi Lachs

Although Mr. Harry Barnet had been married for twenty years, he never for one moment forgot the debt his wife owed him.

He was owed a thousand pounds! It was actually owed by his father-in-law, but because his father-in- law was long dead, he claimed the debt from the daughter. However, as the daughter, his wife, didn't even own a thousand pence, she paid him in another way.

Paying him back was hard, but Mondays were harder than ever, because on Mondays the landlord came round to collect the rent.

The landlord was a gentile who hated "foreigners." He said he didn't care that the Barnets were Jews, but he didn't want any "foreigners" in his house. What's more, they paid him very little rent, otherwise he might even have got used to "foreigners" too. And while he couldn't throw them out because the house was under legal control, he took revenge in other ways.

On Monday morning Mrs. Barnet dragged herself back and forth from the bedroom to the kitchen, limping on her bad leg. She woke her husband.

"Harry, it's already nine o'clock! You'll lose another customer!" she called to him from the kitchen while she washed the dishes, saw the coffee didn't boil over, boiled the milk, cut the bread, and spread a checkered, starched tablecloth over a white wooden table, all the while glancing into the bedroom to see if there was any movement – but no such luck!

Harry was happily snoring away, smacking his red lips and blowing steam through his nostrils like a horse. Mrs. Barnet wrung her hands.

"Mrs. Michael needs those things. He'll lose another customer, and there aren't too many of them."

Finally, a creak from the bed and a loud yawn informed Mrs. Barnet that Harry had got up at last.

Harry sat down on the bed, dangling a pair of legs like thick white logs. His stomach protruded over the edge of the bed as, lazily and sleepily, Harry scratched his soft, almost womanly breast. He gave a long, drawn-out yawn.

His wife came in.

"Just look at you. You'll catch cold like that, God forbid. Why don't you put on your slippers?"

She took out a pair of leather slippers from under the bed.

Harry didn't pay any attention to her. He immediately put his quadrangular skullcap on his thick head and muttered something, then, realizing that his wife was right, he slipped into his slippers.

Remembering it was Monday, he started getting dressed. His trousers had got a bit too tight for him, his braces were too short, his shoes squeezed him, and the corn on his left foot hurt.

He washed his hands and face. He wiped his face with one hand, and with the other he took out his prayer shawl and *tefillin* from the wardrobe.

The leather straps of his *tefillin* also seemed to have shrunk. His red lips began muttering. He yawned and mumbled on. Reaching the *Aleynu* concluding prayer, he spat on the ground according to custom and finished praying.

He went into the kitchen where the boiled egg, black bread thickly spread with butter, and the smell of freshly boiled coffee made him feel happy.

"Go and wash, Harry. You'll be late!"

"Mind your own business! Don't presume on your miserable little dowry! A right fool you made of me! I dragged myself round yeshivas and split my head open with algebra and German, all for that lousy dowry. But you couldn't catch any young peddler with your gammy leg, huh? Oh, the ground should fling him out of his grave, the thief. He promised me fifteen hundred pounds and gave me five. And what became of the five? Huh? I'm asking you! Have you lost your tongue? A nightmare!"

They heard a knock on the door. Harry turned as white as the walls. His puffy cheeks began to shake like jelly.

"Listen Mr. Barnet. I'm giving you notice for the very last time! I'll put you out onto the street if you don't clean up the flat. I won't have any foreigners here, and that's it."

Harry nearly choked on his food. He simply couldn't answer him. It was no use picking a quarrel with a gentile – furthermore Bob, the landlord's big brown dog, suddenly leapt forward. With his shiny long lion's mane, Bob gave a jerk toward the table, trying to rub up against Mr. Barnet.

Mr. Barnet jumped backward, nearly hitting the wall.

The landlord, a tall, sickly man with three deep wrinkles in each of his shrunken cheeks, took his pipe out of the corner of his mouth. A sly, angry smile appeared on his thin-pressed lips, and he cheerfully ordered the dog:

"Go on, Bobby! Get hold of him!"

The dog barked and put both its front paws on the table, almost knocking the breakfast to the floor.

Meanwhile Mrs. Barnet paid the rent. The landlord signed the rent book and left.

Harry sighed, wiped the sweat from his face, and set about finishing his breakfast despite everything.

"Yes, I had to get married to a cripple," he thought, cursing his father-in-law, his wife, and the gentile landlord.

His wife shuffled over quietly from the stove to the table and poured him another cup of coffee. She thanked God that he was silent.

After finishing the grace after meals, he picked up a suitcase stuffed full of goods and left the flat without saying goodbye. He lowered his heavy body quietly down the stairs, listening anxiously in case the gentile came out again.

Once on the street, he felt relieved, and on the 47 tram he bumped into a young man he knew:

"Hey, how are you doing? I was planning to come and see you. How about a game of chess this evening? What, you're not playing chess anymore? Never mind, we can play dominoes. You don't find dominoes interesting? Sure, chess is more intellectual. You know what, we can play sixty-six. Cards are better, actually. You get absorbed, and the evening flies by! You won't be at home tonight? Where will you be? So, I'll come round to your friend's place! A group of three is more cozy."

The young man saw that he wouldn't be able to shake off Harry, so got off a stop earlier.

"What, you're getting off already? Just give me your friend's address!"

Harry jumped up, trying to grab the young man's sleeve, but he was no longer on the tram.

When the conductor shouted "Whitechapel," Harry got off and set off down the narrow streets. Here he felt at home.

Nearly all his customers were outside. In these narrow alleys it seemed like with outstretched arms you'd be able to touch the houses on both sides. Fat women stood on the front doorsteps with close-shorn, thinning hair and deeply lined faces. And there were young women standing around with shining faces and tight-fitting dresses that revealed triple-layered bosoms and other disproportionate parts of their bodies.

Harry licked his lips, threw a cheerful "good morning" to the young women, and began unpacking his wares. A circle of women surrounded him, their eyes beginning to shine. The colorful rayon and knitted underwear appeared enticingly from his suitcase: light green, red, yellow, purple, and pink.

The women pulled out the wares: this one a pair of pajamas, that one a petticoat, another held a swimsuit to her bosom, each asking the others if it suited her.

Harry kept a vigilant eye open. A Jewish man, sitting astride a squeaky bench with his legs wide apart to give his stomach more room, became angry:

"Hey, hey mister, beat it! Get out of here or I'll call a policeman! Look how crazy they get when they see him!"

The man knew that Barnet was a pest who sold his wares on installments. The women flocked to him, lost their heads, and took more than they could afford. So Harry went there once a week without a suitcase, with only his payment book, and refused to leave until he was paid his installments. He didn't even go when they threw hot water over him. Now even the angry Jew's wife was trying on a pair of pajamas!

Harry paid no attention to the man. He wasn't a gentile, after all. Harry helped the young women try on silk blouses, took hold of their bare arms, and asked other women for their opinions.

The women helped him, praising the goods:

"It really suits you, Mrs. Michael – I should be so lucky!"

"She looks like a queen in that jersey, bless her!"

When he got home, Harry crept up the dark staircase as quiet as a mouse and, over a piece of roasted meat and a large plate of grated potatoes, told his wife that he hadn't made a penny all day. She didn't answer, just sighed and carried on knitting a pair of socks for Harry. He remembered how pretty the women had looked wearing his clothes. It just annoyed him that the young man on the bus didn't want to have him round. He took out his chessboard, set up the pieces, and played on his own, cursing his dead father-in-law bitterly as he made the moves.

"That's all I needed – a cripple for a wife! With a dowry like that, she couldn't even have got a young peddler! Oy, gentiles or Jews, they're all the same. Is he any better?" And remembering the young man, his face burned with resentment. He threw over the chessboard in resignation. "That's all I needed," he said aloud, "a cripple for a wife!" His wife didn't answer him.

She was used to it.

Variant Translations

The New World

די נײַע וועלט

Translated by Barbara Harshav

From the start, I didn't like lying in my mother's belly. Enough! When it got warm, I twisted around, curled up and lay still....

But, five months later, when I felt alive, I was really very unhappy, fed up with the whole thing! It was especially tiresome lying in the dark all the time and I protested. But who heard me? I didn't know how to shout. One day, I wondered if perhaps that wasn't how to do it and I started looking for a way out.

I just wanted to get out.

After pondering a long time, it occurred to me that the best idea would be to start fighting with my Mama. I began throwing myself around, turning cartwheels, often jabbing her in the side; I didn't let up but it didn't do any good. I simply gave myself a bad name so that when, for instance, I'd grow tired of lying on one side and try turning over, just to make myself a little more comfortable, she'd start complaining. In short, why should I lie here cooking up something, it didn't do any good – I had to lie there the whole nine months – understand? – the whole period.

Well (not having any other choice), I consoled myself: I'll simply start later! Just as soon as they let me out into God's world, I'll know what I have to do.... Of course, I'll be an honored guest, I have a lot of reasons to think so. First of all, because of what I often heard my Mama tell some woman who (as I later found out) was my Grandma:

"It does hurt a little but I almost don't feel it," Mama would say. "I'm glad! I was so scared I was barren. A trifle? It's already two years since the wedding and you don't see or hear anything.... Minke the barren woman also said she would yet have children. And why should I be surer of it?"

"Well, praised be the one who survives. With God's help, it will come out all right; and God forbid, with no evil eye," Grandma would always answer.

From such conversations, I assumed I would be a welcome guest.

I knew that, here in the other world, where I lived ever since I became a soul, when an important person came, he was supposed to be greeted with great fanfare. First of all, a bright light was to be spread over the whole sky. Angels (waiting for him) were to fly around; merry, beautiful cherubs who spread such holy joy that the person only regretted he hadn't...died sooner. It was quite a novelty that I, an honored, long-awaited guest, expected to be born into a big, light home with open windows, where the sun would illuminate everything with a bright light....

Every morning I waited for the birds who were supposed to come greet me, sing me a song. And I was to be born on the first of *Adar* – a month of joy. "When *Adar* begins, people are merry."

But right here "it" comes – the first disappointment.

Mama lay in a tiny room, an "alcove." The bed was hung with dark draperies, which completely screened out the light. The windows were shut tight so no tiny bit of air could get in, God forbid; you shouldn't catch cold. The birds obviously don't like screened out light and closed windows; they looked for a better, freer place to sing. Meanwhile, no happiness appears either; because I was a girl, everybody in the house, even Mama, was disappointed.

In short, it isn't very happy! I am barely a half hour old but, except for a slap from some woman as I came into the world, nobody looks at me. It is so dreary!

Grandma comes in and smiles at Mama. She looks happy – probably because her daughter has come through it all right. She doesn't even look at me.

"*Mazel tov*, dear daughter!"

"*Mazel tov*, may we enjoy good fortune!" Mama smiles too but not at me.

"Of course I would have been happier if it were a boy," says Mama. Grandmother winks roguishly with a half-closed eye and consoles her.

"No problem, boys will also come...."

I listen to all that and it is very sad for me to be alive. How come I was born if all the joy wasn't because of me! I'm already bored to death. Oh, how I want to go back to the other world.

All of a sudden, I feel a strange cold over my body. I am jolted out of my thoughts; I feel myself clamped in two big, plump hands, which pick me up. I shake all over. Could it be – a dreadful idea occurs to me – is she going to stuff me back in for another nine months? Brrr! I shudder at the very thought.

But my head spins, everything is whirling before my eyes, I feel completely wet, tiny as I am! Am I in a stream? But a stream is cool, pleasant, even nice. But this doesn't interest me as much as the idea of what the two big, clumsy hands want to do with me. I am completely at their mercy.

Thank God, I am soon taken out of the wet. I am brought back to the alcove, already violated, sad. I am carried around the alcove: everybody looks at me, says something. At last, I am put back to bed. Mama does put a sweet liquid thing in my mouth: I am really hungry for what is in the world.

Mama looks at me with her nice, soft eyes, and my heart warms. A sweet fatigue puts me to sleep and I am blessed with good dreams....

But my happiness didn't last long, a dreadful shout wakes me with a start. I look around. Where did it come from? It's Mama!

People gather round.

"What happened? Where did that shout come from?"

Mama gestures, tries to point, her lips tremble, want to say something and can't. She falls back onto the pillow, almost in a faint.

Seeing they won't get anything out of Mama, they start looking for the reason in the closet, under the bed, in the bed.

All of a sudden, a shout is heard from the nurse, who keeps

repeating in a strange voice, "Cats, oh dear God, cats!" The people look up, can't understand what she's saying.

But, except for the word "cats," they can't get anything out of her – so upset is she.

Grandma is also very upset. But she takes heart, makes a thorough search in the bed and, laughing to hide her fear, she calls out, "*Mazel tov,* the cat had kittens. A good sign!"

But apparently, this isn't a good sign. The people are upset.

"On the same day, in the same bed as a cat? Hmmmm, a person and a cat are born the same way," says one brave soul. They calm Mama. But again, nobody looks at me. Mama falls asleep. And with that, my first day comes to an end. I am, thank God, a whole day old and I have survived quite a bit.

The third day after my birth was the Sabbath. This time, a big, red gentile woman puts me in the bath. I wasn't so scared anymore, already familiar with the way it smells.

Once again, I lie in bed with Mama. Mama looks at me more affectionately than yesterday. I open my eyes, I would like to look around a bit at the new world. I am already used to the darkness. All of a sudden – it grows darker for me than before.

A gang of women burst into the alcove. I look at them. They're talking, gesturing, picking me up, passing me from one to another, like a precious object. They look at me, they look at Mama, they smile.

Meanwhile, Grandma comes with a tray of treats.

The women make her plead with them, pretend they don't want to try any of the cookies, whiskey, preserves, cherry brandy, berry juice or wine; but, Grandma doesn't give up, so they open their beaks, and finally consent to do her a favor.

Males also stuck their heads into the female alcove. They talked with strange grimaces, gestured, shook their beards, went into a fit of coughing.

With them, Papa succeeded, not Grandma. And I am named Sore Rivke, after some relative of his.

Now they need a wetnurse. Mama is weak, pale, with such

transparent, narrow hands without sinews, she can hardly pick me up. A middle-class woman, she cannot breastfeed me. I am the opposite: a healthy, hearty gal, greedy, I restrain myself from shouting all I want is to eat.

"Not to a goyish wetnurse," says Grandma. Not for all the tea in China. And she can't find a Jewish one. The pharmacist says I should get used to formula, which is better than mother's milk. But I say I don't want to get used to it and I throw up all the time.

This is bitter! Grandma is upset. Mama even more. But Papa consoles them, saying the Holy-One-Blessed-Be-He will help. And He does.

Our neighbor remembers a wet-nurse named Reyzl. She has the voice of a sergeant-major and two red eyes that scare me. She can't come to our home. She has six children of her own but there is no choice.

All the details are worked out, she is given an advance and may everything work out all right.

Reyzl picks me up out of the cradle, takes out a big, white breast, which looks like a piece of puffed up dough and gives it to me to suck, as a test. Well, what should I say? I didn't drown. Even my eyes fill with the taste of a good wet-nurse.

Reyzl looks happily from one to the other, "Well, what do you say?"

Mama and Grandma glance at each other furtively and are silent....

I have the good fortune to be a tenant at Reyzl's! Not that she needs another tenant because she lives in a flat not much bigger than a large carton. When Reyzl brings me home, her husband comes to greet me carrying their smallest one in his arms and the other five heirs swarming around him. He seems to be pleased with my arrival.

"Well, what do you say about this, eh? Ten gulden a week, my word of honor! Along with old clothes and shoes. Along with the fact that, from now on, they'll give all the repairs only to you! You hear, Beyrish?"

Beyrish is silent. He turns around so his breadwinner won't see his joy.

"You're more of a man than me, I swear. You can earn a gulden faster...." he thinks to himself. But right away he becomes serious. "Where will we put the cradle?" They ponder a long time.

But Reyzl's husband, who is an artist at arranging things in his tiny flat, smacks his low, wrinkled forehead with his hard hand and calls out joyously, "Reyzl, I've got it! Under the table!"

So in a tiny cradle, I am shoved under the table.

With open, astonished eyes, I look at the filthy wood of the table, covered with a host of spider webs, and think sadly, "This is the new world I have come into? And this is its heaven?"

And I weep bitter tears.

The New World

די נײַע וועלט

Translated by Joshua Fogel

Even when I was still in my mother's belly, something didn't feel right to me. But look here! It was warm so I twisted and folded myself up, and there I lay perfectly satisfied.

But, since it was over five months and I had already sensed life, I became not too terribly happy. I was disgusted with the whole business! More than anything else, the constant lying in darkness became so wearisome to me – and I protested. But who heard me? After all, I couldn't scream. One day I deliberated: I'm going about it the wrong way – and I began to look for a way to escape.

I just wanted to get out.

After thinking about it long and hard, it occurred to me that the best advice would ultimately be to engage my mother in battle. So I started to wriggle, to squirm, and often I gave her a poke in the side; I stopped for nothing, but it didn't help. I only managed to make a bad name for myself. So, for example, in the event that wearily I sought to lay down on one side and to turn myself around, just to make it a bit more comfortable, they would start grumbling. In sum, to make a long story short, nothing helped – I had to stay there the whole nine months – do you understand? – to the very end!

Well, not having any other recourse, I took comfort in the fact that I would be delivered later. They had to bring me into God's world, so I could find out what I was destined to do.... I knew that I would be a respected guest – I had many reasons to believe this. First of all, I used to hear my mother very often say to some woman who was (as I was later to discover) my grandmother: "It hurts a little, but I can hardly feel it," my mother would say. "I'm so happy. Oh, how I used to dread the very sound of the words 'barren woman.' Trifling matter, eh? Two years after my wedding and nothing to hear or see.... Minke the Sterile also thought she would have children. And why was I so much surer?"

"Well, blessed is the Lord. If only God helps, good fortune prevails; and, God forbid that the evil eye takes control," my grandmother would nearly always reply.

From these and similar chats, I gathered that I would be a welcome arrival.

I knew that once a respected man passed over into the "other world" where I was living while I was still a soul, they would prepare to receive him with great fanfare. First off, they spread an immense brightness over the entire sky. Angels used to fly around (anticipating his arrival) joyously, beautifully, completely enveloped in the brilliant sun. He was encircled by fiery cherubs who had themselves turned down many blessed joys for this opportunity. The man's only regret was that he had not earlier...died. A remarkable thing it was that I, a dear, long-awaited guest, expected to be born in a large bright room with open windows through which the sun would shine with great rays of light.

I expected that every morning birds would come rustling to greet me, to sing a song of praise. In addition I was born on the first of Adar – a month of joy. "He who enters in Adar will multiply in happiness."

And here "she" came – the first disappointment.

My mother lay in a tiny room, a "cubicle." Her bed was protected by dark curtains which blocked the light well. The little window was shut tight so that, God forbid, not a drop of air would invade the room; and no one would catch a cold. The birds, it seemed, did not care for light obstructed by a closed window, and they went to look for better, freer places to sing. Happiness, for the time being, also failed to appear, because I was a girl, and every one in the room, even my mother, was disappointed.

In a word, there was nothing to be joyous about! I was nearly a half hour old, but aside from a few slaps from an old woman when I came into the world, no one so much as looked over at me. It was so lonesome.

My grandmother peeped in and smiled at my mother. She seemed to be full of happiness – probably because her daughter had survived the ordeal unharmed. To me she paid no attention.

"Congratulations, my daughter!"

"Thank you, Mama, for everything."

Mama was also smiling, but not at me.

"I would certainly be happier if it were a boy," said my mother. Grandmother gave a roguish wink with a half-closed eye and consoled her: "It's okay, you'll also have boys...."

I listened to all this and found it difficult to comprehend. Why was I born if there's no happiness at all because of me?! I was already thoroughly bored. Hey, how'd you like it if I went back to the other world?!

Suddenly I sensed some sort of strange chill pass over my body; I woke up from my imaginary thoughts; I felt myself clamped in two large, fleshy hands that lifted me high up. I was trembling all over. Perhaps – a dreadful notion occurs to me – they're taking me back to stick me inside for another nine months? Brrrr! I shudder at the mere thought of it.

All of a sudden something is turning me by the head, it's making me dizzy, I feel drenched through and through – how big I am! Am I in a river? But isn't a river cool, delightful, and much wider than me? This didn't bother me so much as the thought of what two huge, clumsy hands might do to me. I was completely at their mercy.

But, thank God, they removed me from the wetness, they brought me back into the "cubicle," undressed, dry. They carried me around the little room: everyone looked at me, said something. Finally they laid me back down in bed. Mama placed something sweet, liquidy in my mouth: I was starving and went at it strenuously.

Mama looked at me with her good, soft eyes which warmed my heart. A sweet fatigue put me to sleep and I dreamt of something happy....

However, the happiness did not last long: a horrifying shriek aroused me. I woke up. I looked around. Where did it come from? Who screamed? My mother was the first one!

People came running.

"What happened? Where did that scream come from?"

Mama tried to indicate something with her hands, her lips quivering, wanting to say something but unable to do so. She fell back down on the sofa, practically in a faint.

It was clear that they were not going to elicit a thing from her, so they began to search for the cause in the closet, under the bed, in the bed.

Suddenly a cry was heard coming from the maid, but as if she hadn't screamed with her voice. She repeated continually:

"Cats, help, cats!"

They all exchanged glances, unable to understand. What did she mean? They could exact nothing more from her than the word *cats* – so completely rattled was she.

Grandma was also very upset. But recouping her courage, she began her own proper search in the bed and, laughing, ostensibly in order to conceal a cry, proclaimed:

"Congratulations, the cat gave birth to kittens, an auspicious sign!"

It didn't seem like a good omen. Everyone was troubled.

"On the same day and in the same bed, with cats? Hmmm. So that's how a person and a cat are born," said someone.

Mama was comforted. No one looked over at me. Mama fell asleep. And so ended my first day. I was already, thank God, a whole day old, and had already experienced a great deal.

The third day after my birth was Shabbos. This time some large, ruddy gentile woman conducted me to the bath. Now that I knew what it smelled like, I was no longer frightened.

Once again I was with my mother in bed. Mama looked at me with more tenderness than she had the previous day. I opened my eyes wide and looked around a little bit at the new world. I had already lived in darkness. Then, all at one – it became darker, as it had been earlier.

A flock of wives invaded our little room. I gazed at them. They spoke about something or other, waved their hands about, grabbed me in their arms, passed me from one to the next like a precious object. Looked at me, looked at Mama, smiled.

Meanwhile, Grandma came in with a tray of goodies. The women had to be asked, pretending to want a taste neither of the cakes nor of the whiskey nor of the preserves, the cherry brandy, the berry juice and mead. But since Grandma didn't indulge them, they began to pout, ultimately became amenable, and did her the favor of helping themselves.

The men also stuck their heads into the women's cubicle. They said something with odd looks on their faces, waved their hands, shook their beards, and went away.

In short, my father prevailed this time, not Grandma. And I was named after a relative, Sorah-Rivke.

Now everyone had to have a wet nurse. Mama was weak and pale, with such transparent, blue-veined, dainty hands that she could scarcely lift me. A well-to-do housewife, she couldn't breastfeed me herself. I was just the opposite; a healthy, tough little girl, a glutton, and I was always crying. The only thing I wanted was to eat.

"Not to any gentile wet nurse," said Grandma, indicating that she would not give me away if she could avoid it. She couldn't find a Jewish wet nurse. The druggist said that it would be better for me to get accustomed to powdered milk than to my mother's own milk. But I "said" that I didn't want to get used to it and I constantly threw up.

It was bitter! Grandma was all astir. Mama even more so. But

Papa consoled them: "God will surely bless us with help." And He really did help.

One of our female neighbors remembered something and brought us a wet nurse. Her name was Reizl. She had the voice of a soldier, with a pair of red eyes that terrified me. She couldn't come home with us because she had six of her own children. There was no other option.

Everything was settled, an advance paid to her, and all wished her well.

Reizl lifted me out of the cradle. She took a large, white breast which looked like a piece of fermented dough, and gave it to me to suck on as a trial run. Well, what am I supposed to say to you? I nearly drowned. Even my eyes could feel the taste of this wonderful wet nurse.

Reizl assumed a look of success and said from one to the other: "Ha, anything else you'd like to say?"

Mama and Grandma threw furtive glances at each other and remained silent.

So I was lucky enough to become a resident in Reizl's home! As if she was in need of another resident. For she lived in a small apartment, not much larger than a boarding house room. When Reizl brought me to her home, her husband, carrying the smallest child in his arms, together with the remaining five heirs, all came out to greet me. He truly looked happy at my arrival.

"Well, what else can you say? Ten zloty a week, like I was a real Jewish woman. And also some clothes and shoes. And what's more, from today on they'll give all their repair work only to you. Do you hear me, Berish?"

Berish was silent. He turned aside so that his wife and provider might not see his joy.

"She's more of a man than I am, she can earn money quicker than I can," he thought to himself. But he soon became serious. "Where shall we put this little crib?" They thought about it for awhile.

Reizl's husband, who was an artist at arranging things in their tiny apartment, smacked himself with a calloused hand on his wrinkled, low forehead and exclaimed with delight:

"Reizl, I've got it! Under the table!"

So they slid me, with my tiny cradle, beneath the table.

I looked with wide-open, astonished little eyes at the filthy underside of the table top covered with numerous cobwebs, and sadly thought: "So this is the new world that I've descended into? And this is its heaven?"

And I cried bitterly.

The Relic
אַטלעסענע קאַפּאָטע

Translated by Morris Kreitman

The Gliskers had lived in the open country, on the fringe of the forest, for ages. Yudel Glisker inherited a store which for generations had supplied the needs of the peasantry in the countryside for many a mile around. And he ran it quite single-handed. A tall and broad-shouldered Jew, who was well capable of standing his own ground, he held the respect of the peasants.

Of an independent nature, he did not even allow his wife to lend him a helping hand, except at such times as he went to town to replenish his stock. A woman's place, contended Yudel, was in the home beside her children. It was safest for both parties. …

However, Rachel, his wife, thought otherwise. Knowing full well, though, that when Yudel said no, he meant no, and he was by no means the worst of husbands, she left him to his own devices. To find some outlet for her dormant energy, she took to dairy-farming on her own account.

Yudel raised no objection. So long as she did not meddle in his affairs, she was free to do as she pleased. He was all the more willing to agree, because it would give those idle wenches of his something to do. He even went so far as to help her pick a few head of cattle, paying the peasants their due and chinking glasses with them over a bottle of vodka.

Rachel carried on business no less efficiently than Yudel. Like her husband, she refused to depend on others, doing everything herself. She milked the cows, heated the basins of sour milk, lifted the heavy stone slabs on to the cheeses, churned the butter – all unaided. She even sewed the cheese-bags herself.

Her daughters merely grazed the cattle in the meadows, seeking out the deepest and the lushest grasses. As a consequence, when the cows came home in the evening, their udders were fit to burst with milk. And it was with a sense of deep satisfaction that Rachel would seat herself upon the three-legged milking-stool and nimbly finger the rosy and brownish nipples, until the udders became as flabby and elongated as they had been in the early hours of the afternoon.

Gratefully the relieved animals would lick her hands with their moist, heavy tongues. The warm milk in the pails, the odor of manure in the barn, would infuse Rachel with even greater vigor than usual. At such times she felt herself capable of moving mountains.

As for her daughters, spending the livelong summer day in the meadows, under the untrammeled sky, caressed and tanned by the bright sunshine, they shot up tall and erect as the pines on the fringe of the neighboring forest.

Visiting Jews from the surrounding villages, who drove up in dilapidated little carts drawn by decrepit old horses, for supplies of milk and butter and immense cheeses, could not but notice how remarkably carefree was this "wild" life led by the Gliskers. And it pained them. These callers, who never even ventured near the cowshed, for fear of being tossed by the animals, could not endure the thought of Glisker's three daughters growing up robust and simple as peasant wenches, with the mother herself looking and behaving like a sturdy peasant woman, and with Yudel, the head of the family, wholly engrossed in earthly matters, without a thought for the eternal life to come.

Thus it was that whenever Rachel was adamant in refusing to reduce her prices, these excitable little fellows would turn their attention to Yudel and point out the error of his ways.

"Think of your daughters, Reb Yudel! Where is this sort of life going to lead them? Here you are, a man of standing, and you allow your daughters to graze cattle in the company of peasant lasses and lads. Fine morals they'll learn in the fields, we don't think! You won't find it too easy to marry them off afterwards, when the time comes, Reb Yudel, and you such a fine man and all!"

Yudel was not a bit impressed, except that on occasion he felt greatly tempted to take hold of the speakers by the scruff of their scraggy necks and give them such a shaking, that never again would they make bold to poke their noses in other people's business. He saw through their harangues as so much empty, spiteful talk. Now, themselves without the slightest scruple about charging the poor of the nearby villages fantastic prices for a pint of milk or a few ounces of butter, they expected Rachel to part with her wares for a song and were sorely grieved at her firmness. Their torrent of words was but an expression of personal sorrow not a little inspired by the flourishing condition of his affairs, for which praise be to God!

Yudel, patient man though he was, would surely have ended up by throwing these irascible little fellows out neck and crop. And he might have finished his life peacefully in the cottage where his forefathers had lived before him, had he not one evening chanced upon his eldest daughter, Rosa, locked in embrace with the district chief's son out in the open fields – "for all the world like an animal," as Yudel afterwards told his wife. Thenceforth, Yudel no longer treated the dairymen and their unasked-for advice with the same contempt as of old. Indeed he listened attentively to all their prattle, pondering and brooding over every chance remark that slipped their tongues.

And one fine day towards the end of summer, instead of going to town as mere visitors for the High Festivals, the Gliskers parted with their lonesome cottage, stowed all their belongings into roomy carts with latticed frameworks, and, the cattle roped up behind them, plodded into close-by Bojonitz, to make their home there for good.

Only when his old homestead was out of sight, and the procession of carts was passing through the cone-strewn pine forest, did the last lingering regrets pass from Yudel's heart, and stories he had heard long ago came back to him of Jewish lads and girls who, reared in solitude in the country, had become embroiled in love affairs with Christian friends and had brought shame on their parents – shame beyond repair.

These feelings caused him to seek the friendship of his new neighbors in the village and to place more confidence in them. It was in quite a new light that he now regarded those selfsame Jews who used to come to his cabin in the old days to purchase timber (that being one of Yudel's side-lines). In fact, he even modified his opinion of the dairymen who had been in the habit of haggling so obstinately with his wife. Here in the village he saw that some of these men would spend their evenings in study at the synagogue. What it was they droned out of the huge yellow-leaved volumes, he did not know, but the beadle told him that one of the dairymen – the fellow with the scraggiest neck of all – was extremely pious and learned. As for the others, they knew a thing or two as well.

Yudel would peep furtively over their shoulders, and to his dismay he found that not only could he not understand a single word, he was not even able to read the script. He experienced a sensation that was new to him – a feeling of inferiority. And in spite of himself, this humiliation of being a stranger, a foreigner among his neighbors, clung to him and grew acuter the longer he dwelt in Bojonitz, until it became a veritable obsession with him.

He decided to take a tutor, only not a soul must know: it would never do for him to be thought a simple peasant. He had a reputation to live up to.

In the village it was common knowledge that Yudel was a man of means. And he was treated accordingly. On the very first Sabbath following his arrival, when he presented himself at the synagogue for the morning service, the beadle assigned to him a place of honor. which he occupied ever after.

Even so, Yudel was not quite happy. Honored though he was, he had a disconcerting feeling that he did not fit in. It grieved him above all that alone among the worshippers occupying the front seats in the synagogue, he wore a woolen gaberdine, while the others were all clad in silk. With his great height and mighty back, which concealed behind it a whole cluster of worshippers, he was surely most obtrusive in that woolen gaberdine of his, like some nonentity from the back rows who has pushed his way to the front so as to rub shoulders with the notables of the community.

On the face of it, it seemed a simple enough matter. He could certainly afford a new gaberdine, praise be to God! All he need do was order a few yards of silk, send for "Silly" Gimpel, the skilled village tailor, and that would be that! Surely nothing could be easier.

Nevertheless, Yudel, who was capable of overcoming the most difficult of obstacles, faltered over such a trifling matter, and allowed a secret yearning to come into his life for the first time.

So, on the Sabbath, instead of going straight home after the service as it had always been his custom to do, he would fold his toil-worn hands behind him, the ends of his red-spotted handkerchief clutched between his iron fingers, and, with cramped stride, would pace up and down the front seats of the synagogue like a frightened man who is bracing himself for a plunge into the unknown, and endlessly he would repeat in a wistful sing-song, partly to himself and partly to the notables all clad in silk and satin:

"Sabbath greetings, Sabbath greetings, Sabbath greetings to you!"

Like most of the things Yudel did, this behavior was ill received. On one occasion it evoked a slight, but visible sneer from one of the notables, who muttered an incomprehensible remark into his notable beard, added an equally incomprehensible remark through his notable nose, putting an altogether vulgar interpretation on Yudel's strange conduct.

And one lad of about thirteen, Simcha, the Talmud master's youngest son, was even quicker in the uptake than the grown-ups; he construed without a moment's hesitation the meaning of that delicate twitch of a notable snuff-filled nose. A roguish smile on his pinched features, his fragile body erect, he placed himself behind Yudel, followed him up and down, chanting ever so softly:

"Sabbath greetings, Sabbath greetings, Sabbath greetings to you, and yea, Sabbath greetings to all the eats we are going to have for dinner!"

After Yudel's departure, all the notables chortled mirthfully, reprimanding Simcha the while:

"You ought to be ashamed of yourself. Fancy making a Jew the laughingstock of the congregation, especially on the Sabbath, you impudent brat!"

Never did Yudel hear their laughter. Nor was it in his nature to suspect it. Yet, somehow, it contrived to hurt him.

At home, too, his Sabbath comfort was both enhanced and disturbed. After dinner he took his weekly lesson – and who was his secret tutor, if not Simcha, the thirteen-year-old lad that had entertained the congregation at Yudel's expense? In the afternoon, when the village was always deep in Sabbath slumber, the boy would steal across to the new cottage on the outskirts of the village, to earn his weekly pay of two guldens.

Simcha usually found Yudel in the same posture: seated bolt upright in his bed, with a contented, restful look on his still sleepy face. And Yudel, pretending not to notice Simcha's entry, would address his second daughter, Faiga, with fatherly peremptoriness:

"I say, Faiga, hand me a glass of water, will you. I want it clearrr as crrrystal – and mind there are no flies in it!"

These words invariably tickled Simcha. At the same time, they conjured up a vision of flashing crystal, of limpid water in a running brook, and side by side with it, another vision – of a stagnant pool with dead flies floating on top.

He felt all the more deceived, therefore, when Faiga returned with a ribbed tumbler of the most ordinary water, and he would mimic the man spitefully under his breath:

"I want it clearrr as crrrystal – and mind there are no flies in it!"

Only after Yudel had scrutinized the water, sipped it to the last and swept the palm of his hand over the glistening silvery drops that had settled on his beard, would he discover Simcha's presence, and, greeting him amicably, call to his wife:

"Wake up, Rachel, he's here!"

On the opposite side of the room there was another carved bed, an exact replica of Yudel's, and here Rachel lay, crosswise and fully dressed, her feet resting on a scoured four-legged stool. She was very nearly as big as Yudel, and almost as well built.

Simcha could not help noticing how firmly her bosom heaved behind her white linen blouse, how numerous were the folds in her reddish tartan skirt. She certainly looked a peasant woman with that string of scarlet beads round her throat, and with that red kerchief on her head, from which – contrary to Jewish law – her natural hair showed, black and glossy.

She roused a confusion of feelings in Simcha, which he was afraid to examine, allowing only one to linger in his mind. Was she truly a Jewess, he wondered. He was not alone in his perplexity. The whole village wondered. These strangers certainly gave themselves out as Jews – pious ones at that – and yet their ways were not the ways of Jews.

Simcha turned his eyes from the mother to the three daughters. Everywhere temptation. And he was obliged to cast his eyes on the sand-strewn floor. When Rachel had finished making the beds, he sat down at the table.

Yudel, clearing his throat, asked suddenly:

"I say, Simcha, how many yards of silk d'you think I'd require for a gaberdine, eh? Got any idea, have you?" – as if the lad were a tailor.

Simcha glanced up as though to measure Yudel, and it occurred to him that the man would need quite thirty yards.

"Why, I should say about fifteen," Simcha blurted out, flushing hotly.

Yudel said no more, only regretting his weakness in asking. He saw that he had made a fool of himself. Abruptly he went up to the bookcase, picked out a Pentateuch bound in calf-leather, with large golden lettering on its crimped back. Turning up the weekly portion, he carried the open book to the table reverently and with an air of importance.

The lesson began, with Yudel seated at the head of the table,

Simcha beside him, and opposite them – Deborah, the youngest daughter, her elbows resting on the table, her closed fists firmly embedded in her fleshy checks, and not for a moment did her bright eyes stray from Simcha's pinched features.

Simcha pretended to be unaware of her presence, and nervously moved his tiny forefinger over the print:

"*Vayaitsa Yakov mibeer Shiba*, which means – And Jacob went out from Beer-Sheba, *vayelich Charana*, and went towards Charan."

That was simple enough, thought Yudel. Jacob left one place to go to another just as he, Yudel, had left the country to go and live in Bojonitz. The only difficulty was that he could not distinguish the meaning of each separate word. Reluctant to ask, he floundered badly, growing more and more confused, much to the dissatisfaction of Simcha, who struggled heroically to send the shafts of knowledge home, but all in vain. He talked himself hoarse, like a real grown-up tutor – the very image of his father! Yudel bore it patiently, trying again and again. When at last he contrived to get it right, he beamed all over, and Simcha was so heartened, he actually gave Deborah a triumphant look.

Deborah gaped back with her large simple eyes. She could not understand the cause of all this sudden rejoicing, much less why her father – fine man that he was – allowed himself to be taught by a mere slip of boy.

Meanwhile Rachel came in from the kitchen bearing a large tray of sweetmeats, which Simcha became aware of, even though his back was turned. His slender fore-finger began creeping ever faster and faster over the black print; errors were glossed over, and soon the lesson was ended.

"Well, well," said Yudel, his red face losing a little of its taut expression. "Well, well!"

When his wife had respectfully replaced the book, his features relaxed altogether, and with sudden gaiety he clapped his hands together with such a violent sound, that Simcha jumped, almost scared out of his wits.

"Come along now, let's all have a bite. Don't be backward, Simcha. You mustn't let yourself be beaten by the girls."

At such times it was wonderfully pleasant in that big dusky room, with the furniture a mass of polished shadows, the tiled stove gleaming, and with the dainties on a peasant-made tray vanishing rapidly into large healthy mouths. Simcha felt that assuredly Yudel's cottage was at the moment the happiest in the entire snow-covered village.

With nightfall, which was not far off, the Sabbath came to a close.

When Yudel returned from the evening service, he found a fire already glowing brightly in all four compartments of the kitchen-range, with a huge pot of potato-peel – the cows' supper – in position at one end, and another almost equally huge pot of potatoes – the family's supper – in position at the other end.

Rachel was already mixing the chicken food, while the hens came fluttering down from their shelves or emerged from under the beds, surrounding her like angry demons. They had gone without food all day, except for some crumbs off the table, and they clucked wildly, demanding their due. When she finally set the food down, they all started off on a mad pecking and gobbling race, often ending up in a fight – although there was more than enough to go round – with feathers flying thick and fast,

However, when Rachel began to scold, the fowls ceased their scramble, as though understanding her every word, and they settled down to eat more quietly.

Saturday night was the busiest time of Rachel's life, especially when Yudel made his mind up to drive to town overnight, to replenish his stock, and she would be overwhelmed with work. She kept calling on her daughters to lend a hand; but they were never at home. Immediately after Simcha went, they all slipped out unobserved, and left everything to their capable mother

But it was even more than Rachel could cope with. She always got quite flustered, and when Rachel became confused, she was never able to remember things by their proper names, and she would call all objects, both animate and inanimate, "whatsaname."

"Whatsaname," she cried, meaning Faiga, whom she hoped against hope to find somewhere about the place, "drain the whatsaname and give it to the poor starving whatsanames," obviously meaning: "Faiga, drain the potato-peel and give it to the poor starving animals."

Yudel often wondered where those wenches of his got to of an evening. However, they must be somewhere in the village and would surely come to no harm there.

Immediately after supper he would harness his pair of horses and drive off towards the forest, with a large sum of money in his pocket. Rachel often protested it was foolhardy of him. A snowstorm might come on and cause him to lose his way. Then there was the real danger of bandits. But Yudel went unafraid, and he always returned the following day unharmed.

Winter passed, and Yudel, who never gave up when he set his heart on a thing, was so persevering in his lessons with Simcha, that finally the village marriage-broker, a man who knew everybody's business, got wind of it, and he at once had a brainwave. He would match Yudel with Reb Isaac, the Talmud master, and thus it was that in due course a marriage was arranged between Rosa, Yudel's eldest daughter, and Mordecai, Simcha's sixteen-year-old brother.

No sooner was she betrothed, than Yudel discovered that "that wench of his" was rather a delicate girl, not a bit strong, in fact poorly, and must do not a thing in the house, as befitted a gentleman's daughter.

"Give her no more rough work to do," Yudel adjured his wife, "because she must not exert herself and will have to be well cared for. Besides, now that she's engaged to the Talmud master's son, she'll have plenty of dainty work to keep her busy."

Perforce Rosa spent days on end tracing monograms on lace-fringed pillowcases for herself and her husband-to-be. (Needless to say, Yudel was providing the couple's entire home at his own expense.) She knitted and sewed, embroidered and crocheted all for her future home, not forgetting numerous presents for her in-laws. Rosa toiled and moiled, while Yudel kept raiding his fat wallet, for Reb Isaac, the village Talmud master, was a most learned man, a most particular man, a most ill-tempered man and a most hopelessly penniless man.

In truth, it proved no easy matter to persuade Rosa that she was a delicate girl, in poor health, for she loved to be hale and hearty, as indeed she was, and she loved to do coarse work, even though she loved still better to give her mother the slip on a Saturday night and meet the district chief's son in secret at their tryst outside the village. She hated it like poison pricking her fingers over dainty needlework, she hated it walking about forever dressed up like a mannequin, she hated being genteel, and she hated Mordecai, the Talmud master's son, with an overpowering hatred. But gradually she grew accustomed to her new role (or so it seemed). After a time she began taking it for granted that not only her father, but she too, was a person changed beyond recognition.

Spring came and with it– floods, which drove the villagers on to the rooftops, where they stayed for almost a week. Then the hot weather set in.

Oppressive though the broiling sun was, Bojonitz was full of bustle, for the day of Rosa's wedding was drawing close, and no event in the village, neither death nor birth, was comparable to a wedding.

Yudel's affairs had prospered exceedingly in his new home. His stock of timber had multiplied, so that it overshadowed his entire cottage, and the cows had to graze far away, by the river, while the smell of resin rising in the sun from the sawn logs dominated the length and breadth of the village.

In the evening, when the womenfolk congregated on the benches outside the whitewashed walls of the cottages, under the shadowy eaves, to gossip, Yudel was their unfailing topic. Perhaps it was the odor of his timber which always brought him to their minds and tongues.

Or perhaps it was the sight of him passing through the high street on his way to the synagogue, accompanied by his new-found crony, Baruch "Headpiece," a man remarkable for his wisdom in matters of the Talmud and more remarkable still for his stupidity in everyday affairs.

They were truly an ill-assorted pair. Baruch, with his tiny head a mass of moist hair hanging over his ears, his beard reaching up past his cheekbones to his black little eyes, above which the brows met in one bushy tangle, and his mouth extending from ear to ear, would trot along beside Yudel like a dressed-up monkey or a circus dwarf beside the circus giant. And their shadows in the setting sun – one huge, the other so tiny – would look positively grotesque.

At such times Hannah, the village shrew, often passed nasty remarks even before Yudel was out of earshot.

"Look at him. There he goes! D'you mean to tell me that he's a Jew? Ho, ho, what a Jew! May hair grow on the palm of my hand if that man was not born a Christian.... There!" she exclaimed, triumphantly displaying the palm of her skinny hand, as though that in itself offered proof of the truth of her words.

No one really believed her; but the women, and even some of the men who were in the habit of hanging round the gossipers, listened with the most intense pleasure to Hannah's endless flow of words. Nimble feminine fingers manipulated needles in preparation for the forthcoming wedding, and greedy ears drank in envy-quenching words in the freshening evening air.

"They're a funny lot, those Gliskers. Got the luck of the devil. No harm ever comes their way. If they were real Jews, they'd have troubles and cares of some sort. No harm ever comes their way, No harm ever comes their way...."

Hannah's words had a mournful ring in the evening air.

On the Sabbath of Consolation, only a few days before the wedding, Yudel experienced one of the happiest moments in his life. As he entered the synagogue in the company of Baruch, no less a person than the Rabbi came forward to welcome him.

"Sabbath greetings, Reb Yudel!"

The sun was still high in the skies, and the little house of worship was steeped in sunlight. A golden beam of dust specks was pouring in through the closed window, playing upon the pulpit and ending with a glitter of splendor upon the candelabrum.

Yudel was enveloped by so joyful a sensation, that the vexation caused him in the past by malicious tongues melted like a cloud in a sudden burst of hot sunshine.

"Sabbath greetings, Sabbath greetings, Sabbath greetings to you!" Yudel broke forth into an uncontrollable sing-song, overwhelmed as he was by the honor done him by no less a person than the Rabbi, and overjoyed as he was by the sight of the sunshine resting like a crown upon the candelabrum, which none other than Yudel himself had recently donated to the community. As fine and massive a piece of silver as was to be seen anywhere, and no wonder, thought Yudel, that the golden sunshine had chosen it as its resting-place. Indeed gold and silver always went well together....

This feeling of triumph remained with him up to the very day of the wedding.

The moment had come. Yudel's large front room was bare of all furniture, except for a few long wooden benches lining the walls. Suspended from the center of the newly whitewashed ceiling was a huge paraffin lamp, and hanging all round it were colorful Chinese lanterns. On the walls fluttered a multi-colored assortment of paper ribbons, plain and curled, coiled and crimped – a dazzling mixture of reds, greens, yellows and blues! The floor was strewn with fine golden sand.

Rachel was not wearing her usual red kerchief, but a luxuriant wig with a wide parting in the middle and a white silk bow fastened at the side, such as she used to put on only for the High Festivals.

Yudel was clad in a new and silken gaberdine, donned in honor of the occasion. Marrying into a family that was poor, but of high repute, he had found it in him to discard his woolen gaberdine and change into silk. Its silken rustle filled his ears. It was a sound he would have to get used to. Magnificent was the sheen on his bulky body, and bashful the rosy sheen on his peasant face. Having formed a connection with a family of such refinement, he could at last afford to assert himself, and indeed, the new gaberdine suited him well. It rested on his broad back a perfect fit, and it bore an air of rejoicing – truly the gaberdine was rejoicing!…

Rachel was helping a hired woman to arrange the cut cake on the trays, also the other sweetmeats. She was not a bit flustered, and never lapsed into calling things "whatsaname." Faiga and Deborah were wearing yellow batiste frocks trimmed with innumerable frills and ribbons. They also had white bows in their hair.

Upon a white cushion on an upholstered armchair the bride was seated, all clad in white, her feet resting on a little stool. The guests were beginning to arrive. First the village maidens, their faces reddened by hard washing, bodies tightly laced up, stiff and starchy, in the company of their mothers – pious old women dressed up to the nines.

The musicians held their instruments in readiness: "Silly" Gimpel (the village tailor) with his fiddle, Hersh Laib with his violoncello, little David with his flute.

The bridegroom was due to arrive any moment now. He would be accompanied by the most notable young men of the village and by fellow-students from the distant *yeshiva*, Simcha in their midst, for he was over thirteen and considered a man now.

Yudel was unable to keep still, so full of happiness was he. He paced about the as yet empty room reserved for the menfolk, stopping now at the spread tables, now at the paraffin lamps, whose light he turned full on, then down again, to satisfy himself that the wicks were not smoking. He took out his red-spotted handkerchief to dust the place of honor where the bridegroom would soon be seated, then he stole into the women's room, to have another look at the bride.

But here was an unexpected sight. The bride was squirming unnaturally on her seat, and was groaning softly into her white veil. If there was anything amiss, none of the womenfolk had noticed it. For they showered profuse kisses upon her, embraced her and blessed her, drowning her piteous, muffled moans. Unmarried girls, especially the more elderly ones, were examining with much inquisitiveness her white frock, the veil over her head, the white shoes on her feet, and were blind to the agony distorting the bride's face, which changed from a white pallor to a livid green. And now the orchestra had started up, to the accompaniment of shouts:

"Mazel tov! Here comes the bridegroom! Now play us a merry tune. Here comes the bridegroom!"

Women clapped their hands to time:

"He comes, he comes, to fetch his bride,
The angel of joy shall be their guide."

Yudel left Rosa writhing on her armchair, and hastened forward to meet the bridegroom, who had only just crossed the threshold. A pale, thin, dainty young man, not much taller than his small brother Simcha, and with the same sort of pinched longish nose, he stood hesitating in the corridor, surrounded by a cluster of young men, all wearing silk gaberdines like himself.

The music played merrily.

Rosa was bent double. Nevertheless, she glimpsed her husband-to-be as he was conducted down the corridor, past the open door, towards the men's quarters – so miniature, a mere doll dressed up in silk.

She was seized all at once by a sense of pity for that slip of a boy, pity that mingled strangely with a towering rage. But a pain in the very pit of her stomach overwhelmed all other sensations, and she howled out aloud.

The womenfolk instantly surrounded her. A great uproar and tumult arose. The bride kicked out in agony. She wept like a small child. Hannah the shrew, pushing her way to the front, broke down completely and cried piteously. Rachel kept shouting "Call the whatsaname!" indicating the doctor, although she knew quite well that there was none to be found in the village.

The bridegroom, scared to death, was hustled into a back room. Someone ordered the musicians to join him there and to play up for all they were worth.

His mother was so distraught, that suddenly, while pulling at her hair, she tugged her wig off and stood, baldheaded amid a crowd of bewildered, jabbering, helpless guests.

The only person who did not lose his head was Yudel. As he watched his daughter, a terrible suspicion entered his mind, so terrible that he would have been glad to see the whole nightmare cottage collapse there and then, crushing to death his own flesh and blood and all the loathsome assembled guests.

The Rabbi advised him to have the bride put to bed, to give her a hot compress and to go on with the ceremony at the bedside, for by putting his trust in the Lord, he would assuredly be the witness of a miracle and a speedy recovery. Reb Isaac, the Talmud master, chose this particular moment for losing his notorious temper.

But Yudel paid no heed. Instead, still wearing his silken gaberdine, he ran off to the stable, brought out two black, sleek, rested horses, hitched them up, wrapped the bride in an eiderdown, carried her out in his arms and placed her in the cart. Before even Rachel could grasp the situation and join them, he had climbed up on to the seat, cracked his whip and was off in the direction of the forest.

An eerie silence fell on the cottage. All eyes were turned on the cart with its strange load, with Yudel, the back of his silken gaberdine glistening in the evening sun, whipping the eager horses like a man possessed.

A cloud of dust hid the cart, then that vanished too, leaving nothing behind. The forest in the distance stood motionless and unconcerned as before.

The forest was haunted. No one in Bojonitz doubted that. Demons dwelt in it. In summer they revealed themselves in the form of witches floating over the treetops on broomsticks. In winter they disguised themselves as hungry wolves. Strange tidings were forever coming out of the forest. But nothing was stranger than the tidings Yudel brought back with him after only half an hour's absence.

The tumult in the cottage was hushed, malevolent tongues struck dumb, when his cart reappeared, enveloped in the same cloud of dust as that in which it had disappeared.

Rosa was sitting beside him on the seat. The color had returned to her face. She climbed down unaided.

"The wedding is off," said Yudel to Reb Isaac, quite simply and without any explanations.

The tumult which followed these words was such, that no one afterwards clearly remembered quite what happened. The demons, which the villagers all agreed had swayed Yudel to take this unprecedented decision, seemed to take possession of everybody.

But Yudel was not to be moved.

No one could make it out. Yudel kept his secret even from his wife, of what had passed in the forest. He alone knew of the thoughts that had tormented him as he had driven furiously away from his cottage. He alone knew how near to death his terrible suspicion had brought him. He alone had a vision of that bough upon which he had meant to hang himself. He laughed and wept at his own folly when he found that the suspicion had been unfounded.

That same night, when he had finally succeeded in driving the last of the guests off his premises, when he had said no to the Rabbi himself, he barred the door of his cottage. He flung down his silken gaberdine and donned the woolen one again. The family ate their supper out of a common bowl as they had done in the days when Yudel had considered himself nothing better than a simple, happy peasant.

And to this day his silken gaberdine lies neglected in a heap up in the loft of his cottage. At sunset it catches the scarlet afterglow with the same sheen that tinged it scarlet on that memorable evening when he had driven Rosa off in the cart towards the forest. But it lies there in the loft motionless, forgotten, like the ghost of a folly that had once enveloped Yudel and that Yudel has discarded forever....

A Satin Coat

אַטלעסענע קאַפּאָטע

Translated by Ellen Cassedy

The Gliskers had lived in the village since the beginning of time. Yidl Glisker's store, which had been in the family for generations, supplied the peasants of the surrounding countryside with everything they needed. Yidl ran the business single-handedly. Tall and broad shouldered, he could hold his own against all comers, and for this the local people respected him.

He wouldn't allow his wife in the shop, except when he had to go out of town to replenish his stock. A Jewish woman, Yidl believed, should stay at home and look after the children. That way was best for all concerned.

His wife, Rochel, believed just the opposite. But when Yidl said no, he meant no, so she didn't argue. Instead, she started her own dairy as an outlet for her energies.

Yidl didn't stand in her way. As long as she stayed out of his affairs, he didn't care what she did. Indeed, he was glad – the milk business gave his three girls something to do. He helped Rochel select several head of cattle, paid for them, and drank a celebratory glass of whiskey with the farmers to seal the deal.

Rochel managed her business no less successfully than Yidl. Like him, she took care of everything herself. Alone she milked the cows, warmed the pans of sour milk, lugged the heavy stones used for pressing the cheeses. Alone she churned the butter and sewed the cheese bags.

All her daughters did was tend the cows in the field. After feasting on the tallest and most succulent grasses, the cows would make their way home every evening with their udders full to bursting. Then, with the greatest satisfaction, Rochel would seat herself on the three-legged milking stool. As her nimble fingers tugged on the pink-and-brown teats, she would scoot forward on the stool and shift the bucket with every release of the overflowing abundance. The cows would express their thanks by licking her hands with their wet tongues. The warm milk in the buckets and the smell of manure in the stable awakened all of Rochel's powers. At such times she felt she could bend iron with her bare hands.

All summer, the girls lay in the meadow under the heavens. Warmed and browned by the bright sunshine, they shot up like the pines in the neighboring forest.

The dairymen from town who drove up in their rickety horse-drawn carts to buy Rochel's milk, her butter, and her immense cheeses – they saw the way the Gliskers were living, and they were not pleased. Themselves afraid to venture too close to the stable for fear of being caught on the horns of some animal, they couldn't bear to watch the three Glisker girls growing up like peasants, Yidl paying heed only to his business and Rochel looking for all the world like a healthy peasant woman – instead of a daughter of the Jewish people.

Particularly on those occasions when Rochel refused to lower the price of her milk or cheese, the customers would take Yidl aside and attempt to point out his transgressions.

"What will become of the children, Reb Yidl?" they would say. "How can a Jew permit his daughters to grow up in the field? Are they gentiles? Jewish children are not meant to tend cattle, Reb Yidl – especially not the children of a fine man like you. If things go on like this, Reb Yidl, you'll never be able to marry them off when the time comes. And how will that be, Reb Yidl? Eh?"

Yidl paid them no attention. He had half a mind to grab these sorry townsmen by their withered throats and shake them until they lost their appetite for meddling in the affairs of others. He knew perfectly well that they didn't mean a word they said; they were simply irked that his wife wouldn't sell to them at half price – even though back in town they didn't think twice about gouging the poor women who came to them for half an ounce of butter or a quart of milk. They couldn't bear the sight of the Gliskers' prosperity: that was why they yammered on.

And Yidl would have continued to pay them no mind – had he not happened upon his oldest daughter, Rosa, lying in the open field like a beast with her arms around a gentile boy. After that, he no longer laughed off his wife's customers but instead attended with great seriousness to every word out of their mouths, brooding over even the most trivial remarks. And at the end of the summer, when the Days of Awe drew near, instead of heading into the town on the other side of the forest for only a brief visit (like the little pears, the *yengalkes,* that appeared so fleetingly in the shops at this time of year), the Gliskers sold their house in the village, packed their belongings into high, latticed wagons, roped the cattle to plod along behind, and moved to a cottage on the outskirts of town – for good.

Once there, Yidl allowed himself to recall the many stories he had heard about Jewish girls and boys who took up with peasants in the countryside. A friendship began, one thing led to another, and by the time the parents took notice, it was too late. Thinking along these lines made Yidl feel closer to his new neighbors in town, especially the more "respectable" ones. He looked upon these folk more favorably than he had when they'd come to him to buy timber (for he also traded in wood). Even his wife's customers, the dairymen, now appeared in a different light. Here in town, he noticed that some of them sat every evening in the house of prayer and studied – studied what, he didn't know, but the sexton told him that the fellow with the scrawny neck was quite a scholar, and the others, too, were learning a chapter of the Commentaries.

Yidl cast a furtive glance into the volumes of the Talmud lying on the long scratched table that was greasy with tallow. He understood not a word – couldn't even make out the letters. Suddenly he was seized with a fierce desire to know what was contained in the yellowed pages of these tattered books. He would find himself a teacher, he decided, and pay whatever it cost – more – on condition that no one must know. He was tired of being a country bumpkin.

Everyone in town knew that Yidl was a wealthy man. On the very first *Shabbes,* the sexton showed him to one of the most prominent seats, and he was honored by being called up to the pulpit during the reading of the Torah.

Life in town pleased Yidl. Business was good. He had a teacher and was already making progress as a student of the Torah. Why, then, he wondered, should he be the only one in the front rows who was clothed in a worsted-woolen coat? As he swayed in prayer among the silk and satin, he worried that his six-foot frame, his broad shoulders, must surely look out of place clad in wool. It was a simple matter. All he had to do was order a few yards of silk, send them to Fishl the tailor.... But for Yidl, who could do almost anything in the world, putting on a silk coat was no small matter.

Every *Shabbes,* after praying, he would stretch his legs by pacing back and forth in the space near his seat and mumble a quiet, wistful tune, half to himself and half to the men in silk and satin: "*Gut Shabbes! Gut Shabbes! Oy, gut Shabbes! Gut Shabbes!*"

One eminent member of the congregation smiled into his eminent beard and muttered something through his nose, offering a rather vulgar commentary on Yidl's striding with his great fists clasped behind his back and his red country-style handkerchief tangled in his iron fingers.... At this, Simchele, the Talmud master's son, a pipsqueak of thirteen, took to falling in step behind Yidl's broad shoulders, turning his skinny little body to and fro, lifting his long nose in the air, and droning: "*Gut Shabbes, gut Shabbes! Oy,* good stuffing, good stuffing! *Gut cholent, gut cholent!*"

Once Yidl had taken off his prayer shawl, handed it to the sexton, and gone out, the congregation chortled openly, while scolding the

Talmud master's son: "Shame on you, you little rascal! Imagine making fun of such a man – and on *Shabbes* too!"

Little did they know that it was Simchele who was Yidl's secret teacher. Every *Shabbes* afternoon, the boy earned two gulden for instructing him in the weekly Torah portion. Each week, Simchele would steal through the blue-white shadows to Yidl's house, which stood waiting for him under the vast sky, buried in the snowdrifts at the very edge of town.

There he would find Yidl sitting up in bed, wide-awake and well rested, issuing a fatherly command to his middle daughter, Feyge: "Bring me a glass of water, Fetche. And clearr as crrystal, please – no worms!"

Before Simchele's eyes there appeared first the limpid sparkle of a running brook – then a stagnant mud puddle crawling with worms. But when Feyge returned with a thick, smudged glass of ordinary water, he came down to earth with a thump. He mimicked Yidl under his breath: "Do you hear, Fetche, clearr as crrystal – no worms!"

Still sunk deep in his *Shabbes* repose, Yidl neither heard nor saw. With every sip, he held up the glass between his cracked fingers and examined it closely for worms. Finally he put the glass on the floor, wiped the silver drops from his beard with the edge of a sheet – and suddenly took note of Simchele's arrival.

"Ah, Simchele, *gut Shabbes*!" he cried with delight, and went to awaken his wife. "Rochel, get up – he's here!"

Across the room, on a high bed with carved posts just like Yidl's, Rochel lay crosswise, her legs sticking out and propped on a milking stool. Nearly as big as Yidl and almost as solidly built, she lay fully dressed in a white linen blouse with a red-checkered skirt, a red kerchief tied under her chin, and at her throat a long string of red coral beads. She looked like a country woman who came to town only on Sundays.

At Yidl's cry, Rochel began to stir, and the stool began to slide. With every creak it moved farther away, until finally, when the tips of Rochel's heavy shoes were barely holding on, it wobbled and toppled over with a crash.

At this Rochel awoke, heaved her ample frame into a sitting position, and smiled, "Ah, Reb Simchele!"

"*Gut Shabbes*!" Simchele replied. He pretended not to look but couldn't help observing that her red kerchief had slipped down, disclosing her black hair and the broad white stripe where it was parted – something he had never seen on a married Jewish woman. He was astonished. Almost every *Shabbes* it was the same. She never seemed to notice that her uncovered hair was in plain view.

Simchele was not the only one who was surprised at Rochel's bold behavior. The whole town was bewildered by the Gliskers. They were Jews – and pious ones at that – yet at the same time they were not Jews at all. The man was more robust than a peasant, with daughters as tall and straight as trees – giants, really, with massive shoulders and bosoms and eyes so bright it was actually unpleasant to look upon them. They worked harder than any Jewish children ever seen. The mother was equally strapping, healthy and robust, and her eyes shone like the girls'.

Here in town, Yidl entrusted the store entirely to Rochel. All week she stood in the shop, counting herring. The peasants would patronize no other store. It was "Rochela this!" and "Rochela that!" Who knew why they were so taken with her – unless (God forgive the thought) she was actually one of them. "Rochela this!" and "Rochela that!" – and through it all Rochel paid them no attention whatsoever, except perhaps when a greedy peasant woman damaged the herring while searching for the best pieces or concealed something in her bosom and tried to walk out with it.

When Rochel stepped away from the herring barrels to her green upright scale, she would lift the heavy sacks as if they contained nothing but feathers, rather than the lumpy soda and coarse salt that the peasants bought for their horses and cows. She carried the casks of kerosene, cod liver oil, and cooking oil over the slippery black floor of the store as though they were empty. If, as sometimes happened, a load got stuck on a loose board, she simply gave a tug and pulled it free without effort.

Since the girls worked as hard as their mother, it didn't matter that there was so much to do. With all the customers running to Rochel's, the other shopkeepers sat empty-handed, eating themselves up with jealousy. The floors in their little stores were barren, the herring grew soft, and the brine along with the hoops on the barrels turned red with rust. The salt shrank and hardened in the bags, even the oil seemed to dry up, and the women's envy grew all the more bitter.

Meanwhile, the Gliskers became more prosperous with every passing day. It was not long before the store was so stuffed with merchandise that there was not room for one more item, and the *Shabbes* at Yidl's became all the more festive, the *Shabbes* repose all the more luxurious, the *Shabbes* treats all the more delicious.

And so, on this *Shabbes*, as Simchele waited to begin the lesson, Rochel got down from bed, smoothed the quilt back into place, and went to the front room to wash her hands. Yidl meanwhile had finished dressing and gone to the front room, too, leaving Dvoyre, the youngest, who was twelve years old but looked twenty, to make his bed, smoothing out the wrinkles just like her mother. Upon his return, he stretched and picked several feathers from his beard, rolled them into crumbs and flicked them away, and smiled at Simchele.

They sat down at the table.

"Eh, Simchele," Yidl asked, as if the boy were a tailor, "how many yards of silk do you figure I'd need for a coat, hmm?"

Simchele looked Yidl over, sizing him up at a glance. About thirty yards, he estimated to himself.

"I'd say maybe fifteen," he said, and blushed a fiery red.

Yidl said nothing. He was sorry he'd asked. He went to the glass cabinet and took down the Pentateuch bound in calfskin with big gold letters engraved on its spine. He located the weekly reading, laid the stiff red ribbon between the pages, and carried the open book to the table, where Simchele was seated at his right side. Dvoyre sat opposite, her elbows planted on the table and her fists dug into her cheeks. Not once did she take her eyes off the teacher.

Simchele pretended he didn't know she was there. He ran his skinny index finger over the text "*Vayeytsey yankev mib'eyr shova*," he read, "And Jacob went out from Beer Sheva – *vayeylech chorono* – and went toward Haran."

This Yidl could understand. What was not to understand? Jacob went out from Beer Sheva, just as he, Yidl, had moved out of the village of Bozshenits, but what he couldn't fathom was the meaning of each individual word, and he was ashamed to ask. When he made a mistake, mixing up one thing with another, Simchele was annoyed. Like a born teacher, he did his heartfelt best, attempting to pound into Yidl's head the meaning of each and every word, but all too often his efforts were in vain.

Yidl was patient. He tried and tried again, and when he finally succeeded, he beamed all over, and Simchele was so pleased that he forgot himself and threw a look at Dvoyre, a flash of teacherly triumph in his eyes.

Dvoyre stared back with her grey gentile eyes. She couldn't imagine what the two were so excited about. Why all the rejoicing all of a sudden? And why was her grown-up father allowing himself to be instructed by a mere boy?

Meanwhile, without turning around, Simchele could tell that Rochel was passing by with a platter of delectable things to eat. He moved his thin finger more rapidly over the page.

"*Vayeytsey yankev mib'eyr shova* –"

"Mmmm!" Yidl rubbed his hands together. "Let's have a bite to eat, shall we?" He replaced the stiff ribbon between the pages and gave the holy book to Rochel, who carried it reverently to the bed. She laid it down on the green quilt as tenderly as if it were a coddled child and began to serve the *Shabbes* treats.

"Eat, Simchele! Don't be bashful! What does it say in the book?" Yidl became a lost soul once again. "How is it written?" He furrowed his brow fiercely, as if expecting to extract the answer from his forehead.

Simchele helped him out: "*Im ein kemach, ein toyre* – Without bread there is no Torah."

"But of course!" Yidl slipped Simchele a poppyseed cookie "Enjoy!" Brimming with pleasure, he began to eat with gusto.

"Eat, Reb Simchele." Rochel placed a piece of golden-brown strudel before him. "Here you are." She added a few slices of almond bread to his plate and poured him a glass of tea.

On winter days, immediately after the lesson, Yidl and Simchele would go to the house of prayer together. That is, Yidl went in first, and then came Simchele, far enough behind that the two appeared to have nothing to do with each other. Meanwhile, Rochel barely had time to stumble through the "God of Abraham" prayer for the end of *Shabbes* before dark. Then a yellow fire flickered in all the compartments of the stove. On one burner bubbled a big iron pot of potato peelings for the cows, on another, almost as large a pot of potatoes for the family. A red borscht filled the room with a tart warmth, and as Rochel set herself to mixing a bowl of bran, the hens came fluttering down from the shelves and out from under the beds, clustering around her like a band of demons, clucking, pecking, gobbling, and snatching the food out of one another's beaks, even though there was more than enough to go around. Sometimes a fight broke out and feathers went flying, but as soon as Rochel showed her temper, the birds settled down and behaved themselves, as if they could tell that their mistress knew best.

By now the cows in their stalls were bellowing, especially Rochel's favorite. She had always raised fine-looking cows, but never such a blessed beauty as this one, which she had brought up from a calf. The animal's hide was brown, with white spots that glistened glamorously in the sun. Truly, she looked like a princess – and such udders! No limp rags these, but as firm and healthy as could be, and milk as rich as cream.

On these Saturday nights, Rochel was nearly out of her mind with work. "Feyge, more wood!" she would call, hoping against hope that her daughter was around somewhere. "The potatoes aren't cooking! Feyge, the cow is starving! Have pity on the dumb thing! Feyge – one what-do-you-call-it is enough!"

Feyge tried not to be at home on Saturday nights. She took off after the midday meal and came back only long after dark. As for Yidl, he would often hitch up his horses as soon as *Shabbes* ended and go off on business. So the minute the sun went down, Rochel had to feed her husband along with the cows and the chickens. Not knowing whom to attend to first, she became more than a little scattered, and when Rochel became scattered she lost the ability to call things – cows, horses, husband, children – by name.

"Yidl, did you give the what-do-you-call-it to the what-do-you-call-it?" she would ask, meaning, "Have you fed the horse?"

"Whatsit, the thingums are what-do-you-call-it" meant "Feyge, the potatoes are getting soggy." (Rochel had another weakness as well – no sooner had she put a pot of potatoes on the range than she became convinced they were overcooking.)

In time, Yidl had been studying Torah with Simchele for so long that the town matchmaker came up with the idea of marrying off his oldest daughter, Rosa, to Simchele's older brother, Menashe, who was sixteen.

As soon as the two became engaged, Rochel gave up ordering her daughter to help with the household chores. The bride-to-be was a delicate creature, Yidl declared, who must not be allowed to do any rough work whatsoever. As the future wife of the Talmud master's son, she was to perform only dainty work – and plenty of it.

So Rosa sat all day long tracing monograms on pillowcases for herself and the groom (naturally, Yidl had agreed to outfit the two of them entirely at his own expense). She embroidered matzo covers for herself and her in-laws, knitted challah cloths, sewed a bag for the groom's prayer shawl, and stitched an intricate linen apron for her future mother-in-law. Rosa worked and Yidl paid, because the groom's father, the Talmud master, was quite an important fellow, a learned scholar, fastidious, with a mighty temper – and an utter pauper. It was no easy task to convince Rosa that she was a fragile flower, because as it happened she took great pride in her iron constitution.

She loved hard work and the *Shabbes* rest that followed, and she loved more than life itself the Saturday nights after *Shabbes,* when she was supposed to be at home helping Mother but instead sneaked out to go walking with a gentile boy. She hated like poison to prick her fingers with the embroidery needle. She hated to loll around the house dressed in fancy clothes like a mannequin. She hated being a lady. And more than anything on earth, she hated her future husband.

Bit by bit, however, she became reconciled to her fate – or so it seemed. One thing was certain: She had become a new person, no longer under her mother's thumb

So Rochel did the work of ten, especially during the winter. In the summertime the daylight lasted so long that after the end of *Shabbes* there was nothing left of Saturday night. In summer she would wait for Yidl to come home from the evening prayer and end the Sabbath; she would say the "God of Abraham" prayer, followed immediately by the "Hear, O Israel" bedtime prayer – and then it was off to sleep. In summer she didn't need to cook potato peelings or mix bran. The cows were content to graze all day in the meadow, and she almost never saw the chickens, which spent all day outside laying their eggs. Yidl didn't need to rush off at sundown, and life was good.

Yidl, too, loved the summer *Shabbes* even more than the winter. In summer, he did not go with Simchele to the house of worship after his lesson – it was far too early for afternoon prayers. He was not one to refrain from the enjoyment of *Shabbes,* so he sent Simchele away on some pretext. Behind the back wall of the spacious wooden house, his tall stacks of lumber took up more and more of the yard. There he strolled among the boards, measuring them with his eye.

Counting was forbidden on *Shabbes,* he reminded himself as he cast an appraising look at his holdings and swelled with pride. No evil eye! Soon the tall stacks would completely cover the grass. Already they'd overtaken part of the pasture and forced the cows to graze all the way down by the river – which was all for the best, Yidl figured; the grasses were juicier there.

But why was it forbidden to count? Let's say he were to count just one stack; then he would be able to estimate the rest. Well. He could see he had too much pine – but the alder and the birch – why shouldn't he count them? He felt such a powerful urge to do so that he quickly clasped his hands behind him and went over to pat the cow, so as not to commit a sin.

The cows were begging to be milked, poor things. The grass was so lush here, Yidl thought tenderly, that their udders must be stinging as the Sabbath lingered. He went back to his lumber. There certainly was a lot of it, no evil eye! He walked the narrow passageways between the stacks. How he loved his timber. He adored the scent of it, especially on hot days, when the resin was as soft as honey and smelled as if it had just been cut from the stump.

A man is only human, however. So Yidl shuttled back and forth, here giving the cow a slap on the back, there making quick calculation with the boards. Who knew – maybe it was a permitted to count, after all? He would ask the rabbi, who would no doubt be surprised at his ignorance. "Of course one must not count wood on *Shabbes*," he would say. "By no means! Not with the mouth and not with the eye." The rabbi would smile in a friendly way but inside would think Yidl a fool for asking a question a little child would be able to answer, and no doubt he would take him for a rube....

Yidl sighed and turned onto the road leading to the house of prayer. The chickens followed as if he'd invited them along. Annoyed, he swatted them away with his red handkerchief "Shoo! Shoo!" He looked around to see whether anyone was watching. "Shoo!"

He hated looking like a peasant. Nonetheless, who should appear at his side nearly every *Shabbes* but Boruchel the pinhead – Boruchel, who also loved to spend a summer day strolling through Yidl's timber, sniffing the sweet smell of the resin, and gazing up into the cheerful blue sky.

"*Gut Shabbes*, Reb Yidl!" Boruchel extended his small hairy hand from a paper cuff, his black eyes glittering beneath the damp thicket of hair that extended over his ears into his paper collar. His little beard and bushy black sideburns jiggled when he smiled.

"*Gut Shabbes*! *Gut Shabbes*!" Yidl grabbed Boruchel's scrawny little hand, swallowed it up in his massive paw, and administered a friendly squeeze that lifted Boruchel into the air.

"Owww! How are things with you, Reb Yidl?" Boruchel tried to free his bones from Yidl's iron grip.

"Not bad, praise be to the Almighty!"

"And when is the wedding, God willing?"

"And what is it to you, if I may ask?"

"Nothing – but a good friend would like to know."

"It's not yet arranged," answered Yidl. "Perhaps later in the summer, God willing, after Tishe Bov." And they made their way across the scuffed and trampled lawn that looked like a balding head with its parched grass, heading for the afternoon prayers. Boruchel cast a glance at Yidl's giant shadow, which stretched almost across the entire length of the field, and then at his puny one, which danced along daintily as he strained to keep up with Yidl's colossal strides. Much to his dismay, his head didn't even reach as high as Yidl's shoulders. Perspiring heavily, he raised himself up on tiptoe and spoke into Yidl's ear, his tiny hands making crazy shadows on the scruffy grass.

Almost every *Shabbes* found the two of them proceeding in this fashion to the afternoon prayers. Each time, Yidl was in agony because he could not work up the courage to ask even Boruchel the question that was tormenting him: whether one was or was not allowed to count lumber on *Shabbes*. Boruchel suffered, too, on account of his pitifully small stature.

This *Shabbes,* Yidl had yet another source of distress to contend with. On the way to the house of worship, he had overheard a group of women chatting with Chana-Rochel on the long bench outside her house. They were gossiping about him and his household.

"Here he is in the flesh," Chana-Rochel had said as she'd pointed him out with a skinny finger. "I ask you, does that man look like a Jew? Would a Jew be so successful? Would a Jew have such good fortune? And the rest of them – are Jewish girls so big and strong? Does a Jewish woman kiss the cow? Hair should grow on my hands if those people are Jews." And here Chana-Rochel displayed her palm, as if in so doing she could prove that the Gliskers were not Jews at all, but peasants who had converted to Judaism.

The sun was still high in the sky when Yidl and Boruchel entered the house of prayer. The rabbi himself came over to pay his respects. "*Gut Shabbes*, Reb Yidl."

The little house of worship was splashed with light. A sunny column of dust slanted in through the window and extended all the way to the pulpit, where the menorah stood gleaming.

Yidl felt a wave of joy overtake him. His troubles floated away like a cloud melting in the hot sun.

"Gut Shabbes! Gut Shabbes!" he roared, delighted that the rabbi had honored him with a greeting and that the golden sun had chosen to rest atop the menorah like a crown. It was Yidl himself who had donated the menorah to the congregation – a solid silver one of considerable size. If the sun had sought out the menorah, well, no wonder: gold was always drawn to silver.

And so Yidl lived in wealth and in honor, succeeding in everything that he did. Even the Torah lessons went smoothly; with each passing week, Simchele was increasingly pleased.

Late in the summer, the special day arrived at last. Yidl's big front room was cleared, and long wooden benches were placed around the walls. From the freshly whitewashed ceiling hung a large twinkling lamp and a dozen little lanterns. The floor was spread with fine sand and the walls trimmed with paper streamers, smooth and curled, twisted and crimped. Green, red, yellow, orange – the swirl of colors was dazzling to the eyes.

Instead of her usual kerchief, Rochel was wearing a lustrous black wig with a white silk bow tied at the bun, as on Rosh HaShana.

As for Yidl, in honor of his daughter's union with a gentle and silken young man from a fine family, he had finally managed to take the plunge. Having cast off his old worsted-woolen coat, he now made his entrance – in satin. The fabric shimmered on his massive body. His shy, open face was red and shining. Indeed, the coat suited him. It lay across his broad shoulders as if it had been poured on and seemed to rejoice along with its owner.

Rochel was helping the hired woman to fill the platters with cakes and other sweetmeats. Perfectly composed, she called everything by its rightful name: no "what-do-you-call-it" on this day. Feyge and Dvoyre were wearing white ribbons in their hair and yellow batiste frocks trimmed with myriad ruffles and pleats.

On a stuffed armchair sat the bride, dressed all in white, with her feet resting on a small stool.

The guests began to arrive – young women starched and shampooed, bedecked and berouged; pious matrons dressed to the nines. The musicians stood by with their instruments: Gimpel with his fiddle, Hersh-Leyb with his bass, Dovidl with his bow.

The groom was due to arrive any minute in the company of the finest young men: local boys as well as fellow students from his yeshiva, including Simchele, who was, after all, already a bar mitzvah boy.

Yidl was so full of joy that he couldn't sit still. He paced from room to room, pausing before the overladen tables, checking the lamps to assure himself that they were burning properly, taking out his red handkerchief to give another swipe to the place of honor where the groom would soon be sitting, peeking one more time at the bride.

But what was this? The bride was writhing in her seat and moaning softly into her white veil. At first no one took any notice. Her piteous stifled moans were drowned out by the shower of kisses, embraces, and blessings from the women. Young girls conveyed their good wishes, inspecting her wedding gown, her long veil, and her white shoes – without noticing that her face was contorted with agony, first a chalky white, then a sickly green – and now the band struck up a tune, and the cries rang out:

"Mazel tov! The groom has arrived! Musicians, a merry tune!"

Women clapped their hands and chanted: "Here comes the groom! Here comes the groom!"

Leaving Rosa moaning on the white armchair, Yidl hurried to welcome the young man as he crossed the threshold.

He was pale and painfully thin, no taller than his brother Simchele, with the same pointy nose. Covered completely in satin, he stood surrounded by the throng of youths, who were also in satin. The music played on.

Twisting and turning on her stuffed seat, Rosa stared through the open door as the groom was led by. Such a tiny scrap of a thing! He looked like a doll – a doll swaddled in satin.

All at once a sense of pity for the poor boy took hold of her – pity mixed with a savage rage. She almost broke out into a strange laughter, but then a fearsome pain in the pit of her stomach overwhelmed every other sensation, and she howled at the top of her lungs. At this the women rushed to her side and a great commotion filled the room. In her anguish, the bride kicked and wept like a child. Chana-Rochel, the town gossip, was sobbing. Rochel kept begging someone to run for the "what-do-you-call-it," forgetting entirely that the town had no doctor. The groom, scared to death, was led from the room. His friends were flabbergasted. What was happening was simply inconceivable.

Someone commanded the musicians to play for all they were worth.

The groom's mother plucked at her gaunt cheeks and pulled at her hair. Giving a sudden tug to her satin bonnet, she stood bald-headed in the middle of the frightened, babbling, helpless crowd.

The only one who did not lose his wits was Yidl. He looked closely at his daughter, and a terrible suspicion entered his mind, so terrible that he would gladly have seen his accursed house tumble to the ground and bury him along with his own flesh and blood and every last one of the hateful guests.

The rabbi advised that the bride be put to bed with hot compresses. If a canopy was set up and the wedding performed on the spot, he said, the Lord would provide and the bride would recover.

At that moment the Talmud master lost his famous temper and began to holler.

Yidl spoke neither to the rabbi nor to the father of the groom. Still in his satin coat, he ran to the stable and harnessed two glossy black horses. Then he bundled his daughter into a white down quilt snatched from the bridal bed, carried her out in his arms, and tucked her into the wagon. Before Rochel had time to understand what was happening and try to jump in herself, he leapt up into his seat, cracked his whip, and set out for the forest.

A deathly stillness fell upon the crowd. All eyes were fixed on the wagon with its bizarre load. Across Yidl's broad shoulders, the satin coat reflected the setting sun as he wielded the whip like a man possessed . Finally a cloud of dust enveloped the wagon and it vanished from view.

The forest stood in the distance, as silent and mysterious as ever. As the whole town knew full well, the forest was home to a host of evil spirits. In the summer they rode through the treetops on broomsticks, and on winter days they took the form of wolves.

Outlandish tales had been told about the forest, but none stranger than what Yidl had to say when, after half an hour, he came riding back home

The cottage was hushed and evil tongues fell silent when once again the wagon appeared with its cloud of dust.

Rosa was sitting beside her father. The color had returned to her face. She climbed down from the wagon without assistance.

"The wedding is off," Yidl announced to the groom's father without ceremony. The tumult that followed these four words was such that later no one could remember exactly what happened. But one thing was clear to all. The woods had exerted their demonic power over Yidl. It was the evil spirits that had made him commit such a grievous sin on his own daughter's wedding day. And when demons were mixed up in things, there was no point trying to resist.

Only Yidl knew what had occurred in the forest. Only he could see in his mind's eye the bough of the tree where – driven by the terrible suspicion that had turned out not to be true – he had come perilously close to committing a most dreadful act.

Again and again that evening, Yidl broke out into a wild weeping mixed with laughter. Rochel was convinced that her husband had lost his mind.

That same night, after he had finally driven away the last guest, he barred the door to the front room, tore the satin coat off his back – and became his former self once more.

The family ate their supper from plain earthen bowls, the way they used to back in the village.

And to this day, the satin coat languishes in Yidl's loft, abandoned among other useless things. Every evening, the rays of the sun steal over the discarded garment and cover it with a golden blanket of dust. There it lies, silent and neglected, a relic of a forgotten dream.

Essays

Translated by Anita Norich

On the Publication of *Parisian Writings*

אַ פּאָר ווערטער צום דערשיינען פֿון 'פּאַריזער שריפֿטן'

[*London Vaytshepl*, December 1945, pp. 20–23]

I've just finished reading the literary-social journal, *Parisian Writings*. I stare at this weighty publication sitting on my desk and am astonished. Where does our strength come from? We are said to be a wandering people, but in truth, we are a wonder. Aren't all those who contribute to or are responsible for the appearance of the first post-war journal in Paris giants? Shouldn't we simply bow our heads out of respect for them?

Yes, they must be giants to reach such heights, to be able to create, even to simply be able to think and still seek to create a bridge between European Jews, to be able to worry about the future of our people when their bloody wounds are still open and oozing.

I look at this collection and my heart wants to sing of its glory. I want so much to be able to express my deep thankfulness to my comrades for being so strong and able to overcome what they have endured.

During the bloody war, bombs flew here in London. Death itself flew. I remember how my heart stopped when the radio told us of new disasters, of the millions of our sisters and brothers sent to gas chambers. Everything in me froze and I could not express any of my feelings. I stopped believing in people. I became almost too cynical to believe in anything. Hatred was the only feeling left to me. It's a shame, but it is the truth.

The knowledge that life and death were chasing one another in a game of blind-man's-bluff didn't worry me. What's the point of such a life? I didn't even go to the shelters to protect myself from the bombs. Let come what may.

And now, in this journal, we have writers who didn't learn about what was happening to the Jewish people from the radio. Rather, their own bodies experienced it. They lived through all the seven circles of hell. And still they remained strong.

Parizer shriftn begins with a memorial. And how could it not?

There is a list of those murdered in the concentration camps, those killed in battle against the bestial Nazis, those who were deported and did not return. My own comrades and friends are among those named, and my eyes pour blood instead of tears. I must confess that I am incapable of writing a review of this important journal. I am too close to it all! And I have too much respect for the quantity and quality of its contents to allow myself to write in haste, on one foot as it were.

I just want to congratulate you, editors and contributors to the journal! First, because of the united front you have created amongst yourselves. You saw the most important need: to unite, to work and create together for our people's future.

I congratulate you and wish you great success in your important work. May your hands be blessed!

I look at this journal and thoughts arise that will not let me rest.

I think that if this ancient, clever people – the People of the Book – had been more practical (which, for no good reason, we are said to be), had understood the need for unity in all generations and times and not just in times of trouble, then we might not have had such poems as M. Shulstein's[1] "I Saw a Mountain." There would have been no mounds of shoes marching in his poem. Empty shoes that make one shudder in horror.

Moyshe Shulstein is a young man and perhaps, instead of

1 Moyshe Shulstein (1911–1981) was in the French resistance during the war and imprisoned by the Gestapo in Paris.

abandoned shoes of immolated brides and grooms, he would have seen boys and girls singing and dancing as they walked in open fields under sunny skies. And he probably wouldn't have written this ending to his poem:

> Listen, all who once refused to hear
> As we crossed death's threshold.
> Listen now, in every town and city.
> We are going.
> Dead echoes of a life.
> We will never let you rest.
> We are going, going, going.

And we probably wouldn't have heard Avrom Ber[2] tell us this in his poem:

> Groups of Jewish mothers
> All the Rachels and Leahs
> Millions of funerals
> Every mother carries shards of a child
> Lays it down and disappears.
> Every shard reports:
> Not death, but Nazi murders!

Instead, Avrom Ber might have told us about Jewish mothers who lead children to fields, lay them down with a kiss for them to sleep a healthy sleep on the fragrant grass under a bright sky while they gather vegetables somewhere in Palestine or Birobidzhan.

And Benyomin Shlevin[3] might not have told us in his novel, *Jew-*

---

2 Avrom-Ber Tserata [possibly] (1900–1963) was a typesetter deported to concentration camps, who returned to Paris in 1945.

3 Benyomin Shlevin né Sheynman (1910–1981) went to Paris in 1934 and was imprisoned as a French soldier during the war.

ish Belleville, of pale, frightened youths led away, suitcase in hand, and worked to death in some remote corner of Paris.

Perhaps he would have only told us of Jewish youth who come to Paris on vacation – just like young people elsewhere – simply to enjoy themselves.

It is physically impossible to cite here, or even to name all the articles, poems, essays, etc., that are in this important collection. They are important because of their high caliber, but even more important because writers of every kind united in order to slough off the Nazi filth; they staunched their external wounds, stood erect, and published this momentous work.

I read and am astonished. For four years Paris lay under the Nazi axe – the axe that fell first on Jewish heads and murdered our writers and speakers. I am amazed that Paris could accomplish this!

How high must a people's spiritual level be? How high must they be not to go mad after so many dreadful troubles but, instead, maintain their spirits even when they are tortured in concentration camps, when they must witness with their own eyes their own mothers and fathers, sisters and brothers, little children burned in gas chambers, buried alive?

How much respect, how much reverence can – must – a people have for itself when it has such spiritual strength? One is simply proud to have the honor of being a child of this ancient, tested people.

Yiddish Culture in Paris

אַ בליק אויפֿן פּאַריזער יידישן קולטור

[*Loshn un lebn*, Feb 1948, pp. 48–51]

The trip was nicer than the nicest dream. I hadn't seen my brother in eighteen years and now I was traveling with him to my most beloved city: Paris. That's no small thing! Is there a tourist who doesn't dream of Paris? And who doesn't long to go again once they have been there?

That's especially true now that the Germans – may their memory be erased – are gone.

(In 1940 we could not have anticipated being able to once again take a trip to Paris just for the fun of it.)

When you first get to Paris, there's no sign of anything having happened there. The streets are lively and all lit up at night. The stores are full of the nicest and best rich, elegant chic Parisian wares. They draw the tourist's eye, their opulence speechlessly calling to all who pass by.

The Americans are buying. The English and others want to buy. What's the Hebrew verse in the Talmud? "*Makhshava tova hakadosh barukh hu metzarfa lemaase.*" God links a good thought to an action. Especially if you can buy everything without coupons.

I think Yiddish Paris is just as lively!

When you come into a Yiddish editorial office, it looks like a holiday is being celebrated. My first visit was to the *Naye prese*. The place is large and lovely. The offices are roomy. I was brought in to my old friend, G. Kenig.[1] He met me with the same warm smile he had during the good, pre-war years. At first everything seemed like it had been in the past. But though we chatted a bit and tried to look happy and upbeat for one another, we both knew that beneath the pretense at happiness lay a deep sorrow, one that even a thousand years could not heal.

Munye Nadler[2] is no longer there! Many are missing. Still, our comrades don't belong among the sighers, but rather are those who work. And in work it's possible to forget one's sorrows. And there is a lot of work! I met the current editors: Mr. Vilner, the literary editor, Mr. Litvin,[3] and more. All of them are smart and intellectual people, humble and talented. They give us hope for the future and make sure that the newspaper loses nothing, neither in wisdom nor in quality.

The journal, *Oyfsnay*, under the editorship of the talented Lili Berger,[4] must also appear regularly, and that requires labor and money.

Now, what about the "Union?"[5] It's a large, four-story building in which are united so many Yiddish cultural organizations. May they prosper!

"Wisdom Shall Go Forth from Zion."

This quotation from Isaiah can now be applied to Paris.

Paris has eleven supplementary Yiddish schools for children (and more are being opened); there are several Yiddish theaters; there are several Yiddish libraries where avid Yiddish readers can borrow books.

---

1 *Naye prese* [The New Press] was a Communist newspaper published in Paris. G. Kenig (1909–1972) was its editor.

2 Munye Nadler (1908–1942) wrote in Hebrew and Yiddish for many publications. His turn from religious works to leftist politics was famous. He wrote for *Naye prese* and was a partisan until the Nazis caught and killed him.

3 Mordkhe Litvin (1906–1993) was a partisan in the French Resistance, a cultural critic, and a prolific translator of French, German, and Russian poetry into Yiddish.

4 In addition to being a renowned novelist, short story writer, and critic, Lili Berger (1916–1996) wrote for *Naye prese* and edited a leftist monthly periodical, *Oyfsnay* (Anew), that ran from 1947 to 1948.

5 *Union des Juifs pour la Résistance et l'Entraide* (Union of Jews for Resistance and Mutual Aid) created in 1943.

There's a literary and journalism association in which Chaim Grade is active. There's an association for Polish Jews (and for others). I was amazed when I attended one of the gatherings that take place there every Friday evening. The auditorium was so packed you couldn't have stuck a pin into it. People were even standing in the hallway in order to hear a Yiddish word. And they were young people. Boys and girls. It was reminiscent of the good old days of the Jewish youth in Poland who drank in Yiddish literature and culture so eagerly.

I went to one of the many orphanages for Jewish children. In the middle of a forest with huge golden autumn trees there is a house or, rather, a palace. In this palace, enveloped in a reddish sunset, sat children enjoying their supper.

The director greeted us warmly and asked us to wait a bit because the children could, under no circumstances, be disturbed. Once they had eaten, they came to us, some playful, some deep in earnest thought, with a question in their dreamy eyes. They looked somewhere far away into the night and waited.

I think these children will always gaze somewhere with an unasked question.

But when the secretary, Mr. Farber, appeared[6] the children forgot everything. They ran to him as if he were their very own father. They surrounded him and took turns holding his hands. It's such a shame that the man doesn't have hundreds of pairs of hands instead of just one.

Once he'd held hands with and kissed every one of them, some of the children went back into the house for a class before bedtime. Others accompanied us out.

Before I left, I was able to visit the offices of the *Arbeter vort*, Worker's Word.[7]

And once again the editors greeted us warmly: L. Domankevitch

---

6 Sh. Farber was head of the *Commission Central de l'enfance* (Central Commission for Children).

7 "*Arbeter vort* [Worker's Word] was a Labor Zionist weekly Yiddish newspaper.

and Yosef Fridman.[8] Once again, one sees serious, intensive work and a good relationship among Yiddish writers and the Yiddish word.

I was very sorry that my illness prevented me from getting closer to more of Yiddish life in Paris and its range of Yiddish cultural work. What I've conveyed here is only the view from one corner and only a partial view of that corner.

There is a great deal to be written about the Yiddish painters in Paris. While I was there, several exhibits of individual artists and groups of famous Jewish painters were on display. Marc Chagall had an exhibition. At another, the works of Mané-Kats and Gerah were shown, as were many others, from Picasso to Esther Carp. At a third, there were only Jewish painters, and this one was at number 14.[9] Preparations were underway for an exhibit of the early work of Markiel.[10]

And what about the fine artist, Benn? I'll write about him on another occasion. (Benn's wife, is also a painter, primarily of landscapes.) [11]

Just before my departure I went to a rehearsal of Chaim Sloves's play, *The Revengers*, directed by Yonas Turkov, who is well-known for his cultural work. (It's opening this year's winter season in Paris's YKUT Theater.) Along with Turkov's wife, the talented Diana Blumenfeld, and Yedidia Epshtein,[12] they offer a slew of concerts. I took great

---

8 L. Domankevitch (1899–1973).

9 The *Union des Juifs pour la Résistance et l'Entraide* was at 14 Rue de Paradis.

10 Mané-Kats (1894–1962). Gerah refers to Benn's wife, referenced below; Esther Carp (1910–1970). They may not be as well-known as Marc Chagall (1887–1985) and Pablo Picasso (1881–1973), but they were all contemporaries and sometimes had joint exhibitions. Jacob Markiel (1911–2008) was a painter, born in Lodz, Poland.

11 Benn (Bentziyon) Rabinowicz (1905–1989); in 1974 he was awarded the French Legion of Honor.

12 Chaim Sloves's (1905–1988) plays were staged throughout the Yiddish-speaking world. Yonas Turkov (1898–1988) was an actor and director. He and his wife, the singer Diana Blumenfeld (1903–1961), were active in the cultural life of the Warsaw Ghetto and the Displaced Persons' camps post-war. YKUT (*Yidisher kunst teater*, Yiddish Art Theater) operated in Paris from 1945–1950.

pleasure in them. In short, Paris is lively! You can't get bored there! You're simply not allowed. And the winter season hasn't even begun.

What about the writers? One would need to write a separate chapter about each of them. I just want to mention such giants as Chaim Grade, Moshe Shulstein, Mordkhe Shtrigler, B. Shlevin, to name only a few.[13]

Our Khil Aronson[14] occupies a special place in Paris's cultural life. He absolutely swims in the world of art. He is a fine art critic himself, a wonderful essayist who feels like a fish in water in the galleries and museums of Paris. He searches for art, looking at canvases, literature, museums. When he finds something of artistic value, he won't rest until he has given it the life it deserves.

"When are you coming to us in London?" I ask him.

"When the British Museum brings back its treasures that were evacuated during the war," he answers.

A strange Jew? He's settled, taken care of, as much as a Yiddish writer can be taken care of. And the only thing he lacks is the British Museum with its art treasures!

---

13 Chaim Grade (1910–1982) has been heralded as one of the most important poets and prose writers of the twentieth century; Moshe Shulstein (1911–1981) was a poet; Mordkhe Shtrigler (1921–1998) was a prolific writer who edited the Yiddish *Forverts* newspaper for a decade before his death; Benyomin Shlevin (1910–1981) was a poet, prose writer, and essayist. Each of these men were in Paris after the war and contributed to *Di Naye prese.*

14 Yekhiel Aronson (1896–1966) was an art critic and contributor to *Di Naye prese.*

Esther Kreitman's Autobiographical Notes

אסתר קרײַטמאַנ'ס נאָטיצן וועגן זיך אַליין

[*Yiddishe Shtimme*, London, June 25, 1954]

NB: On June 9, 1947, Kreitman sent the following notes to Yosef Frankl who was preparing a biographical and bibliographical lexicon of London-based Yiddish writers. These notes were only published after her death.

I come from a famous rabbinic and literary family. I and my brother, Yehoshuale – I. J. Singer – were born in the home of my grandfather, Reb Yakov Mordechai Zilberman, (may the memory of the righteous one be a blessing). He was the Bilgoray rabbi, and my parents were living with him after their marriage. When I was five years old, my father became the rabbi in Leoncin and we moved there.

I began writing when I was about sixteen years old. I had quite a few stories in manuscript form. When I left for Antwerp, my father was afraid the czarist officials might suspect that they were socialist writings. Without giving it much thought, I left the manuscripts at home. I hadn't yet shown them to anyone except my mother and brother.

I didn't give writing another thought.

It was only in 1929 that my son – who was still a child – simply forced me to begin writing because he liked the tales I used to tell him.

I came to London with my husband, Avrom, and son, Moyshele (who was then a year old), in 1914. (We fled Antwerp during the First World War.) Here I began writing professionally, as it were, in 1929. I visited Poland twice and saw my brothers, I. J. Singer and Yitzhak (Isaac) Bashevis, long may he live.

By then, my third brother, Moyshe Singer, was a rabbi. He was so religious that he didn't want to come see me because I no longer covered my hair. My father (may the memory of the righteous one be a blessing), who was also a rabbi, did come and so did my mother. They spent some time with me in Singer's summer house in Katsizne's villa.

Later I received letters from my brother Moyshe. They were sent from Russia, to which he and my mother had been evacuated. It has been almost two years since I last heard from them.

I also visited Belgium and France several times before the Second World War.

P.S. My father's name was Reb Pinkhas Singer.

My mother's name was Batsheva.

And another thing: Yitzhak Bashevis and Moyshe were born in Leoncin.

[NB: Following a list of her published works, Kreitman added that her translations from Yiddish into English were completed in ten months in 1929 while visiting Warsaw.]

Appendix

Kaddish For My Mother, Esther Kreitman

קדיש מײַן מוטער, אסתר קרײַטמאַן

[*Loshn un lebn,* June 1954]

Translated by Anita Norich

Who knows a person better than a son knows his own mother? My mother was a person who thought and felt deeply, profoundly. I'm not only saying these words from my aching heart, but from cool common sense. I don't want to say a single word that exaggerates, that is even a hairsbreadth removed from the unadorned truth. Yes, my mother was a profound person in whom the most difficult human conflicts vied with one another. These conflicts were seen in her works, which illuminate and gleam with the most marvelous warmth in all of Yiddish literature. Her pen would fly freely and powerfully, expressing her sharp, positive view of life, people, and the strange world in which we live.

Some acquaintances, who knew my mother only superficially, used to be surprised that this person, subject to such stormy internal struggles, was the writer of the quiet, grand novel, "*Der sheydim tants*" (that I translated and published in English); the broad-ranging, worldly-wise novel, "*Brilyantn*"; the series of beautiful and muti-faceted stories, some gathered in her book "*Yikhes*," some in the Yiddish press throughout the world. These acquaintances could not understand the gap between the personality of the author and her work. They sought all sorts of answers, including incorrect interpretations, because nothing in the world is as disturbing as something one doesn't understand. Human history is a long chain of trying to reach the truth despite an inability to understand. Often these interpretations are based on superstition or fantasy, more often on nothing more than a feeling. People ask how my mother developed such difficult inner conflicts. To give a full answer to this, we would need to know my mother's entire life and, even more, to look back through many generations in the history of our family. I mean our extended family, called the Jewish people. But, in brief, here lies a partial answer: my mother had a tremendously rare sensitivity.

When life was good, she could reach the heights of ecstasy and enthusiasm, heights to which others could not accompany her. She could not tolerate the evil in life, and especially injustice, the lack of honor which unfortunately constitutes the majority of our contemporary, so-called civilization. Like a bad egg that lies heavily on the stomach and can be poisonous, so lay all the ethically negative evils of her surroundings on my mother's head. Often, I would argue with her, saying, "Such is the world! Did we create the world? Is it our job? Isn't it nice enough as it is? If others injure themselves, let them worry about it. If we injure ourselves, let's try to forget the pain as quickly as possible." But my mother couldn't do that. She couldn't tolerate injustice. She felt responsible and all but guilty about the entire world. The tragedies of the years that have just passed – and let's hope that they have really passed – and the coldblooded murder of six million Jews, was a blow that all but destroyed her. The victims' sufferings were reflected in her soul. They were so unbearably painful that, in the end, they changed her, overshadowing all else.

My most wonderful, sweetest memories of my mother are from my childhood, and mostly from Saturday afternoons. My mother wasn't at all religiously observant but, as she herself used to say, she was "bound with a thousand threads" to *yiddishkeyt*, to the lovely Jewish way of life. She told stories with an indescribably humane warmth and depth, precision and phenomenal range – stories of her home in the city of Bilgoray, Poland, where she was born in her rabbinic grandfather's house. She'd tell of her father, the rabbi, the righteous and impractical man, her sharp – too sharp – mother, her accomplished brothers, the surrounding people, other cities and towns, Warsaw, bygone days, the folkloric treasures that were the only riches in the family to grow from generation to generation. If I have even a crumb of that spiritual treasure, if I accomplish a little and marvel at much of Yiddish language and literature despite being raised in London, it's because I inherited it from my dear mother.

My mother did not leave a written will, but I know what she wanted: to place herself in life's battles on the side of humaneness, fraternity, and peace, and to fight against the disturbing, venomous, filthy powers that threaten life. Sordidness, it must be said, can be found not only among other peoples, but also in great measure among Jews themselves. With every breath in her being, my mother identified with the endless battle for a better, purer, and happier world. With every breath in her being, she saw that as the mission of people in general and of Jews in particular, and she knew that without this mission, *yiddishkeyt* was nothing and all our past grotesque, dreadful sacrifices were meaningless.

May the bright memory of my dear, beloved mother live on eternally.

Moyshe Kreitman (Maurice Carr)

My Grandmother Esther

To me, my grandmother wasn't the writer Esther Kreitman but Buba. My first memories of her are in my grandparents' house in London; a house I remember being dark, damp, cold, and dreary. My grandmother was a dumpy figure, always dressed in dark clothes, black hair flaring out on either side of a white part in the middle, and blue eyes so pale they were almost transparent. She was a frightening figure to me; my grandfather Zeyde was more jovial.

We used to huddle in the kitchen in front of a fire that didn't seem to warm anything. There must have been bright sunny days, but I don't remember them. I also don't remember her paying any particular attention to me. Not the rosy-cheeked kind of Jewish grandmother who makes you *apfelstrudel.* Come to think of it, she must have regarded me as a bit of a disaster because I was the reason her son married my mother. And Esther had always thought her son would live with her for the rest of her life, that they would sit together at the kitchen table writing. So my mother's eruption into their cozy life was a tragedy she never accepted. This tragedy happened because of the First World War.

My mother Lola was born in Vienna where her father, A. M. Fuchs, was a well-known Yiddish writer and journalist. He wrote articles for *Forverts* (The Jewish Daily *Forward*). But when Hitler's army marched into Vienna, my mother and her parents were arrested and put into prison. *Forward* paid to get them out. They took a train to Paris and then to London, where my grandfather's two brothers lived.

One day, Fuchs put on his hat and his gloves (he was a bit of a dandy) and took his daughter Lola along to pay his respects to that other well-known Yiddish writer, Esther Kreitman. Royalty paying a visit to royalty. My father was bowled over by Lola's beauty and also the *chutzpah* with which she talked back to her father, he who was always very deferential to his own mother. At the time, Lola had a husband who had stayed in Vienna, so Esther thought it was safe to suggest her son show Lola around London. There would be no danger in his having a relationship with a married woman.

There she made a bad mistake... because I happened.

Lola got a divorce, and my father, standing in the kitchen where everything happened, put his arm round my mother's shoulder, which in those days meant, "We're getting married."

So I was born during the war, not a cheerful time. I remember Lola in a blond halo of hair and Esther in a dark frizz of curls saying nasty things to one another around the fire while my father perched uncomfortably on a stool between them. A long, thin, timid, and uncertain young man, he didn't know how to deal with these two female furies, one feeling she'd rescued him from an overbearing mother, and the other feeling that her son had been stolen away from her.

And Esther was indeed very possessive, not of her husband whom she didn't even like, but of her only son Moishele. When my father was invited to become a member of the prestigious Pen Club after writing his novel, *The House of Napolitano,* his mother insisted on going with him to the first meeting. He never went back. But he loved his mother and felt his mission in life was to look after her and protect her, so that falling in love with Lola was a bit of a tragedy for him too. I think he felt guilty about it all his life.

After the war, *Reuters* sent my father to Paris as foreign correspondent. I was told much later that he had requested this because he felt he had to pull Esther and Lola apart. I was also told that the reason we lived for years in a small hotel was because that way it would be impossible for Esther to come and stay with us.

I always remained frightened of Esther. The last time I saw her, I was about twelve years old and alone in the flat we had eventually moved into. The doorbell rang and there she stood looking paler than ever. "Let me in," she said, "I'm going to faint." I was surprised; nobody had ever told me not to let her in. I asked her to lie down and she waited for my parents. I felt rather hurt, that she felt she needed to be so theatrical, as if I'd close the door on my own grandmother.

My father told me how when Esther and Avrum first got to Antwerp from Berlin, where they had gone through this unwilling and arranged marriage, she and her husband revolted against tradition. Esther threw away her wig and my grandfather shaved his beard. When Avrum's father, Reb Gedalya Kreitman, who had been sending them money, found out about this, he was furious and cut them off without a penny. So they were poor all the rest of their lives. Avrum fixed clasps on lady's handbags, Esther did embroidery, and at one point even opened a small grocery shop. This hurt her pride.

My father remembered how Esther, who was Hindele to her family, would endlessly tell him stories of the *alte heym* (old home) and all of her "wild dreams." As a young girl terrified of the evil spirits that roamed in the dead of night, and wanting company, she would entice her younger brother Yitzhak to climb into her bed with the promise that she'd tell him a story. She knew he couldn't resist. He grew up to become Isaac Bashevis Singer and told his own stories, and who knows, maybe some of them were inspired by those his sister told him so many years ago.

My father also wrote about his mother's death, how she turned round in her bed, disbelieving this was happening to her, and died with her feet on the pillow. She asked to be cremated so that the devils would not get at her body. And later in his own life, before he himself died, he would remember, he actually seemed to relive the scene in Antwerp, when he and his mother were on their way to Poland and she fell down in front of a tram foaming at the mouth in an epileptic fit. And he would weep uncontrollably. My mother and I wouldn't know what to say to comfort him.

Maybe now, Maurice and Esther are sitting together at a heavenly kitchen table … writing.

Hazel Karr

Letter From Stefan Zweig Referring to *Der sheydim tants*

[in YIVO's Esther Kreitman archive]

Translated from German by Anita Norich

49 Hallam Street,
London, W. 1.
Langham 3693
30 June, 1939

Dear Mrs. Kreitman,

Happily, it turns out I was able to read your novel much more quickly than I anticipated. It is an excellent depiction of its milieu and gives a vivid picture of the Eastern world in a tragic moment – or, better put: in one of the tragic moments that keep repeating there. The main character is fully alive and in every sense Jewish, and I understand the great success the book has had in its own language and in its own circles. Don't be discouraged if, at this moment, you have trouble with English publishers. I know from my own experience that publishers here are hesitating to undertake new things as long as the political environment remains so unclear. And there is a certain prejudice against books depicting Jews because there have actually been too many of them in recent years; it is notable that it is precisely Jewish readers and buyers who want to hear no more of Jewish problems after they have had to think about them all day long.

So don't be discouraged if things don't happen on the first try. I hope, with all my heart, that your book will succeed.

With best wishes,
Your devoted
Stefan Zweig

George Bernard Shaw to Esther Kreitman: Handwritten card sent to 56 Lordship Park, N. 16

[in YIVO's Esther Kreitman archive]

9th February, 1940

Dear Madam,

It is not possible for me to read MSS and introduce them to publishers. That is a long and special business which, for various professional and business reasons, an author must not undertake. It is performed by literary agents. It is, however, quite unnecessary to employ an agent. All publishers have readers on whose reports they act; and to seek reports from anyone else is a waste of time.

The leading Jewish publisher in London is Mr. Victor Gollancz. You had better send your MS to him, especially if it has a left wing tendency.

I am much obliged to you for letting me see your translation of my *Intelligent Woman's Guide* into Yiddish; but as I cannot read a word of it (not knowing the language) and you may possibly find a publisher to reprint it at some future time, it had better stay in your hands. In mine it would be buried alive.

Tomorrow my secretary will return the two books to your address.

Faithfully,
G. Bernard Shaw

Bibliography

Prepared by Anita Norich

Yiddish Books by Esther Kreitman

Brilyantn: roman. London: Foyle, Ltd. Hebrew Department, 1944.

Der sheydim-tants: roman. Warsaw: H. Bzshoza, 1936. [serialized as *Dvoyrele* in *Di post,* London) August 10, 1934 – December 7, 1934]

Yikhes: dertseylungen un skitsn. London: Narod Press, 1949.

Table of Contents:

"Atlesene kapote"
"Di naye velt"
"Reb Meyerl"
"Shloymeke"
"Yikhes"
"Zeygers"
"Blits"
"Dzshim"
"Hint"
"Opgefast zikh"
"Gevorn a tremp"
"Tsu shpet"

"Bibliotekn"
"Zi iz nisht blind"

Short Stories by Esther Kreitman

"A farshterter yuntuf," *Dos fraye vort,* December 28, 1934, pp. 8–12.

"Afn Place de la Republique: a skitse," *Loshn un lebn,* July 1946, pp.35–38.

"Ah, peysakh," *Dos fraye vort,* March 30, 1934, pp. 10–13 ("Shloymeke" in *Yikhes;* "Shloyme" in *Blitz).*

"Beshas a seder," *London Vaytshepl,* no. 51, April 1944, pp. 11–12 (included in *Brilyantn*).

"Blitz," *Vaytshepl lebt,* 1951, pp.133–37 (in *Yikhes;* "Blitz" in *Blitz*).

"*An atlesene kapote,*" *Forverts,* Feb. 15, 1948 ("*Atlesene kapote*" in *Yikhes;* "A Silk Gaberdine" in *Blitz;* "A Satin Coat" by Ellen Cassedy in *Beautiful as the Moon, Radiant as the Stars;* "The Relic" by Maurice Carr in *Jewish Short Stories of Today.*)

"Der vanderveg," *Loshn un lebn,* June–July 1955, pp. 4–9.

"Der nadn," *Di Yidishe Shtime,* August 24, 1951, p. 2.

"Di hunger-marshirer," *Dos fraye vort,* March 9, 1934, p. 12.

"Di hungerike," *Belgishe bleter,* vol. 3, no. 2, Feb. 1937, p. 4 (expansion of "Di hunger-marshirer").

"Di naye velt," *Loshn un lebn,* no. 74, March 1946, pp. 7–12 (in *Yikhes;* "The New World" in *Blitz* ; "The New World" by Barbara Harshav in *Lilith* 16, and reprinted in *Found Treasures;* "The New World" by Joshua Fogel in *Yale Review* 73.).

"Di shayle," *Di post,* January 6, 1928, p. 3.

"Doktoyrim," *Belgishe bleter,* November 1936, p. 3.

"Dzshek," *Dos fraye vort,* February 2, 1934, pp. 8–11 ("Dzshim" in *Yikhes;* "Jim" in *Blitz*).

"Gevorn a tremp," *Loshn un lebn,* May 1949, pp. 32–37 (in *Yikhes;* "Becoming a Tramp" in *Blitz).*

"Hint, Hint, Hint," *Dos fraye vort,* December 1, 1933, pp. 13–14 (expanded in *Yikhes;* "Dogs" in Blitz).

"Nakht falt tsu," *Dos fraye vort,* Oct. 19, 1934, pp. 16–17; reprinted in (Lublin) *Oventblat,* July 28, 1939, p. 5 as "Nakht falt tsu ibern Temze."

"Opgefast zikh: A skitse," *Dos fraye vort,* September 29, 1933, pp. 8–10; reprinted in *Vaytshepl lebt almanakh,* 1951, pp. 125–28 (in *Yikhes;* "Breaking the Fast" in *Blitz*).
"Reb Meyerl," *Loshn un lebn,* July–August 1954, pp. 3–11 (in *Yikhes;* "Reb Meyerl" in *Blitz*).
"Tsubislekh mit blut," *Dos fraye vort,* February 22, 1935, pp. 8–9.
"Zeygers," *Di tsayt,* July 31, 1944; reprinted in *Vaytshepl lebt,* 1951, pp. 129–33 (in *Yikhes;* "Clocks" in *Blitz).*

Non-Fiction by Esther Kreitman

"A por verter tsum dersheynen fun 'Parizer Shriftn'," *London Vaytshepl,* December 1945, pp. 20–23.
"A blik afn Parizer Yidishn kultur-lebn," *Loshn un lebn,* February 1948, pp.48–51.
"Der shabes gevidmet der royter armey," *Yidishland,* March 1943, p. 8.
"Etlekhe verter mekoyekh Moyshe Shulshtain," *Loshn un lebn,* January 1946, pp. 30–31.
"Frume gezangen un lirishe poemes fun Yosef Hillel Levi," *Loshn un lebn,* December 1949, pp. 32–35.

Translations by Esther Kreitman Into Yiddish

Di froy in sotsyalizm un kapitalizm. Warsaw: Sh. Goldfarb, 1930. Translation of George Bernard Shaw, *The Intelligent Woman's Guide to Socialism and Capitalism.*
Vaynakht. Warsaw: Helios, 1929. Translation of Charles Dickens, *A Christmas Carol.*

Previous Translations of Kreitman into English (Books)

Blitz and Other Stories, [*Yikhes*] translated by Dorothee von Tendaloo, edited by Sylvia Paskin, London: David Paul, 2004.
Table of Contents:
The New World ("Di naye velt")
A Silk Gabardine ("Atlesene")
Reb Meyerl ("Reb Meyerl")

Shloyme ("Shloyme")
Jewish Nobility ("Yikhes")
Jim ("Dzshim")
Breaking the Fast ("Opgefast zikh")
Becoming a Tramp ("Gevorn a tremp")
Too Late ("Tsu shpet")
Two Libraries ("Bibliotekn")
She Is Not Blind ("Zi iz nisht blind")
Clocks ("Zeygers")
Blitz ("Blits")
Dogs ("Hint")

Diamonds [*Brilyantn*], translated by Heather Valencia, London: David Paul, 2010.

Deborah [*Der sheydim tants*], translated by Maurice Carr, London: Foyle, Ltd., 1946
reprinted London: Virago Press, 1938
reprinted New York: The Feminist Press, 2004
Reissued as: *The Dance of the Demons*, translated by Maurice Carr, N.Y.: Feminist Press, 2009.

Short Stories

Cassedy, Ellen. "A Satin Coat" ("Atlesene kapote"). *Beautiful as the Moon, Radiant as the Stars*, edited by Sandra Bark, New York: Warner Books, 2003.

Fogel, Joshua A. "The New World" ("Di Naye Velt"). *Yale Review* 73, Summer 1984, pp. 525–532.

Harshav, Barbara. "The New World" ("Di Naye Velt"), *Lilith* 16, no. 2, Spring 1991, pp. 10–12. Reprinted in *Found Treasures: Stories by Yiddish Women Writers*, edited by Frieda Forman, Ethel Raicus, Sarah Silberstein Swartz and Margie Wolfe. Toronto: Second Story Press, 1994.

Kreitman, Morris (aka Maurice Carr). "The Relic" ("Atlesene kapote"), *Jewish Short Stories of Today*. Edited by Morris Kreitman. London: Faber & Faber, 1938.

Lachs, Vivi. "The Question" ("Di shayle"), *East End Jews: Sketches from the London Yiddish Press*, translations by Vivi Lachs and Barry Smerin. Detroit: Wayne State University Press, 2025, pp. 113–15

———. "The Dowry" ("Der nadn"), *East End Jews: Sketches from the London Yiddish Press*, translations by Vivi Lachs and Barry Smerin. Detroit: Wayne State University Press, 2025, pp. 116–19.

Selected Critical Bibliography: Yiddish

Anon. "*Der sheydim tants*," (Review), *Belgishe bleter*, Jan. 1937, p. 6.

Anon. "Esther Kreitman, E'H," Obituary, *Di Yidishe Shtime*, June 18, 1954.

Anon. "The Moral of a Novel" (review of *Deborah*), *The Jewish Chronicle*, October 4, 1946, p. 16.

Botoshanski, Yankev. "Tsvishn yo un neyn: Ester Kreytman o'h." [Between yes and no] *Di prese* August 20, 1954, p. 4.

Cahan, Ab. "Bamerkungen vegn "Di atlesene kapote' fun Ester Kreitman, [Comments about the story] *Forward* Feb. 22, 1948, Section 2, p. 5.

Carr, Maurice. "Kadish mayn muter Ester Kreytman," [Kaddish for My Mother],

Loshn un lebn June 1954 pp. 8–10.

Domb, Moshe. "Ester Kreytman: ayndruk fun a bazukh," [E.K.: Impressions of a Visit], *Di Yidishe Shtime*, Dec. 25, 1953, p. 2.

Goldberg, Izak. "An epizod mit an eyntsikn manuskript" [An episode with the only copy of a manuscript] *Yoyvl almanak, Loshn un lebn*, 1956, pp. 97–97.

Katz-Handler, Troim. "Di shvester: Hinde-Ester Zinger-Kreytman." [The Sister] *Yidishe Kultur*, 59, no. 5–6, May–June 1997, pp. 47–49.

Kohn, Hilel. "Vegen Ester Kreytman o'h [letter to the editor]." [About E.K.] London, *Di Yidishe Shtime*, June 25, 1954: 4.

Kreitman, Esther. "Ester Kreytman's Notitsn Vegn Zikh Aleyn." [E.K. Notes About Herself] London, *Di Yidishe Shtime*. July 9, 1954: 3.

Leksikon fun der nayer Yidisher literatur. New York: 1981, vol. 8, col. 260–261.

Levi, Yosef Hilel. "A roman fun Yidishn lebn in Antverpn" [review of *Brilyantn*], *Fraye arbeter shtimme,* Aug. 24, 1945, pp. 5, 8.

———. "Shtrikhn tsu Ester Kreytmans literarishe portret." [E.K.'s Literary Portraits] *Loshn un Lebn* 118, November 1949, pp. 27–31.

Ravitch, Melech. "Ester Kraytman." *Mayn leksikon,* Montreal: 1982, vol. IV:2, pp. 254–256.

Selected Critical Bibliography: English

Boyden, Michael. "The Other 'Other Singer': Linguistic Alterity in Esther Kreitman's Transit Fiction," *Prooftexts,* vol. 31, no. 1–2, Winter-Spring 2011, pp. 95–117.

Carr, Hazel. "My Grandmother, Esther," Afterword in *The Dance of the Demons,* NY: Feminist Press, 2009, pp. 301–303.

———. Foreword to Maurice Carr's *The Forgotten Singer: The Exiled Sister of I.J. and Isaac Bashevis Singer,* Amherst, Mass.: White Goat Press, 2023, pp. 7–12.

Carr, Maurice. *The Forgotten Singer: The Exiled Sister of I.J. and Isaac Bashevis Singer.* Amherst, Mass.: White Goat Press, 2023.

———. "My Uncle Yitzhak: A Memoir of Isaac Bashevis Singer," *Commentary,* December 1992, pp. 25–32. (Reprinted as "Afterword" in *Blitz and Other Stories*; and as "*Biographical Essay*" in *The Dance of the Demons.*

Clifford, Dafna. "From Diamond Cutters to Dog Races: Antwerp and London in the Work of Esther Kreitman," *Prooftexts,* vol. 23, no. 3, pp. 320–337.

Goldman, Ari. "The Long-Neglected Sister of the Singer Family," *New York Times,* April 4, 1991, pp. 15, 20.

[I.B.S.?]. "An Older Polish Jewry: Documentary Novel," review of *Deborah,* The Jewish Chronicle, Sept. 20, 1946, p.13.

[I.J.B.?]. "Yichus," review, *The Jewish Chronicle,* Nov. 25, 1949, p. 15.

Jones, Faith. "An Ester Kreytman Bibliography," *The Mendele Review,* No. 148 (Sept. 2004), https://yiddish.haifa.ac.il/tmr/tmr08/tmr08009.htm

———. "Esther Kreitman, *Jewish Women's Archive,* https://jwa.org/encyclopedia/article/kreitman-esther

———. "Esther Kreitman: Renewed Recognition of her Work." *Canadian Jewish Outlook* 38, no. 2, Mar/Apr 2000, pp. 17–18.

Legutko, Agi. Review of *Diamonds, The Jewish Quarterly,* no. 217, Spring 2011.

Norich, Anita. "Afterword," *The Dance of the Demons,* New York: Feminist Press, 2004.

———. "Esther Singer Kreitman in the Spotlight," review of *The Forgotten Singer,* by Maurice Carr, *Lilith,* November 2, 2023.

———. "The Family Singer and the Autobiographical Imagination," *Prooftexts* 10, 1990, pp. 91–107.

Paul, David and Sylvia Paskin. "Fifty Years On: Introduction to *Blitz and Other Stories,*" (London: David Paul, 2004).

Prager, Leonard. "Esther Kreitman." Yiddish Culture in Britain (Frankfurt: Peter Lang, 1990): 382–3.

Prawer, S.S. "The First Family of Yiddish," *Times Literary Supplement,* April 29, 1983: 3–4.

Sinclair, Clive. "Esther Singer Kreitman," *Lilith,* March 11, 1991.

———. "Esther, the Silenced Singer," *Los Angeles Times,* April 14, 1991.

———. "Esther Singer Kreitman: The Trammeled Talent of Isaac Bashevis Singer's Neglected Sister." *Lilith,* Spring 1991, pp. 8–9.

———. Introduction to *Deborah,* London: Virago Press, 1983.

Singer, Isaac Bashevis. "My Sister," *In My Father's Court,* New York: Farrar, Straus & Giroux, 1975, pp.151–155.

Stavans, Ilan. "Introduction," *The Dance of the Demons,* New York: Feminist Press, 2004.

https://sztetl.org.pl/en/biographies/4459-kreitman-ester

Weinman, Sarah. "Unsung," *Tablet,* June 24, 2009.

Wise, Yaakov. "The First Jewish Feminist?", *Jewish Quarterly,* Spring 2015. vol. 62, no. 1, pp. 44–47.

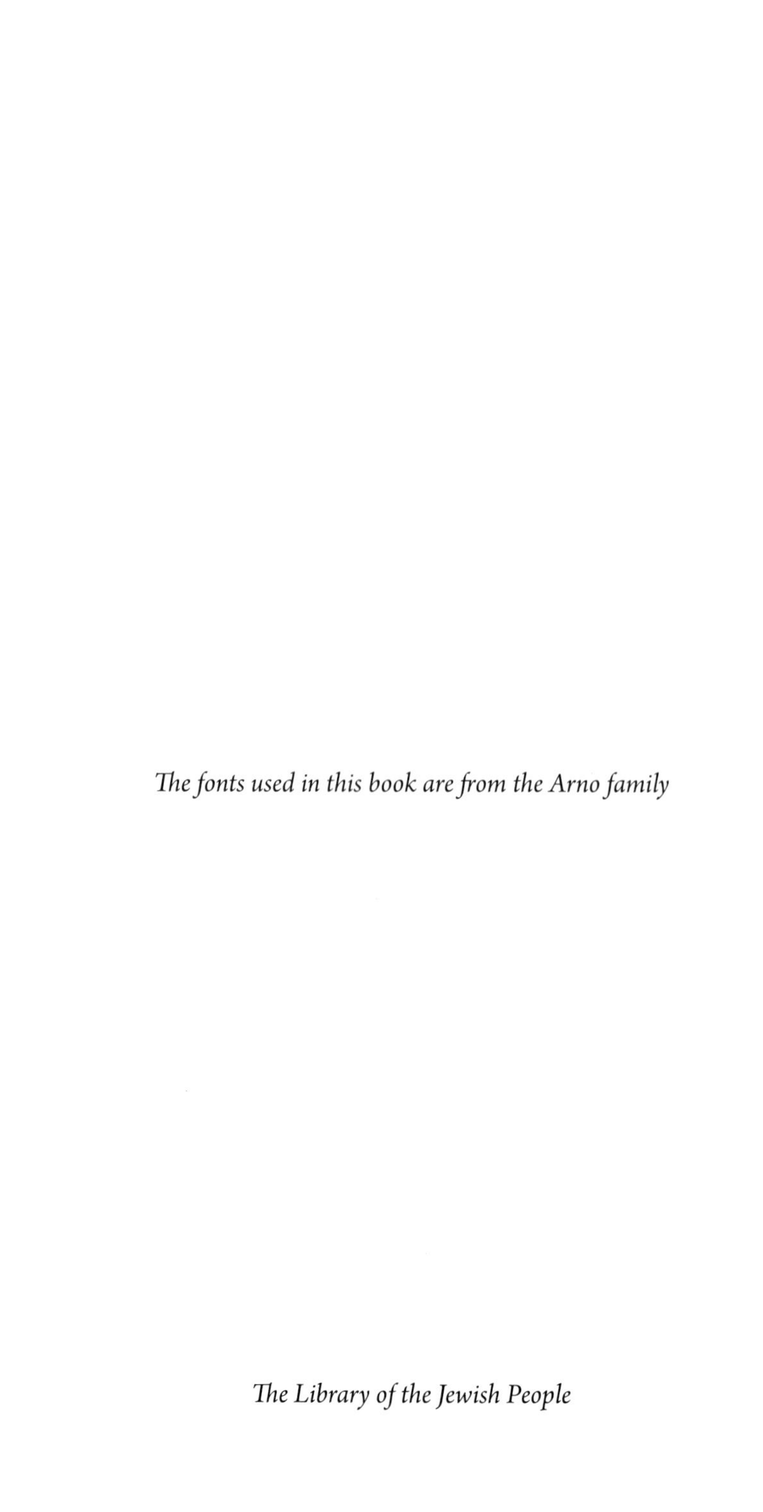

The fonts used in this book are from the Arno family

The Library of the Jewish People